Published by

LIVINGSTON PUBLISHING HOUSE
NEW YORK, LONDON, AMSTERDAM, LLC

www.onelandtwostories.com

ISBN: 978-0-9851961-0-3

Gabbay, Shaul M. and Kazak, Amin M.
One Land Two Stories
Shaul M. Gabbay and Amin M. Kazak
First Edition

Library of Congress Control Number
2012933532
Manufactured in the United States of America

First Edition February 2012

ABOUT THE AUTHORS

The authors of this book are academic pioneers. For a Jewish Israeli and a Muslim Palestinian to debate each other is one thing. It is quite another paradigm to stand together in classrooms to teach and present together, and now to cooperatively publish this book. Their courage to work ensemble goes against the grain of those who are opposed to peaceful coexistence. Those who disagree with their narratives denounce them. Sometimes the criticism comes from their own people who question their voices of moderation. No matter. Professors Shaul Gabbay and Amin Kazak remain resolved to speak their truths. They are determined to promote peaceful resolution to the Israeli-Palestinian conflict.

In their words, "the conflict has existed for far too long. We must move beyond it for the sake of future generations on both sides."

Now living in the United States, Gabbay and Kazak were born in the Holy Land as adversaries. Meeting for the first time in Denver, Colorado in 2003, these professors put their differences aside and have become friends.

In this book, the reader will find something different. Gabbay and Kazak have put their differences front and center. *One Land Two Stories* presents Gabbay and Kazak's opposing viewpoints on every page while taking the reader step-by-step through the history of the conflict.

Kazak was born in Haifa during the British Mandate of Palestine. At age six, during the 1948 War, he became a Palestinian refugee. His father, Moustapha Kazak, took his family across the border to find safety. What was anticipated to be a month or two away from home turned into a lifetime in exile. Kazak spent his formative years impoverished and disposessed in a UN Palestinian refugee camp in Lebanon. With extended family members scattered throughout the Middle East, including Israel, Kazak first realized he was stateless as a boy when his family was forbidden from visiting his aunts and uncles in Syria.

Overcoming obstacles, Amin succeeded in gaining higher education at the American University in Beirut. Earning a Ph.D. in political science, his life changed dramatically when he immigrated into the United States to begin his academic career at the University of Colorado.

Never having met an Israeli Jew in his lifetime, Kazak was introduced to Israeli Professor Shaul Gabbay in 2003. From that encounter, their friendship evolved. As mutual trust developed, mutual respect followed. Learning from each other led to cooperative teaching opportunities at the University of Colorado and the University of Denver.

"Our students are surprised by our friendship," states Kazak. "They realize quickly that Palestinians and Israelis do not have to be enemies. There are important lessons we teach naturally by example. Agreeing to disagree respectfully through civil discourse is probably the most important."

Shaul Gabbay was born and raised in Tel Aviv, the son of Jewish refugees from Arab countries. His father, Eliyahu Gabbay, fled from Baghdad in 1952. He was airlifted with 120,000 other persecuted Iraqi Jews to Israel. His first residence in the Holy Land resembled teepees assembled in the desert. The Israeli Ma'arbara camps accommodated hundreds of thousands of Jewish refugees exiled from their homes in Arab countries.

By the time Shaul was born in 1961, Eliyahu Gabbay had long since left the Ma'arbara camp, graduated from Tel Aviv University and had become a successful business executive. Speaking seven languages, he was able to provide the Gabbay family with a comfortable lifestyle in northern Tel Aviv. For Shaul, coming of age in Israel filled him with a profound sense of belonging and pride in the Jewish homeland.

When it came time to perform his military service, Gabbay did so knowing Israel's security challenges. As a commander in the Israel Defense Force, he led troops in battle during the 1982 Lebanon War. He and Kazak were

ABOUT THE AUTHORS

unknowingly a block away from each other in Beirut when Israeli troops occupied the city.

Gabbay's academic career commenced with a BA from Bar Ilan University and an MA from Tel-Aviv University. In 1991 he received a Presidential Fellowship from the United States to continue his studies. In 1995 he completed the Ph.D. program at Columbia University followed by an invitation from the University of Chicago to complete his post-doctoral studies there. In 1998, Professor Gabbay returned to Israel to teach and conduct research at the Technion-Israel Institute of Technology.

As fate unfolded, Gabbay met Kazak during his welcome to the University of Denver as the Executive Director of the Institute for the Study of Israel in the Middle East in the Korbel School of International Studies, a position he began in 2001.

Arriving in Colorado immediately following the 9/11 terrorist attacks, Gabbay's expertise was sought by local and national news broadcasts. Since then, he has been a frequent commentator on the Middle East for CBS, NBC, FOX and MSNBC.

Over the past decade, Kazak and Gabbay have taught dozens of classes to undergraduate and graduate students. Due to popular demand, the professors have taught classes for the general community and adults as well. All eager to understand the complex issues of the conflict, their students have served as an inspiration to them and have encouraged them to complete *One Land Two Stories*.

Gabbay and Kazak have a lot to teach us about Israelis and Palestinians. Although their stories are quite different and their interpretation of history falls on opposing sides of the conflict, these men resonate in their desire to build a better life for future generations. They believe *One Land Two Stories* lays a foundation of understanding that can do just that.

ACKNOWLEDGEMENTS

This book would not have been possible without the dedication of Pam Solomon, our Managing Editor and Director of Communications. We thank her for years of perseverance in preparing our manuscript for publication.

Our deep appreciation and gratitude goes to Katherine Graham of Art Only, Inc. for her creative design and commitment to this book.

We also thank: Vivienne Chew, Sandy Fazeli Fard, Erik Geib, David Gillespie, Andrea Jacobs, David Kazzaz, Peri Klein, Matthew Markman, Rebecca Otis, Gill Romano, Alla Rubinstein, Deborah Rohan Schlueter, Rachel Smith, Roberta Spivak, Hidde Anthony Stauthamer, Joe Verrengia, and Martin Widzer.

Lastly, we thank our students, from whom we garner inspiration—and our colleagues, who have helped us throughout the years.

TABLE OF CONTENTS

PREFACE | SHAUL GABBAY

I come from Israel where I was born to Jewish parents who were refugees from Arab countries.

I've prayed at the wall of Solomon's Temple in Jerusalem, and I visited Abraham and Sarah's gravesites near Hebron. I've stood where David fought Goliath and I've been awestruck by the starlit skies of the desert where God spoke to our Jewish patriarchs: Abraham, Isaac and Jacob.

My love for Israel resides in the core of my being. It represents who I am and gives my life purpose and meaning.

Jewish values are ingrained within me to work for "tikkun olam" (God's expectation of us to repair the world.)

So working towards resolving the Palestinian-Israeli conflict comes naturally to me.

Meeting my friend and co-author Professor Amin Kazak in the United States has enriched my life. Through the years of building mutual trust, I have been inspired by his ability to see beyond our differences. There is no question that our friendship is a blessing that I immensely treasure and enjoy.

I hold no animosity towards the Palestinian people and truly believe that Palestinians deserve a homeland of their own. However, I am not willing to sacrifice the security of Israel in order to realize the establishment of a Palestinian state.

As you will read, I believe Israel is vital to the survival of the Jewish people.

I embrace this opportunity to deliver what I believe to be the deep-seated essence of the conflict. I believe that Israelis and Palestinians continue to be at odds—first and foremost—because they do not understand each other. For good reason, they—we—hold perceptions about history that are not only different but fuel prolonged animosity.

Without understanding and respecting the perceptions of others, we cannot move forward. And that is exactly what we need to do.

This cooperative venture has only been possible because Amin and I agree to disagree. We appreciate each other's perceptions—which for all practical purposes—represent our realities.

We don't try to convince each other that one side is right and the other is wrong. Instead, we strive to understand each other's hopes and dreams while understanding the past and present difficulties for both our peoples.

Israelis and Jews know they cannot speak for all their people. I have done my best to portray the views of most of us. Opinion polls taken in Israel regularly validate that the vast majority of Israelis are willing to give up land for peace. We are eager to move the peace process forward and to establish a Palestinian state along the borders of Israel. With guarantees of security, I know that Israel is a trustworthy partner for peace.

Of course, much work still needs to be done to heal both cultures from past hostilities.

I dedicate this book to the blessed memory of my father, Eliyahu Gabbay.

I also dedicate this book to my children, Gabrielle and Daniel, and all children of the Middle East. When I look into their eyes, I'll continue to promise them that I will leave no stone unturned in the pursuit of peace.

PREFACE | AMIN KAZAK

I am a proud American who values and upholds the responsibilities of American citizenship. While living this American dream, my Palestinian roots deep inside of me cry out for a better life for *all* Palestinians.

Therefore, my story is dedicated to Palestinians everywhere.

I also dedicate this story to my father, Moustapha Kazak, who spent the last stage of his long life yearning to return to his land and the land of his ancestors—the land of Palestine. Like many Palestinians, my father was forced to flee Palestine and give up his land after losing the war against the Zionist Jews, who declared their own state of Israel in my homeland in 1948. It was a profoundly painful experience that my father never forgot.

The loss of Palestine was al-Naqba—a catastrophe for the Palestinian people. But my father differed from many others because he believed that non-violence was the only legitimate path towards justice for the Palestinians. Therefore, although believing in the Palestinian struggle, my father never engaged in armed conflict against the Jews in Palestine.

Moustapha Kazak was a pacifist and member of the *Shazuliya*, a Sufi group founded by Imam Shadhili from northeast Africa. The *Shazuliya* (or *Shadhiliya*) is a Sufi *Tariqa* (the way or path to reach God) that does not preach isolationism from other segments of society. Instead, *al-Tariqa al-Shazulia* permits all its members to enjoy life, believing in the principles of tolerance and peaceful coexistence even with enemies. My father was strongly influenced by this philosophy.

Although I was deeply influenced by my father's religious beliefs and principles, I have evolved into a secular, non-religious man. None-the-less, I inherited much of what I believe today—that tolerance and non-violence are the only authentic means of resolving the conflict between Palestinians and Israelis—from my father. The principles of *al-Shazuliya* have had a profound impact on me. That's why I dedicate my story to the memory of my father.

I must admit there were times during my life when I doubted whether non-violence could achieve Palestinian freedom. The burdensome memories I carried from my childhood, including my escape from war in Haifa and my formative years in a Palestinian refugee camp—were difficult to reconcile and completely abandon. The hatred I felt against the Zionist Jews then, remains palpable. Like everyone around me I blamed the Jews for my family's poverty and statelessness. I resented Israelis for stealing my homeland and I hated them for not letting us return to our families' homes in the beautiful land of the Carmel Hills outside of Haifa where my established and well-to-do, large Palestinian family had lived for centuries.

I questioned, why did the Jews insist on settling in Palestine? I didn't agree with the Zionist argument that Palestine was part of a Jewish state a thousand years ago, as the concept of nationalism and states began in modern times and does not apply to Zionist claims. I do agree that a Jewish (Hebrew) dynasty existed during the second century BCE in the land of Canaan (historically known later as Palestine). But many other dynasties ruled the land of Canaan. To me, the Zionist rights to the Holy Land stem from fallacious, and unsubstantial arguments.

Meeting Professor Shaul Gabbay in Denver has changed my perspective over the past eight years. Before working together with him, I had never worked with a Jewish person. Although it has taken us some time to develop trust between us, we realize our subsequent friendship represents the possibilities for peace between our peoples. Through lengthy discussions, it has become quite clear that our goals for our children are the same. We both want an end to the conflict and peaceful coexistence.

Working together has allowed me to see beyond our differences, that are clear from our contradictory opinions about the past. Recognizing that our interpretations of history reside on both sides of the conflict, we see no other way than to see our future "beyond" the conflict.

Nurtured by my father's love and his peaceful convictions, I have come to accept that the only solution to the Israeli-Palestinian conflict—for both people—is coexisting, side-by-side, shoulder-to-shoulder, in one state and one land.

I hope that my efforts in writing *One Land Two Stories* will allow my father's soul to rest in peace.

ONE LAND
TWO STORIES

INTRODUCTION

On November 29, 1947, amid dark shadows of World War II and the Holocaust, the United Nations voted to partition the Holy Land into two nations—one for the Jewish people and one for the Palestinians. As Jews crowded into the streets of Tel Aviv, shouts of jubilation were heard worldwide.

At that same moment, millions of Palestinians from the Holy Land wept over the political seizure of their homeland. Once again they were a people dispossessed by foreign powers.

Jews refer to the creation of Israel as a miracle.

The Palestinians call it al-Naqba—the disaster.

One Land Two Stories explores the Israeli-Palestinian conflict through the contrasting narratives of Professors Shaul Gabbay and Amin Kazak. Gabbay, an Israeli, and Kazak, a Palestinian, are natural adversaries by birth, by definition and by experience—yet they have forged a close friendship without surrendering their individual political convictions or mutual hopes for a peaceful resolution.

Kazak was born in Haifa during the British Mandate of Palestine. At age six, during Israel's 1948 War of Independence, he became a Palestinian refugee. His family crossed the border into Lebanon, which granted them the negligible status of refugees, and spent his formative years dispossessed and stateless in an impoverished UN refugee camp.

"We had a series of temporary residences," he says. "It was hard. I lived in troubled surroundings. Unable to go home weighed heavily on our hearts." Kazak, who never fought for his country because there was no country to defend, pursued his doctorate at the American University in Beirut in his 30's.

Gabbay is the son of Jewish refugees who were evicted from Arab countries.

In stark contrast to his stateless colleague, his coming of age in the Jewish homeland filled him with a profound sense of belonging and pride. As a 21-year-old commander in the Israel Defense Forces, he fought in the 1982 Lebanon War. He saw friends die. Youthful idealism transformed into a commitment to pursue peace.

During the Lebanon War, Gabbay and Kazak, unknowingly, were just a few blocks away from each other on either side of the Beirut Museum Alley checkpoint. Strangers separated by circumstance and antithetical ideologies, fate inevitably brought them face-to-face at the University of Denver in 2003.

Gabbay and Kazak endlessly discussed and debated the eternal Arab-Israeli struggle—but they didn't stop there. The professors decided to teach their divergent historical narratives in tandem to undergraduate and graduate students.

One Land Two Stories was inspired by lessons taught and learned inside these academic borders. Demonstrating mutual respect and great civility, these two educators left indelible life-lessons in the hearts and minds of their students. "No matter what content they remember, we know that students will always remember a Palestinian and an Israeli teaching together to encourage greater understanding," Gabbay says.

The book, which untangles Kazak's pro-Palestinian and Gabbay's pro-Israeli narratives, traverses personal, religious, cultural and historical dimensions. Well-researched and documented, the professors delineate the history of their people. The reader will note early on that their interpretations of identical events present two very different stories.

One Land Two Stories is neither a comprehensive history of the Israeli-Palestinian conflict nor an exhaustive geopolitical analysis. The authors have

INTRODUCTION

no agenda to prove each other wrong. They know that archives are laden with one-sided analyses of this well-researched and documented conflict.

This book is for readers who are willing to explore two distinct and divergent narratives of two peoples, both of whom claim the Holy Land as their own. Presented in historical order, readers have an opportunity to explore the "truth" as perceived by Israelis and Palestinians—one epoch at a time, side-by-side. Soon, readers will notice that the truth about the historical record is in the eye of the beholder. And, in this case, the truth does not align. Hence, there are two stories.

Although Gabbay and Kazak possess opposing viewpoints, they have agreed to disagree—and therein lies the genesis of decency among these professors. By acknowledging each other's truth, even though it contradicts their own, they have moved beyond the conflict into mutual respect and friendship. Within this amiable framework, these men continue to pursue peaceful co-existence.

"In order to understand the ongoing conflict between our people, we must know what each side perceives to be the truth," Gabbay says. "Only then can we achieve peace."

"It all starts," Kazak affirms, "with two human beings."

One land. Two peoples.

It is an ancient land divided by politics and faith, where thousands have died for their beliefs over the millennia, and where the monotheistic religions with the same ancient roots continue to spar over the same ground and remnants of the same sacred sites.

Jews believe God promised the Land to Abraham, Isaac and Jacob. This "Promised Land" was the land of the ancient Israelites. Beginning more than a century ago, European Zionist settlers reversed 2,500 years of Jewish exile and immigrated to this scrubby desert crossroads. In 1948, they declared it to be Israel, the modern home of the Jews. In the six decades since, Israel has fought seven wars with its Arab neighbors over the sovereignty and security of the Jewish homeland, including their capital city, Jerusalem.

Palestinians consider the same land to be the homeland of their ancestors. Jerusalem and its surroundings contain some of Islam's holiest sites, including the rock from where Muhammad ascended to visit heaven. Now, millions of Palestinians find themselves without their own state, dispersed from the land they called home for thousands of years. In recent decades, they have relied both on the military intervention by Arab states and their own insurrections against Israel to secure their own future, with little to show for it.

Being an Israeli Jew

I am a citizen of Israel.

I believe in the God of my ancestors. The Land of Israel belongs to the Jewish people—my people—because thousands of years ago God promised the land directly to our patriarchs: Abraham, Isaac, and Jacob. The Jewish Bible, the Torah, was granted by God to the Jewish people at Mt. Sinai through Moses, who taught Judaism to the Israelites when he led them out of slavery in Egypt to the "Promised Land" of Israel more than 3,000 years ago.

For me, it is as simple as that.

Of course, in practice it is far more complicated and it has been particularly so since the creation of the modern State of Israel.

Jewish History

When the Israelites were freed from Egyptian slavery and settled in the Land of Israel more than 3,000 years ago, they lived in tribes scattered throughout the land, with Jerusalem as their capital. For generations their leaders were known as the Judges. Between 1020–586 BCE, 44 Jewish kings led the Israelites. Shaul, my namesake, King Saul was the first King of Israel followed by the Kingdom of David which flourished between approximately 1010 and 970 BCE. King Solomon (David's son) built the first Jewish Holy Temple in 827 BCE on the Temple Mount in Jerusalem, the site considered by Jews to be the most sacred place on earth.[1]

In 586 BCE, this Temple was destroyed by conquering Babylonians who exiled most of the Jews of Israel into slavery in Mesopotamia. Within a century, the Second Temple was rebuilt on the same holy ground when a new King of Persia, Cyrus the Great, encouraged the Jews of Babylonia to return to the Holy Land and reconstitute their Jewish way of life in Jerusalem. For approximately 600 years, Jews lived in Jerusalem and comprised the majority of the population. In 70 CE, the final devastation occurred when the Romans destroyed the Second Jewish Holy Temple, sending the majority of Jews into an approximate 2,000-year period of exile known as the "Diaspora."

The main remnant of the Temple complex left standing above ground today is the Western Wall, commonly referred to by Jews as the Wailing Wall. Throughout history, including today, Jews from around the world can be found every day, all day long, praying to God at the Wall while continuing the custom of writing notes of requests to God and placing them in the cracks of this sacred fortification of the ancient Temple.

Holy Jewish Sites Replaced by Muslims

Today the Islamic Dome of the Rock shrine sits directly upon the Temple Mount. Adjacent to the Dome is the al-Aqsa Mosque, where Muslims pray five times a day. How did this happen? When Muhammad and his Muslim followers conquered the land of "non-believers," it was customary for them to destroy the sacred sites of others, like the Holy Jewish Temple, and build mosques on the identical site. Therefore, when Jerusalem was captured in 638 by Muslim Caliph Umar, the Dome of the Rock was intentionally built upon the Temple Mount where it stands today. Another way to explain this phenomenon is to realize that three Abrahamic faiths sanctify the same sites. Jesus Christ was a Jew who revered sites of ancient Judaic significance, just as Muhammad revered Jewish and Christian figures as Islamic prophets.

By virtue of this commonality, one can understand the significance of Jerusalem to all three religions. It is clear that conflict has occurred throughout the ages because changing powers have often claimed supremacy and/or exclusivity to holy sites, fomenting hostilities between groups who have often denied each others' ties to the land of their ancestors.

Gazing upon Jerusalem from the surrounding hilltops, one quickly comprehends the roots of the conflict: three different religions consider the exact same physical sites as sacred to their faiths. For example, most visitors to Jerusalem are struck by the beauty of the gold Islamic Dome of the Rock standing prominently above the Jewish Wailing Wall.

Jews Respect the Holy Sites of All Faiths

Jews acknowledge, accept and affirm Jerusalem's historic and religious significance for all: Jews, Christians, and Muslims. We pride ourselves on protecting all religious sites and allowing access to them by people of all faiths. What Jews worry about is that if and when Jewish sites are transferred to Arab or Muslim jurisdiction, Jews will be forbidden from praying at these Jewish holy sites—including the Western Wall.

This concern is based on what happened to the Jewish people after the establishment of the State of Israel. When Jordan seized Jerusalem at the beginning of the 1948 War

1 | The Western Wall (Wailing Wall) and directly above the al-Aqsa Mosque and Dome of the Rock

of Independence, Arabs immediately destroyed 58 synagogues in the Jewish section of the Old City. While under Jordanian rule from 1948 to 1967, Jews were prohibited from entering the Old City of Jerusalem and barred from the sacred Temple Mount and Wailing Wall. In other words, for the first 19 years of Israel's existence, Jews could not enter the Old City of Jerusalem and they could not pray at its most sacred site.

When one considers the division of Jerusalem to establish peace with the Palestinians, it is important to envision the potential result. Palestinians demand control over East Jerusalem and want to establish East Jerusalem as their capital city. They are demanding jurisdiction over

2 | President Obama submitting prayer into the Western Wall, July 23, 2008, when he was a Senator

the Old City of Jerusalem. From our recent experience, Jews know that if Jerusalem is ever to be divided again, the result would most likely restrict or prohibit Jewish access to the Old City, the Wailing Wall and the Temple Mount. For most Jews, this concession is impossible and non-negotiable. Therefore, the final status of Jerusalem remains a contentious issue for Israelis and Palestinians.

Denial of Jewish Heritage

Today, there are organized campaigns that deny Jewish claims and access to Jewish holy sites. As recently as October 2010, Jews were appalled when the Palestinian Authority and the United Nations Educational, Scientific and Cultural Organization (UNESCO) declared that Rachel's Tomb in Hebron was not considered an authentic Jewish site. UNESCO stated that the tomb of our Jewish matriarch, Rachel, is instead a solely Muslim historical site called the Bilel Ibn-Bilel Mosque. The denial of the Jewish historical claim to Rachel's gravesite is disrespectful and destructive to my people.

UNESCO's denial of Jewish heritage is but one indication of the bias against Israel within the United Nations, where 48 out of 56 nations voted in favor of removing Rachel's Tomb from Israel's list of Jewish heritage sites. At the same time of this declaration, UNESCO also demanded that Israel remove its claim over Ma'arat Ha-Machpelah. As will be

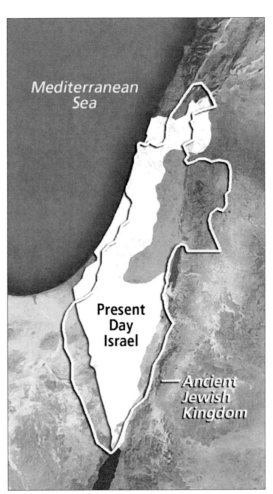

Map 1 | Ancient Jewish Kingdom

described later, Ma'arat Ha-Machpelah is the Cave of the Patriarchs in Hebron, purchased by Abraham as a family burial site. As chronicled in the Torah, this sacred cave is where Abraham, Isaac and Jacob and their wives Sarah, Rebecca and Leah are buried.

While Israelis respect the religious significance of Muslims' sacred sites, we refuse to allow others to deny our heritage, including our claim to Rachel's Tomb, Ma'arat Ha-Machpelah and the Temple Mount. Therefore, we refute the declaration of UNESCO and anyone else who attempts to deny the historical record of our Jewish ancestors.

Denial of our historical attachment to the Holy Land is being used by Israel's enemies to restrict Jewish access to, and negate the significance of, ancient Jewish ties to the Land of Israel. Many Muslims contend that the Jewish Temple never existed.

Nothing can be further from the truth. In my opinion, these attempts at erasing Jewish history, including measures sanctioned by the United Nations, create adversarial positions that drive further wedges between our peoples rather than advancing paths towards peace.

Jewish Ties to Israel

There are approximately 13.5 million Jewish people in the world today. They account for less than one-fifth of one percent of the world's population. Jews trace their heritage to biblical times in the Middle East between 3,500 and 5,000 years ago. Jewish kingdoms, which lasted for more than 10 centuries, included those of King David and Solomon. These empires not only stretched across Israel's current boundaries, the West Bank, and Gaza but sections of Jordan, Lebanon, Syria and Iraq as well. Although not consecutive, the reign of these Jewish kingdoms lasted for nearly a millennium.

While Jews around the world share a common religious heritage, they are not bound by similar practices. Instead, they are individuals in communities living on different continents, subject to different governments and cultures, climates and landscapes. Yet despite this diversity, they are all tied to the Land of Israel. Some have family members living in Israel today. Others are attached through deep historical and religious threads. To understand the various Jewish viewpoints about our homeland, I have categorized them into four perspectives: religious, historical, national and existential.

Religious–Biblical Ties

I am a religious Jew. Obviously, I share the religious perspective. At the core of Judaism is our faith in God, our study of Jewish history as spelled out in the Torah and other primary Jewish texts, and our adherence to Jewish values, norms, and laws.[2]

Jewish history, along with our social and spiritual values and norms, is meticulously chronicled in the Jewish Bible. The ultimate sacred text is the Torah, also known as the Five Books of Moses, and referred to by Christians as the Old Testament. The Torah is written and preserved exactly as it was thousands of years ago—on scrolls made of parchment. They can be found in every synagogue, (Jewish house of worship) throughout the world.

3 | Shaul Gabbay, age 13, at the Wailing Wall for his Bar Mitzvah, 1974

4 | Shaul Gabbay reads from the Torah for his Bar Mitzvah

The Torah elucidates the history and moral laws of the Jewish people. Additional sources of Judaic laws and values include such sacred texts as the books of the prophets, the Kings and the Writings. Important Jewish insights can be found in the Talmud, and the Midrash.

The Land of Israel is referred to in the Bible as Eretz Yisrael, Zion and Yirushalayim (Jerusalem). There are 809 references in the Jewish Bible to the Land of Israel and Jerusalem, signifying the divine Jewish connection to the land.[3]

For the Jewish people, Israel and Jerusalem are sacred and synonymous. The Land of Israel is inseparable from Judaism. In contrast, the Quran does not mention Jerusalem or Israel verbatim even once.

Promises in the Torah to the Jewish Patriarchs Abraham, Isaac and Jacob

The origin of the Israelites began with the Jewish patriarch Abraham, who was born 4,000 years ago in Ur, a Middle Eastern town along the Euphrates River in what is now modern day Iraq. The prevailing religions in the period when Abraham lived included polytheism, paganism and idolatry. Before Abraham, a monolithic faith—the belief in one God—did not exist.

Abraham

In the Book of Genesis, the first book of the Torah, we learn that God selected Abraham and told him that he was to become the leader of a great nation that would become a light among nations. God spoke to Abraham and told him to go to Canaan, "a land which I will show you, and there I will make you the father of a great nation . . . I will bless you and make your name great."[4]

Following God's instruction, Abraham left the comfortable land of his birth and embarked on the journey through the Fertile Crescent to Canaan, which is today's Israel. The stories of Abraham's life in Israel are written in great detail. These details provided followers of Judaism with descriptive maps of the Land of Israel and intricate narratives of Abraham's family and his travels.

Most importantly, Jewish scripture offers evidence of God's intention to grant the Promised Land to Abraham and his descendants.

God frequently spoke to Abraham about the Land of Israel, telling him that the Jewish people would inherit the land for eternity and that in this divinely-granted parcel of earth the Jewish people would become a great nation. "Lift up now your eyes, and look from the place where you are northward, and southward, and eastward, and westward: For all the land which you see, to you will I give it, and to your seed forever."[5]

5 | Torah scroll

6 | Genesis 12:1–3 Hebrew

The Promised Land is geographically described in Gen. 15:18: "Unto your seed have I given this land, from the river of Egypt unto the great river, the river Euphrates."

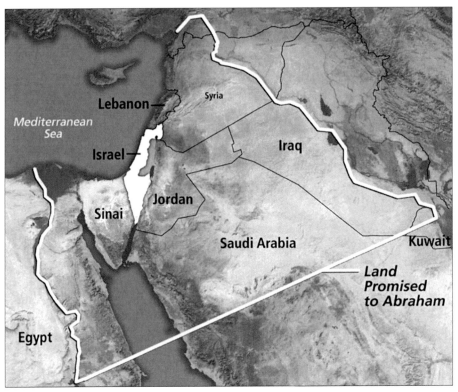

Map 2 | Land promised to Abraham in Genesis 15:18

In addition, God promised to bless the Jewish people in Israel and watch over them forever:

> And I will give unto you and to your seed after you, the land where you are a stranger, all the land of Canaan, for an everlasting possession; and I will be their God."[6]

For Jews, these ancient biblical writings designate our right to this land and our legitimacy as a Jewish nation.

We can trace Abraham's journeys in the Torah. Abraham traveled to many places which remain important to Jews today. He went to Shechem, which now is Nablus in the West Bank and is presently governed by the Palestinian Authority. He went to Jerusalem, which remains the Jewish capital. And he settled in Hebron, another city in the West Bank. It was in Hebron where Abraham bought a cave called Ma'arat Ha-Machpelah and buried his wife, Sarah. Subsequently Ma'arat Ha-Machpelah also became the burial site of Abraham himself as well as his sons Isaac and Jacob, and their wives Leah and Rebecca.

7 | Ma'arat Ha-Machpelah

Jews consider Ma'arat Ha-Machpelah in Hebron to be the second holiest Jewish site on Earth after the Temple Mount in Jerusalem. Since the Palestinian Authority currently maintains jurisdiction over Hebron, access to Abraham's burial site is difficult for Jews. As previously discussed, in 2010 the United National Educational, Scientific and Cultural Organization (UNESCO), declared Ma'arat Ha-Machpelah to be a Muslim holy site, thus denying a Jewish connection to Ma'arat Ha-Machpelah.

Today, Israelis and tourists can visit this significant gravesite under the protection of Israeli guards. If they go unaccompanied, they do so at great risk to their safety. A rabbi in Denver recently told me, "When I was single, I was willing to take the risk of visiting Ma'arat Ha-Machpelah in Hebron in order to visit the holy gravesites of our patriarchs and matriarchs. Now that I am a father, I do not feel that I can take that risk."

Monotheism

The covenant between Abraham and God initiated the beginning of monotheism. Promising to renounce the practices of paganism and idolatry, Abraham is recognized as the first monotheist, a believer in one, singular God. Today, Abraham's monotheism is considered to be the cornerstone of the three Abrahamic faiths; Judaism, Christianity and Islam.

Monotheism is a widespread spiritual practice today, but it was revolutionary in Abraham's time.

Isaac

Abraham's wife Sarah had remained childless. When she was 76, well past her natural child-bearing years, she and Abraham decided to use a surrogate to continue the Jewish legacy. Sarah chose her Egyptian maidservant, Hagar, to be the surrogate mother. Hagar gave birth to Ishmael, Abraham's first son.

Fourteen years later, at the age of 90, Sarah miraculously conceived and gave birth to Isaac. Abraham was 100 years old. The Torah teaches us that Sarah was suspicious of Ishmael because she foresaw future conflicts between the two half-brothers.

To protect Isaac, Sarah convinced Abraham to send both Hagar and Ishmael away from their household. Abraham, who disagreed with Sarah's suspicion about Ishmael's nature, did not want to banish his firstborn son. God intervened and encouraged Abraham to heed Sarah's wishes: "Listen to her (Sarah's) voice in all that she tells you. It is through Isaac that you will gain posterity."[7]

Isaac became the second patriarch of the Jewish people, following his father. He also had a personal relationship with God who promised him the inheritance of the Land of Israel, and the establishment of a great nation there. "And the Lord appeared to him (Isaac)… and said I am the God of Abraham your father: fear not, for I am with you, and will bless you, and multiply your seed for my servant Abraham's sake."[8]

In the Torah, we read that Abraham's faith was ultimately tested when God instructed him to sacrifice his son Isaac. The story is told in great detail. Right before Abraham was to perform the sacrifice, God intervened and stopped the process. Isaac's life was spared and God's trust in Abraham's complete devotion was sealed.

Consequently, Hagar and Ishmael were ordered to leave Abraham's house. When they arrived in the Negev desert, God spoke to Hagar, who felt frightened and betrayed. God comforted her and promised that her son would *also* become the leader of a great nation.

Jews believe that Ishmael received the blessing from God to lead the Arab Nation. From an Israeli perspective, Ishmael and his 12 sons became the Ishmaelites, who were destined to lead the Arab people.

The Torah does not mention much more about the life of Ishmael except that he reunited much later with Isaac when they both buried their father Abraham in Ma'arat Ha-Machpelah.

Jacob

Jacob, Isaac's son, and Abraham's grandson, is the third Jewish patriarch. God also promised him blessings of wealth and national greatness for himself and his descendants. In Genesis, God gave Jacob his new name, "Israel," and from that point on the "Promised Land" was referred to as the "Land of Israel."

God spoke to Jacob, saying, "Your seed shall be as the dust of the earth, and you shall spread abroad to the west, and to the east, and to the north, and to the south: and in you and in your seed shall all the families of the earth be blessed. And, behold, I am with you, and will keep you in all places wherever you go, and will bring you again into this land; for I will not leave you…"[9]

Moses: The Exodus

Jacob and his sons moved to Egypt where they are treated well due to the fact that his son Joseph is favored by the reigning Egyptian ruler. However, over the years, a subsequent Pharaoh of Egypt turned on the Jews and forced them into slavery, an oppression endured by the Israelites for several centuries.

Most Westerners are familiar with the story of Moses for he was the Jewish leader chosen by God to lead the Israelites from slavery in Egypt to the Promised Land. Moses taught the Israelites the principles of their faith, which he received from God at Mount Sinai.

In the book of Exodus, the Torah chronicles the life of Moses and God's selection of him to free the Israelite slaves from more than 400 years of slavery in Egypt. Following their exodus, Moses led the Israelites across the Red Sea, through the desert, to the Land of Israel. Their journey took forty years of wandering in the desert. Moses and the oldest generation of Israelites did not enter the Promised Land. However, God

8 | Jew with Torah at Wailing Wall

was always with the Israelites saying, "And I will bring you into the land which I swore to give to Abraham, Isaac, and Jacob; and I will give it to you as a heritage..."[10]

Today's Torah

The Torah is studied and read today just as it was in ancient times. No matter where a Jew resides in the world, the practices and customs derived from the Torah are parallel. Daily Jewish prayers include reverence for Eretz Yisrael (the Land of Israel.) Prayers asking God for peace in Israel are recited morning, noon and night.

When Jewish people pray, they are supposed to cover their heads and face Jerusalem. In my home in the United States I know in which direction I should pray, and when I go to a synagogue all of the congregants face Jerusalem. However, when I travel, it's not always apparent to me which direction faces Jerusalem. Therefore, when I travel, I always carry a compass so I can face Jerusalem when I pray. When I am in Israel, I face Jerusalem—more specifically, the Wailing Wall. I also always carry a "kippah" (the Jewish head-covering also called a "yalmulkah") in my right pocket so I am prepared to pray properly no matter where I am.

From these examples, one can see that for traditional Jews like me, the biblical ties to the modern State of Israel are fundamental and unbreakable. We believe that the land belongs to us because God gave it to our ancestors. We believe the creation of the State of Israel in 1948 was a modern miracle, one that God intended, created and delivered thousands of years after he first told Abraham to go there. Moreover, we also believe that despite the existential challenges to the survival of the Jewish State throughout its history, divine intervention has been on Israel's side due to God's promise to always protect the Jewish people. And because of this scriptural link spanning millennia, it is up to every one of us, including me, to live according to God's laws and to build, protect and preserve Israel for future generations.

9 | Shaul Gabbay wearing Jewish tallit and kippah

Secular Jews: Historical-Cultural Ties

Not all Jews are religious Jews. This was not the case before the 19th century, when all Jews lived observant lives. The Jews I am describing in this section are secular Jews. They do not necessarily adhere to all Jewish laws and they may not believe the words in the Torah were delivered from God. I refer to this group as secular Jews with historical and cultural ties to Israel. They typically do not defend the legitimacy of the State of Israel by invoking the argument that God gave the land to the Jewish people.

However, their lack of adherence to strict religious practices does not weaken their attachment to the State of Israel. Secular Jews typically see the legitimacy of the existence of Israel through ties other than the Torah. Instead, they cite academic evidence accumulated through scholarship in the social sciences: history, anthropology, sociology and archeology. These Jews are connected to Israel because it is where their ancestors lived and thrived until being exiled by one foreign power after another. Instead of claiming their rights to Israel based on the Torah and covenants granted by God, these Jews respect their lineage as a distinctive, tenacious and religious people. They carry forward an indelible connection to the homeland of their ancestors and they have maintained Jewish traditions and culture for thousands of years despite extreme hardships, not the least of which is having been dispersed throughout the world.

Nationalism—Modern Israelis

For the six million Jewish citizens in the State of Israel, (out of 7.5 million Israelis) Israel *is* their home. (Twenty-four percent of Israeli citizens are non-Jews. Twenty percent are Arabs. Seventeen percent are Muslim. Four percent are Christian.) Someone like me, who was born a "sabra" (an Israeli-born Jew) grew up with an affinity for the land, the country and all that it represents. We are proud to be a fully functioning democracy in the Middle East, a region that is now bubbling with uprisings against non-representative rulers. We take our responsibilities as a safe haven for all Jews worldwide very seriously by embracing the return of Jews to the Land of Israel. From a very young age we learn that the foundation of the State of Israel rests on two principles: security for the Jewish people worldwide, and the ingathering of the Jewish people to Israel.

As modern nationalists, we defend our right to live freely and securely in a region consisting of 25 Arab countries and territories on two continents with a combined population of 358 million people. While we are thankful today to have peace treaties with Egypt and Jordan, we do not take peace for granted because we realize our region is not politically stable, nor is it cohesively democratic. Our hopes and prayers are that we will one day be able to live in peace with *all* of our neighbors, most importantly, with the Palestinian people.

As I've grown older, and especially now that I live in the United States, I realize that being born a "sabra" gives me a unique affinity for the land. My parents were from Bagdad and Aden (now Yemen). If they did not have a safe haven—a Jewish homeland—to escape to in the middle of the 20th century, I may never have been born.

Existential Threat

When I teach my students about the importance of the Land of Israel to the Jewish people, I describe it using a combination of examples from the biblical, historical, and nationalist perspectives—but I don't stop there. It is impossible to describe the feelings Jews have toward Israel today without understanding the scars carved into the Jewish psyche because of thousands of years of spiritual, cultural and physical persecution culminating in the horrors of the Holocaust.

The world changed following World War II. In the United States, our "greatest generation" fought an evil enemy and won. As a result it gained superpower status militarily and economically, a position which it still retains today.

But for Jewish people, the world did not merely change. The Jewish world was indelibly transformed by the Holocaust. Out of nine million European Jews, six million Jews were murdered—that's virtually equal to the entire Jewish population of the State of Israel today. The number of victims is so extraordinary that it is difficult for others to grasp and,

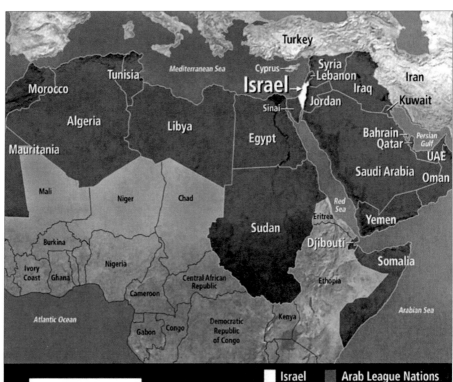

Israel   Arab League Nations

California
158,302 sq. mi.

Israel would fit into the state of California more than 19 times.

Israel's Size Compared to Arab World

- Israel's territory is 8,019 square miles
- Israel's land mass is about 1/625
  (1/6 of 1 percent the size of the Arab World)
- 5.5 million Israeli Jews; 300 million Middle Eastern Arabs and Muslims

World Religions

Christianity..............2 billion people
Islam........................1.3 billion people
Hinduism.................900 million people
Buddhism................260 million people
Judaism ....14 million people

Map 3 | Israel and its neighbors

consequently, some have difficulty understanding why this tragedy is such a core issue for Jews worldwide. Yet for us, the specter of annihilation is very real. Why? Because it happened to us in modern times and it was perpetrated by Germany, a country with one of the most advanced societies of the 20th century.

Those who are not Jewish may have difficulty understanding this. The human cost was so high and the methods so cruel that the specter of total annihilation became a reality engraved deep in the psyche of Jewish people.

10 | Mass grave, Bergen-Belsen

Sheer numbers do not adequately explain this fear of extinction. The proximity of this genocide is equally unsettling. This is not a dark chapter relegated to a history book on the library shelf. Nor was it carried out by a few ignorant or psychotic zealots in some far-off place centuries ago. This is not like the Spanish Inquisition, the Dark Ages, or the 11th century Crusades where Jews were murdered because of their religious beliefs. Nor was it like the pogroms of agrarian Czarist Russia in the 19th century.

The Holocaust happened less than 70 years ago. Adolf Hitler rose to power in part because the majority of people in the 20th century's most educated and advanced societies agreed with him. Even if they did not personally kill Jews, they did not object to his use of Jews as scapegoats for Germany's ills or his plan to systematically exterminate Jewish people.

The Holocaust was executed not only by soldiers, but also with the complicity of judges, doctors, lawyers, university professors, shopkeepers, engineers, elementary school teachers and citizens in all walks of life. Those who didn't explicitly carry out Hitler's Final Solution supported his plans either through action or by remaining silent observers. As we often say, "It takes a village to raise a child." For the Nazis to achieve this unprecedented and systematic extermination of the Jews, it took Germany's collective national consent to set the unspeakable in motion—and they nearly succeeded.

Today, the Holocaust is etched into the Jewish psyche, an indelible fact that can never be erased. We are forever thankful to the Allied Forces who defeated the Nazis in 1945. Jews realize that had the Nazis won the Second World War, world Jewry would likely have disappeared from the Earth. After seeing gruesome photos and newsreels documenting and detailing the Nazi death camps, no Jew believes that Hitler would have limited the genocide to Europe's borders.

That's why, as World War II fades into history, the Holocaust is still a living memory for the Jewish people. It is a constant reminder of our vulnerability and the need for perpetual vigilance.

Jews inhabit a new paradigm of thought and behavior now. Gone are the days when meek Jews, like

11 | Holocaust victims, Dachau

the character of Tevya in "Fiddler on the Roof," merely pray to God to deliver them from evil. Nor are Jews willing to adopt the quiet despair of the condemned souls who walked with their children "like sheep to their slaughter" in the ravines of Russia and the death camps of Eastern Europe. Today's Jews—especially Israeli Jews—are determined to protect ourselves with our own military strength to guarantee our survival. Not only Jewish survival in Israel, but Jewish survival everywhere.

Israelis in the 21st century—my people—encapsulate the commitment to protect, preserve and defend their land and their people. Our slogan is "Never again!" Whether or not they believe in God, whether or not they adhere to the beliefs and teachings of the Torah, the Jewish people will fight to the death to protect Israel as the Jewish homeland—the *only truly* safe haven for Jews around the world belonging to the Jewish people.

This defiant reality is enacted specifically through Israeli policy in the "Law of Return for Jews," which I believe is one of the most important laws in the modern State of Israel. The law entitles every Jew, regardless of where they live, to automatic citizenship in the State of Israel. It guarantees a safety net for Jews and symbolizes the collective responsibility of world Jewry to protect and defend Israel from its enemies.

So when people ask me, "Why is Israel so important to the Jews?" or "Why is Israel such an emotional issue for the Jewish people?" I have a simple answer.

Israel is not *just* land that God promised, not *just* land where our ancestors lived, nor *just* the land of my birth. Israel personifies the actual survival of the Jewish people.

As is customary for some 18-year-old Israeli men and women who enter the Israeli Defense Forces, our graduation ceremony took place at the top of a natural fortress called Masada, across from the Dead Sea.

During the first century CE, Romans surrounded the Jews at Masada, who had fled to this elevated natural fortress to protect themselves from the slaughter. When they realized there was no chance of escape, the Jews of Masada committed suicide, as a free people, rather than surrender to the Romans.

As the sun rose over Masada on my graduation from basic training in 1982, my entire unit simultaneously chanted, "Masada will not fall again!" We felt a deep bond with our ancestors of 2,000 years ago and pledged to defend modern-day Israel from all its enemies.

We shall never break this pledge.

12 | Israel Defense Force flies over Auschwitz, 2003

13 | March of the Living, Auschwitz, takes place yearly, to remember those who perished in the Holocaust.

Being a Palestinian

I am a Palestinian refugee.

I was born in Haifa, Palestine, just a few years before the establishment of Israel in 1948. I embrace the beauty of the ancient Islamic traditions and culture in which I was raised. The fabric of my personality and character is imbued with the traditions of my people. But I also bear contemporary scars that remind me of my status as a political refugee.

While I am an Arab, a Palestinian, a Muslim and a refugee, first and foremost I consider myself to be a secular intellectual. Personally, politically and ideologically, I am committed to forwarding an understanding of peace between Israelis and Arabs. Although I greatly respect the personal religious beliefs of all others, I strongly feel that the administration of religious beliefs belongs in the hands of religious leaders, not political institutions. The ongoing use of religion for political purposes is but a divisive tool that prevents peace in the Holy Land.

Believing in non-violence has remained one of the greatest influences imbedded within me by my father, Moustapha Kazak, who was a member of the Shazili Suni sect of Islam. The pacifist values I obtained from my father remain with me today. I also am convinced that this conflict is not only about land. Instead, I believe our struggle as Palestinian people is to gain human dignity and freedom.

For me, the story begins not in the ancient civilizations of the Euphrates or the land of Canaan. Instead, this story begins in the later years of the Ottoman Empire, which ruled the Fertile Crescent, historically known as bilad al-Sham. This area of the Middle East included Palestine, where I was born in the city of Haifa in the early 1940s during World War II.

My birth coincided with two events that shaped and influenced my thinking on wars, conflicts, and the rights of all peoples for self-determination irrespective of their origin, race or religion: World War II and the conflict between Palestinian Arabs and Jews over the land of Palestine.

As a young man, I never imagined that my childhood experiences as a refugee from my home in Palestine would culminate in a book entitled *One Land Two Stories*. The substance of this book reflects both personal aspects of my life and my commitment to find peace for the people in Palestine.

It is important to remember that until Israel was created in 1948, Palestinian Arab society was comprised of Muslims, Christians and Jews. In this simmering mix of peoples, it is often sadly forgotten that there were Palestinian Arab Jews living in the land of Palestine well before Zionist European Jews began to legally (and illegally) emigrate from Europe into Palestine under the British Mandate. In the late Ottoman period, "native" Palestinian Jews often were described as abnaa al-balad (sons of the country), compatriots or awlad al-Arab al-Yahud (Jewish sons of Arabs).[1]

14 | Christian Arabs in Jerusalem, circa 1936

During the late Ottoman era, many European Jews began storming Palestine to escape European discrimination. While these immigrants were Jews, they were considered foreigners who brandished the ideology of Zionism, which is considered a counterpart of Arabism in the land of Palestine. Consequently and naturally anti-Zionist sentiments were almost totally non-existent prior to this wave of immigration. In other words, anti-Zionist sentiments developed among Arab Palestinians due to the European Jewish wave of immigration into Palestine during the beginning of the 20th century.

It is also important to remember that when the First Palestinian Congress of February, 1919, issued its anti-Zionist manifesto rejecting the illegal Zionist immigration into the land of Palestine, it unequivocally maintained an open hand and an open heart to Arab Jews who had lived there for centuries. Arab Jews were considered native to the land of Palestine, as were the Palestinian Arab Christians and Palestinian Arab Muslims who for centuries had lived in peace side by side, harmoniously, and without hostilities. In this context I should remind the reader that the root of today's conflict between Israelis and Palestinians is not religious. Rather, it is due to the ideology of nationalism—Jewish Zionism and Palestinian Arab nationalism.

After 1948, the native Jews of Palestine co-mingled with the newly arriving Zionist Jews emigrating from Western Europe, Russia and other parts of the Middle East. Together, these Jews coalesced into a new identity. They assimilated, both native Palestinian Jews with their Diaspora cousins, and created a new definition of the so-called "native" Jewish inhabitants of Palestine.

For Palestinians, the new collective Jewish identity was a shocking and detrimental turn of events. For me it is clear that the cohesion of the Jewish identity came at the expense of the Palestinian identity that enabled native Jews, Christians and Muslims to live as neighbors and friends in the land of Palestine for centuries.

The actual moment when I realized I was a Palestinian refugee was when I was 13 and we tried to visit my uncles in Damascus, Syria. We had fled to Lebanon in 1948 to escape the Haganah, which later became the Israeli Defense Force. We always talked about going home to Haifa, and how my father would get his old job back in Palestine. But when we tried to visit my uncles, my mother said we would have to get a permit. I realized for the first time that I was not Lebanese, that I was different from my Lebanese friends who held passports and citizenship allowing them the freedom to travel. Without a passport, my family was restricted from traveling to visit our family. Suddenly, I realized that this conflict was about me.

Importance of the Land to Three Monotheistic Faiths

Throughout antiquity, the people who lived and settled in Palestine integrated the three monotheistic faiths: Judaism, Christianity and Islam. Comprised of Jews, Christians and

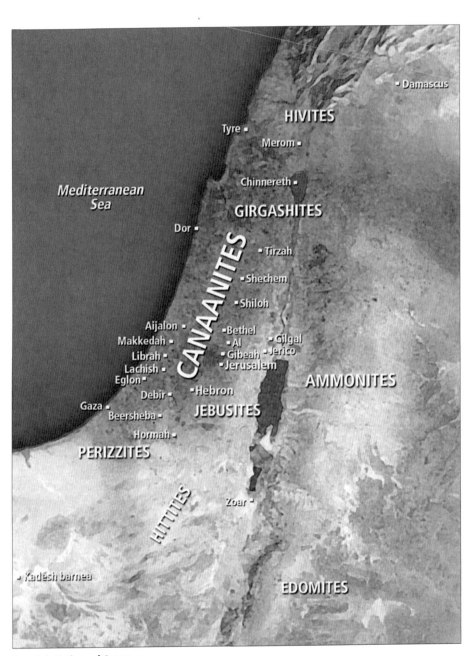

Map 4 | Nations of Canaan

Muslims alike, the people of my homeland, Palestine, proudly trace their historic roots in the land to the time of ancient Canaan. These deep religious ties to the land are equally shared. Each holy place in the land has a unique and important historical and spiritual significance, and the ancient city of Jerusalem is central to the peoples of all three monotheistic faiths. In addition to being the place where the earliest monotheistic peoples—the Jews—once lived alongside their pagan counterparts, Palestine is equally significant to modern Christians and Muslims. Jerusalem, for example, is not only the site of the persecution and death of Christ. It is home to the revered site of the prophet Muhammad's nighttime ride to Paradise. For Muslim Palestinians, Jerusalem is considered to be the third holiest site of Islam after Mecca and Medina.

The Dome of the Rock and the al-Aqsa Mosque are venerated. For Christian Palestinians, the Church of the Holy Sepulchre, the Via Dolorosa, and the Church of the Ascension are sacred holy sites. Unlike the Jewish population in Israel today, the Muslim and Christian Palestinian communities take particular pride in their once-great Arab-Islamic empire.

Unfair Citizenship Laws

It is tragic that while any Jew from any part of the world is entitled to automatic citizenship in Israel today, that right of citizenship is denied to Muslims and Christians who once actually lived in the land of Palestine and had to escape.

Muslims and Christian Arab Palestinians take great pride in their history and respective ancestral ties to the land. No one religion or ethnic group has a monopoly on these feelings. Similarly, since we all shared the land, no single group "owns" or has an entitlement to this land.

It is not my intention to refute or deny ancient Jewish claims to the land, including the Holy Land of Orchalim (Jerusalem). However, I find it imperative to repeat that no religious, historical or racial claim to the land (whether ancient or contemporary) entitles anyone to claim this land to the exclusion of anyone else. Such claims follow a slippery slope to human rights violations and an undeniable downward path toward ethnic cleansing.

The Importance of the Land for Arab Palestinians

For Arab Palestinians, Palestine is a sacred place of paramount importance. This attachment to Palestine has inspired Arab efforts to preserve control over the land throughout history. From Saladin's capture of Jerusalem during the Crusades in the 12th century to the present day, the significance of the Holy Land has been a persistent, indisputable Muslim claim. Therefore, Palestine is significant to all Muslims.

The Integration of Islam

Although the Islamic religion began following the life and teachings of the prophet Muhammad, the religion encompasses teachings of previous prophets shared by Judeo-Christian theology. For instance, Muslims believe the original prophet and patriarch was Abraham whose descendants were Ishmael and Isaac.

Muslims believe that Abraham established the city of Mecca where he and Ishmael built the Kaaba according to God's will. The Kaaba is a sanctuary built more than 4,000 years ago where many believe Adam lived with Eve in the Garden of Eden. Today all Muslims turn toward Mecca and the Kaaba when they pray five times a day.

Nearly 20 percent of the world's population, more than a billion people, are followers of Islam which dictates not only their faith, but their way of life.

United by their common faith, Muslims now live across the globe. Less than 20 percent of them live in the Middle East. Most African countries are Islamic societies. Indonesia claims the world's largest population of Muslims, and many countries of the former Soviet Union are Islamic.

One of the tenets of Islam is the belief in the divine guidance of human prophets and messengers. Unlike Jews and Christians, Muslims consider Islam to be the true and final continuation of the earlier monotheistic traditions. Many key figures in the Jewish and Christian traditions are considered very important prophets of Islam. The full list of prophets of Islam is a bit contentious because different schools of Islamic thought offer different criteria for the title of "prophet." However, there are 25 prophets mentioned by name in the Quran, many of whom are integral in Judaism and Christianity. They are:

Adam
Enoch (Idris)
Noah (Nuh)
Eber (Hud)
Shail
Abraham (Ibrahim)
Ishmael
Isaac (Is'haq)
Jacob (Yaqub)
Lot (Lut)
Joseph (Yusuf)
Jethro (Shuayb)
Job (Ayyub)

Ezekiel (Dhu al-Kifl)
Moses (Musa)
Aaron (Harūn)
David (Dawud)
Solomon (Sulayman)
Elijah (Ilyas)
Elisha (al-Yasa)
Jonah (Yunus)
Zechariah
John (Yahya)
Jesus (Isa)
Muhammad

Additionally, the Quran honors other prophets who have been identified by Muslim scholars. These prophets once held prominent positions as pious men and leaders in the

Judeo-Christian tradition—and several spent the majority of their lives in Jerusalem and the surrounding land of Palestine.

For Muslims, reverence for the many prophets of Islam naturally extends to the places where they lived and died, creating a sacred tie to these sites. For example, the city of Jerusalem witnessed the life and works of the greatest prophets and messengers of God (Allah), including Dawud, Sulayman and Isa. They walked in Jerusalem's stone streets and outlying valleys.

> I prefer to use the term "God" rather than "Allah." The former offers a universally recognized understanding of the spiritual entity that is common to Judaism, Christianity and Islam. The latter, on the other hand, is simply the Arabic word for the same "God"—the God of all three faiths. In my opinion, using "Allah" mistakenly implies that Islam's conception of God differs from the other monotheistic schools of thought, which is erroneous. It can also prove detrimental for success in discussing solutions to the Israeli-Palestinian conflict.

Similarly, Mecca and Medina are important and sacred cities in Islam because of their rich historical association with the prophets Ibrahim, Ishmael and Muhammad. Historically and spiritually, the Islamic tradition embraces the land, places and monotheistic systems of religions that preceded it. Because Islam reveres and upholds the places and prophets of the Holy Land, it is easy to see why Muslims do not view the Holy Land as the exclusive property of Jews or Christians.

Like the Jews, Muslims and Christians believe that God called the Israelites the "Chosen People" and favored them in the number of prophets he gave them. In Islam, one of the earliest prophets was Ibrahim, or Abraham, who is often referred to as the father of the three monotheistic faiths. However, Islamic thought considers Abraham to be a hanif, referring to an Arabian person in pre-Islamic times known as Jahiliyya (the time of ignorance) who followed a monotheistic faith but was not Jewish or Christian.

Abraham's status is explicitly described in the Quran: "Abraham was not a Jew nor yet a Christian; but he was true in Faith, and bowed his will to Allah's (which is Islam), and he joined not gods with Allah.[2] Abraham is perceived by many to be the first monotheist. Jews see Abraham as the first Jew, but some Muslims consider Abraham to be the first Muslim.

Muslims also believe in the future Day of Judgement and in life after death. The word "Islam" in Arabic means submission, and it refers to the Muslim submission to the will of God. The Arabic name for God is Allah.

Religion plays the central role in a Muslim's life as God's law, known as Shari'a Law, dictating the way to live according to Islamic values.

The Prophet Muhammad

In 570 CE, Islamic prophet Muhammad was born in Mecca where he was raised by his uncle from the respected tribe of Quraysh. Muhammad was known for his generosity and sincerity. Due to his trustworthy disposition he was often called upon to arbitrate disputes.

Muhammad was deeply religious, and he rejected the decadence of his society. He often meditated in the Cave of Hira near Jabal al-Nur, the (Mountain of Light) near Mecca.

When Muhammad turned 40 he received his first revelation from God when the angel Gabriel delivered the teachings of the Quran directly to him. Following this divine revelation, 114 chapters (Suras) of the Quran were written by scribes 1,400 years ago. Not one word of its 114 Suras has been changed over the past 1,400 years.

The Quran instructs every Muslim to live according to God's intentions. In addition, the Quran delineates guidelines for proper human behavior for creating a just society. Muslims adhere to the "Five Pillars of Islam," which include faith, prayer, concern for the needy, self-purification and the pilgrimage to Mecca.

When Muhammad first preached the truths of the Quran in Mecca he was persecuted by non-believers. Accordingly, in 622 God commanded that he and his small group of followers leave Mecca and move to Medina, a city 260 miles north.

Years later when Muhammad returned to Mecca, he forgave his enemies and formally established Islam. During his lifetime, nearly all of Arabia had embraced the Islamic faith. The religion spread quickly. Within 100 years following Muhammad's death, Islam had spread across continents from Spain in Europe to the Far East in China as evidenced by the building of glorious mosques such as the Taj Mahal in India and the Hi Shen Mosque in China.

With the proliferation of Islam came great civilizations. Universities flourished as seeking knowledge was a cornerstone of the religion. Great advances in medicine, mathematics, physics, astronomy, geography, architecture, art, literature, and history ensued. Algebra, Arabic numerals, and the mathematical concept of zero were transmitted from Islam to medieval, Christian Europe. In addition, sophisticated instruments such as the astrolabe, the quadrant and improved navigational maps were invented, propelling the advance of European discoveries.

Abraham and Ishmael

According to Islamic tradition, Abraham was responsible for great feats of faith, and his story is well known among the followers of all three faiths, although variations exist in each religion. In the story told in the Quran, Abraham and his wife, Sarah, were very old and childless. Abraham took Hagar (Sarah's handmaiden) as his wife and soon after, Hagar gave birth to a son named Ishmael. When Ishmael was about 13 years old, Sarah, who was past her childbearing years, miraculously gave birth to her son Isaac.

Abraham took Hagar and Ishmael to Mecca to resettle them. Over his lifetime, Abraham made five trips to Mecca to visit Hagar and Ishmael, forming a connection between Jerusalem and Mecca.

Interestingly, God's command to Abraham that he sacrifice his son is a point of contention among the followers of the Abrahamic faiths. The Judeo-Christian tradition affirms that *Isaac* was the one to be sacrificed, while Muslims believe that *Ishmael*, Abraham's first-born son, was the intended sacrifice.

Moreover, there has been great disagreement among religious scholars of each faith regarding the site of the sacrifice. Some have claimed that the site was near Jerusalem, but several Muslim scholars of Islam have determined that it occurred in Mecca. However, the son was spared from death in both depictions, leading many to believe that Abraham's willingness to sacrifice his son is the *real* important issue.

From the Islamic perspective, the allegory illustrates the importance of Ishmael as the firstborn son of Abraham. According to Islam, it was Ishmael who should have inherited the Holy Land which had been given to Abraham by God.

As such, Ishmael is considered to be the patriarch of the Arabs and the righteous recipient of the land. According to ancient Arab culture, the first born of a man is the one who inherits the land of his father. Therefore, what was promised to Abraham by God naturally should have gone to Ishmael upon Abraham's death and to Ishmael's descendants after him.

Islamic Holy Sites

The Islamic tradition describes another great feat of Abraham and Ishmael that occurred on one of their journeys to Mecca. God commanded Abraham and Ishmael to build the Kaaba on the exact site where Adam had previously built the sacred house of worship. God then ordered Abraham to instruct Muslims to make a pilgrimage to the Kaaba.

The pilgrimage (hajj) to Mecca is now one of the five pillars of Islam. Muslims are expected to make this pilgrimage in their lifetime, if they are able. Also Muslims worldwide pray facing the Kaaba in Mecca as it is revered as the center of Muslim worship.

Forty years after building the Kaaba, God commanded Abraham to build a second holy shrine, which is where the al-Aqsa Mosque in Jerusalem now stands. In Islam, these stories serve not only as a connection to Jerusalem as a sacred site but also strengthen the bond between Mecca and Jerusalem for the Muslim people.

The city of Hebron is considered by many Muslims to be the fourth holiest site in Islam because the Cave of Machpelah or the Tomb of the Patriarchs (al-Haram al-Ibrahimi) is located there. It is believed that the cave is the burial site of Abraham, Isaac and Jacob, along with their wives Sarah, Rebekah and Leah. Some Muslims also espouse the idea that the cave was visited by the prophet Muhammad during his mystic night journey to Jerusalem. A shrine complex was built on top of the caves under Herod in the first century BCE, and the Crusaders constructed additions to it in the 12th century CE. Over time, the shrine was modified as control of the area changed hands among the political leaders aligned with the three monotheistic faiths.

In 1266, under the once great Arab-Islamic Empire, the al-Haram al-Ibrahimi became a mosque and an exclusively Muslim holy site—but during the 1967 Six Day War, Israeli forces seized control of Hebron and partitioned the mosque into Muslim and Jewish sections.

Beyond Hebron, a vast collection of sites that are significant to Muslims permeate the Holy Land. Although Jerusalem is the focal point, there are varied interpretations of how far the land extends in each direction. Some Muslims describe the geographic area as reaching to Damascus in the north, to the border of Sinai in the south, Jordan in the east and to the

15 | Church of the Holy Sepulchre

Gaza Strip and the Mediterranean Sea to the west. As described here, the land is replete with religiously significant sites inside and outside of Jerusalem, including Hebron and Gaza. For example, the "sacred valley of Tuwa," as it is referred to in the Quran, is near Mount Sinai in Egypt. It is believed to be the site where God called Moses to challenge Pharaoh and liberate the Israeli people. In Gaza, the Mosque of Sayyed Hashem is built around the mausoleum of its namesake, who was the great-grandfather of the Prophet Muhammad and a well-known Arab trader who died in Gaza in 637 CE. Gaza also is home to The Great Mosque (al-Omari Mosque), which is thought to stand on the site of an ancient Philistine Temple. Even the Church of the Holy Sepulchre in Jerusalem is significant to Islam. The site of Jesus' burial, it is therefore the burial site of a prophet of Islam.

Understanding the Prophet Muhammad's Night Journey

According to Islamic tradition, the Prophet Muhammad traveled from Mecca to Jerusalem in the year 619 CE in what is famously known as the Night Journey (al-Isra) and the Ascension (al-Miraj). It is written in the Quran in the Surra al-Isra, Verse 1:

> Glory to God (Allah) Who did take His servant for a Journey by night from the Sacred Mosque to the farthest Mosque, whose precincts We did bless,—in order that We might show him some of Our Signs: for He is the One Who heareth and seeth (all things).[3]

The Angel Gabriel appeared to Muhammad and led him to a white spirit horse with wings. The Angel Gabriel was bringing the revelation of the Quran to Muhammad. The spirit horse carried Muhammad and the other prophets to Jerusalem, where he met such prophets as Abraham, Moses and Jesus. From Jerusalem, Muhammad was lifted up to Heaven, where he passed through seven heavenly realms and saw many of the prophets of Islam. The Quran details how Muhammad saw Adam, Jesus and John, the son of Zachariah; Joseph, the son of Jacob; and Idris, the prophet from before the great flood. He saw Moses' older brother, Harun, and then Moses himself.

When he arrived in the seventh realm, Muhammad saw an old man seated next to the gate of Paradise, where 70,000 angels pass through each day but do not return until Judgment Day. Gabriel identified the man as Abraham, and then took Muhammad into Paradise where he spoke to God. During his meeting with God, Muhammad also learned the importance of daily prayers.

Muhammad returned to Mecca to reveal the Second Pillar of Islam—that a Muslim must pray five times each day. Another essential theological consequence of Muhammad's Night Journey was the confirmation of the coming of Judgment Day, which demonstrated the significance and existence of Heaven to believers and non-believers alike.

16 | Al-Aqsa Mosque, 1940–1946

17 | Al-Aqsa Mosque, 1898–1914

Jerusalem was already significant to Islam due to the work of the various prophets in the city before Muhammad's journey. Following Muhammad's ascension to Heaven from Jerusalem, Jerusalem became even more central to the Islamic faith as a result of this profound event. Jerusalem became known as the masjid al-Aqsa (distant sanctuary.) This distant sanctuary describes the main mosque in Jerusalem. The al-Aqsa Mosque, the place from which Muhammad ascended to Heaven, is of upmost importance to Muslims.

The Islamic tradition recognizes that Isaac's son, Jacob, was the first to construct a house of monotheistic worship on or near to the site of the al-Aqsa Mosque. In Islam, this holy site is recognized as a "mosque," although Jews consider it to be the location of their "Temple." In both cases, it was an indisputable site of worship. The al-Aqsa Mosque was originally built as a small prayer house by the Rashidun Caliph Umar. It was rebuilt and expanded by the Ummayad Caliph Abd al-Malik, and it was finally constructed by his son al-Walid around 710 CE.

The Night Journey is believed to be Prophet Muhammad's only trip to Jerusalem. This journey irrevocably connected Mecca and Jerusalem and marked Jerusalem as a holy city for all Muslims. According to Dr. Muzammil Siddiqi, former president of the Islamic Society of North America, "The Night Journey was a great miracle that Muslims believe was given to Prophet Muhammad as an honor and as a confirmation of Mecca's spiritual link with Jerusalem."

More details about the Night Journey are specifically described in the Hadith (the sayings and deeds of the prophet). The Isra begins with Muhammad resting in the Kaaba in Mecca, where he was visited by the archangel Gabriel. Gabriel presented Muhammad with the Buraq, a mythological winged steed from the heavens used to transport the prophets. Buraq delivered Muhammad to the Sacred Rock (al-Sakhrah al-Musharrafah) on what is also known to the Jews as the Temple Mount.

After this point, versions of the account and the order of events vary, but Muhammad is believed to have ascended from the Sacred Rock into heaven. After encountering earlier prophets, Muhammad was taken to the Throne of Allah, where he received instruction from Allah for Muslims to pray 50 times a day.

However, on his way down, Moses told Muhammad to go back to Allah to receive a reduction in the number of prayers because followers could never bear the burden of 50 prayers daily. After making several trips to Allah upon Moses' insistence, Muhammad received the final command of five daily prayers for the followers of Islam, which is the customary practice of Islam to this day.

Muhammad returned to Jerusalem where, according to many narratives, he led the other prophets in the prescribed prayers. Muhammad was then taken back to Mecca, where he shared the story with his followers.

Jerusalem and the First Qibla

Upon his return to Mecca, the Prophet Muhammad formally recognized the sacredness of Jerusalem. He shared God's commandment for five daily prayers (Salah), and instructed his followers to pray facing the direction of Jerusalem, thus making Jerusalem the first Qibla (direction of prayer) in Islam. The indication of Jerusalem as the direction of Muslim prayer was of enormous significance because the Qibla is regarded as the most sacred site in Islam. However, several months after Muhammad's migration (Hijra) from Mecca to Medina, a revelation changed to the Qibla from Jerusalem to the Sacred Mosque in Mecca.[4]

Most followers of Islam believe the change of the Qibla from Jerusalem to Mecca means that each faith could have its own Qibla. There is also speculation that the Jews objected to Jerusalem being shared, even then, as a city of importance to other faiths.

Hadith on Jerusalem

Further explanation of the importance of Jerusalem can be found in the Hadith. According to several Hadith, the al-Aqsa Mosque is the third holiest site for prayer. For example, a prayer in the al-Aqsa Mosque is worth 500 prayers in any other mosque. A prayer offered in the Mosque of the Prophet is equivalent to 1,000 and a prayer in the Sacred Mosque is worth 100,000 prayers. The Prophet Muhammad also preached that religious journeys should only be taken to one of the three mosques—in Mecca, Medina and Jerusalem.

From this tradition, Muslims believe visiting Jerusalem and the al-Aqsa Mosque is vital when making their pilgrimage to Mecca and Medina. Many also believe that going to Jerusalem is the one stop in the pilgrimage that will bring complete forgiveness of one's sins.

Still others believe that Jerusalem will play a pivotal role on Judgment Day. Some believe that Jerusalem will supersede Mecca and Medina and will be exalted as part of heaven. Finally, a trumpet call in Jerusalem will mark the end of the world.

Islamic Waqf

Due to the holy status of Jerusalem and the land surrounding Jerusalem, the city and the region are considered to be Islamic Waqf. The Waqf is a concept in Islamic law that is similar to a common law trust. It is seen as an inalienable religious endowment (usually of land or property) in which the use of the land and its benefits are designated by the benefactor to the inheritor forever.[5]

Dr. Siddiqi describes how Jerusalem became Islamic Waqf:

> Muslim rulers and philanthropists built many hospitals, schools, and religious centers in and around Jerusalem. They purchased land in and around the city and dedicated

it as a Waqf (endowment) for religious purposes. The whole city is virtually Waqf land that is non-salable and nontransferable.[6]

The consequence of this view is profound. Muslims could insist that nobody has the right to cede, sell, or control the land of Palestine because it is a Waqf. Though politics and economics play a crucial role in the Palestinian attachment to the land, there is no doubt that faith is a dominant and non-negotiable element. The Holy Land is established in the hearts of every Muslim, and it clearly cannot be erased or substituted.

Conclusion

Tragically, religion has been used as a divisive tool that will continue to shape the Israel-Palestine conflict on both sides. As a proponent of secularism, I feel that the sense of proprietary rights that both sides claim at the expense of the other promotes hatred rather than tolerance and peaceful coexistence. I don't espouse it; neither do I promote it.

For me, embracing my homeland is more significant than the language and manner in which I—or my Jewish neighbors—happen to pray.

Being a Palestinian, I am proud of my identity. I resonate with this poem by Palestinian Edna Yaghi:

To Those Who Torture and Oppress Me

My brethren are the doves, hummingbirds and seagulls
That fly unhindered above my sea.
I am Palestinian,
Therefore, I am.

No one can take my identity
Away from me,
Not tanks or guns or bombs
Meant to desecrate me and kill me.
My country lives in me.

I am the cry of liberty
No matter what they take from me,
They can take away my identity
Or my dignity
Palestinian am I.

Diaspora is a Greek word meaning "to scatter."

In this chapter it refers to the forced expulsion of a people from their homeland and their establishment of expatriate communities.

Diaspora also evokes the heartbreak and suffering of displaced and dispersed people, and their longing to return to their homeland.

Jews and Palestinians each have their own diasporas, and their unique dispersals are at the heart of their cultural identities.

For Jews, it began nearly 3,000 years ago and ended only with the creation of the State of Israel. Over millennia, they were banished, persecuted and killed by regimes ranging from the Babylonians and Romans to Czarist Russia and Nazi Germany.

For many Palestinians, it began with Israel's birth in 1948. While most Palestinians today live under restricted conditions in historic Palestine and surrounding Arab countries, millions of Palestinians are dispersed around the world. Like most displaced peoples, their pattern of flight and exile has been aggravated by wars, economic hardship and international isolation.

Babylonian Exile

Following their exodus from slavery in Ancient Egypt, the Jewish Kingdoms maintained sovereignty in Israel for nearly a thousand years. But when the Babylonians invaded in 586 BCE, it began eras during which Jews suffered at the whim of their conquerors.

The majority of the Jewish population was exiled from the Land of Israel following the destruction of the First Jewish Temple in Jerusalem by Nebuchadnezzar of Babylon. Leaving the poor behind, the most prominent Jews were forced to leave the Jewish kingdom for Mesopotamia.

This was the first Jewish Diaspora when, nearly 2,500 years ago, Jews no longer lived as a majority in Israel, but rather as a minority outside of Israel in predominantly non-Jewish societies.[1] Naturally, some of the Israelites melded into their host cultures, and assimilated into other nationalities and religions. However, most of them maintained their religious and cultural practices, never forgetting their identity with, and attachment to, the Land of Israel. Until the 20th century, these Babylonian Jews spread their roots among indigenous cultures throughout the Middle East including what is now modern Iraq, Syria, Lebanon, and Jordan.

Seventy years after their exile, the Persian Cyrus the Great conquered Babylon. He favored the Jews and encouraged them to return to the Land of Israel offering them resources to rebuild their Temple in Jerusalem. By then not all of the descendants of the dispersed Jews wanted to leave Babylonia, but thousands did return led by biblical figures including Daniel, Ezra, and Nehemiah.[2] Within a century the Jews who returned had completed the construction of the Second Temple.[3]

Roman Exile

The Babylonian conquest and exile was only a prelude of what was to come. The most devastating defeat of the Israelites occurred when the Roman Empire destroyed the Second Jewish Holy Temple in the Land of Israel in 70 CE.

The Roman Emperor Hadrian was determined to eradicate not only Judaism, but also every remnant of Jewish history including the holy city of Jerusalem. To complete the erasure from history, the Romans renamed Jerusalem "Aelia Capitolina" and erected a Roman Temple for Jupiter on top of the ruins of the Holy Jewish Temple. In addition, Israel's name was changed to "Palestine." Most historians believe the name Palestine was selected to insult the Jews as the name was derived from the ancient Philistines, who had been the historical and contentious adversaries of the biblical Israelites.

18 | Destruction of the Temple, 70 CE

The destruction of the Second Temple at the hands of the Romans in 70 CE was among history's bloodiest conquests in human history. Close to a million people were reportedly killed during the siege, and nearly 100,000 Jews were captured and enslaved.[4] The Romans had to climb over mounds of dead bodies as they tore apart the Temple, pilfering the treasures inside. On the 9th of the Hebrew month of Av, the Second Temple was set ablaze. The city of Jerusalem was never returned to its former splendor.

Historian Flavius Josephus recorded the barbaric Roman behavior of the 1st Century in his book, *The Jewish War.* "To give a detailed account of their outrageous conduct is impossible, but we may sum it up by saying that no other city has ever endured such horrors, and no generation in history has fathered such wickedness."[5]

The destruction of both the First and Second Jewish Temples is commemorated each year by Jews on the 9th day of Av (Hebrew calendar) and is considered to be the saddest day of each year. "Tisha B'Av" occurs annually for Jews worldwide and is designated as a religious and national day of mourning in Israel.

In fact, the first third of the month of Av is considered a period of mourning according to Jewish tradition because in this specific month Jews have experienced several historic tragedies throughout the years including the Edict of Expulsion from England in 1290, expulsion of the Jews from Spain in 1492, and the mass deportation of Jews from the Warsaw Ghetto in 1942.

History recorded the Roman victory in Israel when Emperor Titus was heralded back in Rome arriving to a ceremonial parade bearing the Jewish sacred vessels taken as the "spoils of war" from inside of the Jewish Holy Temple in Jerusalem.

> Even though on simple political and military levels there were far more significant victories for the Roman Empire than the destruction of Judea, they saw fit to commemorate this event and preserve it for future generations by building the famed monument, the Arch of Titus. The Arch celebrates the capture of Israel (Judea) and the victory parade of the plundered Temple vessels arriving in Rome during the first century. On the Arch of Titus, which still stands in Rome, one can see the depiction of this devastating event in Jewish history sculpted within this dramatic structure. During the course of the long and bitter Diaspora, this scene became the symbol of Jewish exile...[6]

All that remains today of the Second Temple complex is a portion of the Western Wall in Jerusalem, also known as the Wailing Wall, which surrounded the Holy Temple as fortification. Today you will find Jews praying at the Wailing Wall all day and at night. It is customary for people to write private prayers to God and to insert them in the cracks of this ancient stone structure, considered to be the holiest Jewish site in the world. Paradoxically, Islamic holy sites—the Dome of the Rock and al-Aqsa Mosque—were built directly upon the site of both Jewish Temples and remain standing above the Wailing Wall.

The Wailing Wall is today the most important historical symbol and religious site for Jews around the world. When a Jew visits Israel or an Israeli visits Jerusalem, they usually stop by the Wailing Wall for prayer. Many Jews around the world, including Israelis, celebrate their sons' Bar Mitz-

19 | Ultra Orthodox Jews in Jerusalem, 2005

vahs at the Wall. My own Bar Mitzvah ceremony took place there when I turned thirteen. I celebrated this "becoming an elder in my Jewish community" by reading from the Torah together with my father and my uncles at the Wailing Wall in Jerusalem.

As the reader may have seen, religious Jews often wear similar black suits and black hats. The origin and purpose of this attire includes the Jewish tradition of wearing black during the period of mourning following the death of a close family member. Today, those wearing black outfits every day do so, in part, to symbolize their constant grief over the destruction of the Temple 2000 years ago.

The Diaspora

For 2,000 years the Land of Israel shifted from one empire to another. These foreigners who swept across the region brought new rulers, cultures, and attitudes towards Jewish inhabitants. Tolerance toward the indigenous Israelites varied from ruler to ruler and from century to century. Due to their different religious and cultural practices, which were diametrically in conflict with pagan worship of ancient civilizations, Jews maintained a way of life that set them apart from the prevailing customs. Their communities remained insular, within which they practiced different traditions, including: observing the Jewish sabbath (Shabbat), wearing head coverings (kippahs), wearing prayer shawls (tallit), eating differently, (keeping kosher) and, most profoundly, they prayed to one God. Their unique cultural norms often kept them at a distance from their neighbors.

Consequently, intolerant rulers demanded Jews submit to their gods and their religious customs and practices. Discrimination followed and the Jews were oppressed, enslaved, banished from their homes, and even killed for their faith. Sometimes by force, and other times through self-determination to find a more tolerant place to live, the Jews began centuries of wandering and resettling throughout the Middle East, north into Europe, east into Asia and later across oceans.

For Jews, living among strangers is as natural as adapting to changing seasons. The Torah teaches tolerance and acceptance of differences and Jewish religious commandments insist that one treat neighbors and strangers with respect, hospitality and friendliness. "Love your neighbor as yourself"[7] comes from the Torah and is considered one of the pillars of Jewish values.

In addition, Jews aspired to integrate into the societies where they lived. Jewish tradition prescribes adherence to the laws of the land. Known in Hebrew as "Din Hamakom Dina" (the law of the land is the law), Jews are commanded to be law-abiding citizens wherever they live. Their history proves that they were patriotic citizens who participated, to the extent that they were allowed, in all sectors of society, including serving in their nations' armed forces and defending their homelands in times of war.

Au contraire, the fate for Jews living in the Diaspora among people of different cultures and religions have historically resulted in persecution, exile, and often death.

Anti-Semitism in the Diaspora

For 2,000 years in the Diaspora, Jews accepted their situation as temporary "strangers living in the land of others." Assimilation occurred during the good times. When and where ruling powers were tolerant, Jews advanced in their adopted countries, participating fully as respectful, law-abiding, productive citizens.

However, the Diaspora was punctuated by several anti-Semitic leaders and societies who made life difficult and often dangerous for Jews within their jurisdiction. Persecution and repeated exile became a familiar pattern for Jews whose literature is full of references to the "wandering Jew" having to "move on" and settle from one place to another. Such was the appeal of the Broadway Musical, *Fiddler on the Roof*, a modern depiction of exile and acquiescence.

In the musical, the endearing community of Jews living in a small village called Anetevka, experienced the cruelty and injustice of pogroms (violent mob attack, characterized by killings and destruction of their homes and properties) fueled by Russian Czars' hatred of the Jews. When their tiny shtetl (village) was ransacked and burned, the frightened, defenseless Jews asked their elder:

> "Rabbi, we've been waiting for the Messiah all our lives. Wouldn't this be a good time for him to come?"[8]

> "We'll have to wait for him someplace else," replied the mild and meek elder of the community. "Meanwhile, let's start packing…"[9]

And so it was. From village to town, from country to country, from one continent to another, over the course of 2,000 years, Jews spread away from Israel, putting down roots wherever they could grow them, if only for a short time, until the next wave of violence erupted.

Yearning for The Land of Israel

A major component of Jewish life is enjoying life in the present. Of equal importance is remembering the past. With this culture of reminiscence a yearning evolved that flowed like rivers throughout Jewish culture. You can read it in Jewish literature and hear the poetry of musical lyrics. Libraries of books, poems, stories, and songs speak of Jewish hearts longing to return to Israel, dreaming of the "land of milk and honey," remembering the promise that someday we would be "home" in the "homeland of our ancestors."

The words of Jewish poet and philosopher Judah Ha-Levi from Toledo, Spain exemplify the longing Jews felt for the Land of Israel. Spanning his lifetime from 1085–1114, much of his poetry reflected his love for Israel and his desire to one day return to Zion—the Promised land. Near the end of his life, Ha-Levi settled in Jerusalem to fulfill his dream. Tragically, soon after he arrived, he was murdered by an Arab as he knelt praying at the Wailing Wall. His poem: "My Heart is in the East" became a traditional piece of Hebrew literature.

A Longing to Return to the Land of Israel
A poem by Yehudah ha-Levi

My heart is in the east,
and I in the uttermost west.
How can I find savor in food?
How shall it be sweet to me?
How shall I render my vows and my bonds,
while yet Zion lieth beneath the fetter of Edom,
and I in Arab chains?
A light thing would it seem to me to leave all the good things of Spain
Seeing how precious in mine eyes to behold the dust of the desolate sanctuary.

Jews did their best as "outsiders" in foreign lands. Willing to move away from persecution without fighting or retribution, Judaism reminded the Jewish people of their history and their covenant with God. Remembering the oppression of slavery experienced in Egypt by their ancestors, gave Jews hope of redemption someday in Eretz Yisrael.

My earliest holiday recollections include my family's "Seders" held at Aunt Rachel's house south of Tel Aviv every Passover. Like Jews worldwide, we celebrated with family gathered around the elaborately prepared table retelling the detailed story of our people's exodus from slavery in Egypt to freedom in Israel. At the Seder meal, it is the responsibility of the elder to tell the story of the exodus from Egypt to our younger children so that they always remember that we were once slaves. Passover also enables us to be with family and give our collective thanks to God for the blessings of freedom.

As a child, Passover was my favorite holiday when my aunt's house sat 40 to 50 of us—aunts and uncles, my parents, and more than 20 first cousins. I'm not sure what I liked best during this holiday. There was so much to enjoy. I can still smell the aromas of delicious Iraqi Jewish foods simmering in the kitchen. I can remember the feeling of pride I felt when it was my turn to recite the four questions. When I think back on it now, my large Sephardic family solidified my love of family, tradition, and Judaism. It was a joyous feeling to be all together around the Seder table.

Passover traditions allow us to remember and teach important messages to our children. First and foremost, we remember that once, thousands of years ago, the Jewish people were slaves in Egypt. Having experienced the bitterness of oppression, Jews teach their children and remind themselves to continually work towards freeing people around the world who are still living under oppression. A second and equally compelling value accentuated during Passover is thanking God for all of the freedoms we enjoy today. And living in modern times, now that the State of Israel exists as our Jewish homeland, we thank God for giving us the Land of Israel.

At my family's Seders, the older generation would inevitably reminisce about their "good old days" in Baghdad. I loved listening to my aunts and uncles who would recall beautiful memories of Iraqi Jewish life and culture. And every year, one of my cousins would ask: "Why did you leave if life was so wonderful back in Iraq?" The teachable moment for those of us who were born in Israel began, as we'd learn about Arab anti-Semitism, and the persecution of my family amidst their Jewish community in Iraq. Then we'd ask to hear once again how they escaped and came to Israel.

The storyline of Jews escaping their Arab native lands and finding freedom in Eretz Yisrael ran parallel to the Jews of Egypt, bringing history to life for all of us.

Now, with my own children, living in the Diaspora, I always try to retell some of the stories of my family at our Passover Seder. Although our current history of being Jewish in America is filled with the blessings of democracy and freedom, it is important that my children know that our people were once slaves in Egypt, just as my parents were oppressed and were compelled to flee from Arab Lands. Jewish tradition encourages us to teach our children to never take freedom for granted and to continually seek justice for oppressed people around the world.

Every Seder finishes with the closing prayer, "Next year in Jerusalem." For thousands of years Jews around the world promised to return to Jerusalem—one year after another. Knowing that Jews around the world are praying for their return to Jerusalem on this important holiday is a continuing collective and personal reminder of the ever-lasting significance that Yerushalayim maintains in Jewish theology and tradition. Even though Jerusalem is governed today by the State of Israel, we are forever aware of our vulnerability.

Modern Day Vulnerability: Denial of Jewish Historical Roots

As recently as 2010, the Palestinian Authority released a report which denied Jewish historical roots in Jerusalem.[10] A Palestinian official posted an article on an official website of the Palestinian Authority that claimed the Western Wall in the Old City of Jerusalem was neither sacred to Jews, nor did it belong to the Jewish State. Instead, the article claimed the Temple Mount—Judaism's holiest site— is more rightly the Noble Sanctuary of Islam and belongs exclusively to the Palestinians.

The Israeli government quickly condemned the article. A few days later, the U.S. State Department echoed Israeli indignation, stating it amounted to denying absolute Jewish historic and religious connections to Israel and, in this case, to Jerusalem.

The offending five-page article was subsequently removed from the Palestinian Authority website. But the incident highlights the daunting differences of opinion about Jerusalem. Israelis see this as an example of attempts by Palestinians to deny history.

And, it raises a fundamental question: "Who will control Jerusalem's holiest site?"

20 | Yehuda and Rachel Ben-Zion. Gabbay's grandparents escaped from Aden (now Yemen) following a pogrom against Jews in 1947, when his grandfather's business was burned to the ground. They became Arab Jewish refugees in Bombay, India and later, immigrated to London. Finally, they immigrated to Israel.

Jewish Persecution: Anti-Semitism in Europe

As Jews moved northward, they left Arab countries behind and entered into Europe where periods of tolerance turned into persecution at the hands of Christian European leaders who blamed Jews for killing Jesus Christ. Exiling and persecuting Jewish populations became commonplace for Christians who were indoctrinated to hate Jews.

It seemed as if no place was secure. Jews were unjustly blamed for everything that went wrong, including the Black Plague, poisoning water wells and even the murder of Christian children. Jews were falsely accused of using the blood of Christian children for making matzah (unleavened bread) for Passover. This notion is obviously preposterous. But it is even more outrageous when realized that dietary laws forbid Jews from eating anything that resembles a drop of blood (such as an egg with a red spot). Nevertheless, these libels were widespread and they were believed, making life intolerable and dangerous for Jews throughout Christian Europe.

Examples of Jews being exiled from countries are abundant in the European historical records. In 1290, 16,000 Jews were expelled from England, 100,000 were exiled from France in 1396 and thousands were expelled from Austria in 1421. The Spanish Inquisition in 1492 commenced an era of exile for hundreds of thousands of Spanish Jews, followed by tens of thousands who were forced to leave Sicily in 1496.[11]

From most of these exiles, Jews fled north to Poland and Russia where, in the 18th century, most European Jews assembled in small villages in a region called the Pale of Settlements in the agrarian Russian empire. By the late 1800s Jews found themselves at the mercy of anti-Semitic Russian Czars who periodically burned Jewish shtetls (villages) during pogroms (state-sponsored attacks), sending Jews seeking refuge time and again.[12]

When Jews were not exiled, they suffered from discrimination and persecution in Europe. They were mostly forbidden from owning land, and were prohibited from becoming professionals. Schooling was limited and attending universities was forbidden. As their cultural norms had typically kept Jewish communities separate from neighbors, laws were enacted that forbade Jews from living or working among the prevailing culture. Thus began the ghettoizing of Jews, where walled neighborhoods limited Jewish movement and commerce. In cases where citizenship might have been granted, often, citizenship privileges were revoked, resulting in widespread state-sanctioned persecution.

Even in the United States, which became a safe-haven for worldwide refugees, permission for Jews to immigrate was not always granted, equality for Jews was not always in place, and anti-Semitism was pervasive.

For example, in 1790 legal restrictions in the United States prevented non-Christians— including Jews—from holding public office and voting. Although the Bill of Rights enacted in 1791 reversed this discrimination, in some states these barriers did not officially fall for decades: Rhode Island (1842), North Carolina (1868), and New Hampshire (1877). During the American Civil War, tensions over race and immigration, as well as economic competition between Jews and non-Jews, combined to produce the worst American outbreak of anti-Semitism of the century. Americans on both sides of the slavery issue denounced Jews as disloyal war profiteers, and accused them of driving Christians out of business and of aiding and abetting the enemy.

Major General Ulysses S. Grant, who was later elected President, expelled Jews from areas under his control in western Tennessee:

> The Jews, as a class violating every regulation of trade established by the Treasury Department and also department orders, are hereby expelled…within twenty-four hours from the receipt of this order.

This order was quickly rescinded by President Abraham Lincoln but not until it had been enforced in a number of towns.

Grant later issued an order "that no Jews are to be permitted to travel on the road southward." His aide, Colonel John V. DuBois, ordered "all cotton speculators, Jews, and all vagabonds with no honest means of support" to leave the district. "The Israelites especially should be kept out...they are such an intolerable nuisance."[13]

In the years before and during World War II, Congress, the Roosevelt Administration, and public opinion all expressed concern about the fate of Jews in Europe, but consistently refused to permit large-scale immigration of Jewish refugees.

U.S. opposition to immigration in general in the late 1930s was motivated by the Great Depression. But for Jews, there was an additional layer of opposition. Anti-Semitism, which had increased in the late 1930s, continued to rise in the 1940s. It was an important ingredient in America's negative response to Jewish refugees. Only about 100,000 German Jews were able to obtain visas to enter the United States in the 1930s, escaping Hitler's persecution. It persisted even during the war itself. In a report issued by the State Department, Undersecretary of State Stuart Eizenstat noted that the United States accepted only 21,000 refugees from Europe and did not significantly raise or even fill its restrictive quotas, accepting far fewer Jews per capita than many of the neutral European countries and fewer in absolute terms than Switzerland.

SS St. Louis

The story of the SS St. Louis is a reminder of Jewish vulnerability, even in the United States. Carrying 936 Jewish refugees, this ship sailed from Germany in May,1939. Not only was this ship and its passengers denied entry to Cuba, on June 4, 1939, it also was refused permission to unload in the United States. President Roosevelt, knowing full well of the dangers facing German Jews, decided to turn the ship away from American shores.

This embarrassing action by the United States was in reaction to strong public opinion against Jewish immigration. The result was that these 936 Jewish refugees who could have been saved, were returned to soon-to-be Nazi-occupied Europe.

The United States' restrictive immigration policies were not lifted until 1948, three years after the Holocaust. Scholars estimate that at least 200,000 Jews could have been saved during World War II had it not been for U.S. obstacles to immigration.

Examples like the American political decision to return the refugees on the SS St. Louis, knowing of disastrous conditions awaiting these German Jews, propel Jewish people to conclude that Jews need a homeland where they can control their own destiny and provide their own security.

Israelis know that having our own land, protected by our own vigilant defense forces is *essential* to Jewish survival. We need to be able to protect ourselves from our enemies and we need to maintain a safe-haven for Jews in the Diaspora who might find themselves in harm's way.

From ancient history to recent history, Jews have learned that there is no assuredness of safety anywhere due to pervasive anti-Semitism. We cannot rely on anyone else to protect us or act on our behalf. Instead, we must be strong in our own homeland to protect ourselves and our fellow Jews around the world.

This is the main reason why Jewish communities around the world support the State of Israel. World Jewry realizes that although they live outside of Israel, some day they might need a refuge, too. Therefore, the State of Israel does not only exist for the Jews who currently live there. Instead, Israel exists for all Jews around the world.

The elected government of Israel supports Jewish causes and goals around the world and there is a strong bond between global Jewish communities and Israel. The following exemplifies Israel's outreach as it has taken responsibility for saving fellow Jews worldwide.

Saving the Jews of Ethiopia

An inspiring 20th century example of modern day redemption is the history of a lost tribe of Jews known as the "Beta Israel" in Ethiopia. In 1974, the Jews of Ethiopia suffered under the pro-communist military junta, known as the "Derg" (committee), which had seized power from the emperor Haile Selassie. The Derg installed a totalitarian government supported by the Soviet Union.

21 | Ethiopian Jews arrive in Israel

The new regime was anti-religious and anti-Israel, which quickly included hostilities against the Jews of Ethiopia.

Within a decade, Ethiopian civil wars had killed hundreds of thousands and Israel became increasingly concerned for the Beta Israel community in Ethiopia. Few in Israel knew that the Beta Israel existed. However, these tribal Jews were living Jewish religious lives in the bush of Africa yearning for the day that they could return to the Land of Israel, not even aware that the modern State of Israel existed. To escape tyranny, tens of thousands of these tribal Jews had set out on bare feet across the desert of northern Africa in a modern Exodus to reach their "promised land."

Throughout their long history Ethiopian Jews yearned to return to Jerusalem, which for them symbolized all of the Land of Israel. The Return to Zion was central to Ethiopian Jewry's identity and religious practices. For many, however, their journey home from exile to redemption was fraught with peril and tragedy.[14]

Between 1984 and 1991, the Israeli government began top-secret rescue missions to save the Ethiopian Jews. Israeli military aircraft landed in war-torn North African countries to pick up and deliver Ethiopian "olim" newcomers and settle them in Israel. These secret operations now are known as "Operation Moses" and "Operation Solomon." In a single event in 1991, Israel airlifted 14,200 Ethiopian Jews to Israel in 36 hours. Israelis and worldwide Jewry continue to bring struggling Jews home to Israel.

Anti-Semitism and the Printing Press

22 | Prime Minister Benjamin Netanyahu welcomes Ethiopian Jew to Israel

Rumors and falsehoods became "truths" during the Middle Ages and the Renaissance. When the printing press was invented, horrific lies became codified in anti-Semitic texts. Perhaps the most egregious book was *Protocols of the Elders of Zion*, which was written in 1903 in the Russian Empire. This popular book described a non-existing Jewish plan for world domination.

The book was a total fabrication, of course. Despite its assertions, Jewish leaders from around the world never met in Paris to prepare a global takeover. Nevertheless, European societies fell prey to these accusations of "Jewish conspiracies" and the falsehoods spread. Even in the United States, influential leaders like Henry Ford widely republished these lies and the text was translated into numerous languages.

To this day, anti-Semites continue to rely on its content, spreading lies about Jews through speeches, texts, websites and other methods of anti-Israel propaganda. Sadly, this book remains on the popular best-seller list throughout the Arab world, promoting anti-Semitism, and of course, anti-Zionism.

Televised dramatizations of *The Protocols* appeared on Egyptian television in October-November 2002 and on *Al-Manar* (Hezbollah) television in 2003. The latter version included scenes depicting Jews draining the blood of a Christian child as an ingredient in *matzah*. In 2003, the manuscript library in Alexandria, Egypt reportedly displayed an Arabic edition of *The Protocols* as an example of a Jewish holy book. In 2005, Iranian booksellers displayed copies of *The Protocols* and *The International Jew* at the Frankfurt Book Fair, the world's largest publishing event.

In the United States, the book is distributed widely by Louis Farrakhan's Nation of Islam. In 2002, the Paterson, New Jersey-based Arabic-language newspaper, *The Arab Voice*, published excerpts from the Protocols as true. The paper's editor and publisher Walid Rabah defended himself from criticism with the protestation that "some major writers in the Arab nation accept the truth of the book."[15]

Returning to Israel

Whenever it was politically safe and physically feasible, Jews did return to Israel throughout the centuries joining other Jews indigenous to the region. In fact, since the biblical time of Moses, (when he led the Israelites from slavery in Egypt back to the promised land, which the Israelites then settled) there have always been Jewish communities in Israel. It is important to note that a different national, or sovereign entity has never existed in the Land of Israel except for the ancient era of Jewish Kingdoms (between 500 BCE and 70 CE) until the creation of the modern State of Israel in 1948. (Instead, the Land of Israel became possessions of vast conquering empires throughout this nearly 1900-year period of Middle East history.)

It is true that Arabs lived in Israel before the Israelites arrived from Egypt and during the 2,500-year period of Jewish exile. But these Arabs never organized a separate, sovereign state, nor did any ruler choose Jerusalem as a capital city. Instead, the Land of Israel was conquered by prevailing emperors who ruled the land from far-away capitals, including Baghdad, Rome, Constantinople and Damascus. The indigenous Arabs were part of the empires that ruled the Land of Israel.

Throughout these many centuries, there was never a Palestinian state. In 1948, the Arabs in Israel considered themselves to be living in Greater Syria.

When reading or listening to today's rhetoric, it is easy to be misled and to think that the Palestinians have had a national state which was "taken from them" by Israelis. In fact, there was never a Palestinian state or any other sovereign entity in the Holy Land from the time of the Jewish Kingdoms to the establishment of the modern State of Israel. There were numerous external occupiers of the land, but there was never a separate sovereign entity.

The Rise of Zionism

Things continued to get worse for Jews in Czarist Russia. "Between 1881 and 1906, Jews in Russia were slaughtered, their homes and towns were destroyed, and their women were raped.[16] In Kishinev, "The mob was led by priests and the general cry, 'Kill the Jews' was taken up all over the city. The Jews…were slaughtered like sheep… Babies were literally torn to pieces by the frenzied and bloodthirsty mob."[17]

The need for escape routes for millions of Jews in Europe was critical. Zionism, the desire among Jews to return to the land of their ancestors, evolved during this time period.

Theodore Herzl Leads the Zionist Movement

A young Viennese journalist, Theodore Herzl, was sent to France to write a story about a French military officer who was being tried for treason. There, Herzl witnessed ominous anti-Semitism and it became clear to him that the accusations against Alfred Dreyfus were not simply false, they were conjured up solely because Dreyfus was a Jew.

As he wrote about the details of this infamous case of kangaroo court justice, Herzl became convinced that the Jews of Europe could only survive if they established a safe, sovereign homeland for the Jewish people. Thus Modern Zionism was born—and it evolved into a national liberation movement for Jews to reclaim the Land of Israel as their Jewish national homeland.

Herzl became the Zionist leader, not due to religious zeal—(he himself was not a religious man) but because he saw no other way for Jews to survive the fervor of anti-Semitism he witnessed, first-hand, during the Dreyfus Affair. He realized that deep hatred of Jews not only permeated the mobs in the streets, but its tenacles reached deep within the French government and judicial system as well. Seeing France as a microcosm, Herzl and other Zionist leaders were well aware that the anti-Semitism in France reflected the dangerous realities facing Jews throughout Europe.

The Zionists worked diligently to establish the modern State of Israel. In a pamphlet he published in 1896 titled Der Judenstaat (The Jewish State) Herzl declared, "I consider the Jewish question neither social nor a religious one, even though it sometimes takes these and other forms. It is a national question, and to solve it we must first of all establish it…"[18]

Dreyfus and European Anti-Semitism

The Dreyfus affair was an anti-Semitic military and political scandal, which divided French society in the 1890s and the early 1900s. In November 1894, a young French Jewish artillery captain named Alfred Dreyfus was sentenced to life imprisonment for treason for supposedly passing French military secrets to the German Embassy in Paris. He was sentenced to prison and held in solitary confinement in a prison in French Guiana.

Two years later, evidence emerged exonerating Dreyfus and identifying the true culprit, who was a French Army major. However, high-ranking French military officials suppressed this new evidence and the major was unanimously acquitted in military court.

Meanwhile, Dreyfus languished in solitary confinement for crimes he did not commit. The French Army subsequently accused him of fabricating documents. Those who believed in Dreyfus's innocence included French writer Emile Zola who wrote a vehement public expose in January 1898. His influence led to the re-opening of the case.

When Dreyfus stood trial a second time he was found innocent of all charges.

Dreyfus was exonerated and reinstated as a major in the French Army in 1906. He later volunteered to serve his country in World War I, during which he was promoted to the rank of Lieutenant Colonel.

For reporters who covered the Dreyfus trials, including Herzl, the Dreyfus Affair was an act of vicious anti-Semitism. While the reporters witnessed the false accusations and the obvious bias against Dreyfus due to his Jewish heritage, it became obvious that Dreyfus was originally accused of treason for nothing else but the fact that he was Jewish.

The Dreyfus Affair changed Hertzl's life. While not particularly religious, Herzl's epiphany arose from witnessing the prejudices that permeated Western society. If a decorated soldier like Dreyfus could be unfairly condemned in France, he concluded, the rest of the Jews of Europe had no hope of surviving there.

In the 19th century, France had risen as a beacon of democracy, fairness and justice to people yearning to be free worldwide. Witnessing the darkness and dangers of anti-Semitism first hand propelled Herzl to act—and act he did, quite quickly following the second Dreyfus trial.

Herzl founded the World Zionist Organization and called for the creation of a Jewish State in Palestine. He wrote the pamphlet that became the blueprint for Zionism. Under his leadership, Jewish people worldwide were inspired to quickly reestablish a safe, national homeland for the Jews of Europe.

The rise of Hitler was less than three decades away. Herzl and the World Zionist Organization had a great deal of work ahead of them, not the least of which was to encourage Jews to immigrate to the Holy Land. Although persecuted and facing many evils, it was not easy to convince Jews to leave countries where they had lived and thrived for many centuries. It would take the unspeakable crimes of the Nazis to convince those that survived that they must get out of Europe.

From my own family's history, the Jews of Baghdad persevered through several decades of unbearable persecution before they realized that in order to survive, they must escape from Iraq. In doing so, they left behind their culturally rich, 2500-year-old Jewish community, as well as all of their land and possessions. In *Mother of the Pound* by Dr. David Kazak, it is documented that during a window of opportunity to escape, Iraqi Jews could carry no more than the equivalent of $50. The rest of their assets were confiscated.

This reflection about Alfred Dreyfus and his trials in France have resonated within me in a deep way and I am touched by what Herzl must have felt being a witness to this great injustice. Having been a soldier, I imagine how Dreyfus must have felt when he was so wrongly betrayed by France, where he had served as an officer in the army and was willing to give his life for his country. There was a time in my own life when I had to answer the question, "Am I willing to risk my life for my country?" Like Dreyfus, I made that decision as a young man by joining the military forces of Israel, determined to protect and preserve the Jewish homeland.

Dreyfus volunteered to do the highest deed a citizen can do for his country: to be willing to give his life for its defense. Subsequently, he was accused of the worst crime that a citizen can commit—treason. And why? Not because of evidence but, just because Dreyfus was a Jew.

From this experience, I believe there can be no greater betrayal than for a loyal military officer to be wrongly accused of treason. Dreyfus knew he was innocent. He knew that he was being prosecuted for being Jewish.

The Dreyfus Affair, perhaps more than any other, encourages me to tell the Jewish story, as I am writing in this book. As Herzl knew that he must establish the State of Israel for Jewish survival, I believe that I must do everything possible for the survival of my country—Israel—so that Jewish people will continue to survive.

Ironically, after Dreyfus was freed following his second trial, he continued to serve as an officer in the French Army fighting with the Allies during World War I. Sadly, anti-Semitism in France did not end when the Dreyfus Affair concluded and it continued to touch the Dreyfus family. The French Vichy Government included old anti-Dreyfus cronies and their descendants, who assisted in the deportation of French Jews who were then murdered by the Nazis. Dreyfus's granddaughter, Madeleine Levy, was rounded-up and deported from France to Auschwitz during World War II, where she was exterminated in the Holocaust.

It must be noted anti-Semitism has not ended and heinous crimes against Jews continue. In February, 2006, Illan Halimi, a 23-year old Jew in Paris, was kidnapped, tortured and murdered by anti-Semitic hoodlums. Illan endured three weeks of torture. His body was found naked and handcuffed to a tree near a railway track. Why? Because he was Jewish.

Anti-Semitic rhetoric and crimes continue to take place in the modern Arab and Muslim world. *New York Times* journalist Daniel Pearl was kidnapped and beheaded by extremists in Pakistan in 2002. He, too, was Jewish.

23 | Illan Halimi, a Jewish young man, who was tortured and murdered in Paris, 2006

Zionist Choice of Israel

From the historical records of the Zionist Congress which commenced in Basel, Switzerland in 1897, we know that the Land of Israel was just one of several places discussed as possible locations for the Jewish State. Other recommendations included Uganda and Argentina. In the end, the majority voted to reestablish a homeland for the Jewish people back in the Land of Israel. Contrary to common belief, the Zionist movement was not a religious movement. Instead, Zionism took hold in the late 1800s to combat rising and seemingly unstoppable acts of anti-Semitism.

The European Zionists proceeded to raise funds, and purchased land from the ruling Ottoman Empire, which had conquered and governed the Palestine region since 1517. Like homesteaders across the American West, Jews from Europe traveled to Palestine, settled on purchased land, and became Israeli pioneers in what had been the ancient Land of Israel. Their hard-working spirit and their determination to rebuild the Jewish homeland by hand were put to good use as they set out to re-nourish the barren land which had been neglected for centuries. In doing so, Jews, once again, became Jerusalem's majority population.

Aliyahs

The Hebrew word for immigration to Israel is "aliyah" which means "going up." There were five distinct aliyahs before World War II. The first Aliyah occurred between 1882 and 1903, when 25,000 Jews came to Israel mainly from Russia, Romania, Kurdistan, and Yemen. The second Aliyah brought 40,000 Jews from Russia and Poland between 1904 and 1914. Between 1919 and 1923 the third Aliyah brought 35,000 Jews to Israel mostly from Russia and Poland, but also from Lithuania, Romania, and western and central Europe. The fourth Aliyah consisted of 67,000 Jews, mostly from Poland. During the decade leading up to World War II, while Hitler ascended to power, the fifth and largest Aliyah took place; 250,000 Jews mainly from Germany and Austria survived the Holocaust because they escaped to Palestine between 1929 and 1939.[19]

The largest Aliyah took place when the Iron Curtain unraveled and the Soviet Union collapsed, allowing 700,000 Soviet Jews to emigrate to Israel by 1996. These Jews whose ancestors had survived the Czars, World War II and Soviet Communism, now have become the single largest national group of Jews in modern Israel. Since living under communism stifled religious practices for a generation, the majority of these Soviet immigrants are secular Jews.

Though one would think that most Israelis are religious, the majority of Israelis today define themselves as traditional Jews with a secular orientation, which means on the practical level that they do not live their daily lives in accordance with strict Jewish religious laws. For instance, many do not adhere to religious Sabbath practices, and many do not adhere to strict Jewish dietary kosher laws.

For historians, there is no question that the Jewish people have been a religious civilization that survived despite insurmountable odds. As a sociologist, I find it interesting that the Tibetan Buddhist leader, the Dalai Lama, met with a group of six prominent Jewish leaders in 1989 to learn about their "secret technique" for survival. He said, "We always talk of the Jewish people scattered in so many countries, speaking so many languages… Yet the Jews keep their traditions. It's something admirable."[20]

The Dalai Lama was correct. Always relatively small in number, oppressed for their religion and "different culture," and continually persecuted, killed and exiled, Jews throughout ancient and modern history have managed to adapt and integrate into societies worldwide while maintaining their Jewish identity. While I'm not certain all social scientists agree upon a single reason for Jewish survival, it is interesting, in its purest form, that the Dalai Lama has asked the question—seeking answers for the future of his Tibetan followers.

I conclude this chapter with the Israeli National Anthem written in 1886 by Jews from Bohemia and Moldavia. The lyrics of this song demonstrate the yearning by Jews to return to Israel.

Ha Tikvah
(The Hope)

As long as the Jewish spirit is yearning deep in the heart,
With eyes turned toward the East, looking toward Zion,
Then our hope—the two-thousand-year-old hope—will not be lost:
To be a free people in our land,
The land of Zion, Jerusalem.[21]

The History and Birth of Arab Palestinian Nationalism

Critics of Palestinian nationalism argue that the land of Palestine was an uninhabited desert awaiting its salvation by Zionist Jews arriving from Europe in the late 19th century. This viewpoint is a myth forwarded by Zionist propaganda.

Yet these transparent efforts cannot deny the fact that we, the Palestinian people, not only have a distinguished and important history of our own, but our brand of nationalism exists in the same way that we exist—as a people with just as much right as anyone else to live peacefully and prosperously in our historic homeland.

Arab-Palestinian nationalism is not an isolated movement. The late 19th and early 20th centuries bore witness to the rise of nationalism around the world. Local struggles for self-determination and independence during this European Colonial period developed traditions that coincided with the creation of new indigenous, independent states. Many of the traditions that we consider ancient in origin are in fact recent developments.[1] While fascinating in study, there is nothing remarkable about the need for human beings to seek and find coherence in a common identity through the creation of stories and myths. They actually work to bring societies together.

What is astonishing about the establishment of the State of Israel in 1948, is the way in which the creation of a distinctly Israeli story serves to invoke the denial of the Palestinian people's existence.

24 | Amin Kazak's grandfather born in Haifa, circa 1900

It is best reflected in the frequently repeated and shockingly misinformed public comments of Israeli Prime Minister Golda Meir, who claimed, "There is no such thing as Palestinians. When was there an independent Palestinian people with a Palestinian state? ...It is not as though there was a Palestinian people in Palestine considering itself a Palestinian people and we came and threw them out and took their country from them. They did not exist."[2]

Ancient Ties of Contemporary Arab-Palestinian Nationalism

Long before the Hebrew people first migrated to the land of Canaan around 1800 BCE, the people who lived there were known as Canaanites. The Canaanite civilization encompassed much of the land that is known today as Israel, the West Bank, Lebanon, Syria and Jordan. Mark S. Smith, a scholar in the department of Hebrew and Judaic studies at New York University, notes in his book *The Early History of God* that in many areas, the culture of the Israelite society drew very heavily, if not indistinguishably from, Canaanite culture and society. He writes,

> Early Israelite culture cannot be separated easily from the culture of "Canaan." The highlands of Israel in the Iron Age, circa 1200–587 BCE, reflect continuity with the "Canaanite" (or better, West Semitic) culture during the preceding period both in the highlands and in the contemporary cities on the coast and in the valleys."[3]

As the direct descendants of these earliest Semitic peoples, it cannot be disputed that the Palestinian people of today (Arab, Christian and formerly Jewish) originated in this land with the dawn of civilization and were there to witness the arrival of the Hebrews. During the relatively brief Jewish occupation of the area, the indigenous non-Hebrew peoples remained. The Palestinian people of today consider ourselves to be descendants of the Canaanites, the Edomites and the Philistines who inhabited the area before the arrival of the Jewish biblical Israelites. We have lived continuously in Palestine ever since. The Jewish capture of the land from the Canaanites is well-documented in the Hebrew scriptures.

When Zionist supporters claim that today's Palestinians are from lands far beyond Palestine and not from Canaan, they are perpetuating the notion that only Jewish people are native to the land. This is a false and disingenuous assertion.

The archeological record indicates that Jews and Palestinians have something fundamentally in common pertaining to their relationship to the land. They both came into existence through a blending of local and outside groups following invasion and the mixing together of native inhabitants and invaders.

The Ottoman rule of Palestine saw the growth and prosperity of all of the communities of Palestine, including Christian, Jewish and Muslim peoples. However, the year 1914 marked a paradigmatic and dramatic shift in the Palestinian way of life. The Ottoman Turks' decision to declare war on the European Allies in 1914 led to a series of events that would affect

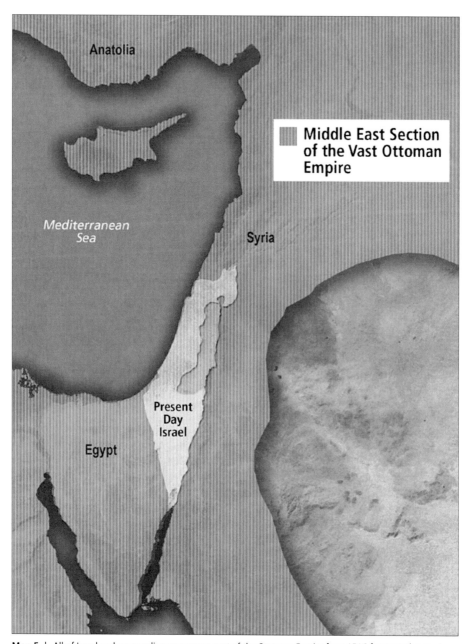

Map 5 | All of Israel and surrounding areas were part of the Ottoman Empire from 1516 for several centuries.

the people of Gaza, as well as all Palestinians, in that century. As one observer noted, "The work of months often proved more effective than the neglect of centuries in destroying the agricultural foundations of village life. Nearly all the improvements of the previous 50 years were swept away."[4] On behalf of the war effort, food and livestock were commandeered, trees were cut down for fuel, and whole villages were quartered off for troops.

The term "Palestinian," resurrected by the British, became associated with the Arab peoples living in Palestine during the British Mandate era. In 1948, the Arab Jews of the region discarded this term in favor of the term "Israeli."[5]

Nevertheless, for the Arabs of the land of Palestine, the term "Palestinian" indicated not only a physical place of origin on the map, but also an increasing sense of a shared past and future and an emerging national identity like those of other modern nations. Even when one asks an Israeli citizen of Arab origins—Christian or Muslim, they refer to themselves as Palestinian Israelis to denote their original ties to the Palestinian people. In the words of Dr. Raed Mualem, "I am a proud Israeli, Christian and Palestinian." I employ the term "Palestinianism" to show that the Arab population originating in the area of the British Mandate of Palestine is distinct from other Arab groups due to its shared history and distinct feelings about its future.

Roots of Arab-Palestinian Nationalism

Just as the land of Palestine is located at the crossroads of three continents regularly vanquished by invaders, the contemporary political ideology that frames Palestinian nationalism today is best represented by the confluence between past confrontations and the unrealized future of a people chronically tormented by their own rulers and external aggressors.

As stated by one of the most respected and revered Columbia University professors, the late Edward Said, in *The Question of Palestine*, it was at the end of the 7th century when Palestine became a predominately Arab and Islamic land. Said writes that almost immediately after the Muslim expansion into the region, the boundaries and characteristics of Palestine—including its name in Arabic, *Filastin*, became known to the entire Islamic world, as much for its fertility and beauty as for its religious significance to the three monotheistic faiths.

In 1516, Palestine became a province of the Ottoman Empire. Even so, the people living in this part of the Holy Land believed they belonged to a place called Palestine. While they were members of a large Arab nation or collectivity, they were distinctly Palestinian. I would also add that despite religious differences—whether a member of the Christian or Jewish minorities, or a Muslim—Arab peoples indigenous to the land were considered Arab Palestinians who were inherently a part of the greater Arab world, culture, history and collective identity.

Of course, throughout much of the duration of the Ottoman Empire, a defined Palestinian national consciousness had yet to further develop. It is simple to explain. For almost six centuries, the Ottoman rulers effectively merged many different regions as well as diverse ethnic and political groups within one framework. Thus, the loyalty of the Turks, Greeks, Arabs and Palestinians among them—was to the house of Osman and the Islamic *umma* over whom the empire governed.[6] Nevertheless, the people of Ottoman Palestine were identified directly in relation to the land in which they lived, and this land was called Palestine. From rural sheikhs, urban notables, merchants and artisans to peasants and farmers, the people living in this land developed a rich culture and an extremely diverse social structure that would lay the foundation for the contemporary definition of a distinct Palestinian identity and a modern sense of nationalism.[7] For over 1,300 years, the Arab people of Ottoman Palestine developed their own unique, autonomous social and political structures.

The cities of Jabal al-Jalee (Galilee), Jabal al-Nablus (Nablus), Jabal al-Quds (Jerusalem), and Jabal al-Khalil (Hebron) were all distinct cultural and economic centers of Ottoman Palestine.[8] During Ottoman rule, these geographic and social centers evolved into thriving urban developments containing a strong Palestinian "national" presence. For example, the city of Nablus represented a geographic region governed by native Palestinian families who developed a prosperous production industry of textiles, soaps and other products, which continues today. Its robust economic capabilities made Nablus a stronghold of prosperity and development, buttressed by a well-delineated division of labor as well as social and power structures. Over time, the city's inhabitants organized themselves into guilds, formed professional organizations and utilized fully functioning trade networks.[9]

25 | Nazareth market, circa 1935

26 | Vintage pre-Israel Palestinian coin

Other cities established similar economic and social systems throughout the Palestinian domain. In the hilled cities, inhabitants had distinct mechanisms of economic production and social organization based on tribal alliances and networks. Families lived together in clans. These clans paid tribute to tribal sheiks. Sheikdoms were interconnected within the geographic districts of Palestine, and trade and communication within Palestine and throughout the region flourished. Trade routes extended from Jerusalem, Nablus, and Acco, through Damascus, south into Egypt, and east along the ancient path of the Hajj (pilgrimage) caravan.[10]

Agricultural production was highly diversified. Cotton was cultivated on the lands of the western plains, olive groves were planted on the terraced hills, and wheat, corn, barley and sesame grains were produced along the eastern plains.[11]

The Arab inhabitants of what was then classified as southern Syria (*Bilad al-Sham*) were an inter-connected part of the social and economic structure of the Middle East. The unique identity of what it meant to be Palestinian was defined by geographic location in

27 | Jaffa, circa 1900

the region and connection to the land in which the people of Palestine lived and worked since the beginning of recorded history. Over the course of its existence, the Ottoman authority had little direct influence over the growth and development of the Palestinian identity. The people of Palestine were left to autonomously celebrate the traditions of their past and shape their society for the benefit of future generations.

Palestinians and Islam

For the Palestinian people of modern days, the history of Palestine is also the history of Islam. Palestine is the land of the prophets of Islam. From Adam, the first prophet, to Muhammad, the last prophet, Palestine was the one place on earth where the prophets were sent to teach mankind the message of Islam. The al-Aqsa Mosque (*al-Masjid al-Aqsa*) and the Dome of the Rock (*al-Masjid al-Haram*) are holy sites in Islam where many of the prophets were born or died, including Ibrahim, Lut, Dawud, Sulayman, Musa and Isa. After the death of the Prophet Muhammad, the land of Palestine and its people were brought under Muslim control at the time of *Umar ibn al-Khattab*, the second Muslim caliph. Palestine was then made part of the Islamic state and ruled by Islamic law.

The new laws of the Islamic state were welcomed by the people of Palestine—Muslims, Jews and Christians—who had suffered under the harsh and despotic Byzantines. The Byzantines were especially known for their persecution of the Palestinian Christians because they belonged to a different Christian sect, despite the fact that the Christians of Palestine were the original disciples of Christ. The Muslim rulers, on the other hand, guaranteed all Christians freedom of religion regardless of their sect. Similarly, Jews were granted the right to live and freely practice their religion in Palestine as well as in all parts of the Ottoman Empire. Thus, there is a reason why Palestine is called the Holy Land—it is the "cradle of monotheism, and its inhabitants consider themselves the 'People of the Holy Land.'"[12] The people of Palestine practiced an abiding pluralism, "which, although differing from 'democratic pluralism', enabled Palestinians to live cooperatively within their diverse community long before that term was coined."[13]

In 1099 CE, Palestine was invaded by the European Crusaders and subsequently occupied for nearly a century. During this occupation, massacres and great injustices were committed against the Muslim, Jewish and native Christian residents of the area. But by 1187 CE, Palestine was again liberated by the Muslims under the leadership of *Salah ad-Din al-Ayyubi* (Saladin) who brought back Islamic law to the area. With Muslim rule restored, the land of Palestine prospered significantly. In 1516, the Ottomans conquered Palestine, and the country was incorporated into the dominions of the Ottoman Empire. Local governors were appointed and sent to Palestine from Constantinople (Istanbul). Palestinians were forced

28 | Camel caravan, circa 1918

to send annual taxes from Palestine to the distant capital. Public works were undertaken in Palestine, such as the rebuilding of the walls of the Old City of Jerusalem by Suleiman the Magnificent in 1537.

During the centuries that followed, Palestine became a safe haven for the expelled Muslims and Jews from Spain, who fled persecution and ethnic cleansing by Catholic monarchies. In fact, the categorization of "Sephardic Jews" originated from the Spanish Jews who escaped from Spain to Jerusalem during the 15th Century. Now "Sephardic Jews" are considered to be those who originated from all Arab countries.

The Beginning of Palestinian Dispossession

The establishment of British rule in Palestine in 1917 marked the demise of Islamic rule in Palestine.[14] Following pressure from notable Jewish leaders upon the British government in 1917, the British government issued the Balfour Declaration, which unilaterally declared a Jewish homeland in Palestine..

29 | British Field Marshall Allenby in Jerusalem, 1917

At the time, Jews living in Palestine made up less than 10 percent of the total population of Palestine and owned merely 2.5 percent of the land.[15] Despite their overwhelming majority status, under British rule, the native Arab population was reduced to second-class status in the land of their ancestors. Today few remember that until the "advent of Zionism, the Palestinians constituted the cumulative human residue, ethnic layer upon ethnic layer, of the admixture of peoples, (including the ancient Hebrews and their descendents), who had entered and left Palestine since time immemorial."[16]

The outbreak of World War II in Europe dramatically altered Palestine yet again. For the local people, the outbreak of war in Europe translated into severe political repression by the British.[17] The British banned virtually all forms of political activity. The regime also implemented a new system of "police and military tribunals which were given extensive powers to search homes, seize suspects and detain them without trial for unlimited periods."[18]

More and more Jews fled Europe and came to Palestine with the intent of building a Jewish-only state under the Balfour Declaration. This is how the current state of Palestinian dispossession truly began; when, as Arthur Koestler put it, "one nation had solemnly promised another the territory of a third."[19]

As the Zionists covertly organized themselves, the British forcefully prevented the return of our exiled Palestinian national leaders. Later the British retreated from the 1917 Balfour Declaration with the passage of the 1939 White Paper, but that did little to stem the wave of Jewish immigrants coming to the land illegally.

The Jews were also upset with British policies. They began secretly forming their own underground terrorist groups and prepared to fight against anyone who stood in the way of the creation of a Jewish State. By the war's end in 1945, Jewish political culture had become increasingly militaristic. W.F. Abboushi notes that following the failed Arab Revolt, the Arabs were too exhausted by the rebellion to oppose the Zionists.[20]

If the events between 1936 and 1939 added up to something unique in Palestinian history, some of the tactics used in the revolt and its social character grew out of the fundamental changes in Palestinian society and the growing challenge posed by Zionists in the five preceding years. While responding to the transformation of their society in different ways, Palestinians applauded the creation of a national [Arab] movement, sharing an ideology that totally negated any Jewish political right over the country.[21]

30 | Arab Palestinian, circa 1910

The Resilient Palestinian People

Historically subjected to an onslaught of foreign invasion and conquest, the people of Palestine developed a singular and resilient national character of resistance that has been passed down through the generations.

During Ottoman rule, the majority of the land was owned by a small land-owning class, and inhabited by peasant farmers who comprised a majority of the population. Meanwhile, the

31 | Palestinian leaders, circa 1915

inhabitants of the hilled areas—much like today—were well organized and difficult to rule.[22] As a result, the Ottomans utilized and empowered local leaders, sheiks in rural districts and notable families in developing and administrating urban centers.[23]

As Muhammad Muslih writes, "'Ottomanism' emphasized a common Ottoman citizenship and loyalty to the *umma*, which served as the reigning ideology until the early years of the 20th century. However, as Turkish nationalism blossomed, the Arab response was, "If the Turks were a nation, so were the Arabs, who were predisposed, by virtue of their legacy, to think of themselves as a distinct ethnic and cultural group within Islam and Islamic civilization."[24]

32 | Palestinian farming, date unknown

By the end of World War I, Arab nationalism was fast becoming a viable ideology. As corruption and suffering proliferated under Ottoman rule, the coalition between local leadership and Ottoman rule grew increasingly estranged.

After World War I and during the British occupation Palestinians suffered from significant restructuring of the Palestinian economy which led to a large, landless underclass of Palestinian natives.[25] Of course, their increasingly impoverished living conditions added insult to injury for Palestinian Arabs experiencing these economic hardships.

According to Muslih, in the aftermath of World War I, several small groups of younger Arab nationalists emerged who were attracted to the goal of pan-Syrian unity between the people of modern Palestine and Syria.[26] Particularly between 1917 and 1920, this new guard began to envision a Syrian-Palestinian alliance—a pan-Syrian unity that would fight for Palestinian rights. Attempting to eclipse the conservative ideology that typified the older, aristocratic class of Palestinians who had long enjoyed the benefits of local control at the behest of the outside ruler, the younger guard attempted to dominate the local political scene in Palestine and advance the new language of Arab nationalism.

The Zionist and British perceptions of Palestine as an "empty" land ignored historical reality. From the perspective of the Palestinian people, their rights as a people were disregarded, their nation was ignored, and their future became prostrate and subjugated to the interests and needs of the advancing Jewish nation.

33 | Palestinian family in Ramallah, circa 1905

As Professor Edward Said writes, "Much of what we call Palestinian self-assertion was articulated in response to the flow of Jewish immigrants into Palestine since the 1880s, as well as to ideological pronouncements made about Palestine by Zionist organizations."[27] In addition, the Palestinian people were constantly deluged by foreign invaders. As a result, the Palestinian Arabs grew together as a community during the interwar years and became the modern incarnation of the Palestinian people.

The only thing missing was a country.

From a Pan-Syrian Ideology to Palestinian Nationalism

As Khalidi writes, "Although the Zionist challenge definitely helped to shape the specific form Palestinian national identification took, it is a serious mistake to suggest that Palestinian identity emerged mainly as a response to Zionism."[28] In the initial years of the British Mandate, the ideological split between older and younger Palestinian leaders was central to the question of who would govern the future state of Palestine. On February 5, 1919, representatives from 14 Palestinian cities and villages submitted a petition to the Paris Peace Conference, demanding that Palestine or "Southern Syria"—as it was fleetingly called—be "inseparable from the independent Arab Syrian government that is bound by Arab unity, and free from all foreign influence or protection."[29]

The initial push for the union of Palestine and Syria was predicated on the vision of bringing the people of the region together to build a common future based on strong mutual cultural, linguistic, religious and familial attachments. One must also remember that despite the artificial construction of these demarcated states in 1917, the people living in Palestine were also considered to be politically part of greater Syria.

Paris Peace Conference

The victorious Allies met at the con-clusion of World War I at the 1919 Paris Peace Conference. Led by the United States, France and England, the Allies set the peace terms for the defeated Central Powers. Diplomats from more than 29 countries deter-mined a set of treaties that reshaped the map of Europe.

Among these agreements was the Faisal–Weizmann Agreement. This document was signed on January 3, 1919, by Emir Faisal, son of the King of Hejaz, and Chaim Weizmann, later to become the President of the World Zionist Organization. Although this agreement was short-lived, it created a blueprint for Arab-Jewish coopera-tion in the Holy Land and called for the creation of a Jewish homeland in Palestine and an Arab nation in a larger portion of the Middle East.

34 | Chaim Weizmann (left) and Emir Faisal (right), 1918

Another contentious and secret document was the Sykes-Picot Agreement, which called for the establishment of a confederation of Arab States under the leadership of King Faisal who, in many ways, betrayed his fellow Palestinian Arabs by agreeing to a Jewish State in Palestine.

Unfortunately, the results of the Faisal-Weizmann Agreement came at the expense of the Arab desire for unified Palestinian-Syrian nationalism. Faisal, the son of Sharif Hussein, had played a pivotal role in the Arab revolt against the Ottomans. At the same time, he established cordial relations with Zionist political leader Chaim Weizmann. This led to the agreement he signed on January 4, 1919, in Paris, which appeared to support Zionist aspirations as well as Faisal's hopes of establishing an independent Arab state. According to Kimmerling and Midgal, Faisal, "...declaring that Palestine should have its own guaranteed status as a Jewish enclave, was unequivocal in his acceptance of unfettered Jewish immigration as long as he received his promised independent state."[30] Subsequently, when the truth of Faisal's concessions became known to the people, Palestinian notables were horrified and declared that they would "not agree to be sacrificed on the altar of independence."[31]

Faisal's fall from power in July, 1920—when the French took military action to have him exiled—underscored what already was abundantly evident to many Palestinian political activists at the time. The vision of Palestine becoming a region of the Syrian Arab state was dead.[32]

By the end of 1920, the regional division between Syria and Palestine was complete.[33] The Palestinians called for the historic land of Palestine and the people living within it to become its own independent state. Locked in a battle for self-determination and freedom from imperial and Zionist encroachment, Palestinian nationalism advanced into a concern for the future of the Palestinians and their equally important homeland. But British control of the country, coupled with the intent to create a Jewish national homeland, ultimately worked to disregard the rights and wishes of the Palestinian majority.[34]

Arab-Palestinian Nationalism Today

From 1948 to 1967, the Palestinian predicament was aggravated by being an Arab entity separated from the greater Arab world. In fact, it was during these middle decades of the 20th century that the Palestinian people developed a "self-identity as a people set apart."[35] Governed in the West Bank and East Jerusalem by Jordanian authorities and in the Gaza Strip by the Egyptian administration, a new generation of Palestinians grew up in this nebulous state of limbo and exile. For them, the 1967 War served as the defining moment in the Palestinian movement for self determination. The Palestinian quest for national identity took on concrete goals: ending Israeli occupation and demanding a Palestinian independent state.

As Said writes, "Within the framework of possible solutions to the whole regional imbroglio, Palestinian self-determination has come to rest by and large on the need for an independent state on a liberated part of the original territory of Palestine."[36]

The year 1967 also marked a turning point in Palestinian leadership. Although the Arab League founded the Palestinian Liberation Organization (PLO) in 1964 as a way of institutionalizing Palestinian aspirations, after 1967 the PLO became the vehicle and true voice of the Palestinian desire to liberate the people from Israeli military occupation and to fight for their rightful Palestinian homeland.

Being born a Palestinian and being stripped of my national identity in 1948 by the establishment of a Jewish state on the homeland of my grandfathers and my ancestors has enabled me to understand personally why national identity is inherently significant to each and every human being living on this planet. National identity has been an essential aspiration for people throughout the world. This is true for the Palestinian people as well.

Throughout the course of the last century, the Palestinian people have faced extraordinary difficulties and hurdles in our unfolding national story.[37] In particular, statelessness has been the most distinctive mark in the Palestinian narrative. In the absence of statehood and institutions, a unique and sharply defined sense of "who is a Palestinian citizen" has appeared. This long-term ambiguity has developed into a viable national story that has strengthened Palestinian self-awareness.

In addition, the ongoing Israeli military occupation has served to emphasize the common, oppressive and repeated fate of the Palestinian people. As Said writes, "To deny the existence of Palestinians makes sense epistemologically if one believes that Palestine is still an empty desert waiting to be cured of its neglect."[38]

The State of Israel came into existence on this once shared land that was entirely known as Palestine. Yet, despite grave threats to our human rights and attempts to deny our reality, my people, the Palestinian Arabs, continue to exist.

I have always lived with the words of Palestinian poet Tawfiq Zayyad in my mind and in my heart:

We Shall Remain
By Palestinian poet Tawfiq Zayyad in "Baqun"

Here – we have a past, a present
and a future.

Our roots are entrenched
Deep in the earth.
Like twenty impossibles
We shall remain.

Having defeated the Germans and the Central Powers in World War I, the Allies (including the United States, Great Britain and France) drew a new map of the Middle East. The carcass of the Ottoman Empire in the Middle East was carved into the modern-day countries of Iraq, Lebanon, Syria and Hashemite Arabia (later to be named Saudi Arabia.) While these states were beset by conflict during decades of colonial occupation by the British and French, the nationalistic identities of their Muslim populations was never in doubt. Nor was their land contested by immigrants of a rival faith.

But there was one more area that fell into a separate category—the British Mandate of Palestine.

Following World War I, the Land of Israel was once again occupied by a foreign power. This time, the ruler was Great Britain. The year was 1921. It was inhabited by Palestinians and Jews, both of whom claimed its future. While all sides enjoyed brief periods of relative harmony, the seeds of today's conflict can be clearly traced to the Mandate period.

British Control

Jews around the world welcomed British rule over Palestine as Great Britain had voiced support for a Jewish homeland in Palestine in the Balfour Declaration of 1917.

The condition of "the land" at that time of history was less than desirable. In fact, it was described by the League of Nations as "a sparsely populated, impoverished, barren area."[1] Even the famous American writer Mark Twain described his visit in the later part of the 19th century:

> ... For the sort of solitude to make one dreary, come to Galilee ... Nazareth is forlorn ... Jericho lies a moldering ruin ... Bethlehem and Bethany, in their poverty and humiliation... untenanted by any living creature... We never saw a human being on the whole route ... Hardly a tree or shrub anywhere. ... Palestine sits in sackcloth and ashes ... desolate and unlovely...[2]

Foreign Office,
November 2nd, 1917.

Dear Lord Rothschild,

I have much pleasure in conveying to you, on behalf of His Majesty's Government, the following declaration of sympathy with Jewish Zionist aspirations which has been submitted to, and approved by, the Cabinet

"His Majesty's Government view with favour the establishment in Palestine of a national home for the Jewish people, and will use their best endeavours to facilitate the achievement of this object, it being clearly understood that nothing shall be done which may prejudice the civil and religious rights of existing non-Jewish communities in Palestine, or the rights and political status enjoyed by Jews in any other country"

I should be grateful if you would bring this declaration to the knowledge of the Zionist Federation.

35 | The Balfour Declaration, 1917

The bleak descriptions of the long-neglected land did not deter the Jewish pioneers who arrived prior to World War I with the utopian dream of reinvigorating, and physically re-cultivating the land of their ancestors. Jews emigrated to Eretz Yisrael, purchasing uninhabited land mainly from absentee landlords.[3]

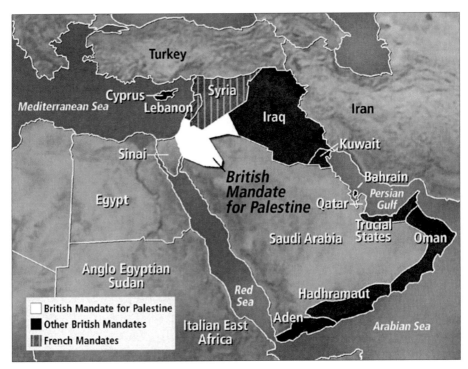

Map 6 | Regional Mandates Post-WWI, circa 1919

Purchasing Land in Palestine

In practice, the new Jewish homeland emerged in Palestine decades before World War I and the resulting Mandates after that war.

When Jews began immigrating into the region from Europe in the late 19th century, they bought uninhabited land directly from the sultan (King) of the Ottoman Empire after land ownership laws and purchase agreements were drastically revised. And it wasn't just Jewish settlers who were affected by these revisions, known as the Tanzimat Laws.

Primarily, the Tanzimat Laws permitted"…wealthy land owners, bankers, business owners, and money lenders anywhere in the Turkish empire to buy land formerly owned communally and inalienably…" by the Arab fellahin peasants. "Wealthy Arabs (effendis) from Cairo to Beirut, Jaffa to Damascus…" purchased large tracts of land which left former land-owning Arab fellahin as "landless serfs who had to work on what was once their own land for the benefit of their new overlords."[4]

The Turks forced non-Muslims (primarily from Circassia, Greece and the Balkans) into the area to become peasants on the land. Following the first wave of Jewish immigration from Russia, Egyptian and Turkish rulers responded by forcing Bulgarians, Circassians, and Arabs from surrounding areas to relocate into the region, changing the demographics of the Holy Land. It was the indigenous Arab fellahin whose culture and economic prospects were diluted.

36 | Pioneers trapping locusts, 1915

Combined, these new populations created considerable competition for employment and the sparse resources in the undeveloped area.

"The Palestinian Arab peasantry watched helplessly as their own land was bought out from under them, often by their own people."[5]

The Tanzimat Laws adopted during Ottoman Rule paved the way for Jewish pioneers who were returning to their land. They purchased land legitimately from the absentee landlords. In the Hope-Simpson report written in 1930, it was concluded that approximately 800 Arab families had to move due to Jewish land purchases. One can understand the misplaced anger that exists among hostile Arabs even today who claim that the Jews illegally took their land.

37 | Jewish farmer, circa 1911

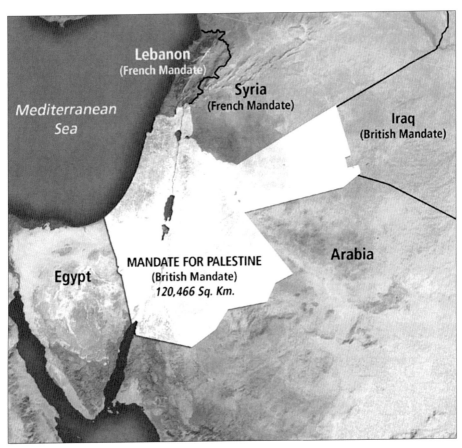

Map 7 | British Mandate of Palestine, circa 1920

But that wasn't the case. Under the Tanzimat Laws, Jewish immigrants purchased the land from Arab landowners. If the redistribution of the Arab fellahin's land could be traced to unscrupulous landlords, the legal sale to Jewish pioneers brought a crucial difference in settlement strategy as compared to other immigrants into Palestine—and sowed the early seeds of today's ongoing Palestinian discontent.

Unlike the absentee Arab landholders who kept the fellahin working on the land as sharecroppers or serfs, Jewish landlords preferred to work their land themselves. There were cases when the Zionist pioneers paid the Arab land owners to compensate the fellahins, enabling them to relocate.[6] This gave these Palestinian Arabs the option to purchase land of their own, which they did on occasion, on adjacent tracts where they could live and mutually benefit from the modernization the Jewish settlers pursued.[7]

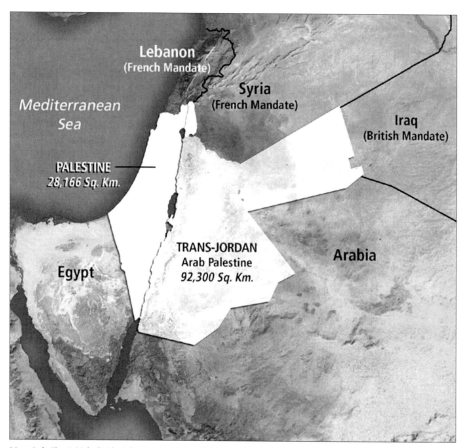

Map 8 | The British divide Palestine; creation of Trans-Jordan for Arabs only, circa 1922

Jewish Pioneers

For Zionists yearning to rebuild the golden era of Jewish life in Eretz Yisrael (the Land of Israel) the end of World War I created an open door for making aliyah (immigrating) into Palestine. During the next 20 years, 363,000 Jews seized this opportunity to escape religious persecution and return to their ancestral homeland where they would be able to live freely as Jews reinvigorating the land.

These Jewish settlers of Palestine had much in common with the hardships faced by the homesteaders of the American West. Both started with nothing but dry, barren land, without irrigation, plumbing, electricity, or roads. In Palestine, painstaking labor went into toiling the desert soil and draining malaria-infested swamps to provide agriculture and housing. Creating irrigation systems was essential for planting crops, which sustained new communal villages known as kibbutzim.

Within a decade, the land began to change, as did its inhabitants. Vegetables sprouted and fruit ripened. Diverse Jewish pioneers shared a common religion. However, they came from diverse cultures and spoke nearly 50 different languages. These Jews worked together to build and develop their new communities. Coming from generations of persecution in their former countries, they wanted to live in peace and friendship with the Arabs who lived in nearby villages.[8]

Within a few more years, the frontier nature of these communities began to fade, and modern infrastructure for social, economic and cultural growth ensued. The Jews developed factories and electrical power plants. Hospitals opened and newspapers were printed. By 1919, the Education Department was established and within a year the Zionist Organization had established 110 schools and three universities.[9]

The Technion, originally called the Technikum, in Haifa was one of these universities. It was founded in 1924. Interestingly, it was at the Technion—now the Israel Institute of Technology—where I held my first position as a professor following the completion of my PhD at Columbia University in New York and post-doctoral studies at the University of Chicago.

The Hebrew Opera debuted in 1922. The first Israeli Philharmonic played in 1936. It wasn't only Jewish settlers who benefitted. By the 1920s this modernization had prompted the immigration of nearly 100,000 Arabs from surrounding countries into Palestine. The standard of living for these Arabs improved significantly due to the increased prosperity of the region. Jews provided employment opportunities and advanced healthcare to their Arab neighbors. "The inflow of Arab immigration, which provided about 7.5 percent of the increase in the Arab population, offers significant evidence of the better performance of the Arab economy in Mandatory Palestine, in comparison to neighboring Arab countries."[10]

Arab Hostilities

Unfortunately, peaceful coexistence did not last long. The Jewish immigrants and most of the Arab inhabitants desired to live adjacent to each other in peace. But Arab extremists who did not want Jews on Arab land began a barrage of attacks against the Jewish population. Violent raids terrorized the unarmed Jewish civilians—men, women and children—in their villages, towns and kibbutzim.

The violence escalated during the anti-Jewish riots of 1919 and 1920 "in which scores of Jews in Jerusalem and Jaffa were attacked, raped and killed."[11]

The hostilities became an ever-increasing challenge for the British who maintained the responsibility of law enforcement for all inhabitants of Palestine. The Jews merely asked the British for protection. Arab demands were much more potent: immediate termination of Jewish immigration into Palestine, prohibition of any Jewish land purchases, and return of land to the Arabs for Arab ownership exclusively.[12]

The British acquiesced to Arab demands within a year of taking power in the region, and began a pattern of appeasement that was repeated several times during the Mandate Period.

In 1922, 74 percent of the original British Mandate of Palestine was relinquished to Amir Abdullah, the King of the reigning Hashemite tribe in Transjordan.[13] All of the land which was east of the Jordan River was given to Transjordan.

The British believed at the time, that this enormous compensation would certainly satisfy the Arabs as they now possessed 74 percent of the British Mandate of Palestine exclusively as a homeland for Arabs. No Jews could live on, nor purchase land in Transjordan.[14]

In turn, Jews accepted being restricted from 74 percent of the British Mandate of Palestine, but the deal was not without hardship. Jewish settlers who had purchased land east of the Jordan River were uprooted and exiled from the East Bank. Future Jewish land purchases and development were limited to the west side of the Jordan River.[15]

Less than a year later, Jews lost more of the Holy Land when in 1923 the Golan Heights, highlands on the Syrian border of Palestine, was relinquished to France, the mandatory power in Syria.

38 | Jewish colony set on fire, circa 1929

With hopes that this division of land would satisfy their neighbors and stop the Arab attacks on their villages, the Jewish settlers focused on their immediate and equally difficult tasks: building their communities, absorbing and integrating more poor and unprepared Jewish immigrants arriving from Europe and preparing for their own Jewish statehood. Losing 74 percent of the land was tolerable as long as they had hope of establishing their Jewish homeland, no matter how small.

Grand Mufti and the Jewish Settlers

In the face of Jewish modernization, the Palestinian Arabs found a leader in Haj Amin al-Husseini, whose influence exponentially expanded beginning in 1921 when he became the Grand Mufti of Jerusalem. Without ever having national sovereignty or any centralized Palestinian governing body, the Grand Mufti served not only as the Arab Palestinian spiritual leader, but also as the designated political leader of the Palestinian Arabs. As an ardent anti-Semite, al-Husseini organized vicious riots and massacres targeting Jewish civilians. In 1929 alone he masterminded attacks against Jews in Jerusalem, Safed, Jaffa and Kfar Darom, (a kibbutz in the Gaza Strip.)

39 | Hebron Synagogue destruction, 1929

The same year, al-Husseini spearheaded the destruction of the ancient, 3,000-year-old Jewish town of Hebron. British authorities described the barbaric nature of the hostilities which ultimately killed 67 Jews.[16] Describing these atrocities, the British High Commissioner John Chancellor wrote, "I do not think that history records many worse horrors in the last few hundred years."[17]

The Hebron Massacre may have been the worst instance of Arab violence, but it was not the last.

Seven years later, the Grand Mufti initiated the Great Arab Revolt. Between 1936 and 1939, Palestinian Arabs launched attacks that killed more than 400 Jewish settlers. The British were ineffective and inattentive; the Nazi rise to power was diverting the Crown's attention and military resources.

While not being able or willing to stop the Arab atrocities, Britain went a step further and double-crossed the Jews by implementing policies that prohibited Jewish ownership of weapons, leaving Jews totally vulnerable. In 1937 a British Commission was created to investigate the Arab Revolt and to recommend an end to the Arab-Jewish hostilities. Led by Lord Earl Peel, an investigative team determined that peaceful coexistence was not a viable option. In its official report the Peel Commission recommended to the British Prime Minister

Neville Chamberlain that the best resolution of the conflict would come through a partition of Palestine into separate Jewish and Palestinian states.

Astonishingly, while the proposal was accepted by the Jews, it was categorically *rejected* by the Arab leadership, who staunchly declared that a Jewish state should not be created on one square inch of Palestine. It is significant to note that from a Jewish perspective, this British offer represents the beginning of the Arab rejection of any and all future offers for the establishment of a Palestinian homeland. Rather than being willing to establish a Palestinian homeland next to a Jewish homeland, Arabs have always rejected the establishment of a Jewish homeland on *any land* in the British Mandate of Palestine. To Jews, the Arab argument against Israel as the homeland for Jews has never been about borders or size; it has been categorically against the Jewish people establishing a Jewish homeland.[18]

This intransigent rejection of Jewish homeland on any parcel or portion in the Holy Land of their ancestors troubled the Jews in Palestine as it alarmed Jews around the world. Yet, this dismal situation had to be put aside as the West was faced with a much larger threat—the rise of Nazi Germany.

Hitler and the Third Reich Rise to Power

Adolph Hitler came to power blaming his country's defeat during World War I on the Jews. He also blamed Jews for the Communist Revolution in Russia and the Great Depression in Europe. To Hitler and the Nazis, the Jews were a criminal race to be annihilated. In his political manifesto, *Mein Kampf*, Hitler outlined Germany's only path to recovery: destruction of the Jewish race.[19]

Hitler's approach was systematic and meticulous. In 1933, Jews were expelled from the German civil service. Later, Jews also were denied employment and education. Violence, arrests and public humiliation against Jews ensued. In 1935, the Nuremberg Laws stripped Jews of German citizenship and prohibited intermarriage, among other restrictions. The construction of concentration camps began.

For German Jews, the only hope was to leave Germany. However, most Jews did not have the necessary contacts abroad or the financial resources to gain entry into another country. And most countries, including the United States, had strict limits on immigration, and had little or no sympathy for the Jews of Europe.

Why Couldn't Jews Immigrate Into Palestine?

Most Jewish settlers in Palestine had relatives living in Jewish communities throughout Europe. They were terrified for their European relatives' safety and survival. At a minimum, the Jews of Palestine begged the British to ease Jewish immigration restrictions so their relatives could leave Europe and find refuge in Eretz Yisrael.

HOLOCAUST VICTIMS 1939–1945

Country	Pre-WW II Jewish Population	Jews Killed
Austria	185,000	50,000
Belgium	65,700	28,900
Bohemia and Moravia	118,310	78,150
Bulgaria	50,000	0
Denmark	7,800	60
Estonia	4,500	1,500-2000
Finland	2,000	7
France	350,000	77,320
Germany	566,000	134,500-141,500
Greece	77,380	60,000-67,000
Hungary	825,000	550,000-569,000
Italy	44,500	7,680
Latvia	91,500	70,000-71,500
Lithuania	168,000	140,000-143,000
Luxembourg	3,500	1,950
Netherlands	140,000	100,000
Norway	1,700	762
Poland	3,300,000	2,900,000-3,000,000
Romania	609,000	271,000-287,000
Slovakia	88,950	68,000-71,000
Soviet Union	3,020,000	1,000,000-1,100,000
Yugoslavia	78,000	56,200-63,300
Total	**9,796,840**	**5,596,029**

Source: Yad Vashem, 2012

But their hopes to rescue Jewish brethren from the perils of Europe were squelched when the British government issued the British White Paper of 1939—often cited as Britain's worst betrayal of the Jewish people. This new edict limited Jewish immigration into Palestine to merely 10,000 immigrants per year. It also prohibited Jews from purchasing land in Palestine. If the doors of Palestine had been open to the entrapped Jews of Europe, millions of Jews might have been saved from death in the Holocaust.

Despite this betrayal, Jews in Palestine volunteered to fight with the Allies to defeat the Nazis.

40 | Amin al-Husseini (left) with Adolf Hitler, circa 1941

The Jewish Infantry Brigade was a group of more than 30,000 Jews from Palestine who volunteered under the command of the British to fight the Nazi advance into Africa. David Ben-Gurion, the leader of the Jewish Agency encouraged the Jews of Palestine to enlist with the British to fight the Nazis stating; "We shall fight the War as if there was no White Paper, and the White Paper, as if there was no War."[20]

This tragic chain of events hurts deep in the hearts of nearly every single Jew around the world today. When Jews hear or use the phrase "never again" they inevitably conjure up images of the horrific death camps and feel a visceral sense of loss and vulnerability. We know that had Israel existed in the 1930s, the Jews of Europe would have had a safe haven because they could have immigrated into Israel. As I described in Chapter One, for Jews around the world, Israel represents the safe haven that didn't exist prior to World War II. "Never Again!" has become a rallying cry for Jews who are determined to ensure Israel's survival, so that Jews will never again be left unprotected in the world.

Today, the State of Israel is their safe haven.

Arab and Nazi Connections

Back in Palestine, the Nazi threat was reflected in more ways than Britain's appeasement. A nefarious alliance between the Grand Mufti and the Nazis was intensifying, with proof to be seen in virtually every neighborhood and village. The Palestinian youth organization established by the Mufti used Nazi emblems, names and uniforms.[21] Arab youth addressed each other chiming "Heil Hitler." The Nazi Propaganda Ministry regularly supplied al-Husseini with fresh anti-Semitic rhetoric for use by the Palestinian Arabs.[22]

Hitler financially supported al-Husseini, putting him on the Nazi payroll as early as 1937 as an agent and a propagandist. "By 1938, al-Husseini fielded some ten thousand fighters, an active propaganda unit and modern weapons…."[23]

Eventually the British realized the Nazi alliance with al-Husseini and decided to drive him out of Palestine.[24] In 1941 al-Husseini worked and lived in Berlin where he aided the Third Reich. He was instrumental in instigating the pro-Nazi coup in Iraq, as well as in organizing the Muslim Nazi Brigade, which was responsible for the murder of nearly 90 percent of the Bosnian Jewish population.

During World War II, al-Husseini's voice was commonly heard delivering anti-Jewish propaganda on Germany's Arabic radio station, convincing Muslims throughout Europe to support the Nazis.[25] On March 1, 1944, al-Husseini stated:

> Arabs! Rise as one and fight for your sacred rights. Kill the Jews wherever you find them. Kill them with your teeth if need be. This pleases God, history, and religion. This saves your honor."[26] In exchange for his allegiance, the Nazis promised Grand Mufti al-Husseini that no European Jew would enter Palestine again.[27]

After World War II, the Nuremberg trials revealed that the Grand Mufti had planned to build an Auschwitz-style death camp in Palestine, near Nablus, for the genocide of Palestine's Jewish population.

Al-Husseini was condemned as a war criminal in Nuremberg and was sentenced to a French prisoner-of-war camp. After escaping to Syria from France, he returned to not only lead the Palestinians, but to convince fellow Arab heads of State to reject the U.N. Partition of Palestine. His reign as the Grand Mufti ended in 1948 and his influence over Palestinian Arabs waned. He died in Beirut in 1974.

Palestine During World War II

As World War II continued, the Jews of Palestine persisted in building what they still hoped would become their sovereign Jewish state. They knew nothing about al-Husseini's grand plans in their own backyard, but they heard terrifying rumors about Europe's death camps and crematoria. They feared the Nazi advancement into Africa knowing that Palestine and the Middle East would likely be next in line for invasion.

Having lived in fear their whole lives, these Jews garnered their strength, and prepared themselves for the ultimate defense of their children and future generations. Whether facing the despicable Nazis or hostile Arabs, they remembered the plight of their ancestors and prepared to defend their homeland at all costs.

It became increasingly clear to the Jews of Palestine that sovereignty for the Jewish State of Israel would not be delivered peacefully. To protect themselves from increasing Arab hostilities, informal Jewish militias were formed. The largest militia under the leadership of David Ben-Gurion (who later became Israel's first Prime Minister) was the Haganah. Other smaller, sometimes renegade groups included the Irgun, and the Stern Gang.

With the fortitude of a people who knew their survival depended on their strength, the Jews of Palestine prepared to protect themselves. Through a network of resistance fighters in Europe, illegal smuggling of European Jews into Palestine became a top priority. When the British interfered, they, in turn, became the enemy. Arms of any kind, any vintage, and any caliber were smuggled into Palestine. Zionist farmers transformed themselves into fighters for the inevitable war rising on the horizon.

To encourage the development of a Jewish homeland in the British Mandate of Palestine, the British had to deliberately reject the rights and wishes of the majority indigenous Arab population that had held the territory since the conquest of the second Islamic Caliph Omar in 638 CE.

As late as 1922, despite an organized and purposeful influx of immigrants from Europe and Russia, the population of Jews numbered less than 90,000 out of a total population of over 750,000.[1] Yet in spite of a 9 to 1 majority, the aspirations of Palestinian Arabs were ignored. The momentum of the Zionist relocation continued.

To the British, the Jewish homeland was an important tactical measure in its broader strategy of establishing its imperial dominance in the Middle East. Offering the Jews a homeland in the land of Palestine meant winning over world Jewry to the British campaign and assuring the Jews' support and allegiance to the Crown's broader post-war ambitions.

In contrast, the British viewed the Palestinian Arabs as lacking the right to assert their independence or achieve statehood. The British expected complacency from the Arab Palestinians and marginal participation in joint Jewish-Arab political institutions. This attitude failed to reflect Arab aspirations or represent the Arabs' vast numerical superiority in the Holy Land.

In light of the British support for Zionism, the Palestinians were in a no-win situation. On the one hand, to participate in unequal political institutions would mean their permanent subjugation to Jewish interests and the end of democracy in Palestine before it even began. But on the other hand, non-participation would allow the British to work even more closely with the emerging and internationally supported Jewish power which would increase the pace of Jewish development in Palestine.

False Alliance: Great Britain's Great Betrayal

To fully understand the challenging situation facing the Arab Palestinians in the era of the

British Mandate, it is important to step back and examine the general political atmosphere in the Arab region during World War I. While the Ottoman Empire proclaimed its neutrality, the combination of expanding hostilities in Libya and the Balkans proved too much for the Ottoman Sultan to resist. Put succinctly by military historian David Woodward,

> Participation in what had begun as a European war might seem to outside observers, therefore, to have been suicidal, but key elements in the government, impressed by German industrial and military power and motivated by dreams of imperial glory, greeted the expanding war as an opportunity to regain lost territories and incorporate new lands and nationalities into the empire.[2]

And so the Ottoman Empire allied itself with the Germans and declared a jihad (holy war) against the Russians, French, and the British in November of 1914. Naturally, the new alliance was cause for great alarm to France and Russia, but particularly to Great Britain, which now faced a powerful foe with a real capability to significantly threaten its interests in the region.

As the war expanded into the Arab world both sides aggressively tried to win the sympathies of the region's leaders. For both the Germans and the British, the primary target was Sherif Hussein, King of the Hejaz in Mecca. Great Britain gained favor by promising to support the establishment of a united Arab state in the whole of the Arabian Peninsula—including Palestine. Authorized by the British Government, Sir Henry McMahon preyed on the Arabs' desire for independence, and made promises in a series of letters known as the McMahon-Hussein Correspondence spanning from 1915 to 1916. In one letter addressed to Hussein dated October 24, 1915, McMahon declared that, "Great Britain is prepared to recognize and support the independence of the Arabs in all the regions within the limits demanded by the Sherif of Mecca," and that "Great Britain will guarantee the Holy Places against all external aggression and will recognize their inviolability."[3]

Naturally the Arabs trusted this declaration and therefore fought and sacrificed their resources and blood contributing to the defeat of the Ottoman Empire. For their efforts the Arabs were certain that they would be granted sovereignty over their own land. However, after the war ended, Arabs began to witness an extremely disappointing scenario. One after another, Britain occupied cities which were important to Arabs and Islam. These included Baghdad, Damascus, and Jerusalem. Then in 1916, the British and French signed the Sykes-Picot Agreement, which cancelled promises made in the McMahon Correspondence and effectively divided the former Ottoman territories between Britain and France. This paved the way for the regional Mandate system, and thwarted Arab independence there.

Nowhere did this duplicity betray the Arab cause more than in Jerusalem.

On December 11, 1917, unaware of the Sykes-Picot agreement the previous year, Palestinian

Arabs welcomed British troops led by General Edmund Allenby with fanfare and celebration. Allenby's own proclamation to the Palestinian people, said nothing of the Sykes-Picot agreement and seemed to honor the Crown's pledge to the Palestinian Arabs in exchange for their military service. In his own words:

41 | British Allenby enters Jerusalem, circa 1917

> Since your city is regarded with affection by the adherents of three of the great religions of mankind, and its soil has been consecrated by the prayers and pilgrimages of devout people of these three religions for centuries, therefore do I make known to you that every sacred building, monument, holy spot, shrine, traditional site, endowment, pious bequest or customary place of prayer…will be maintained and protected according to the existing customs and beliefs of those to whom [these] faiths are sacred.[4]

It wasn't the only example of British lip service to the Palestinians in 1917. In the Balfour Declaration, Great Britain also made promises to the Zionists to establish a Jewish national home in Palestine in spite of the large non-Jewish majority of Palestinian Arabs already living there. Continuing the contradictions, however, the Declaration stated:

> His Majesty's Government views with favor the establishment in Palestine of a national home for the Jewish people, and will use their best endeavors to facilitate the achievement of this object, it being clearly understood that nothing shall be done which may prejudice the civil and religious rights of existing non-Jewish communities in Palestine, or the rights and political status enjoyed by Jews in any other country.[5]

Although the text of the Balfour Declaration was ultimately vague in defining the nature of a Jewish national home, Britain's intentions were clearly to establish a significant Jewish national and political presence in Palestine with the eventual result of Jewish statehood at the expense of the 90 percent non-Jewish inhabitants of the region. The British promises for Arab independence were quickly proven empty—this is in spite of the fact that Allenby himself once described the Arab revolt and subsequent allegiance of the Arabs to the British as "invaluable" to the British cause in dismantling Ottoman rule.[6]

The British Betrayal

Ultimately, the British occupation over the next 30 years did not just result with the end of Ottoman oppression. Nor was it simply a replacement of one ruler by the next.

Instead, the subsequent Mandate period ushered in something profoundly more devastating for the Palestinians.

Supported by the foreign British authority, Zionists began arriving and establishing a Jewish national home squarely in the midst of the territory's majority Arab population. The Palestinian dream of national self-determination—dismissed by one British official as "pipedreams of a backward people"—would continue to be silenced while imperial Europe allowed more and more Eastern European Jews to take Palestinian land. As such, the war for Palestine did not really begin in 1948, but during the British Mandate period when the Palestinians were faced with the enveloping Jewish conquest. How this existential war was fought, whether militarily, financially, or politically is insignificant. During the British Mandate, not only did the Palestinians find themselves betrayed, but in a new fight for survival as well.

Grounded in a series of three inherently contradictory documents—the McMahon Correspondence, the Balfour Declaration, and the Sykes-Picot Agreement—the British Mandate of Palestine went into formal operation on September 29, 1923. Palestine was placed under the jurisdiction of the British. The Mandate recognized "the Jewish Agency as a public body for the purpose of advising and cooperating with the administration of Palestine in such economic, social and other matters as may affect the establishment of a Jewish national home." The British agreed to work with the Jewish Agency "to construct or operate any public works, service and utilities, and to develop any of the natural resources of the country."[7]

In addition to establishing a Jewish homeland in Palestine, the Mandate shredded the Arab identity throughout the region and replaced it with new arbitrary national boundaries that politically separated peoples linked by religion and culture for thousands of years. Suddenly, the Arab people—who were once defined by the land in which they lived and by the villages which they created—were now classified as Iraqis, Syrians, Jordanians, Lebanese, and separately—the Palestinians.

By embracing the fiction that the Holy Land was inhabited only by a small number of people or by disparate religious sects, it became easier for the British to re-draw the country's political and territorial borders in such a way that the Arabs of Palestine were separated from their kinsmen and compatriots living in the neighboring areas. Stuck between the French and British realms of control in the region, new regulations governing citizenship and nationality left many Palestinians living abroad stateless.

Tribesmen who possessed lands on both sides of the Jordan Valley were forced to pay taxes to two different governments. With borders drawn according to the interests of the separate European powers, Palestinian Arabs held a unique identity within the Arab world, while lacking the benefits of statehood.

Meanwhile, as local Arab Palestinians began to feel abandoned, any new Jewish immigrant into Palestine could become a citizen under the Mandate following his/her residence in the land for 24 months.

It is not as if the Arab Palestinians didn't try to establish their own political structure. For example, the people of Ottoman Palestine had elected representative parliaments responsible for local governance in 1877, 1908, 1912, and 1914.[8] In 1919, in an effort to come together and establish a common political identity, a Palestinian Christian-Muslim alliance convened the First Palestine National Congress which established the Palestine Arab Executive as the nationalist representative body of the Palestinian people. Sadly, their efforts were disregarded by the British.

Meanwhile, the Jewish Agency grew into a state with the support of the British. By March 1918, Dr. Chaim Weizmann (later the first President of Israel) arrived in Palestine. Of his major cultural initiatives that changed the landscape of Palestine, perhaps the most influential was the sizable growth of schools for Jewish students and the introduction of the Hebrew language into the curriculum. The landscape changed with the flying of the blue and white Israeli flag, while the Zionist National Anthem could be heard at gatherings throughout the land.

Finally, from the indigenous Arab perspective, the most patent abuse of all lay in Weizmann's attempt to demolish part of the approaches to the Western Wall, which the Muslims regarded as desecration to their sacred holy site. This most egregious act was a blatant violation of Allenby's promise to the Arab Palestinians that their Muslim places of worship would be maintained and protected.

To the indigenous Arabs, who invariably were described as "the non-Jewish communities" in the Balfour Declaration or merely as "the other sections of the population" under the British Mandate, it was resoundingly clear that the British policy towards the Jewish community was to support the nationalist aspirations of the Zionists in Palestine while demonstrably refusing to recognize the national existence of Palestinians. Especially provocative was the decision to "give the Jewish Agency a special role in formulating Mandatory policy while the Arabs were denied any representation at all, except through their religious leaders."[9] Despite the overwhelming demographic majority of the native Arab population, the failure to recognize their existence was exacerbated by the failure to acknowledge, much less uphold, their civil and political rights as human beings.

42 | Palestinian Arab leaders, 1929

Losing the Land: The Beginning of the Struggle for Palestine

It's important to note that the initial relationship between Palestinian Arabs and Jewish immigrants was not entirely hostile. The Palestinian Arabs were curious about the Jewish newcomers and initially benefitted from their need for Arab labor. But as the British Mandate commenced, it became apparent that the Jews were pursuing a primarily separatist agenda, with an economic system dependent solely on Jewish labor and a political apparatus to serve Jewish interests. As the Jewish population increased and the need for Arab labor diminished, the beginning of Palestinian displacement commenced. Therefore, the initial Jewish victory in Palestine was not won through the use of force, but with the power of finance and political organization—with support from Great Britain and affluent world Jewry.

To accommodate the influx of new Jewish immigrants, the Jewish National Fund worked with Keren Ha-Yesod (Foundation Fund), the Palestine Land Development Company, and other Zionist organizations to begin purchasing land in Palestine, particularly from absentee landlords. In 1918, Palestinian non-Jews owned 98 percent of the land, and constituted over 90 percent of the population. But during the first decade of British rule, Jewish ownership of land nearly doubled, increasing from 650,000 dunums in 1920 to 1,163,000 in 1929. Between 1920 and 1939, more than 846,000 dunums (76,150 hectares) were bought by Jewish organizations and individuals. Combining this with the small amount of Jewish-owned land before World War I, this brought the total amount of Jewish-owned land in Palestine to

1,496,000 dunums (134,775 hectares). While this is certainly a sizeable increase in Jewish landholdings, it only equated to about five percent of the total land area.[10]

Meanwhile, the Jewish population increased. From 1918 to 1939 the Jewish population of Palestine expanded from an estimated 60,000 to 460,000. Whereas Jews represented one-tenth of the population in 1918, they became one-third of the population by 1939. Further, 40 million pounds of sterling silver came into Palestine from Jews abroad between the years of 1917–1929. The number of Jewish agricultural settlements also doubled. Altogether, the amount of capital brought into Palestine by Jewish immigrants between 1920 and 1935 was estimated to have amounted to more than 80 million Palestinian pounds.[11]

Due to the steady purchase of land by Jews, the prices of real estate soared, preventing Palestinians from affordable land ownership. This created severe hardships for many Palestinians who had lived and worked on the land for centuries. Now these natives were forced to leave their homes. They not only lost their houses, their communities disappeared and their jobs as laborers ceased.

According to Middle East historian Benny Morris, the conflict became a battle between

> The Arabs who sought to retain the Arab and Muslim character of the region and maintain their position as its dominant inhabitants; and the Zionists who sought to radically change the status quo, buy as much land as possible, settle it, and eventually turn an Arab populated country into a Jewish Homeland.[12]

The monumental progress of Jewish land ownership and population growth for the Zionists resulted in catastrophic consequences for Palestinian Arabs. Jewish purchase of Palestinian land from the Arab land owning class predominantly living in Lebanon and Syria triggered a subsistence crisis for local Palestinian peasantry. By 1930 an estimated 30 percent of Palestinian villagers were landless, and as many as 75–80 percent held insufficient land to meet basic subsistence needs.[13] Arab demands to remedy their situation were ignored by the British. Supported by the Mandate, the Zionists secured more and more land, while developing a strong and independent economy.

Resistance

By the 1930s, the clear beginning of a popular, political Palestinian movement was in the making. It was "one with significant intellectual ferment and diverse notions of its future" in response to the Zionist expansion.[14] The Palestinian people began to enact measures that reflected the evolution of their social identity and the sentiment of their own Palestinian story of nationalism. Between 1936 and 1939, the Great Arab Revolt took place after the killing of two Jews. In retaliation, two Arabs were killed. In the aftermath of these killings, violence escalated.

Thousands of Palestinians from every part and social strata of Palestine were mobilized and unified by a single voice that called for national self-determination against the British and the Zionists. Yet, just as the Palestinian nationalist movement rose to this temporary zenith, thousands of Palestinian protesters were killed and wounded, while those that survived were rounded up, hanged, imprisoned or exiled by the British.[15]

Violence in Palestine: Riot to Revolt

According to Benny Morris, "by 1929 the Arabs understood that disproportionate growth of the Jewish community, nurtured and sustained by Mandatory government measures, promised to turn them into a minority in their own land."[16] And after nearly a decade of crises and of Palestinian failure to limit the emergence of a separatist Jewish entity through non-violent measures, the discontented Arab masses began to target the British governing authority and the emerging Jewish population.

43 | Arab protest delegation to London, 1929

Widespread violence between Jews and Arabs in Palestine erupted in 1929, with what has become known as the Wailing Wall Riots.[17] Violence broke out in Jerusalem and spread to Hebron, Sfaad, Tel-Aviv, and Jaffa. At the time the British had only 292 policemen in Palestine—not nearly enough officials to stop the increasing violence.[18] During a week of bloodshed, 133 Jews and 116 Arabs were killed and 339 Jews and over 232 Arabs were wounded.[19]

44 | Arab women's protest delegation to the British High Commissioner, 1929

As a result of the uprising, on October 21, 1930, the British government issued The White Paper advocating limits on Jewish immigration and land ownership in Palestine, signaling a shift away from the Balfour commitment to the Jews.[20]

Yet the trends of the past several decades continued at an alarming rate. In part as a result of persecution of European Jewry and a limit on immigration into the United States, Jewish immigration into Palestine drastically increased in the early 1930s. From 1929 to 1931 Jewish immigration into Palestine totaled 4,000 to 5,000 people per year. In 1932, 9,500 Jews arrived in the region; in 1933, 30,000 Jews; in 1934, 42,000; and in 1935, 62,000 Jews emigrated to Palestine.[21] As Jewish immigration into Palestine continued to increase, and more and more land fell from Arab to Jewish control, the Arabs' economic situation continued to deteriorate.

After 1930, the situation for the Arab peasantry drastically worsened as land prices were driven up by the influx of Jews from Germany and Eastern Europe. The rise in capital drove up land prices. This, in conjunction with increasing inflation made the prospect of land ownership for the common Palestinian out of their reach as wages kept diminishing. The disenfranchised and frustrated Arabs of Palestine became increasingly more agitated and violent as

45 | Palestinians mobilize taking oath against Jews and British, circa 1936

46 | Awkashi Mosque, Jerusalem, circa 1928

47 | Awkashi Shrine Desecrated, 1929

they saw their options fading away. This loss of their land and livelihood, eventually led to the Great Revolt of 1936–1939, when the Arabs collectively participated in organized strikes, boycotts, demonstrations, and in an avid campaign of armed struggle.

For the Arabs, who saw no alternative but to revolt, the uprising fueled their determination to achieve national independence.

The revolt led to several decisive actions by Palestinian Arabs. First, the sale of land to Jews was strictly forbidden. Those who were found guilty were tried in independent courts and executed. The Arabs of Palestine also made three significant demands. First was the immediate cessation of Jewish immigration. Second was the prohibition of the transfer of Arab lands to Jews. Thirdly, they demanded a democratic government in which the Arabs would have a majority role due to their demographic majority.

In the end, Palestinian Arab appeals, protests, and demonstrations all failed.

PALESTINE

Statement of Policy
by His Majesty's Government
in the United Kingdom

Presented by the Secretary of State for the Colonies
to Parliament by Command of His Majesty,
October 1939

LONDON:
PRINTED AND PUBLISHED BY HIS MAJESTY'S STATIONARY OFFICE

1939

Cmd. 6019

48 | British White Paper of 1939

49 | Jews led out of Jerusalem during Arab Revolt, 1936

50 | British search Palestinians in Jaffa, 1936

The British brutally suppressed the Palestinian Arabs and crushed the revolt. Three years of consistent uprisings, combined with internal divisions led to measures implemented by the British government, which left the Palestinian people economically ruined, politically divided, and militarily destroyed. The opportunity to achieve national independence and prevent the creation of a separate Zionist state was lost.

Conclusion: The Partition of Palestine

The outbreak of World War II significantly altered the status quo of Palestine. The Zionists funneled as many Jewish refugees into Palestine as possible and developed a strong underground Jewish paramilitary. Although illegal, the Jewish units were brazenly armed, trained and deployed at strategic sites around Palestine, ostensibly in defense of the land against the potential invasion by Axis powers. Secretly, the British feared that Jewish troops would inevitably turn against Britain to obtain independence once the hostilities ended.[22]

The Peel Commission of 1936, was officially known as the Palestine Royal Commission. It was a British Commission of Inquiry sent to Palestine in November of 1936 to investigate conditions on the ground, which caused the deadly 1936 Arab Revolt.

On July 7, 1937, Lord Peel published a report recommending that to end the hostilities between Arabs and Jews, the Holy Land needed to be partitioned into separate entities.

The Peel Commission called for the partition of Palestine into three separate states, one for the Jews, one for the Arabs, and a third consisting of Jerusalem, Bethlehem and the towns of Tiberias, Safed, Nazareth and Acre, to be placed permanently under British rule.

The plan for the three-state partition was inevitably dropped due to fierce resistance against it. In fact, the recommendation for partition was rejected due to Arab objections in 1938. But limitations on Jewish immigration were upheld (in writing, at least) by the 1939 White Paper, which called for the admission of no more than 75,000 Jewish immigrants per year from 1939–1945.

The Jewish response was to actively resist British policies. Well-armed extremist groups such as the Stern Gang and the Irgun Zvai Leumi, headed by Menachem Begin, (later Israel's sixth Prime Minister) carried out a campaign of terror against both civilian and military British targets in Palestine.

As the horrors of the Nazi German concentration camps became known to Jews living worldwide, the conviction of Zionists to establish a Jewish-only state in the land of Palestine grew ever more passionate. At one point, a conference of American Zionists met in New York and called for "a complete end to all controls on immigration, the granting of authority to the Jewish Agency to develop the uncultivated lands in Palestine and the establishment of a 'Jewish Commonwealth' in the whole of Palestine."[23]

IRGUN ZWAÏ LÉUMI BE-EREZ JISRAËL
ORGANISATION MILITAIRE NATIONALE JUIVE D'EREZ JISRAËL
JEWISH NATIONAL MILITARY ORGANISATION OF EREZ JISRAËL

An Irgun poster for distribution in Central Europe.

51 | Irgun Zwei Leumi propaganda

Map 9 | Peel Commission Proposal, 1937

As the war drained the resources of the British Empire, its desire and capacity for imperial control over the Middle East dwindled. In 1947, unable to maintain stability in Palestine and manage the opposing interests of the Jews and Arabs in Palestine, the British handed the question of Palestine over to the newly established United Nations.

In November 1947, the UN called for the end of the British Mandate and the establishment of two independent states, one Jewish and one Arab to be carved from the land of Palestine, with Jerusalem to be governed by an international administration.

The UN partition gave control over 55 percent of the territory in Palestine to the Jews who inhabited five percent of the territory. Moreover, they were granted the most fertile, arable land in the country, while the Arab majority was banished to the most infertile and unwelcoming regions. From a population of only 5,000 in 1800, by 1947, the Jews had grown to 608,000 and had been given authority over the majority of Palestine.

52 | Haj al-Husseini and members of the Arab Higher Committee, circa 1936

Palestinians and the entire Arab world denounced the unjust decision. As Columbia University professor Rashid Khalidi wrote, "…for the Palestinians, partition was half a baby."[24]

It also meant that, for Palestinians, war in defense of Palestine against the Zionists was painfully inevitable.

For the Arabs, the UN plan meant that the world's most powerful countries agreed to turn their backs on Arab sovereignty. They therefore felt betrayed once again by imperialist powers. The Arabs categorically rejected the partition, protesting that the decision went against the United Nations Charter, which gives people the right to decide their own destiny.

Arab Palestinians were left to ask, "Why they should be made to pay for the Holocaust…

why it was not fair for the Jews to be a minority in a unitary Palestinian state, while it was fair for the indigenous majority on its own ancestral soil to be converted overnight into a minority under alien rule?"[25]

For the Jews, the partition of Palestine was a significant victory on the road to greater territorial conquest in the land of Palestine. A people marked for annihilation by the Nazi regime had in just two short decades achieved nationhood and a homeland.

For Arab Palestinians, who had experienced the devastation of one occupation after another, the defeated Ottoman Empire was replaced by British rule, only to make way for the Zionist occupation. Unlike the long precedent of occupations in Palestine, however, the Zionist mission was not to occupy the country, but to expel the non-Jewish indigenous inhabitants from their homes, lands, livelihoods and history.

Jews yearned and prayed for a return to their homeland for thousands of years. But it wasn't until the full extent of the Holocaust emerged at the end of World War II and the establishment of the United Nations that a safe haven for Jews in the Holy Land was established.

Palestinians had struggled for their own state since the fall of the Ottoman Empire and the end of World War I. But instead of realizing their own nationalist dream, they found their homeland being partitioned again by the world powers.

Within months, the region would be engulfed in war once more. This time it was not a world war between empires, but a bitter street fight for survival between former neighbors.

For Jews, the result of this conflict was a miracle. For Palestinians, it was "al-Naqba—the disaster."

It wasn't until Nazi Germany was defeated in 1945 that the world realized the magnitude and the horror of the Holocaust.

Reports about Nazi camps drifted out of Europe during the war years like an eerie fog. But at that time, no one grasped the enormity of Hitler's savage design to systematically exterminate Jews in gas chambers and then burn their remains in crematoria to hide the evidence and deny future culpability.

53 | Holocaust victims, Dachau, 1945

Only when the absolute horror of what had transpired, at the hands of the Nazis, was witnessed firsthand by the liberators did the world take notice. Although the combat-hardened troops had witnessed plenty of death and destruction, the butchery seen and smelled inside the concentration camps would haunt American soldiers for the rest of their lives.

Among the witnesses was General Dwight D. Eisenhower, Supreme Commander of the Allied forces. Astonished by what he observed during camp inspections, Eisenhower publicly declared that the atrocities were "beyond the American mind to comprehend."[1] He was determined to have the world acknowledge these unspeakable crimes declaring, "I never dreamed that such cruelty, bestiality, and savagery could really exist in this world."[2] Not only did he command all his troops and citizens of towns to see for themselves what the Nazis had done, he ordered all civilian news media and military combat camera units to visit the camps so that they could generate recorded proof of these crimes against humanity for perpetuity.

54 | Eisenhower, Ohrdruf, 1945

He explained in a letter to General George S. Marshall, "I made the visit deliberately, in order to be in a position to give first-hand evidence of these things if ever, in the future, there develops a tendency to charge these allegations merely to 'propaganda.'"[3] In 1999, the Dwight D. Eisenhower Memorial Commission was created to memorialize President Eisenhower for his service in the Allied Forces in Europe during World War II and his commitment to rectifying the injustices committed during the war.

Holocaust Denial

Little did Eisenhower know that in years to come Israelis and Jews around the world would be confronted by growing groups of scholars and world leaders who deny the Holocaust happened. This modern, sophisticated, anti-Semitic movement of Holocaust Deniers still accuses Jews of inventing and aggrandizing the Holocaust to generate political and financial support for Israel. Their malicious falsehoods propagate throughout broadcasts, published books, the Internet, as well as within corridors of some Western universities. As recently as December 11, 2006, a conference dedicated to the Denial of the Holocaust was organized by Iran. The conference took place in Tehran and was attended by representatives from 30 countries around the globe.

Even Palestinian President Mahmoud Abbas, a man whom I believe wants to end the conflict in the Holy Land, conducted research as a young doctoral student in the Soviet Union questioning the number of deaths during the Holocaust and raising questions about the relationship between Zionism and Nazism. His thesis, *The Connection between the Nazis and the Leaders of the Zionist Movement 1933–1945*, discussed what some critics consider to be Holocaust Denial. This work was published in a book in Arabic, *The Other Side: the Secret Relationship between Nazism and Zionism* (Arabic: al-Wajh al-Akhar: al-'Alaqat as-Sirriya bayna an-Naziya wa's-Sihyuniya.)

However, Holocaust Denial is not merely an intellectual exercise. Perhaps the most extreme perpetrator is the President of the Islamic Republic of Iran, Mahmoud Ahmadinejad, who regularly denies the Holocaust and routinely calls his supporters to "wipe Israel off the map."[4] This same regime is developing nuclear warheads for missiles that can reach Israel's major cities.

Post-World War II

While people worldwide began to recover and rebuild after World War II, merely *living* beyond the trauma was a monumental hurdle for Holocaust survivors. The logistical nightmare of being physically and emotionally depleted, while penniless and homeless, challenged their very existence.

Unable to return home, where property and possessions had been confiscated, where entire Jewish communities had vanished, and where neighbors at a minimum had cooperated with the Nazis, the survivors who had the strength to think about the future were determined to leave Europe. However, most countries restricted Jewish immigration due to anti-Jewish sentiments, xenophobia, and post-war economic hardship. Even the United States enforced strict immigration policies. No country welcomed the survivors with open arms.

Most of the 900,000[5] Holocaust survivors ended up alone in Displaced Persons Camps administered by the Allied powers in occupied post-war Europe.

It was during these desperate circumstances that the need for a Jewish homeland for the Jews in Palestine gained sympathy and political traction around the world.

55 | Survivors of Bergen Belsen become DPs

In Palestine, the British continued with their policies of the 1939 White Paper that strictly limited Jewish immigration. Underground Jewish resistance groups in Palestine increased the smuggling of Holocaust survivors into Palestine. Although tens of thousands of refugees were successfully smuggled from ports in Europe on crowded, mostly unseaworthy vessels, an equally large number of Jewish Holocaust refugees were rejected from Palestinian shores. However, instead of turning the refugee ships back to Europe as had been done prior and during World War II, the British built detention camps, first in Palestine on the Mediterranean coast, and eventually larger camps built on the island of Cyprus. In all, more than 50,000 Holocaust survivors were imprisoned by the British in these camps for three years.[6]

This was an extremely difficult period for refugees who had managed to survive and escape Europe only to be imprisoned again behind barbed wire and unable to reach "the Promised Land." For the Jews in Palestine, to sit by and watch the unjust treatment of their people being held in British detention camps after surviving the horrors of the Holocaust, was far more than they could tolerate.

Jews in Palestine supported by world Jewry, as well as others who understood the Jewish plight,

56 | Jews in DP Camp, Germany circa 1947

concluded that the British laws, which restricted Jewish immigration to Palestine needed to be broken. The time for Jewish statehood was overdue. Jews were more determined than ever to do everything necessary—even fight—for their independence so that all Jewish people could find refuge in their own sovereign Jewish homeland.

57 | Exodus, ship carrying 4,500 Jewish Holocaust survivors to Palestine, was denied entry by the British and returned to Germany, 1947

Building an army became a necessity for the Jews in Palestine. Except for young children and the elderly, every able-bodied Jew was considered to be a soldier in the pursuit of independence. Holocaust survivors smuggled in by the Haganah were immediately handed a weapon and mobilized as protectors of the Jewish homeland. As they joined this Jewish militia, one can only imagine how this hodgepodge of bewildered and persecuted

58 | Jewish Holocaust survivors in British Detention Camp, Cyprus, circa 1947

people must have appeared—untrained, of all different ages, male and female, wearing different clothing and speaking an assortment of different languages.

Even more than amassing a force, the Haganah's primary challenge was obtaining weapons. Due to the heavily policed arms embargo imposed by the British, weapons smuggling increased.

I recently interviewed Jewish men in Denver, Colorado who clandestinely participated, although 8,500 miles away, in garnering weapons for the Jews in Palestine. Their smuggling activities included purchasing guns of all varieties from sporting goods stores throughout Colorado, especially in small rural towns outside of Denver. The stockpile of arms was left in an abandoned cave in the foothills of the Rocky Mountains. Although the men never knew exactly how the weapons were shipped from the United States, or even who or how they were transported into Palestine, they believed the weapons were taken to Nebraska for packing, and they heard that farming barrels, which typically held produce, were used to ship the weapons to Palestine.

Britain Wants Out: UN Partition Plan

With the displaced persons camps of Europe overflowing with 900,000 Jewish refugees the world did not want, and the plight of Holocaust survivors languishing in British detention camps in Cyprus under scrutiny by Western powers, the British looked for an exit strategy from their governing role in Palestine.

Britain itself was economically drained from its significant role in defeating the Nazis during

World War II. The British needed to concentrate on matters closer to home. They recognized that a simple solution to the problems in Palestine was not on the horizon. Subsequently, in 1947 they handed the British Mandate of Palestine over to the jurisdiction of the nascent United Nations.

The United Nations Special Committee on Palestine (UNSCOP) proceeded with due diligence by immediately sending fact-finding missions to Palestine. During many meetings with the Jews of Palestine, UN emissaries determined that the Jews needed an independent country of their own, primarily because coexistence was not an option for the Arab Palestinians who refused to recognize the right of Jews to their own Jewish State in any part of Palestine.

In fact, the Palestinian Arabs refused to meet with these UN officials, insisting that the United Nations had "no jurisdiction over Palestine." The opinion of Grand Mufti al-Husseini was straightforward. It really didn't matter what the UN decided. Arabs would never accept a Jewish homeland in Palestine.[7] They expressed their intentions openly: when the British relinquished control of Palestine, the Arabs would push all the Jews into the sea.[8]

On November 29, 1947, a vote was taken at the United Nations headquarters in New York. By a narrow margin, with 33 votes in favor, 13 against, and 10 abstaining, UN Resolution 181 was passed, establishing two separate states in Palestine. There was not a single vote in favor of partition from the Arab world.[9]

The Jewish State was designated on land that had mostly been purchased, and revitalized

59 | *The Palestine Post*, 1948

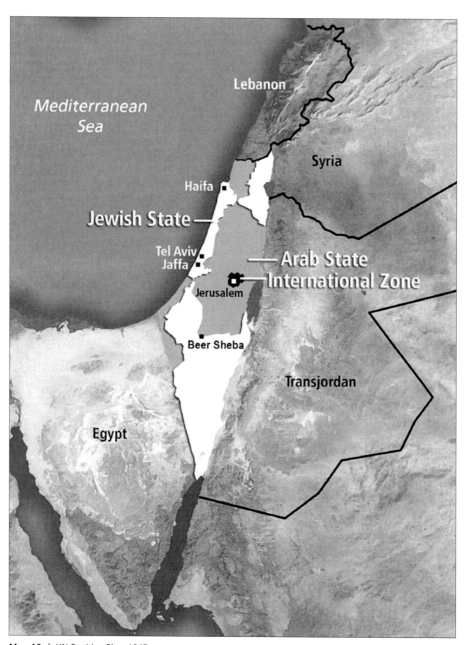

Map 10 | UN Partition Plan, 1947

by Jewish immigrants. Jews constituted a majority of the population in this small portion of the original British Mandate of Palestine. Sixty percent of the land designated for Israel was the Negev desert, an area considered to be uninhabitable.[10]

The Palestinian homeland named "Palestine" included "much of the coastal plain from the Sinai border up to Jaffa, all of the West Bank's central hill country, and most of Western Galilee."[11] Arabs represented the majority of the population in "Palestine."

The UN also created separate governance for Jerusalem, determining that it would be neither Israeli, nor Palestinian land. Instead the city of Jerusalem was to be an "international city" governed by the UN.[12] It was clearly specified that Jerusalem would be an open international entity insuring that holy sites would remain open and accessible to people of all nationalities and faiths.

60 | Al-Husseini with Nazi SS troops

Although the land granted to the Jews in this UN Partition Plan was a mere fraction of the ancient Land of Israel, Jews in Palestine and around the world celebrated this international decision.

The hostility felt by the Palestinian Arabs was palpable in the wake of the UN vote. They had sided with the Nazis during World War II, and their defeat bred calls for vengeance. Al-Husseini expanded his calls to "kill the Jews."[13]

Palestinians along with fellow Arabs in surrounding countries unequivocally rejected the Partition Plan. In doing so, they in effect rejected having a homeland of their own. Had they done so at that initial stage, approximately half of the British Mandate of Palestine would have been theirs. Instead, Arabs immediately declared war on the newly designated State of Israel. This "War of Annihilation," as they called it, was not just between the Palestinian people and Israel. Instead it was a war between the entire Arab world and the newly created Jewish State of Israel. Soon it would be labeled the Arab-Israeli conflict.

In a six-month period following the UN vote, Britain prepared its withdrawal from Palestine. The Arabs in Palestine quickly took advantage of this interlude and began a series of Arab attacks upon the Jews. Arab countries sent in thousands of fighters to assist the Palestinians.[14] The Haganah took the lead as the Israeli Defense Force, while hastily mobilizing other Jewish militias to defend the Jews of Israel. However, Jewish defense was greatly impaired by the British who strictly enforced the detainment of Jewish refugees in Cyprus. There were more than 8,000 able-bodied young Jewish men in the detention camps who would undoubtedly have been helpful to the Haganah. Nonetheless, Britain did not release Holocaust survivors, even though the odds of Jewish survival in a war against the powerfully armed Arab world appeared to be practically nil. Even more insidious, in many documented instances the British confiscated weapons from Jews and turned these arms over to the Arabs.[15]

These British betrayals of the Jewish people prompted Jewish paramilitary groups to launch sabotage attacks against the British during the pre-1948 War period.

Palestinian Arab Flight

Fearing the inevitability of a full-scale war, up to 300,000 frightened Palestinian Arabs fled Palestine to avoid the violence.[16] Palestinian leaders used scare tactics to encourage the flight of the Palestinians. They intentionally spread false rumors of widespread savagery by the Jewish forces to ignite panic among the Palestinians, who inevitably fled from their villages to neighboring Arab countries. All of this

61 | Palestinian flight

was done in order to clear the area of Palestinians so that the invading Arab armies could annihilate the Jews without killing Palestinians during their onslaught.

Most of these Palestinians who fled believed what Arab leaders had promised them. They believed they would be able to return to their homes quickly following an inevitable and swift Arab victory.[17]

Siege of Jerusalem

Probably the most intense fighting of the pre-war period occurred during the Arab "Siege of Jerusalem" which began on December 1, 1947, and lasted through July 10, 1948. This Arab blockade of Jerusalem prevented food and supplies from reaching the holy city, isolating 100,000 Jewish residents. By barricading the road to Jerusalem from Tel Aviv, neither food nor supplies could enter the ancient city where Arabs and Jews had recently lived cooperatively together.

The Arabs also bombarded the blockaded Jews by firing shells indiscriminately into Jerusalem neighborhoods, killing hundreds of civilians and leaving hundreds wounded without medical provisions. During this siege, Arabs also succeeded in cutting off the flow of water, leaving Jews in Jerusalem on the verge of starvation and death.[18]

Convoys of trucks attempted to reach the stranded Jews in Jerusalem, but to no avail. A notorious attack occurred against a Jewish medical convoy on its way to Hadassah Hospital in Jerusalem on April 13, 1948. The convoy was vulnerable because the British had stopped providing military escort. Moreover, the British failed to intervene and stop the deadly attack. In the end, 79 Jews—mostly unarmed doctors and nurses—were murdered."[19]

Stranded in Jerusalem, an American student at Hebrew University, Zipporah Porath, wrote a letter to her family back in the United States on March 29, 1948:

> Dearest Each of You,
>
> Jerusalem has been holding its breath for two days. A shayarah (convoy) returning from Kfar Etzion was ambushed in the hills of Hebron by thousands of Arabs lying in wait all along the road. For thirty hours our boys fought for their lives before the British Army made any effort to get through to liberate them…The people in this country are simply made of iron. It is unbelievable what they have to endure and how much they'll yet have to endure before this is over. I am not alone in my feeling of foreboding. Everyone senses that there are very difficult days ahead.
>
> We aren't fooling ourselves. Jerusalem and its 100,000 Jews are in for it. Everyone knows there is no defending the city from a strategic point of view. Our only hope is international intervention in some form—a UN militia or some other neutral force. I can't believe the entire world would abandon the Holy City without making provisions for safeguarding the sacred places or trying to prevent an outright attack…[20]

All in all, more than 1,000 Jewish civilians were killed during the 1948 Siege of Jerusalem.

Deir Yassin

During the pre-war period, another notorious incident occurred in an Arab village known as Deir Yassin on the barricaded road to Jerusalem.

What happened in Deir Yassin is intensely contested between Arabs and Jews, Israelis and Palestinians. The Jews agree that civilians were killed, but refute that there was a massacre.

After investigation, Israelis report that on April 9, 1948, members of the Irgun, a splinter group of the Israeli forces, entered Deir Yassin. Their intention was not a secret. They planned to drive out Iraqi troops who had entered the village in March to cut off the road to Jerusalem. The Israeli military fighters encouraged the Palestinian villagers to escape, and prior to the battle, approximately two-thirds of the population of the village took the opportunity to flee.

But Iraqi soldiers had disguised themselves as women (concealing weapons beneath the flowing robes of the chador) and had hidden among women and children in the village. Consequently, fighters of the Irgun found themselves taking fire from "women." In the fight that ensued, many innocent women were killed. The Irgun forces suffered more than 40 percent casualties before succeeding in killing or capturing the Iraqi fighters.

Later, when the Haganah troops arrived in the village they found dead civilians. So did the Red Cross. However, there was no evidence of a "massacre." More recently, Arab scholars from Beir Zeit University in Ramallah concluded that while 107 Arabs were killed in Deir Yassin, including some civilians caught in the crossfire, a massacre had not occurred.

62 | Medical convoy en route to Jerusalem, 1948

These Arab scholars concluded, that "Arab spokespersons at the time hugely exaggerated the Deir Yassin fight, making up stories of gang rape, brutalities committed against pregnant women, unborn children cut from their mothers' wombs, and massive murders with bodies thrown into the nearby quarry. These same Arab sources admit that their purpose in these exaggerations was to get Arabs to flee the area and also shame the Arab nations into entering the conflict with great alacrity."[21]

The accusations by the propagandists did succeed in terrifying the Palestinians as tens of thousands fled after hearing the rumors about what had (allegedly) happened in Deir Yassin. They had no way of knowing that the rumors were untrue.

To date, Palestinians continue to commemorate the Deir Yassin "massacre" on American campuses throughout the United States.

Israeli Independence

On May 14, 1948, control of Palestine by the British ended and British troops left the land. At four o'clock in the afternoon, Israel's first Prime Minister, David Ben-Gurion, declared Israel's Independence to the entire world. From the basement of the Tel Aviv Museum, Ben-Gurion read the Israeli Declaration of Independence over a loudspeaker as hundreds of Jews gathered to hear his words and thousands more poured into the streets to celebrate.

The day signified the end of 2,500 years of Jewish exile and the return of the Jewish people to Israel, their ancestral homeland.

> ERETZ-ISRAEL [(Hebrew)—the Land of Israel, Palestine] was the birthplace of the Jewish people. Here their spiritual, religious and political identity was shaped. Here they first attained statehood, created cultural values of national and universal significance and gave to the world the eternal Book of Books.
>
> After being forcibly exiled from their land, the people kept faith with it throughout their Dispersion and never ceased to pray and hope for their return to it and for the restoration in it of their political freedom.
>
> WE EXTEND our hand to all neighboring states and their peoples in an offer of peace and good neighborliness, and appeal to them to establish bonds of cooperation and mutual help with the sovereign Jewish people settled in its own land. The State of Israel is prepared to do its share in a common effort for the advancement of the entire Middle East.[22]

As the Jews of Israel took to the streets in celebration, carrying flags of the new born state, Ben-Gurion spoke in a voice tinged with trepidation. "They celebrate now, but they will have to bleed tomorrow," for as the Jewish population celebrated their newfound freedom in the streets of Tel Aviv, Arab countries including Syria, Lebanon, Iraq, Egypt, Saudi Arabia, and Jordan simultaneously declared war on the State of Israel and mobilized nearly 100,000 troops for an attack on the fledgling nation.

Jews not only faced a war for their independence, but a veritable war of survival. With well-equipped and superiorly armed Arab forces from Egypt, Jordan, Syria, Lebanon, and twice as many professional soldiers, attacking from three fronts, Arab leaders rallied with the battle cry, "Annihilation of the Jews. We will push them into the sea."[23] While the Arab forces had modern-warfare weapons, the Jewish Army had only insufficient rifles and artillery, and at the war's onset did not possess any tanks or airplanes.

Many believe this attack by Arab countries did not occur six months earlier so that the British would not interfere

63 | Ben-Gurion declares Israeli statehood, 1948

with their plans to massacre the Jews. It also gave the Arab Palestinians time to flee so they wouldn't be caught in the cross-fire of the war to come. The Arab population had been told by General Azzam (first Secretary General of the Arab League) to "leave so that we can more easily exterminate the Jews. You'll be back in your homes within a month…" and "This will be a war of extermination and a momentous massacre which will be spoken of like the Mongolian massacres and the Crusades."[24]

Immediately following the British departure, Jordan invaded Jerusalem and occupied all of the Old City including the Temple Mount, the Western Wall, and the West Bank. Egypt grabbed and occupied the Gaza Strip and bombed Israel's largest civilian center, the city of Tel Aviv. An Associated Press account on May 17,1948, described the attack: "Arab Planes Hit Tel Aviv, Tiberias. Invader Hammering Jewish Outposts."[25]

The Israelis fought a defensive war, knowing their survival rested on the results of this "genocidal war of extermination" launched against them.[26]

Altalena: Controlling the Irgun

As a result of rogue militia mistakes like the one in Deir Yassin, the new Israeli Government led by Prime Minister David Ben-Gurion took on the arduous task of combining the Israeli troops into one defense force—the IDF. The Altalena Event is an example of Israel's determination to stop the Irgun paramilitary group (commanded by Menachem Begin) from operating independently of the Israel Defense Force.

Following the Declaration of Independence in May, the Irgun planned to ship weapons and nearly 1,000 volunteer fighters from Europe to Israel on a ship called the Altalena. David Ben-Gurion ordered an attack on the Altalena when it's captain refused to follow orders from the IDF on the shores of Tel Aviv. Sixteen Irgun fighters were killed during the hostilities.

This example, although still contentious, reveals some of the necessary steps that need to be taken by the government of a country in order to consolidate militias under one command. Israelis expect no less from the Palestinians whose numerous fighting factions have persistently been unregulated and uncontrolled by Palestinian leaders, allowing terrorists to commit attacks against innocent Israelis.

Arab Palestinian Refugees

As in all wars, the plight of innocent civilians is tragic. For Arab Palestinians, their escape from Israel to surrounding Arab lands caused one of the twentieth century's greatest quagmires. Exact numbers are not available but the estimates include up to 700,000 Palestinians escaped the fighting by fleeing Israel between November 1947 through May 1949, with the intention of returning to their homes after the anticipated Arab victory. However, due to the Israeli victory, most of these Palestinian refugees have not been able to return to Israel.

A great deal of debate continues six decades later. How many Palestinians fled? Why did they leave? Did they listen to Arab leaders who told them to get out of the path of the invading Arab armies? Did the Israeli army chase them out?

We know for certain that during the pre-war period, many affluent Arabs of the north, from Acco to Haifa, including villages between the two towns, closed up their homes and waited out the war in Lebanon and Syria. Seeing their political and social leaders flee alarmed an estimated 100,000 Arab peasants (fellahin) who gathered their belongings and walked to Lebanon and Syria.

Some argue that many were chased out by the Israeli army. Israel admits to encouraging civilian Palestinians to move from areas where Jews were surrounded by Palestinians fighters. For example, Jews encouraged innocent Palestinians to leave Jaffa, Jerusalem, and the western Galilee, to avoid being caught in the inevitable crossfire.

In other documented examples, Jewish leaders and neighbors pleaded with the Palestinians to stay, telling them they would be welcomed as friendly neighbors in the new State of Israel.

In April 1948, "at the risk of his own life, the senior Jewish official in Haifa, as well as the Haganah's high command, drove through the Arab section of the city with a loudspeaker on April 26, 1948, calling out in Arabic to the residents of his city to remain on their land and in their homes." The British police noted, "Every effort is being made by the Jews to persuade the Arab populace to stay and carry on with their normal lives, to get their shops and businesses open and to be assuaged that their lives and interests will be safe."[27]

Israelis have admitted there were instances when the Haganah used scare tactics, attempting to make the Palestinians believe that the size of Israel's defense forces had become massive. Starting rumors about the "extraordinary might" of the Haganah panicked some Palestinians who decided to escape. But the Jews never threatened, nor intended to kill peaceful Palestinian civilians.

On the other hand, Arab leaders made it clear in their broadcasts to the Palestinians that they should leave the area so that "Arab armies would have a clear field in which to perpetrate their genocide of the Jews. We will smash the country with our guns and obliterate every place the Jews seek shelter in," stated the Iraqi prime minister, Nuri Said. "The Arabs should conduct their wives and children to safe areas until the fighting has died down."[28]

Admitting complicity five years after the war, the Jordanian newspaper Al Urdun published an article which included, "For the flight and fall of the other villages it is our leaders who are responsible because of their dissemination of rumors exaggerating Jewish crimes and describing them as atrocities in order to inflame the Arabs... By spreading rumors of Jewish atrocities, killings of women and children etc... they instilled fear and terror in the hearts of the Arabs in Palestine, until they fled leaving their homes and properties to the enemy."[29]

Palestinian Authority President Mahmoud Abbas admits Arab culpability in the flight of the Palestinians when he wrote: "The Arab armies entered Palestine to protect the Palestinians from the Zionist tyranny, but instead they abandoned them, forced them to emigrate and to leave their homeland…"[30]

Due to the lack of census data, we will never know the precise number of Palestinian refugees, nor exactly why each one of them left their homes from 1947 through the six months of the War of Independence in 1948. In any case, the tragedy for these Palestinians is that they lost their land. It is something that refugees have endured in the aftermath of war throughout human history, including my own parents.

Israeli Victory: Offers of Land, Reparation, Reunification Rejected by Arabs

The result of the 1948 War of Independence surprised the world. Under what seemed like insurmountable odds, the Israelis won the war in six months. During this time no country came to the aid of Israel. By November 1948, the Israelis defeated all of the Arab armies and recaptured not only Israel's portion of the UN Partition Plan, but they also occupied portions of the land, which had been designated by the United Nations for the Palestinian homeland. (Remember, the Palestinians had rejected this land partition.)

In the aftermath of the 1948 War, Egypt occupied and fully controlled the Gaza Strip. Jordan controlled Jerusalem and the West Bank. More than 10,000 Jews became refugees from these areas now occupied by Egypt and Jordan—as Jews were immediately expelled from living in these areas. Arab armies razed Jewish communities and killed or expelled all Jews.

Jewish holy sites were destroyed as well. In East Jerusalem alone, 57 synagogues, libraries and houses of learning, many of them centuries old, were desecrated and destroyed. The Jordanians used the stones from these desecrated and destroyed buildings to later build urinals, sidewalks and roads.[31]

Israelis extended several offers to give back captured territory during the armistice talks of 1949. In its armistice with Lebanon, Israel agreed to withdraw from the portion of southern Lebanon it had captured during the war. With Syria, Israel agreed to several demilitarized zones and a cease-fire as well as international borders at the cease-fire lines.[32]

Armistice talks were held on the Greek Island of Rhodes in 1949. At that meeting, Israel offered to return the land that had originally been given to the Palestinians in the Partition Plan and a proposal was offered to reunite Palestinian Arab families separated during the war, in exchange for a peace treaty.[33] "This would have allowed hundreds of thousands of refugees to return to their homes. The Arabs categorically rejected these offers because, as they have admitted, they were on the verge of mounting a new offensive that would involve some nine thousand terrorist attacks, mostly from Egypt, over the next six years and help ignite another war in 1956."[34]

At the Lausanne conference in the summer of 1949, Israel offered to repatriate 100,000 Palestinian refugees even without a peace treaty. Israel also offered financial restitution to Palestinian refugees several times. "Later, Israel again offered restitution and the return of frozen bank accounts and the contents of safe deposit boxes. Under pressure from Arab governments, (Palestinian) refugees refused to fill out forms needed to verify ownership because the mere paperwork might imply recognition of Israel. So Israel rewrote the forms to placate the refugees, but only a tiny fraction ever submitted the requests. In 1960, Israel was still trying to find ways to pay reparations to refugees via secret contact through Cypriot authorities, but Arab states intervened and shut down this option. As late as 1964, the U.S. Department of State compiled a comprehensive evaluation of refugee property, which Israel agreed to use as the basis for negotiations for just compensation. Again, the Arab states refused to negotiate, keeping the lost opportunity secret from the refugees."[35]

64 | Hurva Synagogue, before destruction

These offers by my country typified our earnest desire to live side-by-side in peace with the Palestinians in the Holy Land. Israel required only one condition: that the Arabs finally accept our right to exist as the homeland of the Jewish people.

Each time Israel offered land, reparations and repatriation, the Arab states rejected their proposals. The Palestinians and Arabs rejected outright all peace offerings from Israel and never provided counter-proposals except for their call for the destruction of the Jewish State.

From the Israeli perspective, the Arabs consistently chose war instead of peace.

65 | Hurva Synagogue, 1948, after destruction

This catalyzed more than 60 years of death, turmoil, and devastation, and solidified the Jewish notion that "if tomorrow the Arabs lay down their weapons there will be peace; but if tomorrow Israel lays down its weapons, there will be no Israel." The Arab refusal to accept Israel's right to exist as a Jewish homeland, lies at the very core of all roadblocks to peace negotiations—then and now. If Arab leadership had ever accepted Israel's right to exist, the Palestinians would have had a homeland of their own. This was as true in the proposal offered in 1937 by the British in the Peel Commission, and again in the 1947 proposal presented by the United Nations in Resolution 181, as it is today.

Arab hostility towards Israel continues. Egypt, which signed a peace treaty in 1979, and Jordan, which established peace with Israel in 1994, are presently diplomatic exceptions. The remaining 19 Arab countries have never formally made peace with Israel. In 2011, toppled regimes throughout the Middle East and the volatile Arab "street" illustrate the dangerous instability that continues to exist throughout the region.

Not only have these neighboring Arab states ever agreed to peace with Israel, they have never even signed basic cease fire agreements following military engagements. For example: Iraq never signed the 1949 Ceasefire Agreements following the 1948 War. While direct hostilities ended long ago, there is an argument to be made that Israel officially remains in a state of war with these countries. And it's not mere diplomatic trivia. These circumstances cause real complications. Israelis cannot travel to Arab countries. Even Americans who have been to Israel and carry an Israeli stamp in their passports cannot enter these countries.

When Iraq was liberated and Saddam Hussein's regime was ousted, I was contacted by a colleague about helping the Iraqis build a democratic society. Coincidentally, I had always wanted to visit Iraq, since it was the homeland of my father. But of course, it was not possible due to my Israeli citizenship. With democracy emerging in Iraq, I became more hopeful about seeing my father's homeland and exercising my rights to obtain an Iraqi passport.

According to the new Iraqi constitution, a son of an Iraqi citizen is entitled to Iraqi citizenship. Since my father was an Iraqi citizen before escaping to Israel, I hoped to attain Iraqi citizenship. But my hope quickly evaporated when I was reminded that even post-Hussein Iraq is still considered to be at war with Israel. I remain hopeful that I will someday be able to visit Baghdad, where my father's family traced its lineage back thousands of years.

Postwar Palestinians

Palestinians after the 1948 War of Independence can be divided into two groups. First are the Palestinians who stayed on their land in Israel. The second are those who became refugees in Arab lands outside of Israel.

The Arab Palestinians who did not flee kept their homes and their land in Israel. As Israel developed into a democracy, these Israeli Palestinians became known as "Arab Israelis" (or "Palestinian Israelis") and received full Israeli citizenship. From 170,000 in 1949, they now number more than 1.4 million people. These Israeli Arabs fully enjoy the freedoms of Israel's democratic society. They serve as elected officials in the *Knesset*, the Israeli parliament. They are mayors. They hold prestigious posts as faculty members in Israeli universities and work as educated professionals. And "they enjoy a standard of living, political and personal freedom, and economic opportunity unparalleled anywhere in the Arab world."[36]

Unlike all other citizens in the State of Israel at the age 18, Arab Israelis are exempt from military duty in the IDF. Indeed, it is not in the interest of the Israeli government to place Arab Israelis in a position where they would have to fight against other Arabs. However, Arab Israelis can volunteer for the military. And thousands do. Druze number more than 100,000 in Israel and the majority of them proudly serve in the IDF. There are thousands of Sunni Muslim Circassians in the army. A significant number of Bedouin Israelis volunteer for military service. My colleague and friend, Dr. Raed Muaem, who is the Senior Vice President of Nazareth Academic Institute, knows several Arab Israeli IDF soldiers from his village in the Galilee who hold high ranking positions in the Israeli Defense Force. In that same village, Arab Israeli citizens celebrate Israel's Independence Day.

Palestinian Refugees

Unlike Israeli Arabs, most Palestinian refugees who fled to neighboring Arab lands, including Lebanon, Jordan and Syria, have been denied citizenship in their new host countries. Without citizenship, they have been relegated to inequitable status. They are restricted from entering occupations, and from obtaining work permits and educational opportunities.[37]

Most of the Palestinian refugees have been confined in Palestinian Refugee Camps in Lebanon, Jordan, Gaza, and the West Bank. They have been housed in refugee camps governed by the United Nations Relief and Works Agency (UNWRA), an agency established exclusively by the United Nations to assist the Palestinian refugees.[38]

Refugee status has been bestowed on the Palestinians for the longest period of time recorded in the history. Moreover, according to the UNWRA definition of refugee status for Palestinians, a Palestinian refugee includes children born to a Palestinian refugee. Consequently, Palestinians are the only refugee group in the world whose population continues to multiply. According to UNRWA, there are 4.7 million registered Palestinian refugees.[39]

The living conditions in these UNWRA refugee camps are deplorable. One cannot deny the human suffering endured by Palestinian refugees who have been lingering without citizenship in such unacceptable living conditions. In addition, incitement against Israelis is prevalent. There is no question that anti-Semitism and anti-Western attitudes breed in this hopeless environment, and that these attitudes have often manifested themselves in acts of violence and terrorism.

Jewish Refugees from the Arab World

When Israel declared its independence, there were large populations of Jews living in Arab states elsewhere in the Middle East. Jews from Iraq and Egypt had lived in those countries for more than 2,500 years. Those from Lebanon, Syria, and Yemen had lived in communities for a millennium. In 1948, 850,000 Jews lived in Arab and Muslim countries.

66 | Yemenite Jews fleeing to Israel, circa 1948

67 | Ma'abarot Israeli refugee camp for Jewish refugees from Arab lands in Israel, 1948. Shaul Gabbay's father lived in a Ma'abarot camp after being rescued from Iraq.

At first, Arab leaders believed that the infant State of Israel would be crushed in battle, but after Israel defeated the combined Arab armies in the 1948 War of Independence, Jewish citizens of Arab countries found themselves in untenable living conditions. Guided by anti-Jewish sentiment and increasing Arab nationalism, Jews from the Arab world were easy targets, subjected to degrading civil codes, imprisonment, and property confiscation—even death.

By 1974, the Jewish population in the Muslim world was only a few thousand.[40]

Although we don't know the exact numbers, it is estimated that between 700,000–900,000 Jews were forced to flee. They abandoned homes, property and accounts worth around $2.5 billion. About 80 percent of these Jewish refugees found safe haven in Israel. These Jews from Arab lands now comprise nearly 50 percent of the Israeli population.[41]

Following the 1948 War of Independence Israel faced the arduous task of taking care of hundreds of thousands of Jewish refugees arriving penniless and homeless from Arab countries as well as those who had survived the Holocaust. The population of Israel in 1948 was 650,000 Jews. Within three years, it was 1.3 million. The State of Israel was fulfilling its main mission of being a safe haven for Jews around the world. "No influx like it had been witnessed in modern times. It was an "open door" from which older and vastly wealthier nations would have recoiled in dismay.[42]

Despite the tremendous challenges, Jews rejoiced in ending thousands of years of exile and the rebirth of their ancestral homeland. For Jews worldwide, the creation of the State of Israel was the answer to their prayers. For thousands of years, Jews prayed to return to Eretz Yisrael.

In a matter of decades—and despite the presence of hostile states on their doorstep—my people arduously built one of the world's most advanced and prosperous democracies.

For me, for fellow Jews in Israel as well as for Jews around the world, the establishment of our own Jewish State in 1948 was not a catastrophe.

It was a miracle.

The War of 1948: al-Naqba—The Catastrophe

I was six years old, a happy-go-lucky child–enjoying my days in Rowdat al-Atfal Preschool in Haifa, the beautiful city of my birth on the Mediterranean Sea. I remember vividly the first time I heard gunfire. The conflict began and everything in my life changed. The fighting ended my days of enjoying the neighborhood playground. In essence, the war stopped my childhood—and childhood is something that cannot be replaced. There is no substitute for it…

I remember becoming a Palestinian victim of al-Naqba—The Catastrophe.

On May 14, 1948, a Jewish state was created in a land once inhabited almost entirely by Arabs. From the emergence of Zionism and the beginning of Jewish immigration into Palestine, the Palestinians had consistently lost land and civil rights. To the dismay of the Palestinians, the Jews agreed to a series of international agreements that gave them a foothold in the region for future expansion and control—all at the Palestinians' expense. In 1948, the Jews realized their long-sought victory and the Arab community of Palestine was shattered.

When the combined Arab forces fought the new Jewish state in the War of 1948, hundreds of thousands of Palestinians lost their homes and more than 350 Palestinian villages were destroyed. Although the plight of the Palestinian people was

68 | Amin Kazak (left) and brothers, 1947

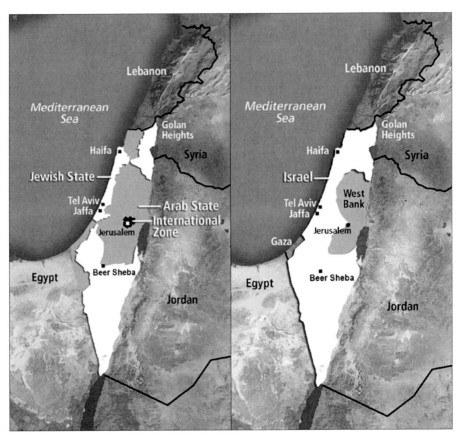

Map 11 | Jewish expansion, pre-1948 and post-1948

overshadowed by the Arab invasion of Israel, an important distinction must be made between a war that was initiated by the Arab states and the atrocities committed by the Jews against the Palestinian people during that war in order to solidify their control of Palestine. These were the events (such as the Deir Yassin massacre) that produced al-Naqba, the "great catastrophe" for the Palestinian people. Al-Naqba remains central to the Palestinian belief that we are victims of a devastating conspiracy and a monumental injustice.

Prelude to War

The Palestinians' opposition to the new State of Israel was not simply rooted in a hatred of the Jews. The Palestinians have a long history of opposition to colonial authority and had been seeking their own homeland since the fall of the Ottoman Empire. Any partition of Palestine was seen as a violation of the rights of Arab Palestinians who were the indigenous people of the land. But for Jews, partition was the first significant achievement of the Zionist dream of Jewish statehood.

In the November 1947 Partition Plan (also known as UN Resolution 181), the United Nations sought to establish a Jewish state with a population of 500,000 Jews and 400,000 Arabs, and an Arab state that was to include 725,000 Arabs and only 10,000 Jews. A sizable population of both Jews and Arabs was to occupy the international zone of Jerusalem.

The plan gave the Jews control over 55 percent of the territory, even though they comprised only 37 percent of the population. As the UN unjustly granted the Jewish minority control over the majority of territory in Palestine, understandably Palestinians and the Arab states of the region rebuffed the Partition outright, and committed themselves to the prevention of the establishment of a Jewish state in Palestinian land. In the eyes of the international community at the United Nations, the plan was marginally enough to secure peace in the Holy Land. It did not, however, seek reconciliation between the two sides of what was clearly becoming a civil war between the Jews and the Palestinian Arabs. Indeed, the plan fostered unprecedented violence.

By May 1948, the Zionist forces were well organized, well-armed and prepared to declare the State of Israel. They claimed 78 percent of the land of Mandate Palestine, far more than the 55 percent of land allocated to it by the 1947 UN Partition Plan.[1] Their forces included the Haganah, famous for its professionally trained and experienced soldiers, and the Haganah's strike force, the Palmach.

These groups were mobilized during the British withdrawal. Inter-ethnic harassment and rioting soon developed into sniping, village raids, and street combat. Under the impotent watch of the fleeing British, civil strife in Palestine between the Arabs and Jews had already become a deadly cycle of take-no-prisoners ambushes, terror bombings, and village depopulation. However, before they left, the British had been careful to give the Zionists an advantage over the native Palestinians. Palestinian leaders were banished, leaving the Palestinians displaced and disorganized. Against the now-organized and militant Zionists, the Palestinians never

69 | Jews attack British, 1945

established a political foothold or focused their communities to effectively respond to the vast changes overtaking them. Of course, as wealthier Arabs fled the area for safer ground when the fighting began, those left behind were alarmingly rudderless, and "fell easy prey to rumor and to the alarm which soon overcame all parts of the Arab population."[2]

The Arab-Israeli War of 1948, which erupted after the November vote at the UN, occurred in two distinct stages. As the British withdrew, those who remained in Palestine stood face-to-face for the first time, neighborhood by neighborhood, without third party protectors or intermediaries. The result was chaotic fighting and skirmishes. Once the British were gone entirely, the conflict expanded into a full-scale war with invasions by Lebanon, Iraq, Syria, Jordan and Egypt.

For its part, the Arab League had already formed a force called the Arab Liberation Army (ALA). The ALA consisted mostly of volunteer foreign Arab soldiers. Some Palestinians also joined the ALA as volunteers or through the faza'a system in which village leaders formally provided men and supplies. Placed at the helm of the ALA was Fawzi al-Qawuqji, who first came to the country to command the 1936 Arab uprising. Qawuqji represented "a pan-Arab solution to the challenge of Zionism, implicitly downplaying the significance of the Palestinian national movement in favor of a vision reflecting his own rich experiences in Syria, Saudi Arabia and Iraq."[3] As a result, Qawuqji was a thorn in the side of the Mufti of Jerusalem, Hajj Amin, who had his own political plans for an independent Palestine. The Mufti protested the role of the ALA and the pan-Arab determinism it entailed. He also questioned Qawuqji and his designation as the supreme military commander of Palestinian military operations.[4]

70 | Al-Hussayni (center) and brigade, 1948

Despite the inner factionalism, the ALA was the best equipped and largest of the Palestinian fighting forces. Other local fighting brigades emerged, the most famous of which was led by Abdal-Qadir al-Hussayni.

Meanwhile, the Zionist forces numbered some 35,000 part-time fighters, many of whom had been trained by the British during the Second World War and the Arab Revolt.[5] As tensions rose, the Haganah increasingly relied on full-time soldiers. Politically and militarily, the Arab opposition fell short and the Palestinian civilian population grew more vulnerable to severe Jewish attacks.

The War for Palestine
Terror and the Beginning of the Refugee Problem

By the time full-scale war began in May 1948, the Jews had established a strategically advantageous position within Palestine, and a significant portion of Palestinians were forced to flee from their homes by armed groups of Zionist foot soldiers. With the approved UN Partition and the inevitable withdrawal of the British from Palestine, the Jews changed from the defensive posture they had adopted during the Arab Revolt of 1936-1939 to an aggressively militant posture. From the initial Jewish acceptance of the Partition, it was never the Jewish intention to remain within the prescribed borders.

With the goals of expanding their territory, the Jews spent a decade gathering intelligence on Palestinian villages and towns, and developed strategic military plans, which would allow them to establish their state utilizing land that far surpassed the territory allocated to them by the 1947 Partition. Central to these plans was the forced transfer of the indigenous Arab population so that a purely Jewish state could be established and maintained.[6] David Ben-Gurion, who oversaw the Jewish war strategy and implementation, previously revealed his designs for the Arab population within the projected Jewish state in a letter to his son in 1937:

> The Arabs will have to go, but one needs an opportune moment for making it happen, such as a war.[7]

And discussing the ideas set forth in the Peel Commission of 1937 he remarked,

> The debate has not been for or against the indivisibility of Eretz Israel (the Land of Israel). No Zionist can forego the smallest portion of Eretz Israel. The debate was over which of the two routes would lead quicker to the common goal.[8]

These plans were put into effect on March 10, 1948, when the Jewish leadership adopted Plan Dalet, the order for "Jewish forces to ethnically cleanse the areas regarded as the future Jewish state in Palestine."[9] By December of 1948, 700,000 native Palestinians had evacuated their homes inside the new Jewish state, never to return again. Their expulsion and the subsequent destruction of their lands provided the spark that ignited the continuing Arab-Israeli conflict.

Ethnic Cleansing in the Jewish State
Deir Yassin Massacre

As the pressure for war increased, Jewish militias launched terror activities aimed against both the British and Palestinian civilians.

Regarding the British, the most infamous incidents were the hanging of two British officers and the bombing of the King David Hotel in Jerusalem on July 22, 1946. However, it was the purely genocidal actions aimed at Palestinian civilians, particularly in the village of Deir Yassin, which left an ever-lasting imprint on the Palestinian people for generations to come.

Importantly, not all of the Jewish para-military groups agreed with the idea of a Jewish state and a Palestinian state existing simultaneously in the land of Palestine. Opposing the Jewish accep-tance of the UN Partition, some Jews believed that the future State of Israel should include all of Palestine and neigh-boring Transjordan.[10] The right-wing ("Revisionist") forces of the Haganah, the Irgun Z'vai Leumi (National Military Organization), the Lochemei Herut Israeli (Lehi), and the Fighters for the Freedom of Israel, (Stern Gang) pursued this all-or-nothing agenda by targeting Arab civilians. Despite the fact that the Jewish Agency had previously labeled them as "dissidents," they were allowed to join the ground forces on behalf of the Jewish cause in early 1948.[11] The entry of the Irgun and Stern Gang into the ground fighting in early 1948 pre-cipitated the Deir Yassin massacre.[12]

The small village of Deir Yassin lay just two kilometers south on the Tel-Aviv highway, the main road to Jerusalem from Tel Aviv. As an Arab Muslim village of stonecutters, it was home to approxi-mately 750 people. The terraced, stone-cut homes of the village descended eastward to meet a quarry-studded pathway that led to Givat Shaul, a

71 | Jewish bombing of King David Hotel

72 | King David Hotel destruction

western suburb of Jewish Jerusalem. Importantly, Deir Yassin lay inside the "international zone," an area in and around Jerusalem designated by the UN Partition Plan to be under international control. It was also the area of Palestine that counted one-sixth of Palestine's Jews at that time.[13]

Along the same route of Deir Yassin was the town of Kastel (Qastal), which occupied a strategic hilltop, coveted by both sides for the significant military advantage it afforded whoever controlled it. In early April, Kastel ultimately fell to the Haganah in Operation Nachshon. Jewish forces immediately began blowing up the houses of the village.[14] Next, the Palmach set about to depopulate and destroy the hostile neighboring Arab villages existing along the main artery road from Tel Aviv to Jerusalem.

Deir Yassin, however, was not a hostile village in 1948. Although armed attacks had previously emanated from Deir Yassin against Givat Shaul during the Arab-Jewish-British strife of the 1920s and 1930s, by 1948, Deir Yassin was "studiously honoring a Haganah-sponsored agreement to refrain from hostilities with neighboring Jewish areas in exchange for protection from Jewish attack."[15]

Notably, the village leaders of Deir Yassin refused to offer refuge to Arab armies in their streets and homes out of fear of attack from the Jews. In fact, the villagers provided intelligence to the Haganah and repeatedly repelled the Arab ALA's attempts to occupy the village, even while the Haganah took the nearby strategic Sharafa ridge and effectively isolated Deir Yassin from the ALA base at Ein Karem.[16]

Yet on the morning of April 9, 1948, two far-right revisionist divisions of the Jewish military apparatus, the Irgun and the Stern Gang, surrounded the town in order execute all of the military-aged males. Although instructions were given in advance to minimize casualties at Deir Yassin, insider accounts demonstrated a premeditated conviction by the guerrillas —many of whom were teenagers lacking in military training—to incite panic throughout Arab Palestine by their actions that day.[17] They were under the command of the future Israeli Prime Minister Menachem Begin.

However, the violence spiraled, and the villagers of Deir Yassin were targeted to pay the ultimate price in revenge for the atrocities committed by other Arab groups during the civil insurgency. Jewish guerrillas began to brutally kill every villager in sight. Witnesses later testified to seeing children being lined up and shot. Women carrying babies were stabbed to death in cold blood. Those who tried to run away were gunned down, and men were lined up and executed in the town quarry.[18]

Beyond the fact that the attack was characterized by unmitigated violence and rage, it seemed that the simple execution of the villagers was not enough to satisfy the guerrillas' blood thirst. Survivors' accounts described how prisoners were brutalized and women were sexually assaulted as they were stripped of their traditional modest attire and their family jewelry was torn from their bodies.[19] Even elderly women were attacked.

The following day, the Haganah leadership sent operations officer Eliyahu Arbel to inspect the destruction. Twenty-four years later, he wrote, "I have seen a great deal of war, but I never saw a sight like Deir Yassin," largely comprised of "the bodies of women and children, who were murdered in cold blood."[20]

According to Jerusalem Shai (Internal Intelligence) Commander Yitzhak Levy:

> The conquest of the village was carried out with great cruelty…LHI members tell of the barbaric behavior of the IZL toward the prisoners and the dead. They also relate that the IZL men raped a number of Arab girls and murdered them afterward.[21]

Mordechai Gichon reported on April 10th,

> The adult males were taken to town in trucks and paraded in the city streets, then taken back to the site and killed with rifle and machine-gun fire. Before they were put on the trucks, the IZL and LHI men searched the women, men, and children [and] took from them all their jewelry and stole their money. The behavior toward them was especially barbaric [and included] kicks, shoves with rifle butts, spitting and cursing.[22]

Initial reports estimated the dead to number above 200, but the actual number of Arab casualties totaled between 100 and 110, with some reports estimating the death toll as high as 140.[23] Those lucky enough not to be slaughtered were "ignominiously paraded through Jerusalem and then sent to the city's Arab sector."[24] Understandably, the horrific massacre at Deir Yassin had a profound psychological and political effect on Arab-Jewish relations.

For their part, Jewish leaders responded to worldwide outcry about the massacre by sharply criticizing the actions of the Irgun and the Stern gangs. However, many more disastrous examples occurred during the ensuing months of forced expulsions of entire villages and the destruction of Palestinian homes. One commander in the southern front, Yitzhak Pundak, reported the scope of their operations:

> There were two hundred villages and they are gone. We had to destroy them, otherwise we would have had Arabs here as we have in Galilee. We would have had another million Palestinians.[25]

Later, leaders of Israel have tried to justify what occurred. Menachem Begin wrote there would not have been a State of Israel without the "victory" at Deir Yassin.[26] The calculated intent of Jewish intimidation was to cause mass panic in order to entice Arabs to flee from their homes.[27] And, indeed, the Jews took advantage of every opportunity to encourage, intimidate and often force Palestinians to evacuate their homes and territory.

The Legacy of Deir Yassin Massacre: Perpetuation of Ethnic Cleansing

The events of Deir Yassin were seen as a turning point in the 1948 War. More than anything, the brutalization of its villagers came to "epitomize the Zionists' willingness to commit atrocities in order to establish a state." No doubt, the news of Deir Yassin precipitated the flight of Palestinian Arabs. Meanwhile, the Haganah's Plan Dalet initiated a campaign for the systematic expulsion of Palestinians from large areas of the country.[28] The Jewish military objective was not merely survival, but to achieve an ethnic cleansing of Palestine in order to establish a secure and more viable Jewish state.

Menachem Begin, the head of the Irgun (Zionist militia,) recalled:

> In Jerusalem, as elsewhere, we were the first to pass from the defensive to the offensive... Arabs began to flee in terror... Haganah was carrying out successful attacks on other fronts, while all the Jewish forces proceeded to advance through Haifa like a knife through butter. The Arabs began to flee in panic shouting "Deir Yassin." In months preceding the Arab invasion, and while the five Arab States were conducting preparations, we continued to make sallies into Arab territory. The conquest of Jaffa stands out as an event of first rate importance in the struggle for Hebrew independence early in May, on the eve of the invasion by the five Arab States.[29]

An officer of Jewish forces at the time, Shulamit Aloni, recalled how special political officers would visit military units the day before an operation. They would demonize the Palestinians and recall the Holocaust as a point of reference for the ensuing operation.[30] Jewish forces attacked and expelled Arabs and the forces defending them in the Galilee, in the Jordan and Jezreel Valleys and in Tiberius. First attacking the village of Kherbet Nasir ad Din, Jewish forces again committed atrocities that sent panicking villagers to Arab Tiberius, which the Jewish forces also attacked soon afterwards. Arab leaders of the city were forced to order an evacuation after Jewish forces rejected offers for a truce.[31] Some Palestinian villages, such as Nazareth were spared destruction because of their historic ties to Christianity and a lack of desire to provoke Christians worldwide.

In Haifa, 70,000 Arab inhabitants fled after Arab notables in the town ordered an evacuation on April 21. Though Haifa's Jewish mayor pleaded with the Arabs of the city to stay, he was unable to control the indiscriminate shooting of the Irgun and the Stern Gang against Arab civilians.

As my father was a pacifist, he did not volunteer to fight the Israelis. All of his life my father had been a part of al-Yashrotiyya, a Sufi religious group that believed in piety, peace, and nonviolence. When the fighting escalated near my home in Haifa, my father decided to move us from Haifa to a safer place. There was daily fighting by this time. From our home, I heard the echo of bullets and explosions. It was terrifying for me as a little boy, just as it was for my sister.

Most of what I heard about the fighting I learned from my Uncles. They were volunteers in the Palestinian army, who, from what I understood, fought the Jews near Mount Carmel. In my mind, I can still see them returning at night very tired and sweaty. I can picture them carrying their weapons. They spoke openly and emotionally about the combat to my parents. I remember listening from afar with my sister. We heard them emphatically repeat over and over, "We are not going to let them take our land and our homes. It is our land and it means everything to us."

73 | Amin Kazak (center) and older brothers

74 | Amin Kazak's uncle became a Palestinian refugee in Syria, 1948.

The Arabs tried to negotiate better terms for a truce proposal, but the Haganah demanded the unconditional surrender of the Arabs. Palestinians also unsuccessfully pled with the British to intervene, which they refused to do. Due to the sheer panic of their people, Palestinian leaders relented and ordered their people to evacuate from Haifa.

75 | Amin Kazak's uncle became an engineer in Saudi Arabia

76 | Amin Kazak's aunt and her family in Haifa, who stayed in Israel in 1948 and became Israeli citizens

To the south, IZL units bombarded the northern part of Jaffa sending additional terrified Palestinians into the southern part of the city of Haifa. The British, under pressure from Arab leaders to stem the tide of massive exodus of Arabs throughout the country, occupied Jaffa once again and drove out the IZL, but the Arab inhabitants, knowing the British would be leaving Palestine in another two weeks, did not return to their homes.

Expulsion and murder by way of ethnic cleansing was systematically practiced against the native Palestinian communities throughout the spring and into the summer of 1948. Mirroring the events at Deir Yassin, the massacre of Tantura, a "trophy" village located along the Mediterranean coast near Haifa, was another example of Jewish military brutality. The village of 1,500 inhabitants was attacked on May 22, 1948, nearly a week after the birth of Israel. The village men were separated from the women and taken for execution on the beach. After the rampage against the village was over, two surviving Palestinians were ordered to dig mass graves that would hold 230 bodies.[32]

Famously interviewed by Teddy Katz, all of the Palestinian witnesses (some 30 survivors) of Tantura, in addition to seven former Palmach soldiers, confirmed the slaughter took place after the villagers had surrendered to the Israeli military forces.

In addition, psychological scare tactics were employed by the Jewish forces to carry out the "transfer" of Arab populations. For example, Haganah radio broadcasts warned of "supposed" smallpox cases breaking out in Jaffa due to the arrival of Syrian and Iraqi fighters carrying the infectious and deadly disease.

Arab men were determined to protect Palestinian women from Israeli abuses, due to sensationalized reports, which indicated that women were being violated by attacking Jewish forces. "Attacks on women were carried out with the full knowledge and anticipation that Arab notions of honor would incite Palestinians to remove their families from the path of danger."[33]

The truth is the Zionist intention to remove or forcibly expel the Palestinian people from their homes and villages was most successful when the Zionists used intimidation and rumor to hasten the process. Frightened and unarmed Palestinians abandoned entire villages due to flying bullets and outright fear.

> My family's situation demonstrates this reality. We had moved from Haifa to Acco (Acre) near the Lebanese border to find refuge from the fighting in the city. However, Acco was soon besieged by the Israelis. Many of our villages were being taken over by the Zionists. We were especially fearful of the Irgun. We heard stories of how they killed innocent women and children. I was absolutely terrified of them. When Palestinians heard the Irgun might be coming, they fled from their villages fearing a massacre like Deir Yassin. I constantly worried that I might be killed, and I feared for the safety of my sister.

The ethnic cleansing of Palestine took just six months.

Despite the overwhelming evidence to the contrary, official Israeli sources have always maintained that the refugee problem was not one of their making, but rather the responsibility of the Arab leaders, who had called on the Palestinians to clear out of the way for the invading Arab armies. While it is true that some Arab leaders indeed ordered evacuations, it is also clearly evident that Jewish leaders and the military establishment encouraged the Palestinian exodus.

Similarly, it was well known that new Israeli villages were built to replace Arab villages in the aftermath of the Palestinian flight. Quoted in Ha'aretz on April 4, 1969, Moshe Dayan addressed an audience of students at the Haifa Technion,

> Villages were built in place of Arab villages. You don't even know the names of these Arab villages, and I don't blame you, because the geography books disappeared. And not only do these books no longer exist, but the Arab villages don't either. Nahalal rose on the site of Mahloul, Kibbutz Gvat on the site of Jibta, Kibbutz Sarid on the site of Huneifis, and Kfar Yehoshua on the site of Tel al-Shuman. There isn't a single place built in this country where, before, there wasn't an Arab population.[34]

77 | Amin Kazak's father, Moustapha Kazak (center), and his brothers

Moshe Dayan's admission of the historical facts indicating Israeli use of force against the native Arab population in 1948 is rare. Instead, Jews have held a longstanding denial of Israeli culpability in the disastrous events of al-Naqba, the expulsion of Palestinian refugees and the intentional destruction and replacement of Palestinian villages. Even today, Israelis refuse to accept responsibility for the historical Palestinian calamity. From one administration to the next, Israeli leaders have expressed rudimentary denial and no accountability for the Palestinian refugee problem.

Nevertheless, the facts speak for themselves. During the period between the Partition of Palestine and the outbreak of war in 1948, some 400,000 Palestinians were driven from their homes and became refugees. This meant that more than half of 700,000 Palestinian refugees fled or were forced to leave Palestine prior to the outbreak of full-scale war between the newly declared State of Israel and the armies of the Arab states.

What I find to be most misleading is that in defending themselves and excusing their actions, the Zionists continually insist that they bought the Land of Israel through legal transactions. In fact, for 87 percent of the lost Palestinian land, this was a fabrication.[35] Moreover, when Jews claim that the Palestinians left their lands voluntarily in 1948, they attempt to absolve Israel of responsibility for the refugee problem that gets worse every year. Therefore, when Israelis claim that the refugee problem is one for the neighboring Arab countries to resolve, they are choosing to forget that they played a sizable role in the destruction of Arab communities and in the forceful, expulsion en masse of Palestinian refugees from Palestine.

This kind of denial and perpetuation of untruths adds fuel to the fire for Palestinians who have suffered displacement for six decades.

By the time of the British withdrawal, all hopes turned towards our brothers in the large Arab armies of Egypt and Jordan to save us and return us to our homes. To keep us safe, my father decided that our family should escape across the border from Acco (Acre) into Lebanon to avoid the on-coming fight. I remember a big truck, which our family shared with other families to take as much of our belongings as possible. I can still picture all of our personal belongings loaded on the truck. What we left behind was far more than our possessions. Two of my aunts stayed in Acco (Acre). Others in my extended family escaped to Syria and it would be many years before we saw them again.

My parents, my sister, and I ended up in a refugee camp in Lebanon near the Beirut airport. We often heard the adults around us talking about how the Arabs would win the war and we would soon be able to go back home to Haifa.

However, as history would reveal, none of their predictions became true.

Instead of going home, my father agonized over seeing his family living in the squalor of a Palestinian refugee camp for seven years—until I was thirteen.

The Arab Invasion
King Abdullah's Dual Agenda

Palestinians were disappointed by the Arab nations that had promised to defend them.

Certainly, massacres and the systematic destruction of ancient villages stoked the wrath of the surrounding Arab nations and prompted their coordinated invasion of the Jewish state in 1948. The fact that these nations' militaries were wholly unprepared for a coordinated attack of this scale suggests that Arab leaders may not have believed an invasion would be necessary.

On May 12, the political committees of the Arab League approved a war plan, but they were unable to find a military commander willing to carry it out. Many Palestinian Arabs hoped that Jordan's monarch, King Abdullah I would lead the Arab armies to victory and return the Palestinian people to their land. However, the King had already been secretly meeting with the Jewish

78 | King Abdullah of Jordan

Agency (and the British before them) for quite some time. As early as 1937, Abdullah was a proponent of the partition of Palestine into two distinct regions, which would allow for the merger of the Palestinian region into Jordan (then Transjordan). It has since become well known that Abdullah met with Golda Meir on May 11, 1948, four days prior to the Declaration of Israeli Independence. The account of this meeting demonstrates that the King warned Meir and the leaders of the Yishuv (Jews in Palestine) of an imminent invasion by the Arab states.[36]

79 | Haifa and the sea from Carmel, circa 1927—the area of Haifa where Amin Kazak's family lived prior to 1948

Playing a double game between the Palestinian people and their Jewish aggressors, Abdullah secretly entered into an agreement of non-aggression with the Jews on the island of Rhodes in April 1949. The agreement stipulated that King Abdullah would cede all disputed territory in the border areas and in Jerusalem to the Israelis, while

80 | Palestinian refugees fleeing from Israel in 1948

preventing "all land, sea, or air military or paramilitary forces… including non-regular forces from committing 'any warlike or hostile act against the military or paramilitary' forces of Israel."[37] Meanwhile, Great Britain, in "addition to sanctioning the partition of Palestine and the absorption of central Palestine by Abdullah, agreed in March 1948 to come to the King's aid should he be attacked."[38]

Only adding fuel to the lost cause of Palestine and dashing the dreams of independent Palestinian statehood among his most ardent Palestinian supporters, Abdullah sought to make the best of a bad situation and annex the West Bank for himself, thereby living side-by-side with Israel. Abdullah's secret negotiations "led to the collusion that barred the creation of an Arab Palestinian state."[39]

With or without the brewing war, Abdullah's ambition was to annex the West Bank and seize control of Jerusalem, not to help create a Palestinian state. As the first Secretary-General

81 | Cover of Amin Kazak's Palestinian Refugee Travel Document

82 | Inside pages of Amin Kazak's Palestinian Refugee Travel Document

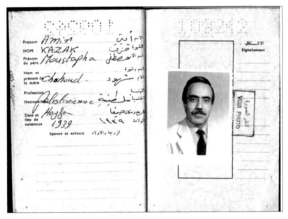

83 | Inside pages of Amin Kazak's Palestinian Refugee Travel Document

of the Arab League, Abdel Rahman Azzam, once admitted to a British reporter, the goal of King Abdullah of Transjordan "was to swallow up the central hill regions of Palestine, with access to the Mediterranean at Gaza. The Egyptians would get the Negev. Galilee would go to Syria, except that the coastal part as far as Acre (Acco) would be added to Lebanon."[40] Not coincidentally, on April 26, 1949, King Abdullah officially changed the name of his kingdom to the Hashemite Kingdom of Jordan, having decided to "drop the word 'Palestine' both from the name of the country and from the list of his own titles as King."[41]

By December of that year, Palestinian residents of the Jordanian-controlled areas of Palestine (as well as in Jordan proper) were declared Jordanian citizens. By April 24, 1950, the West Bank of Palestine was formally annexed and henceforth referred to as the West Bank of the Hashemite Kingdom of Jordan.

Abdullah's ambitions were just one reason for the Arab League's failure in successfully fighting for the Palestinians against Israel. King Farouk of Egypt realized Abdullah's designs on the West Bank and sought an Egyptian land-grab in Gaza and other parts of Palestine. The Lebanese joined the coalition as a gesture of membership in the Arab League. All of their armies possessed more equipment and munitions on paper than what was available to them on the battlefield.

Critically, the Arab armies were fighting for an abstract cause, far away from their homes and their families. Palestinian aspirations were marginalized by the national interests of the individual Arab states. It was common knowledge that the May 1948 pan-Arab invasion of the nascent State of Israel was more a greed-based scramble for Palestinian territory than anything remotely akin to a legitimate fight for Palestinian national rights.

In hindsight, defeat was all but inevitable.

> The result for my family was devastating. We ended up staying in the refugee camp in Lebanon for six years, from 1948-1954. My father had been a railroad inspector in a station operated by the British in Haifa, which provided a good living. My large, prominent Kazak family was well known in the Carmel region overlooking Haifa and the Mediterranean. Leaving our upper-class Arab lifestyle in our beautiful city on the sea, surrounded by our rich culture and extended family, and ending up in the meager tent-life of a UN Palestinian refugee camp, totally transformed our lives. Words cannot describe the devastation of the escape, nor can they express the feelings of betrayal we lived with when we realized that we could never return home. For me, a traumatized 6-year old, I would live in a Palestinian refugee camp until I was 12 years old. I doubled my lifetime in the squalor of that camp.

Since then, the Arab states have repeatedly failed to put the Palestinian population on the road to independent statehood. They have demonstrated little regard for Palestinian human rights or even improving the quality of life for Palestinians in the occupied areas—which is part of the reason why 120,000 West Bank Palestinians moved to the East Bank of the Jordan River (into Jordan) and about 300,000 others emigrated abroad.[42]

Since 1948, Jordan, Lebanon and Syria have been responsible for the massacre and expulsion of Palestinian people on their own soil. Saddam Hussein of Iraq is yet another example of Arab leaders manipulating Palestinian suffering for their own gain while casting asunder the fate of the Palestinian people. Following the Persian Gulf War, the Kuwaitis set about punishing their Palestinian citizens for Hussein's actions. The Kuwaiti retribution against the Palestinians was so severe that Arafat was forced to acknowledge that, "what Kuwait did to the Palestinian people is worse than what has been done by Israel to Palestinians in the occupied territories."[43]

As an Egyptian diplomat once remarked about the Palestinian refugees, "We couldn't care less if all the refugees die. There are enough Arabs around."[44]

Conclusion

For the Jews who saw the simultaneous invasion of six Arab fighting forces against them as a battle of apocalyptic proportions, their victory in the 1948 War was nothing short of miraculous. For the Palestinians, who survived the brutality, terror, massacre, rape, humiliation and betrayal of 1948, the events of that year were nothing short of a total disaster.

84 | Amin Kazak, age 20, when he started his teaching career in an UNWRA girl's school in Lebanon

Outside of the new Jewish state, hundreds of thousands of refugees crowded into the Palestinian refugee camps administered by the United Nations in the Gaza Strip, the West Bank, Syria, Lebanon and Jordan. Despite primitive living conditions and the physical fragmentation of the Palestinian community, the people emerged with a new understanding of statelessness and thus, the beginnings of an emergent Palestinian identity. At the heart of this identity was their suffering al-Naqba, the great catastrophe that befell the Palestinian people in 1948.

My father found employment in Saudi Arabia, which enabled my mother to move us out of the UNWRA Palestinian Refugee Camp when I turned 12. Although my father lived far away from us, our lives improved dramatically. He sent money every month. The most important issue for both of my parents was that we all received a good education. After high school, I was enrolled at the American University of Beirut when my mom and my younger siblings left Lebanon to join my father in Saudi Arabia. Most of them became Saudi citizens. I remained in Beirut to finish my studies.

Forty-five years later, I returned to the place of my birth. It was 1993, after I became a citizen of the United States and finally belonged to a country, even if it wasn't my homeland. When I entered Israel, a young Jewish soldier asked me for my identity card and I showed her my American passport. She was very polite. I couldn't help wondering what she would think if she knew my story. Did she even know that the birth of her country had caused me and my family to be stateless human beings for decades? She stamped my passport, smiled at me and I said nothing...

I went directly to Haifa to see my aunt and cousins who I had not seen for 45 years. I asked my cousin if he would take me to our old apartment building where we had grown up together. He asked if I was sure. I said, "Of course! It is the place of my birth." Reluctantly, he took me to my old neighborhood. It was then that I realized why my cousin hesitated to bring me there. To my dismay the buildings I had remembered were gone. My childhood Palestinian home had become a city park.

I was disappointed and angry that my Arab neighborhood had vanished. At that moment, I realized it was as if Israelis wanted to make certain there was nothing that a refugee like me could return to claim.

Following defeat in the 1948 War, Arab states seethed for decades and launched a pair of wars on Israel to avenge their lost honor and recapture territory. But neither strike was successful. Instead, their continuing pattern of defeat in 1967 and 1973 redrew the political map of the Holy Land, ending hopes of a Pan-Arab empire stretching from Morocco to Iraq.

For Israel, victory on the battlefield secured the young nation as borders were altered to more defensible positions. But victory also transformed Israel into a dominant power over stateless Palestinians. This problematic role would complicate its future. Peace with Arab neighbors remained a difficult and elusive goal.

For the Palestinians, their destiny in Gaza and the West Bank for the first time would be in the hands of Israel rather than Arab states and colonial empires. But rather than achieving statehood, what followed was a period of exile, suffering and resistance. Global Palestinian leadership emerged, while conflict over the Holy Land deepened.

After 19 years of independence, Israel once again faced a coordinated Arab invasion by the armies of Egypt, Syria, Jordan, and Iraq. As if living a recurring nightmare, more than 250,000 enemy troops surrounded the Jewish homeland threatening another "War of Annihilation." The battle cry of Arab leaders was familiarly venomous.

In the words of Iraqi President Abdul Rahman Arif:

> The existence of Israel is an error which must be rectified. This is our opportunity to wipe out the ignominy which has been with us since 1948. Our goal is clear—to wipe Israel off the map.[1]

In the words of Egyptian President Gamal Abdel Nasser:

> The basic objective [of the Arab Armies] will be the destruction of Israel. The Arab people want to fight.[2]

The words of Syrian Defense Minister Hafez al-Assad were the most chilling:

> …Strike the enemies' civilian settlements, turn them into dust and pave the Arab roads with the skulls of Jews.[3]

While the threatening rhetoric of Israel's adversaries was familiar, the actual threat posed by the Arab armies was greater than in 1948. Their military forces had acquired nearly 1,500 tanks and aircraft from the Soviet Union. In addition to increased military strength and training, the Arabs were more motivated. The Arab humiliation encumbered due to their defeat in 1948 had festered for decades. And since honor is a value their culture holds higher than all else—the Arabs were riled by their determination to destroy Israel.

Led by the charismatic President Gamel Abdel Nasser, Egypt mobilized its entire army, deploying 150,000 soldiers to the Israeli border.

Egypt defied international law by conducting illegal reconnaissance missions over Israeli territory. Even more egregious, Egypt closed the Straits of Tiran to Israeli shipping, ordering

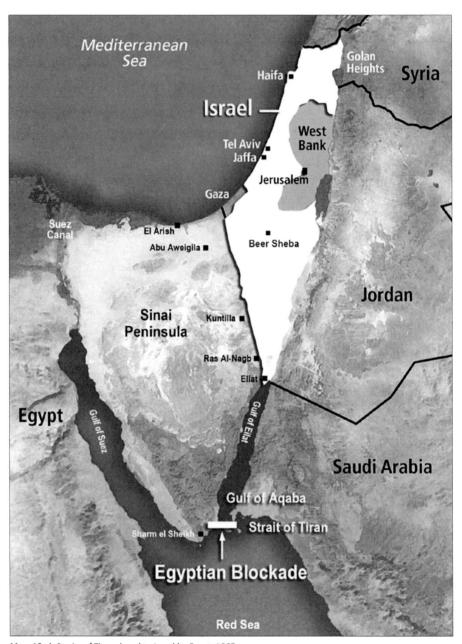

Map 12 | Straits of Tiran closed to Israel by Egypt, 1967

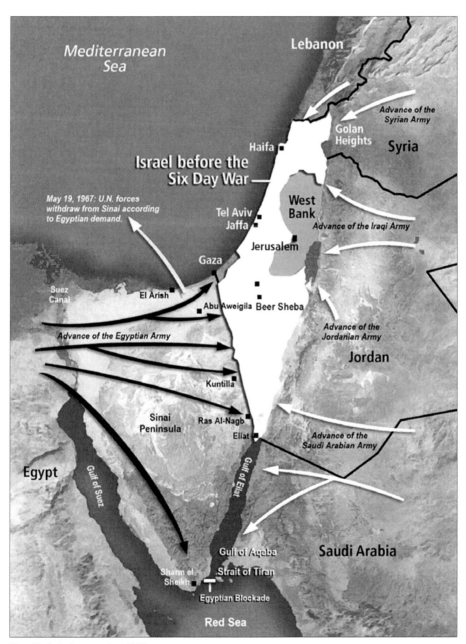

Map 13 | Arab aggression, 1967

Egyptian troops to fire upon any Israeli vessel sailing in or out of the waterway. This clear act of war according to international law blocked Israeli access to the Gulf of Aqaba, severely limiting Israel's sea access to the outside world. Israel relied on this route for vital oil imports from Iran.

On May 16, 1967, President Nasser ordered the immediate withdrawal of the United Nations Emergency Force (UNEF), which had been stationed in the Sinai Desert following the 1956 War to safeguard the Egyptian-Israeli border. Following departure of the UN troops, Nasser made his intentions perfectly clear:

> As of today, there no longer exists an international emergency force to protect Israel... The sole method we shall apply against Israel is total war, which will result in the extermination of Zionist existence.[4]

Simultaneously to these Egyptian acts of war, Jordan signed a five-year mutual defense pact with Egypt, pledging support for waging war against Israel. In addition, Syria joined the Arab coalition and immediately mobilized 50,000 troops along Israel's northern border.

At this point, nearly 207,000 enemy troops sat on three fronts of Israel's borders. Close to 130,000 Egyptian soldiers with 900 tanks were positioned in the Sinai Peninsula on Israel's southern border. Egypt also had 140,000 additional troops capable of joining the battle with 300 more tanks. Syria had 75,000 soldiers with 400 tanks stationed on the Golan Heights, a geographically strategic position for the enemy as soldiers and tanks on these hills had the military advantage of overlooking Israel's northern border near the Sea of Galilee. More than 32,000 Jordanians with 270 tanks were deployed in the West Bank, within a few miles of Israel's holiest city, Jerusalem and barely 20 miles from Israel's largest civilian population in Tel Aviv.[5] Another 150 tanks were moving into Jordan from Iraq, which was determined to join what was being called in the Arab world "the final battle."[6] The collective Arab fighting force also included at least 700 combat aircraft.

On the Israeli side, with full mobilization of its civilian reservists, there were 264,000 soldiers, 800 tanks and 300 aircraft. Israel prepared for a defensive war. All men and women in the IDF were called up to active duty. In preparation for the impending war, Israelis were clearing hospital beds for the wounded.

In her memoirs, Golda Meir wrote,

> There were also the grim preparations that had to be kept secret: the parks in each city that had been consecrated for possible use as mass cemeteries; the hotels cleared of guests so that they could be turned into huge emergency first-aid stations; rations stockpiled against the time when the population might have to be fed from some central source; the bandages, drugs, and stretchers obtained and distributed.[7]

Jews around the world were listening to broadcasts by Arab leaders who reaffirmed the Jewish fear of annihilation:

From the radio in Cairo:

> With the closing of the Gulf of Aqaba, Israel is faced with two alternatives either of which will destroy it; it will either be strangled to death by the Arab military and economic boycott, or it will perish by the fire of the Arab forces encompassing it from the South from the North and from the East.[8]

From Syria, Defense Minister Hafez al-Assad:

> Our forces are now entirely ready not only to repulse the aggression, but to initiate the act of liberation itself, and to explode the Zionist presence in the Arab homeland. The Syrian army, with its finger on the trigger, is united....I, as a military man, believe that the time has come to enter into a battle of annihilation.[9]

King Hussein of Jordan announced unity among Arab countries to engage in Israel's demise:

> All the Arab Armies now surround Israel. The UAR [Egypt], Iraq, Syria, Jordan, Yemen, Lebanon, Algeria, Sudan, and Kuwait...There is no difference between one Arab people and another, no difference between one Arab army and another... We have reached the stage of serious action and not declarations.[10]

Ahmed Shukairy, the Chairman of the Palestine Liberation Organization (PLO) pronounced:

> This is a fight for the homeland—it is either us or the Israelis... It is my impression that none of them will survive.[11]

Israel Exhausted Every Diplomatic Option

Even though the Arab attack was imminent, the Israeli government led by Prime Minister Levi Eshkol left no diplomatic stone unturned. Working with the United States, it pleaded with the Arab world—especially King Hussein—to stop the aggression.

But all Israeli diplomatic efforts failed. The Arab world was determined to restore its honor by wiping out the Jewish State. On June 5, Israeli Defense Minister Moshe Dayan ordered Israeli air force fighters to target Arab air force bases. Undetected, Israeli fighter jets attacked while the Egyptian planes were still on the ground. Quickly, most of Egypt's air force and runways were destroyed. By the end of the first day of the war Israeli fighter aircraft had also struck the Jordanian, Iraqi, and Syrian air forces. These surprise airstrikes crippled Arab air capabilities. It was a decisive blow that military analysts agree enabled a swift, Israeli victory.

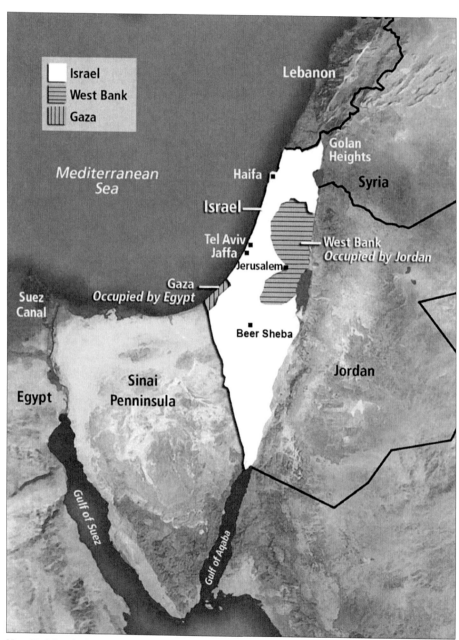

Legend:
- Israel
- West Bank
- Gaza

Lebanon

Golan Heights

Mediterranean Sea

Haifa

Syria

Israel

Tel Aviv
Jaffa

West Bank
Occupied by Jordan

Jerusalem

Gaza
Occupied by Egypt

Suez Canal

Beer Sheba

Sinai Penninsula

Jordan

Egypt

Gulf of Suez

Gulf of Aqaba

Map 14 | Israel, 1948–June 5, 1967

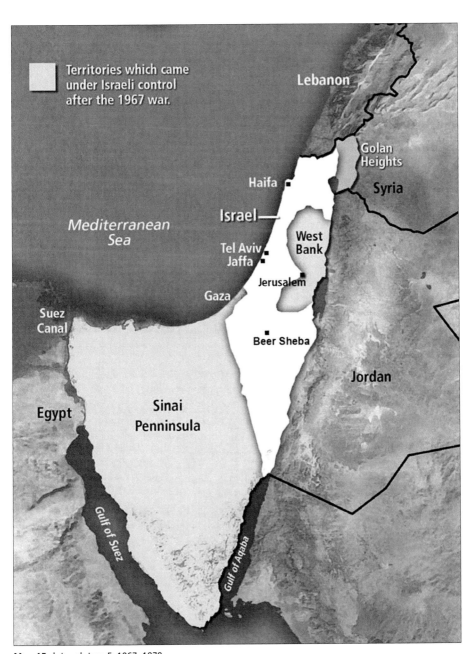

Territories which came under Israeli control after the 1967 war.

Lebanon

Golan Heights

Syria

Haifa

Mediterranean Sea

Israel

West Bank

Tel Aviv Jaffa

Jerusalem

Gaza

Suez Canal

Beer Sheba

Jordan

Egypt

Sinai Penninsula

Gulf of Suez

Gulf of Aqaba

Map 15 | Israel, June 5, 1967–1979

Immediately, the Jordan Legion bombarded the civilian population of Jerusalem and Petah Tiqva. Trying to avoid war with Jordan, Israel sent another message to King Hussein via the Romanian consulate (which had offices in both East and West Jerusalem) that was brief but unambiguous:

> If you stop the bombardment now, we will consider it to have been your "salvo of honor" paying lip service to the Arab world's demand for your participation. Stop the bombardment now and we will not invade the West Bank.[12]

Israel also sent an emergency message to King Hussein through U.N. representative General Bull, asking Jordan to refrain from engaging in war "…stating that Israel would not attack if Jordan kept out of the conflict."[13]

But King Hussein had received a phone call from Egyptian President Nasser, who lied that his air force was over Tel Aviv and his armor was advancing on Israeli positions. Hussein believed the Egyptian President, who was considered to be the champion of all Arab nations, and so he rejected Israel's overture.

> Had he heeded Israel's request, the West Bank and East Jerusalem would have remained under Jordanian rule. Instead, Hussein plunged into the war, ordering his artillery to target West Jerusalem, hitting civilian locations indiscriminately and firing on the Israeli parliament building (Knesset) and the prime minister's office.[14]

The Arab attack was ineffective. In less than one week, Israel defeated all four Arab armies on three separate fronts and captured the Sinai Desert, the Golan Heights, and the West Bank —including Jerusalem. In what was soon named the Six Day War, 759 Israelis were killed, and another 3,000 were wounded. Total Arab casualties were estimated at 15,000.[15]

Israeli Victory: Land for Peace Offers

Israel had defended itself and survived. It also captured territory, which it offered to relinquish to the Arabs in exchange for peace. Israel offered Egypt withdrawal from the entire Sinai Peninsula. It offered to return the Golan Heights to Syria. Most of the West Bank was offered back to Jordan. Israel merely asked for "normalization of relations, and a guarantee of free navigation through the Straits of Tiran."

In his address to the United Nations, following the Six Day War, Israel's UN Ambassador Abba Eban, asked Arab countries to come to the peace table "informing them unequivocally that everything but Jerusalem was negotiable. He reiterated the fact that territories taken in the war could be returned in exchange for formal recognition, bilateral negotiations, and peace."[16]

It was an extraordinary gesture. Arab leaders delivered their answer at the subsequent Arab Summit Conference in Khartoum, Sudan. They unanimously rejected peace offers from Israel, by reciting what has come to be known as the "Three No's: No Peace, No Negotiation, and No Recognition of Israel."

Following the Khartoum rejection, Israel continued to pursue diplomatic channels. In secret talks with King Hussein, Golda Meir offered Jordan the majority of the West Bank, excluding Jerusalem. The King refused. Later, in his memoirs, Palestinian leader Yasser Arafat wrote, "…had Hussein taken back the West Bank from Israel, Hussein certainly would never have permitted a Palestinian state to rise on the West Bank."[17]

On November 22, 1967, the UN Security Council passed Resolution 242, which called for the warring parties to "work for a just and lasting peace in which every state can live in security." It called for Israel to withdraw from occupied territories in exchange for peace, "free from threats or acts of force" and a "just settlement to the refugee problem."

85 | IDF paratroopers pay respect at the Western Wall, Jerusalem, when it was liberated from Jordan, 1967

Israel accepted this UN resolution, emphasizing the specific wording "from occupied territories" not indicating all occupied territories. This distinction, from an Israeli point of view, meant the resolution accommodated the principal of land for peace, and acknowledged it did not need to return all the territory it captured during the 1967 War.

In contrast, this resolution was categorically rejected by the PLO and every Arab state.

Celebration of Reclamation of Jerusalem

Although the Six Day War was traumatic, Israel and Jews around the world rejoiced. The victory allowed Israel to reclaim its 3,000 year-old capital city, Jerusalem.

By now, the reader undoubtedly realizes that Jerusalem is more than just a city to the Jewish people. It is sacred to them beyond measure. Referred to as Yerushalayim and Zion in Hebrew, Jerusalem has always been considered to be the most holy of holy Jewish sites. The ancient Jewish Temple of King David and Solomon stood on the Temple Mount in Jerusalem thousands of years ago. During ancient times, Jews made pilgrimages to Jerusalem four times a year. To this day, Jews around the world pray facing Jerusalem reciting prayers, which idealize Yerushalayim. In the Hebrew Bible, Jerusalem verbatim is referred to 669 times. The Quran, in contrast, does not mention Jerusalem once."[18]

In the words of Jerusalem's former Mayor Ehud Olmert, Jerusalem represents "...the purest expression of all that Jews prayed for, dreamed of, cried for, and died for in the two thousand years since the destruction of the Second Temple"[19]

Following the occupation of Jerusalem and the West Bank by Jordan in 1948, Jews had been forbidden from praying at the Kotel, (Western Wall) which is the only remaining remnant of the Second Jewish Temple destroyed in 70 CE.

Jews also were prevented from visiting their holy sites throughout Jerusalem and the West Bank such as Ma'arat Ha-Machpelah, (the burial sites of Abraham and Sarah) and Hebron, where King David is buried.

During Jordanian rule, 57 synagogues were destroyed in the Old City of Jerusalem and the West Bank. Jewish tombstones were desecrated in the ancient Jewish cemetery on the Mount of Olives. Shamefully, pieces of these tombstones were found embedded in the newly constructed roads and Jordanian army latrines.[20]

Unlike the desecration during Jordanian rule, Israel has faithfully protected the holy sites of not only Jews, but those of Christians and Muslims as well, even going so far as to relinquish jurisdiction of religious sites to different faiths. For example, Christians now control the Ten Stations of the Cross. Muslims were given control of the Dome of the Rock shrine, and the al-Aqsa Mosque, sites where Muslims built religious structures upon the exact location of the former Jewish Temples.[21]

Managing the Territories

However, victory did not bring peace. Following the 1967 War, Egypt launched its "War of Attrition," continually bombarding Israeli positions along the Suez Canal and in the Sinai Peninsula. This campaign of violence cost hundreds of Israeli lives.

Probably the most significant challenges for Israel stemmed from its occupation of the Gaza Strip and the West Bank, inhabited by nearly one million Palestinians.

Jews believed then, as they do now, that 1967 would have been the perfect time for the Arab nations to take the land offered by Israel to build a sovereign Palestinian homeland. Jordan and Egypt could have created a Palestinian homeland when they occupied the West Bank and Gaza from 1948–1967. But the Palestinians did not demand it and there were no inter-Arab negotiations for that outcome. In fact, the leader of the Palestinians in 1964 stated in the newly created PLO Charter the following:

> Article 24. This Organization does not exercise any regional sovereignty over the West Bank in the Hashemite Kingdom of Jordan, or the Gaza Strip or the Himmah Area. Its activities will be on the national popular level in the liberation, organizational, political and financial fields.

Nor did the other 21 Arab countries of the Middle East demonstrate an interest in creating a Palestinian state or otherwise resolve the Palestinian issue. "On the contrary, most of the surrounding Arab states… perceived the Palestinian cause especially as embodied in the Muslim Brotherhood, as a threat to Arab stability in the region."[22]

Improvements for the Palestinians

Israel had no choice but to take responsibility for these disputed territories and the people who lived there. But governing approximately 1.3 million[23] Palestinians in the West Bank and Gaza proved to be more problematic than most imagined in 1967 and created additional security challenges and economic liabilities for Israel.

Beginning in late 1967, Israel built roads, sanitation and medical facilities for Palestinians in the West Bank. The standard of living for the Palestinians rose to 20th century standards when Israel provided the infrastructure to bring telephones and electricity into the West Bank and Gaza. "…The gross domestic product of the West Bank grew at rates of between 7–13 percent per year over the next 25 years…."[24] Economic conditions greatly improved through exchanges of tourism, retail sales, and restaurants. Israelis shopped in Palestinian shops and ate in restaurants in the territories, while Palestinians from the territories worked and shopped freely in Israel.

Under Israeli governance the Palestinians of the territories had the highest standard of living of any Arab country with the exception of the oil rich states. Between 1967 and 1993 the Arab population of both areas "…tripled from around 950,000 to more than three million and 260 new Arab towns were built. West Bank students studied in Haifa. Seven new universities were built in the territories for the Palestinians."[25] Perhaps most telling is the fact that life expectancy significantly increased while infant mortality greatly decreased due to improved medical care provided by the Israelis to the Palestinians.

I was a teenager during this period, and I remember these were happy years of peaceful coexistence.

There were no checkpoints or barriers and both Palestinians and Israelis freely crossed the borders from Palestinian areas into Israel. I remember frequent family shopping trips into the territories, where my parents bought us our favorite candy and fruits.

I still remember the sweetness of the fruits, dates, and figs we ate in Gaza. My mouth waters thinking about the "knafe,'"a kind of crusted cheese, we bought from Palestinians in Nablus. My favorite shoes were purchased in the West Bank near the towns of Jericho and Nablus. My sisters and I would marvel at the leather goods and sheepskin coats.

I had a friend from Gaza named Omar who joined the neighborhood soccer games. He was a few years older than me and he often accompanied his Dad who worked in my Tel Aviv neighborhood. I remember enjoying summer days together and our teenage boy conversations over sweet tea. We spoke primarily Hebrew to each other, and here and there, we spoke Arabic, the native language of my father.

Perhaps the most tender memories are those of the day my family drove our Volkswagen Bug 30 minutes from my home to visit Jerusalem for the first time. I can still see my parents' tears when they touched the Wailing Wall. As I looked around at the masses of Jews weeping and praying with so much emotion, I knew, even at the age of six, that this was a forever-to-be remembered moment for the Gabbay family. When I visit Israel now, more than 40 years later, I always go to the Wall to pray. While there, I cannot help but recall my first time in East Jerusalem with my family. Now that I think of it, it was the only time I ever saw my father cry. He was 37 years old.

For me, as for most Israelis, these years following the 1967 War were good times. Perhaps it was not only that I was a child with limited knowledge of the conflict. In my world, I remember the calm of peaceful coexistence. Two peoples living in peace.

PLO Leader Yasser Arafat

That is not the Gaza of today. So what changed? Twenty-six years later, as a result of the Oslo Accords, Israel agreed to relinquish control of the territories to the Palestinian Authority led by Yasser Arafat in 1993. As a young doctoral student at Columbia University with relatively liberal views, I was happy to see the transfer of power. None of my colleagues was in favor of the Occupation. All Israelis wanted sovereignty for the Palestinians. We wanted the Palestinians to have what we were building: a vibrant growing democracy in the Middle East.

It was not to be. Arafat was the most charismatic Palestinian leader. His legitimate determination to liberate the Palestinian people and bring them a homeland of their own was—unfortunately—laced with hatred, incitement, and terrorism.

Following Arafat's assumption of power in the West Bank and Gaza, conditions for Palestinians in both the West Bank and Gaza declined rapidly and vociferously. The GNP dropped to "one-tenth of what it was under Israeli control."[26]

Using the plight of Palestinians languishing in UNWRA Refugee Camps, Arafat chose to ignite hostility by blaming Israel for the misery of the Palestinian refugees. Israel did what it could to improve the lives of refugees, even offering land and reparations through diplomatic channels, and raising the standard of living for Palestinians when the camps were within their jurisdiction. Most Israelis wanted the Palestinians to have their much-desired homeland. It was mostly the Arab countries that caused the endless squalor of their Palestinian Arab brethren. Egypt, Jordan, Syria and Lebanon prevented Palestinians from attaining citizenship in their countries, leaving Palestinians virtually stateless. The Arabs used the Palestinians as pawns in the Arab-Israeli conflict.

Article 24 of the PLO's original Charter clarified that the Palestinians did not lay claim to the West Bank, nor the Gaza Strip. Following the Six-Day War and Arafat's mentoring, the PLO revised its Charter by removing Article 24 and claiming the West Bank and the Gaza Strip as Palestinian land.

But it should be noted that Arafat did not single-handedly create a reign of terror against the Israelis. For instance, Egypt's secret police engineered the creation and deployment of the fedayeen, or terrorist infiltrators, who carried out over 9,000 terror attacks against Israel from 1949-56, killing more than 600 Israelis and wounding thousands.[27]

Soviet Influence and Intervention

During this period, the Soviet Union meddled intensely in the region to destabilize it as part of their broader Cold War struggle with the United States. In 1964, the first PLO Council consisted of 422 Palestinians who were "handpicked by the KGB," the Russian secret police.[28] U.S. intelligence reported that the Russians were arming and training thousands of Palestinian terrorists.

The Soviets propagated their influence through educational indoctrination as well. Palestinian "freedom fighters" were trained in Moscow at the Patrice Lumumba People's Friendship University…which served "as a base of indoctrination and training" for PLO leaders.[29] For instance, Palestinian Authority President Mahmoud Abbas graduated from this program. His thesis inspired his book, *The Other Side: the Secret Relationship between Nazism and Zionism*, which attempts to discount and obfuscate the Holocaust:

> It seems that the interest of the Zionist movement, however, is to inflate this figure [of Holocaust deaths] so that their gains will be greater. This led them to emphasize this figure [six million] in order to gain the solidarity of international public opinion with Zionism. Many scholars have debated the figure of six million and reached stunning conclusions—fixing the number of Jewish victims at only a few hundred thousand.[30]

Palestinian Liberation Organization (PLO) Takes the Lead

Israelis were tormented by PLO terrorism in the 1960s much like the world is currently tormented by al-Qaeda. For years, unfederated terrorist groups had been attacking Israel. Now, under Arafat's leadership, Fatah, the Movement for the National Liberation of Palestine joined the PLO, consolidating the most feared terrorist organization known to the modern world.

After the Six Day War, Arafat established the PLO as a state-within-the-state of Jordan and a haven from which the PLO could launch lethal attacks into Israel. While in Jordan, Arafat successfully recruited Palestinian refugees into his fold, which multiplied the size of his terrorist organization.

King Hussein of Jordan had tremendous difficulties with the PLO operating within his country and threatening his authority. Nearly a thousand skirmishes occurred between Arafat's PLO fighters and Jordanian soldiers between 1967 and 1970.

In 1970, U.S. Secretary of State William Rogers developed a plan to turn the West Bank and Gaza over to the Palestinians in exchange for peace. Arafat proceeded to try to sabotage the initiative by inciting riots throughout Jordan, and then escalating the terrorism with new methods. Instead of attacking institutions of power, terrorists turned to hijacking and bombing civilian airliners. The first of these attacks occurred on February 21, 1970, when Swiss Air flight 330 bound for Tel Aviv was bombed in mid-flight killing 47 innocent passengers including 15 Israelis.

86 | PLO hijacking, Dawson's Field, Jordan

International condemnation ensued when terrorists hijacked three more flights—two American and one Swiss. Two of the planes landed in Jordan. The ensuing hostage crisis was resolved when seven PLO prisoners were released from European prisons, but the PLO then blew up the aircraft.

Consequently, world opinion hardened against Arafat and the PLO terrorists. Jordan attacked the PLO in a military action known as Black September. It took 55,000 Jordanian soldiers with 300 tanks to finally force Arafat and his forces out. Arab leaders from Egypt, Kuwait, Lebanon, Libya, Saudi Arabia and Sudan sided with King Hussein against the PLO and Arafat.

Arafat and the PLO forces fled to Lebanon to set up new headquarters. Due to Lebanon's weak central government, the PLO once again established a state-within-a-state and was able to operate from Lebanon with the backing of the USSR. "Russian-trained PLO operatives were manning a dozen terror-training camps in Syria and Lebanon, and deploying terror cells across the globe from Germany to Nicaragua, Turkey to Iran." By 1973, Arafat had become a Soviet accomplice, a relationship that continued for nearly two decades until the final fall of the Soviet Union in 1989. "His adjutants, including Mahmoud Abbas, were being trained by the KGB in guerrilla warfare, espionage, and demolition; and his ideologues had gone to North Vietnam to learn communist propaganda techniques.[31]

Propaganda War

Arafat also was influenced by the Romanian dictator, Nicolai Ceausescu—who was a Soviet proxy. Under Ceausescu's tutelage, Arafat began changing his tactics to shift attention

87 | Headline story of Munich Massacre, 1972

87 | Israelis pay tribute to the fallen athletes killed during the Munich Massacre

away from PLO terrorist attacks to generate international sympathy by calling for Palestinian liberation rather than blatantly demanding Israel's destruction. He proclaimed his people were victims of human rights violations by the "evil Zionist occupiers."

Arafat created nothing less than a new Middle East paradigm. The change in tactics garnered support for Palestinians still languishing in UNWRA Refugee Camps without a homeland of their own. Attacking Israel in this propaganda war as "human rights abusers" began to take hold not only in the Arab world, but also throughout Europe and even among human rights advocates in the United States, including academic circles. Due to this designed deception, the international perception of Israel began changing from that of a victim of Arab aggression to an imperial bully that oppressed helpless Palestinians.

At the same time, Arafat continued to oversee the PLO's terrorist campaign from Lebanon. The targets expanded from commercial airliners to an attack on the Lod International Airport in Tel Aviv where 27 people were killed. The PLO also launched attacks in northern Israel, including holding children and babies hostage, and then killing them in cold blood.

But perhaps the most abhorrent act of PLO terror was the 1972 Munich Massacre, where eleven Israeli athletes were murdered at the summer Olympic Games in Germany. The group who carried out this targeted attack was called Black September, which operated under Arafat's command.[32] A horrified world watched the attacks on television. Once again, Western leaders spoke of increasing security and rooting out terrorism much like the current War on Terror, but the public felt increasingly helpless in combating this rapidly enveloping guerrilla warfare.

Timeline of Arafat's Campaign Against Israel[33]

Late 1950s: Arafat co-founds Fatah, the "Movement for the National Liberation of Palestine."

January 1, 1965: Fatah fails in its first attempted attack within Israel—the bombing of the National Water Carrier.

July 5, 1965: A Fatah cell plants explosives at Mitzpe Massua, near Beit Guvrin; and on the railroad tracks to Jerusalem near Kafr Battir.

1965–1967: Numerous Fatah bomb attacks target Israeli villages, water pipes, railroads. Homes are destroyed and Israelis are killed.

July 1968: Fatah joins and becomes the dominant member of the PLO, an umbrella organization of Palestinian terrorist groups.

February 4, 1969: Arafat is appointed Chairman of the Executive Committee of the PLO.

February 21, 1970: SwissAir flight 330, bound for Tel Aviv, is bombed in mid-flight by PFLP, a PLO member group. 47 people are killed.

May 8, 1970: PLO terrorists attack an Israeli school bus with bazooka fire, killing nine pupils and three teachers from Moshav Avivim.

September 6, 1970: TWA, Pan-Am, and BOAC airplanes are hijacked by PLO terrorists.

September 1970: Jordanian forces battle the PLO terrorist organization, driving its members out of Jordan after the group's violent activity threatens to destabilize the kingdom. The terrorists flee to Lebanon. This period in PLO history is called "Black September."

May 1972: PFLP, part of the PLO, dispatches members of the Japanese Red Army to attack Lod Airport in Tel Aviv, killing 27 people.

September 5, 1972: Munich Massacre—11 Israeli athletes are murdered at the Munich Olympics by a group calling themselves "Black September" and said to be an arm of Fatah, operating under Arafat's direct command.

March 1, 1973: Palestinian terrorists take over Saudi embassy in Khartoum. The next day, two Americans, including United States ambassador to Sudan, Cleo Noel, and a Belgian were shot and killed. James J. Welsh, an analyst for the National Security Agency from 1969 through 1974, charged Arafat with direct complicity in these murders.

April 11, 1974: 11 people are killed by Palestinian terrorists who attack apartment building in Kiryat Shmona.

May 15, 1974: PLO terrorists infiltrating from Lebanon hold children hostage in Ma'alot school. 26 people, 21 of them children, are killed.

June 9, 1974: Palestinian National Council adopts "Phased Plan," which calls for the establishment of a Palestinian state on any territory evacuated by Israel, to be used as a base of operations for destroying the whole of Israel. The PLO reaffirms its rejection of United Nations Security Council Resolution 242, which calls for a "just and lasting peace" and the "right to live in peace within secure and recognized boundaries free from threats or acts of force."

November 1974: PLO takes responsibility for the PDFLP's Beit She'an murders in which four Israelis are killed.

November 13, 1974: Arafat, wearing a holster (he had to leave his gun at the entrance), addresses the UN General Assembly.

March 1975: Members of Fatah attack the Tel Aviv seafront and take hostages in the Savoy Hotel. Three soldiers, three civilians and seven terrorists are killed.

March 1978: Fatah terrorists take over a bus on the Haifa-Tel Aviv highway and kill 21 Israelis in the Coastal Road Massacre.

1982: Having created a terrorist mini-state in Lebanon destabilizing that nation, PLO is expelled as a result of Israel's response to incessant PLO missile attacks against northern Israeli communities. Arafat relocates to Tunis.

October 7, 1985: Italian cruise ship Achille Lauro is hijacked by Palestinian terrorists. Wheelchair-bound elderly man, Leon Klinghoffer, was shot and thrown overboard. Intelligence reports note that instructions originated from Arafat's headquarters in Tunis.

December 12, 1988: Arafat claims to accept Israel's right to exist.

September 1993: Arafat shakes hands with Israeli Prime Minister Rabin, inaugurating the Oslo Accords. Arafat pledges to stop incitement and terror, and to foster co-existence with Israel, but fails to comply. Throughout the years of negotiations, aside from passing token efforts, Arafat does nothing to stop Hamas, PFLP, and Islamic Jihad from carrying out thousands of terrorist attacks against Israeli civilians. With Arafat's encouragement and financial support, groups directly under Arafat's command, such as the Tanzim and al-Aqsa Martyrs Brigade, also carry out terror attacks.

1973 Yom Kippur War

During this expanding terror campaign, Arab states were planning their own conventional attack, convinced that Israel was preoccupied and weakened.

In 1973 on Yom Kippur, the holiest day of the Jewish calendar, Egypt and Syria launched a coordinated surprise invasion of Israel.

On Israel's borders, the Arab states massed forces that were equal in size to the total number of forces of NATO in Europe. On the Golan Heights alone 180 Israeli tanks faced an onslaught of 1,400 Syrian tanks. Along the Suez Canal, 436 Israeli defenders were attacked by 80,000 Egyptians.[34]

Egypt and Syria were aided by Iraq, Saudi Arabia, Kuwait, Libya, Algeria, Tunisia, Morocco, Lebanon and Jordan. Supporting this third war of annihilation was the Soviet Union, which supplied weapons, tanks and aircraft to penetrate further into Israeli territory than during any previous war. The attack killed 2,688 Israelis and wounded 7,250. The IDF lost 40 percent of its tanks.[35]

Yet the outcome of this assault was similar to the previous two wars. Israel ultimately repelled the Arab invasion and established significant military positions in the Sinai Peninsula and on the Golan Heights.

This surprise attack by the allied Arab forces occurred on Yom Kippur, the holiest day of the Jewish year. I was 12 years old and like most religious Jews, I was with my family in the synagogue. As is customary, the country shuts down on Yom Kippur. People do not use electricity, nor do they use telephones. The streets are empty as Jewish people do not drive on this Day of Atonement. Instead, Jews, including my family, spend the day fasting and praying at the synagogue.

My older sister, Aliza, was not with us on that day as she was an officer in the IDF and was on active duty on an air force base in the south.

We learned we were at war while in the synagogue. A young soldier entered and interrupted our prayer service to speak to our Rabbi. Quickly, our Rabbi told us that Israel was under attack and the soldier read a list of code names indicating the military units which needed to report immediately for active duty. The Rabbi sent all of us home.

Hurriedly, my family walked with the other congregants to our homes, where we immediately turned on the radio. Of course, we were thinking, "Where is Aliza and is she safe?" The broadcasts were filled with news that our air force bases had taken sizable hits and that many aircraft were destroyed. Not knowing Aliza's location, but knowing that her job entailed air force air control, we knew that she was in grave danger.

Shortly, the phone rang and my father was called to duty and he immediately left the house. We raced to fill sacks with sand to place around our bomb shelter, while neighbors scurried to stock food and water, blankets and bedding into the shelter for our apartment building.

At home in northern Tel Aviv, I helped my mom and younger sister cover our windows with dark paper, while listening to the radio reports indicating how devastating the first hours of the attack had been. Israeli planes were shot down and many young Israeli pilots were killed. It was clear that the IDF was caught totally off-guard, and the survival of the country was in question.

As more and more units were called into action, we realized that the strike against us on Yom Kippur weakened our capacity to mobilize quickly.

The more we listened the more frightened we became. For the first time in my life, I feared the Arabs might win.

Meanwhile, when Aliza returned home, she appeared to have aged from her experiences as a 19-year-old soldier. She described the devastation to her air force base, where she had worked around the clock dispatching planes from an underground military compound.

Aliza survived, thank God, but suffered the loss of many friends in that war. This loss is something nearly every Israeli shares. No matter your age, if you are older than 18, you understand the responsibilities of military service in Israel, and you know someone close to you who has died protecting the Jewish homeland.

Jewish Settlements in the West Bank and Gaza Following the 1967 War

Following the Six Day War, Israelis began to build villages in the territories captured in Judea, Samaria, and Gaza. Initially for security reasons, Israel allowed citizens to establish settlements in the territories; particularly, to protect the narrow Tel-Aviv to Jerusalem corridor, where the majority of the Israeli population lived. Within a decade, a sizable group of ideological settlers emerged within Israel. These groups believed that winning the 1967 War reflected "an act of God and indicated divine providence that the historic Land of Israel should be restored to the Jewish people."[36] This wave of settlements were promoted primarily through the economic incentives offered by Prime Minister Menachem Begin, whose Likud Party opened the pathway for these mostly religious Jews to develop villages in the West Bank. For these settlers, the territories needed to be reclaimed by Israel because they were a part of the biblical Holy Land, promised by God to Jewish ancestors: Abraham, Isaac, and Jacob.

Today, some of these settlements are thriving. Nearly 300,000 Jewish settlers live in 127 settlements in the territories. Sixty percent of the settlers live in five settlement blocs: Ma'ale Adumim, Modiin Ilit, Ariel, Gush Etzion and Givat Ze'ev, near the 1967 border. These settlements are virtual suburbs of Tel Aviv and Jerusalem[37] and they comprise between 4–6 percent of territorial land of the West Bank. In previous peace offers, these suburban settlements have been part of the "settlement blocs" that even Yasser Arafat is said to have "grudgingly accepted" at Camp David. Israelis assume—and Palestinian moderates understand—that these suburban settlements will remain within Israel's new defensible borders in any future peace agreement. Most Israelis believe that when the Palestinians are willing to seriously negotiate, Israel will make a "land swap" with the new Palestinian State to provide 4–6 percent of additional Israeli land for the Palestinian State.

The development of Israeli settlements is almost always to provide housing for the Jewish residents in these suburban settlements and to accommodate for natural growth within their municipal boundaries. While Palestinian rhetoric contends that Israel consumes a vast amount of land in the territories, in reality more than 80 percent of the territories in the West Bank are solely under the control of the Palestinians and are governed by the Palestinian Authority. The remaining area in dispute is extremely small, covering less than 40 square miles.

However, not all of the settlements are along the 1967 Green Line and they do not fall into this suburban category. Moderate and liberal Israelis understand that ideological Jews living in these settlements located further into the West Bank probably will need to be relocated into Israel following a peace settlement. Of course, this is a sensitive issue among the religious right in Israel. Even the Knesset, Israel's parliament, is divided on the topic.

However, there is absolutely no tolerance for violent acts, including any committed by rogue settlers against Palestinians in the territories. Most Israelis believe the settlements have become a nuisance that receives too much media coverage. Expensive to keep secure, and a liability in the campaign of public perception, Jews have been willing to give up the settlements in exchange for a viable peace agreement with the Palestinians and Arab world. In 2001, Israeli Prime Minister, Ehud Barak, offered 93 percent of the territories, including parts of East Jerusalem to the Palestinians. The Palestinian rejection of this offer not only shocked the rational world, it was followed by the bloodiest and most vicious Palestinian terrorist attacks on Israel, now known as the Second Intifada.

Another example of Israel's willingness to trade settlements for peace was the Gaza Disengagement in 2005, when Israel left the area unilaterally. But that step did not convince Palestinian leaders to negotiate. And consequently, it reinforced the conservative Israeli view that offering land for peace is naïve, if not a gross mistake. In essence, Israel exchanged territory for more terror. The terrorist organization, Hamas, subsequently came to power in Gaza through democratic elections and physically forced the more moderate but weaker Palestinian Authority into the West Bank. The Gaza Strip declined into an enclave of fanaticism and terror.

The Palestinian Nationalist Movement

The consequences of Israel's victory in the 1967 War were more far-reaching than anyone could have anticipated.

Formerly, the Palestinians had coalesced into a unique nationalist movement that separated them from the greater Arab world. The catastrophic events of 1948 had in effect transformed three-quarters of a million people in the region from Palestinian Arabs into Palestinian refugees, with swelling communities throughout the surrounding nations of the Middle East and the United States. The Palestinian Diaspora remained bonded together by a distinct sense of exile and displacement that only refugees can share. In time, these refugees—and their children born in exile—began to reignite nationalist aspirations for a Palestinian homeland.

The years leading up to the Six Day War of 1967 witnessed a surge in Palestinian "togetherness" and the resolve to take their cause into their own hands—to reclaim the land they had called home for nearly 1,300 years.

By winning the war, Israel had conquered the Palestinian territories of the West Bank, East Jerusalem and the Gaza Strip, ushering in new policies of military occupation and settlement that resulted in wider and more direct Israeli contact with the Palestinians. For the modern Palestinian movement, it was a new opportunity with a new controlling power. But the Israeli occupation became a source of conflict and unrest.

89 | UN Secretary General Thant

This ominous view was shared by world leaders.

> I do not want to cause alarm but it is difficult for me not to warn the Council that, as I see it, the position in the Middle East is more disturbing…indeed more menacing than at any time since the fall of 1956. UN Secretary General U Thant, Security Council meeting – U.N. S/7906 26th May 1967.

The Palestinians initiated the clear goal of liberation in the Palestinian National Charter:

> The Palestinian Arab people possess the legal right to their homeland and have the right to determine their destiny after achieving the liberation of their country in accordance with their wishes and entirely of their own accord and will…The Palestinian identity is a genuine, essential, and inherent characteristic; it is transmitted from parents to children…The liberation of Palestine, from a human point of view, will restore to the Palestinian individual his dignity, pride, and freedom. Accordingly the Palestinian Arab people look forward to the support of all those who believe in the dignity of man and his freedom in the world… The liberation of Palestine, from an international point of view, is a defensive action necessitated by the demands of self-defense. Accordingly the Palestinian people, desirous as they are of the friendship of all people, look to freedom-loving and peace-loving states for support in order to restore their legitimate rights in Palestine, to re-establish peace and security in the country, and to enable its people to exercise national sovereignty and freedom.[1]

National Identity

Put succinctly by religious scholar Juliane Hammer, "Palestinian national identity cannot be understood separate from the emergence of the Palestinian national movement."[2] However, in part because of their dispersal throughout the Middle East, the Palestinians lacked a trusted leader who could articulate their needs and deliver the return to their homeland.

So they turned to their new host countries such as Jordan, Egypt, and Syria for support. In turn, the Palestinians allied themselves with the Pan-Arab nationalist movement. After all, the Palestinians as a people shared many of the same goals as the visions of Pan-Arab nationalism: primarily, the eradication of the newly founded State of Israel. Furthermore, the Palestinian identity was essentially tied to a larger Arab identity, making the alliance appear to be an easy fit.

Arab Agendas

For King Abdullah of Transjordan, the absorption of the Palestinian identity into a more general pan-Arab identity was important for his personal ambitions to eventually absorb the West Bank into the Hashemite Kingdom of Transjordan. A loss of Palestinian self-identity meant that he could bring the population under his control and foster a collective Jordanian identity. The sheer numbers associated with this plan were enticing; the Palestinians living in refugee camps represented a quarter of Jordan's population. But their conditions were a stumbling block. The Palestinians remained isolated and under-represented, and were the most detrimentally affected populace of Jordan's economic depression after 1949, known as "the years of famine."[3]

Not all Arab states shared Jordan's view. Lebanon feared its large and rapidly growing Palestinian refugee population and the threat the refugees posed to the country's already fragile demographic and political equilibrium.[4] Palestinian refugees, therefore, were barred from jobs, healthcare, owning land and citizenship.

Syria, too, denied Palestinians from claiming Syrian citizenship in order to preserve its so-called Syrian identity.

In the years between 1948 and 1960, Palestinian aspirations were held subservient to those of the Arab nationalist movement and to the leaders of their host countries. Indeed, it was Arab unity that was to be preserved at all costs. The goal of the time was to establish a Pan-Arab nationalist enterprise, not to secure a Palestinian homeland.

Refugee Transformation

As a people without political or economic power, the Palestinians lacked any type of political advantage or social capital either in Israel or in the surrounding countries. Those who fled remained homeless, stateless and destitute. Meanwhile, those who remained in Israel were "actively prevented from cultural expression of their identity and were completely repressed in terms of political activity."[5]

These conditions proved to be the grounds for dramatic nationalist transformation. Refugee camps became self-dependent societies unto themselves. The experiences of the Palestinian refugee population came to define what it meant to be Palestinian.

Institutions began to emerge in the camps. Through the development of UNRWA and other international relief organizations, children attended elementary school and young adults participated in preparatory programs for college and vocational training within the refugee camps. UNRWA's educational programming initiative was so effective that it was once noted in a study that, "never before in the Arab Middle East has there been as inclusive an educational system as that of the UNRWA, reaching as it does to all classes and both sexes."[6]

This resulted in the creation of a new generation of literate Palestinian youth for whom learning became synonymous with liberation. Armed with specialized degrees and a growing impatience with the status quo, this became the generation of Palestinian nationalists who

90 | Refugee camp in Nablus

were no longer encumbered by the political reticence of old village chiefs and what they perceived as political impotence of their forbearers. Indeed, educated Palestinians began to look towards the possibility of creating a new entity representing the Palestinian cause.

The camps also spawned a new generation of leaders. Before the great catastrophe of 1948, the land-owning elite were the notable leaders of the people. Now a new generation of university-educated leaders arose. Many were the descendents of non-landowning merchant and small-business class Palestinians who were forced from their towns along with the tenant farming communities during the war. During the 1950s, this younger generation of Palestinian activists set in motion a "culture of resistance" even as their host countries prohibited the development of nationalist organizations.

This culture of resistance began the development of a Palestinian diasporal identity, effectively raising awareness of the plight of the Palestinian people. Inside Israel, Palestinians still living in Israel were beginning to realize they could affect their own destinies. Secret organizations were forming, such as the General Union of Palestinian Students, which became "the basis for the new political movements that would re-forge Palestinian national identity in the exile."[7]

Between 1959 and 1963, as many as 40 secret organizations were formed, "with anywhere from two to 400 members, expressing frustration with the passivity of their parents", along with a clear dissatisfaction with the Arab states' "propensity to use the Palestinian issue for their own purposes."[8]

In 1959, a fledgling newspaper called *Filastinana* ("Our Palestine") was advocating for the liberation of Palestine and its people. And on January 1, 1960, Fatah (Palestinian Resistance Movement) was born.[9] It was to become "an entirely independent, wholly Palestinian, purely nationalist movement in the Diaspora, dedicated to regaining Palestine."[10] Emerging leaders such as Yasser Arafat, who was educated at Cairo University, became the co-founder of the Fatah movement. George Habash, educated at the American University of Beirut, became co-founder of the Popular Front for the Liberation of Palestine (PFLP).

91 | Palestinian overlooking West Bank village

As the new generation of Palestinian nationalists emerged, a recognizable difference between them became definable. One group advocated for a pluralistic Palestine, harkening back to old customs and traditions of village and town life. The other group called for a secular, pan-Arab approach for Palestine and the region.[11] The leaders of both political viewpoints came from similar social origins in the lower-middle and middle classes. Entry into universities transformed them into a post-1948 class of new professional elites.

The Fatah movement

The Fatah movement became the core of the first, more traditional group. Led by conservative intellectuals their leaders were: Arafat, Salah Khalaf and Khalil al-Wazir. Bridging the ethos of the lower-middle classes, the leadership of Fatah articulated a nationalist consciousness that emphasized the importance and uniqueness of Palestinian history, culture and traditions. The recently vanquished peasant and village identity was an orientation for Fatah's symbols and discourse. Most famously, Arafat adopted the peasant "uniform" in a very stylized manner. By wearing the black and white checkered keffiyya headscarf, Arafat invoked the "Palestinian-ness" of ties to family, religion and tradition as the foundation of national solidarity. In effect, Arafat "apotheosized the peasant-as-heroic-guerrilla who rose up to avenge and reclaim the land."[12]

Arafat forged the backbone of a new Palestinian nationalism; one which integrated the diverse constituencies of Palestinians who were all equally affected by the tragic refugee experiences of 1948 and 1967.

Departing from the promoters of pan-Arabism, Arafat and his contemporaries emphasized "a strictly Palestinian nationalist orientation, viewing the liberation of the Palestinian homeland as the royal road to Arab unity."[13] Convinced that the Arab states and their leaders were not focusing enough on liberating the Palestinians, Khalaf recounts the development of Fatah:

> At the beginning of the 1960s, then, discontent was rife among Palestinians faced with the indifference of Arab regimes. Increasing numbers of my compatriots, inspired among other things by the campaign we were waging in the Filastinana magazine, began to feel a pressing need for a purely Palestinian fighting organization.[14]

Fatah was to be a revolutionary force bound and determined to seize their homeland from Israeli control. And Fatah was to be a military force, as military action was the archetypal means to galvanize and mobilize the Palestinian people. According to a Fatah memo, "We, the people of Palestine, are in need of a revolutionary upheaval in our daily lives after having been afflicted by the Catastrophe of 1948 with the worst diseases of dependency, division, and defeatism. This upheaval in our lives will not occur except through our practice of the armed struggle and our assumption of responsibility for it and leadership of it."[15]

Fatah began a series of guerrilla attacks, knowing full well that it could not truly overcome Israel's military superiority. However, it was able to establish a growing presence as a distinct Palestinian group. Each Fatah attack signed up hundreds of recruits. Gaining support from Palestinians from across the Arab world, Fatah evolved into a mass movement, a globally recognized image of the new Palestinian generation fighting for Palestinian liberation.

Arab leaders began to show concern. They recognized that a Palestinian revolutionary movement could threaten their interests and the status quo. They sought to relieve themselves of responsibility for the displaced Palestinians and therefore avoid a direct confrontation with the "Palestinian albatross."[16] As Khalaf remembers, "Various governments, taking note of the situation, believed that this 'vacuum' should be filled by the creation of a movement that would channel the growing anger and make sure it didn't turn against them."[17]

The PLO

And so, in 1964, the Palestinian Liberation Organization (PLO) was founded and spearheaded largely by Egyptian President Gamal Abdel Nasser. Nasser proposed the PLO as an "independent" institution, which would give Palestinians a representative conduit through which they could struggle on their own behalf for their own rights. Launched in the first Arab Summit in 1964, and led at the time by Ahmad Shukeiry, the PLO was to become the political and legal front for the activities of Fatah and other militant groups. For hopeful Palestinians, the organization rejuvenated their long, silenced voice. And by its own accord, it was to uphold the "legitimate rights of the Palestinian people."

But the PLO also validated the original concerns of Khalaf: "When, in 1964, the PLO was established, it was intended to be an instrument of Arab nationalists. And although it had wide Palestinian support, its primary achievement was legitimacy in the Arab world, particularly Jordan."[18] However, as Hammer notes, "Founding the PLO to represent the Palestinians in the absence of a state, and the start of wide-scale military activities, mainly carried out by Fatah cells since 1965, marked a new phase in the development of Palestinian national identity."[19] From the perspective of the Arab leaders, the creation of the PLO would give the Palestinians the "illusion of determining their own destiny while simultaneously ensuring Arab state control over it."[20]

Whatever the geopolitics, for the Palestinian people these new developments were exciting. Palestinians took to the streets in a new campaign against Israel; they even conducted a couple of demonstrations. They convened the first Palestine National Congress in May 1964 in Jerusalem with an assembly of 422 Palestinians from ten Arab countries.[21] In addition to putting forth a Declaration of Independence, the new assembly established the key institutional structures of the organization, such as the creation of the Palestinian Arab Liberation Army, and the drafting of the Palestinian National Covenant.

This important Palestinian document included three principles: National unity, national mobilization and liberation."[22] Equally important was the call to denounce Zionism as a "colonial movement in its inception, aggressive and expansionist in its goals, racist and segregationist in its configurations, and fascist in its means and aims."[23]

Despite the fact that the PLO was neither independent nor capable of armed struggle, its Covenant was a call of revolution to the Palestinian people, to whom the only acceptable outcome would be the liberation of the Palestinian people and the return to their homeland.

As fervor among Palestinians began to grow, so did suspicions of the PLO, largely among the leaders of Fatah and the Arab Nationalists Movement (ANM). For one, members of Fatah were increasingly becoming aware that the PLO was simply a ploy by Arab nations to curb revolutionary aspirations among Palestinians and to set up a unified Arab military force. As Khalid al-Hasan remarked, "We considered the PLO to be an Arab instrument and its military wing a part of the Arab armies. In view of our experiences with Arab leaders, especially in 1936, and our deep lack of trust towards them… we feared that the PLO would kill or divert the awakening of our people."[24]

In time, it became widely recognized by the Palestinian leadership that the PLO was "created by Egypt, controlled by Egypt, and functioned mainly as an instrument of Egyptian diplomacy in Arab politics."[25] At the same time, however, as a matter of politics, members of Fatah also were quite aware that the PLO did enjoy Arab legitimacy—an issue of utmost importance. Since military action against Israel was considered vital, the PLO operated to elevate international attention to the plight of the Palestinians.

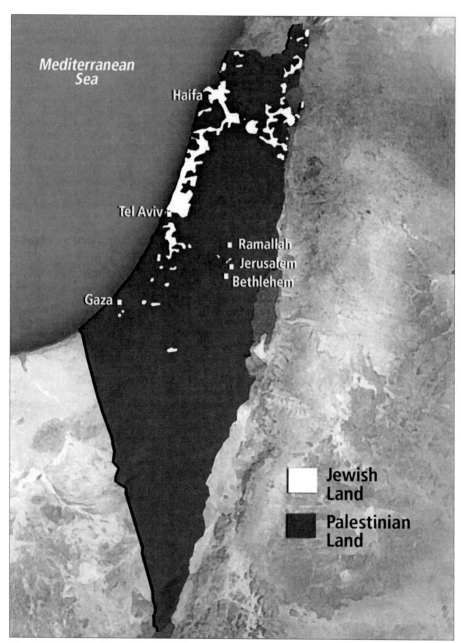

Map 16 | 1946 Palestinian and Jewish land

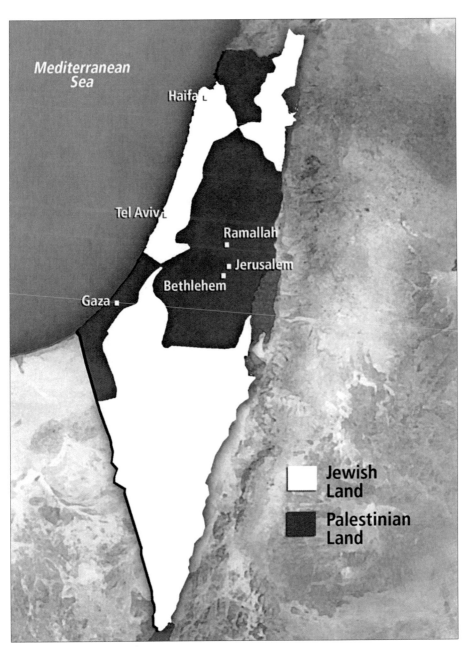

Map 17 | 1947 UN Partitian Plan

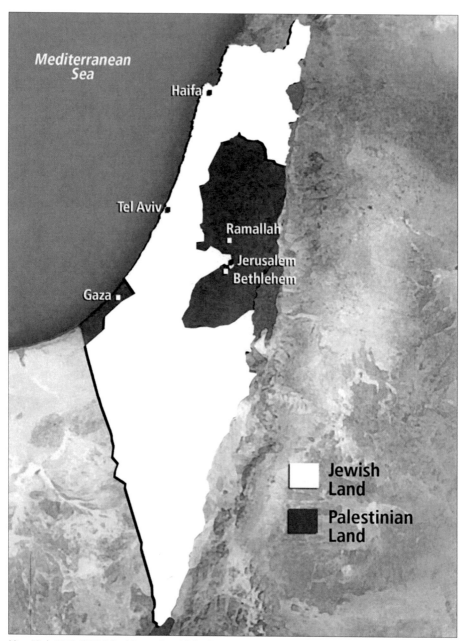

Map 18 | 1949–1967 Palestinian and Jewish land

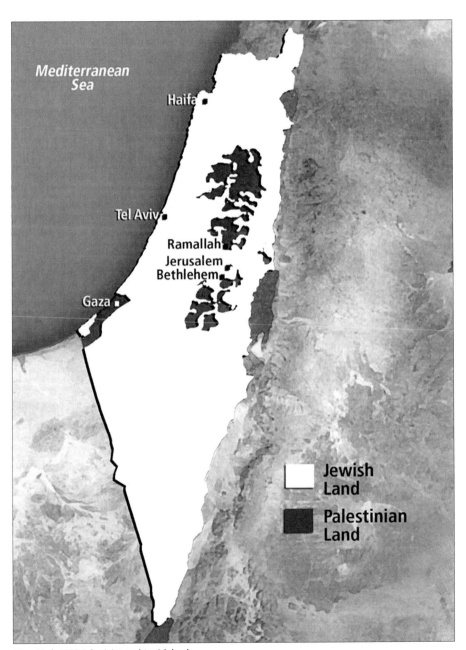

Map 19 | 2000 Palestinian and Jewish land

92 | Palestinian homes in Old City Wall, Jerusalem

Beginning in 1965, over the objections of President Nasser, Fatah began carrying out guerrilla operations in Israel. By 1967, Fatah attacks against Israel escalated. With the backing of Syria, the PLO was able to increase its military activity by attacking Israel from across the Lebanese and Jordanian borders in the first six months of the year. The rate of Fatah operations jumped fourfold between March and April."[26] Due to its success in guerrilla warfare, Fatah began to win over members of the ANM and the PLO. The comparatively conservative ANM, for example, began imitating goals initiated by Fatah: "Constant raids on Israel would scare away immigrant settlers, weaken the economy, and paralyze vital installations, while readying the Palestinian, Arab, and international conditions for the final and decisive battle of liberation."[27]

By 1969, the PLO was an autonomous organization with eight distinctive resistance groups under its network.[28] Fatah was the most populous and dominant. Arafat became chairman of the executive committee and the visible leader of the PLO. Throughout the Palestinian communities—both in the Occupied Territories and beyond—the PLO became "the symbol of Palestinian nationalism and the embodiment of Palestinian hope."[29]

Yet, for all of their aspirations and struggle for fair and adequate representation, the Palestinian people were vilified as terrorists by the rest of the world.

The Six-Day War of 1967: Defeat and Hope

As the summer of 1967 approached, another Arab-Israeli war seemed inevitable. By many accounts, Arabs and Palestinians alike believed that Israel had deliberately provoked the war in order to gain more territory and further exert its Zionistic aspirations in the region.

No one will ever know for sure if Egyptian President Nasser fully intended to attack Israel or whether, as many historians speculate, he was caught in a trap by his Syrian partners.[30] Nevertheless, Nasser, as the champion of pan-Arabism, repeatedly boasted of his ability to lead the Palestinian people to victory by reclaiming their homeland.

PLO leader Ahmed Shukeiry went even further, reportedly saying, "It will be us or Israel. There will be hardly any Jewish survivors in Palestine."[31] When Nasser blockaded the Strait of Tiran on May 22, 1967, and amassed Egyptian troops in the Sinai, he may have been bluffing. However, Israel considered his actions to be an unequivocal threat to the survival of the Jewish State.

For the Palestinians, the possibility of war was an opportunity to finally regain their homeland. Yet after only six days, whatever expectations the Palestinian people may have entertained were demolished. While the Six Day War proved to be a triumph for the Israelis, it was yet another catastrophic event for the Palestinian people.

The swift Israeli victory came as a crushing and demoralizing shock to the Palestinian people. Nasser had led his people—and the entire Arab world—into "the most serious defeat since the end of colonization."[32] And among many Palestinians, it was becoming quite clear that the Arabs, for all of their perceived might and dignity, could not, and would not be able to liberate their people. As Fatah co-founder Khalaf (also known as Abu Iyad) remembers upon hearing of the defeat:

> And Nasser had surrendered! Who could ever have imagined such a thing? The great leader of the Arab nation, the man sent by destiny, the hero who was going to help us recover at least part of our usurped country, had plunged headlong into an enterprise without so much as a minimum of preparation! Bitterness mixed with anger. The Arab armies, all the Arab armies put together, hadn't been capable of keeping the little Israeli army at bay. Worse they had yielded more territory to the Israeli expansionists.[33]

What the 1967 War meant for Israel was territorial expansion. Paraphrasing historian Isaiah Berlin, Israel always had "more history than geography. Now, however, it had history, geography and two distinct and opposing populations to control."[34]

Occupation and Destruction

Israeli acquisition of so much land through war translated into an immediate and coercive military occupation of the Palestinians, and the incorporation of Jerusalem under Israeli sovereignty. Not surprisingly, the days and weeks that followed Israel's June 5th so-called preemptive attack resulted in the creation of between 250,000 and 300,000 more Palestinian refugees. Again, Palestinians suffered. This time they were driven out of the West Bank and the Gaza Strip. Most of these 1967 refugees had already been refugees from the 1948 War.

Immediately, Israel took control over the Old City of Jerusalem, by annexing Arab sections of the city. The entire Arab municipality was closed, the mayor of the city was expelled to

Jordan, and full operations of all political and social entities were transferred to the Israelis in West Jerusalem. As Sari Nusseibeh, President of al-Quds University and a Palestinian living in Jerusalem recounts, "We were not just getting a new ruler to tax and control us. We faced a state with a military and civil bureaucracy with claims to our land."[35]

And walking in the city just days after the war, he described his findings in the Mughrabi Quarter near the Western Wall: "Within days of the war, the sappers, wrecking squads and bulldozers arrived. The quarter's wretched inhabitants were given two hours to clear out, and the entire quarter was razed, including two 12th-century mosques, to make room for a plaza in front of the Western Wall."[36] Within weeks of the war's end, the Israeli authorities also destroyed the Palestinian villages of Imwas, Beit Nuba, and Yalu in the Latrun area. The residents of these areas were expelled. And within months after the war's end, construction began on the first Jewish settlements in the West Bank.

Post–1967 Israeli Occupation of the West Bank, Gaza Strip and East Jerusalem

To be sure, the situation looked bleak for the Palestinians who had pinned their hopes and heart-harbored dreams of liberation on the Arabs. Visions and renewed memories of the 1948 catastrophe began to resurface among those in the occupied territories as well as in the greater diaspora. Only a generation after al-Naqba, what was to become of the Palestinian people now? Were they ever to regain their land and establish a nation?

Certainly, the international community wondered the same thing. Attempts were made by the United Nations to promote a just and lasting peace in the region. On November 22, 1967—in a rare unanimous vote—the UN Security Council passed Resolution 242, which called for Israel's withdrawal from the territories occupied during the War. To this end, Resolution 242 stressed the inadmissibility of the acquisition of territory by way of war. In reference to the Palestinians, the resolution problematically called for achieving a "just settlement of the refugee problem."[37]

Although neither side was particularly happy with the "oblique and fuzzy formulas" proffered by Resolution 242, the reason for the initial Palestinian rejection was due to the fact that the Palestinian issue was reduced to merely that of the humanitarian plight of the refugees.[38] As Schlomo Ben-Ami (later Israel's Foreign Minister under Ehud Barak) wrote, "The relegation by Resolution 242 of the Palestinian problem to the margins of peacemaking in the region signaled the beginning of a new phase in the history of Palestinian nationalism."[39]

Israel Seizes Jerusalem

Instead, the Israelis chose to ignore the authority of the UN, and focused on upholding their own laws of the land. Within days of destroying the Mughrabi Quarter to create the Western

Wall complex, Israel's Interior Minister signed a decree extending Israeli sovereignty to East Jerusalem. The decree also enlarged the municipal boundaries by 28 square miles at the direct expense of existing Palestinian lands in the West Bank.[40] Following this, the Knesset passed legislation, which unilaterally called for the "reunification" of Jerusalem, effectively calling for the de facto annexation of Jerusalem and its surrounding environs to the West.

Also disparaging, when Israel annexed the city, the Palestinian inhabitants of Jerusalem were not granted citizenship in Israel like the Arab minority who had remained in Israel after 1948. Instead, the Arabs of Jerusalem were issued residency cards, which gave them inferior status. Additionally, the Arabs of Jerusalem were considered inferior to the Palestinians of the West Bank and Gaza.

Israeli occupation altered and catastrophically affected Palestinian society, including Palestinian cultural expression and the economic and political rights of its people. As Ben-Ami writes, "Israel's sin in the aftermath of the war lay in her total misunderstanding of the conditions that were created by her victory."[41] Perhaps given the Israeli sense of euphoria and hubris following the 1967 War, Israelis became blinded to what was really happening to the Palestinian people.

> Israelis liked to believe, and tell the world, that they were running an "enlightened" or "benign" occupation qualitatively different from other military occupations the world had seen. The truth was radically different. Like all occupations, Israel's was founded on brute force, repression and fear, collaboration and treachery, beatings and torture chambers, and daily intimidation, humiliation and manipulation.[42]

Defeated, but not broken, the Palestinians retained hope, and, if anything, their resolve for liberation was strengthened. In addition, the events of 1967 set the Palestinian national movement on a new course, one with distinct independence from outside Arab leaders and diplomatic guile.

For the first time in the history of the Middle East, "the Palestinians were about to disengage from the status of a tool in the hands of the Arab states to that of an independent subject."[43] They now knew with certainty that they, alone, would have to liberate themselves.

The Arab states had failed them one too many times. And perhaps ironically, the War of 1967 aided in galvanizing the Palestinian nationalist movement.[44] Without a greater Arab military option, Palestinians had no alternative but to forge their own identity and purpose. They were no longer Palestinian refugees. They were Palestinians.[45]

Aftermath of 1967: A Movement in Exile

In the aftermath of 1967, the PLO began to revolutionize. Yasser Arafat became chairman of

93 | Battle of Karama, 1968

the PLO, and led the reorganization of the ideological and practical aspects of the organization. By transforming the PLO into the "sole legitimate representative of the Palestinian people," Chairman Arafat became "the leader of the struggle for an independent Palestine."[46]

Immediately, Fatah began planning attacks to show the Israelis and the world who they were, and what they were made of. Hope had once again been ignited in the hearts of the Palestinian people. Pride replaced the disgrace of being a refugee. The new Palestinian identity meant being a guerrilla—fidai—a heroic fighter for the Palestinian people and the cause of nationhood.

The PLO became the vanguard of the Arab struggle against Israel. In July 1968, a new form of Palestinian resistance was revealed in the hijacking of an El Al jet to Algiers. Car bombs were activated in Jerusalem and Tel Aviv's central bus station, and the passengers of an El Al flight were targeted in the Athens airport. Israel responded with a raid on the Beirut airport, destroying fourteen jets belonging to Arab countries.

Soon, the West Bank and Lebanon became the battleground for what had quickly escalated into a war with no end in sight. As Ben-Ami writes, "Fatah struck roots throughout the occupied West Bank and dragged Israel into a war that is still going on today."[47]

The new, combative stance of the PLO under Chairman Arafat relied upon several sources of inspiration. First was the now legendary battle at Karama in March, 1968, at the site of Fatah's military base. Karama, which means "dignity" in Arabic, was the site on the East Bank of Jordan where a massive Israeli incursion encountered a bitter clash against Palestinian and Jordanian forces. The Palestinian units performed under Yasser Arafat's command, and the acts of their heroism and bravery against the IDF brought wide-scale recognition to the Palestinians' struggle for international recognition. As Khalaf remembers from his participation in the battle:

The battle of Karama…was hailed as a stunning victory throughout the Arab world. Legends were woven around it. Tens of thousands of people, including the highest civilian and military officials of the Jordanian regime, descended on the town to pay their respects to the mortal remains of our martyrs…[48]

For many, the small victory at Karama signaled the rise of the PLO to prominence. Despite the fact that the Israeli forces eventually defeated the Palestinian and Jordanian forces, what mattered more was that they put up a strong fight, and the Israeli victory came at the cost of Israeli bloodshed. Among the Palestinians, Karama came to be known as the fedayeen fighters suppressing an Israeli intrusion into Jordan. Showing that victory was possible, even against overwhelming odds, thousands of young Palestinian fighters joined the Palestinian resistance groups.

Secondly, the PLO was inspired by the FLN's successful struggle against French rule in Algeria. Seeing the Algerian defeat of the French as a mirror to the Palestinian struggle against the Israelis, the "implication was that the Zionist occupation would be dismantled by exactly the same type of popular struggle."[49] From the Palestinian perspective, Zionism could not be considered anything other than a colonialist movement, which, in time, would be forced out just as the battle of the Algerians against the French led to the forced evacuation of more than a million European settlers.

According to Ben-Ami, "Just as the defeat of the French was made inevitable, among other reasons, by their demographic decline, so the Israelis were likewise doomed to lose the demographic race."[50]

Beyond Algeria, the revolutionary struggles in Vietnam and Cuba provided the Palestinians and their leadership with inspiration and context for successful techniques of resistance in their own struggle. Specifically writing about the post-colonial struggles of the time, the work of revolutionary writer, Frantz Fanon, inspired the refugee generation of '48 with his promise that violence "frees the native of his inferiority complex" and "restores self-respect."[51]

Elsewhere, the Cuban Revolution inspired the tactic of using military action as political propaganda. Marxist-socialist revolutions throughout the Third World were the order of the day, and the means and ends of these revolutionary struggles were not lost on the Palestinians.

Arafat and the PLO armed the Palestinian people with a clear voice and a mission. At last, it seemed, the Palestinian people were swiftly approaching the brink of liberation, and a final return to their home of 1,300 years. But as their disheartening history might have predicted, emancipation was not going to be easy. While a mass uprising seemed inevitable in the days and weeks following the Six Day War, Fatah and other groups had also suffered great losses and the gulch between those living in Palestine and those living in the diaspora widened.

In addition, the PLO was facing its own limitations. Having been effectively ousted from the West Bank by the Israelis in 1968, the PLO attempted to reassemble in Jordan, only to be exiled again in 1970. Then, due to the Israeli invasion of Lebanon in 1982, and the Lebanese Civil War, the PLO was forced to move to Tunisia. These events were "a blow to Palestinian institution building in the diaspora, and the move to Tunisia geographically disconnected parts of the Palestinian diaspora from Palestine."[52]

Still, these events did not bring about the demise of the collective Palestinian identity, nor did it halt the determination of the Palestinian diaspora. If anything, Israel's continual oppression and denial of the political significance of the Palestinian national movement created an outcome contrary to what was intended. Rather than crushing the PLO, the Israeli denial of the PLO made it stronger. Like it or not, the Israelis and surrounding Arab states had colluded to create a vacuum in which Arafat became the de facto leader. All of this gave way to the metamorphic period for the development of Palestinian national consciousness and identity.

They had once been "Palestinian Arabs" and were forced in 1948 to become "Palestinian refugees."

In 1967, they simply and finally became Palestinians.

Conclusion

For the Palestinians and the PLO, the years between 1967 and 1982 can be characterized as the years of Palestinian resistance and rebirth. After the 1967 War, a new form of Palestinian resistance formed. Whether it was the Israeli military occupation in East Jerusalem, the West Bank and the Gaza Strip, or the slaughter of thousands of Palestinians in Jordan in 1970 and south Lebanon in 1982, or the series of attempts launched by Israel to destroy the PLO, the Palestinian people and their leaders remained steadfast.

Even with their leadership in exile, the widespread mobilization of the Palestinians into political organizations of the PLO translated into a multi-national network of resistance and national consciousness. The PLO institutionalized this consciousness, bringing Palestinian nationalism into a new age of organization and intent.

Translating hardship into success has always been the Palestinian way, and the PLO exemplified this in the 1960s and 1970s. Given all of its difficulties, the PLO managed to survive and perpetuate itself as the only recognized voice of the Palestinian people. Its exile was symbolic of the Palestinian struggle, and it nurtured a national mythology of heroism and sacrifice portrayed by the image of the Palestinian refugees and their descendents. The leaders of the PLO understood and captured the imagination of their followers far and wide, proving even in temporary defeat that the Palestinian national movement would not only grow, but also live on to be a force to challenge Israeli hegemony in the decade to come.

As much as al-Naqba stole the dreams of my childhood, the 1967 Arab defeat in six days also influenced me dramatically. Many Palestinians and many Arabs called the defeat of 1967 "The Second Naqba." But for me, the 1967 Arab defeat was not a Naqba. Instead, it was a trigger for my own awakening with a new perspective about the Palestinian-Israeli conflict.

For me, it became clear that Palestinians should pursue a different direction—to rely on themselves rather than the protection of Arab brothers, the international community or the United Nations. It was time, in my opinion, for Palestinians to pursue their own path to attain independence and self-determination.

Unfortunately, the Palestinians did not take this opportunity to act independently after 1967. Rather, it acted in accordance with the authoritarian mentality of other Arab regimes.

In the 1980s, the Arab-Israeli conflict swung north to Lebanon, a country plagued by a decade-long civil war. Sectarian violence among differing factions in Lebanon left a weak central government. When Arafat and the PLO fled from Jordan, the PLO easily moved their operations into Lebanon.

For Israel, the establishment of PLO headquarters in Lebanon caused trouble on its northern border, as the PLO used its new location to launch frequent deadly attacks on Israelis across the border. With the support of Syria, the PLO entrenched itself throughout the south of Lebanon. After enduring years of terrorist attacks on innocent Israeli civilians, Israel launched an invasion in 1982 to weed out the PLO terrorists from southern Lebanon.

For Palestinians, the Lebanon invasion was a disproportionate use of force by Israel causing death and destruction, including more than 17,000 Lebanese casualties. The expulsion of Palestinian leader Yasser Arafat and fellow PLO operatives was a blow to the hope for Palestinian liberation.

The murder of Palestinian refugees, including women and children, in Sabra and Shatila refugee camps ignited additional hostility towards Israel for its complicity in the inhumane actions. With their leadership in Tunisia, Palestinians became more determined to free themselves from Israeli occupation.

Arafat in Lebanon

Following Black September, when the PLO was chased out of Jordan, it soon entrenched itself in the villages of southern Lebanon and embarked upon a campaign to establish its political stronghold. At the Arab League's 1974 conference in Rabat,[1] the PLO won the formal status as the "sole legitimate representative of the Palestinian people."

Consequently, Israel had to secure its northern border. The PLO had not only initiated a campaign of relentless raids and rocket-fire into Israel from Lebanon, but had launched a number of attacks against the citizens of southern Lebanon. Many of these citizens were Christian Lebanese.

Divided Government Leads to Lebanese Civil War

The PLO's ability to quickly use southern Lebanon as a retreat from Jordan illustrated the prevailing weakness of the Lebanese government. Since gaining independence from its Ottoman, and then French rulers, successive Lebanese governments had struggled to maintain the country's sovereignty and territorial integrity. In particular, Syria, its neighbor to the East, has

Map 20 | Lebanon

never recognized Lebanon as a sovereign nation. On the contrary, Syria maintained its desire to dominate "Greater Syria," which included Lebanon.

Internally, Lebanon's layers of ethnic, cultural, and religious factions made it extremely difficult to govern as well. Competing interests in Lebanon represented Sunni and Shi'ite Muslims, Druze, and Christian (Maronite, Catholic, Greek Orthodox) populations. Additionally, there were also 200,000 Palestinian refugees in Lebanon, most of whom were in UNWRA-administered Palestinian refugee camps. Most of these refugees had been in Lebanon since the Israeli War of Independence in 1948.

> *My co-author, Amin Kazak, was a Palestinian refugee. Readers will see in his companion section that he never received Lebanese citizenship. In the spring of 2005, after the assassination of Lebanese Prime Minister Harriri, I had an opportunity to meet with Farid Abboud, the Lebanese Ambassador to the United States. When I asked him when Palestinians residing in Lebanon could achieve Lebanese citizenship, I was astonished when he bluntly suggested that "they should all go back to their homes in Israel."*

Each sectarian group in Lebanon promoted diverse political ideologies. Coupled with the lack of military security, Lebanon remained in a constant state of chaos. No leader could please the multiple and fractious groups within the country. When the PLO entered Lebanon, it quickly established a foothold in southern Lebanon for its nefarious activities and faced no effective resistance from any national authority or local law enforcement. By the middle of the decade, these fractious conditions provided the fuel for a 15-year Lebanese Civil War. It wasn't just Jews living across the border in Israel who were victims of this chaos. Minority religious groups in Lebanon were persecuted during this Civil War as well.

Told poignantly, former Lebanese Christian citizen, Brigitte Gabrielle, writes of her family's hardships in two books, B*ecause They Hate: A Survivor of Islamic Terror Warns America* and *They Must Be Stopped: Why We Must Defeat Radical Islam and How We Can Do It.* Ms. Gabrielle has emigrated from Lebanon to the United States and devotes her life to warning the West of the dangers of radical Islamic Jihad. In her fascinating book she describes how her country was practically stolen by terrorists and how she was robbed of her childhood. In her own words:

> I was born in Lebanon and raised as a Christian. When the Lebanese Civil War broke out, our family and our Maronite community came under vicious attack by Islamists. They promised to destroy us, and some 100,000 Christians died as a result. I was nearly

Map 21 | PLO "Fatahland" threatens Israel

killed by a mortar. Our home was destroyed. We lived in a bomb shelter for seven years. Most of my childhood friends were killed. That's how I know about this fight.

PLO Establishes "Fatahland"

By 1972 Arafat had established a state within a state—"Fatahland"—in southern Lebanon.

The PLO's "Fatahland" gained unfettered access to Lebanese seaports as well as the airport near Beruit. Arafat acquired unlimited access to Lebanese international banking as well as national Lebanese communication facilities. In the south of Lebanon the PLO had all but replaced the state, taking over essential governmental functions. Arafat's "Fatahland" was so all-encompassing that it provided security and social services not only to Palestinians, but to Lebanese civilians as well. The PLO collected taxes, and issued identification and travel documents. It established a military base for the unregulated importation of weapons, all free from Lebanese law enforcement or international constraints.

The PLO also capitalized on its dominance in the south to cultivate "revolutionary" myths based upon a wide range of communist and anti-Western ideologies. In turn, this propaganda campaign attracted throngs of new recruits who were trained, armed, and dispatched throughout the nation, utilizing unregulated and uninterrupted advanced communication technology. Soon southern Lebanon became the "terrorist capital of the world."[2]

PLO Attacks Israel Across Lebanese Border

Seeking to restore some semblance of order and to avoid an escalating conflict with the State of Israel, the Lebanese Army attempted to restrain the PLO and engaged in a series of clashes with PLO forces. The PLO was unrelenting, however, refusing to accept any constraints on its activities against Israel.[3] Unable to control the PLO or its Syrian sponsor on his own, Lebanese President Charles Helou asked Egyptian leader President Nasser for help.

Nasser viewed the PLO as the primary vehicle for advancing Pan-Arabism, and he turned down President Helou's plea for assistance. In defeat, the Lebanese government capitulated and accepted an agreement in which the Lebanese government would ignore PLO strikes into Israel in return for a PLO commitment to refrain from interfering in the internal domestic affairs of Lebanon. The PLO quickly violated this agreement, taking free rein in perpetrating terrorist attacks against Israel while at the same time working to undermine the legitimacy of the Lebanese government.[4]

The strategy and path to success of the PLO vis-à-vis the Lebanese government was its ability to take advantage of Lebanon's cultural and social fragmentation. Various parties in Lebanon began forming their own militias for self-protection and pursuing their individual interests. The Lebanese Army, one of the smallest and weakest armies in the Middle East, quickly disintegrated as soldiers defected to the sectarian militias. Chaos ensued. Mafia-styled militants seized control of villages and towns and engaged in extortion, robbery, smuggling, drug trafficking and other criminal activities as a means to support their private wars.

Lebanese authorities in turn, were rapidly being pushed into irrelevancy as the PLO transformed into Lebanon's most potent, organized fighting force. It was under these conditions that the 1982 War in Lebanon broke out as various factions chose either to ally with or against the PLO, while others pursued their own agendas garnering outside assistance.

Lebanese society was largely fragmented along religious lines with sub-divisions within those groups. The outline presented here follows that pattern with the notable addition of secularist groups and outside influences.

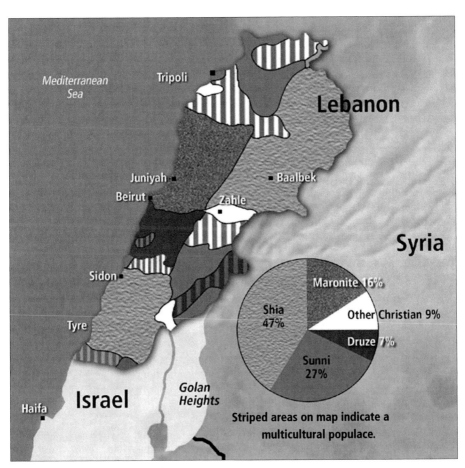

Map 22 | Fragmented Lebanese society

Druze

The smallest of all religious groupings in Lebanon, the Druze had no natural allies and thus were forced to forge partnerships with external actors. With modest nationalistic aspirations, this small sect of less than 700,000 people in the Middle East, typically are loyal to the ruling power wherever they reside. Under the leadership of the Jumblatt family, the group in Lebanon formed the Progressive Socialist Party (PSP) and developed strong ties with the Soviet Union. When Israel subsequently occupied southern Lebanon and Syria withdrew from the area, the Druze also aligned themselves with the Israelis. Despite its minority status, the PSP was able to amass one of the most powerful militias in Lebanon, which it used against its primary adversary, the Phalangists.[5]

Muslims

Muslims, particularly those residing in the north of the country controlled by Syria, initially sanctioned the influx of Palestinian militants. The Muslim leadership believed the demographics of Lebanon had swung to their favor and they called for a constitutional amendment that would award them the power that their population merited. As the PLO became evermore entrenched and radical, however, the Muslim population began to view the PLO as a threat rather than an asset.

Sunnis

Being that the majority of PLO members were Sunnis themselves, the Sunni population of Lebanon naturally allied with the PLO. Of the numerous Sunni militias formed, however, only al-Mourabitoum had a strong following. Fighting alongside the PLO under the banner of Freedom-Unity-and-Socialism, the group touted the Nasserist line of Pan Arabism and sought to preserve the secularist Arab character of Lebanon.[6]

Shi'ites

Initially, many Shi'ite Muslims welcomed Israel's efforts to rid Lebanon of the PLO. Not only did the PLO's secularist stance clash with their traditional and conservative religious views, but as residents of southern Lebanon Shi'ites feared the repercussions of continuous PLO raids and rocket attacks into northern Israel knowing that such behavior placed them on the front lines of Israeli reprisal. Backed by Syria, the most significant militia to emerge from this faction, Musa al-Sadr's Amal, sought to elevate the profile of Shi'ites in Lebanese society and to rid the country of any foreign occupiers (Initially the PLO, and then later turning against Israel.)[7] It is from this group, moreover, that the radical Islamist group Hezbollah emerged when a faction of hardliners broke away in 1982 with political, moral, military and financial support from Syria.

Christians

Christian militias drew their support primarily from the north of the country and relied on Europeans and Israel for arms, aid, and support. Nearly all the Christian militias which emerged promoted some form of nationalist political agenda and were generally dominated by Maronite leaders. The Maronites regarded themselves as descendents of the Phoenicians and thus historical allies of the Tribes of Israel. Therefore they developed an alliance with the State of Israel.[8] The two most notable factions included the Phalangists and the South Lebanese Army.

Phalangists

Headed by Bashir Gemayel, the Phalanges was the most powerful of the Christian militias. Sharing the common aim of ridding Lebanon of its PLO parasite, the Phalanges emerged as a strong Israeli ally. They went on to found the Lebanese Forces in 1977, established strongholds in East Beirut, and became a natural enemy of Syria which was intent on claiming Lebanon as its own.[9]

South Lebanese Army (SLA)

Originally members of Lebanon's national army, the group emerged when the Lebanese military Major Saad Haddad formed the Free Lebanon Army in the south of the country which eventually became the SLA. Although many of its members were Druze and Shi'ites, its officer corps was Christian dominated. Serving as Israel's proxy, by the 1980s the group had gained control of much of southern Lebanon where the SLA fought to root-out various opposing forces including the PLO, Hezbollah, and Amal.

Secularists

Primary among this grouping was, of course, the PLO. With an annual income of approximately $90 million from Arab oil money donations, the PLO quickly became the most potent fighting force in Lebanon.[10] Yet, while the various factional leaders liked to portray themselves as united, they were not. It seemed that the only subject on which they all agreed was their mutual determination to eradicate Israel. Aside from Israel's demise, the various factions that made up the PLO often came to loggerheads over political agendas, tactical approaches, and the whims of their external supporters (primarily Syria which sought to keep the umbrella organization's power in check). Accordingly, as Arafat struggled to maintain unity, over time the PLO squandered much of its sympathy both within Lebanon and abroad.[11]

The growth of the PLO in Lebanon coincided with an increased restlessness among the Muslim population for greater participation in the Lebanese government. The PLO in Lebanon forged close ties with the Lebanese Muslim community by promoting radicalization and violence over reconciliation or compromise. Fearing a PLO revolt backed by Syria, Christians in Lebanon began to arm, which in turn, prompted the remaining factions to do likewise. By 1975, the country was fully militarized with more than 20 private armies just waiting for a spark to ignite a civil war.[12] That spark came in the spring of 1975.

Civil War Begins

Although there are several accounts of the specific events, which ignited the Lebanese civil war, what is clear is that by early 1975, Muslim demonstrations and strikes had become widespread. In addition clashes had broken out in Sidon between PLO militants and Christian Phalangists who could no longer bear the Lebanese government's impotence in constraining the PLO's actions.[13]

As violence spread throughout Lebanon, it was the PLO who quickly gained control over the whole of southern Lebanon. The success of the PLO was largely due to its access to large caches of quality weapons, which had been received from PLO supporters, including Syria and Iran. They also engaged in a strict adherence to the rules of guerrilla warfare—which decidedly focused attacks on *civilians*, always avoiding battle with an equal or superior force, and never at a time and place of the enemy's choosing.[14]

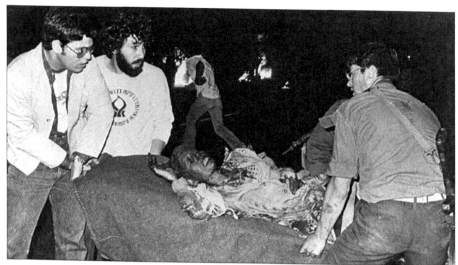

94 | Victim of Coastal Route Massacre, 1978

Israeli Restraint

Despite the unrelenting spree of murderous attacks Israel had endured since 1968, Israel's response to the build-up of PLO forces in southern Lebanon was remarkably restrained. Aside from operation "Spring of Youth," which was in part a response to the 1972 Olympic Massacre of Israeli athletes by the PLO in Munich and a brief incursion into Lebanon during the Yom Kippur War of 1973, Israel's actions against the PLO in Lebanon were largely confined to the clandestine pursuit of terrorist operatives overseas, and quick sorties into southern Lebanon intended to destroy PLO launching sites and weapon arsenals. All of this changed, however, when Palestinian terrorists infiltrated Israel and demonstrated their capability for brutality.

The attack was timed to derail the historic peace negotiation between Israeli Prime Minister Menachem Begin and Egyptian President Anwar Sadat. On March 11, 1978, eleven Fatah terrorists led by an 18 year-old female operative infiltrated Israel from the Mediterranean Sea. The group immediately killed an American tourist when they came ashore. Intent on killing as many Israelis as possible, the group then hijacked a bus on Israel's coastal road and headed south towards Tel Aviv. The terrorists shot at and threw grenades indiscriminately at passing vehicles, fired upon the kidnapped passengers aboard the bus, and threw at least one body from the bus as it sped down the highway to Tel Aviv.[15] In what many consider to be the first modern case of suicide terrorism in Israel, the Coastal Route Massacre was brought to a tragic end just north of Tel Aviv after 37 Israelis and tourists were murdered including 13 children. This terrorist attack left 76 Israeli civilians wounded.

This horrifying terrorist attack is etched in my memory. I was 17 years old. My high school friends were playing soccer outside in our neighborhood. Doron's mom came running to us shouting, "Everyone go back home immediately!" I was terrified. Images of what might be happening raced through my mind. When I entered my house, I told my mom to turn on the radio. We listened in horror while journalists attempted to piece together what had happened on this bus, now surrounded by Israeli security forces, just a few miles from my home in the northern part of Tel Aviv. Leaders informed us to stay inside because a terrorist incident had occurred in this bus. Reports included several casualties and that the IDF was investigating the possibility of multiple attacks in separate locations. I remember hearing the barrage of sirens, and the hovering helicopters above as we stayed glued to the radio for more information.

The hijacked bus from which terrorists had inflicted a death spree was stopped within walking distance of my childhood neighborhood. I perfectly remember the sinking feelings of fear and vulnerability which came over me that day. I had never thought of the war zone edging into my neighborhood. For me, the feelings I experienced were similar to those described by New Yorkers who experienced 9/11.

Until that moment in my life, I had believed that my country could always protect me with its powerful and determined security forces. With this new reality of terrorists willing to kill themselves in their mission to kill Jews, I began to understand true fear, and I recognized the vulnerability of every Israeli. Little did I know then the role I would play in defeating these terrorists years later in Lebanon.

Israeli Invasion: Operation Litani

Israel's response was swift and stringent. Speaking to the Knesset on March 13, Prime Minister Begin declared, "Gone forever are the days when Jewish blood could be shed with impunity. Let it be known: The shedders of innocent blood shall not go unpunished. We shall defend our citizens, our women, our children."[16]

The following day "Operation Litani" was launched to force PLO militants out from their entrenched strongholds in southern Lebanon to positions north of the Litani River. Unprepared for face-to-face confrontation with the IDF, PLO forces in southern Lebanon where quickly overwhelmed by the Israeli soldiers and within eight days, we Israelis had achieved our mission of pushing the militants twenty miles deep into Lebanese territory and away from our northern border.

95 | UNIFIL Commander and Arafat in Beirut, 1978

Responding to this defensive measure, on March 19, 1978, the UN Security Council adopted Resolutions 425 and 426 calling for the withdrawal of Israeli forces and the establishment of a United Nations Interim Force in Lebanon (UNIFIL). The mandate of this mission was threefold: a) to confirm Israel's withdrawal from southern Lebanon; b) to restore international peace and security, and; c) to assist the Lebanese Government in restoring its effective authority by ensuring that no military assets other than those of UNIFIL or the Lebanese government existed south of the Litani River.[17]

The Israeli government agreed to the Security Council's terms: yet not before our UN Ambassador Chaim Herzog delivered a scathing assessment of the Council's performance thus far. His indignation reflected the sentiment of the Israeli people:

> Having failed for 30 years to adopt a single resolution condemning the murder of innocent Israeli civilians, this Council long ago forfeited its right to pass judgment on actions stemming from terrorist outrages.

> When tens of thousands (some 50,000 dead and 100,000 wounded) were being slaughtered and a million became refugees in the bloody war in Lebanon—during two years of continuing bloodshed—this Council did not meet even once.

Since 1968, we have witnessed some 1,500 separate acts of international terrorism throughout the world. Not once was the Security Council jarred into response.

This world organization showed where it stood last November when, ignoring President Sadat's momentous visit to Jerusalem, it chose to continue indulging in sterile condemnations of Israel…

The Security Council has seen fit to seat at this table the observer of the organization which openly and proudly proclaimed its responsibility for the cold-blooded and meticulously planned murder of children 3 and 5-years-old, of a 14-year-old clarinetist, their parents, brothers and sisters, of a female photographer from abroad [In reference to the PLO being granted UN Observer Status].

How can this body expect to retain any prestige or moral standing after inviting to its councils the observer of an organization that has announced that these inhuman acts would continue?[18]

Herzog then outlined the illegal and immoral actions undertaken by the PLO over the past decade and concluded his speech by expressing hope that, maybe, this time, the Council would not fail in its duties:

Let this Council, by its behavior and by its reaction to these events, ensure that the forces of terror will not be encouraged, and that the sacrifices brought by Israel in the last few weeks will not have been in vain.[19]

Despite Herzog's eloquently and clearly delineated concerns, Israel complied with UN Security Council Resolution 425 and withdrew all of its forces in early June and turned control of southern Lebanon over to Major Haadad's Free Lebanon Army and UNIFIL forces.

UN Incompetence

Following the UN decision, indeed, UNIFIL stationed 4,000 soldiers throughout the area. PLO leaders quickly understood that if UN forces were allowed to fulfill their duties its militants would be deprived of access to any territory contiguous with Israel from which to launch attacks. The PLO militants launched an attack on a contingent of UNIFIL soldiers stationed in Tyre, killing three UN soldiers. The loss of three UN troops brought the entire UNIFIL mission to a halt, practically freezing any opposition to the PLO. Within a year the PLO had reinserted 700 militants and their support units into the UNIFIL zone.

More troubling still, the UN forces subsequently negotiated an agreement which effectively gave PLO forces free reign within the UN zone in return for a commitment that the PLO would refrain from attacking UN bases. UN forces also agreed to never approach PLO outposts,

96 | Terrorist attack at Israeli Kibbutz Misgav Am, 1980

while releasing captured PLO militants and returning seized PLO weapons.[20]

In Israel we realized that putting our welfare in the hands of the UN forces was an act of self-destruction.

By December 1980, 69 terrorist operations had been launched against Israelis from within the UNIFIL zone. That was not all. Within Lebanon, dozens of attacks by PLO terrorists were perpetrated mostly against the Christian Lebanese population creating a situation so dire for the Christians that Prime Minister Begin compared these attacks against the Lebanese Christians to the systematic extermination of the Jews in Europe.[21]

In turn, when Israel pursued the perpetrators of these attacks, UN commanders were quick to vehemently condemn Israel's actions. In truth, UN policies allowed the militants to surrender themselves to UN officials who would inevitably return the terrorists back to the PLO.

To make matters worse, UNIFIL forces made no attempt to halt PLO supplies and in the end "the PLO was granted a free hand in the building up of weapon caches within the 20-kilometer cordon sanitaire that the UN had guaranteed Israel."[22]

Israel's newly appointed Ambassador to the UN, Yehuda Blum, summarized our Israeli delegation's frustrations as follows:

> It is difficult to grasp how some members of the Council can ignore the fact that UNIFIL is now being blatantly used as a cover behind which PLO terrorists can shelter whilst planning and launching their attacks and then hide their tracks after carrying out their criminal acts. It is equally difficult to grasp how in the fight of this wholly reprehensible record of direct challenges to and abuse of UNIFIL, the PLO can be portrayed here in a favorable light and requested merely to continue its over-all cooperation as an essential condition for the effective discharge by UNIFIL of its duties. What is really called for is a forthright condemnation of the PLO's flagrant violation of UNIFIL's mandate.[23]

Israel's Challenge in the UN

We Israelis never found the United Nations to be supportive of our country and our interests after Resolution 181. The numeric disadvantage of Israel is obvious since every country in the UN General Assembly has one vote. Given that the United Nations consists of 22 Arab countries (Arab League) and 57 Islamic countries (Organization of Islamic Countries) Israel's challenges are immediately apparent. Israel stands alone as the only Jewish state in the world. Primarily, the only support Israel can count on is the special veto power that the United States sometimes exercises on its behalf in the Security Council. However, even this veto is limited to Security Council resolutions. There is no veto option for decisions made by the UN General Assembly. Moreover, Israel cannot always count on the United States for support. For example, much later, when the Israeli Air Force attacked and destroyed Iraq's nuclear facility in 1981, the United States did not prevent the UN resolution condemning Israel's actions.

The UN's opposition to Israel was not limited to UNIFIL actions in Lebanon. Israel was the only member state of the UN that had been systematically denied the right to sit on the Security Council, while being routinely subjected to politically motivated condemnation by this same body. Israel and the South Lebanese Army (formerly the Free Lebanon Army) found themselves in the 1980s constantly on the diplomatic defensive, even when the facts on the ground clearly affirmed their positions.[24]

A blatant example of UN bias against Israel took place on April 7, 1980. Five PLO terrorists entered kibbutz Misgav Am along the Lebanese border. The terrorists shot their way into the nursery where they killed the secretary of the kibbutz and an infant. They held the rest of the children hostage and demanded release of 50 Palestinian terrorists being held in Israeli prisons. Our army responded, killing the five terrorists. Four children and eleven soldiers were also injured. Israeli units entered southern Lebanon to eliminate the terrorist stronghold from which this terrorist unit had operated, a task which seemingly neither the Lebanese government nor UNIFIL forces were either capable or willing to do.

97 | Children staying in bunkers at Kibbutz Gadot during Syrian attack, 1967

The UN's response to this horrific attack against children soon came to exemplify its bias against Israel. Rather than condemn the PLO's actions in the most emphatic terms, members of the Security Council welcomed the convening of a meeting made at the behest of the PLO. Then, without any mention of the murders and the taking of children at the kibbutz as hostages—members of the Security Council summarily summoned Israel's delegation to their chamber and proceeded to castigate Israel's actions against the PLO terrorists in southern Lebanon.

> During these years I was serving as a Commander in the IDF. When we turn 18 years of age, every Israeli must perform compulsory military service. Usually during this period of training, cadets could return home to their families once every two weekends for the Jewish Shabbat. Due to the increased security needs of Israeli towns, villages and kibbutzim located along the Lebanese border, instead of a respite at home, members of my unit volunteered every weekend to provide security for Avivim, an Israeli village located on the Lebanese border.
>
> The Israelis in this town were mainly Jews from Morocco. These kind people worked the agricultural fields during the day. The terrorist attacks had occurred nearby and they were frightened. These Israelis were haunted by their memories of a PLO terrorist attack on their village in 1970 when terrorists infiltrated across the border from Lebanon and attacked their school bus. That atrocity resulted in the deaths of nine children and three teachers. Nineteen others were wounded.
>
> The families in Avivim were comforted by the presence of young IDF soldiers, like myself, who volunteered to provide security during the weekends.
>
> I remember feeling like it was the least we could do for these poor immigrants who were living so close to the border, merely trying to live their lives in peace. Their agricultural fields ended at the barbed wired border with Lebanon, exposing them physically to sniper shootings and terrorist infiltration. The reality of their lives was that their children had to sleep in bomb shelters every night and they had to constantly look over their shoulders as they picked the produce from their fields during the day.

Israeli Ambassador Blum echoed my personal sentiments when he expressed the prejudice of United Nations towards Israel:

> Here at the United Nations attempts are being made to manipulate the Security Council, as well as other organs of the Organization, to suit the whims and wishes of

the terrorist PLO. This travesty has reached such proportions that, in the meetings of the Council held last week, at the instigation of the PLO, no speaker—not one speaker saw fit even to mention the atrocity perpetrated by PLO thugs at Misgav Am, let alone condemn it. Incidentally, the PLO boasted that criminals of various nationalities from Syria to Pakistan participated in this outrage. I am sure all those countries must no doubt be exceedingly proud of this contribution to humanity.[25]

Over the next two years, from 1980 to 1982, emboldened with the knowledge that UN forces would do little to thwart their nefarious plans, PLO operatives significantly escalated their attacks on innocent Israeli civilians living along the Israel-Lebanon border. In the spring of 1981 alone, PLO militants launched 1,230 rockets into Israel before agreeing to a U.S.-brokered ceasefire—an agreement to which the terrorist organization immediately reneged. During the next year PLO militants carried out 290 additional attacks against Israel in which 29 people were killed and an additional 271 were wounded. Compounding the fears of many Israelis was the fact that during this same time period the PLO had accumulated substantial weaponry including tanks, Katyusha rocket launchers, anti-tank cannons, 100 or more large-caliber mortars, and a number of SA7-Strella anti-aircraft missiles.[26]

In public and media interviews, as well as in my classes, I am often asked, "Why does Israel consistently oppose what seems to be a simple solution to border skirmishes—placing UN Peacekeeping Forces, as a buffer, between Israel and PLO operatives? Moreover, I am asked, "Why does Israel revert to retaliatory actions instead of calling on UN forces for protection?" These are legitimate questions. My explanation is that the United Nations forces often are in the same bind as Israel and the United States when fighting terrorists. It is not conventional warfare, such as one nation's army fighting another's. Instead, terrorist organizations can easily infiltrate UN forces and perpetrate their attacks from the proximity of UN positions. This happens frequently.

Terrorists shoot rockets, for instance, from places adjacent to UN facilities, or next to a UN vehicle. This enables terrorists to not only succeed in attacking Israel, they win the "victim sentiment" when Israel fires back at the same location. Often, by the time of the counterattack, the terrorists have escaped from the launching site, and it is innocent UN officials or volunteers who receive the counter strike. Therefore from the Israeli point of view, instead of being a buffer zone of "peacekeeping," the UN forces often unwittingly become a safe haven for the terrorists.

Most importantly, in fighting terrorists, Israel finds itself in a relative disadvantage.

As an official member of the United Nations Israel has to obey UN policies in its operations but terrorists do not have such limitations and constraints. So while terrorists attack Israeli civilians from their locations across the Lebanese and UN lines, Israel is prohibited from pursuing these terrorists once they escape behind the UN forces.

Furthermore, our enemies are aware that Israeli military operations go to great lengths to warn civilians and humanitarian groups, such as the UN, about impending strikes. Israel also utilizes extraordinary precision as well as restraint to prevent the deaths of civilians. The terrorists use this Israeli value of preserving innocent life, by using civilians and the UN as human shields. Again, the terrorists operate within and from schools, hospitals, UN facilities, even from homes of ordinary Palestinians.

Lastly, during investigations of UN Peacekeeping Forces, Israelis have witnessed that a great deal of terrorist activity, such as massive rearmament, occurs within sight of UN Peacekeeping Forces and typically without UN intervention. So we are left with no other alternative than to act in defense of our own citizens.

1982 Lebanon War

By 1982 the Israeli public was demanding action from their government to protect them. Israelis expected their government to fulfill its most primary obligation towards its citizens: the security and safety of its population. This, in turn, gave Defense Minister Ariel Sharon widespread support to stop the PLO attacks by eradicating the PLO's military, political, and economic overarching hold over Lebanon. Under Sharon's leadership, Israel was determined to eliminate the PLO presence in Lebanon in addition to evicting Syrian forces from Lebanese territory. The ultimate goal was to facilitate the creation of a stable Christian-led Lebanese government which would sign a peace treaty with Israel.[27]

In defense of this position, former U.S. Secretary of State Henry Kissinger later remarked, "No sovereign state can tolerate indefinitely the buildup along it borders of a military force dedicated to its destruction..."[28]

On June 3, 1982, terrorists attempted to assassinate Israel's Ambassador to the United Kingdom, Shlomo Argov, at the Dorchester Hotel in Park Lane, London. The IDF launched retaliatory attacks on the PLO in Lebanon. Palestinian militants responded by unleashing a wave of rocket and artillery fire into civilian populated northern Israel. Israel responded with a long overdue, full-scale military operation called "Peace for the Galilee," later known as the 1982 Lebanon War.

Israel's primary target, the PLO, posed a formidable threat with 15,000 well-armed troops positioned in three concentrations. In addition to the PLO, the Syrians were also a force to be reckoned with having over 30,000 troops located primarily in the Bekaa Valley; including several armored and commando divisions, as well as numerous surface-to-air missile batteries. The Lebanese Army consisted of merely 10,000 troops, while local militias contributed another 50,000 to 60,000 combatants. In addition to these forces were a number of foreign sponsored mercenaries consisting of approximately 6,000 fighters in the battle against Israel.

Israel fielded less than 78,000 men and women, but their troops were far better equipped and trained in conventional warfare.[29]

Operation Peace for the Galilee was launched on June 6, 1982. Supported by naval and air force units, our ground forces swept through southern Lebanon quickly; capturing nearly all PLO positions.

Once the PLO threat was largely contained, we turned our attention to the Syrian forces. Again, victory was swift. Within three days, the IDF captured the Russian-made anti-aircraft batteries, clearing the way for an air assault. In the air-to-air confrontation, the Syrian Air Force operating in Lebanon was almost totally destroyed.[30]

Israel had achieved its stated military objectives within the first 5 days of combat. The United States clearly signaled its support of Israel's defensive act by vetoing UN Resolution 509, which demanded Israel's unconditional withdrawal from Lebanon.

> My unit in the infantry was a part of this IDF operation. We entered the battle in June, during the second-wave. As a Commander, my unit cleared PLO outposts, and captured PLO operatives, while gathering intelligence information from the civilians we encountered and PLO captives. When my unit reached Beirut, we were stationed in Museum Alley, a neighborhood of Beirut. Nineteen years later, after meeting my colleague Amin Kazak in Denver, Amin and I realized that we had been within a few blocks of each other in Beirut. When I was a Commander in the IDF in a war to chase the PLO out of Lebanon, Amin was a Palestinian refugee (originally from Haifa) and a graduate student studying at the American University of Beirut.

Israel's military campaign in southern Lebanon ended in late June. At that time the majority of Syrian forces retreated deeply into the Bekaa Valley, and no longer posed an imminent threat to Israel. The Beirut-Damascus highway was under Israeli control as was most Lebanese territory to its south. Most important, the PLO had been defeated, demoralized and were about to be deported.

What had taken the PLO 12 years to amass was lost in less than 12 days.[31] Despite these victories, Israel understood full well that if the IDF were to withdraw its forces the PLO would immediately reestablish its bases in the south. The goal of eradicating PLO threats from Lebanon and the signing of a peace treaty with the legitimate Lebanese Government remained elusive.

No PLO Surrender: Taking Beirut

Seeking to solidify its gains, on July 1st Israel laid siege to the PLO's only remaining stronghold—the city of Beirut. Employing a combination of force and incentives, Israel offered to prevent the bombing of Beirut in exchange for surrender by the PLO and Syrian forces in the city. In essence, Israel gave the militants an exit route. Surrender and the citizens of Beirut will be saved. Unfortunately, the PLO refused to surrender. The civilians of Beirut were doomed.

Heavy fighting commenced immediately in and around Beirut. Simultaneously, over the course of six weeks Israel never stopped its efforts in seeking a resolution through diplomatic paths with one clear and legitimate condition: the surrender of the PLO and their expulsion from Lebanon. Finally, realizing the futility of continuing the battle, Syria agreed to withdraw its remaining forces from Beirut on August 14. Less than one week later a badly battered Yasser Arafat, seeking not only to save face but perhaps his own life, gave in and agreed to evacuate his forces.

Our siege of the PLO and the Syrian forces in Beirut was an unpopular move, not only among the majority in Lebanon, but also around the world and even within our own Israeli society. There were heavy civilian casualties throughout the city of Beirut. Israel hoped that with the PLO gone, Lebanon's moderate factions could form a coalition government and finally end their agonizing years of Civil War. For Israelis it was the first time in history where a unified consensus was not totally behind our war effort.

98 | PLO expelled from Beirut

A quarter-century later, this Israeli narrative would parallel the goals and struggles of the United States during its wars in Iraq and Afghanistan fighting al-Qaeda and other radical insurgents. The big difference is that while the United States was fighting thousands of miles away from its own border, Israel was fighting within a few miles of its villages and citizens. To protect itself from PLO terrorism and Syrian-backed enemy forces, Israel's goal was to establish conditions in which the people of Lebanon could form a strong, democratic government free from the stranglehold of the PLO.

However, as Americans are learning, any occupying power is cast internationally as the "bad guys," no matter how noble their goal. The minute there are civilian casualties the world seems to induce amnesia and blame turns upside down from the terrorists to the occupying power.

The widespread criticism of Israel as the "villain with superior military power" had become an international image nightmare. Israelis were demonized as hostile occupiers of the Palestinians in the West Bank and Gaza. Israel's negative image exponentially increased when international media broadcast images of civilian casualties and bombed-to-rubble neighborhoods of Beirut.

Israelis were blamed for all Lebanese suffering. For the Israeli government, ridding Lebanon of the PLO was a necessary evil. Left to its own devices, even with the assistance of the UN, Lebanon today would be either governed by Syria or it would be Fatahland. By facing the unavoidable task of defeating and exiling the PLO and removing Syrian forces, Israelis believed they had given the moderate Lebanese a chance to end their civil war and move forward into a serious process of nation building. Most importantly for Israel, exiling the PLO from Lebanon secured safety for Israelis living along the border.

The United Nations did step up their involvement by enlisting a multi-national force, which arrived in Beirut on August 21. Comprised of American, French and Italian troops, Israelis rested easier thinking that "reliable" forces had been stationed nearby to keep the peace.

As the leaders of the PLO began their escorted exile to Tunisia, people worldwide watched as Yasser Arafat and his forces drove out of Beirut in jeeps waving Palestinian flags, cheering and displaying victory signs. Seemingly untarnished, the leader of the PLO smiled for international camera crews who filmed the PLO departure more like a victory parade rather than an exile.

By the end of August more than 14,000 PLO forces had left Beirut and relocated their head-quarters in Tunisia. An unfamiliar calm took hold throughout Lebanon for the first time in nine years. The sense of euphoria in Israel was almost palatable as the central components for peaceful resolution were rapidly falling into place. Unfortunately, they were about to fall apart.

Assassination of Lebanese President

Whereas the month of August 1982 had been one of success for Israel and the people of Lebanon, calm turned to despair with the assassination of newly elected Christian Lebanese President Bashir Gemayel. Prompting fears of a renewed bloodbath in Lebanon—or worse yet, a reassertion of PLO infiltration—the Israeli government decided to temporarily occupy West Beirut. To protect Lebanese civilians from renewed civil war, Israeli forces under the command of General Amos Yaron took responsibility for establishing and maintaining calm on September 15, 1982.

An investigation revealed that PLO militants responsible for the assassination of President Gemayel were hiding among refugees in two Palestinian refugee camps near Beirut. Intelligence indicated that rogue PLO operatives had avoided exile by hiding among civilians. These terrorists needed to be extracted from the camps.

Sabra and Shatila Refugee Camps Raided

On September 16, 1982, Israeli Major General Amir Drori met with Lebanese Phalangist leaders to work out the details of entering the Palestinian Sabra and Shatila refugee camps to rout out the remaining PLO operatives. It was determined that Israeli soldiers would control the perimeters of the refugee camps, avoiding the need to enter into the camps themselves. The Lebanese Phalangist forces were to enter the camps, drive out the PLO fighters and then hand them over to Israeli forces as prisoners of war.

What transpired during this mission and its aftermath is one of the most regrettable military episodes in Israeli history. The Phalangist forces that entered Sabra and Shatila refugee camps killed approximately 1,000 people over a 48-hour period.[32] Most of the casualities were civilians. What became apparent was that the Lebanese mission was most likely motivated by vengeance for the assassination of President Gemayel, who was a Christian Phalangist.

The aftermath was widely described as a massacre in Sabra and Shatila. Fingers pointed at Israel for these atrocities, when it was clearly the Lebanese Christian Phalangists who committed the terrible crimes.

The act of blood revenge is culturally prevalent in Lebanon and across the Arab world, often referred to as "honor killing." Honor is the highest value in Arab culture. When a family member—and in this case, also a political leader, President Gemayal—is assassinated, kinsmen are obligated to take revenge upon those responsible. This is what occurred in the Sabra and Shatila refugee camps.

Unfortunately, this type of revenge killing seemed interminable during the Lebanese Civil War. The best way for me to describe this mindset is to compare it to the mentality of urban gang warfare or Mafia killings in the United States. Law enforcement experts and security personnel, familiar with gang warfare will confirm that there is a never-ending vicious cycle of violence. What is so tragic for the Lebanese people caught in the middle of this type of continuous warfare is that these honor-motivated killings continue, even today.

When the Israeli public learned about the atrocities that occurred in Sabra and Shatila, a loud public cry of outrage erupted. More than 10 percent of the Israeli population gathered in Tel Aviv's city square to demand a judicial inquest as well as an end to the war in Lebanon. Indeed, Israeli President Yitzhak Navon echoed these sentiments by immediately calling for an investigation. In his own words:

99 | U.S. Marine barracks terrorist attack, 1983

> I believed that we had a responsibility to investigate what happened in Sabra and Shatila. If we are guilty, we need to take responsibility. If we are not guilty, let the world know that we are not.

In response to the outcry, on September 28, 1982, the Israeli government established the Kahan Commission to investigate the Sabra and Shatila massacre.

When the Commission's report was published in February 1983, its severity surprised even the most cynical of observers. Having gone to Beirut to interview over two hundred witnesses, taking statements from dozens of the others, the Commission found that while it was Phalangist forces which perpetrated the massacre, Israel as the power in charge of the camps at the time, bore indirect responsibility for not foreseeing the possible outcomes and for not preventing the tragedy. In a passage which has come to have a lasting impact on the ways in which civilized democracies and their commanders engage in modern urban warfare, the Commission explained:

> If it indeed becomes clear that those who decided on the entry of the Phalangists into the camps should have foreseen—from the information at their disposal and from things which were common knowledge—that there was danger of a massacre,

and no steps were taken which might have prevented this danger or at least greatly reduced the possibility that deeds of this type might be done, then those who made the decisions and those who implemented them are indirectly responsible for what ultimately occurred, even if they did not intend this to happen and merely disregarded the anticipated danger.[33]

With regard to Defense Minister Ariel Sharon, the commission found:

It is our view that responsibility is to be imputed to the Minister of Defense for having disregarded the danger of acts of vengeance and bloodshed by the Phalangists against the population of the refugee camps, and having failed to take this danger into account when he decided to have the Phalangists enter the camps. In addition, responsibility is to be imputed to the Minister of Defense for not ordering appropriate measures for preventing or reducing the danger of massacre as a condition for the Phalangists' entry into the camps. These blunders constitute the non-fulfillment of a duty with which the Defense Minister was charged.[34]

As a result of the Commission's finding, Defense Minister Ariel Sharon resigned his position immediately.

Israeli Withdrawal

In the aftermath of the Sabra and Shatila massacre and following worldwide condemnation of what had occurred, our IDF forces withdrew from western Beirut and the multinational force reentered the area. The United States began brokering a series of discussions to facilitate the withdrawal of all foreign armed forces from Lebanon, including troops from Syria, the PLO and Israel. In talks between Israel and the new Lebanese government, headed by Bashir's brother, Amin Gemayel, a peace agreement was reached. Without strong leadership who could control the warring factions? Progress was minimal at best. Israel believed that without its military presence, the vacuum of power would quickly be filled by terrorist infiltrators.

For Israel, the civil war not only continued in Lebanon, but the previously waring factions now aligned themselves together against Israeli presence in their country. And more concerning, the rising power filling in the vacuum left by the PLO exile became the Shi'ite Hezbollah forces. Like Americans who are growing weary of U.S. involvement in the Middle East, Israeli public support for staying in Lebanon waned and increasingly louder voices were heard expressing the desire to bring Israeli troops back home.

As the IDF troops gradually retreated southward, they suffered heavy losses from Hezbollah and several sectarian militias in Lebanon who had aligned themselves with Hezbollah in order to force the IDF completely out of Lebanon.

U.S. Marine Barracks Terrorist Attack

Major attacks against western interests transpired during this period of time. IDF head-quarters in Sidon was attacked killing 36 Israeli soldiers. Then, on October 23, 1983, 241 Americans and 58 Frenchmen were killed when terrorists attacked the United States Marine barracks outside of Beirut. These barracks housed the multinational forces sent into Lebanon to secure the peace. "It was the single deadliest day for U.S. Marines since the Battle of Iwo Jima."[35] Unwilling to endure further casualties, the multinational force quickly disbanded and withdrew in the spring of 1984.[36]

Only Israel stayed the course to halt the continuous atrocities engulfing the Lebanese people. Staying in Lebanon was neither easy, popular, nor safe. In the Chouf Mountains, our troops were forced to engage in continuous clashes between Christian and Druze Lebanese, the latter led by Walid Jumblatt. Israel's entanglement in Lebanon became known as "the Lebanese mud" as IDF losses increased and the fighting dragged on. The Lebanese government found itself unable to rein in the opposing forces and the region tragically descended into anarchy once again.

Israeli popular opinion indicated a growing desire to leave Lebanon. Israeli mothers wanted their sons and husbands out of harm's way and back to their homes and families. Politically, the continued War in Lebanon caused the resignation of Prime Minister Begin on August 23, 1983, bringing in a new government led by Prime Minister Yitzhak Shamir, of the Likud party, who stayed in power until general elections were held in the fall of 1984. The 1984 elections brought about a National Unity Government in which Shamir served as Vice-Premier and Minister of Foreign Affairs for two years. Shimon Peres of the Labor party served as Prime Minister until the two leaders rotated positions in 1986 and Shamir began his second term as Prime Minister.[37]

In January 1985, the Israeli government voted to gradually withdraw from Lebanon in stages and by the end of that year most Israeli troops had retreated to the international border. A limited number of soldiers remained behind, however, as part of the IDF's cooperation with Lebanese troops to try and maintain the buffer zone in the south.

Ehud Barak, who was elected Prime Minister in 1999, led his government to vote for a complete Israeli withdrawal from Lebanon, which indeed occurred in 2000.

Continuous Attacks On Israel From Lebanon

Though Israel had completely withdrawn its forces from Lebanon in 2000, Israel's northern towns and villages continued to suffer from rocket attacks by Hezbollah, the new fast-growing and religiously motivated terrorist organization. From 2000 until 2006, 4,000 rockets were fired upon Israeli citizens.

It is beyond the scope of this book to detail the Second Lebanon War, which was between the Lebanese Hezbollah terrorist organization and Israel and not directly related to the conflict between Israel and the Palestinians. However, it is still important to note that in the summer of 2006, following the kidnapping of Israeli IDF soldiers by Hezbollah, Israel launched the Second Lebanon War in order to safeguard its northern border just as it had done in 1982. The 2006 War ended with the placement of international forces along the border between Lebanon and Israel to prevent further attacks from Hezbollah into Israel.

Though it seemed that Hezbollah suffered a great defeat in the Second Lebanon War, it was only a short time before Hezbollah had rearmed and reestablished its military power in Lebanon. In a few months, as if history had repeated itself, Israel faced tens of thousands of rockets supplied to Hezbollah by Syria and Iran.

Hezbollah remains in Lebanon as a formidable foe. Beyond merely filling the militant role that the PLO once played, Hezbollah has gone on to monopolize the political and economic sectors of Lebanese society by forging a precarious alliance with Israel's two most dangerous enemies—Syria and Iran.

To date Hezbollah has risen to prominence within the Lebanese parliament. The terrorist organization controls Lebanon today with Iran's support. For example, it is only following the consent of Hezbollah that prime ministers and presidents are ushered into their posts.

The First Intifada

Israel's north was not its only military challenge. In 1987, Palestinians of the West Bank and Gaza took to the streets in protest. By the mid-1980s civilian-on-civilian violence within the Territories became the primary method of Palestinian actions. With tensions mounting, Israel sought to stem this latest tide of violence by implementing "Iron Fist." As a result of this policy, individuals were routinely stopped and asked to present their identity cards. Israel's military and security operations were stepped up in the Territories, and the government increased the arrest and expulsion of those inciting and/or perpetrating violence.

Simultaneously, the Israeli government increased economic initiatives to improve the lives of Palestinians in the Territories. Many Palestinian civilians did take advantage of the new economic and business opportunities and were able to earn a decent middle-class wage.[38] Unfortunately, the Palestinian leadership had come to reject the idea of economic integration on the basis that such an arrangement would, in their minds, be equivalent to conceding defeat to Israel.

By 1985, there was a lack of leadership within the Territories for the Palestinians. This vacuum contributed to the success of radical fringe elements who seized control of the Palestinian street inciting evermore venomous rhetoric and bloodshed against Israel and Jews.

The Reagan Initiative

The United States President Reagan Initiative of 1982 outlined a series of steps to be taken in order to implement UN Security Council Resolution 242.[39] Adopted by the Council in the wake of the Six Day War, UN Resolution 242 called for Israeli withdrawal from the occupied Territories in exchange for peace and recognition. In order to attain this goal Reagan proposed the following:

- A transitional period of five years be established during which time full autonomy would be extended to the Palestinians of the West Bank and Gaza. This period would begin after an election of a self-governing authority.

- A freeze on the construction of Israeli settlements during this transitional period.

- Determination of the final status of the West Bank and Gaza to be decided through multi-party negotiations with Jordan assigned to represent Palestinian interests.

- For peace to be established Israel would withdraw from the West Bank and Gaza, except from sections required to assure its security. The extent to which Israel should be asked to give up territory will be heavily affected by the extent of true peace, normalization and the security arrangements offered in return.

- Jerusalem was to remain undivided; its final status would be decided through negotiations.[40]

To an outsider, the Reagan Plan seemed innocuous. In fact, one would expect Palestinians to embrace such a proposal in that it set out a direct path to self-rule. Yet far from fostering harmony, the Reagan Plan caused deep divisions within the Palestinian factions.

The more moderates led by Yasser Arafat and his Fatah associates praised the plan for its implicit acceptance of Palestinian claims. Exhibiting both diplomatic and political flexibility the moderates signaled their willingness to accept the establishment of a Palestinian State alongside an Israeli State, but were careful not to ostracize supporters in the Territories who may have been skeptical of such a plan. As a result, the Fatah movement quietly engaged countries in the region to advance movement on the diplomatic front, while at the same time Fatah activists in the Territories heightened the level of anti-Israel rhetoric causing an increase in violent attacks perpetrated against Israeli targets.[41]

On the other side of the Palestinian political spectrum were the rejectionists. Comprised of elements within the Popular Front, Democratic Front, General Command Palestinian Popular Struggle and Sa'iqa, the rejectionists argued that the Reagan Plan did not guarantee Palestinian sovereignty, would require Palestinians to accept the Jewish State and thus abandon the dream of establishing an Arab State in all of historical Palestine. Finally, adding insult to injury, they argued that the plan placed the fate of the Palestinians in the hands of King Hussein of Jordan—an unpalatable thought to many of these militants who since Black September, still retained an intense animosity towards the King.

So strong was the sense that negotiations with Israel must be avoided that a faction of rejectionist members set out to remove Arafat from office.[42] This internecine conflict was not confined to the political echelon. Palestinians took up arms against Palestinians as the various factions jockeyed for power. Now exiled in Tunisia and consumed by their own internal rivalries, PLO leaders seemed oblivious to the deteriorating circumstances on the streets of the West Bank and Gaza. This disarray provided the perfect atmosphere for a new group to assert itself—one capable of going beyond the PLO's traditional roles.

100 | Hamas poster calling for an armed battle to liberate Palestine

Rise of Hamas

For Palestinians in the Territories, the PLO was perceived as a secular diaspora organization seeking to assert its authority on the Territories from the outside. On the other hand, Hamas residing in the Territories emerged as a popular grassroots movement. Hamas was an outgrowth of the Muslim Brotherhood which had been present in Gaza and Egypt since 1928, propagating its religious ideology.

Hamas leaders lived among Palestinians, maintained daily contact with them, and shared in their hardships. Being "native Palestinians" born and raised in the Territories gave them a certain advantage over the PLO, which was widely viewed as corrupt. Even more significant was the fact that, while the PLO was outside of Israel, Hamas quickly coalesced its popularity within the Territories through a combination of religious appeals, organizational efforts (particularly on university campuses), and most importantly, the provision of much needed social services.[43]

In the early 1980s, Israel not only tolerated Hamas and its leadership, but at times actively fostered its growth as well as other Islamic movements in the occupied Territories. Israel believed that these religious organizations could serve as a counterweight opposition to the PLO's popularity. Accordingly, many in the Israeli political establishment and, more

This rumor sparked violence throughout the Gaza Strip and West Bank as demonstrators burned tires, threw stones and hurled Molotov cocktails at Israeli soldiers and civilians. PLO operatives escalated this spontaneous uprising by spreading rumors of vengeful Israeli attacks and organized campaigns of violent activities in cities throughout the Territories. Random acts of violence and rioting gave way to organized demonstrations by Hamas and Islamic Jihad.

Similar to its experiences in Lebanon, the IDF was forced to use military force to combat civilian violence, often perpetrated by youth in the streets.

When one recounts the First Intifada, one generally thinks of young boys throwing stones at Israeli soldiers. But this image is not entirely accurate. To begin with, remember the Israeli forces were mostly teenage Israeli soldiers themselves, not trained for guerrilla warfare. Secondly, far more than rocks were being thrown. Between 1987 and 1991, Israelis documented having been attacked by 3,600 Molotov cocktails, 100 hand grenades and at least 600 attacks causing the deaths of 16 Israeli citizens and 11 Israeli soldiers. Another 1,400 Israeli citizens and 1,700 IDF soldiers were wounded.[45]

Additional violence occurred between Palestinians. There were numerous documented accounts of Palestinians who were stabbed, hacked with axes, and shot by other Palestinians. *The New York Times* (October 24, 1989) described the discovery of "a cache of detailed secret documents showing that the PLO hired local killers to assassinate other Palestinians and carry out "military activity" against Israelis." One document described how the PLO wanted the attacks credited to fictional groups so as not to disturb the US-PLO dialogue."[46]

Yasser Arafat endorsed the killing of Palestinians when they were considered to be "collaborating with Israel."[47] Indeed, he ordered executions of fellow Palestinians. After numerous murders, the local PLO commissioned an investigation of those who had been killed. The results were delivered to the PLO headquarters. "We have studied the files of those who were executed, and found that only two of the 118 who were executed were innocent," Arafat said. The innocent victims were declared "martyrs of the Palestinian revolution" by the PLO.[48]

All together more than 1,000 Palestinians were murdered at the hands of fellow Palestinians for collaborating with Israel. This reign of terror affected Palestinians who worked for the Civil Administration in the West Bank and the Gaza Strip. Any contact with Jews could warrant a PLO death sentence. More Palestinians were killed by fellow Palestinians during the First Intifada than were killed by IDF forces.

Everyday life for Palestinians was in turmoil. Palestinian streets and marketplaces became common battlefields. Getting to and from jobs was dangerous. Education schedules were often interrupted by many organized Palestinian demonstrations during the Intifada.

It was during these years that many Palestinians who could leave the Territories, did so to avoid the turmoil and violence. Palestinian emigration peaked during the Intifada.

By 1992 the Intifada was waning. Many of the young leaders were arrested and jailed by the IDF. Ironically, many of the Intifada's young leaders like Marwan Barghouti later became officials in the Palestinian Authority where they continued their violent opposition to Israel.

Between 1987 and 1992 Israel was engaged in protecting its citizens against the violence of the First Intifada. Certainly Israel had the military capability to curb the uprising by using its full military might. However, Israel was not facing another country's army. Instead it was facing men, women and children whose inflamed actions caused demonstrations in the streets that inevitably turned violent. It was practically impossible for Israeli soldiers to distinguish between terrorist foes and innocent civilians who were merely exercising their rights of free speech. In fact, most of the violence was among Palestinian factions. Whenever defensive moves were made by Israeli soldiers, their actions were condemned as hostile Israeli acts of violence against innocent Palestinians.

The images emerging from the Territories told a damning story against Israeli forces. Instead of media coverage holding the terrorists responsible for perpetrating violence against the Jews, the Israelis were depicted as the powerful aggressor tormenting the poor Palestinian people. It was the David and Goliath story turned upside down.

The negative impact of worldwide media coverage which assigned the blame for the violence in the streets on the "Israeli occupation" was Israel's greatest challenge. Israel's deteriorating international image became a PR problem that continues today.

Arafat Changes Course

In the midst of the Intifada turmoil, the PLO Chairman shocked everyone. On December 13, 1988, Arafat stood before the United Nations assembled in Geneva, and surprised the world. Having been the champion of armed struggle, he suddenly and unexpectedly denounced the use of terrorism, and accepted the existence of Israel.

While Israel reacted with hope and optimism, it understandably questioned Arafat's sincerity. Recalling the infamous "peace in our time" remarks by Chamberlain after returning from signing a non-aggression pact with Hitler, Israelis proceeded with the hope that Arafat's intentions were honorable and sincere.

But Arafat had ulterior motives. Seeking to topple Hamas and regain his status as the principal representative of the Palestinian people, Arafat capitalized on the growing unrest within the Territories, utilizing the Intifada to elevate his own popularity and take back the leadership role of the Palestinian people. By adopting the 1988 Algiers Declaration importantly in its security apparatus, sought to prop up these groups (particularly Hamas) in the hope that they would fulfill three vital objectives:

- They would fill the local political void in the Territories (which had come about as a result of the PLO's exile to Tunisia);

- They would continue and expand the provision of essential social services for Palestinians, including hospitals, education, and welfare;

- As religious organizations the movement's adherents would be less likely to engage in violence.[44]

For Israel, these assessments were wrong and unforeseeable consequences arose.

Indeed, Hamas did rise to fill many of the political roles formerly carried out by PLO representatives. In Gaza and most of the West Bank Territories, it did expand social service outreach and it did use religious appeal to attract evermore supporters. Yet rather than preaching a peaceful form of Islam as Israeli strategists had hoped, Hamas leaders quickly learned that they could gain a political advantage over the PLO by questioning its authority as well as its secularist vision.

Moreover, by inciting and carrying out acts of violence, Hamas leaders who were native to the Territories, were able to present themselves as the true vanguard of the Palestinian cause. Much to the dismay of Israel and to the PLO, Hamas and other Islamic groups categorically rejected Israel's right to exist; calling instead for the establishment of an Islamic State in all of Palestine. At the outbreak of the 1987 First Intifada a visible struggle for power was evident between the more "pragmatic" PLO and the "rejectionist" Islamic and revolutionary factions.

For years, prior to the 1987 First Intifada, frustration in the Territories had been mounting as the Palestinian leadership was unable to provide tangible economic and/or political progress. Much of this frustration was exacted upon innocent Israelis. But whereas the political parties could claim such attacks as victories, they did little to improve the livelihood of the average Palestinian—in fact quite the opposite. The Arab Summit of November 1987 convened in Amman making absolutely no mention of Palestinian suffering. This omission became the tipping point. Many Palestinians felt as if they had been completely abandoned. Not only had their own leaders been proven unreliable, but it seemed as if no one in the entire Arab world was championing Palestinian statehood.

The years of simmering and growing discontent with the status quo exploded in December 1987. An Israeli businessman was stabbed to death on the streets of Gaza. On the same afternoon an Israeli truck driver lost control of his vehicle near the Erez Crossing between Israel and Gaza. The accident resulted in the death of four Palestinian laborers and rumors quickly spread that the event was, in fact, an "act of Israeli revenge."

which called for a two-state solution to the conflict with Israel, Arafat's political power play represented a 180 degree turnaround.

Addressing the UN General Assembly in Geneva he stated:

> We want peace... We are committed to peace, and we want to live in our Palestinian state and let others live...The PLO will seek a comprehensive settlement among the parties concerned in the Arab-Israeli conflict, including the State of Palestine, Israel, and other neighbors, within the framework of the [proposed] international conference for peace in the Middle East on the basis of resolutions 242 and 338 and so as to guarantee equality and the balance of interests, especially our people's rights, in freedom, national independence, and respect the right to exist in peace and security for all...[49]

Responding to Arafat's UN declaration, Secretary of State George Shultz quickly announced U.S. support for the creation of a Palestinian State and arranged for immediate diplomatic meetings between the Israelis and Palestinians in Tunisia. These talks ultimately led to the 1991 Madrid Conference.

As he had calculated, Yasser Arafat would rise to the position of chief negotiator for the Palestinian people.

The decision to pursue peace through negotiations with Arafat and the PLO carried great risk for Israelis. It meant placing our security in the hands of a group which had previously demonstrated its ultimate intention to eradicate the Jewish state.

For Arafat, it was his path back to power.

In 1992, the Labor Party won the election and Prime Minister Rabin formed a governing coalition. In 1993, he signed the Oslo Peace Agreement with the PLO.

On July 1, 1994, Arafat and his cadres stepped off a plane in the Gaza Strip.

Israel's troubles were about to increase.

The PLO Relocates to Lebanon

The PLO needed a home to serve as the base of its operations when it left Israel. In Jordan, the Palestinian population already exceeded 60 percent of the country, and so it seemed logical to build a base of operations there. But Jordan—due to King Hussein's interests in preventing a sovereign Palestinian state—was the last of the Arab nations to recognize the PLO as the sole representative of the Palestinian people. His reluctant support of the PLO stemmed from fear. For the Jordanian king, the PLO's organizational strength and large demographic might posed a significant threat to his rule and the stability of the kingdom. More than anything, Hussein felt personally threatened by Yasser Arafat's popularity and power. He feared that Arafat might overthrow him.

Israeli raids on the PLO refugee camps within the sovereign jurisdiction of the Hashemite Kingdom caused additional instability.

Again faced with a historic opportunity to be the champion of the Palestinian cause, King Hussein, like his grandfather Abdullah, chose the opposite course of action. Hussein was unwilling to be dragged into another war with Israel on behalf of the Palestinian people. Moreover, Hussein recognized the internal fragility of his own rule in Jordan.

King Hussein launched Black September in 1970, a sweeping campaign against the PLO that resulted in the deaths of some 20,000 Palestinians and the expulsion of a portion of the Palestinian community from Jordan.

Libyan leader Muammar al-Qaddafi opposed Hussein's cold-blooded massacre of the Palestinians, saying: "We are faced with a madman like Hussein who wants to kill his own people. We must send someone to seize him, handcuff him, stop him from doing what he's doing, and take him off to an asylum."[1]

> *Eventually, the PLO was defeated in Jordan and moved to Lebanon where I had lived since my family escaped Palestine in 1948. I was not as enthusiastic as others were about the PLO arriving in Lebanon. I was skeptical about the possible results because I felt that the PLO would eventually become mired in the swamps of Lebanese politics and might forget its main objective of taking back the Palestinian homeland by fighting the Israeli enemy.*

Some 235,000 Palestinian refugees greeted the PLO in its new Lebanese home. Arafat set up his headquarters in Beirut, but the real presence of the feday (literally translated as "one who sacrifices himself") rested near the border with Israel, where much of the Palestinian population lived without the political and civic rights of their brethren in Jordan, or even Syria and Egypt.[2] Despite the prevailing political and ethnic struggles already plaguing Lebanon, the PLO created a "virtual Palestinian 'para-state' in Lebanon."[3]

This PLO-led state-within-a-state successfully initiated and delivered humanitarian services to the Lebanese people. They created an extensive system of hospitals and clinics for healthcare, and delivered public water sanitation and electricity to serve Palestinians and native Lebanese alike.[4] Palestinian political organizations flourished under the PLO, bringing together all sectors of Palestinian society. While the Lebanese Civil War flared between 1975 and 1976, the PLO remained stable due to its self-reliance and ability to withstand military incursions from the weak Lebanese army.

Indeed, a strong sense of organized and resurgent Palestinian nationalism flourished in Lebanon.

Palestinian History in Lebanon

In the not-so-distant past, Lebanon and Palestine were not separate entities. During the Turkish Ottoman administration, there were "no borders or checkpoints, no sovereign states with their 'security dilemmas,' no chauvinistic nationalisms."[5] With a single administration governing the region, it was not uncommon that people in the Galilee were drawn to the charms of Beirut, or that an individual could be born from a marriage between a woman from Jerusalem and a man from Tripoli.

There is a long, documented history of integration and communalism between Palestinians and Lebanese prior to the arrival of the British and the French, and most especially before the insertion of Israel in the close-knit neighborhood of the Middle East. Sharing social, cultural and ethnic similarities, the Palestinians and the Lebanese also have shared in their extreme suffering through the wars and military infractions by the Zionist state.

But when Israel was established, this communalism dissipated. In 1948, some 104,000 Palestinian refugees fled from northern Palestine into Lebanon.[6] Unlike other Arab countries, Lebanon was divided among several ethnic communities. The Christian leaders of Lebanon strongly sympathized with the Israeli Zionists, and viewed the Palestinians as a "fifth column" with the potential to upend their country's fragile sectarian political landscape.

When they arrived, these Palestinian refugees (including my family) made the unfortunate discovery that the historically warm welcome from Lebanese brethren no longer existed. Although they were among fellow Arabs, the Palestinians were dis-

101 | Arafat posters on display in al-Bass Refugee Camp in Tyre, Lebanon

criminated against at every level of society. Their conditions in refugee camps were the worst in the diaspora, the attitudes between Palestinians and the Lebanese were hostile and mutually reinforcing.

Life in Lebanon for Palestinians was bleak, and conditions were made harsher by authoritarian measures set in place to control their movement and activities."[7]

Nevertheless, Lebanon became the location for the PLO to regroup, rebuild its forces and, ultimately, redouble its strength. From this base, it managed to survive several confrontations with the Lebanese military, Christian Lebanese militias and even the Syrian army.[8]

> Arafat was now a head of state in all but name, more powerful than many Arab rulers. His was no longer a humble revolutionary movement, but rather a vigorous para-state.[9]

Palestinian strength in Lebanon came from lessons learned from the events of Black September in 1970. For example, they realized the need for the resistance movement to be more firmly rooted among the people. The PLO sought to establish stronger allies among the local Shi'ite Muslims in southern Lebanon, despite the strong animosity and organized violence from the Christian Maronites. The effort was not entirely succesful. Even the marginally stronger relationship with the Shi'ites was tenuous at best and support from the Lebanese Sunni's was solid but only marginal, and therefore easily exploitable.

The outbreak of the 1975 Lebanese Civil War furthered these intercommunal tensions, by using the Palestinians as the scapegoat. And, when Israel launched its first invasions into southern Lebanon in 1978, "it was able to leave behind a pro-Israeli, anti-Palestinian militia and population in place."[10]

1982 Israeli Invasion

With its full-scale invasion of southern Lebanon in 1982, Israel convinced some that it was a welcomed liberator of the native Lebanese from the abusive Palestinians, who had evidently overstayed their welcome.

On June 6, 1982, the Israeli army invaded Lebanon in retaliation for the attempted assassination of Israeli Ambassador Shlomo Argov in London two days earlier by a PLO breakaway group known as Abu Nidal Organization (ANO). ANO was a dissident Palestinian organization backed by the government of Iraq, and known as a militant Palestinian faction that had bitterly split with Fatah and the PLO years earlier. The organization was led by Sabri Khalil al-Banna (aka, Abu Nidal—or Father of Struggle), who's political extremism and proclivity for violence made him an enemy of the PLO and unpopular among the more moderate Palestinians.

By 1982, it was well known that the PLO in Lebanon had nothing to do with Abu Nidal or his organization. However, following the ANO attack on Ambassador Argov in London, Ariel Sharon, then Israel's Defense Minister, used the incident as a pretext to invade Lebanon. Sharon called the Argov attack "the spark that lit the fuse." Yet it was clear among the Lebanese and Palestinians alike that the Israelis used this as an excuse to conduct a well-planned military incursion. Sadly, this was precisely the response that Abu Nidal had intended to provoke, and the Palestinian people viewed him as a murderous traitor to his people and their cause.

The 1982 invasion into Lebanon known as Operation Peace for the Galilee resulted in 18,000 deaths and 30,000 injuries, mostly to non-combatants. Initially, Israel stated that it planned to penetrate only 40 kilometers into Lebanese territory and Israeli troops destroyed all Palestinian and Lebanese resistance near the border. However, Sharon's attack became far more ambitious and cruel, akin to General Sherman's "March to the Sea" in the U.S. Civil War. Israeli troops persisted forward and committed a series of atrocious human rights violations against the unarmed civilian population. The destruction proceeded as far as Beirut.

By June 18, 1982, the Israelis had surrounded PLO forces in west Beirut. After two months of fighting, U.S envoy Philip Habib negotiated a cease-fire. The Habib Accords outlined the future of west Beirut to be under the control of the Lebanese Army. Meanwhile, the Americans pledged that civilian Palestinians living in the Lebanese refugee camps would be protected following the PLO's departure.

The PLO left Lebanon on September 1. On September 10, the multinational forces that oversaw this withdrawal left Beirut as well. It was a mistake for which the remaining Palestinian civilian population would pay a heavy price. Less than 24 hours later, Sharon declared that 2,000 terrorists remained in the Palestinian refugee camps.

Sabra and Shatila Massacre historians and journalists agree that it was during a meeting between the Israeli and Phalangist leaders in Bikfaya on September 12th that an agreement was made authorizing the Lebanese Phalangist forces to "mop up" the remaining Palestinian civilians who remained living in the refugee camps around Beirut.

On September 14, Lebanese President Bashir Gemayel was assassinated, presumably by Syrian agents. The following day, Israeli forces re-occupied Beirut by encircling and sealing off the two large refugee camps there: Sabra and Shatila.

It is no secret that Sharon had met with President Gemayel months earlier, telling him that Israeli forces were planning an invasion to force the PLO out of Lebanon. This was the beginning of an insipid plan derived by Sharon in which Israel would effectively conquer Lebanon, liquidate the PLO and put a "friendly" Christian regime in power as its neighbor to the north.[11] In doing so, this would effectively scatter even more Palestinians to the wind.

102 | Sabra and Shatila Massacre, 1982

In the early morning hours of September 15, Israeli fighter-bombers streaked low over west Beirut. Israeli troops already were on the ground. By 9 a.m., Sharon was personally directing the Israeli half of the two-prong mission with the Phalangists. The IDF surrounded the refugee camps with Israeli tanks and soldiers while Phalangist troops entered the camps.

During the late afternoon and evening, the Israeli forces began to shell the camps with heavy artillery. Meanwhile, Sharon and his entourage were positioned at the Kuwaiti Embassy junction situated at the edge of the Shatila Refugee Camp. From the roof of this tall building with its panoramic view, it was possible for Sharon to clearly observe the destruction of the Sabra and Shatila camps.

Under the guise of rooting out so-called "terrorists" Phalangist forces slaughtered as many as 1,500 Palestinian civilians.[12] Israeli troops guarded the exits of the camps and Israeli snipers fired upon civilians in the streets. Systematic roundups, reinforced by the Israeli army, resulted in dozens of disappearances.[13]

> I lived not far from Sabra and Shatila—maybe one mile. It was about 9 o'clock at night. I went out on my balcony. My neighbors asked, "Do you see the lights?" The sky was lighting up. It looked like fireworks. The next morning, we woke up and heard people screaming in the street. We went down and saw women in their nightgowns and old men in their pajamas. The women were not even covering their faces. They were all screaming "The Jews… they attacked us!"

Nearly 3,000 Palestinians may have been murdered in the Sabra and Shatila massacres.

The news began broadcasting images of the civilians slaughtered—women and children. I could see faces of the Israeli soldiers. They were shocked at what happened. That's when I thought, "This is it. I'm not going to live in this country anymore." Luckily, I got out of the madness. Within two or three days, the American Embassy gave me a tourist visa to the United States."

Sabra and Shatila Massacre

Although the U.N. Security Council condemned the massacres and even determined them to be acts of genocide, the victims and survivors have never received restitution for the crimes committed against them. As Israeli journalists Schiff and Ya'ari concluded in their sobering reflection of these events: "If there is a moral to the painful episode of Sabra and Shatila, it has yet to be acknowledged."[14]

Twenty years later, the bitter memory of this impunity rests in the hearts of all Palestinians. Both for the victims—who already were refugees from Israeli aggression in 1948—and for Palestinian refugees elsewhere, the events serve as yet another reminder of the "despoliation and direct domination imposed on Palestinians by Israel."[15] The tragedy has become synonymous with the Israeli refusal to acknowledge Palestinian identity and the right to self-determination.

Impact of Palestinian Dispossession and the 1982 War

The 1982 Israeli invasion of southern Lebanon resulted in its occupation of half of the country and the effective termination of the PLO's para-state in Lebanon.[16] The departure of Arafat and the official PLO forces left over 350,000 civilian Palestinians in Lebanon besieged by Shi'ite Amal militia (supported by Syria) in the infamous "War of the

Camps."[17] Although many Palestinians were once again displaced, the effect of these events strengthened and restored unity among the long-divided Palestinian factions. Moreover, the massive human toll reinvigorated Palestinians to demand restitution for their besieged homeland.

The dire circumstances of Palestinian refugee life and permanent statelessness among Palestinians generated hostility and demands for freedom. In particular, the subjects of Israel with no national citizenship—the Palestinians of the West Bank and Gaza Strip—lacked political representation. Their economic development was limited and social conditions deteriorated. The Palestinian national consciousness began to dwindle as well. The PLO was the only representative of the Palestinian people, yet for 20 years failed to achieve national liberation. Now it was exiled to Tunisia after being forced from Lebanon. The people of Palestine were isolated and desperate for recognition.

It was really the sense of disillusion and unrest during the 1982 Israeli invasion of Lebanon, which made me search for another place to live far away from the insanity of the conflict. So I made my choice to move to the United States. It was my second diaspora, but this time it was my choice!

Being in the United States has offered me an opportunity to examine the conflict from a different perspective. In Lebanon, the conflict was part of my daily life. My thinking was heavily clouded by my daily experiences and emotions.

Living away from the conflict in the United States, I am now capable of seeing the conflict differently. I do, however, continue to seek justice and the right of self-determination for the Palestinian people, just like I did while in Lebanon, as that passion for statehood remains in my soul and in my heart.

The difference for me now is that I have the privilege of "distance" from the hostilities. I have the time and the space needed to intellectually dissect the complexities of the seemingly insurmountable conflict. Writing this book with my friend and co-author, Shaul Gabbay, is a part of my on-going determination to assist both peoples in finding the path to peace. Could I have written this book if I was still living in the midst of the conflict? It's a good question. Probably not.

The Intifada

Out of this dense milieu of conditions, the spontaneous eruption of massive civil resistance in 1987 was a desperate cry from the Palestinian people of their earnest desire for freedom and independence.

Defined by historian Rashid Khalidi, the Intifada was the "grassroots popular uprising, which occurred in the occupied Palestinian Territories in December 1987."[18] The term "intifada" is most commonly translated into English as "uprising," but this definition ignores a whole host of deeper meanings.

In Arabic, intifada literally means "shaking off," as in shaking off the Israeli occupation. However, in terms of Palestinian consciousness the word has come to mean the shaking off of one's own passivity and leaping to one's feet in defense of Palestinian rights.[19]

Several prevailing factors steered the way to the Intifada. The effects of the 1982 Israeli War against the PLO in southern Lebanon effectively forced the PLO to Tunisia, where it remained a leadership in exile. The trauma of the massacres in the Sabra and Shatila refugee camps stirred both anger and resolve for statehood among Palestinians in exile. Yet, these tragic events also led the Palestinians towards a normalization of affairs between the Palestinians, the greater Arab world, and Israel.

During the years of Israeli occupation, the Palestinians who remained in the Occupied Territories were discouraged when the PLO left Israel. To prevent a mass exodus by those living under the harshness of military occupation, provisions from outside supporters came into the Territories. One means of support was the creation of a project by the Arab states called the Steadfastness Fund (Sunduq al-Sumud).[20] This fund, established at the Baghdad Arab Summit in 1978 delivered close to $90 million per year for nearly five years to the Palestinians.

Meanwhile, everyone living within the Occupied Palestinian Territories faced the disturbing reality of being second-class citizens. They blatantly had fewer rights than the Jews or—at best—a separate set of rights. The Palestinian people found that occupation had turned into hardened military rule.

By 1985, the term "Iron Fist" entered the Israeli lexicon, in reference to the approach taken to the occupation by then Prime Minister Yitzhak Rabin.

Exacerbating the effects of living under military occupation, the expansion of Israeli settlements into the Palestinian Territories was gradually erasing Arab Palestine. Contrary to UN Resolutions 181, 242, and 338, which set forth the idea of an Arab and Jewish State and the notion of "land for peace" (i.e.: Israeli exchange of territory for Arab peace), the Jewish population of Israel initiated the slow takeover of land it failed to conquer prior to and during the war of 1948. During this time, the ominous notion of "transferring" the Arabs became a part of the social and political ideology of Israel. Whether through economic incentives or forced deportation, the Israeli intent to marginalize the Palestinian population as much as possible was under way.

Military occupation of East Jerusalem, the West Bank and the Gaza Strip brought several benefits to Israel, while strengthening the sense of euphoria among some Israelis in the aftermath of 1967. For one, the rich water resources of the Territories were diverted to Israel or to its settlers, who, despite controlling some 0.4 percent of the land in the Territories, consumed approximately 28 percent of the water.[21] Secondly, an onerous system of permits dictated how Palestinians could travel, set up businesses, and import materials. These permits controlled what Palestinians could and could not produce and each included a service fee. Palestinians needed to carry a permit to conduct even the most routine activities. Israel also prevented Palestinian products from competing with Israeli products in the world market, while preventing imports from outperforming Israeli products in the Territories.

Moreover, Israel's construction and agricultural industries gained sizable profits from the use of cheap Palestinian labor. Palestinians had effectively become a supply of cheap labor and had little choice but to work for the occupier by building Jewish settlements, aiding the Israeli military and even working for police officials. For Palestinians, all of this was alienating and offensive.

For the Palestinians, Israeli occupation translated into paying taxes in exchange for living under the occupier. As Palestinian resentment grew in the Territories, a common bond developed among the Palestinians. Songs were composed to express a growing sense of community among all Palestinians, including those who remained inside Israel, the Territories and scattered beyond. A literature of Palestinian resistance appeared and quickly expanded as East Jerusalem became the center of the Palestinian press—"a major tool in creating national consciousness"—with newspapers distributed semi-illegally in the West Bank and Gaza, Israel, and abroad."[22] Of course, the Israeli authorities attempted to quell political organizing by outlawing meetings, discussions and all Palestinian political activities. The display of the Palestinian flag was even forbidden under the military occupation. However, none of these crackdowns could stop the generation of Palestinians born under occupation from becoming advocates for its end.

Amid this backdrop of Palestinian anguish and dissatisfaction, the massive civic demonstration of the Intifada was initially sparked by a terrible, yet fateful, traffic accident. On December 9, 1987, an Israeli truck driver struck and killed four Palestinian residents of the Jabaliya Refugee Camp in Gaza. Rumors circulated that the incident was not an accident, and that the truck driver was avenging the death of his brother who had been stabbed to death two days earlier in the Gaza market. By that afternoon, denunciatory leaflets about the incident circulated in the streets. By the time of the funeral that evening, thousands of mourners pummeled the nearby Israeli army post with stones.

The following morning, the Intifada (later known as the First Intifada) was inaugurated with full-scale violence that broke out between the Jabaliya Camp residents and the IDF when the residents of the camp awoke to find their streets and alleys blockaded with quickly-constructed military barricades. The protests began in the Gaza Strip and quickly spread throughout the Palestinian Territories.

The rumor inflamed Palestinian passions and set off disturbances in the Jabaliya camp and in the rest of the Gaza Strip. From Gaza the disturbances spread to the West Bank. Within days the Occupied Territories were engulfed in a wave of spontaneous, uncoordinated, and popular street demonstrations and commercial strikes on an unprecedented scale. Equally unprecedented was the extent of mass participation in these disturbances: tens of thousands of ordinary civilians, including women and children.[23]

Israeli politicians and military commanders initially dismissed the uprising as the latest in a series of small conflicts that Israel had continually fought with its Arab neighbors for 40 years. However, the Intifada actually was a unique, homegrown movement born of the history of Palestinian oppression in Gaza, the West Bank, and East Jerusalem.

103 | Unarmed young fighter versus Israeli occuption

Compared to the failures of the 1936-39 Arab Revolt, the meaning and expression of the Intifada was collective and widely shared, as opposed to being focused only among those with particular grievances. As Rashid Khalidi explains, "the spontaneous outbreak of the Intifada gave a much needed boost to a Palestinian national movement that was clearly flagging, and most importantly it reestablished 'the inside,' of Palestine itself, as the center of gravity of Palestinian politics, rather than 'the outside,' the Palestinian Diaspora, where it had been located for so many decades."[24]

From this uprising, a new form of Palestinian emerged—a young fighter who was unarmed and determined to confront the Israeli occupation and its soldiers head-on.

Although spontaneous acts of violent defiance occurred, what is most significant about the Intifada was that it was predominantly a non-violent uprising. It consisted of social solidarity, group organization, national loyalty, and determination among every sector of the Palestinian people, including women and children. There was no prevailing Palestinian desire to conquer the territory of Israel, or to push the Jews into the sea. It expressed more of a desire for statehood, equality and human rights. The unarmed Palestinians courageously stood up against the region's strongest military in protest against the oppression of the Israeli occupation. The fighters of the Intifada were not trained guerrillas, but group organizers and willing participants in acts of nonviolent civil disobedience.

During the Intifada, Palestinian scholar and sociologist Salim Tamari, wrote:

> The side that has always been known about Palestinian resistance is the military side, but during the Intifada, another form of resistance emerged with the formation of popular committees, strikes, and civil disobedience. This is significant... it gave the Palestinian individual faith in his ability to stand against one of the most important military authorities in the world. The Palestinian individual stood against this force with his body unarmed.[25]

Non-violent Efforts

Within two months, community organizers from within the Territories began drafting leaflets and setting goals in an attempt to channel the Palestinians' anger into a productive outlet for the struggle. Among these organizers were Arab intellectuals from East Jerusalem, who became major actors in drafting non-violent strategies of resistance.

One such intellectual was Sari Nusseibeh, a Harvard graduate of philosophy. Nusseibeh sought to communicate to Israelis that the occupation in its current form would only serve to deepen the hatred between Israelis and Palestinians. He called on the international community to recognize the right of the Palestinians to self-determination, and to convene a conference that would oversee the establishment of a Palestinian state ruled by Palestinians, peacefully co-existing with Israel. Knowing that such demands would never be noticed in the world unless accompanied by heavy media coverage, he drafted a document called the "Jerusalem Document," which spelled out how Palestinians must stand up and communicate to the world that they do not accept occupation:

> The relationship of the Palestinian people to the occupation consists of a vast network. The majority of this network includes procedures, transactions, and regulations requiring tacit consent from the Palestinian side, whereas the remaining part of it forms

104 | Civil protest, Ramallah, 1988

an Israeli, one-sided coercive relationship…[E]nding the occupation necessitates [our] national will to break off all the relationship's ties to the occupation system, whose existence depends on our tacit consent, so that nothing remains of the occupation except the part only relying on coercion and violence by the other side.

Despite aggressive and coercive measures taken by the Israelis, Palestinians maintained their commitment to nonviolence. Mayor of the town, al-Bireh, Abd al-Jawad Saleh (who was deported for ten years), recalled his efforts during the Intifada:

We formulated…a new form of struggle: voluntary work and a movement of nonviolent struggle against military occupation. The Israelis considered this very dangerous.[26] In revolt against the Israeli occupation, the Palestinians armed themselves against the most highly technical army in the region with nothing but stones and strength of mind; and in comparison to the great number of Palestinian fatalities, there were no Israeli fatalities from the several million stones that must have been tossed.[27]

The Jerusalem Post and Reuters confirmed, "In two months of unrest, Palestinian protesters have not fired a single bullet or used explosives other than petrol bombs."[28] During this time period, the IDF found numerous caches of AK-47s, explosives and hand grenades that remained unused. Palestinians realized that they would face large human losses if they used tactical weapons. Nevertheless, the element of fear that had kept the Palestinians quiet for twenty years disappeared during the 1987 uprising, as children became willing to defy the Israeli army by throwing stones."

Israeli Response to the Intifada

The initial Israeli response to the Intifada was one of fear, then brutality and violence. Almost immediately, the Israeli military reserves were called up for duty, and Israeli military presence in the Occupied Territories significantly increased. In an attempt to suppress the Palestinian uprising, local schools, colleges, and other centers of cultural and social activism were shut down. As this happened, however, the Palestinian people were ever more mobilized with revolutionary fervor. For example, they found creative ways to circumvent the school closures by setting up their own clandestine classrooms for their children. Economically, they became increasingly self sufficient. Despite Israeli measures to thwart the uprising, nearly every member of the Palestinian population continued to participate. Urban and rural populations alike came together in protest of the occupation and to stand up for their cause.[29]

As the initial weeks of the Intifada turned into months, thousands of Israeli soldiers were deployed to serve as military police in the Occupied Territories. It is important to note that Palestinians in the Territories were not Israeli citizens. Israeli military law certainly reflected that fact. Felicia Langer, an Israeli lawyer who defended Palestinians in Israeli courts, spoke of countless confessions that were extracted or manufactured out of bruised and broken Palestinian prisoners in Israeli-run prison camps.

She described the situation in terms of the popular novel, Dr. Jekyll and Mr. Hyde. Israeli soldiers were normal citizens in a democratic state, but once in uniform inside the Occupied Territories, they would transform into remorseless aggressors.[30] Israeli government officials spoke of defeating the threat with "force, power, [and] blows."[31] Yitzhak Rabin, acting Minister of Defense during the Intifada, authorized soldiers to "break [the] bones" of Palestinian troublemakers as an underlying facet of his plan to crush Palestinian nationalism with an "iron fist."[32] Rabin would later deny having said any such thing, but Ha'aretz revealed that 197 Palestinians had been treated for fractured limbs within three days of Rabin's orders.

In further attempts to suppress the Intifada, and to further fragment Palestinian society, the Israeli occupation authority gave Military Orders 854 and 947 to control what material could be used for Palestinian educational curricula and set up a "civil administration" to address the "civil affairs of the inhabitants." This civil administration was an attempt to supplant the local leadership with a network of armed, handpicked representatives who would cooperate with Israel.[33] Military order 854 soon pushed further, imposing curfews on the Occupied Territories and closing the schools outright. These measures naturally triggered a massive Palestinian response outlined in Leaflet Number 24, which stated:

> All teachers, high school pupils and students, and especially elementary school pupils, to mobilize for the success of the popular education operation…in order to foil the

authorities' policy of closing the schools and inculcating ignorance in our children. Popular education is a national responsibility.[34]

A collective effort was undertaken to continue the basic education of Palestinian children in secret, without any Israeli interference or restrictions on what could and could not be taught. Teachers and intellectuals began their own community work, as they were restricted from entering their academic environments. With this, boys and girls of all ages were co-educated in private homes.

Effectiveness of the Intifada

As the doors of the universities clanged shut, theoreticians and university instructors joined together with the families, popular committees and the youth of the uprising, preventing a disjuncture between the "thinkers" and the greater Palestinian community.

This was a particularly riveting moment when the university president defended his students in the streets and the physics professor worked with the baker to plan food distribution.[35] The Palestinian population focused on one goal: self-determination and the establishment of an independent Palestinian state. Added to this, the Intifada brought the plight of the Palestinians a greater degree of international attention and recognition. For the first time in history, the humanitarian toll and reality of life in the Palestinian Territories was publicized to the world community. In effect, it created more political momentum toward Palestinian independence than 20 years of armed struggle before it.

Television coverage of IDF soldiers attacking stone-throwing young Palestinians generated worldwide sympathy. People were appalled by images of armed and riot-geared Israeli soldiers attacking women and children who had nothing but stones to protect themselves.[36]

For his part, Nusseibeh realized the importance of communicating this message to the Israelis. "Our own road to statehood is through Israel, through Israeli public opinion…it is our responsibility as Palestinians to emphasize to the Israelis that it is peace that we seek and coexistence, not the destruction of Israel…not for Israel's sake but for our sake."[37] Although it was difficult to convince the Palestinians of their intent, nonviolent intellectuals like Nusseibeh and Mubarak Awad eventually made progress with the PLO leadership.

While still isolated in Tunisia, Arafat and his comrades recognized that individual leaders in the Palestinian Territories were truly leading the Intifada. Therefore, Arafat and others increasingly supported nonviolent action and civil disobedience. For Arafat, a successful course of revolutionary action gave him needed legitimacy.

One of the intellectual leaders inside Palestine at the time of the first Intifada, Daoud Kuttab spoke of the new phenomenon:

Leaders of the various PLO factions were able to fend off criticism by saying "this is the wish of the uprising leadership."...The Intifada thus gave the PLO a new and more powerful [ability] to make concessions-not from a position of weakness-but from that of strength...If anyone came to the PLO and said why are you accepting 242 or recognizing Israel, Arafat would say, this is what my people, who are fighting the Israelis daily, want.[38]

Even as the leader of the Palestinian people, Arafat's approach to giving way to the needs and wants of his constituency was a rarity in the history of the Palestinian struggle. As Hanan Ashrawi adds, "the focus shifted from a leadership in exile to a people under occupation, and rebellion began to take on the shape of nation building."[39]

The mass mobilization of the Palestinians during the Intifada paved the way for the Palestinians to convene the 19th Palestinian

105 | Palestinian support for Arafat, 1991

National Council on November 15, 1988. At this historic meeting in Algiers, Arafat declared the establishment of the state of Palestine on the basis of UN Resolution 242, requiring Israel to withdraw to the pre-1967 borders. Resting firmly on Resolution 242 helped Arafat to reiterate the stance of the Palestinian people and the PLO:

> The inadmissibility of the acquisition of land by war and the right of all states to live within secure and recognized borders, thus calling for a just solution to the Palestinian refugee problem.[40]

Most importantly, this landmark declaration of Palestinian statehood was also a formal recognition of the State of Israel and the start to a mutual path towards a "two-state" solution.

Recognition of Israel

Prior to this moment any recognition of Israel was an unthinkable move for any representative of the Palestinian people. However, the Intifada effectively brought the Palestinian people out of the mindset that they could turn back the clock to pre-1948. Although truly a strength, the ability to compromise was viewed by some as capitulation and weakness. Yet many who engaged in the struggle for freedom from Israel saw compromise and a normalization of affairs as the only option for their future. Those who were willing to compromise for peace realized that there was no need to replicate the injustices of the past.

To this end there could be no compromise solution that would displace 3.5 million Jews, even if twice as many Palestinians remained displaced as a result of the creation of Israel. The armed struggle was laid to rest when it appeared that an alternative and viable diplomatic endeavor was underway.

The change in the PLO political position vis-à-vis Israel and the new political conditions that the movement created forced the United States and Israel to change their policies towards the Palestinians. Suddenly, Arafat was seen as a legitimate partner in peace for accepting Resolution 242 as a means to Palestinian statehood. At the UN General Assembly meeting a month later in Geneva, Arafat addressed the Assembly as the undisputed leader of the Palestinian people. He also clearly delineated his objective for peace by "totally and absolutely [renouncing] all forms of terrorism, including individual, group and state terrorism."[41] The U.S. accepted Arafat's new position, but the Israeli administration flatly rejected it.

Israel tried to impede American-PLO cooperation by saying it would not agree to the 1967 borders. Israel also maintained that the PLO needed to change the wording of its charter and the United States must not accept a Palestinian state.[42] The aim of Israel was to freeze negotiations with the Palestinians while insisting on including Jordan as a negotiating partner. However, Jordan's trusteeship of the Palestinian cause had long since dissolved. And, the change in American attitude under U.S. Secretary of State James Baker was instrumental in bringing the Israeli and Palestinian leadership face-to-face at the negotiating table.

Conclusion

The overall experience of the Palestinian people from 1948 onwards was one of demonization. The continual repression of Palestinian refugees in Jordan and Lebanon, coupled with continued Israeli military aggression against Palestinian civilians only served to promote the dream of Palestinian self-determination. Despite the events of Black September and the enormous loss of life in the 1982 Israeli war on Lebanon, Palestinians remained determined not to be erased by the forces of history. By 1987 the Israeli military occupation of East Jerusalem, the West Bank and Gaza Strip quickly deteriorated into a dehumanizing morass for both the occupied and the occupier. In their attempts to suppress Palestinians with an "iron fist," the Israeli military implemented the deportation of political activists, political assassinations, mass arrests, curfews, punitive economic policies and the break-up of communal structures.[43]

In the first year of the Intifada, 318 Palestinians were killed, 20,000 wounded, 15,000 arrested, 12,000 jailed, 34 deported, and 140 houses demolished.[44] Under the Israeli siege, however, the new Palestinian nationalism was reborn guided by a vastly younger, highly educated and astute population known collectively in Arabic as the "Children of the Stones." For the first time, Israel faced a modernized and socially cohesive Palestinian nationalist movement guided by an ideology of self-awareness, steadfastness and self-reliance.

As the years of the Intifada progressed, Palestinian determination for statehood was matched by the intensity of Israeli violence and oppression. Between 1987 and 1993, 1,540 Palestinians died—including 353 children under 16—130,000 were wounded, 116,000 detained for different periods of time, 770 houses demolished and 120,000 olive and fruit trees uprooted.[45] Internally, the Palestinian community of the West Bank was shaken, rattled, and stirred in every direction during repeated Israeli attempts to suppress their endeavors to achieve freedom.

But history has shown that not even the mighty Israeli military could silence the will of the Palestinian people. Their continued efforts and resilience during the Intifada started a new era in history. Israel and the United States recognized the PLO as the political representative of the Palestinian people. The PLO renounced their continuation of armed struggle, terrorism, and accepted the existence of two states. Jordan renounced their claim over the Palestinian Territories of the West Bank.

Had it not been for the spontaneous events of the Intifada, the people of Palestine may very well have been forgotten by history, and the Catastrophe of 1948 might have been completed.

Peace in the Middle East has been elusive. The Holy Land has been the subject of internationally brokered agreements for the past 100 years, yet hostilities persist. Most people wonder if peace there is a hopeless venture.

Israelis contend their first choice is peace with all of their Arab neighbors and a Palestinian State alongside of Israel. They have reached agreements with Arab nations, notably Egypt and Jordan. But they have not secured a lasting peace with the Palestinians. For Israel, any peace must include an acknowledgment of Israel's right to exist as a Jewish State with Jerusalem as its capital and a renunciation of violence from the Palestinians. Without these assurances, Israel pursues security measures that, to Palestinians, appear at odds with the peace process.

Palestinians feel equally wary of the peace process. Their history is littered with examples of colonial powers, and even Arab states, ignoring their needs and betraying them during negotiations. Palestinians have been accused of being slow and disingenuous at the bargaining table. But they see little interest on Israel's part toward three essential Palestinian objectives: the right of return for Palestinian refugees, Jerusalem as their capital, and the establishment of an independent Palestinian state.

The pursuit of peaceful coexistence between Jews and their neighbors began long before the establishment of the State of Israel. Peace is one of the most significant pillars of Jewish values and norms. It is an essential ingredient of the Jewish faith. First and foremost, the Torah teaches us to "Love your neighbor as yourself." (Leviticus 19:18) When praying from any Jewish prayer book the word shalom, which means peace, appears on just about every page. In our daily prayers, we ask God numerous times "sim shalom al Yisrael amecha," which means bring peace upon your people—Israel.

Judaism teaches us respect for other cultures. Jewish laws require acts of loving kindness and charity in every human interaction. Jewish people do not judge people of other faiths. Instead, we believe our neighbors are children of God who should be treated with respect and dignity. Unlike other religions, which seek to proselytize others into their religion, Judaism does not seek to convert others into the Jewish faith. Instead, we maintain a divine responsibility to represent a "light" unto the nations, always striving to live according to the laws of the Torah. In essence, we are God's partner in tikkun olam (mending the world) which teaches us to continually strive for peaceful coexistence with our neighbors.

The desire for peace is ingrained in Jewish and Israeli culture and it is pursued through all channels.

David Ben-Gurion, Israel's first prime minister, extended his hand in friendship to the Palestinians and other Arab neighbors on May 15, 1948, in the Israeli Declaration of Independence. Today, nearly 20 percent of Israel's citizens are Arabs and they enjoy a standard of living that far surpasses those in the Arab world. Arab Israelis can go to college and participate in every aspect of Israeli culture and the Israeli economy. They even have representatives in the Knesset.

Arab countries have not reciprocated these neighborly efforts or unprejudiced policies. Instead, Jewish people are not welcome in Arab nations. My father was persecuted in Iraq and had to escape from Baghdad where his Jewish community had flourished for 2,500 years. With Israel stamped in my American passport, I can visit Egypt and Jordan because of our negotiated peace treaties. However, I am prohibited from travelling to almost all other Arab countries. I cannot enter Lebanon, Syria, Iraq or Saudi Arabia. Every year thousands of Arab visitors are welcomed in Israel.

Restrictions against Israelis have been instituted in the Palestinian Territories as well. Whenever Israel has relinquished territory to Palestinian jurisdiction, Jews living there have been forced to evacuate. When the British turned over 74 percent of the British Mandate of Palestine to Transjordan in the 1920s, Jews living east of the Jordan River were forced to vacate their homes and were moved into what would later become Israel. When Israelis left the Gaza Strip, Jews living there had to be evacuated. And throughout the peace process, Palestinian leaders have insisted that any future Palestinian state be a country without Jews. This requirement painfully reminds Jews of when our ancestors were evicted from one country after another.

These demands by Palestinians are not only discriminatory. They are in stark contrast to the fairness shown by Israel to more than a million Israeli Arab citizens.

If the Palestinians truly want peace, Israel will do everything within reason to make it happen. But more and more Israelis, as well as Jews around the world, are coming to the sad realization that we might not have an honest, able, peace-motivated partner at the negotiating table.

In Israel we are able to distinguish law-abiding Palestinian people from the extremists among them. We go to great pains to only target those who clearly have blood on their hands when pursuing terrorists and make all efforts to minimize innocent casualties. Regretfully, this approach has not been shared by Palestinian authorities. Sadly, extremist positions have been advanced not only by terrorists, but by Palestinian leaders as well. We understand that without leaders who promote peaceful coexistence, Palestinians will continue to be indoctrinated with prejudicial misinformation about Israel.

Palestinian Media Watch, a non-governmental organization, reports what is being broadcast to the Palestinian people. By watching and listening to "their own words," we know that the media in Gaza and the Territories are distributing a steady barrage of propaganda against Jews and Israel. This extends into children's programming, where Disney-like animal characters call Jews "monkeys and pigs" and children are reminded to rid the world of the "evils of Zionism." Arab schoolbooks do not include Israel on world maps. Instead, they show the borders of a Palestinian homeland and deny Israel's existence entirely. Young Palestinians are taught that when the Jewish occupiers leave, Palestinians will return to their homes because all the Jews will be expelled.

Despite these challenges, Israel continues to pursue peace. From the Israeli point of view, there will be a viable Palestinian state when the Palestinians acknowledge the rightful existence of the Jewish state and they renounce and control violence.

I pray to God daily that this peace will be accomplished in my lifetime. As I continue to work on peace initiatives, I am inspired by my Palestinian colleagues, who, like my co-author Dr. Amin Kazak, also believe that peace is possible.

Peace Offer from the Declaration of Independence

It is instructive to look back through Israel's history to see how this pattern emerged.

In the Israeli Declaration of Independence, Israel expressed its desire for peace to its Arab neighbors and the world:

> We extend our hand to all neighboring states and their peoples in an offer of peace and good neighborliness, and appeal to them to establish bonds of cooperation and mutual help with the sovereign Jewish people settled in its own land.[1]

Regrettably, Israel's Arab neighbors rejected any form of peace with the Jewish state during the first quarter-century of its existence. Arabs spewed bellicose rhetoric and launched coordinated attacks on the vastly outnumbered and militarily-inferior new nation. Israel emerged militarily victorious time and time again. And, time and time again it gained new territory that added to its security. Yet Israel didn't impose the historically recognized principal of victor's justice, i.e., to the victor goes the spoils of war. Instead, Israeli leaders pursued the principal of land in exchange for peace.

In hindsight, it appears Arab governments had no intention of signing permanent peace agreements with Israel, opting instead to continue hostilities. In so doing they blocked what could have been a viable Palestinian state for more than a half-century from coming into being.

Israel's acquisition of territory following its victory in the 1967 War significantly enhanced Israel's security and became the basis of all future peace talks. Having tripled its land size in just six days, including the recapture of East Jerusalem, Israel firmly established itself as a regional superpower. It sought to leverage this newfound status into a viable and lasting peace.

Just ten days after the war's end, Israeli Foreign Minister Abba Eban stood before the UN General Assembly and urged its members to steer clear of mistaken past approaches and compel Arab states to engage in forthright, honest and meaningful negotiations so that lasting peace in the Middle East could finally be attained. As Eban so eloquently stated,

> What the Assembly should prescribe is not a formula for renewed hostilities, but a series of principles for the construction of a new future in the Middle East. With the cease-fire established, our progress must be not backward to an armistice regime which

has collapsed under the weight of years and the brunt of hostility. History summons us forward to permanent peace and the peace that we envisage can only be elaborated in frank and lucid dialogue between Israel and each of the States which have participated in the attempt to overthrow its sovereignty and undermine its existence....

In free negotiation with each of our neighbors we shall offer durable and just solutions redounding to our mutual advantage and honor. The Arab States can no longer be permitted to recognize Israel's existence only for the purpose of plotting its elimination. They have come face to face with us in conflict. Let them now come face to face with us in peace.[2]

Israel subsequently vowed to be generous in exchange for formal acceptance by its Arab neighbors and reliable tranquility. As Eban would later explain in direct talks with Arab countries, "everything is negotiable."[3]

Unfortunately, the Arab World reacted negatively to Israel's peaceful overtures. On September 1, 1967, Arab nations responded in the Khartoum Resolution. In its third paragraph the Resolution states in no uncertain terms: "no peace with Israel, no recognition of Israel and no negotiations with it..."[4]

Fortunately, members of the United Nations Security Council, exercising analytical rigor and well-fashioned reason (and breaking with routine) responded with a far more workable plan.

UN Resolution 242

On November 22, 1967, the UN Security Council unanimously adopted Resolution 242 which ever since has served as the basis for all peace negotiations between Arabs and Israelis. The resolution establishes five principal areas of contention which remain relevant today: the deployment of Israeli forces, peace within secure and recognized boundaries, freedom of navigation, a just settlement of the refugee problem, and security measures including the establishment and policing of demilitarized zones. Of primary importance to the Israeli delegation, 242 firmly established "Land-for-Peace;" a principal which was used successfully by Egyptian and Israeli negotiators at Camp David.

Peace with Egypt

When Anwar Sadat became Egypt's president, he abandoned Nasser's unwavering quest to forge an Arab Nationalist state and embarked on a new and wholly different path. Sparking the ire of many Egyptians, Sadat instituted a multi-party political system, opened the Egyptian economy to foreign capital and ousted Soviet troops from Egyptian soil. In 1977, he offered his hand to Israel in the hope of establishing a lasting peace.

But that was just the beginning of astonishing changes to come. Laying the groundwork for future discussions between the Israelis and Palestinians, Sadat shocked the world with his sudden and dramatic visit to Israel in 1977.

Sadat Makes History

From a black sky above Lod Airport, the glaring lights of an approaching aircraft suddenly appeared. The plane circled once, landed, and taxied to a floodlit area on the tarmac. An honor guard stood at attention while trumpets blared. As the aircraft slowly turned towards the awaiting dignitaries, the writing on its fuselage came into view: "Arab Republic of Egypt."

We were all mesmerized by the unbelievable event about to transpire. It was 1977 and the leader of the Arab world had landed in Israel!

In an atmosphere charged with euphoria, apprehension and fear, Sadat emerged. This was the same man who had attempted to starve Israel into submission through a war of attrition, who had attempted to sweep the Jews into the sea by uniting the Arab world in war against Israel, and who once declared that all of historical Palestine had belonged to Egypt for the past 7,000 years. Now he was at the Israeli international airport standing before the highest echelons of Israel's political and military establishment.[5]

In what can only be described as a surreal setting, Sadat strode down the red carpet where he was warmly welcomed by one Israeli official after another…and then approached Golda Meir.

Ms. Meir grasped the President's hands with one hand and then the other; he did likewise. Kissing her cheek he remarked, "I've been waiting to meet you for a long time." Displaying her brilliant tact, wit and subtext, Golda replied, "And we've been waiting for you for a longtime [emphasis added]."[6]

106 | Sadat(left) addresses Israeli Knesset, 1977

Sadat appeared before the Knesset in Jerusalem on November 20. But he did not direct his remarks to world, Arab leaders, or even the Knesset members seated before him. Instead, Sadat spoke directly to the people of Israel. He urged them to tear down the wall which stood as a barrier to peace and security in the Middle East.

> This wall constitutes a psychological barrier between us, a barrier of suspicion and a barrier of rejection; a barrier of fear, of deception, a barrier of hallucination without any action, deed or decision. A barrier of distorted and eroded interpretation of every event and statement ...constituting 70 percent of the whole problem.[7]

While the immensity of Sadat's visit to Jerusalem was not lost on the international community, for Jews the event was like divine validation. After a 1,900-year quest for peace, security, and cultural freedom through which the Jews had been the primary target of humanity's most vile behaviors, it seemed as if finally the Jewish people would attain full sovereign recognition. After all, if peace could be forged with the greatest of all of Israel's foes, then surely others would follow suit. Or, so it was hoped.

At only 16 years old, it was difficult to grasp the magnitude of this diplomatic achievement, but I remember with total clarity the excitement and sheer joy that permeated my household. What first comes to mind when thinking about the importance of that night, I remember that I was supposed to have a math test the next day, but it was cancelled. My parents, who never let us skip school for any reason, did so the next morning. We had stayed up the night before glued to the television and we continued doing the same thing for endless hours the next day watching every move and listening to every word. We knew we were living history in the making. I'd never experienced such a state of euphoria. It's not like my parents had ever burdened us with their fears of the threats, or the constant state of war we lived in. But the difference on that day was palpable. I had never seen my parents so exuberant. It was as if the weight of our neighbors' animosity was lifted off our shoulders and we could stand taller, safer and happier.

The second he appeared in the door of aircraft, I was mesmerized. To watch our strongest foe and the most prominent Arab leader, President Anwar Sadat, in our Jewish country, Israel, smiling and shaking hands with our leaders was truly unbelievable. It was like a dream.

The die had been cast! Yet despite the tremendous breakthrough, forces seeking the demise of any move towards a peaceful resolution of the Arab-Israeli conflict were hard at work.

107 | Sadat, Carter and Begin sign Peace Treaty between Egypt and Israel, 1979

Not only had PLO forces operating from Lebanon signaled their outright objection to any peaceful settlement with Israel, the Arab community as a whole was also wary of any form of rapprochement with the "Zionist entity." Accordingly, instead of receiving support for his efforts to gain freedom for the Palestinian people and to "liberate" the Sinai Peninsula and Gaza from Israeli occupation, Sadat found himself increasingly isolated.

On December 5, 1977, the governments of Algeria, Iraq, Libya, Syria, and South Yemen jointly condemned Sadat's actions; vowing to "work for the frustration of the results of President Sadat's visit to the Zionist entity."[8]

Sadly, across the Arab world the burning of Egyptian, Israeli and American flags became a routine spectacle.

Framework for Peace in the Middle East

Much more work lay ahead. Of seminal importance with regard to the future of Israeli-Palestinian relations was the *Framework for Peace in the Middle East* signed on September 17, 1978, by the negotiating parties six months earlier at Camp David. It is this document which set in motion the tenuous and often turbulent negotiation process between Israelis and Palestinians by calling for:

1. Egypt, Israel, Jordan, and the representatives of the Palestinian people [to] participate in negotiations on the resolution of the Palestinian problem in all its aspects: To

achieve that objective, negotiations relating to the West Bank and Gaza should proceed in three stages:

(a)...there should be transitional arrangements for the West Bank and Gaza for a period not exceeding five years. In order to provide full autonomy to the inhabitants, under these arrangements the Israeli military government and its civilian administration will be withdrawn as soon as a self-governing authority has been freely elected...

(b)...the parties will negotiate an agreement which will define the powers and responsibilities of the self-governing authority to be exercised in the West Bank and Gaza...

(c)...When the self-governing body authority (administrative council) in the West Bank and Gaza is established and inaugurated, the transitional period of five years will begin. As soon as possible, but no later than the third year after the beginning of the transitional period, negotiations will take place to determine the Final Status of the West Bank and Gaza..."

—*Framework for Peace in the Middle East*, Camp David[9]

Obstacles to Peace

With the assassination of Sadat by Muslim fundamentalists in 1981, Israel's subsequent entry into the Lebanese Civil War, and the resulting expulsion of the PLO's leadership to Tunisia, all prospects for a negotiated peace settlement between Israelis and Palestinians as called for in the Framework at Camp David seemed to be off the table. In Washington, President Ronald Reagan was on edge as a result of the Iran-Iraq war and the Soviets' recent invasion of Afghanistan. He became convinced that the lack of any progress towards a resolution of the Palestinian problem was a formula for the continuing escalation of violence in the Middle East. While the various initiatives brought forth by the Reagan administration throughout the 1980s sparked much debate, they did little to bring the parties any closer together.

Arafat at the UN Reverses Course

Perhaps the most dramatic reversal of policy occurred in 1988 when Arafat denounced terrorism and told the world that he wanted peace with Israel. While Israel reacted with hope and optimism, it understandably questioned his sincerity. Recalling the infamous "peace in our time" remarks by British Prime Minister Neville Chamberlain after returning from signing a non-aggression pact with Hitler, Israelis proceeded with the hope that Arafat's intentions were honorable and sincere.

However, Arafat did have ulterior motives. Seeking to topple Hamas and regain his status as the principal representative of the Palestinian people, Arafat capitalized on the growing unrest within the Territories and utilized the Intifada as the basis for a political process towards a permanent settlement. The PLO's November 1988 adoption of the Algiers Declaration, which called for a two-state solution to the conflict with Israel, represented a 180-degree turnaround.

Addressing the UN General Assembly in Geneva one month later, Arafat surprised the world when he proclaimed:

> We want peace…. We are committed to peace, and we want to live in our Palestinian state and let others live…The PLO will seek a comprehensive settlement among the parties concerned in the Arab-Israeli conflict, including the State of Palestine, Israel, and other neighbors, within the framework of the [proposed] international conference for peace in the Middle East on the basis of resolutions 242 and 338 and so as to guarantee equality and the balance of interests, especially our people's rights, in freedom, national independence, and respect the right to exist in peace and security for all…[10]

Responding to the PLO's public pledges of this policy change, U.S. Secretary of State George Shultz quickly announced that the U.S. conditions for recognition had been met and a United States-PLO dialogue would begin in Tunis followed by the 1991 Madrid Conference.

Madrid Conference

Although the Madrid process amounted to nothing more than ten rounds of futile negotiations, the conference did have symbolic significance—it was the first time that all interested parties had gathered face-to-face. Also, the Madrid conference provided an opening for direct back-channel talks, free from outside influences. In the spring and summer of 1993, under the sponsorship of the Norwegian government, Israeli and Palestinian representatives forged a mutually agreeable proposal for the creation of a Palestinian state.

Oslo Accords, Reason for Hope

On August 25, 1993, Yitzhak Rabin—now Israel's Prime Minister—informed U.S. Secretary of State Warren Christopher that the Israeli government had reached a major agreement with the Palestinians.

The Declaration of Principles on Interim Self-Government Arrangements (commonly known as the Oslo Accords, or DOP) laid out a blueprint for mutual recognition, mutual purpose, and peaceful coexistence:

> The Government of the State of Israel and the P.L.O. team (in the Jordanian-Palestinian delegation to the Middle East Peace Conference) (the "Palestinian Delegation,") representing the Palestinian people, agree that it is time to put an end to decades of

confrontation and conflict, recognize their mutual legitimate and political rights, and strive to live in peaceful coexistence and mutual dignity and security and achieve a just, lasting and comprehensive peace settlement and historic reconciliation through the agreed political process."

In an atmosphere of euphoria and exhilaration, the signing of the DOP, Letters of Mutual Recognition and the subsequent Israeli-Palestinian Interim Agreement on the West Bank and Gaza (delineated subsequently in talks known as Oslo II), the political terrain of the Arab-Israeli conflict was forever transformed. Not only had a framework detailing the areas of negotiation been established, but assignment of the various duties, obligations, and timetables had also been agreed upon.[11]

Every Israeli serves in the military from years 18–21, and so most enter college at an older age than our counterparts in the U.S. For those like me who engaged in combat, we carry the additional weight of participating in war's inevitable death and destruction. The hardest thing I've ever done occurred during the Lebanon War when I served as a Commander in the IDF. One of my most difficult duties was to console the families of my men who had fallen in battle. While visiting each house of mourning, I would look into the eyes of mothers who lost their sons and relive the circumstances of each soldier's ultimate sacrifice.

Nothing can convince someone of the need for peace more than being confronted with such utter family grief and devastation. For me, this visceral agony dramatically convinced me to do everything possible to help build bridges towards peace. When Rabin acquiesced and shook hands with Arafat who we had considered to be a terrorist thug in the past, I put my trust in this wise man, believing that times would change, terrorism would stop, and peaceful days lay ahead for all of us.

I experienced another epiphany when I realized that the Oslo agreement had been spawned by academics rather than by career diplomats. This peacemaker role played by people like me was a revelation and an inspiration. Public opinion often prevents politicians from constructively engaging their enemies. So in this instance, secret negotiations in Norway were conducted on behalf of Israel by my academic peers: Ron Pundack and Yair Herschfeld. These professors achieved what diplomats and elected leaders could not. Their achievement influenced me to pursue peace through academic and people-to-people initiatives.

I am particularly proud of the peace initiatives I led at the University of Denver as the Executive Director of the Institute for the Study of Israel in the Middle East (ISIME). For nearly a decade I helped to facilitate conferences, meetings and connections between Israelis, Arabs and Palestinians on Colorado campuses and among communities in order to promote solutions to the Arab-Israeli conflict. Someday, I hope to continue the work we started in 2009, TeachPeace in the Middle East.

Growing Distrust

Sadly, this triumphant mood was short-lived.

Within months of signing the historic accords, forces conspiring to derail the peace process gained the upper hand. In a series of tit-for-tat events, wide-eyed optimism quickly gave way to condemnation, blame, and a spiral of ever-growing distrust. From Israel's point of view the newly formed Palestinian Authority (PA) failed in its obligations by allowing terrorists to operate from PA-controlled territory and by refusing to extradite known criminals. While Hamas, Islamic Jihad, and other likeminded groups began waging a campaign of suicide bombings in Israel's cities, the Israeli government was hard pressed to withdraw its forces from agreed-upon areas, release prisoners, or hand over additional territory to an untrustworthy PA. It was of little surprise that Final Status negotiations were all but doomed—at least at that time.

Loss of Rabin

Final Status negotiations were scheduled to begin in May 1996, but they would be delayed another four years as the region became embroiled in more violence and tragedy. Shortly after the assassination of Israeli Prime Minister Yitzhak Rabin by an Israeli extremist, another wave of suicide bombings terrorized an already traumatized Israeli public. For those in the peace camp, both Arab and Israeli, it was obvious that the peace process had been dealt a double blow. Yet fate had one more twist in store.

Running in an election campaign dubbed "Peace with Security," Benjamin Netanyahu squeaked past Shimon Peres to win a 50.49 percent to 49.51 percent vote in June of 1996. With the signing of the Wye River Memorandum on October 23, 1998, Netanyahu agreed to transfer an additional 13 percent of the West Bank territory to full Palestinian control in three stages. But his reluctance to honor agreements signed by the previous government, combined with a shocking escalation of Palestinian terrorism, brought the peace talks to a complete standstill.

Yitzhak Rabin was my favorite Israeli leader. He represented sheer hope. I was inspired by his courage and his vision for peace. He was elected while I was an undergraduate at Bar Ilan University. While I was the editor of the student magazine, I had the opportunity to interview Rabin. I remember the feeling of being in the presence of an incredibly special leader.

First and foremost, he came across as honest and sincere, the kind of person who earned instant respect while building trust and confidence. Secondly, that respect and confidence was rooted in his history, which included his military role as Chief of Staff during the Six-Day War of 1967. Everyone knew that he would never jeopardize the security of Israel.

He also demonstrated a pragmatic approach to dealing with Palestinian issues. Rabin's second term brought in an era of hope and belief that peace could happen between the Palestinians and Israel. Seeing his handshake with Arafat on September 27, 1993, on the White House lawn gave me the same sense of euphoria we felt when Sadat came to Israel to make peace 16 years previously. Peace seemed possible with Rabin at the helm.

Then he was gone.

108 | Rabin-Arafat handshake, with U.S. President Bill Clinton

10 שנים לרצח יצחק רבין

חוזרים לכיכר

לזכור יחד.
לשמור על התקווה.

מוצ"ש 12.11.05, בשעה 20:00, כיכר רבין ת"א

109 | Israel commemorates 10 years since the assassination of Yitzhak Rabin

Palestinians Did Not Comply with Agreements

It became obvious very quickly to Israelis that Arafat's talk—and even his signature—did not match his actions on the ground. There were several areas of non-compliance.

1. The PA failed in its obligation to renounce violence and to take all measures necessary to prevent acts of violence and terrorism against Israel.

2. The PA refused to resolve all outstanding issues through bilateral negotiations and to resolve all disputes through peaceful means, and to cooperate in the creation of a joint mechanism for negotiation and dispute settlement.

3. The PA actively engaged in the incitement of violence.

4. The PA refused to apprehend, prosecute, and detain known terrorists.

5. The PA failed in its obligation to ensure that holy sites in the areas under the administration of the Palestinian Authority were to be duly respected and protected.

6. The PA did not adhere to its obligation to ensure that no armed forces other than the Palestinian police and Israeli military forces were to be established or operate in the West Bank and Gaza Strip.

7. The PA did not fully carry out its obligation to confiscate illegal weapons.

8. The PA failed to maintain joint security and other cooperation mechanisms with Israel in order to ensure public order and security.

Peace with Jordan

While attainment of a meaningful and sincere final peace agreement with the Palestinians was out of reach by the mid-1990s, Israel was still able to reach a long overdue achievement with the signing of the Treaty of Peace between the Hashemite Kingdom of Jordan and the State of Israel. In truth, despite Jordan's participation against Israel in the 1948 War of Independence and the 1967 Six-Day War, relations between the Kingdom and Israel could easily be described as amicable. Indeed, since King Abdullah's secret visit with Golda Meir in 1947, dozens of clandestine meetings at the highest level, between representatives of the two countries had taken place.[12]

Despite the fact that Jordan and Israel had been formally in conflict, each of them viewed the other as a source of stability and security. For instance, when Syrian troops threatened to overthrow the Kingdom during Black September, the king called upon Israel for assistance. Israel responded by sending its jet fighters to "buzz" the advancing Syrians, sending them into retreat.[13]

As made patently apparent by the signing of the Common Agenda on September 14, 1993—just one day after the signing of Oslo—the primary obstacle to an Israeli-Jordanian peace was a resolution of the Palestinian issue. Because Jordan was home to the second largest Palestinian population in the world (after the Territories),[14] any substantive move towards détente with Israel prior to a Palestinian agreement risked the triggering of yet another insurrection. Keenly aware of this hindrance and wishing to advance his own peace ambitions, King Hussein relinquished all claims to the West Bank in July of 1988. This paved the way for a future Palestinian state and, consequently, peace with Israel.[15] Less than one year later, much to the delight of a weary Israeli public in dire need of good news, Prime Mister Yitzhak Rabin and King Hussein met on their desert border to sign into law a mutually binding peace agreement on July 25, 1994. Sadly this was to be Mr. Rabin's last official act as peacemaker.

While the Israeli-Egyptian peace treaty maintains an essence of belligerency by emphasizing "respect [for] each other's right to live in peace" and spills much ink on the issue of security, the Israeli-Jordanian treaty is much more cordial. Partnership rather than respect sets its tone, and details about cooperation are far more prevalent then security.[16] The treaty provides a detailed blueprint for ongoing political, economic, social, cultural, and human interaction. Among the key issues covered are the establishment of borders, the normalization of economic and diplomatic relations, Israel's assurance to divert to Jordan 50 million cubic meters of water from the Jordan River each year, and the parties' pledge to cooperate during times of drought. With regards to security and defense, the parties not only vowed to respect each other's sovereignty, but, going much further, promised to jointly combat terrorism and other security threats while working towards the creation of a mutual partnership for common defense. On the topic of Jerusalem, Jordan was granted "special status" over Muslim Holy sites and was promised that Israel would give "high priority to Jordan[s] historic role in these shrines" during Final Status negotiations. Finally, both parties agreed to work with Egypt to find a resolution to the Palestinian refugee problem and would prevent the unauthorized movement of refugees across their mutual border.[17]

Focus on Palestinian Negotiations

With the Egyptian peace holding strong and a long-awaited pact with Jordan now firmly in hand, the Israeli government set its sights on the two remaining holdouts—Syria and the Palestinians. Progress on these fronts, however, remained elusive. Palestinian rejectionists continued their torrent of violence and Syrian President Hafez al-Assad demonstrated, at best, erratic interest in reaching a peace settlement.

Another change at the top of Israel's government brought a new perspective and more opportunity.

Ehud Barak, Israel's most highly decorated military officer, had conducted his election campaign as "Rabin's heir," a man of military stature seeking peace. As Prime Minister, however, Barak's approach to peace was a radical departure from that of his mentor. Whereas Rabin tempered his decisions by taking a gradual approach, Barak sought to cut the Israeli-Arab Gordian knot with one bold stroke.[18] Removing the "phased approach" from the agenda once and for all, the Barak Plan called upon Arab leaders to discuss the full gamut of issues and set a 15-month deadline (until October 2000) on all tracks—including the conclusion of a Final Status agreement between Israel and Palestine, the withdrawal of Israeli forces from Lebanon, a peace agreement with Syria, and the establishment of a regional accord aimed at resolving the pending refugee and water rights crisis.[19]

Barak initiated plans for Israel's May 2000 withdrawal from Lebanon. Barak believed that withdrawal from Lebanon would help jumpstart and facilitate negotiations with Syria.[20] But talks with Syria were deadlocked from their outset. Whereas Assad demanded a return of the Golan Heights up to and including the shores of Lake Galilee, Barak sought to maintain a sliver of land (approximately 200 meters wide) around its northern shore. Although bogged down on this single issue, talks did continue well into the year 2000. The progress made between the two countries came to a halt when Assad, knowing his days were numbered and that his son would soon be taking over as President of Syria, decided to end the negotiations. Assad died in June of 2000.

Then the Barak government set out to jumpstart the all but dead peace process with the Palestinians with a meeting in Sharm al-Sheikh, Egypt. The signed agreement—officially *The Sharm al-Sheikh Memorandum on Implementation Timeline of Agreements and the Resumption of Permanent Status Negotiations* (commonly referred to as the Sharm al-Sheikh Memorandum or Wye II)—was signed on September 4, 1999. Commentators mocked it as "an agreement to reach an agreement already made,"[21] For the Palestinian delegation, it amounted to accepting to renegotiate something they were already legally entitled to under the previous agreement with Netanyahu according to the 1998 Wye Accords. Nonetheless, the new memorandum did provide for one highly prized incentive—a direct path to Final Status negotiations.

With Barak's attention initially turned towards the Syrian track, the conclusion of several rounds of negotiations between Israelis and Palestinians did not result in an accord. However, they succeeded in bringing the Israelis closer to the Palestinian position.

President Clinton Takes Center Stage

On July 5, 2000, President Clinton announced that within the week an historic meeting would take place with the objective of "reach[ing] an agreement on the core issues that have fueled a half-century of conflict between Israelis and Palestinians."[22] The task would be immense. The issues to be discussed would strike at the very heart of Israeli anxieties and Palestinian identity. These included a resolution of the Palestinian refugee question, the establishment of borders and security arrangements, and finally, the most difficult task: that of defining the status of Jerusalem. I will delineate each of these below.

Refugees: Right of Return?

The United Nations Relief and Works Agency for Palestinian Refugees (UNRWA) estimated that, at the time of the Camp David talks, there were more than 4 million Palestinian refugees living in 59 refugee camps and in neighboring countries.[23] Negotiations on the fate of these refugees rested upon respective interpretations of UN Security Council Resolution 242 (2b) and UN General Assembly Resolution 194; clause 11, which states that the General Assembly

> resolves that the refugees wishing to return to their homes and live at peace with their neighbors should be permitted to do so at the earliest practicable date, and that compensation should be paid for the property of those choosing not to return and for loss of or damage to property which, under principles of international law or in equity, should be made good by the Governments or authorities responsible.[24]

Resolving this issue is of the highest priority for the Palestinians who view al-Naqba as a loss of homeland, the disintegration of their society, and the beginning of a hasty process of cultural destruction. Accordingly they declared: Israel must guarantee the right of return to Israel for any refugee desiring such a move. In addition Israel must award compensation for all lost property and assets to Palestinian refugees who have settled over the past half-century in other countries.[25]

For Israeli negotiators, such demands are unacceptable and unwarranted. The Palestinian narrative ignores the fact that it was Arabs who created the refugee problem in the first place by not accepting the Partition Plan of 1947, and following instead the misguided advice of Arab leaders determined to eradicate Israel. In addition, Israelis blame Arab countries for using the Palestinians as political pawns in an effort to prolong the Arab-Israeli conflict and to divert world attention from the atrocities which they commit within their own countries.[26] This reality has definitely been uncovered during the repression of Arab citizens during the Arab Spring in 2011.

As spelled out in the DOP and the Israeli-Jordanian Peace Treaty, the Israelis believe that the Palestinian refugee question needs to be considered in conjunction with the forceful displacement of more than 800,000 Jewish refugees who were displaced from Arab countries.

With rigid lines drawn in the sand, the question of the refugees would become one of the most arduous addressed at Camp David, and by some accounts, was perceived to be the ultimate deal-breaker.

Clinton Parameters

As with all other issues discussed at Camp David, the refugee problem remained unresolved. During the ensuing six months, various attempts to bridge the differences between the parties had been attempted, the most notable of which were the Clinton Parameters. When negotiators reconvened in the Egyptian Red Sea resort of Taba the following winter, these parameters served as the basis for compromise. Sensing the remaining gaps had more to do with formulations relating to the right of return than to fundamental ideological differences; President Clinton proposed the following guideline, which was accepted in Taba as a starting point by negotiators on both sides:

> Under the Two-State Solution, the guiding principle should be that the Palestinian state will be the focal point for Palestinians who choose to return to the area without ruling out that Israel will accept some of these refugees. [The Parties] need to adopt a formulation on the right of return to Israel itself but that does not negate the aspiration of the Palestinian people to return to the area. The agreement will define the implementation of this general right in a way that is consistent with the Two-State Solution. It would list five possible final homes for the refugees:
>
> 1. The state of Palestine
> 2. Areas in Israel being transferred to Palestine in the land swap
> 3. Rehabilitation in a host country
> 4. Resettlement in a third country
> 5. Admission to Israel

In listing these options, the agreement will make clear that the return to the West Bank, Gaza Strip, and the areas acquired in the land swap (discussed below) would be a right to all Palestinian refugees. While rehabilitation in host countries, resettlement in third countries and absorption into Israel will depend upon the policies of those countries.

Negotiators in Taba addressing the refugee issue had made considerable progress. Through an Israeli initiative they had agreed to create joint narratives with regard to the "refugee tragedy," and following the Clinton Parameters they were able to formulate a 15-year absorption plan.[27]

Although an agreement was not reached, it was apparent that both parties exercised a great deal of flexibility: Israel was willing to accept partial responsibility for the refugees and was somewhat accommodating regarding the right of return as long as certain red lines were not crossed, while the Palestinians demonstrated an understanding of Israel's concerns and a willingness to work toward a practical compromise.

Borders and Security

At Camp David, negotiations on borders and security focused on how to safely hand over territory, which Israel had conquered and occupied as a result of the Six-Day War. Israeli negotiators, in concord with their longstanding "Land for Peace" doctrine, insisted that Israel's victory should lead to nothing less than a complete and genuine final resolution of the Israeli-Palestinian conflict.[28] During the talks, controversy immediately arose over the wording of UN Security Council Resolution 242's operative clause calling for…

Withdrawal of the Israeli armed forces from Territories occupied in the recent conflict.

The French version of the resolution has a subtle, but significantly dissimilar wording:

Retrait des forces armees israeliennes des territoires occupes lors du recent conflit.

The difference between the translations lay in the absence of the definite article ("the" Territories) in the English version. Consequently, at Camp David a dispute ensued over whether or not the resolution would require Israel to retreat from all the Territories it had captured, or whether Israel would still be in compliance with the resolution by retreating— on mutually agreed upon terms—only from some of the captured Territories. The later interpretation was eventually adopted.

With a hint of movement on the Palestinian side, Clinton presented several bridging proposals at Camp David which resulted in both concessions and backpedalling, but never a solid agreement. Saeb Erakat had suggested that another round of negotiations should be planned for August or September. The Israeli delegation became incensed. To them it was confirmation of their suspicion that Arafat was not interested in going the extra distance for the sake of peace. He would offer no clarity whatsoever and instead insisted on more Israeli concessions at each round of talks.[29] Needless to say, no progress was made in the Borders and Security Committee at Camp David.

Putting forth a sincere set of viable agendas for the follow-up Taba talks, Clinton invested the next four months mulling over the respective positions and discussing parameters for compromise with his advisors, as well as with Israeli and Palestinian negotiators. On December 23, President Clinton presented his thoughts regarding borders and security:

Territory
Eighty percent of the settlers would remain in settlement blocs to be annexed by Israel. Israel would annex 4–6 percent of the West Bank unless an agreement was reached on the leasing of additional territory. In exchange, Israel would transfer to the Palestinians 1–3 percent of its own territory, and in addition, provide safe passage between the West Bank and Gaza.

Security

To balance Israel's security needs with the Palestinian quest for maximum sovereignty, Clinton proposed that the future Palestinian state would be "non-militarized;" the only military force on its soil would be the Palestinian police, Palestinian security services and an international force that could not be withdrawn without mutual consent. The IDF would continue to hold positions in the Jordan Valley for 36 months while an international force was gradually introduced. After this period a small Israeli contingency could remain for an additional 36 months depending on relevant regional threats. Israel would be permitted three early warning stations to be jointly manned with Palestinian forces; the status of these stations would be re-examined after a period of 10 years. In the event of a concrete threat to Israel's national security, Israel would be permitted to deploy additional forces in the Jordan Valley upon notifying the international force. Finally, arrangements would be made to negotiate Israel's use of Palestinian airspace for military training purposes.[30]

On December 27, 2000, Barak's security cabinet voted to accept Clinton's ideas with minor reservations.[31] The Israeli government as a whole gave the go-ahead the next day—a major breakthrough in Israeli politics. The government, crossing one of its red lines, accepted the end to an IDF presence in the Jordan Valley[32] and ceded 100 percent of the territory Arafat was seeking.[33]

Despite the fact that Arafat could now present an agreement to his people that actually netted real and sizable concessions, he stalled. By requesting clarifications and avoiding responses, he raised the ultimate doubt as to whether the revolutionary could become a statesman. Only after several rounds of discussions with Clinton, Egyptian President Hosni Mubarak, King Abdullah II of Jordan and several European delegates, did Arafat finally accept Clinton's proposal, albeit five days past the original deadline.[34]

Taba

From January 21–27, 2001, direct negotiations between the two sides began in Taba, Egypt, this time without an American presence.[35] For the first and *only* time, the Palestinians presented a map depicting their vision of territorial borders. It seemed as if the respective positions were moving closer together and that a future Palestinian state was beginning to take form.[36] Then tragedy struck. The murder of two Israeli restaurant owners by Palestinian assailants and growing unrest within the Israeli public traumatized by yet another round of obscene violence—the Second Intifada—gave rise to the need to address immediate domestic concerns. Barak suspended talks and returned to Jerusalem to answer to Knesset members. The talks ended on January 28th with no agreement. However, it is noteworthy to realize just how far the two sides had come since the breakdown of talks six months earlier.

Territories

Both parties agreed that the basis for future borders would be the June 4, 1967, lines and that any modifications would be calculated from this baseline. Territory to be annexed was based on the Clinton Parameters, but with different interpretations: the Israeli reading envisioned contiguous settlement blocs; while the Palestinians believed that such blocs would cause significant harm to the needs and rights of Palestinians. Israel presented maps, which reflected its willingness to dismantle settlements in the Jordan Valley as well as in the Gaza Strip. With regard to land swaps, Israel sought six percent of the West Bank (the outer limits of the Clinton parameters) while the Palestinians were only willing to consider 3.1 percent. Finally, the Israelis proposed leasing an additional two percent of land in the West Bank. The Palestinians refused to discuss the matter until after the establishment of a Palestinian state.

Security

The Israelis requested three early warning stations, which the Palestinians were prepared to accept under certain conditions—the exact terms would be detailed later in further negotiations. The Israelis concurred with Clinton's proposal of establishing non-militarized Palestinian security forces, while the Palestinians maintained their claim to a state with limited arms. As for the withdrawal of Israeli forces from the West Bank and the Jordan Valley, the Israelis concurred wholly with the Clinton parameters. The Palestinians, however, believed that a sustained Israeli presence would exacerbate Israeli-Palestinian tension and they therefore proposed 18 months for Israeli withdrawal from the West Bank with an additional 10 months for withdrawal from the Jordan Valley.

There were many who criticized President Clinton for not presenting his ideas earlier. President Clinton later recognized that this was one of his biggest mistakes in the negotiations. The Clinton Parameters marked a decisive turning point in the negotiation process, affording Israeli and Palestinian negotiators the ability to envision territorial concessions based upon a pragmatic compromise. Yet there was one more parcel of real estate, slightly larger than a football field, to which appeals for *pragmatic compromise* would have no persuasive force whatsoever.

Jerusalem

For Jews, "Jerusalem is everything," expressed Ehud Olmert, the Mayor of Jerusalem. "It is the center of Jewish history, the center of Jewish life, the center of the Jewish religion. Jerusalem represents the purist expression of all that Jews prayed for, dreamed of, cried for, and died for in the 2,000 years since the destruction of the Second Temple."[37]

Points of contention over Jerusalem stem from security, and political considerations. Most of all, the controversies emanate from emotional and religious sensitivities.[38] The modern city of Jerusalem rests upon the various ruins of empires past. At its center, dividing east from west, sits the Old City and the Temple Mount, or as it is known to Muslims, Haram al-Sharif. Christians consider it hallowed ground. As delineated earlier, this is Islam's third holiest site—the place from which Muhammed ascended into heaven.

Palestinians claim that al-Quds (The Holy City, i.e. Jerusalem) has been the geographical, political and spiritual center of Palestine for centuries and that since its establishment, Israel has sought to create facts on the ground which favor a Jewish demographic in the city. Once again ignoring the fact that it was the Arab armies which attacked Israel, the Palestinian delegation blamed Israel for violating the UN Partition Plan in 1948, and thereby occupying 84 percent of Jerusalem and forcing thousands of Arabs to flee their homes. Invading again in 1967, it is their contention that the Israelis captured the whole city, including the Old City, and expanded the city's municipal boundary to include 1.3 percent of Occupied Palestinian Territory in violation of international law.[39]

Israelis claim that since 1004 BCE when King David established Jerusalem as the capital of the Jewish nation there has remained a constant and enduring Jewish presence in the city. Jerusalem was, is, and will always be the spiritual center of Jewish life and the political capital of Israel. Despite its numerous conquests, no other nation or state which gained sovereignty over the area had ever made Jerusalem a capital city—not even a district capital.

Since the city's reunification in 1967 under Israeli rule, Jerusalem has remained open and the rights of all religious groups have been protected. With regard to the status of Jerusalem as *corpus separatum*, ("separated body"—an internationally administered zone governed by the United Nations) it should be recalled that this idea was a non-binding proposal which never materialized; having become irrelevant when the Arab states rejected UN Resolution 181 and invaded the fledgling State of Israel.[40]

Accordingly, as the Basic Law of 1980 reiterates: "Jerusalem, complete and united, is the capital of Israel under exclusive Israeli sovereignty."[41] Nevertheless, recognizing its significance in the Arab world, Israel has agreed to address Jerusalem related issues as part of the permanent status talks.

Negotiations on the permanent status of Jerusalem need to deal with three practical considerations: How will it be managed on a day-to-day basis; how will it be managed on a spiritual basis, being holy to the three monotheistic religions and the home to 57 holy sites in the Old City alone; and how will it be managed politically—namely, under whose control will its sovereignty lie?[42]

Seeking direction on how best to approach these talks, Clinton consulted with Arafat about the issue of Jerusalem on the first day at Camp David. Arafat's reply was straightforward; "It's simple. East Jerusalem for us. West Jerusalem for the Israelis. It will be the capital of two states, and there will be a joint commission for water, roads, electricity…"[43] Arafat suggested that the Palestinian state would have sovereignty over both Islamic and Christian holy sites, including the Haram al-Sharif/Temple Mount. It was a vision which can only be characterized as preposterous to the Israelis who at that point were only willing to *consider* a division of the city into two municipalities with special administrative functions assigned to the Palestinians over the holy sites. This, of course, was considered an equally ridiculous proposal to the Palestinians.

Finally, as if endowed with the wisdom of Solomon, the Americans tried a new approach: a vertical division of the Haram al-Sharif/Temple Mount. What was Arab would be Palestinian, what was Jewish would be Israeli. In other words, Palestinian sovereignty over the surface of Haram al-Sharif, Israeli sovereignty over the Western Wall and the Holy of Holies with the inclusion of a commitment by both parties not to excavate beneath the Mount or behind the Wall except by mutual sovereign agreement.[44]

Negotiators at Camp David and Taba came closer to resolving the question of Jerusalem than most people believed was realistically possible. Resolving 90 percent of the issue, however, it was the remaining 10 percent—the spiritual dimension—which constituted 90 percent of the issue. It is worth noting the losing positions at Taba:

1. Sovereignty
Both sides accepted in principle the Clinton suggestion of having Palestinian sovereignty over Arab neighborhoods and Israeli sovereignty over Jewish neighborhoods, but the Palestinian side rejected Israeli sovereignty over Israeli settlements outside the municipal borders of Jerusalem, including Ma'ale Adumim and Givat Ze'ev. Both sides accepted the principle of a land swap with several minor reservations on the Palestinian side. Finally, Palestinians understood that Israel was ready to accept Palestinian sovereignty over the entire Muslim, Christian, and Armenian quarters of the Old City, while Israelis understood that the Palestinians were ready to accept Israeli sovereignty over the Jewish quarter of the Old City and part of the Armenian quarter.

2. Open City
Both sides favored the idea of an open city, but the Palestinians refused to guarantee free access to all holy sites, particularly, Harem al-Sharif.

3. Capital for Two States
Both sides accepted that the city of Jerusalem would be the capital of the two states: Yerushalayim as the capital of Israel and al-Quds as the capital of the state of Palestine.

4. Holy/Historical Basin and the Old City
The Israeli side expressed its interest and raised its concern regarding the area conceptualized as the Holy Basin which includes the Jewish Cemetery on the

Mount of Olives, the City of David, and the Kidron Valley. The Palestinians agreed to take into account Israel's concerns, provided that these places remained under Palestinian sovereignty. Other ideas were suggested including internationalizing the area or creating a joint Palestinian/Israeli regime. The Palestinians rejected both proposals.

5. Holy Sites Including the Western Wall

Both sides accepted the idea of mutual religious control and management. According to this principle, Israel would maintain control over the Western Wall although there remained a dispute regarding the Holy of Holies; the inner sanctuary of the Temple, which today rests on the Temple Mount. While the Palestinians acknowledged Israel's wishes to establish an affiliation to the holy parts of the Western Wall, they all but denied the existence of the Holy of Holies.

6. Haram al-Sharif/Temple Mount

Trapped in deadlock, the Americans suggested that for an agreed period of time Haram al-Sharif/Temple Mount would be placed under the international sovereignty of the five permanent members of the Security Council plus Morocco. The Palestinians would become the custodians of the area during this period during which the parties would either agree on a new solution or agree to extend the existing arrangement. Neither side accepted or rejected the suggestion.[45]

The Ultimate Failures of Camp David and Taba Peace Negotiations

The ill-fated finale of talks in Taba brought the era of Oslo, and seven tumultuous years of searching for a negotiated peace in the Middle East, to an abortive end. The Camp David process was unprecedented, both in scope and in detail, as the issues addressed derived from the core of Israeli and Palestinian identities, fears, emotional attachments and religious convictions. While Ehud Barak had brought the Israel public within reach of their long sought after goal of peace with the Palestinians by going further than any Israeli leader had gone in the past, or would likely go in the future, it is now evident that Arafat was incapable of or unwilling to make the transition from a freedom fighter to statesman.[46] Barak, realizing the trap which was being set for him, justified his "generous offer" on the need to establish whether or not Arafat was a genuine partner for peace. Clearly, to the Israeli people, he was not.

Such sentiment is not merely an expression of Israel frustration. In a post-Camp David interview, President Clinton praised Barak vis-à-vis Arafat, declaring him to be "more creative and more courageous."[47] American mediator Dennis Ross concluded, "when all is said and done...negotiations failed mainly because they ran into a brick wall called Yasser

Arafat."[48] Even Arafat's own allies were shocked. Prince Bandar Bin Sultan of Saudi Arabia, for example, declared, "Barak's position was so *avant garde* that it was equal to that of Prime Minister Rabin," and that, "Arafat's failure to accept the deal in January of 2001 was a tragic mistake—a crime, really…"[49]

Even worse than missing another opportunity, Palestinians burst into a tantrum, which became known as the Second Intifada (or al-Aqsa Intifada). Had Arafat truly been an honest, able broker he would have acted quickly to diminish the impact of this uprising so that an atmosphere conducive to peace talks would have been kept alive. Instead he encouraged it, directed it, and even facilitated its growing intensity.

After refusing the Partition Plan of 1947; banking on misplaced reliance in 1948, 1967, and 1973; failure to act in 1978; acting badly in 1982; failing to abide by agreements in 1993; and failing to seize the prize at Camp David, when will the Palestinians and their leadership finally do what is necessary to establish a Palestinian State? When will the Palestinians and their leaders finally do what is necessary to establish a Palestinian state living side by side in peace with Israel?

More than Ten Years Later: Still Waiting for an End to Violence

More than ten years later, Israelis and Palestinians are about as far apart as they have ever been. Various Palestinian factions have since waged an unrelenting campaign to kill more Jews than their rivals in an effort to win the approval of bloodthirsty terrorists. When the Israelis built a wall to stem the tide of terrorist attacks, Palestinians responded by randomly bombing Israeli towns. When Israel unilaterally withdrew from Gaza as a measure of good faith to promote peace, Palestinians stepped up their attacks—not only against Israel, but against each other as well.

Despite all of these rejections, Israelis will not give up on peace.

Today, Mahmoud Abbas and the Palestinian Authority lead the Palestinians in the West Bank while Hamas continues to rule Gaza. Since Hamas is considered to be a terrorist organization, neither Israel nor the United States considers Hamas as a legitimate partner for negotiations. In essence, all the Palestinians of Gaza need to do is to renounce violence and recognize the State of Israel. Instead, Hamas remains committed to Israel's destruction.

The peace process is now being considered via a "unity government" between the Palestinian Authority of the West Bank and the Hamas government of Gaza. In late 2011, Israel was dubious about the possibility of negotiating with this proposed alliance. However, Netanyahu continues to invite the PA President, Mahmoud Abbas, to the negotiating table—an invitation which Abbas refuses, all the while declaring that Jewish settlements are the main obstacle to peace.

From the Israeli point of view, the only way to achieve peace is for the Palestinians and Israelis to negotiate directly with each other. We ask that our Arab and Palestinian neighbors recognize Israel's right to exist as the Jewish homeland. And we insist that violence be renounced.

Israelis believe that when the Palestinians in the West Bank and Gaza are governed by peace-seeking leaders who are willing and able to stop the violence and eliminate the vengeful and aversive attitudes towards Jews and Israelis, there will be peace.

Obama Administration Attempts

The Presidential election victory of Barak Obama in 2008 brought new energy and hopeful attempts to bring peace to Palestinians and Israelis. These attempts have fallen short, as the Palestinians continue to disregard the essential ingredients for successful peace negotiations.

Progress is being made in the Palestinian Territories of the West Bank where the Palestinian Authority is delivering better economic conditions for its citizens.

The Obama administration believes that institutional and economic development in the West Bank will ease Israel's security concerns and is thus a fundamental prerequisite to peace. This "West Bank First" approach, however, is fraught with several challenges:

1. It has only nominally addressed Israel's security needs.

2. It relies on a mistaken belief that Hamas in Gaza will simply change or go away.

3. It is tantamount to passive approval of sanctions and the isolation of Gaza.

4. Simply stated, there is no single Palestinian government with which to negotiate. The elected Hamas government in Gaza is considered to be a terrorist entity by the United States and Israel because Hamas calls for the destruction of Israel in its Charter and endorses terrorist activities against Israeli civilians. So even if an agreement is made with the Fatah-led Palestinian Authority in the West Bank, Israel would still have to deal with Palestinians in Gaza who are governed by a terrorist organization.

5. Should Hamas join in a unity government with the Palestinian Authority in the West Bank, it would be asking Israelis to negotiate peace with an entity whose stated goal is to eliminate the State of Israel.

Even if one were able to overlook these hurdles, the Obama team has fallen short of facing the realities, complexities and inner-workings of the Palestinian-Israeli conflict. It may also be ignoring the influence and nuances of the turmoil spreading throughout the Arab world. The instability of the Arab region has resulted in turmoil for nearly every Arab country, overthrowing regimes in Tunisia, Libya and Egypt and threatening the viability of others, including Syria.

With more regime changes likely, the region may look extremely different within the coming years and it is uncertain whether new regimes will be more or less amenable to peace. The stakes are especially high for Israel because it exists as the only democratic, westernized, non-Arab country in the region. Whether Israel will be willing to risk extensive agreements with these new and unknown leaders is an important question—and unlikely.

Time will tell whether Obama's desire for a U.S. brokered peace agreement will become a reality during his administration. For most Israelis who would like nothing more, they are not particularly optimistic during these dramatically turbulent times in Middle East.

September, 2011, Palestinian Statehood Request for UN Recognition

The Palestinian unilateral request for recognition of Palestinian Statehood by the United Nations on September 24, 2011, was a move by Palestinian Authority President Mahmoud Abbas to gain recognition of Palestinian statehood directly from the UN rather than through negotiations with Israel. The Israeli government has been offering to reconvene direct peace talks to resolve the conflict between Israel and the Palestinians. Yet, Palestinian President Abbas has continually refused to negotiate directly with Israel and to deal in good faith with the Israeli government in order to resolve the Final Status Issues: borders, Jerusalem, settlements and refugees without any preconditions to the negotiations.

Although the bypass efforts to gain recognition of Palestinian statehood directly from the UN did occur, the Palestinian statehood bid remains in the "back rooms" of the United Nations. Many believe the Palestinians will not gain statehood through the UN because of realities in the Palestinian Territories and Gaza where there is no Palestinian unity. There is, however, a chance that Palestinians will be granted UN "observer status" (similar to that of the Vatican). However, it will not likely gain full UN member status.

Following Mahmoud Abbas's speech at the United Nations, Israeli Prime Minister Benjamin Netanyahu asked him, once again, in front of the nations of the world, to restart the peace talks. Netanyahu even offered to begin negotiations in New York, since both leaders were in the United States for a meeting of the UN General Assembly. In addition he said,

> To the Palestinians I also issue a call. Take Israel's outstretched hand. Seize the opportunities before us to advance down the real road toward peace, a road of solutions not resolutions, dialogue not monologue, and direct negotiations not unilateral declarations.[50]

This request to restart the peace talks through direct negotiations was ignored by the Palestinan PA President.

To us all, Palestine is a composite of history and myth, of memories and dreams, of nostalgia and visions, of possession and loss. Its loss has touched us all and imprinted us with an indelible melancholy and fierceness…With one hand the world covered its eyes, and with the other shoved us aside lest we display our unseemly sores. And yet we dared assault the world with the discourse and vision of peace that only the victim can offer as the quality of redemption, and we gained an audience. And we have been offered back fragments of our dismembered land, to be pieced together slowly, and to be transformed into the quality of healing.[1]

The Palestinian State that the United Nations envisioned in 1947 in its partition of the Holy Land was never established. After the 1948 Arab-Israeli War, the land was carved up between Israel, Egypt, and Jordan. In a gross and collective denial of Palestinian rights, Israel claimed 77 percent of historical Palestine, while Jordan occupied and annexed East Jerusalem and the "West Bank" of the Jordan River, and Egypt took "temporary" control of the small coastal plain known as the Gaza Strip.

We lost more than our bid for statehood.

While the world was hypnotized by the mythological Zionist narrative of an empty Palestine that would serve as a homeland for the world's beleaguered Jews, the Palestinians lost what Edward Said referred to as "permission to narrate."

More recently, when the leadership of various Arab and Muslim states sought to participate in diplomatic negotiations with Israel on behalf of the Palestinian people, many of these negotiations fell short of the desires of the Palestinian people.

Egyptian Peace Agreement

In 1978 American President Jimmy Carter invited Israeli Prime Minister Menachem Begin and Egyptian President Anwar Sadat to begin a new series of peace negotiations between

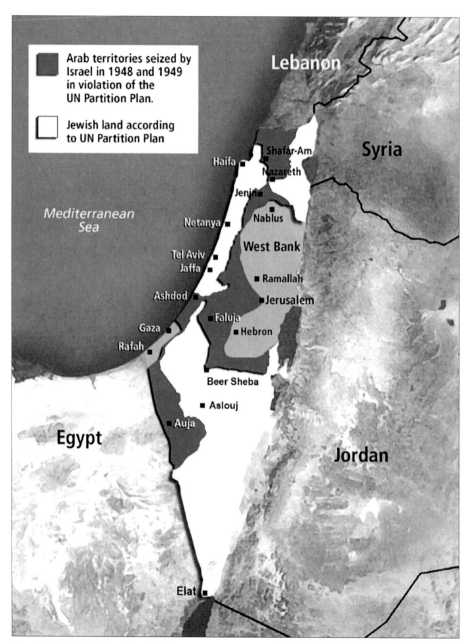

Map 23 | Palestinian loss of land, 1948

110 | Egypt-Israel Peace Treaty, 1978

Israel and Egypt and to establish a framework for resolving the Israeli-Palestinian conflict. Many Palestinians initially thought that Sadat would be the true champion of the Palestinian struggle. Once again, however, the dealings of Arab leaders with the Jewish State brought only more disappointment to the Palestinians. Heralded as a "turning point" in Middle East history, the 1978 Camp David Accords and the Israeli-Egypt Peace Treaty of 1979, failed to achieve a comprehensive resolution of the Palestinian question. Primary responsibility for the failure of the Accords and Treaty lays with Israel, which continued to confiscate Palestinian lands while building new settlements in the Palestinian Territories and even forging a separate peace agreement with Egypt.

For Palestinians, Israeli actions amounted to oppressive measures of war rather than an overture of peace.

111 | Camp David Peace Accords sealed with handshake, 1979

This separate deal between Israel and Egypt did not bring a comprehensive peace to the Middle East. Instead, the treaty enabled Israel to invade Lebanon in 1982, without fear of Egyptian aggression and intervention. The Israeli invasions of southern Lebanon resulted in the destruction of Lebanese towns and villages including Palestinian refugee camps. Hundreds of thousands of Lebanese and Palestinians were evicted from their homes as casualties of Israel's direct intent to destroy the PLO base there and annihilate any support for the Palestinian nationalist movement.

Despite the importance of peace and diplomacy between Egypt and Jordan with Israel, the fact remains that the Palestinian people remain in limbo after three decades of attempted diplomacy with Israel and its leadership. The three basic principles of Palestinian political demands include: the right of return for Palestinians, Palestinian self-determination, and the establishment of an independent Palestinian state.

Despite the lack of progress in negotiations, Palestinians have gained strength and resolve by developing an "inner reliance." Beginning in the late 1980s, rather than depend on the continual diplomatic failure of self-interested Arab intermediaries, the Palestinian people began to negotiate directly with the Israelis and speak to the world on their own behalf.

Central Issues of the Conflict and Its Resolution

Five key issues have animated every attempt at peacemaking between Israel and the Palestinians. They are: 1) Jerusalem, 2) borders, 3) settlements, 4) refugees and 5) security.

Jerusalem

In the debate over Jerusalem, the Palestinians are only asking for half of the city—East Jerusalem, which was controlled by Jordan before being captured by the Israelis in 1967.

The Old City of Jerusalem contains the third holiest site in Islam, the al-Aqsa mosque and the Dome of the Rock, from where Prophet Muhammed visited heaven on his winged steed. The Old City is also home to the Church of the Holy Sepulchre and several important sites to Palestinian Christians.

Meanwhile, the Israeli government is unwilling to divide or share Jerusalem. From its point of view, Jerusalem is the political and religious center of the Jewish people. In 1980, the government of Israel passed a law stating, "Jerusalem, complete and united, is the capital of Israel."[2]

In the history of negotiations for peace, Israel has consistently refused to share the city. Israel continues to confiscate Palestinian homes, displace Palestinian residents, and build Jewish-only housing facilities in historically Palestinian Arab neighborhoods. This causes tremendous tension and hostility between the peoples.

It is undeniable that the issue of Jerusalem will continue to be the heart and soul of Palestinian consciousness and the main cornerstone of any successful peace resolution. It is useless to talk about peace and the likely creation of a Palestinian State without resolving the issue of Jerusalem.

Borders

Since the Palestinian Declaration of Independence in 1988, the people of Palestine have recognized the existence of Israel and the borders of Israel as they were established before the 1967 War. The Palestinians want the peace talks to start from the basic position that all the land occupied by Israel in 1967 belongs to a future Palestine state. Any Palestinian land given to the Israelis would have to be compensated for by a balanced land swap. While Israeli Prime Minister Benjamin Netanyahu accepts that there should be a Palestinian State and that there will have to be an Israeli withdrawal from parts of the West Bank captured by Israel in 1967, Israel is unwilling to give up the large annexations that Israel has taken from Palestinians whose family ties to the land go back for centuries. Israel has already unilaterally withdrawn from Gaza, which, Prime Minister Ariel Sharon said at the time, would be the last and only Israeli withdrawal. Israel wants its own borders to include all of Jerusalem and the major Israeli settlements that have been built in the West Bank.

Settlements

The issue of the settlements has been the most contentious issue since the Oslo Talks. Armed and militant settlers regularly stage violent attacks on Palestinian civilians while the Israeli army stands idly by. Ideally, the Palestinians would prefer that Israel withdraw from all of its illegal settlements in the West Bank as they did in Gaza. However, the Palestinian leadership is also willing to accept the reality that some will have to stay.

With this understanding, Palestinian leaders argue for a minimum number of settlements to remain in exchange for a land swap to compensate for the loss of Palestinian land.

Settlement growth has been the key sticking point in more recent talks. Palestinians have

112 | Palestinian protesting against settlements, 2011

283

113 | Israeli settlement of Beit Ayre, West Bank, 2011

threatened to leave the talks if settlement construction continues. Palestinian Authority President Mahmoud Abbas has even threatened to resign if the building continues. This is especially important given the growth of settlements has escalated exponentially since the Oslo peace process of 1993—a pure violation of agreements in the eyes of the Palestinians.

Of course, the Israeli government insists on keeping the major Israeli settlements in East Jerusalem and the West Bank. Any departure from this position on settlements would break up the coalition on which the Netanyahu government rests. An immediate problem is that an Israeli moratorium on West Bank settlements expired on September 26, 2010, and there has been no immediate solution or extension of the moratorium.

The United States and the international community do not recognize Israel's annexation of East Jerusalem or any of the West Bank settlements as legitimate.

Palestinian Right of Return

Haqq al-awda, (the Right of Return) is considered a sacred right for Palestinians who were forced to flee their homes in the 1948 War. It is considered a political principle to repatriate Palestinian refugees to Israel, irrespective of how long they have been isolated from their homeland. The Right of Return is recognized by the UN General Assembly Resolution 194 which was passed on December 11,1948. Article 11 of Resolution 194 states:

> …that the refugees wishing to return to their homes and live at peace with their neighbors should be permitted to do so at the earliest practicable date, and that compensation should be paid for the property of those choosing not to return and for the loss of or damage to property which, under principles of International law or in equity, should be made good by the Governments or authorities responsible.[3]

The United Nations General Assembly also passed Resolution 3236 on November 22, 1974, which emphasizes the right of return for Palestinian refugees, considering such right as an "inalienable right." The number of Palestinian refugees from the 1948 War is estimated at between 700,000 and 800,000.[4]

Where are the Palestinian Refugees Today?

Generations of exiled Palestinians continue to live in the squalor of Palestinian refugee camps holding the keys to their family homes and deeds to their family land which was confiscated by Israel. The original Palestinian position on refugees was their total "right of return," which meant that the only way to correct this great injustice was to allow these people and their descendants to return to their land and their homes.

However, the fact is, many of these homes have been destroyed, or are occupied by Israeli citizens.

Recently, therefore, Palestinians have softened this position. For many, it would be acceptable to reduce the Right of Return to something less than 100 percent if Israel compensates Palestinians for their suffering and acknowledges that the Palestinians were the victims of Israeli crimes.

Israel rejects the idea that Palestinian refugees from any previous war should be allowed any "right of return" to their former homes in modern Israel. They claim that this is a ploy to destroy the identity of the Jewish State of Israel. For this reason Prime Minister Netanyahu has called for Israel to be recognized as a Jewish State. Palestinians worry that calling Israel the Jewish State is dangerous because it will lead to the expulsion of Arab Palestinians still living within Israel's borders. Palestinians consider this expulsion to be likely as they take seriously the problematic talk in Israel of "transferring" the non-Jewish population in Israel to areas of the Occupied Territories.

Security

Palestinians argue that security will come from the establishment of a viable Two-State Solution and not the other way around. When Palestinians obtain a sovereign state, with territorial integrity, freedom of movement within secure borders, peace will follow. PA President Abbas fears that the client-status of Palestine under Israeli occupation weakens the ability of the PA to govern and opens the Palestinian political arena to a Hamas takeover, as occurred in the Gaza Strip in 2007.

Certainly, Abbas and the Israeli government share the same fear that Palestine could one day fall into the hands of Hamas. Israel opposes Hamas because it intends to eradicate Israel and convert the entire region into Palestine. Israel insists on complete control of the PA, and also argues that a future state of Palestine be demilitarized. The central problem with Israel's demand for demilitarization is that it castrates the PA and the future Palestinian State from effectively governing itself.

The Palestinian Path to Reconciliation

While some Israeli historians wish to argue that Israel has made every effort to reach a peace settlement with the Palestinians only to be rebuffed by Arab rejectionists at every step, the record demonstrates that this is clearly not the case. To the contrary, in the words of former Israeli diplomat, Schlomo Ben-Ami: "Peace was not the priority for the Israeli leaders; settling land and absorbing immigrants was."[5]

Israel's stance on Jerusalem, settlements, borders, refugees, and security was clearly evidenced by its adamant resistance to any erosion of the territorial status quo that has emerged out of its 1967 victory.[6] However, by the late 1980s, it became clear to Israeli leaders that these issues and the Palestinian "problem" in its midst had not only persisted throughout two decades of military occupation, but that it was not going away.

As a result of the mass mobilization of hundreds of thousands of young Palestinians in the West Bank and Gaza Strip during the Intifada, the fall of the Soviet Union and the severe psychological toll taken by the Gulf War, the leaders of the Israeli Likud party accepted the fact that the Palestinian problem needed to be resolved.

The Path to Madrid

By 1991, the Intifada had ebbed and flowed for four years, while the rest of the world was witnessing monumental changes. The Soviet Union had fallen, and the American forces won the First Gulf War. Now allies, Russia and the United States sought ways to establish peace in the Middle East under President George H.W. Bush's mantra of a "new world order." American policy seemed to be shifting.

As early as 1989, the American Ambassador in Tunisia, Robert Pellitreau, over Israeli objections, met with a PLO delegation at the U.S. Embassy in Tunisia. When, in a press conference in Paris on May 9, Arafat retracted the PLO Charter, which called for the eventual disappearance of Israel, more pressure was put on Israel to negotiate. In May, U.S. Secretary of State James Baker told AIPAC (the Israeli lobby) that Israel should abandon its expansionist policies.

Soon American efforts concentrated on holding an international conference between Israel, the Palestinians and the surrounding Arab states on UN Resolutions 242 and 238. Jerusalem, refugees, and settlements were also on the agenda. In effect, the impending Madrid conference on October 30, 1991, was a moment when Palestinians believed their political rights would be realized.

Madrid Conference

Hosted by the Spanish Government and led by the United States and Russia, the Madrid Conference was an international conference conducted outside the auspices of the United Nations. The effort brought together Arab and international partners in the collective undertaking of establishing peace between the Palestinians and Israelis. Although a landmark in the formal recognition of Palestinians and Palestinian rights, the conference was fraught with complications from the start.

To start with, Israel stipulated that it would only attend the conference if the PLO (the now internationally recognized representative body of the Palestinian people) was prevented from participating. Israel also did its best to undermine Palestinian national rights from the start by refusing to discuss the issues of Jerusalem or of Palestinian statehood. To edge the process forward, the United States recognized obstacles to getting the conference started and, therefore, preliminarily accepted Israel's conditions for participating in the conference.

At the same time, the United States assured the Palestinian delegation that the political identity and rights of Palestinian people would be respected. The driving force for peace under the Bush Administration policy was two-fold: peace for Israel and land for Arabs. In effect, it became the first American Administration to explicitly support an independent Palestinian State.

The conservative Likud-led Shamir government, which condoned the expansive Jewish settlement policy in the West Bank and Gaza Strip, flatly rejected the Bush plan. Ultimately, however, Israel submitted to the "land for peace" principle, although it remained not the only party at the conference that stood in opposition to its proceedings.

Like Israel, there were other groups who opposed the Madrid Conference or any direct ne-gotiations for peace between Israel and the Palestinian people. Arab States, especially Syria and internal Palestinian groups such

114 | Madrid Peace Conference, 1991—Israeli negotiator Elyakim Rubinstein (right) shaking hands with Jordanian-Palestinian delegation head Majali

as Hamas, Islamic Jihad and other radical groups, argued that negotiations would not bring restitution to the Palestinians. Hamas argued that armed struggle against Israel was the only way to procure peace because the idea of territorial concessions to Israel and of two states coexisting in Palestine was an anathema to all of the Islamic movements."

Nevertheless, the Madrid Conference was held on November 30, 1991. Against all demands put forth by the Palestinians and delegations of Syria and Egypt, Israel declared that it would not withdraw from lands acquired through war, or according to the UN Resolutions 242 and 338. While this came as nothing new, what was unique about the Madrid Conference was the invigorated U.S.-led effort to implement the UN resolutions and allow the Palestinian people to speak with a single voice.

For many Palestinians, the Madrid Conference was the first serious attempt at creating a Palestinian State since the early 1940s. For both sides of this long struggle it represented the possibility of mutual acceptance and co-existence. It was an earnest undertaking met by few serious supporters. Although the conference legitimized Palestinian national rights and eventually affirmed the leadership of the PLO, it did not bring political parity to the Israelis and Palestinians. Whereas the Palestinians saw Madrid as the necessary step for making peace with Israel and procuring Palestinian Statehood at long last, the Israelis saw it as a tool for containing the Intifada.

Although meaningful expectations were not met in the Madrid Conference, negotiation and diplomacy were now an important aspect of the Palestinian political agenda for peace and statehood. Importantly, mutual recognition of both sides was a landmark moment in the trajectory toward future negotiations.

Madrid Disappointments

For Palestinians, a glaring omission in the Madrid talks was the Palestinian right of return. This critical topic was not addressed at all, even though it was held as the highest priority for the Palestinian people. Instead, the Israelis demanded that the Palestinians formally recognize the Jewish State under Resolution 181, but failed to meet their side of the bargain by refusing to recognize the Palestinians' right of return.

It is also critical to note that the Two-State Solution with Palestine and Israel living side-by-side was broached. Despite Israeli reticence on the issue, the Palestinian diplomatic negotiators continued to push for a Palestinian State along the June 1967 borders, for a homeland where the Palestinian people could live in peace and dignity and for a fair resolution of the refugee problem.

From the perspective of the Palestinian delegation at Madrid, the purpose of negotiating for peace was not to lose more Palestinian land, further negate Palestinian rights, or to continue to suffer the shame and brutality of the Israeli occupation. In working for peace, the members of the Palestinian delegation were tasked with the literal responsibility of saving Palestinian lives. However, "we wanted to save lives, not to be patronized into submission."[7] It was clear from U.S. behavior that it was not free to shape its own policies due to Israeli bullying and manipulation.

Ironically and unfortunately, what has prevailed from Madrid is an image of Palestinian intransigence. It seems the insistence by the Palestinians to be represented by their own chosen representatives (rather than by other Arab nations) has been misconstrued into the notion that the Palestinians were unwilling to pursue peace. This was far from the truth.

To the Palestinians and their chosen representatives, the premise of peace was predicated on the recognition of true Palestinian statehood. That meant that recognition of Palestine as a separate national identity with its own sovereignty was central to the negotiations. In the 1988 Palestinian Declaration of Independence, Palestinian leaders recognized the existence of Israel. In return, the Palestinians were looking for recognition of their own nation. In doing so, the true voice of the Palestinian people emerged.

Palestinian Demands Change

As negotiations continued beyond Madrid, one significant aspect of the Israeli-Palestinian peace process is the notable evolution of official Palestinian positioning vis-à-vis Israel. For example, when the Peel Commission proposed partition of Palestine in 1937 and again when the United Nations did the same in 1947, the concept of partition was rejected by the Palestinians on the principle of their all-or-nothing view of a unitary state over the entire land of Palestine.[8] As the decades wore on, this principle was also central to the Palestinian National Charter of 1968, which insisted in Article 2 that,

> Palestine, within the frontiers that existed during the British Mandate, is an indivisible territorial unit.[9]

Palestinian policy about the division of the land became more accommodating in the 1980s. By 1988, it had dramatically changed when the Palestine National Council (PNC) endorsed the principle of the partition of Palestine. More dramatically, the Palestinians formally agreed to a Two-State Solution.

However, this time it was Israel (under the Likud government) that rejected the idea of a clear partition of the land into two states. Instead, the Israeli Likud government laid claim to all the biblical Land of Israel, including "Judea and Samaria", otherwise known as the West Bank.[10]

In the words of then Prime Minister of Israel Yitzhak Shamir, who led the Israeli delegation at the Madrid Conference, "The past leaders of our movement left us a clear message to keep Eretz Yisrael from the sea to the river Jordan for future generations, for the mass alliya (Jewish immigration) and for the Jewish people, all of whom will be gathered into this country."[11]

Two-State Solution Mutually Accepted

Five years later, the mutual acceptance of a Two-State Solution to the conflict occurred and it was groundbreaking. By casting away this key ideological point of impasse more practical solutions could be negotiated for the sharing of the land and for the good of all of the people living in the Holy Land.

The Oslo Accords

The Madrid Conference of 1991 was co-sponsored by the United States and the USSR. An international peace-seeking assembly, it included several countries in the negotiating process. Hosted in Spain were delegations from Israel and the Palestinians, along with representatives from the European Union, Canada, Japan, Saudi Arabia, Syria, Lebanon and Jordan. However, the most important outcome of Madrid was a series of secret negotiations, which took place in the Norwegian capital, Oslo, and eventually led to the establishment of mutual recognition between Israel and the PLO. This mutual recognition was sealed in the historic handshake between Israeli Prime Minister Yitzhak Rabin and PLO Chairman Yasser Arafat on September 13, 1993, on the South Lawn of the White House. This was a momentous event in the history of the 20th century, and particularly one in which two leaders of the Middle East, "redrew the geopolitical map of the entire region" in one fell swoop.[12]

It almost didn't happen. Early in the negotiations, Israel nearly rejected the Palestinians in order to strike a deal with Syria.[13] During bilateral talks between Israel and Syria in Washington in 1994, under the Madrid Formula, it became apparent Syria was willing to establish peace with Israel in exchange for the total withdrawal from the Golan Heights. Of course, this would have forced Rabin to relinquish land won by Israel in the 1967 War—a move seen by some Israelis as contrary to the belief that the Land was given to the Jewish people by God and therefore could not be given up by Israelis. Even in the name of a real peace with Syria, the dismantling of Israeli settlements in the Golan Heights would prove too politically risky. Instead, Rabin concentrated on a deal with the PLO.

One of the contributing reasons why dealing with the Palestinians was the preferred option was the fact that agreements for Palestinian self-governance would take years to become codified, thus giving Rabin hope that staying in the Occupied Territories and building more settlements would eventually stem Palestinian demands for the land itself.

But if choosing the PLO over the Syrians was politically safer, it was not diplomatically easier. For one thing, talking directly with the PLO meant negotiating the right of return of Palestinian refugees. It also meant negotiating with Arafat.

For Rabin, Arafat was a main obstacle to reaching an agreement with the local Palestinian leadership in the Occupied Territories. Much against Rabin's will, he was "forced to recognize that he could not bypass the PLO and that, if he wanted a deal, a direct channel to Tunis would be necessary and that he would have to address himself to his archenemy, Yasser Arafat."[14]

Oslo I

Divided into phases, the Oslo Agreements took place in 1993 and 1995. The Hebron Protocol was signed in 1997. Known as Olso I, the first Oslo Agreement was signed on September 13, 1993. The agreement involved two key issues: 1) Mutual recognition between Israel and the PLO, and 2) the Declaration of Principles (DOP), which set an agenda for negotiations on Palestinian self-government in the Occupied Territories, beginning with Gaza and Jericho. Two letters on plain paper, without letterhead, were the symbols of mutual recognition.

In his letter to Rabin, Arafat "observed that the signing of the DOP marked a new era in the history of the Middle East." He confirmed the PLO's commitment to recognize Israel's right to live in peace and security, and accepted United Nations Security Council Resolutions 242 and 338. Arafat renounced the use of terrorism and other acts of violence. In addition he agreed to change the Palestine National Charter to align it with these new Palestinian concessions.

To this, Rabin replied with a terse, one-sentence reply to the leader of the Palestinian people. It confirmed that, "in the light of these commitments, the government of Israel had decided to recognize the PLO as the representative of the Palestinian people and to commence negotiations with the PLO within the Middle East peace process."[15]

However, in the continuation of these negotiations, it is vital to note that other significant issues arose from Oslo I. They included: the removal of international law—with the exception of the legal underpinnings of Resolutions 242 and 338—as the basis for resolving the Palestinian-Israeli conflict, the redeployment of Israeli forces from within areas of the Gaza Strip and West Bank, and the unlinking of interim and final status issues.

The linkage of these issues stymied talks at Oslo I, yet the decision to separate them in the name of making peace, ultimately did not serve the interests of the Palestinian people living in the Occupied Territories and beyond.

Certainly, in light of the United States' position that negotiations between Israel and the PLO would not necessarily entail a "land for peace" arrangement, it was clear to both sides that some land would have to be relinquished as part of the deal. However, Israel was bent on its own interpretation of Resolution 242, which meant not regarding itself as an occupying power, and therefore, denying the right of Palestinian statehood with borders, and equality for Palestinians.

115 | IDF soldier in West Bank, 2006

Moreover, although Israel and the PLO exchanged the nod of mutual recognition from the outset, there was ultimately no mutual sharing of power between them in the application of the agreements.

From the outset there were glaring problems with the Oslo I agreement. For starters, the DOP was entirely silent on issues which were vitally important to the Palestinian people, including: the right of return for 1948 refugees, the actual borders of a future Palestinian State, the status of Jerusalem and the future of Jewish settlements in the Occupied Territories. Thus, in exchange for diplomatically recognizing Israel and amending the PNA charter to reflect this change of ideology, the Palestinian people saw Arafat relinquishing all of their core principles in exchange for very small returns.

Palestinians suffered from more and more of their land being transferred into Israeli jurisdiction. Primarily, the West Bank was divided into cantons, favoring Jewish settlers, while diminishing Palestinian autonomy.

This issue was specifically noted in the second Oslo agreement (Oslo II), known as the "Interim Agreement," signed on September 28, 1995. The primary feature of Oslo II was the division of the West Bank into three areas, each of which had varying degrees of control under either the Palestinian Authority or Israel. In Gaza, this translated into the compromise of about a third of the land allocated to Israeli settlers. The remaining two-thirds of Gaza were cut into cantons, wherein 1.1 million Palestinians were forced to live. "This allotted roughly 128 Israelis per square mile in Gaza to 11,702 Palestinians per square mile."[16]

The West Bank was accordingly divided into Areas A, B, and C, which allotted full, partial, or no control to the PA. For example, it was agreed that in Area A, which, in its original state, was composed of seven major Palestinian towns, total civilian and security control was allotted to the PA. In Area B, which consisted of the remaining Palestinian population centers (excluding some refugee camps), control of civilians was placed in the hands of the PA, while security was placed under the control of Israelis. In effect, this placed Area B under Israeli jurisdiction. Finally, in Area C, Israel maintained full control of the area incorporating Israeli settlements and "state lands," including Israeli military bases in the West Bank.

Most important to the Palestinian perspective is that by 2000, the West Bank was cordoned off in such a way that Palestinians were left with very little control over non-contiguous land. For example, Area A comprised 17.2 percent of the West Bank, while Area B contained 23.8 percent.[17] This left 59 percent of the land to Area C. However, in practical terms, this meant that by the time of the Camp David Accords in 2000, Israel controlled nearly 83 percent of the West Bank (Areas B and C combined).[18]

Oslo Accords

Initially, at least, when the Oslo Accords were signed in September 1993, two-thirds of the Palestinian people supported it.[19] The Palestinian people regarded Oslo as the agreement that would bring better living conditions and an end to the occupation. During this time, support for Yasser Arafat leaped to 65 percent and a general embrace of the mainstream secular nationalist movement headed by Arafat was approved at 55 percent across the West Bank and Gaza Strip.[20] But this "golden era" of the peace process did not last long as Palestinian hopes for statehood faded with the election of Benjamin Netanyahu as Israeli Prime Minister in 1996, and by continuing and unrepentant building of Jewish settlements in the West Bank and Gaza Strip.

It is undeniable that the Oslo Accords have "irreversibly altered the legal and political landscape of the Middle East."[21] On the face of it, bringing Yasser Arafat as the emblematic leader of the Palestinian people back to Gaza in July 1994 represented a new beginning for the Palestinian people, which happily translated into governing themselves, in their own land. Even to the people of Gaza, Arafat was a symbol of national liberation and thousands greeted him with cheers. But "the circumstances, conditions

116 | PA guard, Ramallah, West Bank, 2011

and restrictions under which Arafat's regime was established were in fact not so different from the previous PLP administrations he had been heading, particularly the Palestinian state-within-the-state in Lebanon between 1972 and 1982."[22]

At the time of these negotiations, Arafat was confronted from within the PLO with accusations that he was allowing himself to be a pawn of the Israelis in exchange for power. Outside of the PLO, the militant Islamist resistance movements, Hamas and Islamic Jihad, regarded any compromise with the Jewish State as an insult to the Palestinian people and their struggle. As Edward Said wrote in his lambast of the Oslo Accord, "All secret deals between a very strong and a very weak partner necessarily involve concessions hidden in embarrassment by the latter."[23]

"The deal before us smacks of the PLO leadership's exhaustion and isolation, and of Israel's shrewdness."[24] President Assad of Syria even compared Arafat's actions with those of Anwar Sadat, whose separate deal with Israel gave way to Egypt's isolation and vilification, especially when Egypt stood silently by when Israel invaded southern Lebanon in 1982.

The problem with the outcome of Oslo was that the practical solutions for peace were never fair to the Palestinian people. What is worse is that from the standpoint of those living within the Occupied Territories, the Oslo process made it ever more legal for Israel to control the land. More remarkable was that by dividing the Territories into zones of varying jurisdictions, the Palestinians remained isolated in separate self-governing cantons, and therefore were unable to travel freely and unable to engage in effective commerce. By 2002, all Palestinians living in the West Bank lived within less than four miles of the Israeli-controlled territories of Area C.[25]

In the end, the territorial divisions agreed to in Oslo II set the precedent for a framework of the final settlement options in the West Bank that would favor Israeli settlements and expansion and preclude any territorial continuum for a future Palestinian State.[26] Tragically, by accepting the provisions of the Oslo Accord, Arafat accepted the legitimacy of the Israeli settlements in the Occupied Territories. By the time the last part of the Oslo agreement was put into effect with the Hebron Protocol signed into agreement on January 15, 1997, much of Palestinian land was already divided.

Hebron Protocol

The Hebron Protocol represented the first part of the Oslo agreement brokered by Rabin's successor, Netanyahu. Specifically addressing the governance and control of Hebron, a thriving economic center and city in the West Bank of historical importance to all three monotheistic faiths, the protocol effectively divided the city into two parts: H1 and H2. H1 consisted of 80 percent of Hebron, home to approximately 100,000 Palestinians, whereas H2 was composed of approximately 30,000 Palestinians and 250 to 400 Israeli settlers, who were protected by the Israeli army. Additionally, the H2 region encompassed the downtown commercial area of the city.

In a departure from the Oslo agreements, the Hebron Protocol contained no reference to UN Resolutions 242 and 338 as the legal framework for negotiations. More disconcerting however, is a letter appended to the document from former U.S. Secretary of State Warren Christopher, which explicitly pledged U.S. support for Israel's interpretation of its obligations under the accords, and also stipulated that Israel alone would decide on the time and scope of any future redeployments of the Israeli forces. Further redeployments by Israel would be conditioned by the Palestinians meeting their responsibilities—as defined by Israel alone.

Perhaps the most alarming aspect of the Hebron Protocol was that it ultimately appeared to make it more difficult for the Palestinians to achieve statehood, rather than being a step towards Palestinian Statehood.

Palestinian lands were further subdivided. The small resulting territorial enclaves in the Occupied Territories were then surrounded and fully controlled by Israeli forces. Armed Israeli settlers were allowed to remain in an important Arab population center. Finally, since the protocol clearly defined the right of Israel to unilaterally make decisions as to whether the Palestinian Authority was being compliant with the protocol, it appears that these were one-sided obligations.

From the Palestinian perspective, the series of Oslo Agreements made it possible for Israel to establish itself as the single authority, giving itself the power to determine the appropriation of land to the Palestinian Authority. This proved to be to the detriment of the Palestinian people.

Ultimately, the Israeli policy of closure devastated the Palestinian economy and people. By routinely and haphazardly closing roads, Israel totally restricted the free movement of Palestinians from one place to another. Using roadblocks and checkpoints has deliberately hindered the Palestinians from engaging in successful commercial endeavors. It has also prevented Palestinians from accessing necessities for their daily lives: from healthcare and education, to merely visiting relatives and friends in other neighborhoods.

As Sara Roy wrote in early 2002, "Closure has since become an institutionalized system in the Gaza Strip and the West Bank and, almost nine years after it was introduced, has never been lifted, although its intensity is subject to change."[27]

Moreover, in addition to the policy of closure, Israel remained firmly entrenched in the West Bank by placing military checkpoints throughout the West Bank and Gaza Strip, which further implemented its control over and separation of the Palestinian people in the Occupied Territories.

For the Palestinians, these policies became brutal tools for even greater and malicious oppression by Israel. In the end, Oslo effectively legalized Israeli control over the Palestinian people. Even former Israeli Foreign Minister Shlomo Ben-Ami, who served under Ehud Barak as Minister of Internal Security and chief negotiator at the Camp David negotiations, maintained that "in practice the Oslo agreements were founded on a neo-colonialist basis, on a life of dependence of one on the other forever."[28]

By 2000, what remained of the agreements was a Palestinian quasi-state that was far from viable and an unrelenting settler movement in Israel that would never allow for total Israeli withdrawal from the Occupied Territories.

Outcome of the Oslo Accords on Jordan-Israeli Relations

Although Jordan's King Hussein was angry with the PLO for being kept in the dark during their secret negotiations with Israel, the king had long maintained that peace between Israel and the Arab states was not only necessary but inevitable. In serving the strategic self-interests of Israel and Jordan, the 1994 Israel-Jordan Peace Treaty came as a historical continuum of Arab-Israeli negotiations resulting in a warm peace between the two countries that continues to this day. The treaty ended 46 years of tension between Israel and Jordan; however many Palestinians living on both sides of the Jordan River saw it as failing to address their grievances and another betrayal. Palestinians felt particularly betrayed when Jordan was delegated the role of protecting the Islamic shrines in Jerusalem.

Among all of the Arab states, Jordan was the most directly affected by the Oslo negotiations between Israel and the PLO. Strategically, a new alliance between Israel and the PLO could threaten Jordan's political stability if the Palestinians in the West Bank assumed too much power. Moreover, given the preponderance of the Palestinian population already existing in Jordan, the fear of a PLO-led takeover and transformation of the Hashemite Kingdom into a Palestinian Republic had long been the concern of Hashemite kings since the Palestinian refugee crisis began in 1948. Of course, rather than making a direct deal with the PLO, King Hussein preferred to deal with Israel.

During a meeting with King Hussein on a yacht on the Red Sea, Yitzhak Rabin reportedly assured the King that, "Israel remained firmly committed to upholding his regime, that Jordanian interests would be protected in dealing with the Palestinian issue, and that future peace strategy would be closely coordinated with Jordan."[29]

Ultimately, while conspicuously leaving Yasser Arafat out of the agreement process, the agreement between Israel and Jordan set forth a small exchange of territory to make the Jordanian/West Bank border conform to geographical landmarks. The treaty also opened the way for cooperation in trade, tourism, transport links, water resources, and environmental protection. In effect, it also secured Jordan's border with that of the West Bank, although the West Bank itself was still a contested territory between Israel and the Palestinians.

Impact of Oslo Accord to Camp David (2000)

From the start, the Oslo Agreement was rife with asymmetries, ambiguities, and contradictions. It was a systematic oppression of the powerful over the powerless.

Although mutual recognition fundamentally changed the character of the conflict at the diplomatic level, before long it became an obstacle to real peace. As Ian Lustick writes, the opponents of the Oslo peace process see it as a way to "pay lip service to the agreement while ignoring its political content and insisting that it be understood as a legal document and as a basis for pushing Israeli prerogatives and punishing Palestinian 'violations.'"[30]

On one hand, Jewish settlers and their ideological supporters saw any deal made with the Palestinians as a sacrifice of Jewish control and sovereignty over the biblical claims to Jewish lands, especially as their continued expansion of Jewish settlements and hold over East Jerusalem continued unabated.

Camp David Summit 2000

The opportunity to resolve these inequities occurred at the Camp David Summit meetings of 2000. This summit is often described as Ehud Barak's unprecedented and historically generous offer to come close to an agreement and Yasser Arafat's uncompromising response of "no."

While it is said that "the Palestinians never miss an opportunity to miss an opportunity," this remarkably shallow statement, fails to take into account the historic complexities and dynamics of the negotiations process. Offering up Arafat as the sole criminal and culprit of Israeli-Palestinian peace negotiations denies a more nuanced and far more realistic analysis to what was happening in the bigger picture at the time.

Of course, this perception was not helped by U.S. President Bill Clinton, who publically blamed Arafat for the summit's failure. Nevertheless, it has since been argued that the Palestinians were not alone when it came to the failures of the summit meetings. "The failure of the Oslo peace process was largely due to faulty negotiating styles, poor management of the implementation process, and the unwillingness of right-wing Prime Minister Benjamin Netanyahu to honor negotiated agreements."[31] More than anything, however, the peace process did not implement peace. Instead, it "intensified rather than mitigated Palestinian dispossession, deprivation, and oppression, and so precluded a fair and workable settlement of the Palestinian-Israeli conflict."[32]

In the years that stood between the signing of the DOP in September 1993 and September 2000, the real living conditions that existed in the Gaza Strip and West Bank steadily deteriorated. Most remarkable was that in light of these negotiations an influx of nearly 100,000 new Jewish settlers arrived in the West Bank and Gaza, effectively doubling the settler population that existed in previous decades. During this time, the Israeli government confiscated nearly 40,000 acres of Palestinian land for the construction of Israeli settlements and Israeli-only bypass roads to connect the settlements to the Israeli interior, while inhumanely dividing Palestinian population centers.

The majority of the confiscated Palestinian land was viable for farming and agricultural production. While the Palestinian people were starved for food, Israeli forces seized $1 billion worth of Palestinian agricultural land.

Meanwhile, the continued Israeli control over the West Bank and Gaza Strip during this "interim period" led to even greater Palestinian decline. Resulting from arbitrary yet consistent Israeli-imposed curfews and closures in the Occupied Territories there was a rise in Palestinian unemployment, increased poverty, school closures, and a rise in child labor rates.

The continued oppression of the Palestinian people that resulted from the Olso Agreements framed the foundation of the Palestinian perspective of the Camp David talks in 2000. Although the Camp David negotiations largely pertained to territorial swaps between the two parties, the main issues driving Yasser Arafat at the time were jurisdiction over Jerusalem, including the Haram al-Sharif, and the Palestinian right of return. By the time of Camp David, the Palestinian Authority was a "rump authority, dependent on Israel for its every slightest action, presiding over a mere 20 percent of their territory."[33]

However, with hope in their hearts, the Camp David negotiations were to bring about the moment that the Palestinians had longed for: a third phase of Israeli redeployment, in other words, a major military retreat from the Palestinian Territories. Yet going into the negotiations, Yitzhak Rabin's untimely successor, Ehud Barak, aimed to "force Arafat to undertake the final round of negotiations after receiving the fewest possible concessions."[34]

Mistrust and Intransigence

Certainly, Barak's strategy was contrary to the spirit of Oslo, which was namely to build trust. Inevitably, the breakdown of negotiations at Camp David was mired in mistrust and intransigence. From the Palestinian point of view, the devastating occupation had become systemic. By that time, the Palestinians were refusing any further concessions to the Israelis.

From the Palestinian perspective, the failures of Camp David stem from Israel's incomprehension of the Palestinian reality. The tragedy here is that instead of seeing the history of a nation of refugees, and the enduring military occupation that was a result of the creation of the State of Israel as problematic to peace, the negotiators at Camp David saw the political and military presence of Israel in the Palestinian Territories as morally and politically legitimate. The Israeli negotiators failed to take into consideration that the discussion of the Palestinian refugee question had been on the table since the Madrid Conference. At the same time, Israel demanded that Arafat sign an accord in which he would give up further claims.

Thus, the Camp David fiasco truly began when Israeli negotiators had the audacity to think that after all of the horrific machinations of the Oslo Agreements, any Palestinian leader would be able to sign a peace agreement renouncing the rights and recognition of Palestinian refugees living stateless in the Diaspora.

Ironically, the Israeli proposals at Camp David were said to have been the most generous that the Palestinians could ever get. This was evident in Barak's move to final status talks before negotiating the third phase of redeployment. The move put the Palestinian negotiators in the position of having to discuss permanent-status arrangements of the Israel-Palestinian borders, including everything therein while it only controlled 17.2 percent of the West Bank and 66–80 percent of the Gaza Strip in isolated enclaves.[35] In the end, although Barak did talk about Jerusalem, the Temple Mount/Haram al-Sharif, refugees, and the return of Palestinian territory the Prime Minister's negotiations with the Palestinians was not a true compromise. To the contrary, Barak's vision of a final settlement translated to Israel's annexing large settlement blocs in the Territories and retaining total control.

Ultimately, Barak's famous "offer" to return 90 percent of the West Bank was an exchange for annexing Palestinian lands that left a sizeable portion of the Jordan Valley completely under Israeli control. This "generous offer" did not include East Jerusalem, nor did it account for the fact that the majority of the Gaza Strip would be returned to Palestinian control in separated and Israeli-encircled cantons.[36]

It was an overly rigid peacemaking attempt that presented the Palestinians with little room for negotiation. From the Palestinian perspective, the amount of land returned to the Palestinians was not as significant as who had control over each area of land. The primary reason for failure, from the Palestinian viewpoint, is that since the Israelis maintained ultimate power and control over land designations, Israel would continue to negatively impact Palestinian life just as it had done during the occupation.

Road Map (2003)

In the wake of the failure of the Camp David meetings in 2000, a renewed cycle of violence ignited between Israelis and Palestinians. Oslo failed to deliver, and the Palestinians were left far more destitute than when they entered into negotiations with Israel at the end of the First Intifada. Between 2000 and 2003, nearly 3,000 lives—the majority of them Palestinian—were claimed in the new round of violence, and this does not include the 20,000 others injured, many of them children.[37] On the Palestinian side, there was already little faith left in the peace process and many Palestinian groups, including Fatah, prepared for the probable failure of the negotiations and the renewal of attacks. On the Israeli side, the IDF began conducting exercises for the retaking of Palestinian cities.

A new negotiating framework was desperately needed. Rather than relying on Oslo as the only process available, it was now evident that the elements missing or silent in Oslo were the most vital to bringing about an end to the conflict. The issues of land, settlements, Jerusalem, refugees, and borders remained central to Palestinian objectives, which could clearly not be delayed or ignored in any future negotiations.

117 | Red Sea Summit leaders, 2003 (from left to right: Palestinian Prime Minister Abu Mazen, U.S. President George W. Bush, Israeli Prime Minister Ariel Sharon, and King Abdullah II of Jordan)

In September 2003, the United States saw the opportunity to focus on the resuscitation of peace building in the Middle East as a way of bringing peace, stability, and democracy to the region as a whole.

With this, the United States sponsored the "Roadmap" for a peaceful solution to the Israeli-Palestinian conflict. After Clinton's failure at Camp David, the George W. Bush administration saw Israeli-Palestinian negotiations as part of a larger sweeping Middle East strategy. Bush "embarked on a titanic enterprise aimed at dismantling the Iraqi tyranny, restructuring the Middle East, knocking down al-Qaeda, and helping democracy put down roots throughout the Arab world."[38]

Somewhere in this obviously flawed plan, Jerusalem issues were connected with the instability caused by U.S.-enforced regime change in Baghdad. As Schlomo Ben-Ami adds, "an Arab-Israeli peace was meant to emerge almost as an inevitable by-product of an American victory in Iraq."[39]

The "Roadmap" became a document jointly drawn by the "quartet," otherwise known as the United States, Russia, the European Union, and the United Nations, which provided for the establishment of a Palestinian State in the Occupied Territories. Although the notion of bi-nationalism was not a new one, what was unique about the "Roadmap" was that it stated a "goal-driven" and "performance-based" approach to permanently settling the Israeli-Palestinian conflict within a period of two years. In exchange for actual statehood, it required the Palestinian Authority to make democratic reforms and abandon the use of violence. Meanwhile, Israel was required to support and accept the emergence of a reformed Palestinian government and end settlement activity in the Gaza Strip and West Bank.

From the Palestinian perspective, there was no hope for the "Roadmap" without genuine cooperation from both sides. The concept of interim agreements had become utterly obsolete, if only because the Israelis were incapable of paying the political price of true compromise in a piecemeal process.

However, Israeli Prime Minister Ariel Sharon rejected the main requirement of Israeli participation when he rejected the settlement freeze, saying this was "impossible" due to the "need" of settlers to have new houses for expanding their families.[40] Again, settlement growth and perpetuation continued to be a slap in the face of the Palestinians.

By 2003, anything to ameliorate the humanitarian crisis facing the Palestinian people would have been an improvement. Nearly 70 percent of the population was living below the poverty line, existing on $2.00 per day.[41] The situation was not helped by more than 150 Israeli military checkpoints in the Occupied Territories. Additionally there was rapid expansion of Israeli settlements during the Oslo years. Ironically, calling for the strengthening of Palestinian democracy prompted the Palestinian parliamentary elections in 2006, in which Hamas won a surprise victory, giving the Islamist party 76 of the 132 seats in the chamber with the Fatah party trailing the Hamas majority by 43 seats. Any Palestinian will

118 | Bethlehem checkpoint protest, 2005

say that the democratic vote for Hamas was an expression of collective exasperation at the corruption of the Fatah party within the PA, as well as its inability to deliver peace or protect its own people from Israeli control.

Outcome of Roadmap

By 2006, many declared the "Roadmap" dead. While the Israelis appeared to be complying, at a minimum, with the demands of this particular version of peace, it was revealed later that the construction of settlements had continued unabated throughout the "Roadmap" years. This was set against the backdrop of the unilateral Israeli pullout of settlements in Gaza in 2005. Although the disengagement plan from Gaza came as a shock to many, it also was not surprising when Prime Minister Ariel Sharon stated that the disengagement from Gaza would be the only Israeli withdrawal from the Occupied Territories. Sharon denied any intention of carrying out a second unilateral pullout from the West Bank.

Perhaps to ease the relocation of Israeli settlers from Gaza, many new neighborhoods were systematically built by Israel on the edge of areas of West Bank settlement jurisdiction, which expanded well beyond original agreements and, in many cases, was carried out on private Palestinian land.[42] So-called "security" issues were given as the central reason for the growth of settlements. Yet, as Ha'aretz reported, Israel exploited the violence of the Intifada by arguing that the settlers should not be exposed to security risks, while Palestinian farmers were prevented access to their properties as their land had been annexed into Israeli settlements.[43]

Where the Peace Process Stands Today

Today, Palestinian Authority President Mahmoud Abbas, remains in limbo as the leader of a quasi-state still at the mercy of its most pernicious neighbor. As ever before, the issue of settlements and settlement growth remains central to negotiations between the Palestinians and the Israelis. Israel halted most settlement construction for ten months in November 2009, saying it viewed the politically "difficult step" as a gesture to bring the Palestinians into direct peace talks. Abbas consented to the talks nine months later but threatened to abandon them if the freeze was lifted. In light of the failure of more recent talks led by U.S. Secretary of State Hillary Clinton and despite international pressure to discontinue the building of the West Bank settlements, the Netanyahu administration has lifted the ban on settlement construction. In response, Abbas has not only left the talks but he has threatened to resign.

Abbas's resignation could quickly bring about the collapse of the PA. With this, the civil authority of the entire West Bank, including zones A and B controlled by Israel, could be returned to Israel or transferred to the United Nations. As ever before, the "all or nothing" desire for land and real statehood on the Palestinian side remains clear and inviolable from the Palestinian side of negotiations, even as land has been continuously confiscated and built upon by Israel since the Oslo Accords. However, a potential resignation by Abbas may well bring about a third Intifada, and without an internationally recognized Palestinian leader, this will have very serious ramifications on any prospect of peace.

One thing is ultimately clear to Palestinians. Our demand for statehood includes sovereign, contiguous territory, fairness and equality. The recognition of the Palestinian right of return and compensation for refugees, reconciliation on the issue of settlements and the final fate of East Jerusalem remain essential issues for future and successful peace negotiations. I should emphasize that any attempts of not taking these issues seriously is, in my view, a waste of time and not a serious effort to resolve the conflict.

Barak Obama and the Palestinians

In 2008 I was impressed by presidential candidate Barak Obama, who promised to solve the Palestinian-Israeli conflict through mediated negotiations. I believed his efforts were genuine and most Palestinians accepted his even-handed approach to resolving our issues. At the beginning of his administration, we welcomed his outreach to Muslims worldwide as a milestone in U.S.-Arab relations.

However, once Obama became president, it became evident early on that it would be hard for him to fulfill his campaign promises. Under pressure from the Jewish-American community and the Israeli Netanyahu government, he seemed to bend.

It is a shame that Obama has not been capable of accomplishing more for the Palestinians including the right of return, obtaining East Jerusalem as our capitol, and stopping the expansion of Jewish settlements.

As recently as August 2011, Netanyahu indicated his willingness to negotiate the 1967 borders. Sadly, I believe I represent most Palestinians by saying that I will believe it when I see it. We are tired of rhetoric that sounds good. We don't want to get our hopes up too high and then be disappointed once again. The time for action is now.

Mahmoud Abbas Requests Recognition of Palestinian Statehood from the UN

On September 23, 2011, Palestinian Authority President Mahmoud Abbas delivered an historic speech to the UN General Assembly in New York requesting UN recognition of Palestinian statehood. Greeted by cheers, whistles and long-standing applause from most of the UN delegates, he expressed the heartfelt desires of his people. "...After 63 years of ongoing catastrophe, we say enough, enough, enough. It is time for the Palestinian people to gain their freedom and independence..."

This request for recognition by the UN was a proud moment for Palestinians who support PA President Mahmoud Abbas and admire his courage to stand in front of the nations of the world and demand recognition of Palestinian statehood. Palestinians point to the fact that since Israel became a country by a UN vote in 1947, then certainly, after six decades of suffering and oppression at the hands of Israeli occupation, the Palestinian people, including millions of Palestinian refugees, deserve to have their land be recognized by the UN as the sovereign State of Palestine.

With a great deal of pride, Palestinians in the West Bank witnessed Abbas' action at the United Nations as a demonstration of strength. They have continually been disappointed by the peace process that has failed to deliver relief of their suffering, liberation from Israeli occupation, or the establishment of a Palestinian homeland.

Abbas worked stalwartly to gain the support of 122 member states, who pledged their intention to vote in favor of recognition of Palestinian Statehood by the General Assembly of the UN.

Even though Israel and the United States threatened to cut off humanitarian aid to the Palestinian Authority if Mahmoud Abbas requested statehood from the United Nations, the Palestinian leader persevered and gained the admiration of his people and their supporters around the world for his impressive speech at the UN. Indeed, although his efforts at the UN may not result in immediate statehood, his initiative unquestionably raised support for Palestinian liberation and advanced the prospects for the establishment of the State of Palestine.

Mahmoud Abbas wrote in his request to United Nations:

> I have the profound honor, on behalf of the Palestinian people, to submit this application of the state of Palestine for admission to membership in the United Nations.

> This application for membership is being submitted on the Palestinian people's natural, legal and historic rights and based on United Nations General Assembly resolution 181 (II) of 29 November 1947 as well as the Declaration of Independence of the State of Palestine of 15 November 1988 and the acknowledgement by the General Assembly of this declaration in resolution 43/177 of 15 December 1988.

> In this connection, the state of Palestine affirms its commitment to the achievement of a just, lasting and comprehensive resolution of the Israeli-Palestinian conflict based on the vision of two states living side by side in peace and security, as endorsed by the United Nations Security Council and General Assembly and the international community as a whole and based on international law and all relevant United Nations resolutions.[44]

Looking Back

Throughout these decades of negotiations, I have to admit that Arafat was a constant presence. And because of that, one cannot dismiss the influence of Arafat. He was one of the fighters who upheld the objective of the sacred return to Palestine.

But he lost the momentum towards fulfilling the sacred dream of every Palestinian. He was part and parcel of the Arab League establishment and part of the failed rhetoric. When he spoke at the UN, he did not represent the Palestinian people. He wore the keffiyeh as if it was his own symbol. Wearing the keffiyeh means nothing to me. It does not make you more of a Palestinian.

All of his actions were intended to maximize his power. It seemed like a play on the stage. He was the ringmaster.

I'm not sure that anyone in political leadership represented the true will of the Palestinian people.

In terms of Arab leadership, the last figure I can point to who was earnest about the Palestinian people was Nasser. He was honestly concerned about the issue. He fought for the Palestinians. He stood strong to resolve the Palestinian and Jordanian conflict. He couldn't resolve it, and he died the day after he returned from Amman.

Intifada translates into English as "uprising" or "rebellion." But in Arabic it literally means "shaking off." The difference in those definitions reveals how Israelis and Palestinians separately view these events, especially the Second Intifada.

To Israelis, the Intifadas have been well-orchestrated terrorist operations that are more pernicious than the formal wars of the past. In a few seconds, bombs have turned busy markets and quiet neighborhoods into killing zones. That Palestinian leaders would pay their youth to blow up innocent civilians has created a mindset of fear spawning more aggressive security measures.

To Palestinians, the Intifadas have been honest outbursts of nationalistic frustration by oppressed people fighting for their freedom. Betrayed by the Arab nations and Western powers, they have been crowded into squalid refugee camps while Israel expands and prospers. Suicide bombers not only brought a dose of suffering to their oppressors, but the attacks offered terrorists a path to paradise—and Allah. For freedom fighters who'd lost hope for a better future in this world, attacking Zionists offered them martyrdom.

Whatever the interpretation, one thing is clear: trust on both sides was a victim of the Second Intifada.

The Second Intifada was the most reprehensible terrorist campaign against innocent Israelis in our nation's six-decade history. It persisted for five years, until our additional security measures succeeded in ending the barrage of terror in 2005.

Ironically, it occurred on the heels of our greatest hope for peace. In negotiations throughout the 1990s, Israel offered more in concessions to the Palestinians than ever before, more than many Israelis ever thought possible—or even sensible. Even the most generous terms were rejected.

Following these offers of concessions to the Palestinians, Israelis severely suffered from yet another turbulent and deadly uprising.

The Second Intifada

For five consecutive years innocent Israeli teenagers were killed at beachfront gatherings. Parents were struck down in neighborhood pizza parlors. Families were massacred at religious gatherings, and commuter buses were bombed during rush hour. For Israelis, saying goodbye to children and loved ones in the morning became a daily, frightening proposition. When Israel retaliated by targeting the perpetrators of terror as well as their weapons caches in the West Bank and Gaza, Palestinian communities erupted in violence and blamed the Israelis for the deaths of their loved ones caught in the crossfire.

Public opinion, vis-à-vis the Palestinians, took a nose dive during the Second Intifada, known as al-Aqsa Intifada. For many Israelis, the conclusion was inescapable: "We offered them peace, and we got terror in return."

The Second Intifada was significantly different from the first Palestinian uprising of 1987–1993. It was less of a grassroots movement and more of a strategically orchestrated barrage of violence planned and endorsed by the upper echelons of Palestinian leadership. Yasser Arafat called upon the Palestinian people to commit acts of violence. Many analysts believe he was directly involved in the mayhem and used it specifically to deflect attention away from his stubborn performance at the Camp David summit, when he rejected offers for a Palestinian State.

Unfortunately, his strategy worked. Media coverage of Palestinian funeral vigils revealed the hysteria of the crowds. It seemed as if each funeral procession fueled more hatred and increased vengefulness. The recruiting of suicide bombers increased with each display of sorrow. Rumors spread that families of suicide bombers received hefty martyrdom payments directly from Arafat. Time and again, Palestinian leaders glorified those who strapped bombs on themselves to kill as many Jewish civilians as possible.

For Israelis, it was a frightening time and there was no end to the violence on the horizon. Unlike previous wars there were no large Arab armies amassing at the borders. Instead, Israelis viewed the charred and mutilated remains of their relatives and fellow citizens strewn across the streets of their cities. Internal security understandably became a paramount national priority.

During the horrors of the First Intifada, Palestinians targeted Israeli security forces operating in Palestinian centers. By now, however, Israeli forces no longer routinely patrolled Palestinian communities and neighborhoods. As a result, Palestinian terrorists brought their renewed attacks into the heart of Israel's cities. Drive-by shootings, ambushes, mortar attacks and most disturbingly, wave after wave of suicide bombings became the *modus operandi* of Palestinian terror.[1]

The result of this organized chaos was not only the death of thousands, injury of tens of thousands, and the terrorization of millions, but it also encouraged Hamas as an ever-more popular alternative to the PA leadership. It also prompted unprecedented Israeli defensive measures and nearly eliminated the idea of "negotiated peace" from the Israeli-Palestinian dialogue. Trust was virtually eliminated from both sides.

Arafat's Role in the Outbreak

Palestinians blame the al-Aqsa Intifada on Israeli opposition leader Ariel Sharon's visit to the Temple Mount on September 28, 2000. Despite being Judaism's holiest ground, only a handful of Israelis have ever set foot on this 36-acre compound, which has been the site of the Muslim Dome of the Rock shrine and the al-Aqsa Mosque since the 7th century.

When Ariel Sharon walked on the Temple Mount, the Second Intifada ignited. But there are indications that Palestinians had already been planning violence. Arafat played the differing Palestinian factions, often relaying different messages to different groups. Many believe that when Arafat called a halt to violence in speeches heard in the West in English, he was inciting groups to violence in his backyard in Arabic. For example, Arafat used the pretext of Israel's opening of a second entrance to a pre-existing archeological tunnel in Jerusalem in 1996 to incite an uprising. In fact, this tunnel, which dates back to the Hasmonean Era,

119 | Temple Mount

is located hundreds of yards away from Haram al-Sharif and therefore is neither historically nor geographically connected with Islam or the Palestinian people.

Nevertheless, Arafat encouraged a group of security officers in Gaza to go out and fight Israel, stating:

> Our Palestinian people will not stand idly by when their holy sites are being violated... Oh our pure martyrs. Rest in peace, calm and assured. Our blood is cheap for the sake of the goal that had united us in the past...The believers shall inherit paradise. They shall fight for Allah and kill and be killed.[2]

Arafat's speech was subsequently broadcast on Palestinian television along with a recurring message from the Legislative Council urging the population "to move immediately and effectively to meet this criminal scheme."[3] While the appeal did result in the gathering of large crowds throughout the Territories, it did not produce scores of martyrs as Arafat had hoped for. It did improve Arafat's deteriorating standing amongst Palestinians who increasingly viewed the PA as corrupt and abusive. It also provided cover for the release of scores of prisoners, and at the same time, presented a credible threat to Israel.

As such, the tunnel incident set an important precedent, which would later be drawn upon to spark the al-Aqsa Intifada: whenever the need arose, Arafat would incite violence at a level commensurate with the perceived severity of the issue.[4]

Commenting on Arafat's strategy in the fall of 1996, UN Special Envoy to the Middle East Terje Rod-Larsen, a key figure in the Oslo peace process, proclaimed that "Arafat constituted the foremost obstacle to peace, and that the [Oslo] process would be more stable and successful if he disappeared altogether from the political scene."[5]

Taking cues from the First Intifada, Arafat concluded that the best means of gaining leverage in peace negotiations was through the threat of violence and its use. Accordingly, during the months prior to Camp David, dozens of convicted militants were released from Palestinian prisons and terrorist arsenals multiplied. Simultaneously, Palestinian children attending summer camps received military training.[6] Palestinian airwaves were flooded with a daily barrage of incitement through speeches, interviews, sermons, and documentaries detailing Israel's alleged transgressions.[7] All of this provocative choreography contributed to the outbreak of the Second Intifada.

The fact that Arafat was preparing for confrontation could also be construed from analyzing his obstinate performance at Camp David. As was described in detail in the previous chapter, Arafat rejected a Palestinian State on 93 percent of the Territories for the Palestinian homeland.

Later, former commander of the Democratic Front for the Liberation of Palestine, Mamduh Nofal, revealed that by early September Arafat's intentions were clear: "He told us, now we are going to the fight, so we must be ready."[8] Hamas leader, Mahmoud al-Zahar, confirmed such assertions in lectures given at Gaza University. Al-Zahar revealed that "President Arafat instructed Hamas to carry out a number of military operations in the heart of the Jewish state..."[9] In fact, Arafat's own communications minister, Imad Falouji, admitted in a December 2001 speech that, "the Intifada had been planned in July, far in advance of Sharon's provocation."

The overall situation was best summarized by Marwan Barggouti; founder of Fatah's military wing (the Tanzim) and a leader of both the First and Second Intifadas who in an interview with the *al-Hayat* newspaper exposed his role in igniting the al-Aqsa Intifada.

> On the eve of Sharon's visit, I participated in a TV panel on a local TV station. I found this to be the right opportunity to call upon the public to go to al-Aqsa on the following morning because it is not possible for Sharon to arrive at the Temple Mount [El-Haram al-Sharif] "just like that" and walk away peacefully. I was determined and early the next morning I went to al-Aqsa...
>
> I was dissatisfied with the small attendance and when friction did not occur, I became

angry. We tried to create friction, but with no success… War breaks out according to the decision of the president or the commander of the military… At the same time, I saw within the situation a historic opportunity to ignite the conflict. The strongest conflict is the one that initiated from Jerusalem due to the sensitivity of the city, its uniqueness and its special place in the hearts of the masses who are willing to sacrifice themselves [for her] with not even thinking of the cost.

After Sharon left, I had stayed in the area for two hours with other well-known people and we spoke about the character of the reaction and of how people should react in all the towns and villages and not only in Jerusalem. We made contact with all the factions."[10]

Arafat unleashed the instruments of his prearranged conspiracy to provoke an unprecedented armed struggle.[11] As early as September 13, members of Arafat's Fatah movement began carrying out attacks on Israeli military and civilian targets; including the bombing of Sgt. David Biril who was on patrol near Netzarim in the Gaza Strip.[12] While almost no violence occurred the following day when Sharon walked on the Temple Mount, Palestinian activists, religious leaders, media outlets and Arafat's propaganda machine ratcheted up their activities to full capacity—all but insuring an outbreak of violence the second day following Sharon's visit to the Temple Mount.

In an inflammatory sermon delivered on September 29, 2000, during Friday prayers in the al-Aqsa Mosque, Sheikh Hian al-Adrisi told the overflowing crowd of some 22,000 worshippers that "Jews wanted to storm the al-Aqsa Mosque and drive Muslims out of it."[13] He went on to incite violence by declaring:

It is not a mistake that the Quran warns us of the hatred of the Jews and put them at the top of the list of the enemies of Islam. Today the Jews recruit the world against the Muslims and use all kinds of weapons. They are plundering the dearest place to the Muslims, after Mecca and Medina and threaten the place the Muslims have faced at first when they prayed and the third holiest city after Mecca and Medina. They want to erect their temple on that place....

Al-Adrisi called upon worshippers "to sacrifice their lives and blood to protect the Islamic nature of Jerusalem and al-Aqsa!" Reacting to this vilification of Jews and Israel, within four days of the sheik's sermon, thousands were injured and at least 47 were dead in the streets of Jerusalem.[14]

Palestinian worshipers began pelting Jewish worshipers gathered at the Western Wall below them with stones and bottles. Police attempting to evacuate Jews under attack found themselves targeted at a police station located near the Temple Mount. This police station faced a frenzied Palestinian mob. As more Israeli police forcefully arrived to rescue officers trapped inside the besieged station, Radio Palestine broadcast a call to all Palestinians to come to the Temple Mount. As the day progressed and the number of rioters increased, stone throwing gave way to Palestinian gunfire and the launching of Molotov cocktails.[15]

It was Rosh Hashanah, the Jewish New Year. Unfortunately, the events of September 29 were merely a harbinger of what would amount to another year of tragedy.

Muhammad al-Dura's Death

If Arafat and Barggouti had any doubts that a full-scale uprising would take root, those doubts were firmly put to rest by the afternoon of September 30th. Filmed by a Palestinian cameraman working for the France 2 News Agency; the death of 12-year-old Muhammad al-Dura in Gaza, would be played over and over again on Palestinian television. Perhaps more than any other image, al-Dura's death quickly became "a potent symbol" against "Israeli aggression" which incited further violence.

The incident occurred at the Netzarim Junction at 3:00 pm when Palestinian rioters laid siege to an Israel Defense Force (IDF) position. Caught up in the ensuing gun battle were Muhammad and his father, Jamal. Cowering behind a concrete cylinder, the footage showed Jamal begging for the gunmen to stop firing just as his son was struck by a bullet. Approximately one half hour later, Muhammad was struck again and slumped over into his father's lap, apparently dead.[16]

There is no question that seeing the child's death did escalate the violence. It also condemned Israel for killing Muhammad al-Dura. However, Israelis questioned the authenticity of the video footage. There was strong evidence that the footage may have been staged and or tampered with in order to accuse the IDF of intentionally killing this Palestinian child.

Israelis view the death of children as reprehensible, and Muhammad al-Dura's death was no different. It was a tragedy.

As is regularly initiated by Israel in circumstances such as these, an investigation of the incident began immediately. Soon, investigators became suspicious of the original film broadcast by the France 2 News Agency. Analytical evidence began to mount clearly demonstrating that it would have been impossible for Israeli soldiers to have shot Muhammad or his father. Moreover and quite unsettling, careful review of the footage in question and the events it recorded pointed toward conspiracy.[17]

Setting aside the Israeli account of events as determined by an independent IDF investigation, a German investigation chronicled in a TV documentary, *Drei Kugeln und ein totes Kind* (Three Bullets and a Dead Child), found that at a minimum, the Israeli soldiers stationed at the outpost in question could not have killed the boy and that al-Dura may in fact have been shot by Palestinian gunmen.[18]

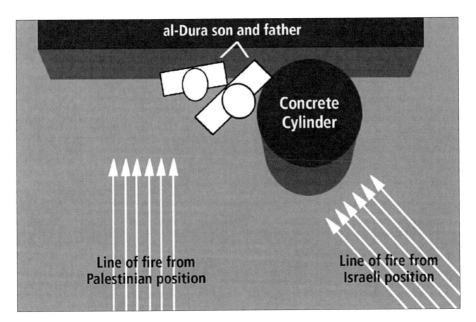

120 | Lines of fire in al-Dura's death

In 2004 Phillipe Karsenty, a French media analyst and founder of Media-Ratings, which monitors the media in France for bias, accused the French Television network France 2 of broadcasting staged footage of the reported killing of the 12-year old Palestinian boy. In response to the accusation, France 2 sued Karsenty for libel. Karsenty won his case in France's highest appellate court.

In the words of French writer Gerard Huber, "The entire event was staged." Reporter Charles Enderlin and France 2 News Network were unable to prove their case in a Paris appeals court. Having exhaustively reviewed the available footage, facts surrounding the case, and taking into consideration the fact that Enderlin and France 2 would not comply with full disclosure (denying the court access to 27 minutes of the original, unedited film), the court found in favor of Philippe Karsenty who declared "the report is a fake." Karsenty blamed Enderlin and France 2 for "fuel[ing] hatred of Israel, the Jews and the West around the world."[19]

This investigation of doctored images and faulty reporting is not the first of its kind. This one, however, dragged on.

France 2 filed a counter-suit asserting that Karsenty libeled the network in his accusation that footage of the death of Muhammad al-Dura was staged. The network initially was declared the winner, but the Paris Court of Appeals overturned the judgment in May 2008 when France 2 refused to release all the footage it had recorded on the day of the incident.

No matter the outcomes of these cases, the issue remains an important one. Are Palestinians staging deaths and fabricating Israeli wrong-doings to gain support for their cause? Or worse, are they staging hostilities to incite hatred and recruit additional terrorists?

Exactly what happened at Netzarim Junction that day will likely remain a controversy, demonstrating another example of each side perceiving the truth differently. Yet, what did become evident was the fact that the media played and continues to play a central role in people's perceptions about the conflict. In fact, Israelis know that Israel often loses the battle of public opinion when it acts against terrorists who operate among civilians, essentially using innocents as human shields.

As Yoram Meital notes in his in-depth study of the Israeli and Palestinian positions surrounding the peace process and ensuing Intifada, "The vicious cycle of brutality and rabid hatred was both self-sustaining and spiraling."[20] In the days following the death of Muhammed al-Dura, furious demonstrations broke out all across the Territories and in several Arab towns within Israel. While these events added more fuel to the fire it was the incidents of mid-October which seemed to signal the beginning of an all-out war encouraged by Arafat and his PA security forces.

Ramallah Murders of IDF Reservists

Up until this point it was Hamas, Islamic Jihad and the Palestinian Front for the Liberation of Palestine (PFLP) that had carried out nearly all deadly attacks on Israeli citizens and soldiers.

That changed on the morning of October 12th when two non-combatant Israeli Reservists (serving as drivers) missed their turn-off, and mistakenly entered the Palestinian city of Ramallah. In the past, Israeli soldiers routinely had been turned back at this point. But when the Reservists reached a Palestinian roadblock at the outskirts of town they were detained by PA policeman and taken to the local police station.

As news of the incident quickly spread, a crowd of some 1,500 gathered at the station and demanded the death of the Israeli prisoners. A group of rioters stormed the building whereupon they began to beat the two captives. Veteran photographer Mark Seager, who has covered atrocities in places like the Congo and Kosovo, described the scene as "the most horrible thing that I have ever seen… It was murder of the most barbaric kind. When I think about it, I see that man's head, all smashed. I know that I'll have nightmares for the rest of my life."[21]

The two soldiers were not only beaten to death, they had been stabbed, their eyes had been gouged out, and they were disemboweled. One of the murderers proudly displayed his bloody hands to the crowd just minutes before a bludgeoned body was thrown from the second floor window and subsequently stamped upon and beaten with metal bars by the enraged mob. The other was dragged out a door and set ablaze. Then, at 10:30, approximately one hour after their initial arrest; the bodies of the two soldiers were dragged

121 | Murderer of Israeli IDF Reservists shows bloody hands to the crowd in Ramallah

to al-Manara Square where members of Arafat's Tanzim militia began an impromptu victory celebration.[22] A stunned Israeli public watched the images of this savage attack in utter disbelief. Even those who had heretofore defended the Palestinians while condemning the IDF for using "disproportional force" were left speechless.

Palestinian Intimidation of International Journalists

Images of the event became the subject of yet another media scandal. It was widely reported that PA affiliates had, either smashed cameras, opened them and removed the film, or threatened to beat foreign reporters attempting to capture images of the incident on film.[23] Nonetheless, an Italian film crew did manage to record the event and the contents of that recording were promptly broadcast throughout the world. Unlike the Muhammed al-Dura footage, however, controversy did not arise over what exactly happened—that much was indisputable. Rather, it was the blatant disregard for journalistic professionalism and subsequent evidence of widespread Palestinian intimidation tactics being used against any journalist daring to publish a negative account of Palestinian activities which became, and remains, the cause of serious concern.

In a letter to *al-Hayat al-Jadida*, the official daily newspaper of the Palestinian Authority, Riccardo Cristiano, the deputy head of the Jerusalem bureau of Italy's state television channel RAI stated:

> My dear friends in Palestine. We congratulate you and think that it is our duty to put you in the picture (of the events) of what happened on October 12 in Ramallah. One of the private Italian television stations which competes with us (and not the official Italian television station-RAI) filmed the events. Afterwards Israeli Television broadcast the pictures, as taken from one of the Italian stations, and thus the public impression was created as if we (RAI) took these pictures.

> We emphasize to all of you that the events did not happen this way, because we always respect (will continue to respect) the journalistic procedures with the Palestinian Authority for (journalistic) work in Palestine and we are credible in our precise work.

> We thank you for your trust, and you can be sure that this is not our way of acting. We do not (will not) do such a thing.

> Please accept our dear blessings.

> Signed,
> Ricardo Christiano
> Representative of RAI in the Palestinian Authority[24]

Effectively implying that he would never again film events which were liable to cast a negative light on the PA, Cristiano's letter passively identified Mediaset (Italian News Network) as being responsible for the footage. This in turn necessitated Mediaset to withdraw its staff from the Territories for fear of Palestinian revenge attacks. Indeed the Italian television station admitted that journalists were attacked for covering other Palestinian riots and thus Cristiano's letter was meant to dispel any notion that the station was responsible for its broadcast.[25] Further investigation revealed that Palestinian broadcast stations were making every effort to hide the disturbing pictures;[26] while Palestinian authorities were carrying out a very successful campaign to control the western media coverage, whether by cajoling them or by overt threats and assaults.[27]

If there exists any doubt that such an assertion is true, recall the words of Palestinian Cabinet Secretary Ahmed Abdel Rahman when he called international news agencies informing them that the safety of their staff could not be guaranteed unless they withdrew embarrassing footage of Palestinian police officers joyfully firing into the air on September 11, 2001.

This practice has since become an official policy.

On August 26, 2002, the Palestinian Journalist Union declared that "news photographers are 'absolutely forbidden' from taking pictures of Palestinian children carrying weapons... taking part in activities by militant groups, [or other images which] hurt the Palestinian cause."[28] As Joshua Muravchik points out, such is the difference between reporting from a democratic regime like Israel and an authoritarian one like Palestine. While this works to Israel's disadvantage, "it is not for Israel's sake so much as for the sake of their readers and viewers and effectiveness of their profession that journalists ought to give systematic consideration to the problems of dealing with warring parties that are so dissimilar in how they deal with [treat] the press."[29]

Mitchell Report

Less than a week after the barbaric acts in Ramallah, President Clinton convened a summit in the Egyptian resort town of Sharm el-Sheik in an effort to negotiate a truce. At this October 17, 2000 meeting, the parties agreed to establish an independent commission to investigate the causes of the violence (the Mitchell Report) and to issue a joint public statement unequivocally calling for an end to the violence. In the end, however, it seemed as if Arafat and other Arab delegates were merely going through the motions. Arab League members meeting in Cairo on October 21st issued a statement "praise[ing] the Intifada."[30] Meanwhile, Palestinian violence not only continued, it became evermore vile. By October 30th it was evident that Palestinian militants intended to continue their rampage when four Israeli women were gunned down in the Israeli city of Hadera. Violence reached its apex on November 20, 2000, when Palestinian militants detonated explosives targeting Israeli schoolchildren.[31]

With violence spiraling and Arafat still refusing to accept the Clinton Parameters as the basis for continuing negotiatons, Prime Minister Barak, who had staked his entire political career on making peace with the Palestinians, had little choice but to throw in the towel. He announced his resignation on December 8th, paving the way for early elections set for February 6, 2001.

From Barak to Sharon

Whereas Barak had garnered support from Israelis based on the promise of peace, newly elected Prime Minister Ariel Sharon promised security. Nicknamed the "Bulldozer," Sharon had served as a military commander in all six of Israel's wars. A hard-liner with a reputation for taking a no-nonsense approach to Israel's security, he was a staunch proponent of the settler movement, believing that only by achieving the dream of "Greater Israel" that included all of the occupied Territories could Israel's security be ensured.

Sharon managed to assemble the largest political coalition the State of Israel had ever seen, with eight separate parties participating in his government. With this wide and broad-based support, Sharon carefully laid out his government's objectives in his inaugural address on March 7, 2001:

> The government, under my leadership, will act to restore security to the citizens of Israel and to achieve genuine peace and security in the area. I know that peace requires painful compromise on the part of both sides. Any diplomatic accord will be founded upon security for all peoples in the regions.

> Despite considerable concessions we made on the way to peace—by all governments of Israel—in the past few years, we still haven't found willingness for reconciliation and true peace on the other side.

> I believe we can gradually advance towards peace through an approach based on mutual respect and confidence building… If our Palestinian neighbors choose the path of peace, reconciliation and good neighborly relations they will find that I and the government I lead are honest and faithful partners [for peace].[32]

With Sharon's hand outstretched in peace, Israelis waited uneasily for a Palestinian response. While a series of mostly minor tit-for-tat attacks did occur in the month of March, it was the events of spring 2001 which clearly signaled the Palestinian intent. It became evident the Palestinians would continue their campaign of terror. Even more disturbing, they apparently had every intention of escalating the level of violence to ever new heights.

In April 2001, Palestinian militants fired mortars from the Gaza Strip directly into Israeli towns and cities. Then on May 7, IDF naval commandos intercepted the *Santorini*; a vessel laden with an estimated $10 million in weaponry en route from Lebanon to the Gaza strip.[33] While these events signaled a new and grave phase of violence, it was the June suicide bombing of a popular Tel Aviv nightclub, causing the deaths of 21 Israeli young adults, which highlighted growing tensions between various Palestinian factions.

Passover Dinner Terror Attack

Despite the cold-blooded nature of this latest wave of armed violence—mostly targeting Israel's youth in restaurants, cafes and nightclubs—the government's initial response was relatively reserved, focusing on police actions rather than military ones. The breaking point came a year later in Spring 2002, when a Hamas suicide bomber killed 30 people and wounded another 140 as they gathered to celebrate the first night of Passover at the Park Hotel in Netanya.

Sharon's response was quick and decisive. Operation Defensive Shield was put into action on March 29, 2002, as the Prime Minster made his intentions clear:

> …to catch and arrest terrorists and, primarily, their dispatchers and those who finance and support them; to confiscate weapons intended to be used against Israeli citizens; to expose and destroy facilities and explosives, laboratories, weapons production factories and secret installations. The orders are clear: target and paralyze anyone who takes up weapons and tries to oppose our troops, resists them or endangers them— and to avoid harming the civilian population.[34]

In the spring of 2002, I was visiting my family in Israel to celebrate Passover together. This joyful holiday is always celebrated in Israel amidst family and friends. Often large families gather in hotels where special meals are prepared for hundreds of guests.

That year we were in a hotel near the coastal city of Netanya. During our seder, we heard the horrific news about a suicide bombing in a nearby hotel, where a terrorist, disguised as a woman, carried a suitcase full of powerful explosives into the crowded hotel dining room. The bombing killed 30 people and severely wounded 140 more holiday guests, some of whom were Holocaust survivors. We were literally sickened by the news of families, like ours, being killed at their Passover seder.

Our feelings turned to fear when we realized how close we were to the attack. As if in a war zone, we were checked and had to present our identity cards each time we came in or out of our rooms. Soldiers could be seen everywhere in the seaside tourist town of Netanya on the Mediterranean coastline, as well as in every other tourist location.

This was the first time I was in Israel when a suicide bombing attack occurred so close to where I was staying. And I was terrified for my family, my wife, and my young daughter. Although I had served as a Commander in the IDF during wartime, I felt terribly vulnerable. As a father, I realized that I could not protect my family from the possibility of being killed by suicide bombers. I also realized, sadly, that this horrifying act of sheer terror could happen to anyone, at anytime and anywhere. Remembering how Americans felt after 9/11, I realized that Israelis had to live with this same sense of vulnerability and fear 24/7.

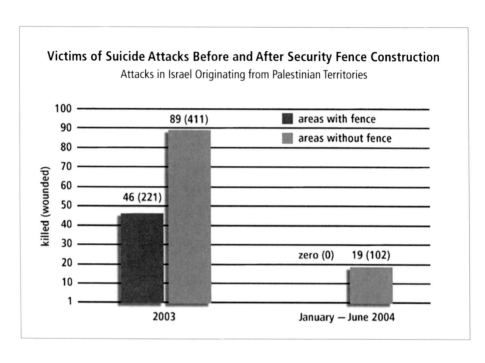

Victims of Suicide Attacks Before and After Security Fence Construction

Attacks in Israel Originating from Palestinian Territories

Operation Defensive Shield

The largest military operation in the West Bank since the War of 1967, Operation Defensive Shield was viewed by most Israelis as a necessary response to the Second Intifada during the preceding 18 months.

Its success cannot be disputed. In a one-month period, terrorist attacks against Israeli targets fell by 70 percent; suicide bombing fell 46 percent, and Israeli fatalities dropped 35 percent.[35] Moreover, the IDF confiscated more than 5,000 illegal small arms and explosives, as well as documents from Arafat's compound which provided ample evidence of the PLO's knowledge of, and collusion with, terrorist organizations attacking Israel.[36]

When Operation Defensive Shield concluded on May 10, 2002, the Sharon government was faced with two immediate objectives. First, Israel needed a plan to ensure the long-term protection of Israel's citizens against future attacks. Second, Israel's international reputation needed repair. Perversely, it soon became clear that in the eyes of the international community, Israel's pursuit of these two goals was somehow antithetical.

Responding to its urgent and immediate needs, the government did what the citizens of any country would expect their government to do if faced with wave after wave of terror attacks against innocent civilians. The Israeli government used all means necessary to end the bloodshed. Seeking to minimize international criticism while achieving its security objectives, the Sharon government embarked on a three-pronged approach designed to end terror at a minimal cost.

The first step was to authorize targeted assassinations against those practicing terror, including the leadership and those facilitating, masterminding or otherwise contributing to terrorist operations. The most significant among these individuals included Sheik Yassin and Abdelaziz al-Rantisi, who were killed in Gaza.

Secondly, the construction of a security barrier was intended to stem the tide of terrorist attacks originating in the West Bank. The barrier surrounding Gaza, which was destroyed during the opening days of the Intifada, was also reconstructed.

From a purely pragmatic perspective the construction of a security barrier seemed to be the most benign approach for stemming the unrelenting waves of terror attacks. Modeled along the lines of those built to separate North from South Korea and India from Pakistan, the plan was to build a long security fence that would be erected at critical points along the West Bank border. In Gaza, the security barrier had proven itself to be one of the most effective tools in the war against Palestinian terror. The idea of extending this defensive measure to the West Bank, therefore, seemed to be the most prudent security measure. It was not until after a flood of deadly attacks in the fall of 2003, however, that the West Bank Barrier was deemed politically and economically viable. As anticipated, the international community immediately chastised Israel's decision.

From Israel's perspective, it seemed as if any defensive measure would be misinterpreted and misrepresented by the international community as a hostile act of Israeli aggression. The Israeli Minister of Housing and Construction, Natan Sharansky, aptly voiced Israel's frustration:

> It seemed that in eyes of many, the Jews had a right to defend themselves in theory but could not exercise that right in practice... Our government understood that there were three options to maintain an acceptable level of security for our citizens. The first was to wage a total war against Palestinian terror using weapons that would claim many innocent Palestinian lives. The second was to keep our reserves constantly mobilized to defend the country. The third option was to build the security fence. Had the Palestinian Authority become a partner in fighting terror, as it was obliged to do under all the agreements that it signed, none of these options would have become necessary.[37]

Despite the spat of international criticism, once again the facts spoke for themselves. In just three years, suicide attacks against Israel practically disappeared; plunging from a high of 60 operations in 2002 to five in 2005. The security fence, moreover, greatly contributed to

Israel's policing efforts. In 2001, only 56 infiltrators from the West Bank had been captured by Israeli security personnel. By the time the first phase of the fence had been completed in 2004, the number of attacks thwarted by Israeli security forces had soared to 367.[38] All of this translated into the undeniable fact that many innocent lives were being saved daily. Indeed, the number of victims directly affected by Palestinian terrorism plummeted from a high of 2,594 people in 2001 to 291 victims in 2007.[39]

Finally, the Sharon government decided to unilaterally withdraw from the Gaza Strip.

Whereas Israel's northern cities had suffered the brunt of suicide bombings and other deadly assaults, for the citizens of the southern city of Sderot, it was the merciless and unrelenting barrage of missile and mortar fire originating from the Gaza Strip which defined their daily life. Using Google Earth to identify targets, Gaza-based militants randomly fired their homemade Qassam rockets into Israel on a daily basis.[40] According to UN sources, the primary targets of these attacks were timed to target children on their way to classes and their schools.[41]

Media Challenges

Although necessary to stop the terror, the military actions during Operation Defensive Shield were often misrepresented in the media. With bias against Israel, scenes were often filmed and aired throughout the world depicting Israel as the perpetrator of violence.

It was common for me when appearing as a commentator for Colorado and international media to be asked to analyze the conflict. I realized that Israel being a full-fledged democracy held an inherent relative disadvantage as free access to the press allowed images of death and destruction to be broadcast instantaneously and many times out of context. It was clear that Israeli reporters held themselves to higher standards than their non-Israeli colleagues did.

For example, immediately following the Jenin Palestinian refugee camp operation, Palestinian spokesmen reported a "massacre of thousands of innocent Palestinian civilians." It usually took me 48 hours to validate information from reliable colleagues in Israel. Following this report, and many others, when I did receive verifiable information, I would ask newscasters to present the accurate facts. What I soon realized was that by this point, the story was "old news." My findings confirmed that instead of thousands being killed in Jenin, there were 52 deaths and that 27 of those killed were suspected terrorists. But none of this would be reported to the public. Neither would the fact that booby traps had been set to kill Israeli soldiers entering the camp, and it was these same booby traps that caused most of the civilian deaths. Sadly and inaccurately, images of dead bodies would be sealed in the minds of viewers as "horrifying Israeli acts of violence" against "innocent" Palestinian civilians.

Unfortunately, live TV and other instant media often spread misinformation, even by journalists with the best of intentions. The consequences for Israel were often damning. This does not include the propaganda spread by Israel's enemies, including false reporting, the doctoring of photographs, and accusing Israel of purposefully killing innocent civilians. In some cases there were even staged acts to provoke the IDF with the sole purpose of attaining photographs of subsequent Israeli actions.

Examples include the tragic death of Muhammad al-Dura in Gaza, discussed earlier. Other examples include the Flotilla incident of 2010, when Israeli soldiers boarded a ship that refused to comply with the Israeli naval blockade of Gaza. With knives and lethal tools, so-called "humanitarians" brutally attacked the Israeli soldiers being dropped by an IDF helicopter to investigate the cargo of the ship. Israelis see these "human rights actions" as concerted efforts to provoke Israeli military reactions with the clear intent of increasing international condemnation of Israel.

The Second Intifada arose from the quagmire of the occupation and its destructiveness.
—Abdel Jawad[1]

The 1990s began as a decade of hope, with peace negotiations making grudging progress that yielded a Nobel Prize and the Oslo Accords. Yet, the decade culminated with the Second Intifada, also known as al-Aqsa. To the rest of the world, such deterioration appeared confusing and disheartening. How could this happen?

Of course, to those on the inside, the foundation of peace was unstable and showed cracks from the beginning. Nearly as soon as they had begun, the Oslo Agreements were invalidated for the Palestinian people because illegal Israeli settlements grew bigger, encompassing more and more Palestinian land. As Israeli infrastructure seemed to continue its unchecked expansion, the economic well-being of the Palestinian people markedly deteriorated.

The peace process was further hampered by the massacre of 29 Palestinians in Hebron in 1994 by an Israeli religious extremist named Baruch Goldstein. In response, Palestinian Islamist extremist groups launched attacks on Israel. It is said that Goldstein's massacre of Palestinians inspired another Jewish religious extremist, Yigal Amir, to assassinate Prime Minister Yitzhak Rabin in 1995.

Rabin was a co-recipient of the 1994 Nobel Peace Prize (with Yasser Arafat and Shimon Peres) for his efforts to create peace in the Middle East. Islamist extremists viewed Arafat as an illegitimate leader of the Palestinian people for making peace with the Israelis. Likewise, Jewish extremists in Israel derided Rabin for his negotiations with the Palestinians. Prior to his death, Jewish extremist rabbis excoriated Rabin for giving up Jewish lands in the West Bank and invoked an arcane Talmudic ruling that condemned Rabin for posing a "mortal threat" to the Israeli people.[2] Remarkably, posters depicting Rabin in a Nazi uniform were distributed at an anti-Government rally in Jerusalem before Rabin was assassinated.[3]

Tunnel Excavation Threatens the al-Aqsa Mosque

Prime Minister Benjamin Netanyahu's 1996 decision to open an ancient tunnel under the Old City of Jerusalem sparked the hostilities leading up to the 2nd Intifada.

According to Netanyahu, the opening of the tunnel was merely an efficient way to bring more tourists to the east side of the Old City. But for Palestinians, the tunnel was a shortcut for Jewish extremists to pierce the heart of Arab East Jerusalem and change its demographic character.

They also worried the excavation would undermine the structural foundations of the Muslim holy place above it.

And of course, since the al-Aqsa Tunnel was Israeli-controlled, Netanyahu's plan for the tunnel was a one-way street in the Israelis' favor. Palestinians would not be permitted to use the tunnel in a similar fashion to travel more swiftly from one side of the city to the other. Due to Israeli control of the contested city, this would be a privilege granted only to Jews.

It was abundantly clear that Netanyahu (and his supporters on the far right) aimed to build the tunnel in order to establish a stronger Jewish foothold in Arab East Jerusalem. This was carried out at the expense of future Palestinian sovereignty and claims to East Jerusalem as the future capital of the Palestinian state. The tunnel was seen as a direct means of implementing the long-standing desire by Jewish religious extremists to control the entire city of Jerusalem and to ethnically cleanse the city of its non-Jewish inhabitants.

More specifically, the tunnel provided a sheltered shortcut to the Western Wall from the site of a Jewish yeshiva located in the Muslim quarter of the Old City, known as Ateret Cohanim, or "Crown of the Priests." Ateret Cohanim is an extension of a U.S.-registered nonprofit agency, which is well known for bringing Jewish people to live in Arab East Jerusalem by buying Arab property and systematically forcing Arabs out. The organization's primary objective is to reclaim Arab East Jerusalem for the Jews by moving in more Jewish families with the same extremist ideological orientation. They believe non-Jewish citizens do not have the right to live in the present day State of Israel, including the biblical lands of Judea and Samaria, as well as in lands now occupied by modern day Jordan and Iraq.

As much as has been exposed about Muslim and Christian religious extremists, it is tragic that Jewish extremists hold radical, destructive views that influence Israeli policymakers. They promote a radical version of politico-religious Zionism that is largely responsible for bringing so much suffering to the Palestinian people, including the rapid expansion of the Israeli settler movement and the 1994 Goldstein Massacre at the Cave of the Patriarchs in Hebron.

Some say it was the pressure of wealthy right-wing patrons of Ateret Cohanim that persuaded Netanyahu and Jerusalem Mayor Ehud Olmert to open the tunnel at their behest. It is noteworthy that before Netanyahu came to power, the previous Labor government declined to open the contested tunnel out of fear that it would incite violence. Yasser Arafat claimed that opening the tunnel was a "big crime against our religious and holy places."[4]

Therefore, it was predictable that the opening of the tunnel would spark widespread outrage among the Palestinian population. Within five days of the tunnel's opening on September 24, 1996, Palestinians and Israeli military forces clashed in the West Bank and in the Gaza Strip. The violence demonstrated Palestinian frustration, not only because the tunnel opened, but more importantly, due to the lack of progress in the peace process—which Palestinians believed had failed to protect the Palestinian people from such encroachments on their religious rights.

Some Israelis, including Netanyahu, floated the argument that Palestinian fears concerning the security of the Haram al-Sharif were unfounded. However, using such a pejorative approach toward deep-seated Palestinian fears only inflamed emotions. There is no question that the long history of threats and outright attempts by Jewish extremists to destroy Haram al-Sharif has traumatized the Palestinian psyche.

In 1969, an Australian named Dennis Michael Rohan set fire to the al-Aqsa Mosque. The

122 | Haram al-Sharif

fire gutted the southeastern wing of the mosque, destroying priceless wood and an ivory pulpit sent from Aleppo by Saladin. Although not a Jewish extremist, Rohan's evangelical Christian background fueled his attempt to destroy the mosque. From a Palestinian perspective, his beliefs derived from the same Jewish intention to rebuild the Jewish Temple on the site of the ancient Temple Mount, or the Haram al-Sharif.

In the 1970s, Jewish extremist groups began a campaign of provocation and violence that included attempts to dig tunnels in order to enter this hallowed area by force. There have also been several botched efforts to plant bombs in the Dome of the Rock and al-Aqsa Mosque.

Between 1978 and 1982, the Islamic Waqf documented 200 acts of desecration and provocation on or near the Haram al-Sharif by Israeli extremists.[5] In 1982, Allan Goodman, an Israeli soldier with an American passport, entered the Haram al-Sharif with an Israeli-issued automatic rifle and opened fire on Muslim worshippers. Although he only killed one person (and wounded dozens of others.) Goodman became the source of inspiration for Baruch Goldstein in the 1994 Hebron Massacre.

Throughout the 1980s, there were several attempts by Jewish extremists to raid and blow up the Haram al-Sharif. One group in particular, known as the "Temple Mount Faithful," formed with a commitment to build a third Jewish Temple on the Haram al-Sharif following the destruction of the existing Islamic buildings in the plaza.[6] The organization continuously petitioned the Israeli government for the right to lay a cornerstone of the projected Jewish Temple on the Haram al-Sharif. Although the Israeli government has consistently denied the group the right to do this, the Temple Mount Faithful has been granted permission to visit the Haram al-Sharif during certain hours on certain days.

On one of these days, Monday, October 8, 1990, rumors spread among Palestinians that the Temple Mount Faithful were coming to the Haram al-Sharif to lay the cornerstone of the third Temple. Across the Palestinian Territories, Muslims were called to Jerusalem in anticipation of resisting the destruction of their holy site by this group of Jewish extremists. Tension and anxiety surrounded the Muslim worshippers that morning, but the crowd began to riot only after a tear gas canister (presumably originating from the Israeli authorities) landed and exploded in the midst of women at the Dome of the Rock.

123 | Inciting Palestinian fear of Haram al-Sharif takeover

As the crowd moved against the tear gas, some participants began throwing rocks.

In response, the Israeli border guards opened fire; 17 Palestinians were killed and more than 150 were injured that day. In less than a week a total of 14 Israelis and 56 Palestinians lay dead.

Once again, Israeli religious extremism and a flagrant overreaction by Israeli security forces resulted in a death toll that was overwhelmingly Palestinian.

The Israeli insistence that the Palestinian people had nothing to fear with the opening of the al-Aqsa Tunnel was seen as an obvious omission of truth. For Palestinians, the facts could be seen on the ground where Palestinian blood had been spilled. It is little wonder why Netanyahu's decision to open the tunnel was seen as an insensitive blow to Palestinian sovereignty. To Palestinians, Netanyahu's pandering to the Jewish religious right only added fuel to the conflict. The opening of the tunnel shattered any Palestinian faith in a peaceful resolution to the conflict.

Extremist Activity

The years leading to the outbreak of hostilities between the Palestinians and Israelis in 2000 can be characterized by the rise of extremist religious-political ideology on both sides of the conflict.

There is no doubt that Hamas and Palestinian Islamic Jihad stood diametrically opposed to the secular-nationalist PLO (Fatah), and its creation of the Palestinian Authority, as well as the Israeli-Palestinian peace process of the Oslo Accords.

However, we also should not forget the increasingly violent and extremist religious ideology that was taking hold of Israel at that time. This Jewish extremist ideology promoted Goldstein's massacre of innocent people at the Cave of the Patriarchs, the assassination of Yitzhak Rabin and the emergence of the far-right religious Zionist groups such as the Temple Mount Faithful and the Ateret Cohanim, which was committed to the ethnic cleansing of Jerusalem.

During this time, were there attacks on Israel by Islamic extremists? Undeniably, yes. As a fringe element of Palestinian politics at the time, the Palestinian Islamist organizations were responsible for conducting a campaign of terror against Israeli civilians, which helped to turn the Israeli public against the idea of making peace with the Palestinians.

The power and influence of the Israeli far right meant Israeli leaders simply would not voluntarily relinquish control over the West Bank and East Jerusalem. This control included the Israeli settlement system, control of the West Bank aquifers, control over the economy of the Palestinian areas, and Israeli "security arrangements" extending over the entire Palestinian area.[7]

To the Palestinian people, these controls—especially the continued construction of the settlements—were just as much an assault on the peace process as were buses exploding in Tel Aviv. To the Palestinian people, land is a cultural symbol of investment in the future.

The expansion of Israeli settlements severely impeded Palestinian socio-economic growth and development, thereby undercutting prospects for a territorially and economically viable state. As such, the continued denial and usurpation of Palestinian lands during the Oslo process was a direct denial of their right of existence.

Ultimately, the confluence of these issues encouraged Palestinian Islamist organizations to act independently from the Palestinian Authority and to engage in a cycle of violence against Israeli targets, bringing more harm than good to the people on either side of this ideological divide. Both had fatal consequences for the peace process.

Settlement Expansion

Throughout the negotiations for peace in the 1990s, the Israeli-only settlements began to appear as elaborate, imposing fortresses on the hillsides of the West Bank. Not only did the settlements (and the infrastructure that supports them) negatively and severely impact Palestinian development, but the extremist makeup of the Israeli settlers became a critical

124 | Lifta, Palestine, until 1948 an active community near Jerusalem, now abandoned while newer Israeli neighborhoods (background) grow.

Map 24 | Israeli settlement expansion in the West Bank

source of instability and violence against largely unarmed Palestinian civilians. Israeli settlers (and even their young children) were frequently known to attack their Palestinian neighbors, and most especially farmers who continued to plant and harvest in what little remained of their ancestral lands.

The restrictions on Palestinian life in addition to the violence committed against them by armed extremist settlers sparked Palestinian resentment. As early as 1991, Secretary of State James Baker explained that Israeli settlement expansion is a form of "de facto annexation... changing the fact[s] and circumstances on the ground in the absence of negotiation between the parties, which would be designed to resolve this Arab-Israeli conflict in a peaceful way."[8]

Israel's settlement enterprise is vast and controls nearly half of the West Bank. It includes land reserves, agricultural and industrial facilities, Israeli-only bypass roads and the "separation" wall, which was built to keep Palestinians out of Israel, but allow Israelis into what little remains of Palestine. Over half of the West Bank has remained under the control of Israel through this extensive infrastructure. All of this was initiated and constructed in a time of ostensible "peace."

The Palestinian uprising in 2000 was also motivated by the Israeli withdrawal from Lebanon in June of that same year. From the perspective of the Palestinians, why should Arafat continue pursuing a treaty with Israel after so many failed negotiations when 500 Hezbollah fighters had effectively forced Israel to pull back to the international border of Lebanon?[9] Increasingly, the Palestinians began to wonder why they were being forced to negotiate a settlement with their own occupier instead of using force to liberate themselves.

The successful model of Hezbollah inspired and created a renewed sense of Palestinian militancy, and, unfortunately, this reached as far as Arafat, who, wanted to be as successful as Hezbollah was in Lebanon. Arafat believed the "Lebanonization of the struggle against Israel...would break the capacity of resistance of the Israelis."[10]

125 | Muhammad al-Dura, seen alive on video

The Outbreak of the al-Aqsa Intifada

Calling the al-Aqsa Intifada "Mr. Arafat's War" greatly whitewashes the responsibilities and failures of both the Israeli and Palestinian leadership. However, from the Palestinian perspective, it was the continued violence and persecution of Palestinian civilians by the Israelis during the Oslo years that led to the outbreak of the al-Aqsa Intifada.

On September 28, 2000, 1,000 Israeli police officers escorted Ariel Sharon to the former site of the Jewish Temple

126 | Young al-Dura, dead at his father's side

Mount on the Haram al-Sharif. For Palestinians, the site of the Dome of the Rock and the al-Aqsa Mosque in East Jerusalem represented the hope of finding a Two-State Solution. Sharon's visit to the site—the same man who was found to bear indirect responsibility for the massacres of Palestinians in the Sabra and Shatila refugee camps in Lebanon—was an assault on this hope and a desecration of a holy site. When Sharon declared that the area would remain under perpetual Israeli control, it was a smack in the face of even the most politically moderate Palestinian. It was also a contradiction of the Israeli announcement that it would respect the status quo of the religious sites in Jerusalem following the Israeli capture of East Jerusalem in 1967.

Palestinians believed there was a growing desire among Jewish extremists to gain a foothold on the Haram al-Sharif. Claiming the Haram al-Sharif as the "Temple Mount," Jewish extremists want to build a new Jewish Temple on the Haram al-Sharif.

Indeed, as Ben-Ami fairly indicates, "Israeli's disproportionate response to what had started as a popular uprising with young, unarmed men confronting Israeli soldiers armed with lethal weapons fueled the Second Intifada beyond control and turned it into an all-out war."[11]

Muhammad al-Dura

On September 30, 2000, only a few days after the outbreak of hostilities in Jerusalem, Israeli forces in Gaza shot and killed an unarmed, 12-year-old child named Muhammad al-Dura. French cameras captured the last terrifying moments of the boy's life as he attempted to hide behind his father from bullets falling upon them. The world watched the boy die on camera as his critically wounded father swayed unconsciously. After enduring so many atrocities inflicted by Israeli forces, Palestinians were incensed by the tragic image of Muhammad al-Dura and his young, innocent son. Watching broadcasts of the victimized father and son's final moments, served to incite the Palestinian people to protest and resist such ruthless, Israeli military aggression.

During the next 39 weeks, Israeli security forces killed 338 Palestinian civilians, 109 of them under 18.[12]

Israel denied responsibility for these deaths, claiming that it only used force when necessary. Sources close to Israel also denied Israeli culpability in the death of Muhammad al-Dura. Regardless of Israel's claims, the casting of stones is less important here than the fact that the aggression between Israel and the Palestinian people claimed yet another life of yet another Palestinian child, and this time in a most visible way. In the end, Muhammad al-Dura became the symbol of the al-Aqsa Intifada.

The simple evidence of extreme and disproportional force used by the Israelis against the Palestinian population is demonstrated by the death toll catalogued in May, 2002 by B'Tselem, the Israeli Information Center for Human Rights in the Occupied Territories.

By then, the Israelis were using F-16 warplanes against Palestinian targets in Gaza, causing extensive collateral damage. B'Tselem reported that the Israeli killing of "children and other innocent civilians, extra-judicial killings of suspects, and complete blockades of Palestinian towns and villages had become routine."[13]

127 | Palestinians wait in line at the Separation Wall

128 | Separation Wall seen from Aida Refugee Camp

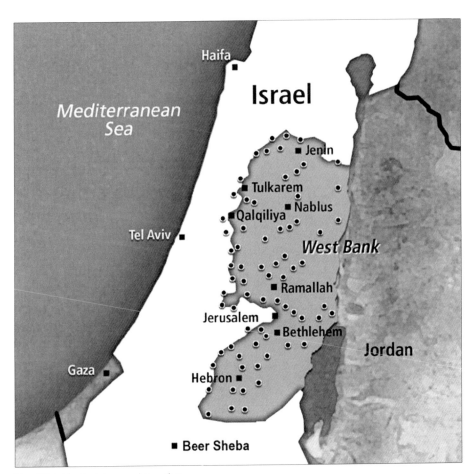

Map 25 | Checkpoints around Jerusalem

By 2002, more than 1,400 Palestinians and 469 Israelis had been killed in this round of attacks. During March 6–16, 2002, more than 200 Palestinians were killed by IDF forces. On March 8 alone, 40 Palestinians died, including two Arab medics killed by Israeli army troops in the West Bank town of Tulkarm.

The Wall

It was during this time that the Israeli government began construction on the West Bank Security Wall—the barrier used to cut off the Palestinian West Bank from Israel while settler-only bypass roads enabled Israelis to travel to and from the Israeli interior to their homes in the illegal settlements in the West Bank. While the barrier was originally designed to follow the Green Line (Israel's pre-1967 border), Sharon decided to alter the plan in order to encompass some of the major Israeli settlements within the West Bank and, of course, all of Jerusalem, regardless of Palestinian claims to the city. Not only was the building of the wall very controversial among Palestinians, but the Israeli seizure of Palestinian land in

129 | Separation Wall, Bethlehem, West Bank

order to do so was seen as yet another assault on Palestinian freedom.

In February 2005, the Israeli cabinet approved the current planned route for the barrier, after Israel's Supreme Court ruled the previous route was needlessly disruptive to Palestinians' lives. Many say that the wall epitomizes everything that is wrong with Israel's occupation of Palestinian land. While the wall can be seen as a de facto border between the two states, it remains that illegal Israeli settlements continue to grow deep inside the occupied West Bank.

The wall effectively separates the Palestinian people away from each other, while Israeli citizens are allowed to travel freely on Israeli-only bypass roads to their illegal places of residence in the West Bank. Israelis argue that the fence can be removed when a negotiated settlement takes place between the two sides. However, the Palestinians see the wall as a precursor to a permanent structure like the one surrounding Gaza. Naturally, they do not want to become hemmed into the West Bank in discontinuous "bantustans."

Recently when I visited Jerusalem, I looked with my own eyes and realized that by constructing the wall, the Israelis have changed the realities on the ground for Palestinians who no longer live in contiguous neighborhoods. This division will make it ever-more difficult for Palestinians to establish East Jerusalem as the capital of the Palestinian state. The wall leaves Arab neighborhoods without any connection to the rest of Arab Jerusalem. In other words, it appears that Eastern Jerusalem has vanished because of the construction of the wall.

Jerusalem can no longer be divided into two capitals for two states.

Map 26 | Existing or approved separation wall, 2005

130 | Mahmoud Abbas(center) and aides, 2005

In 2004, the International Court of Justice ruled against the barrier, saying that it breaches international law and should be dismantled. The Court called it "tantamount to de facto annexation," and said that the barrier inhibited Palestinians' right to self-determination. Like the settlements, however, Israel ignored the calls of the international community and continued to build, build, build.

Arafat Not to Blame

While some prefer to blame the Second Intifada on Arafat, he was in fact under pressure from more radical groups to renew the armed struggle after so many failed negotiations. It's unlikely that he initiated the uprising with specific orders.[14] As in the First Intifada, the 2000 uprising in the Palestinian Territories erupted spontaneously and from the grassroots. However, unlike the First Intifada, it was just as much a backlash against failure of the peace process and continued subjugation by Israeli forces as it was an expression of disappointment with the political bankruptcy of the Palestinian Authority.

The al-Aqsa Intifada "erupted out the accumulated rage and frustration of the Palestinian masses at the colossal failure of the peace process since the early days of Oslo to offer them a life of dignity and well-being, and at the incompetence and corruption of their own leaders in the Palestinian Authority."[15]

The failures of Oslo were more than apparent. Also, the land-for-peace strategy for a Two-State Solution to the conflict was stymied by the disappointing intransigence and failure in leadership of both sides.

Arafat's Death and the Rise of Hamas

In November 2004, Yasser Arafat died. Many optimistically thought that new opportunities for peace would emerge now that he was off the stage. In January 2005, Mahmoud Abbas was elected president of the Palestinian Authority and within weeks had met with newly elected Israeli Prime Minister Ariel Sharon at Sharm-el-Sheikh. Both sides announced an end to the violence. The Israeli parliament approved the disengagement plan from Gaza in February. In March 2005, Palestinian militant groups agreed to a tahde'ah (lull in the fighting). While not a full truce, this was considered major progress and some have argued that it marked the end of the al-Aqsa Intifada.

In retrospect, the most significant result of the al-Aqsa Intifada had to be the rise of Hamas, which unlike the PA is a religiously-motivated organization. The main stronghold of Hamas is Gaza, a densely populated area in the southern part of Palestine.

I should confess here that although I am Palestinian by birth, I have never felt an attachment toward that part of Palestine until I learned about the horrible conditions in Gaza for the Palestinian people. I was horrified to hear about the restrictions on Gazans who could not move in or out of the Strip. This horrible reality for the Palestinians in Gaza stymied life in general and curtailed economic, civil and social progress.

Knowing about this tremendous hardship suffered by my fellow Palestinians in Gaza, I realize that sympathy and compassion towards people who are fighting for justice should not be based only on shared race, ethnic, or religious commonalities. To me, what is more important is not the national identity you share with certain people; rather it is the human bond we share with all human beings.

With this in mind, I continue to search for the most workable solution to the conflict between Palestinians and Israelis who share the same land today while having different stories about the past.

Dating its foundation relics to circa 3,000 BCE, Gaza City is one of the oldest communities in the world and no stranger to conflict.

Strategically situated between Asia and Africa, Gaza connects the Levantine heartland to the Egyptian desert, South Asia to the Arabian Peninsula, and Europe to the rest of the ancient world.

The region has served as a vital link along many of history's most important trade and military routes. But the area also has known much suffering as a battlefield for nearly all of the great ancient civilizations.

For Palestinians, Gazans suffered under decades of Israeli occupation. Since the Israeli withdrawal, more than 1.5 million Palestinians continue to suffer due to Israeli restrictions on their borders, including the naval blockade of their Mediterranean coast. Most egregious are the Israeli military air and artillery strikes, which terrorize civilians and have caused thousands of casualties.

Israel argues that its military actions are to protect Israeli citizens from thousands of missiles launched into Israeli communities from Gaza. Having left Gaza in 2005, Israelis have been faced with elected Hamas leaders who are dedicated to Israel's destruction. There is also great conflict between Hamas and the Palestinian Authority.

And so the conflict continues.

What many outsiders don't realize is that Israelis sympathize with the peaceful Palestinian citizens of Gaza. We understand that the population is living under an oppressive government, which does not allow freedom of speech or association. We understand that terrorists use Gazans as human shields, and use their houses, schools, and community centers as headquarters and weapons caches and as camouflage for tunnels.

What we don't understand is why Gazans don't strive to create an honest and prosperous future and abandon their intention to destroy Israel. Tragically, none of this is likely as long as the forces of radicalism with a clear, and vehement anti-peace agenda remain in power.

Dealing with Islamic extremism in Gaza is challenging. The hatred of Jews and Israel is taught and reinforced in state-sanctioned schools and in Islamic mosques. Suicide bombers are glorified. Mothers believe that their children will be blessed in the afterlife if they carry out a suicide bombing, after which the bombers' families are financially rewarded. This practice is beyond comprehension in Israel, where the Jewish religion values every life, including those of our enemies.

A significant example of opposing values was discussed in previous chapters.

Jews are not welcomed to live among the Palestinians in Gaza, the West Bank, nor in any future established state of the Palestinian people. In Israel, on the other hand, more than a million Arabs, more than 20 percent of the Israeli population are welcomed Israeli citizens who share the same rights as all Israelis and benefit from all that Israel's democracy has to offer.

Another example is the ultimate value of life, and life-saving practices in Israel. For Jews, the value of life stands above all else. The scriptures teach us that "to save one life, is as if you have saved the world." There are numerous and continuous examples of Palestinians who seek life-saving treatment in Israel. Israeli doctors graciously save the lives of Palestinians every day. From infants with terminal illnesses, to adults with complicated heart conditions, Israeli doctors save the lives of Palestinians in Israeli hospitals every day.

In 2010, a documentary film *Precious Blood* examined the true story of a Palestinian infant in Gaza whose life was saved by advanced treatment received at Tel HaShomer Hospital in Israel. The baby's Muslim mother admitted that she would be proud to have her baby son grow up to be a suicide bomber. In essence, she was saying she would be proud if he were to blow himself up to kill Jews. This same mother was equally determined to save the little boy's life by accepting the expensive medical care her son was receiving from Jewish doctors in Israel. The juxtaposition of this woman's belief system was presented in the film, leaving Israelis, including the filmmaker, bewildered and deeply disturbed. It is a totally incomprehensible way of thinking and a troubling value system for us in Israel.

A further example of differing values is exemplified by the death of Sheik Nizar Rayyan in Gaza. Rayyan was a senior Hamas official targeted for assassination by the IDF in 2009. His home in Gaza was to be destroyed because it was being used as a Hamas weapons repository and terrorist communication center. This man was no stranger to violence. He had previously glorified his own son's actions as a suicide bomber in order to kill Israeli civilians.

It was clear to the Israeli military that Rayyan had several wives and 11 children living with him in Gaza. The IDF warned him about their intention to destroy his home as a legitimate military target and asked him to evacuate his wives and his children in order to spare their lives. Instead, Rayyan kept the women and children with him in the house. When the Israeli missile struck Rayyan's home, four of his wives and 10 of his 11 children were unnecessarily killed. In essence, he used his family members as human shields.

During the subsequent funeral procession of the Rayyan family, the bloodied bodies of Rayyan's children were carried through Gazan streets where incendiary crowds of mourners vented their rage towards Israelis. Extremist Palestinian leaders like Rayyan believe that those who die in the fight against Israel will have a special place in heaven. But the Sheik also knew that his choice to allow his family to be killed would inevitably incite more anti-Israeli sentiment and facilitate the recruitment of suicide bombers in Gaza.

To Israelis, this is reprehensible at every level.

Terrorist Activities

The rage and violence of the Second Intifada was not only limited to the West Bank and Israel. It clearly spilled over with a vengeance to the Gaza Strip. Aided and abetted by Iran, Syria and the Hezbollah leadership in Lebanon, Gaza was transformed into a terrorist stronghold from which Hamas and other Palestinian militants launched an unrelenting campaign of terror between 2000 and 2008. More than 1,100 Israeli citizens were killed and thousands more were wounded.[1]

Despite vicious daily incidents, the initial Israeli response in Gaza was unprecedentedly reserved. From 2000 to 2005, Israel appealed to the international community for assistance, made diplomatic overtures, negotiated a ceasefire with Hamas, and even forcibly removed every Israeli citizen and all military assets from the Gaza Strip. Instead of seizing this opportunity to build the foundations of a viable state and to bring about tangible improvements for the Palestinians of Gaza, the Hamas leadership executed a bloody coup d'état against the Fatah Palestinian government, killed and kidnapped Israeli soldiers, stepped up weapon smuggling operations, and intensified its attacks on Israel. At its worst, as many as 100 rockets and mortars were directed at Israeli cities each day.

During this barrage, Israel continually sought peace. Surely no modern nation has endured such extreme hostilities, and demonstrated such self-restraint against terrorists on their border.

History of Gaza

When Great Britain received the Gaza Strip as part of the British Mandate of Palestine, Gaza became part of the Arab-Israeli conflict. However, in Gaza the polarization, which had come to define Jewish-Arab relations in the rest of the British Mandate, was slow to take root. Unlike their European counterparts, the Jews of Gaza were well-established, spoke Arabic, and were not buying land—the primary source of angst elsewhere in the Holy Lands. For

131 | Gaza, 1918

example, when rioting Arabs from the north entered Gaza repeatedly in the 1920s, the Arabs of Gaza formed a protective wall around their Jewish neighbors and whisked them off to safety.

Gaza was the only place in Mandate Palestine where Jews did not suffer a single casualty.[2] But good neighborliness began to evaporate when thousands of Arab refugees from the north fled to Gaza and infused a new anti-Zionist narrative into the local culture.

Jewish-Arab relations remained cordial even when a Jewish farmer named Tuvia Miller sought to establish an orange grove south of Gaza City in 1930. This was the first Jewish land purchase in Gaza. At the time no political significance was attached to the transaction by either the Jewish buyer or by his Arab neighbors.[3] Although the plot was abandoned in

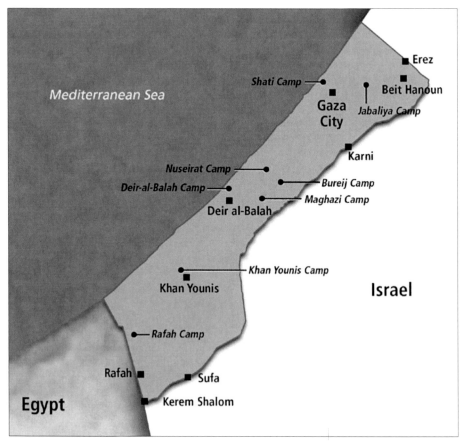

Map 27 | Gaza refugee camps

1939 after repeated attacks, in hindsight Miller's purchase was significant. Not only was it to become the first Zionist settlement in what is now known as the Gaza Strip,[4] it also rekindled internal debates over Jewish claims to the territory. While Palestinian Nationalists never disputed that the Gaza Strip, in its entirety, was an inseparable part of their national homeland, the Jewish narrative could be divided between religious nationalists who viewed the territory as integral to the State of Israel and Rabbis who insisted that the territory was beyond the borders of Eretz Israel.[5]

This debate and its central importance to future Israeli-Gazan relations was abruptly put to the test when Egypt captured Gaza during the 1948 War of Independence.

Conditions in Gaza rapidly declined following the Egyptian invasion and the resulting consequences of the 1948 War. The decline is attributed mainly to the infiltration of Palestinian refugees from Israel who fled south to avoid the fighting. Soon it became apparent that these temporary refugees would not be returning to their homes in Israel.

The United Nations Relief and Works Agency (UNRWA) estimates that during the Israeli War of Independence, the population of Gaza had increased three-fold.[6] The Palestinian exodus from the newly established Jewish state created a challenging humanitarian crisis as relief workers scrambled to feed and shelter close to 200,000 new residents. The situation was further complicated when Egypt took control of Gaza. It soon became clear that Egypt and Jordan had intentions for the land which they had captured—intentions other than Palestinian statehood.

With the backing of the Arab League, Egypt set up the All-Palestine Government in Gaza in September of 1948. This move had two consequential effects. On the one hand, it sent a wave of hope through the Palestinian community in Gaza that they would soon achieve independence and statehood. However, it sparked animosity and distrust between the governments of Jordan and Egypt which subsequently became embroiled in a bitter dispute for the "scraps of Palestine." In February, 1949 the Arab league cut off funding for the All-Palestine Government and denied the Palestinian delegation a seat at the League's next meeting.[7]

Aside from the realization that statehood was a long way off, it quickly became apparent to the Palestinians that Gaza would not be run by civilians and particularly not by Palestinians. Economic hardships immediately took hold as the occupying Egyptian government imposed discriminatory bureaucratic practices, an unbalanced tax structure, and denied nearly all Palestinians the right to travel beyond the boundaries of Gaza.[8]

Despite these difficult conditions, or perhaps because of them, the dream of Palestinian independence was kept alive by Egyptian infiltrators including Hassan al-Banna and Yasser Arafat. For his part, al-Banna, the leader of the Muslim Brotherhood, rallied the Palestinians for the creation of an Islamic state through waging a Holy War against the Jews in Israel.

When Egyptian President Gamal Abdel Nasser blocked the Suez Canal to Israeli shipping in 1956, Israel occupied Gaza, where Arafat and his counterparts joined Egyptian fedayeen militants in direct confrontation with Israeli forces. As a consequence of these actions, the Egyptian government instituted a harsh crackdown on both Brotherhood and fedayeen forces, fearing their attacks could drag Egypt into direct confrontation with Israeli forces. In return, Israel promised a hands-off approach to Gaza and an uneasy peace ensued. As one commentator put it, "the region was never so quiet as the following decade."[9] Nevertheless, it was during this period of relative calm that a new generation of Palestinian activists arose. Drawing inspiration from National Liberation Front (FLN) activities against the French in Algeria, this new breed of militants called for all-out guerrilla warfare against Israel to oust the Jews and destroy Israel in order to create a secular Palestinian State.

Fatah and Arafat Rise to Power

This new movement called itself Fatah, meaning the "Palestinian National Liberation Movement." With secured funding from Kuwait, Fatah members embarked on a series of deadly attacks against Israeli targets. Fatah gradually became the largest and most violent political faction in Gaza. In fact, Fatah forces operating from Gaza could claim to have carried out at least twice as many attacks as those originating from terror bases in Jordan, Syria, and Lebanon.[10] With these "victories" and the Arab League's founding of the PLO in the summer of 1964, the dream of an independent Palestinian state was invigorated. It was not until after the 1967 War, a war which proved to most Palestinians that the Arabs armies could not be counted on to bring about their liberation, that Yasser Arafat was able to seize control of Fatah.

With the Palestinian cause now directed solely by Palestinian leadership, the struggle for liberation became evermore violent. Attacks in Israel were of course commonplace; but now the PLO, under the direction of Yasser Arafat, brought the struggle to the international stage. Palestinian terrorists spread their attacks elsewhere, including hijackings of commercial airliners which affected people around the world, who watched with horror as the Palestine liberation movement terrorized international travelers.

Muslim Brotherhood Influence

While the fate of Gaza had for the most part been directed and determined by outside occupiers, internal influence by the Muslim Brotherhood and the rise of the PLO began to significantly influence the region. Initially, the Muslim Brotherhood maintained a low profile prudently choosing not to challenge the nationalist PLO who enjoyed massive popular support. With the PLO's expulsion and in the wake of the Iranian Islamic revolution, however, the Muslim Brotherhood began a concerted effort to recruit and mobilize the masses in Gaza. Backed by Israel—which hoped that the Muslim Brotherhood would fill the political void in Gaza while promoting religion rather than resistance[11]—the group initially focused its efforts on benign activities such as religious devotion, education and the provision of social services. Over the next decade the group came to wield evermore power in the Gaza Strip through its monopolization of the Strip's social and humanitarian institutions and by appealing to Gaza's traditionalist society which was open to religious teachings and social structures.[12]

Seeking to capitalize on the Brotherhood's growing popularity—the fact that Arafat and the PLO leadership had, by this time, been exiled to Tunisia, and that unrest among the Palestinian populace was growing—in December of 1987, Sheikh Ahmed Yassin, Abdel Aziz al-Rantissi, and Muhammad Taha formed the political movement Hamas (•arakat al-Muqāwamat al-Islāmiyyah, meaning Islamic Resistance Movement) at the beginning of the First Intifada. Separating its command structure from that of its founding organization the Egyptian Muslim Brotherhood, the newly independent movement consisted of two wings. The first of these was socio-political in nature and served to secure support by making the citizens of Gaza ever more reliant on the organization for their well-being. The second of these, the Izz ad-Din al-Qassam Brigades (al-Qassam Brigade) was, and remains, a paramilitary force dedicated to the destruction of Israel through armed resistance.[13]

In retrospect, the rise of Hamas and the ensuing intifada while PLO leader Yasser Arafat was exiled to Tunisia, did more to distance the Palestinians of Gaza from those of the West Bank than any other development.

Arafat Changes Course

To reassert himself as the recognized Palestinian leader, Arafat differentiated himself from Hamas by becoming a "peacemaker." He spoke to the United Nations General Assembly in Geneva on December 13, 1988, renouncing violence and accepting Israel's right to exist.[14] From this point on until 2000, Arafat's Fatah Party and Hamas continued to grow further apart ideologically, strategically, politically and physically.

The ideological differences between Fatah and Hamas were evident early on. The PLO's assertion that any future Palestinian state would be secular and democratic in form—be it leftist, communist, or Baathist—did not rest well with Brotherhood adherents who, according to their ideology envisioned an Islamic nationalist state founded upon Quranic teachings.[15] This, in turn, resulted in a geopolitical rift with Hamas, which then turned towards Islamic extremists in Lebanon, Iran, Indonesia and elsewhere for support. In contrast, the PLO allied itself with moderate Arab states such as Egypt and Jordan. These ideological and political divisions resulted not only in an intra-Palestinian break up, but it also deepened the chasm between the Christian West and the Islamic East. Evidence of this inevitable outcome soon erupted on the streets of Jerusalem and beyond.

From the time the PLO delegates announced their intention to pursue peace talks with Israel, Hamas militants, with the assistance of Iran, embarked on a rapid and unprecedented process of militarization.[16] Although some Hamas leaders recognized the potential recruitment value many of the proposed Oslo institutions could provide, in the end, the Hamas leadership rejected any participation in these institutions and instead joined forces with the Palestinian Islamic Jihad, Democratic and Islamic Nationalist Fronts and other rejectionist factions.[17] Resolute in its intention to derail the peace process, Hamas began a shocking three-year campaign of suicide bombings on April 6, 2004. For its part, endowed with a "strong police force" and in accordance with Article VIII of the Declaration of Principles, the newly autonomous Fatah-led Palestinian government engaged in a military campaign to weaken, if not eliminate its emerging rival—Hamas.[18]

By expelling many Hamas leaders, the Fatah-led Palestinian Authority (PA) increased its influence and control in the West Bank. Compared with Hamas' rejectionist position, the PA was able to maintain a façade of respectability in the eyes of the international community.

However, Hamas was able to successfully undercut Arafat's authority by appealing to a relatively large minority who supported armed resistance over reconciliation with Israel.

132 | Encouraging children to be terrorists

For example, in an interview with al-Jazeera, Ahmed Yassin, the spiritual leader of Hamas, declared that the PA had become subservient to the United States and Israel, and that Arafat no longer represented the true wishes of the Palestinian people.[19] Chief Fatah advisor Muhammed Dahlan, on the other hand, accused Hamas of "playing dirty tricks with the future of the Palestinian people" and argued that Hamas was executing the will of foreign powers—a veiled reference to Iran and Syria—rather than thinking of the best interest of the Palestinian people.

Many Palestinians saw Hamas as an alternative to the Fatah-led Palestinian Authority and respected the organization as a powerful grassroots Islamic force possessing a potent military wing capable of delivering painful blows to Israel through suicide bombings

133 | Palestinian children encouraged to become terrorists

and other forms of terrorism. With help from Iran and Syria, Hamas' al Qassam Brigade fighters were able to intensify their military training, while financial support poured in from the Palestinian diaspora in Iran, Saudi Arabia and other Islamic states.[20] According to one intelligence assessment, Hamas had the potential to someday become a regional power.[21] For this to happen, the U.S. and Israeli-backed institutions created through the Oslo peace process would need to be destroyed first. The Second Intifada provided the perfect conditions for this to occur.[22]

As time went on, it was Hamas which came to enjoy greater and greater popularity. Arafat began to compete directly with Hamas by offering families up to $3,000 for their children's participation in suicide bombings and also rewarding others whose family members died or were wounded.[23] The results of the internal fighting were devastating for the Palestinians and Israelis as well. Meanwhile the Palestinian Authority's annual revenue decreased from over $600 million to a mere $27 million by the end of 2001, as much of the international community gradually lost patience with Arafat and the PA.[24] In contrast, Hamas's popularity continued to rise and its Iranian sponsor continued to back its operations.

When the Hamas suicide bomber killed dozens during Passover in Netanya in the spring of 2002, Israeli Prime Minister Ariel Sharon responded decisively with *Operation Defensive Shield*, a counter-offensive in the West Bank to stop the terrorist violence against Israeli citizens. In addition, during the Second Intifada, targeted assassinations of Hamas leaders were conducted by Israeli forces in Gaza.

Sheikh Ahmed Yassin was perhaps the most significant among those targeted. Yassin was killed on March 22, 2004. He had been the spiritual leader of Hamas and the "Mastermind

134 | Hamas gunmen

of Palestinian Terror."[25] Described by Prime Minister Sharon as "a mass murderer who [was] among Israel's greatest enemies," Yassin had planned and executed suicide bombings in Israel killing children, teenagers and grandparents; Israeli citizens, Arabs and Jews as well as numerous innocent tourists. Within one month of killing the Sheikh, the IDF also assassinated Hamas's second in command, Abdelaziz al-Rantisi, on April 17, 2004.

For the Israelis, targeting and killing the leaders of the terrorists was necessary to combat the suicide bombers causing civilian casualties in Israeli cities. However, these assassinations were widely condemned not only in the Palestinian Territories but throughout the Arab world as well. The photographs of Yassin and al-Rantisi's funeral processions were televised globally. This coverage prompted the recruitment of more radical terrorists.

Israel Leaves Gaza

Whereas Israel's northern cities had borne the brunt of suicide bombings, the southern communities of Sderot and Ashkelon absorbed missile and mortar fire from the Gaza Strip. Gaza-based militants continually fired Qassam rockets into Israel on a daily basis.[26] Shockingly, the primary targets of these horrifying attacks were schools. To make matters worse, the terrorists timed the firing of rockets to hit children on their way to classes.

According to 2008 report by the United Nations Office for the Coordination of Humanitarian Affairs, as many as 10 rockets were fired between the hours of 7:00 am and 8:30 am on an average school day, sending children running for cover.[27] At night, whole families struggled to sleep as they huddled in bomb shelters or on the bottom floors of their homes—the only place considered marginally safe.

Map 28 | Gaza rockets and Israeli vulnerability

"It's like Russian Roulette," said one Sderot resident. "You know that eventually a rocket will land on your house."[28] In fact, 90 percent of Sderot residents reported having a missile land on their street or an adjacent one.[29] As a result of these unrelenting attacks, 75 percent of children ages 4–18 now suffer from post-traumatic stress; 120 of these children are currently in long-term mental health therapy. The problem is, as one trauma intervention specialist put it, "It's [the rocket attacks] ongoing, there is no 'post.' How do you treat post-trauma in this situation?"[30]

In 2009, I supported a Denver group called Action Israel that started a project called "Bikes Under Fire." Israeli children who lived in villages along the Gaza border could no longer play outside, as their neighborhoods were within the range of constant rocket fire from Gaza. These children and their families not only slept in bomb shelters, but their daily lives were also impeded because they had to be within a 15-second distance of a bomb shelter at all times. This fifteen-second rule applied to everything including one's walking to school, shopping at the market, or playing outside.

The "Bikes Under Fire" project built bike trails beyond the firing range of Hamas rockets. It also supplied bicycles so that dozens of children could ride together simultaneously in a supervised bicycle club. With funds to pay for adult supervision, Israeli children living in and near Sderot could ride outdoors once again.

It is heartwarming to receive photos of the kids riding outdoors. The communities often express their gratitude for the people in Denver who care about their kids. For those of us who support this on-going project, we feel a sense of accomplishment. Yet we also feel sad for Israeli children who have grown up sleeping in bomb shelters due to rockets landing indiscriminately all around them. No one should have to raise their children under such conditions. No country on Earth would accept this bombardment from its neighbors.

In 2011, a rocket launched from Gaza hit a school bus in our "Bikes Under Fire" community, killing a boy who had enjoyed our bicycle club. Had the bus been hit a few minutes earlier, scores of children would have been murdered. With Gazan rockets becoming more accurate and sophisticated—thanks to Iranian support and smuggling operations—the range of these rockets now enables them to land in larger Israeli cities such as Beersheva, and Ashkelon. Analysts predict it won't be long until the Hamas terrorists in Gaza will be able to target civilians in Tel Aviv, Israel's largest city.

By the eve of Israel's disengagement from Gaza more than 2,600 rockets had been fired upon the cities of southern Israel; the vast majority of these were Qassam rockets.[31] Fabricated from everyday materials such as steel pipes, aluminum, fertilizer, and sugar, first generation Qassam rockets reached a mere three kilometers (less than two miles), but they caused significant damage.[32] Over the years, Palestinian terrorists made these weapons evermore lethal. Improvements to structural materials, propellants, and the performance of warheads, including the addition of metal shrapnel, have made these homemade weapons an arsenal to be reckoned with.[33] Today's Qassam IV has a range of 17 kilometers (10.5 miles) and can reach Israel's largest port city, Ashdod. With the introduction of Grad rockets nearly 1 million innocent civilians (15 percent of Israel's total population) are now within the firing range of Gazan terrorists.[34]

Causing the IDF further concern has been the steady increase in the smuggling of deadly materials through a network of tunnels dug beneath the Philadelphi Route—a narrow strip of land separating the Gaza Strip from Egypt's northernmost border. Munitions have become a local industry there. Rival factions eagerly compete to supply Hamas and other extremist organizations through the tunnels with black powder, guns, missiles and rockets imported from Iran, Iraq, Syria, Sudan, Libya, and Lebanon's Hezbollah. As a result, the number of tunnels crossing into Egypt increased exponentially.[35] Even the Palestinian Authority, (which under Oslo had been charged with the responsibility of disarming militants), directly engineered, financed, or otherwise aided in the construction of these illegal smuggling routes.[36] Egyptians living along the border with Gaza were bought-off, bribed, or coerced into allowing their homes to be used as "weapons transportation hubs."

In the present uncertain times of the Arab Spring uprisings, it remains to be seen how changing regimes will deal with terrorist activities across borders. It seems as if Egypt's new government is incapable, or unwilling, to monitor the flow of materials across the Egyptian-Gaza border. This predicament enables and facilitates the smuggling of weapons into Gaza.

Gaza–Unilateral Disengagement

By late 2003 it was evident to all but the most optimistic observers that the peace process had reached an impasse. It was in this context that Ariel Sharon and members of his inner-circle began planning for Israel's unilateral "disengagement" from the Gaza Strip and parts of the West Bank. Prime Minister Sharon stated, "I attach supreme importance to taking all steps which will enable progress toward resolution of the conflict, ...however, if the Palestinians do not make a similar effort toward a solution of the conflict, I do not intend to wait for them indefinitely."[37] On February 2, 2004, Sharon announced to the nation, "In the future there will be no Jews in Gaza."[38]

Sharon pointed out that "the Disengagement Plan [would] not prevent the implementation of the Road Map." Rather, "it [was] a step Israel [would take] in the absence of any other option in order to improve its security."[39] Firmly believing that, "only security will lead to peace—and in that sequence,"[40] Sharon's disengagement plan was based on Israel's acceptance of the longstanding principle of "land for peace" and was meant to reduce friction between the two peoples. It was hoped that this show of Israel's good faith would jump start the peace process and accordingly facilitate its long-term security needs.

All of this rested upon what later proved to be the mistaken belief that the Palestinians would take advantage of this historic opportunity to establish their own state.[41] Speaking directly to the Palestinian people, Sharon expressed the intent behind his Disengagement Plan as well as Israel's hope for its eventual results:

> It is not in our interest to govern you...We would like you to govern yourselves in your own country: a democratic Palestinian state with territorial contiguity in Judea and Samaria and economic viability, which would conduct normal relations of tranquility, security, and peace with Israel.[42]

I welcomed the announcement of Israel's intention to disengage from the Gaza Strip as did many Israelis who always hoped for the day when Israel could safely relinquish control of the Territories. I remember teaching my classes that this withdrawal could lead to a national homeland for the Palestinian people. As a child, I remembered my family's frequent trips to Gaza to shop and enjoy our neighbor's restaurants and delicious foods. I also remembered the beautiful beaches and hoped that Gaza would become a new beach resort along the Mediterranean Sea. I spoke of these hopes to my students in classes and to audiences of television and radio broadcasts. It was truly a hopeful and exciting time for us. I must have been overly optimistic because I truly believed Gaza could develop into a peaceful, prosperous homeland for the Palestinian people.

Sadly, the evacuation of all Jews living in Gaza and the Israeli military withdrawal only resulted in Gaza becoming more radicalized. Not only were Israelis uprooted from homes where they had lived for 30 years, the Israeli greenhouses specifically left behind to benefit the Palestinian agricultural industry were destroyed by radicals within a few hours of the Israeli withdrawal.

Instead of peace and prosperity, we received unrelenting rocket attacks on Israeli families.

135 | Gaza beachfront

Result of Gaza Disengagement

In the months that followed Sharon's announcement clashes within the Strip escalated sharply. While the majority of these attacks targeted border crossings, border police, and soldiers operating within Gaza,[43] it was the rocket strike on a nursery school in Sderot which could not be ignored.

Israeli military leaders were well aware that before leaving the Gaza Strip they needed to do everything possible to eliminate the terrorist infrastructure. Operation Active Shield was charged with clearing Gaza's northern border of rocket launch sites and other terrorist operations. Operation Rainbow, on the other hand, was a follow-up to an earlier operation (Operation Root-Canal) and was mandated with the responsibility of "terminat[ing] the transfer of all illegal weapons which passed through the Egyptian-Gaza tunnels." Perhaps the most visible of these Israeli efforts was the "demolition of structures that pose(d) an operative security risk to Israeli forces."[44]

These demolitions were met with tremendous international condemnation as some of these structures were private homes. Nevertheless, Israeli intelligence confirmed that certain homes in Gaza were frequently used for military operations and the smuggling of weapons. Accordingly, because these homes were used by terrorists to smuggle illegal weapons into Gaza and to launch weapons into Israel, these "homes" were legitimate military targets under international law.[45] As Israeli Ambassador to the United Nations Dan Gillerman methodically explained:

> Today Israel stands at the gates of hell in the Gaza Strip. The southern city of Rafah serves as the 'Arms Smuggling Gateway' of the Palestinian Authority and the main pipeline for transporting weapons and ammunition into Gaza...

The Rafah tunnels are typically dug inside residential homes to evade discovery by Israeli security personnel, in blatant disregard for the safety and well-being of Palestinian civilians. They are concealed under bathrooms, living rooms and kitchens. They are intentionally hidden under the beds of children and little babies...

Both customary law and conventional law make it clear that the use of civilian objects and dwellings to support a military attack, constitutes a war crime. The Israeli Defense Force does not demolish structures indiscriminately. The clear policy guiding the IDF is that only those involved in terror and violence against Israeli civilians hold no immunity. When terrorists fire from within civilian structures, activate roadside charges from trees and fields, or use a structure to conceal a weapons transfer tunnel, military necessity dictates the demolition of these locations. Under international law, these structures are considered legitimate military targets. Therefore, in the midst of combat, when dictated by operational necessity, Israeli security forces may lawfully destroy structures used by terrorists...

This is common knowledge—and yet it is too often that this Council is called upon to apply a different standard to Israel...

The Security Council has never dealt with the dangers to peace and security of smuggling arms through the tunnels of Rafah from Egypt. It did not meet to condemn the horrendous desecration of the bodies of Israeli soldiers during a defensive operation to dismantle these tunnels. It did not come together following the hijacking of an UNRWA ambulance by armed elements in Gaza last week. It did not stand up against the murder of a mother and her four daughters in the Gaza Strip or the continuing cultivation of a culture of hate.

Unfortunately, Israel does not have the luxury of pursuing this policy of apathy and inaction....

Israel has done and will continue to do everything it can to prevent harm to innocent civilians. Even during times of war, the death of innocent civilians is regrettable, but we cannot be deluded by false pretense and any ambiguity between the terrorists and those who fight this deplorable scourge.[46]

Tragically, the practice of exploiting civilians as "human shields" has become a recurrent terrorist strategy. It was employed by Hezbollah during the 2006 Lebanon War and once again by Hamas during Operation Cast Lead.[47] The UN Security Council has done little to curb this practice while continuing its condemnation of Israel.[48]

Israel Moves Settlers Out of Gaza

Following military operations to rid Gaza of terrorist infrastructure, the IDF prepared to remove Jewish settlers from their homes in Gaza. During the winter of 2004–2005, a shaky cease-fire was maintained as Israel made preparations for a summer withdrawal. Although attacks against Israel had slowed during this time, Palestinian intra-group conflicts were most notable during this period. The natural death of Yasser Arafat on November 11, 2004, led to a series of clashes as rival factions fought to fill the resulting political vacuum.

In Israel there were non-violent clashes between Israeli groups with opposing positions. The "Blue Flags" represented those who supported the disengagement plan which called for the evacuation of Jewish settlers living in Gaza. The "Orange Flags" opposed the withdrawal from Gaza, demonstrating for the rights of Jews to live among the Palestinians in the Gaza Strip. Although public sentiment was split, plans for Israel's disengagement from Gaza went forward rather smoothly, as most Israelis hoped that leaving Gaza would provide an opportunity for peace with the Palestinians.

Israel's Supreme Court gave the legal go-ahead in June 2005 and by early August Israeli and Palestinian security forces were engaged in the process of coordinating logistics in order to ensure the smooth transfer of territory.[49]

It is important to note that most Jewish settlers in Gaza were opposed to leaving their homes. In their settlements these Jews had turned the desert into agriculturally viable lands over three decades. They not only had to leave their homes and communities, gravesites of their loved-ones needed to be excavated and moved into Israel.

Israelis and Jews around the world anxiously watched as IDF soldiers entered the Gush Katif region of the Gaza Strip to begin the removal of Israeli citizens on August 17, 2005. For five consecutive days, images of unarmed IDF soldiers forcefully removing Jewish Israeli citizens from their homes in Gaza flashed across every television screen in Israel. In some cases, Israeli soldiers had to physically carry them out. The angry Jewish settlers chastised the young, IDF soldiers for forcing Jews from their homes.

It was a heart-wrenching experience for the settlers, the soldiers and Israelis in general.

In all, 42 day-care centers, 36 kindergartens, seven elementary schools, and three high schools were closed, relocating 5,000 schoolchildren. Thirty-eight synagogues were left behind. Forty-eight graves were exhumed and moved to Israel.

It is also important to note that industrial high-tech greenhouses were left intact for the Palestinians to continue the thriving agricultural successes developed by the settlers. Instead of utilizing the greenhouses, which had employed thousands of Palestinians and produced vegetables and fruit within the desert, the facilities were looted and burned immediately following the Israeli withdrawal. Instead of welcoming the use of housing and community centers, the Palestinians insisted that all Jewish structures be plowed to the ground. Synagogues that stood in Gaza were burned down within hours of the withdrawal.

Once all 8,000 Israeli citizens who had resided in the Gaza Strip were safely evacuated, the IDF immediately turned its attention to its own withdrawal. By September 12th not one Israeli soldier or asset remained.

On that day, Maj. Gen. Dan Harel, signed a declaration officially ending military rule in Gaza.[50] It was followed by Israel's Interior Minister, Ophir Pines-Paz signing an order recognizing the Gaza Strip as a "foreign territory."[51] With the ball now firmly in the Palestinian's court, Israelis awaited the Palestinian response. This hopeful yet tense situation was best described by Prime Minister Ariel Sharon at the United Nations' Opening Plenary:

136 | Israeli greenhouses donated to Palestinians

> The State of Israel proved that it is ready to make painful concessions in order to resolve the conflict with the Palestinians.... Israeli society is undergoing a difficult crisis as a result of the Disengagement.
>
> Now it is the Palestinians' turn to prove their desire for peace. The end of Israeli control over and responsibility for the Gaza Strip allows the Palestinians, if they so wish, to develop their economy and build a peace-seeking society, which is developed, free, law-abiding, and transparent, and which adheres to democratic principles. The most important test the Palestinian leadership will face is in fulfilling their commitment to put an end to terrorism and its infra-

137 | Greenhouses destroyed by Palestinians

structures, eliminate the anarchic regime of armed gangs, and cease the incitement and indoctrination of hatred towards Israel and the Jews.

I call on the Palestinian leadership to show determination and leadership, and to eliminate terrorism, violence, and the culture of hatred from our relations. I am certain that it is in our power to present our peoples with a new and promising horizon, a horizon of hope.[52]

Israel's disengagement from Gaza sparked renewed optimism among many in the region concerning the prospects for peace between the Palestinians and Israelis.[53] Yet while Israelis were hopeful for a better, peaceful future, it seemed as if the Palestinians had more nefarious intentions.

Sharon's call for leadership, peace, and progress was answered instead with a volley of rocket fire hitting the city of Ashkelon on September 20th. It soon became evident that the Palestinian leadership in Gaza, rather than seizing upon this unique opportunity for peace, was more intent on declaring itself the victor. Posters appeared showing masked Hamas fighters expelling frightened, ultra-orthodox Jews from the Strip. As Nathan Shachar points out, "There were no such Jews among the Gaza settlers."[54]

Despite this negative response, Israel pushed forward by establishing "new rules of the game" which incorporated both carrots as incentives and sticks as sanctions. On the one hand, Israel opened the Gaza coast to commercial fishing, reopened the Karni and Sufa terminals, and worked out an agreed arrangement to open the Rafah border crossing into Egypt under EU supervision. On the other hand, Israel would live up to Sharon's warning made at the United Nations, that until the Palestinian leadership roots out and combats the terrorist threat, "Israel will know how to defend itself from the horrors of terrorism."[55]

Frustrated with the internal political wrangling that consistently blocked any progress towards a peaceful resolution of the Israeli-Palestinian conflict, Ariel Sharon established a new Israeli party, Kadima, which was centrist in its ideology. Kadima, which means to move forward, set out to do just that. Attracting many career politicians from both the left-leaning Labor party and Sharon's right-leaning Likud

138 | Netzarim Synagogue burned by Palestinians

party, Kadima won the March 2006 elections on a platform which included the following aspirations:

1. A unilateral disengagement from all remaining Palestinian territory under Israeli control (the West Bank) based upon the settling of "firm and mutually agreeable borders with the Palestinians and the dismantlement of Israeli settlements located on Palestinian lands."

2. The making of territorial concessions to the Palestinian Authority with the caveat that Jerusalem and Jewish enclaves in the West Bank would remain under Israeli control.

3. This was essentially the same deal laid out at Camp David. Finally, Kadima members committed themselves to the Washington-backed "Roadmap to Peace" and the creation of an autonomous Palestinian state.[56]

Elections in Gaza: Hamas Victory

In sharp contrast, the political rifts among the Palestinians in the Territories in the winter of 2006 were anything but predictable or peaceful. As noted earlier, since the 1980s Hamas's popularity vis-à-vis the PLO and Fatah-led Palestinian Authority had been steadily increasing. That Hamas would do reasonably well in the January 2006 Palestinian Legislative Elections was not out of the question. An overwhelming victory, however, was as unimaginable as it was destructive. As Khalid Jadu, Hamas's Councilman in Bethlehem, stated five days before the vote, "anything more than 55 seats would be an achievement—and probably a headache."[57] At the time, no one could have predicted just how right Mr. Jadu was.

In a shocking upset, Hamas won 74 out of 132 seats on January 25, 2006, with an additional 4 seats going to pro-Hamas independents. The vote gave Hamas a decisive majority in the PA legislature. Some attributed Hamas' success to its grassroots organizing strategy, its promotion of the "resistance project" and the backing of regional actors.[58] Others explained the unexpected victory by pointing to disillusionment with the peace process, Hamas's role in providing basic social services and as a "revulsion at a decade of Fatah misrule"[59] and widespread corruption. In truth, it is this latter view, which seemingly best explains Hamas's victory.

"Palestinians by and large were not voting for political Islam or the destruction of Israel," says Hamas political leader Ghazi Hamad. "Hamas presented an alternative to rampant corruption, Oslo and the road map... a proper balance between political and military struggle." This approach is what Hamas's supreme leader, Mashaal, has dubbed the "gun and olive branch" strategy.[60]

Either way, Hamas's victory dealt the final blow to any semblance of cordial Fatah-Hamas relations. Hamas's leadership made clear its refusal to accept the basic principles of a national unity government. As called for by Palestinian President Mahmoud Abbas in an address to the new parliament on February 18th, it was expected that the next Palestinian government would:

1) abide by existing agreements with Israel;
2) accept negotiations as the "strategic and credible" way to resolve the conflict; and
3) espouse "peaceful" rather than armed resistance.

Hamas's outright rejection of these principles (particularly the latter two) had several detrimental effects:[61]

First, the Middle East Quartet announced its intention to cut off assistance to the PA unless Hamas:

1) renounced violence,
2) recognized Israel,
3) and accepted previous Israeli-Palestinian signed agreements.

Hamas's refusal to do so resulted in the implementation of Israeli-U.S.-E.U. economic sanctions in which only basic humanitarian assistance was channeled through the PA into Gaza.

Second, Hamas's hard line stance resulted in a series of intra-Palestinian clashes as each faction sought to attain authority. While several attempts were made to create a Palestinian national unity government, cooperative Hamas-Fatah relations disintegrated in the summer of 2007 when things turned violent. Through a bloody coup Hamas seized absolute political and military control of the Gaza strip forcing Fatah leaders to flee from Gaza and settle in the confines of the West Bank.

Due to this violent change of power, and the fact that Hamas was determined to be a terrorist organization by the United States and western allies, diplomatic attempts were implemented to isolate the Hamas government. Simultaneously, Israel, the United States and other countries worked to improve the living conditions for Palestinians living in the West Bank. Instead of moderating its terrorist activities or its determination to destroy Israel, Hamas leaders dug in their heals and turned to Iran, Syria, and Hezbollah for funds and other forms of support.[62] It is now known that Iran contributed as much as $10 million per month to Hamas operations while Syria and Hezbollah facilitated the transfer of Iranian-supplied weapons into Gaza.[63]

For Israeli policymakers, the Hamas victory posed several immediate challenges. First, there was the need to prevent the internecine Palestinian conflict in Gaza from spilling over to the West Bank. Second, Gaza's nearly 1.5 million citizens needed resources, but they had to be provided without giving Hamas and its agents the opportunity to rebuild and enhance its deadly arsenal. Finally and most centrally, Israel's security apparatus was faced with the daunting task of preventing the Gaza Strip from turning into an Iranian-backed terrorist base from which radical Islamists would be free to fire upon Israeli cities at will.

Hamas Takes Control of Gaza

Hamas leaders wasted no time making their intentions known. In a raid into Israel near the Karem Shalom crossing on June 25, 2006, Hamas terrorists killed two Israeli soldiers and abducted IDF soldier Gilad Shalit. From the time of his capture in 2006, Hamas denied any access to Shalit[64] including assessment of his condition and assistance to him by the International Red Cross. Despite the pleas by family members, the Israeli government, and international leaders, Hamas refused to release the Israeli soldier for more than five years.

Perhaps taking a cue from Lebanon's Hezbollah that started the Second Lebanon War the same year, Gazan militants launched an all-out bombardment on southern Israeli towns. As noted earlier, during the first five years of the Second Intifada more than 2,600 rockets and mortars had been fired on the cities of southern Israel reaching a peak in 2004, with a record 284 attacks.[65] In the post-disengagement period, an alarming 6,000 rockets and mortars were fired, with nearly 3,000 launched from Gaza in 2008 alone.[66]

On December 19, 2008, Hamas abruptly and unilaterally announced an end to the ceasefire which had been in place for six months. This was immediately followed by the launching of dozens of Qassams and longer-ranged Grad missiles into Israel.[67] This dangerous provocation was not left ignored.

Operation Cast Lead

On December 27, 2008, the IDF replied with Operation Cast Lead. As Defense Minister Ehud Barak succinctly stated, the aim was clear: "To change the situation fundamentally, until there is no rocket fire."[68] Other objectives included damaging Hamas's smuggling routes, its leadership and tactical operations.[69] Although the latter of these objectives was only partially achieved, and after succeeding in dismantling the terrorist infrastructures in Gaza, Israel began to withdraw its troops on January 17, 2010, in accordance with UN Security Council Resolution 1860.

According to Major General Yoav Galant, "There was nearly not one weapon storage facility, smuggling tunnel and terror operative house that was not hit in the Gaza Strip."[70] The Hamas leadership had been dealt a debilitating blow on several fronts.

Hamas leaders apparently miscalculated the Arab and international response. Moderate Arab States—fearful of Tehran's attempt to achieve hegemony in the Middle

East—discretely welcomed Israel's actions.[71] As one Palestinian human rights activist paraphrased Egypt's stance:

> This war is only superficially about Gaza. It is really about defending the Egyptian regime against its foreign and internal enemies, about sending a message to Iran: "We have been slow to react but here it comes."[72]

Finally, many Palestinians in the Gaza Strip blamed Hamas for Operation Cast Lead. As Michael Slackman and Ethan Bronner of the *New York Times* learned in interviews with scores of Gazan households, very few blamed Israel for the situation. Instead, "they blamed Hamas for their misery, for seizing the Israeli soldier, Staff Sgt. Gilad Shalit, which led to the blockade."[73]

Gazans understand that it was the Hamas regime itself which brought on the war and created their current state of despair.[74]

Aftermath of Operation Cast Lead: The Goldstone Report

Since the end of Operation Cast Lead, the number of terrorism attacks emanating from Gaza has lessened, but it has not stopped. Hamas and Fatah continue to be at odds. And Hamas remains in power, although some believe the citizens of Gaza are unhappy with their authoritarian rulers.

On the other hand, international condemnation of Israel's actions is at an all-time high. Perhaps the most egregious criticism came in the UN Goldstone Report, which condemned Israel for war crimes during Operation Cast Lead. This report accused Israelis of intentionally targeting innocent Palestinian civilians. This accusation cannot be further from the truth. In fact, "Israel did not have a policy of targeting innocent civilians. Indeed, the IDF went to unprecedented lengths to minimize civilian casualties."[75]

Hamas, meanwhile, routinely dressed combatants in civilian clothing. Its operatives fired rockets from inside densely populated civilian areas and used civilians as human shields. Furthermore, Hamas stored weapons in mosques and other civilian structures including homes, schools and community centers.

Furthermore, the Goldstone Report demonstrated its bias through faulty fact-finding methodologies. The report has been widely analyzed and subsequently criticized for misrepresentation of the truth, distortions and general bias against Israel.

In the spring of 2011, South African Judge Richard Goldstone, who led the United Nations investigation, recanted his charge of Israeli human rights violations and war crimes during Operation Cast Lead. His reassessment came from the realization that Israel had not intentionally targeted civilians. Instead, it was clear that Hamas terrorists had hidden themselves and their weapon arsenals amongst civilians who were inadvertently killed due to having been used by Hamas as "human shields."

"If I had known then what I know now, the Goldstone Report would have been a different document," Judge Richard Goldstone wrote in the *Washington Post*.[76]

The Israeli government had condemned the 547-page report from the outset, calling it distorted and biased. Following Mr. Goldstone's retraction, Israeli Prime Minister Benjamin Netanyahu stated: "Everything we said has proven to be true: Israel did not intentionally harm civilians, its institutions and investigative bodies are worthy, while Hamas intentionally fired upon innocent civilians and did not examine anything..."

Unfortunately, Israel's reputation has already suffered as a result of the false accusations in this UN Report. Other members of the investigative team stand by their conclusions, despite evidence to the contrary. Even more damaging, Goldstone was instrumental in referring the case against Israel to the International Criminal Court in The Hague for having allegedly committed war crimes. Israel plans to defend itself against these war crimes allegations.

Israeli Action to Prevent the Killing of Civilians

The government, citizens and military of Israel have tried to defend our country in accordance with the highest of moral standards. No government can fail to react when its towns and cities are subject to deliberate bombardment, nor can a government be expected to provide those who attack its citizens with the means to continue their assaults.[77] When Israel did act, it took extraordinary precautionary measures to prevent, and or minimize civilian casualties.

Israelis provided warnings to Gazan civilians to vacate areas targeted for military strikes. These warnings were sent to Palestinians via the media, on leaflets dropped from aircraft, through the blasting of sirens, and even through phone calls and text messages sent to Palestinians in their homes and on their cell phones.

The military checked and then double-checked sites to ensure that any given target was indeed military in purpose.

Finally, the Israeli military prosecutes any IDF soldier accused of operating outside the realm of operational orders, national law, or international law.[78]

Comprehensive investigations were held in Israel following Operation Cast Lead which dealt with every accusation made in the Goldstone Report, as well as other indications of wrongdoing. The Israeli public demands accountability and has confidence in the reliability of its government's internal investigations.

Israelis are also aware of the general bias against Israel which eminates freely from the

United Nations. Sadly, when the UN decides to head investigations against Israel, most Israelis have come to expect biased investigations and unreliable reporting.

Release of IDF Corporal Gilad Shalit

On October 18, 2011, Gilad Shalit was returned to Israel by Hamas in exchange for the release of 1,027 Palestinian prisoners. Many people have asked me, "Why were Israelis willing to agree to this lopsided exchange?" My answer is that the Jewish value of life—even one single life—is paramount. In fact, we are taught that "to save one life is as if we have saved the world." This value is imbedded in Israeli military practices. Therefore, Israel spares no efforts in bringing home every Israeli soldier from behind enemy lines, as well as in freeing its soldiers held captive by the enemy.

This core value is an important part of every Israeli soldier's psyche. When I served in the IDF, I knew that my fellow soldiers and my country would make every possible effort to bring me back home to my family, whether alive or dead.

It is therefore natural for Israelis to accept this exchange, even though the price was exorbitantly high and potentially dangerous for the citizens of Israel. After all, most of the Palestinian prisoners released had the blood of innocent Israeli citizens on their hands.

Furthermore, the facts indicate that there is great risk of future terrorist attacks being perpetrated by released Palestinian prisoners. During the past twenty years, at least 180 Israeli citizens have been murdered in Israel by former Palestinian prisoners. The public demonstrations in Gaza celebrating the return of Palestinian prisoners indicated the Palestinian desire to kidnap additional Israeli soldiers.

Despite these realities, Israelis are jubilant to have Gilad Shalit home and safe in Israel. At the same time, we realistically acknowledge the need for Israel to be evermore vigilant in fighting terrorism. Our national security and public safety measures need to remain on high alert.

If it is proper to "reconstitute" a Jewish state which has not existed for two thousand years, why not go back another thousand years and reconstitute the Canaanite state? The Canaanites, unlike the Jews, are still there. – H.G. Wells[1]

Gaza has become a significant symbol in the struggle for Palestinian statehood and global human rights; especially when raw images of its shattered buildings and dead children are circulated around the world within minutes of Israeli airstrikes.

That squalid, seething Gaza would become a landmark in the struggle for Palestinian statehood is ironic. Until recently it was never really the center of anything in the Palestinian experience. Hemmed in by the Mediterranean Sea and Israel and sharing only a small border with Egypt, this sliver of land has always been something of an outpost. Unlike the West Bank, it does not contain significant Islamic holy sites. For most of its long history, it has not been closely identified with Palestinian leadership or the wider Arab world.

As recently as 20 years ago, the Palestinian focus was totally fixed on Lebanon and the West Bank. Gaza was, by comparison, an afterthought.

However, Gaza now requires special attention due to its equally unique history, situation, needs and political demands. Under the political control of Hamas, Gaza is the more radical of the centers of the Palestinian ideal. It has become a place of immense suffering and complexity. Questions of statehood can no longer be answered without Gaza. It has now become a cornerstone of the conflict.

The key to understanding Gaza is the composition of Gaza's population. Unlike other Palestinian centers, approximately three-quarters of Gaza's population is comprised of 1948 refugees and their descendents,[2] who live in refugee camps separate from the indigenous population. Due to this refugee problem, the population's political demands are somewhat different from those of the Palestinians living in the West Bank.

For example, in the past, the refugees have opposed the idea of a Palestinian state in the

West Bank and Gaza. Had they agreed to a Palestinian state of their own along side of Israel, they would have relinquished their goal of returning to their homes in Israel—where they had lived prior to 1948. Instead, Gazans have argued that if all of Palestine cannot be regained, the minimum acceptable borders would be those of the UN 1947 Partition Plan.

Gaza represents only 1.6 percent of historic Palestine and has never held any strategic or biblical importance to the Israeli government either. In fact, Israel has long considered Gaza to be a burden. During the 1970s and 1980s, Israeli leaders often talked about Gaza as a bargaining chip in the peace process that they were willing to concede. So it is not surprising that Gaza was the first area that the Israelis handed over to limited Palestinian control under the Oslo agreements in the 1990s. It is well known that Gaza cannot survive by itself as an independent entity. Therefore, it needs to be a part of the future Palestinian nation.

Ancient Ties

The oldest sources referring to Gaza indicate that it was once the residence of the Egyptian governor of Canaan. The Ancient Egyptians ruled over Gaza for 350 years. In 1180 BCE, Gaza became an important coastal city under the Eastern Mediterranean peoples known as the

139 | Gaza Mosque, circa 1918

Philistines. The name "Palestine" is derived from the Philistines who dwelled in these lands. Goliath was a Philistine. In the 5th century BCE, the ancient Greek philosopher Herodotus used the term "Palestine" to describe the entire coastal region from modern Lebanon to Egypt.

Foreshadowing modern times, life in ancient Gaza was never easy. From Sumer and Pharaonic Egypt until the First World War, the land of Palestine was the "obligatory route between the valleys of the Euphrates and the Nile."[3] Along with the rest of Palestine, Gaza was invaded throughout the centuries by the Sumerians, Pharaonic Egyptians, Phoenicians, Assyrians, Babylonians, Persians, Greeks, Romans and Byzantines. It was left in ruins by the Crusaders and it was also the site of Mongol raids. In addition, those living in Gaza regularly suffered from floods and locust infestations.

Yet since the earliest known accounts, Gaza was also a prosperous trade center and home to one of the chief port cities of the Levant. The people of Gaza stoically remained at the important intersection of north-south and east-west trade networks and ever-shifting political alignments. During these ancient times, there were no fences or barbed wire and there was no forced ghettoization of the local people. Ironically, the argument has been made that "there are no Palestinians," or that the Palestinian people of today are not native to the land and therefore, are from somewhere far beyond Palestine.

Claiming only Jewish people are native to this land is false and myopic. The archeological record indicates that Jews and Palestinians have something fundamentally in common in their relationship to the land. They both came into existence through a blending of local and outside groups during times of invasions and periods of native co-existence.

During the Muslim conquests in the 7th century, Gaza City became the first city in Palestine to be conquered by the Bedouin people of the Arabian Peninsula who brought Islam and the teachings of Muhammad to the area. In 635 CE, Gaza quickly developed into a center of Islamic learning and law. Palestine subsequently remained under the Rashidun and Ummayad Caliphates for the next 1,300 years. In the 16th century, Gaza was incorporated into the Ottoman Empire. During the first half of Ottoman rule, the Ridwan dynasty controlled Gaza. Under Ridwan rule the city experienced prosperity and peace.

The Ottoman rule of Palestine saw the growth and prosperity of all of the communities of Palestine, including Christian, Jewish and Muslim peoples. However, the year 1914 marked a dramatic turn in the Palestinian way of life. The Ottoman Turks' decision to declare war on the European Allies in 1914 led to a series of events that would affect the people of Gaza, as well as all Palestinians for the century to come. As one observer noted, "The work of months often proved more effective than the neglect of centuries in destroying the agricultural foundations of village life. Nearly all the improvements of the previous 50 years were swept away."[4] On behalf of the war effort, food and livestock were commandeered; trees were cut down for fuel and whole villages were quartered off for troops.

Modern Occupation

> Zionist colonization must either be terminated or carried out against the wishes of the native population. This colonization can, therefore, be continued and make progress only under the protection of a power independent of the native population—an iron wall, which will be in a position to resist the pressure to the native population. This is, in toto, our policy towards the Arabs...[5]

Before the birth of Israel, Gaza was a remote seaside oasis of citrus groves and Islamic learning, while the rest of Palestine was in a state of nationalist turbulence. It was a small, sub-district of Palestine, which quietly existed beyond the fray of economic and political life. Gazans engaged primarily in agriculture, growing oranges and other citrus fruits along the Mediterranean coast. Its connection to the larger Palestinian movement can be traced to events in 1929, as Gaza became part of the rapid political mobilization of the Palestinian community as a whole. As Kimmerling and Migdal noted, "Practically all the new activism had a militarist, anti-imperialist tone, directed against the British, without exception viewing Zionism as a foreboding menace."[6]

By the 1930s and the Great Arab Revolt against Great Britain and the rising Zionist tide, the clear birth of a popular political Palestinian movement was in the making. The Palestinian people began to enact measures that reflected the evolution of their social identity and the sentiment of their own nationalist Palestinian story.

Under the UN Partition Plan of 1947 that called for two states, Gaza was designated as one of the three core zones of the fragmented Palestinian state. However, in the 1948 War, the fertile grain growing and grazing areas of the east and the lucrative citrus and vegetable fields in the north were lost to the Zionists. As a result of the war, 180,000 refugees poured into Gaza, joining the 80,000 indigenous residents. From this point forward, Gaza became known for its refugee camps such as Beach Camp, Bureij, Deir al-Balah, Jabaliya, Khan Yunis, Maghazi, Nuseirat and Rafah.

The area was named the Gaza Strip because it was a sliver of land that remained unconquered by the Israelis at the cessation of the 1948 War. Gaza was claimed by Egypt.

By December 1949, the United Nations General Assembly established the United Nations Relief and Works Agency (UNRWA) for the Palestinian refugees. UNRWA provided (and continues to provide) basic social, medical and educational services.

For the next 20 years, the Palestinians reeled from the trauma of being displaced from their land in Palestine. They wanted to return home and anticipated the day when they could repossess their houses in Israel. Every Palestinian who fled the hostilities, "no matter what the circumstances, left behind property in the form of land, crops, orchards, industrial plants, quarries, heavy equipment, trucks, banks, bank accounts, houses, furniture, rugs, household effects, stores and warehouses full of goods, livestock (including goats, sheep, hens, and cattle), cash, jewelry, and more." In 1998, it was estimated that the value of Palestinian property lost between 1947 and 1948 was equivalent to $57.8 billion.[7]

Meanwhile, Israel enacted laws in the Israeli legislature, the Knesset, allowing the Israelis to retroactively and prospectively confiscate all properties from anyone defined as absentee. This included all of the property left behind by Palestinians. Everything left behind inside the newly formed State of Israel was "appropriated by Israel and turned over to the Jewish National Fund for administration and disbursement to Jewish immigrants."[8] To date, Israel has not paid financial reparations to the Palestinians whose lands, homes and possessions were absorbed by the state.

While the refugees in Gaza remained in their camps after the 1948 War ended, many attempted to return to their homes and villages to retrieve their property or to find lost relatives. These efforts involved traversing the new boundaries of Israel, which the Israelis considered illegal infiltrations.[9]

According to Israeli historian Avi Shlaim:

> Infiltration was a direct consequence of the displacement and dispossession of [the Palestinians]…The motives behind it were largely social and economic… The infiltrators were [mostly] Palestinian refugees whose reasons for crossing the border included looking for relatives, returning to their homes, recovering material possessions, tending their fields, harvesting… During the 1949–56 period as a whole, 90 percent or more infiltrations were motivated by social and economic concerns…. [As a result of] the "free-fire" policy adopted by the Israeli army, border guards, and police [in this same period]… between 2,700 and 5,000 infiltrators were killed… the great majority of them unarmed.[10]

Inevitably, it was from this "free-fire" policy of shooting to kill any individual Palestinian refugee returning to claim his property, that a policy of massive Israeli retaliation against Palestinians began. This involved "striking at the individual villages and areas from which Israel claimed the infiltrators had come—places that lay inside the boundaries of neighboring states."[11] Such attacks greatly affected the people of the Gaza Strip who were governed by the Egyptian administration. As Rubenberg writes, "The raids were conducted at night, were aimed at civilian targets, and violated the sovereignty of the Arab states."[12]

Specifically, in February 1955, the violent Israeli reprisals in Gaza set in motion a chain of reactions that led to Israel's invasion of Egypt in October of 1956. As many attest, the acts of violence against the Gazans fueled the frustration and anger leading up to the 1967 War.

Unlike the West Bank, which was governed by Jordan after the war, Gaza and its refugee residents fell under Egyptian rule. Consequently, subsequent generations of Gazans do not identify with Jordanians as do Palestinians in the West Bank. Many Gazans not only question the political link with Jordan, but feel no specific cultural ties with Jordan.

During their 19 years of Egyptian rule, the general consensus was that Gazans could move with greater freedom in and out of the region, but had no political freedom. As a result, underground groups such as the Muslim Brotherhood and the Palestinian Communist Party emerged within the refugee camps and gained popularity among young Palestinians. The vast refugee population had little opportunity for economic advancement. Men worked as seasonal day-laborers in the citrus groves, "but at least half of the adults were unemployed, and the per capita gross national product was only $80 in 1966."[13]

By the early 1960s, Arab leaders were interested in avoiding further conflict with the Israelis. But by this time, a revolutionary Palestinian movement was forming under the leadership of Yasser Arafat. As previously described, Arafat was influenced by what had transpired in Algeria and Cuba, the indigenous Vietnamese resistance to the United States and Arab nationalism more generally. In Egypt, President Gamal Nasser proposed the creation of the Palestinian Liberation Organization (PLO). It was to be an independent institution through which Palestinians could advocate for their own rights. However, Nasser's intention in establishing this organization was to create the illusion of Palestinian representation, while in reality, he wanted to ensure Arab control over it. Although famous for his pan-Arab inclinations, Nasser was also determined to suppress any opposition to his rule, including opposition from the Palestinian people under his care in Gaza.

Then, Egypt's humiliating defeat in the 1967 War changed the face and role of Gaza.

Economic Dependency

In the June 1967 War, Israel conquered Egypt's Sinai Peninsula, and the Gaza Strip. An Israeli coercive military occupation of these areas was immediately instituted. Just as in 1948, the Palestinians thought that the occupation would be short-lived. Also as in 1948, thousands of Palestinians were forced by Israel to flee from their homes. In particular, some 250,000–300,000 people fled or were driven from their homes in the West Bank and Gaza Strip.[14] Of this number, many were already refugees of the 1948 War.

> On July 2, 1967, under pressure from the international community, Israel announced that it would permit the return of refugees if they applied no later than August 10 (subsequently extended to September 13). The number of refugees who were aware of Israeli's announcement is unclear, but given the turbulence of their lives in the months after the war, it is safe to assume that the number was limited. Nevertheless, 120,000

persons applied to return; of these, Israel permitted only 14,000 to do so. The refugees from 1967 were officially termed "displaced persons" and they, together with their descendants, are thought to number some 1.1 million today.[15]

In Gaza, an immediate impact of the Israeli occupation was a significant rise in unemployment. Service jobs in the Egyptian army and UN forces vanished. Trade with Egypt stopped, and the shipping port closed. Along with the West Bank, the economy of Gaza was absorbed into the Israeli economy as the occupation continued. This left the people of Gaza dependent on Israel for goods and services. The economic practices of the Israeli occupation permitted "only certain Gaza products to be sold within Israel, flooding the Gaza market with Israeli goods, restructuring Gaza's agriculture, and encouraging Arab laborers to work in Israel."[16] Soon, the Israeli currency became the only legal tender in the Gaza Strip, and local merchants and banks had no way to hedge against soaring inflation.

As the monetary relationship between the Gaza Strip and Israel changed under the Israeli occupation, so too, did agriculture. As a result of the occupation, Israel prevented Palestinian farmers from exporting any produce that would compete with Israeli goods. Restrictions were placed on the Palestinian consumption of water and the growing of certain crops, while Israeli farmers were free to plant according to their preference and consume all of the water they needed for their crops to grow successfully. As a result, agriculture stopped supporting the Gazan economy and an unprecedented reliance on Israeli products and produce ensued, leading to a massive upheaval of centuries-old traditions. Gaza went from independence to dependence on Israel.

With no economic alternative, more and more Gazans became the manual labor force of Israel. Legally and illegally, men and boys of all ages left their homes early in the morning to commute to Israel to build its infrastructure. While the wages were low by Israeli standards, they were actually five times the rate in Gaza, which made employment in Israel attractive. Illegal and unregistered, many of these jobs were exploitative. An adult could expect to earn up to $15 dollars per day, whereas a child would be illegally hired and paid $5–6 dollars.[17]

While Palestinians were paid to work in Israel, they were not permitted to sleep there. It was illegal for them to remain inside Israel between the hours of 1:00 a.m. and 5:00 a.m., and so many were forced to find ways to hide in Israel rather than endure the long commute between home and work. Many Palestinians slept in shacks, or on construction sites. Some spread out on the floors of Israeli restaurants. "There were cases of disasters when workers locked into factories at night were unable to escape when fires broke out."[18] For the refugees of Gaza, working meager jobs in Israel on their own land was not only demeaning—it was a constant reminder of their subservient treatment as non-citizens of the Israeli state. Israeli economic policy implemented by its military occupation of Gaza effectively "turn(ed) the Gaza Strip into a large labor camp."[19]

After 1967, there has always been a sense in Gaza that, eventually, the Israelis would push the Palestinians into the sea. The Israelis encouraged Palestinian emigration and they cut off water and food supplies to the Gazans.

> I have never been to Gaza. Many might find that surprising. People around the world look at the Holy Land as such a small area on the map and they assume it is all interconnected. But when I lived in Palestine, I was a small child living north of Haifa. Gaza was a different place, miles away. We had no connection to it.
>
> Then we moved to Lebanon, where we were refugees. Gaza was under the rule of the Egyptians and subsequently became occupied by the Israelis. So, I could not go to Gaza. However, I knew that the Palestinians there were like me and so I felt a certain kinship with them. They were like cousins in my extended family that I had never met.

Contemporary Colonization

Until 1978, the Gaza Strip had only a low priority in the Israeli settlement movement. Historically, Gaza was not part of the Judea and Samaria regions, and therefore did not appeal to Jews who were seeking to inhabit the ancient biblical lands. As early as 1987, Israeli Foreign Minister Shimon Peres admitted that Jewish settlements in the Gaza Strip did not provide any security benefit to Israel and therefore believed they should be dismantled.

Prior to the Camp David Accords in 1978, the object of Israeli land settlement in Gaza was to "surround and contain the Strip by placing a dozen settlements directly to the south of Pithat Rafiah, rather than placing vulnerable civilian settlements within the congested and volatile Strip itself."[20] This policy changed with the rise of the Likud government and the subsequent signing of the Israeli peace treaty with Egypt. Although Egypt and Israel inevitably normalized their relations, this only made things worse for the Palestinians of Gaza and the West Bank. In particular, one key point of criticism was that the Egyptian peace treaty with Israel failed to demand greater concessions for Israeli recognition of the Palestinians' right to self-determination. After Camp David, the residents of the Gaza Strip and the West Bank found themselves at the mercy of far-right Israeli settlement policies.

The Accords demanded the evacuation of Israeli settlements from Pithat Rafiah along the Egyptian border. This left the Palestinians in the Gaza Strip with a border directly adjacent to Egypt. In essence this meant that the Israeli government could no longer surround the Gaza Strip from all sides. In response, the Israeli government chose to build substantial settlements within the territory. In doing so, the Israeli government "aimed at creating such an interlocking grid of Jewish and Arab communities that they could not be disentangled in any future negotiations. The settlements would both make it impossible for the Palestinians to carve out a state on the West Bank and Gaza and would also isolate the Palestinian towns from each other, preventing coordinated political action."[21]

But unlike in the West Bank, the settlements in Gaza did not have room to grow because it was impossible to find additional land in such a small place, especially as the Palestinian population was already so dense. The Israeli government pressured the Palestinians to sell their property or risk Israeli expropriation. This was in order to enable the building of Israeli settlements in Gaza. As Israeli settlements swelled in Gaza, more and more Palestinian land was expropriated. New settlements sprang up next to refugee camps. Israeli-only supermarkets, banks, recreational facilities, tourist resorts and industry were planned, while the rest of Gaza's population lived in squalor.

To make matters worse, many of the settlers arrived with extreme racial and religious views, and exercised their perceived superiority over the Gazan citizens. Gazans stood helplessly when Israel further imposed its 50-meter wide security zone. From 1982–1983, the residents of the town of Rafah and the Rafah refugee camp were forced to relocate. By the mid-1980s, Israel controlled nearly 30 percent of the Gaza Strip.

The looming confrontation between the citizens of Gaza and the settlers of Israel was predictable. With the impoverished population of Palestinians living in refugee camps, while the Israelis inhabited spacious, modern settlements, it didn't take long to realize the animosity that would ensue.

It was in this cauldron that the nascent ideas of a distinct Palestinian nationalism simmered, and a fierce guerrilla movement spread throughout the Gaza Strip. "Substantial quantities of light weapons remained in the Strip from the Egyptian army and the PLA, and the members of the PLA blended into refugee camps and poor sections of towns or hid in dense orange groves. The guerrilla movement was complemented by a civil disobedience campaign: students demonstrated in the streets and schoolyards, lawyers refused to appear in court, and residents boycotted Israeli goods"[22]

During these years of the growing Palestinian movement, not only did Palestinian men and women take up arms on their own behalf for the first time, but they also resonated with the ideology of "a movement to repossess a land and a history that had been wrestled from us. Our leaders were popular and accountable to us, not hereditary or imposed on us from above."[23]

Israeli retaliation against the Palestinian nationalist movement in Gaza was especially swift and fierce. Round-the-clock curfews were imposed on refugee camps while Israeli soldiers searched houses and interrogated residents in an effort to root out guerrilla fighters and quell the movement. "Many were beaten, their belongings were smashed, and 12,000 relatives of suspected guerrillas were deported to detention camps in the Sinai. At least

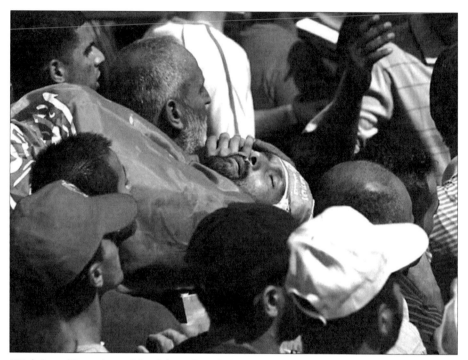

140 | Funeral Procession at al-Ayn Refugee Camp, 2007

13,000 were forced to leave their homes as roads were bulldozed through the refugee camps to facilitate army control and prevent guerrillas from escaping."[24]

On the whole, the Israeli military occupation limited Palestinian political activities in the Gaza Strip to a much greater extent than in the more established West Bank. Greater divisions were particularly evident in Gaza, as many people were attracted to the Islamic fundamentalist movements. This appealed to the Palestinian sense of tradition and faith while also attracting those who were disillusioned with the PA's inability to move the peace process forward.

In the First Intifada of 1987, the Palestinian people of Gaza were angry and well supplied with light arms and rudimentary military training from the Palestine Liberation Army (PLA). "Within months, they turned to guerrilla tactics against Israeli control. Guerrillas hid in orange groves and congested quarters of the towns and camps. They lobbed grenades at Israeli military vehicles, burned buses that transported Gazans to work inside Israel, and attacked the banks, post offices, and markets that symbolized a return to normal life in the Strip."[25] Systemic civil disobedience also supplemented the 1987 Intifada revolt. The students of Gaza protested publically, teachers protested against the

Israeli occupation school system, and women's groups formed in protest. Between the actions of the guerrilla groups and the nonviolent protests, the primary goal was to make Gaza ungovernable.

Instead, Israel responded—as usual—with disproportionate force. Palestinian activists were arrested, deported and imprisoned (if not killed). Refugee camps were placed under lengthy curfews while the Israeli military "searched homes, smashed belongings, and forcibly removed thousands of residents."[26] To facilitate army control, homes were destroyed as roads were bulldozed through the camps in an the effort to break up the alleys where guerrilla fighters sought safe haven.[27]

Using overwhelming force, Israel isolated and destroyed the Gaza uprising. In the end, even though Prime Minister Sharon forced the refugee camps into submission, resentment in the camps burned very deeply, causing individuals to form militant cells that launched attacks against the Israeli aggressors even as the First Intifada came to an end. Palestinian frustrations continued to grow as a result of the obvious lack of improvement in their living conditions and with the continuing decline of their political status.

Initially, at least, when the Oslo Accords were signed in September 1992, two-thirds of the Palestinian people supported the peace initiative.[28] Accordingly, expectations for the results of the Accords were very high. The Palestinian people regarded Oslo as the agreement that would end the occupation and deliver improved living conditions. During this time, support for Yasser Arafat leaped to 65 percent and a general embrace of the mainstream secular nationalist movement headed by Arafat won approval by 55 percent of the Palestinian population across the West Bank and Gaza Strip.[29]

This "golden era" in favor of the peace process did not last long as Palestinian hopes for statehood faded when Benjamin Netanyahu was elected Prime Minister of Israel in 1996. His administration allowed ceaseless and unrepentant building of additional Jewish settlements in the West Bank and Gaza.

On the face of it, the return of Yasser Arafat to Gaza as the leader of the Palestinian people July 1994, represented a new beginning for the Palestinian people. They felt they had a chance of governing themselves, in their own land. Even to the people of Gaza, Arafat was a symbol of national liberation, and thousands greeted him with cheers and jubilation. However, circumstances evolved that made the PLO's success unattainable..

The Rise of Hamas

The label "Islamism" is a relatively recent term coined in the 1970s. In light of the reasons for the emergence of political Islam in the Middle East, the movement gained ground in Gaza after 1967. As Israelis celebrated their swift victory in the 1967 War, Islamist ideas infused the ideological vacuum left behind by the failure of pan-Arabism.

The term Islamism (or "political Islam") was used to refer to the "rise of movements and ideologies drawing on Islamic teachings in order to articulate a distinct political doctrine." In particular, "Islamic themes of collective injustice and equality were mobilized against those regimes that were corrupt, bankrupt and authoritarian, and often supported by the West in the Cold War confrontation with the Soviet empire."[30]

Historically, the activists in Gaza included members from the underground groups that came into being during Egyptian rule. Among these groups was the Muslim Brotherhood, which helped to galvanize protests against Egyptian policies, especially after Israel brutally attacked Gaza in the 1953 and 1955 cross-border raids. In particular, the Muslim Brotherhood pushed to arm the Palestinians, and to engage Egyptian forces in order to protect Gazans from Israeli attacks. It also stood firm against any plans to resettle Palestinians outside the refugee camps. They held firmly to the belief that these Palestinian refugees should return to their rightful homes in Israel.

During the 19 years of Egyptian rule over Gaza, the Muslim Brotherhood was continually harassed, along with other political organizations, such as Fatah and the Communists. The PLO was explicitly secular in its ideology. Since the PLO was composed of Fatah, the Popular Front, the Democratic Front and the Community Party, they all agreed to secular political principles. The Communist party, in particular, was once well rooted in Gaza due to its appeal among the poorest Palestinians who felt discriminated against by the professional class of the Palestinians living in the West Bank.

The religiously based, Muslim Brotherhood, and later, Hamas, had adherents in the Gaza Strip as well. Unlike the secular political platform of the PLO, the Muslim Brotherhood called for the return to religious traditions and the establishment of an Islamic state. In the mid-1980s, since 95 percent of the 633,000 Gazan population was Muslim, there were many who desired to follow the traditional Islamic doctrines of Hamas.[31]

As early as 1980, there was conflict and violence between the Islamists and secular groups in the Gaza Strip. The most extraordinary incident occurred on January 7, 1980, when "some 500 men marched from a mosque in the center of Gaza City to attack the Red Crescent Society, smash liquor stores, burn movie houses, and wreck restaurants that served alcoholic drinks."[32] For the next two decades, as the PLO became steadily weaker, more corrupt, and more incapable of resolving the Palestinian-Israeli conflict, the Islamists emerged as a viable alternative. Their mantra taught that the Palestinian people would ultimately triumph if they would turn to God.

Sheikh Yassin, who later founded Hamas, once said in an interview that unless the PLO adopted Islam as its ideology, "Muslims must maintain a cautious distance: a Muslim who joins Fateh[Fatah] is like a Muslim who drinks wine or eats pork."[33]

For the Israelis, the inner conflict over religion in the Palestinian Territories was seen as a strategic advantage because it turned one faction against the other and sidetracked the Palestinians from struggling against the occupation. Outlawing all political parties, the Israeli government was careful to allow the Muslim Brotherhood (and later Hamas) to exist, but only as charitable organizations.

At first, the public in Gaza was particularly wary of the Muslim Brotherhood because of its perception that the Brotherhood was controlled by Israel. However, once Hamas and Islamic Jihad emerged as independent splinter groups in the Gaza Strip, the formerly secular, nationalist approach was adopted by the Islamists who infused their ideology with religious symbolism and language.

In the name of defending the Palestinian people, Hamas effectively put forth an uncompromising political stance against Israel. In doing so, the political question "Who really represents us?" came to the fore. With this in mind, it is no coincidence that the creation of Hamas in Gaza coincided with the aftermath of the outbreak of hostilities in the

141 | Peaceful Hamas supporters, Ramallah, 2005

1987 Intifada. Indeed, the "formation of Hamas marked a clear shift in the ideological and political attitude of the Muslim Brotherhood in Palestine towards the Israeli occupation."[34]

Pressing and changing circumstances enabled the rise of Hamas out of its roots in the Muslim Brotherhood. Already, other Palestinian groups such as Fatah and Islamic Jihad were undertaking their own acts of resistance against the Israeli occupation. In years prior, the idea of engaging in violent acts of resistance against Israel stood against the Muslim Brotherhood's priority of increasing Islamic education throughout Gaza. However, the creation of Hamas enabled the Muslim Brotherhood to distance itself from violent activities, while also keeping a hand in the action.

The rise of Hamas in Gaza triggered serious competition and rivalry between other political groups in the PLO, especially Fatah. When the Oslo Agreement was signed between the PLO and the Israeli government in 1993, Hamas strongly opposed it. Seeing the PLO as making concessions about Palestinian lives and welfare, Hamas also opposed the creation of the Palestinian Authority on ideological and political grounds. Their claim was that the secular nature of the PA conflicted with Hamas's vision of Palestine as an Islamic state, which would exist on the land occupied by Israel. Hamas argued, "the PA was merely a tool to implement an Israeli-American scheme against the interests of the Palestinian people; it decided, therefore, to resist the Oslo Agreement and to oppose and undermine the PA. It exercised this opposition through violent attacks against Israel, and through an official boycott of the presidential and legislative elections that took place in 1996."[35]

Israeli Withdrawal

By 2005, Prime Minister Sharon and the Israeli government finally recognized the heavy burden of defending the Israeli settlements in Gaza and decided to withdraw from the Gaza Strip. Indeed, the settlements were officially handed over to the Palestinians, but not before the structures within them were demolished by tanks.

During the settlement withdrawal of Gaza, Israeli extremists frequently stated that the global and local opposition to settlements was opposition to Israel itself. Some even equated opposition to illegal settlements with anti-Semitism. However, what is often popularly misunderstood is that the Palestinian opposition to settlements comes not out of a malicious desire to deny Israel's right to existence, but rather, to assure that Palestine may exist side-by-side with Israel.

When Shimon Peres stated that the Israeli Settlements in Gaza were an overextension of Israeli resources, the Gazans interpreted this statement as meaning that armed resistance against Israel had succeeded. Later in 2005, after nearly four decades of military occupation and the encroachment of settlements ended, it did feel like a victory to Gazans to see Israel retreat. "We witnessed a day that was made fact by their blood, struggle, and patience.

They believe today that they harvested what they planted during the last 38 years of steadfastness."[36]

This was not to deny the obvious fact that Ariel Sharon's plan to withdraw from Gaza was a strategic way of maintaining and strengthening settlements in the West Bank. Clearly many of the settlers moved straight from Gaza to the West Bank, suggesting that Israel would continue the building of new settlements in the West Bank until the territory there is entirely confiscated by Israelis.

In the January, 2006 elections, Hamas won an upset victory over Fatah, winning 74 out of 133 seats in the Palestine Legislative Assembly. Despite this victory, under the Palestinian constitution, Mahmoud Abbas remained President of the Palestinian Authority.

Meanwhile European and American leaders abroad pledged not to negotiate with Hamas and not to provide aid to the Palestinians until Hamas agreed to disarm and recognize Israel.

Refusing to compromise its position, Hamas leaders refused to ever recognize Israel and to never give up the Palestinian claim to all of Palestine, despite the fact that a majority of Palestinians voters hoped that Hamas would lead them down the path of peace.

The Hamas-led government of Gaza was sworn in on March 29, 2006. Fatah refused to join the coalition because Hamas would not recognize the PLO as the representatives of the Palestinian people, and would not agree to honor past agreements of the Palestinian Authority and the PLO, including the Oslo Agreements that recognize the existence of Israel and formed the basis for the legitimacy of the Palestinian Authority. With this, the international community and specifically, the United States, suspended aid to Gaza, where Hamas was now in charge.

Prisoner Exchange October, 2011

On June 25, 2006, just as the Palestinian Authority announced the conclusion of an agreement for a truce with Israel, Hamas fighters from Gaza attacked an Israeli army border outpost at Kerem Shalom, killing two soldiers and capturing a third, Gilad Shalit. Hamas offered to exchange the soldier for Palestinian prisoners. Israel refused to negotiate and began a siege of Gaza and later launched an invasion called "Operation Summer Rains" to pressure Hamas to return the soldier alive and to stop the barrage of Qassam rockets that were being launched from Gaza on Israeli civilians.

From the Gazan/Palestinian point of view, Gilad Shalit is a soldier who is subject to being captured by his enemy. He would only be released according to rules of international law or he would be released after diplomatic steps that might take place between the two parties at war. To this end, they ask, "How many Palestinians and Lebanese were and are imprisoned by Israel solely as "bargaining chips"? How many are kept in "administrative detention" without any criminal charge, let alone conviction?"

In reality, Israel has a long history of taking Palestinian hostages in this cycle of violence.

Operation Cast Lead

On December 27, 2008, without warning, Israelis launched a war against Gaza. Calling it "Operation Cast Lead," Israelis killed 1,455 Palestinians including 333 children. The attack included a bombing campaign resulting in the complete destruction of large areas of Gaza leaving many thousands of Palestinians homeless.

The IDF used airstrikes with precision missiles to bomb homes, killing Palestinians as they slept. Tanks and short-range artillery were employed to kill Gazans and deadly white phosphorus was spread over densely populated residential areas. The destructive offensive lasted for 22 days, culminating in unprecedented casualties and destruction, including the obliteration of thousands of civilian homes.

International condemnation of the Israeli attack began immediately by Amnesty International and other humanitarian groups. They demanded an investigation into Israeli conduct in the war. Accusations of Israeli war crimes were rampant, as the death tolls included innocent civilians.

> Much of the destruction was wanton and resulted from direct attacks on civilian objects as well as indiscriminate attacks that failed to distinguish between legitimate military targets and civilian objects. Such attacks violated fundamental provisions of international humanitarian law, notably the prohibition on direct attacks on civilians and civilian objects (the principle of distinction), the prohibition on indiscriminate or disproportionate attacks, and the prohibition on collective punishment.[37]

The Goldstone Report

Following the Gaza War, United Nations Human Rights Council commenced a fact-finding mission created to investigate violations of international human rights and violations of humanitarian laws. Justice Richard Goldstone, former judge of the Constitutional Court of South Africa was chosen to lead this investigation. The Goldstone Report "found evidence that both Israeli forces and Palestinian militants committed serious war crimes and breaches of humanitarian law, which may amount to crimes against humanity."[38]

Goldstone stated, "We came to the conclusion, on the basis of the facts we found, that there was strong evidence to establish that numerous serious violations of international law, both humanitarian law and human rights law, were committed by Israel during the military operations in Gaza…The mission concluded that actions amounting to war crimes and possibly, in some respects, crimes against humanity, were committed by the Israel Defense Force (IDF)."[39]

Although Israeli officials denigrated the Goldstone Report, the international community welcomed its findings. Former U.S. President Jimmy Carter commented, "The Goldstone committee examined closely the cause of deaths of the 1,387 Palestinians who perished, and the degree of damage to the various areas. The conclusion was that the civilian areas were targeted and the devastation was deliberate. Again, the criticism of Israel in the Goldstone report is justified."[40]

Norman Finkelstein wrote, "The findings were consistent with those of the other human rights organizations: Israel is guilty of a very significant number of war crimes."[41]

Prisoner Exchange: Gilad Shalit

On October 18, 2011, 1027 Palestinian prisoners were freed from Israeli jails. The deal was brokered by Hamas, which released Gilad Shalit, in exchange for a thousand Palestinian mothers and fathers, sons and daughters, who were able to return back to their families after years of captivity in Israel.

While the story of Gilad Shalit has been spread across international front pages and broadcasts for five years, the heart-wrenching stories of thousands of Palestinians languishing in Israeli prisons for decades have received very little attention from the world media. Unfairly, Palestinian prisoners have been hidden from view and their human stories have been ignored. Even when prisoners went on hunger strikes, the world ignored their plight. During this prisoner release, the Palestinians were not referred to by name, but by the number 1,027.

Palestinians, including elected members of parliament, were forgotten by the world even though they had been unjustly kidnapped and held, without being charged and without having a fair trial in Israel.

There are thousands of tragic Palestinian stories. Take the fate of 57-year old Fakhri Barghouthi, who was imprisoned in Israel at the age of 24, and who has spent 33 years locked behind bars. Both of his parents and one of his brothers died while he was held captive in Israel. Then there is Hassan Salameh, whose newborn twins, Ali and Sanaa, were only 19 days old when he was arrested in 1982. His release after 29 years in prison brings him back to his family as a grandfather.

There is no question that justice has been denied for Palestinians held captive in Israeli prisons.

Witnessing the celebrations in the Occupied Territories and Gaza, one gets a sense of the jubilation of Palestinians who have been reunited with their families at last.

But the struggle is not over. There are thousands of Palestinians still languishing behind bars in Israel who need to be released. As reported in an editorial in the Saudi Arab News:

> While the Palestinians have every reason to celebrate the liberation of their loved ones, this must draw the world's attention to the plight of thousands of other Palestinians rotting away for years and decades in appalling conditions in the Israeli gulag. Amongst the 1,027 prisoners, 315 have spent more than 20 years for demanding freedom and dignity in their own homeland and protesting against the worst occupation the world has ever seen...[42]

The Future of Gaza

What kind of solution to the Israeli-Palestinian conflict do the Palestinians of Gaza seek? For starters, the option of becoming permanently joined with Jordan appears out of the question. More than the West Bank, the people of Gaza have no historic ties with the Hashemite Kingdom. Moreover, they resent Jordan's past treatment of Palestinians living under its rule. However, Gaza is in desperate need of an economic outlet with its neighbors, especially for its produce. Meanwhile, the port of Gaza is a viable potential hub for trade, should peace with Israel ever be achieved.

Like the Palestinians of the West Bank, the vast majority of Gazans hold to the long-held nationalist aspiration for an independent Palestinian state. Today, the Palestinians outside of Israel are made up of three groups: the Palestinians of the West Bank, the Gazan Palestinians and the Palestinians of the Diaspora. Those in Gaza desire Palestinian statehood as much as Palestinians elsewhere, but due to internal and external political pressures, the means and ends of the Gazan political leadership differ greatly from those of Mahmoud Abbas and the Fatah Party in the West Bank.

The palpable sense of poverty and despair in densely populated Gaza today makes it one of the most dangerous places to live in the world. The economy and living conditions of Gaza have suffered precipitous declines since 1967. Hunger and malnutrition have increased along with the growth of its population.

The increase in the radicalization of the population, along with heightened levels of violence within Gaza hurts the Palestinians. So do the relentless Israeli attacks.

"Final Status" refers to the four issues at the conflict's core—borders, Jerusalem, settlements and refugees.

Can both sides return to these issues yet again and resolve them? To do so, they will have to reach deep within their political systems and cultures to find the flexibility and compromise required to craft a real treaty. Otherwise, peace will be evaded.

So much has happened since 1948. And yet the Final Status issues persist.

Israel has waited many years to establish a lasting peace with the Palestinians. When Yasser Arafat tightly held the reigns of Palestinian leadership, Israel perceived a perpetual unwillingness on his part to honestly accept an independent Jewish state in Israel—even though his statements to the West indicated a desire for peace. His words indicated one thing; his actions demonstrated quite the opposite.

Following Arafat's death, Israel's hope for a reasonable peace partner was revived when Mahmoud Abbas (Abu Mazen) became president of the Palestinian Authority (PA) on January 9, 2005. For a short time the Palestinian leader of the Fatah Party ruled both Gaza and the West Bank from Gaza. Since he adopted a more moderate stance toward Israel, hope for peace was in the air. But Hamas' victory in the democratic Palestinian election held in Gaza in January 2006, dealt two devastating political blows to the peace process. The first occurred within the Palestinian leadership following a fractious transition of power. Hamas waged a vicious military coup against the PA's Fatah leaders, causing Abbas and the Fatah Party cabinet to flee to the West Bank.

Hamas's coup d'etat created a quagmire for the international community because Hamas is an "identified terrorist organization" outlawed by Israel, the United States, the European Union and many other western states. To convince Hamas to change its ideology and end its ongoing terrorist attacks against Israelis, several measures and sanctions were instituted against Hamas. These measures, included a naval blockade of Gaza in order to restrict the flow of weapons into the Gaza Strip.

The international community has repeatedly urged the leaders of Hamas to renounce violence and accept Israel's right to exist. For more than six long years, however, Hamas has adamantly upheld the doctrine of armed struggle against Israel while expressing its determination to eradicate the Jewish people from the Holy Land.

Due to Hamas's intractable position, especially its refusal to end terrorism, the United States and Israel have subsequently ended diplomatic relations with Gaza. Without assistance from the U.S., Gaza has become the proxy of American's adversaries, namely, Iran and Syria. In addition, Hamas has formed a strong alliance with the Lebanon-based Hezbollah terrorists, who also operate under the supportive tenacles of Iran and Syria.

There are now two distinctly different groups of Palestinians—those living in Gaza and those living in the West Bank.

The release of 1,027 Palestinians from Israeli jails by Hamas in 2011 in exchange for the release of a captured Israeli soldier, Gilad Shalit, has further demonstrated the effectiveness of Hamas in dealing with Israel. This, in turn, strengthens Hamas popularity within Palestinian society, thus, perhaps, lowering the status of the PLO and Fatah.

The United States and other nations desiring a Two-State solution have continued to support the economic growth of the West Bank, including funding several nation building initiatives which were implemented by the Palestinian Authority (Fatah Party) in the West Bank.

American administrations have increased this political and economic support hoping that the Palestinians in Gaza (who have been sanctioned due to Hamas' terrorist activities) will be influenced to choose to be led by the more moderate Palestinian Authority instead of the militant Hamas government in Gaza. Since Palestinian Authority leader Mahmoud Abbas in the West Bank has won generous financial support from the West, due to his renunciation of violence and his anti-terrorism efforts, supporters of Israel hope that Hamas will lose its popularity in Gaza.

However, since the facts on the ground have not indicated a more moderate approach by Hamas, there has been little success in forwarding the peace process since the Camp David Summit of 2001. At the time this book went to press, the Final Status Issues remain unsolved.

Instead, President Obama has pressed vigorously for the renewal of negotiations between Israel and the Palestinian Authority in the West Bank. However, PA President Mahmoud Abbas acted against the wishes of the Obama administration when he unilaterally requested recognition of Palestinian statehood from the United Nations General Assembly on September 24, 2011.

Amid these challenging and contentious circumstances, the Israelis continue to pursue peace with the Palestinian Authority in the West Bank. However, President Abbas has been unwilling to restart the peace talks, insisting that he will not negotiate unless Israel stops construction in Jerusalem and the West Bank, an issue which has never been was a precondition for negotiations.

Therefore, the Final Status Issues remain hotly contested and clearly unresolved. Israeli administrations hold the PA leadership responsible for the lack of progress. As Israeli

Deputy Foreign Minister Daniel Ayalon recently said, "Enough stalling, enough excuses. Abu-Mazen (Mahmoud Abbas) knows our phone number and our address. He could be here in 10 minutes. We have been waiting for him for two years. Unfortunately we are left staring at an empty chair."[1]

Israel's positions on the Final Status Issues are as follows:

Borders

Israel Desires to Establish a Palestinian Homeland

Israel has been offering land to the Palestinians in exchange for peace for more than 45 years. Israel will negotiate borders with the Palestinians through face-to-face peace negotiations with Palestinian leaders. Israel has no interest in continuing to occupy the West Bank and has already relinquished control over Gaza.

The Israeli position is to negotiate in good faith with the Palestinians in order to create a viable and sovereign Palestinian state in the West Bank and Gaza with safe passage between the two.

The Pre-1967 Borders are Indefensible

Israel holds the position that the 1967 borders (Green Line) insisted upon by the Palestinians and the Arab League are not acceptable because they are indefensible. In Israel's view, the Green Line should be treated simply as a starting point for future negotiations.

The pre-1967 boundaries are based on temporary ceasefire lines established by the 1949 Armistice Agreements between Israel and Egypt, Lebanon, Jordan and Syria following the 1948 War of Independence and the establishment of the State of Israel. These ceasefire lines were never intended to be permanent international boundaries. Rather they reflected the relative positions of Israeli, Jordanian, Syrian, Egyptian, and Iraqi forces at the end of that war.

Calls for Israel to withdraw to the Green Line reflect the Arab position that the West Bank and East Jerusalem are "occupied" territories. Israel contends that these areas were not under the legitimate sovereignty of another state prior to Israeli control over them. In fact, Jordan captured the West Bank and East Jerusalem in 1948 and occupied them until 1967. As such, Israel and the U.S. have never recognized the legitimacy of Jordan's rule west of the Jordan River.

UN Security Council Resolution 242 is often cited in support of the Palestinian contention that Israel must withdraw from the West Bank and East Jerusalem. Israel's position is that Resolution 242 calls for Israel to withdraw from "territories occupied in the recent conflict." There is no reference to withdrawal by Israel from *all* territories or even *the* territories. Resolution 242 also specifies that any withdrawal by Israel is contingent upon the establishment of secure and recognized (i.e. agreed upon) boundaries. In other words, the resolution does not require Israel to unilaterally withdraw, but foresees a negotiated agreement between the two parties to determine where Israel's secure borders should be drawn.

Israel Requires Secure and Defensible Borders

UN Security Council Resolution 242 recognizes the right of every state, including Israel, to live in peace within secure and recognized borders. Throughout its history, Israel has been forced to grapple with repeated military assaults from neighboring Arab countries, most of which have yet to recognize Israel as a legitimate state. Israel also has suffered repeated terror attacks from armed factions such as Hamas and Hezbollah that seek Israel's destruction. Even if a peace agreement is achieved between Israel and the Palestinians, Israel would still have the inherent right to defend itself against potential threats. What the future will bring largely depends upon the establishment of secure and defensible borders between Israel and a Palestinian State.

Annexation of the Etzion Block

Based upon previous negotiations, Israel has asked to annex the Israeli settlements of the "Etzion Block." These settlements were built as suburbs of Tel Aviv and Jerusalem. They exist close to the Green Line and consist of 4–6 percent[2] of the Palestinian Territories. To compensate Palestinians for the loss of this West Bank land, Israel has offered a "land swap" in exchange for Israel's annexation of the "Etzion Block." In other words, Israel could transfer to the Palestinians an amount of land equal in size and of commensurate value (to the "Etzion Block") from southern Israel to the future Palestinian state.

Annexing the area of the Etzion settlements along the Jerusalem-Tel Aviv corridor will provide Israel with the security buffer zone it needs to protect its narrow nine-mile-wide borders established by the 1947 UN Partition Plan. The 240,000 Israeli settlers in this area will remain Israeli citizens. As a result of this exchange, Israel would be willing to dismantle all the rest of the Israeli settlements in the West Bank. Approximately 100,000 Israeli citizens in these settlements would be uprooted by Israel from the eventual newly created Palestinian state and transferred into Israel.

It should be noted that when one reads about, or hears people talk about, the "pre-1967 borders" this refers to the 1947 UN Partition Plan map that includes the narrow nine-mile width of Israel between Tel Aviv and Jerusalem. In 2011, when

President Obama called for Israel to concede to the precondition of pre-1967 borders, it caused Israelis to fear that the U.S. President endorsed the re-establishment of this indefensible border for Israel. Obama clarified his position later, saying that he meant for that border to be a "starting point" for future border negotiations. However, one can clearly understand Israeli sensitivities and reactions to such a miscommunication.

Demilitarization and Early Warning Detection

For a new map to succeed, Israel must maintain defensible and secure borders—a condition that probably requires the demilitarization of the Palestinian state. It may also require the installation of early warning military systems in part or all of the Jordan Valley (similar to those protecting Israel in the West Bank since 1967).

Jerusalem

Jerusalem is Essential to the Jewish People

Since Jerusalem embodies the sacredness of Judaism and the 5,000-year scope of Jewish history, Israel's position has been to keep a united Jerusalem as its political capital, under Israeli jurisdiction.

Since the Palestinian position also demands rule over East Jerusalem as the future Palestinian capital, there has been talk of dividing the city between east and west. During the 2000 Camp David Summit, Israeli Prime Minister Ehud Barak offered an immense compromise when he suggested dividing Jerusalem as part of a broader peace offer. But even that offer was rejected by Palestinian leader Yasser Arafat. It is far from certain whether such an offer will ever be made again.

Israel Needs to Maintain Sovereignty Over Holy Sites

When Palestinians demand that East Jerusalem be their capital, it must be understood that East Jerusalem encompasses the entire Old City of Jerusalem. This is the area captured by Jordan during the 1948 Israeli War of Independence. It includes the Western Wall and the Temple Mount, which are the holiest of holy sites for Jews. Israelis are extremely concerned that if the Palestinians control East Jerusalem including the Old City, Jewish people would be barred from accessing our holy sites.

Why do we fear this? Because it has happened before.

Israelis were exiled from East Jerusalem during the Jordanian occupation from 1948 to 1967.

Jews were prohibited from entering the Old City and could not even pray at the Wailing Wall. We also remember the devastating destruction of religious sites by the invading Arab armies in 1948, including the razing of 58 synagogues.

Moreover, during Palestinian Authority rule, there have been numerous attacks by Arabs against Jewish religious sites in the West Bank. Since 2000, Joseph's Tomb, Rachel's Tomb and the Shalom El Israel synagogue in Jericho have been desecrated. There are often desecrations of Jewish gravesites on the Mount of Olives. Jews visiting the cemetery are in danger of attack.

Denial of Jewish Claims to the Holy Land

It is not just holy sites that concern Israelis. Jewish claims to the Holy Land are undermined and regularly denigrated by those who write "revisionist history." By denying Jewish historical facts, perpetuators of this misinformation often incite Palestinians to deny Jewish claims to the Land of Israel and particularly to their Jewish holy sites.

Like Holocaust deniers, the revisionists of Middle East history deny the existence of Jewish religious sites. Some even claim there was never a Jewish Temple on the Temple Mount.

As recently as 2010, UNESCO passed a resolution claiming that Rachel's Tomb and Ma'arat Ha-Machpelah (Cave of the Patriarchs) were never Jewish historical sites, but are solely Muslim ones.

In contrast, Israelis not only recognize the significance of the Holy Land to people of all three Abrahamic faiths, they continue to protect Muslim and Christian sites with the same tenacity and respect as they do their own. In the case of Jerusalem, Jews have been protecting Islamic holy sites in the city for nearly 50 years.

This protection extends to people as well. During the First Intifada, Islamic extremists attacked Christian pilgrims and desecrated Christian sites. The Christian population in the Palestinian Territories south of Jerusalem has been harassed for decades. Consequently, East Jerusalem's Christian population has declined significantly.[3] This reinforces Israeli fears that adequate protection of the holy sites and freedom of worship in Jerusalem can only be guaranteed under Israeli jurisdiction.

A final peace agreement with the Palestinians must not only protect Israel's fundamental national and religious links to Jerusalem, but it must also allow Israelis and Jews access to Jewish historical and religious sites existing in the West Bank including Ma'arat Ha-Machpelah, the Cave of the Patriarchs in Hebron, as well as other holy sites throughout the West Bank.

Historical Claims

Jewish claims to Jerusalem date back long before King David made Jerusalem the capital city of the Jewish kingdom thousands of years ago.

Jews have continuously lived in Jerusalem since the time of King David, except during the period of Jordanian occupation from 1948 to 1967. Jewish devotion to the city was unequivocal, even when Jerusalem was controlled by hostile empires. The Jewish people are the only people who have ever made Jerusalem their capital city and they have constituted a majority of the city's population since the 1860s. Today, Jerusalem is the largest city in Israel with approximately 10 percent of the country's population residing there.[4] Jews account for approximately 65 percent of Jerusalem's inhabitants[5] and key Israeli government institutions are located in the city, including the offices of the President, the Prime Minister, the Knesset (Israeli Parliament) and the Supreme Court.

Lawful Claims to Jerusalem

Israeli control of Jerusalem is legal under international law because the city was acquired through acts of self-defense against invading Arab states during the 1948 War of Independence.

In contrast, Jordan illegally occupied East Jerusalem in 1948 through an offensive war, clearly contrary to international law. When Israel was attacked during the Six Day War, Israel took defensive action to protect itself against further Arab attacks, consequently gaining control of East Jerusalem.

Palestinians base their claims to East Jerusalem on a variety of UN resolutions. But none of these claims are legitimate.

Israelis point out that the wording of UN Security Resolution 242 does not require Israel to withdraw from Jerusalem. In fact, Resolution 242 makes no specific reference to Jerusalem, simply requiring that Israel withdraw from "territories" to "secure and recognized boundaries."

Israeli Voters Concerned about Future Partitions

Since 1967, Israel has implemented a series of policies to prevent any future partition of the city. Laws passed by the Knesset in 1967 extended the jurisdiction of the Jerusalem municipality to include East Jerusalem. Although Israel has asserted to the UN that it has not officially annexed East Jerusalem, the Israeli Supreme Court has held that eastern areas of Jerusalem have, in fact, become part of the State of Israel.[6]

Since various Israeli administrations have voiced the possibility of relinquishing Arab portions of Jerusalem, Israeli voters have been concerned about future offers by Israeli officials concerning Jerusalem's future. In 2010, the Knesset enacted a law requiring that any proposal to relinquish any portion of Jerusalem to Palestinians, including East Jerusalem, would require a two-thirds majority approval. If it passed, the Knesset further established that Jerusalem's division would be subject to a national referendum before it could be enacted.

No to International Control

UN Resolution 181 of 1947 proposed that Jerusalem would come under international jurisdiction. By accepting UN Resolution 181, Israel conceded to Jerusalem becoming an "international city." However, this agreement was never implemented because the Arab States immediately declared war on Israel and Jordan quickly captured the city.

Subsequently, Israelis argue that this resolution was non-binding and became irrelevant as a result of the invasion. Since Israel now controls the historic Jewish capital, this resolution, that Arab nations voided by their aggression in 1948, cannot now be cited by Palestinians objecting to Israel's jurisdiction over East Jerusalem.

The notion of an internationally managed, independent Jerusalem has been suggested by third parties several times in the past. But considering the UN's acts of bias against Israel and the inadequacy of its peacekeeping missions in Lebanon and elsewhere in the Holy Land, it is highly unlikely that Israel would entrust the safety of Jerusalem to UN jurisdiction in the future.

What is at Stake for the Jewish People?

Security is at the heart of the Jerusalem question. As recently as March 2011, there was a bus station bombing in Jerusalem. Bordered on three sides by Palestinian territories, Jewish neighborhoods in the city are within the reach of short-range weapons. It is estimated that Palestinians in the West Bank possess about 15,000 such weapons. Since 1967, there have been numerous attacks on Jewish neighborhoods in Jerusalem from the West Bank.

An Analogy to Washington D.C.

Students often ask me, "Why is Israel so obstinate about Jerusalem?" The best way to answer is to pose a fictitious analogy:

Imagine the United States was entangled with a Native American tribe demanding that its ancestral land be returned. The tribe demands that Washington D.C. be divided as part of a peace treaty. This division would award the National Mall to the tribe, including the U.S. Capitol, the Washington Monument, the Lincoln Memorial, the Library of Congress, and the Smithsonian museums.

Congress would never agree to it. The American people would never agree to it.

Now imagine that the United Nations passes resolutions insisting the United States adopt this policy in order to establish a lasting peace with the tribe. And to bring this nightmarish analogy to its fullest, the tribe insists that due to the fact that the *tribe and the U.S. cannot come to an agreement, the tribe decides to unilaterally establish their own country hostile to the United States on the Mall in Washington D.C. They even go to the United Nations General Assembly in New York to ask the UN for recognition.*

Perhaps, through this analysis, readers may get a sense of how strongly Israelis feel about Jerusalem. It may also explain the Israeli determination to keep Jerusalem both undivided and under Israeli jurisdiction.

Settlements

For Israelis, the issue of settlements is a contentious one. There are those who believe the settlers in the West Bank should move back to Israel, acquiescing to the Palestinian demand that Palestinian land be "for Arabs only." There are others who believe that Jews should be allowed to live in the West Bank because it is part of the Holy Land promised by God to the Jewish patriarchs. And finally, there are Jews who are concerned the settlement issue has tarnished Israel's good standing in the international community.

What is clear is that Palestinian leaders have been consistent. They claim that the future Palestinian State will be segregated. No Jews will be allowed to live in the Palestinian State. Today, it is a capital offense for Palestinians to sell land to Jews. In many instances, it is forbidden for West Bank Palestinians to work for Jews. This absolute Palestinian intention to restrict Jews from the future Palestinian State is clear to Israeli citizens, although it is rarely acknowledged by the international community (which often criticizes Israel for discriminating against Palestinians.) Israel, on the other hand, extends the rights of Israeli citizenship to close to the twenty percent of its population who are Arab Israelis.

Jews Should be Able to Live Throughout the Holy Land

Jews have lived in the West Bank since biblical times. The Israeli position is that Jews have a legal right to live there. Following the Six Day War, many Israelis decided to move to settlements in the West Bank because of the area's historical and religious significance to them.

Since the West Bank is regarded by Israel as "disputed territory," Israel's position is that the competing claims over the West Bank, including the Jewish settlements existing there, should be resolved through peace negotiations.

The position taken by successive Israeli leaders has been that the settlements—apart from the outposts, which the government has dismantled—are entirely legal and have been developed according to international humanitarian law.

Israel has valid claims to the West Bank not only due to Jewish historical and religious claims to the land but also because the territory was not under the sovereignty of any independent Palestinian state before coming under Israeli jurisdiction as the result of a war of self-defense in 1967.

Finally, Israelis believe the issue of settlements is more of a Palestinian political maneuver to avoid viable peace negotiations. The insistence by Palestinian President Abbas demanding the freeze of settlement building as a pre-condition to resuming peace talks, which gained support internationally, is an example of such a maneuver. To most Israelis, this pre-condition seems to be a stalling tactic in order to avoid negotiating in good faith directly with the Israelis. It is also seen to be an intentional diversion in order to further condemn Israelis in the international media for the failure of peace negotiations to date.

Settlements Do Not Prevent Negotiations

As far as Israelis are concerned, settlements are not the real obstacle to a peace agreement. Israel has demonstrated its commitment to dismantling settlements when it returned occupied territory to the Palestinians as it did outright in Gaza in 2005.

Israelis argue that even before there were settlements in the West Bank, Arabs were unwilling to make peace with Israel. And settlements did not prevent the establishment of peace agreements between Israel and Egypt in 1979, nor with Jordan in 1994. Notably the Palestinians agreed to sign the Oslo Accords despite the rapid growth of the Jewish settlement population between 1992 and 1996.

Palestinians and other opponents of Israel's settlement activity have accused Israel of violating Article 49 of the 1949 Fourth Geneva Convention Relative to the Protection of Civilian Persons in Time of War. Article 49 prohibits states from transferring parts of their population into occupied territory, and was intended to protect local populations from deportation and displacement. Article 49 however, cannot be applied to Israel's settlement activity. The West Bank and East Jerusalem are not "occupied" territories, but "disputed" territories over which there are competing claims that must be resolved through negotiations. Article 49 does not apply to the voluntary repatriation of individuals to the lands from which their ancestors were expelled.

Despite all this, Israel recognizes the significance of the West Bank to the Palestinians and hopes to return it to the Palestinians in exchange for peace between our peoples.

The Settlements Were Never Intended to Displace Arab Inhabitants

Israeli settlements were only established after detailed investigations ensured that Jewish settlement communities would not be established on private Arab land.[7]

To this day, Palestinians derive significant economic benefits from Israeli settlements. The Manufacturers Association of Israel estimates that some 22,000 Palestinians are employed in the construction, agriculture, manufacturing and service industries that serve the settlements.[8]

Settlement Growth and Construction

Israelis deny that previous agreements with the Palestinians restrict Israelis from building in the West Bank settlements. Instead, Israeli leaders have implemented "settlement freezes" in the West Bank from time to time, as acts of good faith during negotiations. However, since the Palestinians have rejected Israeli offers of peace, construction within the settlements has continued to accommodate for population growth within the settlements, including the building of more apartments and schools. This growth has occurred within the designated boundaries of the settlements and no additional West Bank land has been utilized.

A Possible Solution

In the West Bank, 80 percent of the settlers live in blocks that account for 4–6 percent of the land. The area is called the Etzion Bloc. The five settlements in this bloc house 240,000 settlers near Jerusalem and the Green Line.

These settlements are virtual suburbs of Jerusalem and Tel Aviv, creating a wider buffer zone that enhances the security of the most populated areas of Israel. Prior to building the settlements along this corridor, Israel was only 9 miles wide, leaving it vulnerable to terrorist and enemy attacks. The settlements in the Etzion bloc are: Ma'ale Adumim, Modlin Illit, Ariel, Gush Etzion, and Givat Ze'ev.

Israel has announced plans to build homes in the area between Ma'ale Adumim and Jerusalem, thereby broadening the connection between the two. In response to international criticism over this project, Israelis argue that without this link, Jerusalem would be an island without any contiguity with the rest of the State of Israel. Israelis also contend that the incorporation of the five major settlement blocs into Israel will not prevent the creation of a contiguous Palestinian state.[9]

In exchange, Israel will transfer an equal amount of its own territory to the Palestinians, and provide safe passage between the West Bank and the Gaza Strip to provide for a contiguous Palestinian State.

The other, approximately 80,000 settlers in smaller settlements throughout the West Bank will likely be uprooted and moved into Israel. Israel has made these transfers of their populations in exchange for peace several times. For example, Israeli settlers in the Sinai were uprooted from their villages and resettled in Israel following the 1979 peace agreement with Egypt, and thousands of Israelis left Gaza when Israel ended the occupation of Gaza in 2005.

Will this suffice? It's hard to predict. When Israel dismantled settlements in Gaza and forced Israelis from their homes, Israelis received only more terror in return. This reinforced the

Israeli viewpoint that it is not the settlements that pose the greatest threat to peace, but the violent refusal of Palestinians to accept Israel as a legitimate state.

From the Israeli perspective, the real obstacle to peace has been the Palestinian refusal to recognize Israel as a legitimate Jewish homeland. Denying Israel's right to exist and the years of violence and terrorism inflicted by Palestinian militants against Israeli citizens have constituted the true obstacle to peace.

Until Palestinians collectively recognize Israel's right to exist, renounce violence and successfully stop terrorists within their midst from attacking Israel, Israelis do not find it necessary to dismantle settlements or force hundreds of thousands of Israeli citizens to leave their homes, nor to inhibit growth of their communities existing in the West Bank.

Refugees

Israeli officials deny that Palestinians and their descendants have an absolute "right of return" to Israel. The final status of the refugees should and will be determined through direct peace negotiations.

Establish a Palestinian Homeland for the Refugees

Israelis maintain that the establishment of a new Palestinian state will encompass a successful resolution of the Palestinian refugee problem, allowing Palestinian refugees from around the world to settle in the new Palestinian state.

Reciprocal Compensation

Israel has agreed, in principle, to compensate Palestinian refugees for properties lost in Israel. However, compensation should be conditioned upon reciprocal compensation being paid to hundreds of thousands of Jews who were expelled from Arab countries following Israel's independence.

Finally, Israel insists that any final status agreement must also terminate the refugee status for all Palestinian refugees and suspend all further claims against the State of Israel.

The reasons for these positions on the refugee issue are critical.

"Right of Return" is Demographic Suicide

Israelis cannot afford to accept the "right of return for all Palestinian refugees." The number of Palestinians in 1948 was about 700,000. Now, it is estimated to be more than 10 million worldwide. Their repatriation would turn the Palestinians into the majority in Israel. Israel is the only democracy in the Middle East. If it acquired an Arab voting majority, its existence as the world's secure Jewish homeland would end. All laws pertaining to Jewish issues would inevitably be democratically overturned. Consequently, Israel would no longer exist as a safe haven for world Jewry.

In addition to this existential threat to Israel's survival, should radicalized refugees be allowed to return to Israel, they would most likely constitute a security threat to Israel. They could join with Palestinian extremists to attack Jewish Israeli citizens from inside Israel.

No Legal or International Precedent

Israel does not believe the Palestinian "right of return" exists as an international legal right. Palestinians became refugees as a result of wars. It was Arab nations that triggered the Palestinian Diaspora. Therefore, the refugee problem should be resolved primarily by those who perpetrated the hostilities.

Specifically, it was the Arab States' rejection of UN General Assembly Resolution 181 Partition Plan that initiated the Arab War of annihilation against Israel. Since this war against Israel resulted in the mass exodus of Palestinians from their homes in Israel, it is the Arab States that lost the war, that should absorb the Palestinian refugees who fled from Israel into their countries.

Tragically, Arab states, with the exception of Jordan, have refused to permit the integration of their Palestinian refugee populations into their societies and have denied them basic human rights and freedoms for more than 60 years.

Palestinians born in Arab states have been excluded from acquiring citizenship in Arab nations, resulting in generations of statelessness for the Palestinian refugee population. From the Israeli perspective, Arab states have implemented exploitative and repressive policies to further their own political agendas, including gaining international support for Palestinian statehood.

Israel has set the most positive example for absorbing refugees. Israelis argue the 1948 War brought about a population exchange: when Palestinian refugees who left Israel were replaced by incoming Jews who had been forced, as a result of persecution or direct expulsion, from their homes in neighboring Arab countries. These Jewish refugees sought protection in Israel and were granted citizenship. Arab states should therefore do the same for the Palestinian refugees rather than denying them citizenship and refusing to integrate them into their Arab societies.

The Solution

Israel contends that any future Palestinian state should welcome Palestinian refugees in the manner Israel has welcomed worldwide Jewish refugees since 1948. With assistance of the international community and especially from Arab countries, Palestine should absorb all Palestinian refugees. This would not only improve the conditions for the Palestinian people presently living in UNWRA refugee camps, it should also fulfill their long-awaited dream of a homeland of their own.

Palestinians want to live peacefully. To do so they need a viable homeland in the Holy Land where, after a six-decade hiatus, they can once again pursue their own cultural narrative. It's a narrative that is every bit as old and rich as the Jewish narrative. And to do that, they need a peace agreement with Israel that satisfactorily resolves the four core issues that have defined both the scope and failure of peace talks in the region for generations. Several issues have been at the center of the Palestinian concern: borders, Jerusalem, Israeli settlements in the West Bank, and the 1948 Palestinian refugees right of return.

Borders

Defining territory has been one of the four core issues of the Israeli-Palestinian conflict, and any agreement on the borders of the future Palestinian state has significant consequences for all other final status issues. The central importance of the issue is reflected in Palestinian efforts to determine a "border-first" approach in the 2010 peace negotiations.

Palestinian statehood and the right of self-determination is a fundamental demand of the Palestinian people. The creation of a Palestinian state—a homeland to which many Palestinians will be free to return after more than 60 years in exile—is crucial to ending the displacement and statelessness that generations of Palestinians have been forced to endure. However, what is essential for my people is that the new Palestinian state will be established in such manner as to ensure its long-term political, social and economic viability.

Without this, there can be no just equitable solution to the Israeli-Palestinian conflict, and therefore no durable and lasting peace in the Middle East.

Palestinians have made noteworthy compromises about borders since 1948. The issue of borders has shifted significantly toward what many Palestinians perceive as a historic compromise. Initially laying claim to all of historic Palestine, the Palestinian leadership modified its original territorial demands following the 1988 Palestinian Declaration of Independence and Palestinian acceptance of the Two-State Solution. Since then, Palestinians have sought to establish an independent, viable and sovereign Palestinian state, with East Jerusalem as its capital on the land occupied by Israel after the 1967 War.

Palestinians have indicated their willingness to recognize Israel's borders as encompassing the territories occupied by Israel prior to the 1967 War. This acquiescence to ceding approximately 78 percent of historic Palestine is viewed by Palestinians as an enormous sacrifice as what they are willing to accept—the remaining 22 percent—is a mere fraction of the land that was allocated to Palestine by UN Resolution 181.

In return, Palestinians seek Israel's withdrawal from the entire West Bank, including East Jerusalem, to the pre-1967 borders otherwise known as the Green Line. The Green Line represents the armistice lines drawn pursuant to the 1949 Armistice Agreements between Israel, Egypt, Lebanon, Jordan and Syria.

This position is broadly in line with the proposals laid out in the Saudi Initiative (also known as the Arab Peace Plan). The Initiative, endorsed in 2002 and reaffirmed in 2007 by the Arab League, proposes the creation of a Palestinian state composed of the Gaza Strip and the West Bank with its capital in East Jerusalem. In return, Israel would be recognized by all Arab countries and granted full, normal diplomatic relations. The Palestinian Authority, along with many in the international community, have given full support to the Saudi Initiative. Some factions within Hamas have also indicated a willingness to accept a Palestinian state within the pre-1967 borders, although Hamas has yet to officially support the Two-State Solution.

Moreover, the Palestinian Authority has remained open to the idea of limited land swaps on the basis of the pre-1967 borders. Some Israeli settlements would be allowed to remain intact in exchange for Palestinian acquisition of territory now part of Israel. Palestinian leadership at the Camp David Summit in 2000 were prepared to consider a land swap on a one-to-one ratio, provided that land acquired by Palestine would be of equal value, in areas adjacent to the border with Palestine, and in the same vicinity as the lands to be annexed by Israel.[1]

International support is strong for a viable, contiguous and independent Palestinian state, with East Jerusalem as its capital, on the basis of pre-1967 borders. The international community has consistently denounced Israel's illegal and unilateral annexation in 1967 of the Gaza Strip and the West Bank, including East Jerusalem. Such territories have been regarded by the international community, led by the United Nations, as Occupied Palestinian Territories with Israel as the occupying force. In particular, the UN Security Council in Resolution 242[2] has reaffirmed the illegality of the acquisition of territory by war, and calls for the withdrawal of Israeli forces.

Israel's extensive settlement activity with its accompanying infrastructure—including the ongoing construction of the separation barrier and settler-only "bypass" roads—are widely regarded as a serious threat to Palestinian efforts to create an independent and viable

Palestinian state on the basis of the pre-1967 borders. Palestinians perceive the construction of the separation barrier, together with the annexation of Palestinian land and the severe restrictions placed on freedom of movement for Palestinians in the Occupied Palestinian Territories, as a blatant attempt by Israel to unilaterally determine the borders of the future Palestinian state. If completed, the separation barrier will leave Palestinians with only 54.5 percent of the West Bank, or 12 percent of historic Palestine.[3]

The international community has criticized the unilateral actions taken by Israel to transform the physical and demographic character of the Occupied Palestinian Territories. The UN Security Council has stated that Israel's settlement policies are in "flagrant violation" of the 1949 Fourth Geneva Convention Relative to the Protection of Civilian Persons in Time of War.[4] Similarly the UN General Assembly has called for the immediate and complete cessation of all Israeli settlement activities in the Occupied Palestinian Territories.[5] The International Court of Justice has ruled that Israel's settlements and separation barrier constitute a violation of international law and interfere with the territorial sovereignty and right of the Palestinian people to self-determination.[6]

Indeed, the right of Palestinians to self-determination and statehood has a firm foundation in international legal instruments such as the Universal Declaration of Human Rights, the International Covenant on Economic, Social and Cultural Rights, and the Declaration on the Granting of Independence to Colonial Countries and Peoples. To this effect, UN General Assembly Resolution 54[7] reaffirms the right of the Palestinian people to self-determination, including the option of a State. Similarly, UN Security Council Resolution 1397 refers to the co-existence of the two states of Israel and Palestine, each with secure and recognized borders.[8]

It is undeniable that the issue of borders is a vital and necessary condition for a future Palestinian state. Fair borders ensure the political, economic and social viability of the proposed nation. A just and lasting peace can only be achieved on the basis of a territorially contiguous Palestinian state, in which Palestinians will have full control over their borders and security, enjoy freedom of internal and external movement of goods and persons (including between the West Bank and Gaza), and have access to sufficient land and resources to ensure growth and the development of a sustainable economy.

A Palestinian state that deviates significantly from the one demarcated by the Green Line, and which lacks territorial contiguity and control over its borders and resources, runs contrary to the right of the Palestinian people to independence and self-determination. A Palestinian state in this form would fail to restore and guarantee the fundamental rights of the Palestinian people, and its citizens would unlikely be able to accept its legitimacy.

Not only has the creation of a Palestinian state on the basis of pre-1967 borders gained popular support among many Palestinians, but, as noted above, the concession of approximately 78 percent of historical Palestine is perceived by Palestinians as a tremendous historical sacrifice. Further concessions are unlikely to be acceptable to most Palestinians, and may result in a greater shift in popular support for groups like Hamas. This would undoubtedly have severe consequences for the achievement of an equitable and durable peace in the Middle East.

Jerusalem

Equally, there can be no Palestinian state without East Jerusalem as its capital.

The issue of Jerusalem has proved to be one of the thorniest in the final status negotiations. Jerusalem has deep resonance for both Palestinians and Israelis, and the future of the city lies at the very heart of the current conflict. A resolution that is acceptable to both parties is central to a just and sustainable peace in the Middle East.

For Palestinians, Jerusalem or al-Quds, "The Holy One," is the heart of Palestinian nationality and identity. It is a city of immense strategic, socioeconomic, geographic and political importance, and is regarded by Palestinians as the capital of the future Palestinian state. Jerusalem also epitomizes the struggle of the Palestinian people for their cultural and historical homeland. It is a sacred city that holds tremendous religious and historical significance for Palestinians, both Muslims and Christians alike. An equitable agreement on Jerusalem is therefore pivotal in the minds of Palestinians.

Jerusalem is the center of life for both the West Bank and Gaza Strip. The city lies in the north-south crescent of the West Bank and is a major intersection of vital east-west and north-south transportation routes. Wider East Jerusalem extends from Ramallah to Bethlehem and has continued to serve as the political, administrative, cultural and commercial capital for Palestinians. It remains as the economic center of Palestine, accounting for some 35 percent of the Palestinian economy.[9] East Jerusalem is crucial to the integrity of the Occupied Palestinian Territories, and indeed, the future of the Palestinian state; without East Jerusalem, the possibility of an economically and politically viable Palestinian state is severely compromised.

Jerusalem is also deeply sacred to Palestinian Muslims and Christians. Semitic Canaanite/Palestinian roots in Jerusalem can be traced back 5,000 years. The city's Islamic heritage derives from the fact that it is the site of the Prophet Muhammad's Night Journey, *Isra and Mi'raj*, and served as the first *qibla* (direction of prayer) for Muslims. The al-Aqsa Mosque, located within the Haram al-Sharif, "Noble Sanctuary," Temple Mount, is the site of Islam's third holiest shrine. Jerusalem is also home to the Holy Sepulchre, Christian Palestinian Arab Churches and the Mount of Olives. Free and unimpeded access for Christians and Muslims to worship in Jerusalem is therefore essential to any resolution of the Jerusalem issue.

Palestinians have laid claim to the area comprising pre-1967 East Jerusalem as the capital for a new Palestinian state. Palestinian leadership has also stipulated that Jerusalem must be an open city, with no physical partition that would prevent freedom of movement within its boundaries. Freedom of worship and access to sites of religious significance must be guaranteed. Since most of the religious sites are located within the Old City in East Jerusalem, they would therefore fall under the sovereignty of the future Palestinian state.[10]

During the course of the peace negotiations, Palestinian leadership has indicated greater willingness to discuss, in principle, the establishment of East Jerusalem as the capital of Palestine, and West Jerusalem as the capital of Israel, within the pre-1967 boundaries and with detailed arrangements for the city's administration. From the Palestinian perspective, this would necessarily entail a political, but not a physical, partition of Jerusalem. Sovereignty and control of the city as a whole would be shared between Palestine and Israel.

Integral to the Palestinian position is the demand that Israel completely withdraw from the occupied city of Jerusalem. This constitutes little more than a demand for the implementation of numerous UN General Assembly and Security Council resolutions, and compliance with fundamental principles of international law.

The 1947 UN Partition Plan, accorded Jerusalem the special status of a *corpus separatum*, according to which the city would fall under the administration of the UN. However, this Plan was never implemented and in 1967, following its victory in the Six-Day War, Israel annexed East Jerusalem (which had been under Jordanian rule since the end of the British Mandate in 1948) and in 1980 formally declared Jerusalem to be Israel's "eternal and undivided capital."

Israel's unilateral actions have been denounced by the international community which, led by the UN, has reaffirmed that the acquisition of territory by war is illegal and has called upon Israel to refrain from taking any action that would alter the status of Jerusalem. UN Security Resolution 242 of 1967, for example, mandated Israel's withdrawal from the Occupied Palestinian Territories. Additionally, UN Security Council Resolution 478 declared Israel's 1980 "Basic Law on Jerusalem" to be a violation of international law, and any attempts by Israel as the occupying power to impose its laws, jurisdiction and administration on Jerusalem as null and void.

Despite agreement by both Israeli and Palestinian leadership during the Oslo Accords to refrain from taking any steps that might prejudice the final status issues, Israel has systematically and methodically worked towards the realization of Jerusalem as its "eternal and undivided capital." Through the implementation of a series of policies described by commentators as the "Judea-zation of Jerusalem," Israel has both undermined the peace process and the feasibility of the Two-State solution.

Israel's policies have centered on attempts to ensure exclusive control over East Jerusalem by transforming its demographic landscape through settlement strategies for Israelis, coupled with restrictions on Palestinian land use and ownership, construction and residency rights.

Israel's policies have also included the expansion and redrawing of the city's municipal boundaries to encompass areas in the West Bank, and the construction of the separation barrier and for illegal Jewish settlements in and surrounding East Jerusalem. Large numbers of Palestinians have been evicted from East Jerusalem, their ID cards confiscated, lands appropriated and houses demolished. Palestinian institutions such as the Orient House, the Higher Council for Tourism and the Palestinian Chamber of Commerce in East Jerusalem have been forced to close down.

The effects of such policies on Palestinians have been wide-ranging and severe. Today, more than 185,000 Israeli settlers reside in East Jerusalem, greatly outnumbering Palestinians.[11] Settlement policies and the construction of the separation barrier have resulted in grave hardship for many Palestinians who have been cut off from their fields, jobs, schools, medical facilities and neighbors. East Jerusalem is increasingly characterized by Palestinian enclaves that are surrounded by Israeli settlements and villages, causing West Bank Palestinians difficulty accessing their economic and social center. The overall effect of Israeli policies has been the increasing fragmentation of East Jerusalem and its isolation from the West Bank and Gaza.

Many of Israel's policies in Jerusalem are not just violations of international law, but are also perceived by Palestinians as systematic attempts to unilaterally determine the fate of Jerusalem and diminish the viability for part of the city to become the capital of the future Palestinian state. There is no doubt that through its Judea-zation policies, Israel has been able to assert de facto control over the whole of Jerusalem. However, such strategies are clearly untenable for achieving a just and lasting peace.

As Hassassian elaborates: "[Israel's] strategy is fundamentally flawed. The hope that with the passing of time, the question of Jerusalem will be decided by ongoing de facto demographic and physical changes is simply not plausible. Neither is it a possibility that the world will magically forget that East Jerusalem is a part of the West Bank and that Jerusalem must be a multicultural city and not for Jews and Jews only."[12]

Indeed, for as long as Israel refuses to acknowledge Palestinian sovereignty in (at the very least) East Jerusalem, there is likely to be further bloodshed and conflict. Jerusalem will continue to be a source of immense frustration and regional instability for as long as Palestinians are denied their legitimate rights to the city.

Settlements

Israel's construction of settlements in the Occupied Palestinian Territories presents the single biggest threat to the peace process and the establishment of a viable and contiguous Palestinian state. The construction, expansion and consolidation of Israeli settlements, the accompanying confiscation of Palestinian lands, and the demolition of Palestinian homes are significant causes for instability. They have fueled frustration, tension and violent confrontations between the two sides, exacerbated by radicalized Jewish settlers in East Jerusalem and the West Bank. Settler violence against Palestinians and their property has been widespread and committed with legal impunity, often with the support of Israeli forces. The "price tag" strategies employed by Israeli settlers to prevent the removal of settlement outposts have also contributed to the mass displacement of entire Palestinian communities in the West Bank.

Since the Oslo Accords, Israel systematically transferred large numbers of Jewish settlers past the Green Line and into strategically located settlements in the West Bank, East Jerusalem and Gaza. Today, more than 490,000 Israelis reside in settlements in the Occupied Palestinian Territories; there are an estimated 300,000 settlers in the West Bank[13] and more than 190,000 in East Jerusalem.[14] Between 1967 until the end of 2007, Israel established 121 "formal settlements" in the West Bank, with another 12 settlements in East Jerusalem. In addition, there are estimated to be more than 100 "illegal outposts" in the Occupied Palestinian Territories that have been constructed by settlers in violation of Israeli law.[15]

To Palestinians, all of the Israeli settlements in the Occupied Palestinian Territories are illegal and must be evacuated and dismantled. Any settlers who do not wish to evacuate would

142 | Israeli watchtower above West Bank checkpoint

be subject to the sovereignty of the new Palestinian state. If any settlements are to remain intact, their numbers will be kept to a minimum and will be reflected in any land swap arrangements that may form part of the final peace agreement.

Pending such final agreement, the Palestinians demand an immediate and genuine freeze to all settlement activity, including the "natural growth" of settlements. This would, in accordance with Phase 1 of the Roadmap, include: a freeze on all settlement-related construction; the cessation of all settlement-related planning; the revocation of economic and legal incentives for the relocation of Israeli citizens to the settlements; and the immediate end to all land confiscation and property destruction by Israel.

Palestinians view a settlement freeze as a litmus test of Israel's seriousness towards the peace negotiations and the Two-State Solution. From the Palestinian perspective, Israel is unilaterally creating "facts on the ground" through its settlement activity, thereby prejudicing or pre-empting the outcome of the final status negotiations.

The Israeli settlements vary in size and character, from farming and frontier villages to full-scale cities. The three largest and fastest growing Israeli settlements in the West Bank are Modi'in Ilit, Ma'ale Adummim and Betar 'Illit. Each has populations of 30,000–45,000 settlers.[16] To encourage growth, the Israeli government has offered settlers a number of legal and financial incentives, including housing subsidies, tax benefits and business grants. These sweeteners have been so successful over the past two decades that the population growth rate in the settlements (excluding East Jerusalem) is 4–6 percent, compared with a 1.5 percent growth in the rest of Israel.[17]

In the West Bank, settlements comprise just 1.2 percent of the West Bank territory. However, direct and indirect Israeli settlement control extends over more than 40 percent of the West Bank,[18] including the area's water and electricity supply. It is not so much the size of the territory encompassed by the settlements in the West Bank that has had devastating consequences for Palestinians; rather, it is the way in which such settlements and their accompanying infrastructure have cut through the West Bank, severing geographical continuity for Palestinian communities, curtailing their basic rights and freedoms and destroying their livelihoods. Many settlements have been built on prime agricultural land confiscated from Palestinians, or over valuable water sources such as the Western Aquifer basin.

More specifically, the construction of settler-only "bypass" roads that connect settlements to each other and to Israel have severed territorial contiguity between East Jerusalem and the rest of the West Bank. The ability of Palestinians to use these roads is limited and in some cases prohibited, and the "buffer zones" on either side of bypass roads have resulted in significant loss of Palestinian agricultural land. The imposition of numerous Israeli military checkpoints, roadblocks and other physical barriers have further isolated

Palestinian communities in the West Bank, significantly curtailing Palestinians' freedom of movement and crippling their means of earning a livelihood. Most Palestinian towns and villages are surrounded by Israeli settlements, roads and security forces, and are almost entirely dependent on Israel for water and electricity. If completed, the separation barrier—an integral part of Israel's settlement infrastructure and a "visible and clear act of territorial annexation under the guise of security"[19]—will leave Palestinians with only 54.5 percent of the West Bank.[20]

Human rights abuses associated with Israeli's settlement activities include forcible evictions of Palestinians from their homes in the West Bank and East Jerusalem, the confiscation of their lands and the destruction of their properties. It is estimated that as of July 2010, at least 230 Palestinian structures were demolished in East Jerusalem and Area C of the West Bank in 40 separate incidents since the beginning of 2010. This resulted in the displacement of more than 1,100 Palestinians, including 400 children.[21]

In 2010, there were at least 1,500 currently pending demolition orders against Palestinian structures in East Jerusalem, and over 3,000 in Area C of the West Bank.[22] The impact of displacement on families and communities can be severe; in addition to the trauma of experiencing forcible eviction from and destruction of their properties, families are often deprived of physical and economic security, and face increased difficulty in accessing basic services such as water, health care and education.

Internationally, the settlements are Israel's most controversial ongoing policy.

Settlement activities violate the spirit of the Oslo Accords as well as fundamental principles of international law. In transforming the physical and demographic character of the Occupied Palestinian Territories, Israel has violated Article 31(7) of the Oslo Agreement which states that "[n]either side shall initiate or take any step that will change the status of the West Bank or the Gaza Strip pending the outcome of the permanent status negotiations."

In building its settlement enterprise, Israel is in breach of international humanitarian and human rights law. In particular, Article 49(6) of the 1949 Fourth Geneva Convention Relative to the Protection of Civilian Persons in Time of War states that: "[t]he Occupying Power shall not deport or transfer parts of its own civilian population into the territory it occupies." As the International Committee of the Red Cross (ICRC) has noted, the inclusion of this sub-article by the drafters of the Fourth Geneva Convention was intended to prevent the transfer by states of "portions of their own population to occupied territory for political and racial reasons or in order...to colonize those territories. Such transfers [have] worsened the economic situation of the native population and endangered their separate existence as a race."[23]

The UN Security Council has stated that "Israel's policy and practices of settling parts of its population and new immigrants in [the Occupied Palestinian Territories] constitute a flagrant violation of the Fourth Geneva Convention...and also constitute a serious obstruction to achieving a comprehensive, just and lasting peace in the Middle East."[24] Similarly, the UN General Assembly has demanded immediate and complete cessation of all Israeli settlement activities in the Occupied Palestinian Territories, and has expressed its view that Israeli settlements in these territories are illegal.[25] The UN's Special Rapporteur on the Situation of Human Rights in the Palestinian Territories Occupied Since 1967 has referred to Israel's settlement policy as "a form of colonization in a world that has outlawed colonialism."[26]

The International Court of Justice (ICJ) has also confirmed the illegality of Israel's settlement activity. In its advisory opinion concerning Israel's construction of the separation barrier, the ICJ ruled that Israel's settlements and the separation barrier have been established in violation of international law. The ICJ has called for Israel to cease such activity, and to compensate or provide other forms of reparation for Palestinians whose homes or agricultural lands have been destroyed.[27] Israel however, has refused to accept this opinion.

As an occupying power, Israel is also responsible for ensuring the humanitarian needs of Palestinians under its occupation are met. Despite such responsibilities, Israel's settlement policies have curtailed the basic rights and freedoms of Palestinians, including their right to freedom of movement, work and housing, and their right not to be subject to discriminatory policies.

Many Palestinians believe that for so long as settlement expansion and the forcible acquisition of Palestinian lands is allowed to continue, there is little incentive for Israel to negotiate in good faith towards a final status agreement. For Palestinians, Israeli settlement construction and the Two-State Solution are inherently contradictory; the latter requires an end to Israel's occupation of the Occupied Palestinian Territories while the former is a clear signal of Israel's intention to continue its occupation.

Israel's intransigent stance on the settlements is evidenced by continued Israeli construction in East Jerusalem. With its intention to occupy all of Jerusalem, Israel rebukes international law and even condemnation by their allies by stubbornly pursuing settlement construction policies the rest of the world rejects.

From the Palestinian perspective, the continuation by Israel of its settlement activity amounts, in effect, to the de facto creation of a One-State Solution. In order for there to be a just and lasting peace, Israel must dismantle and evacuate its settlements, and use appropriate incentives to encourage the withdrawal of settlers to within Israel proper.

Refugees and the Right of Return

Of the core issues to be negotiated, the Palestinian refugee problem remains one of the most complex and sensitive in the quest for peace.

Palestinian refugees are the longest standing and largest refugee community in the world. Generations of statelessness and enforced exile, together with repeated cycles of displacement, discrimination, insecurity, and infringement of basic rights and freedoms have characterized the experiences of a significant number of Palestinian refugees for over 60 years. Any final settlement of the refugee issue demands a just and equitable solution that is based on existing United Nations resolutions and that recognizes and addresses the grave historical and ongoing injustices against the Palestinian people.

At the center of any possible resolution of the refugee issue are the following core Palestinian stipulations: an unlimited right of return for Palestinian refugees and internally displaced persons (IDPs); Palestinian statehood; and compensation or restitution. Integral to these stipulations is the assumption of moral responsibility by Israel for the expulsion of Palestinian refugees from their homes in 1948, and for their ongoing displacement.

For Palestinians, an unlimited right of return must include: the right of refugees and IDPs to repatriate to their former properties inside of Israel, the right to return to a new Palestinian state drawn on the basis of pre-1967 lines, and compensation for property confiscated by Israel, as well as for the historical injustices and other non-material loss suffered by the Palestinian refugees.

The right of return itself is predicated on United Nations General Assembly (UNGA) Resolution 194 (II) of December 1948. This provides for the return of refugees to their homes inside Israel and recognizes their right to receive compensation should they choose not to return, or if they have suffered loss of, or damage to, their original properties. Resolution 194 has, in turn, been reaffirmed by the UNGA every year since its passage.

The right of return is enshrined in international human rights instruments and refugee law. For example, Article 13 of the Universal Declaration of Human Rights provides for the right of every individual to leave and return to his or her country. Similarly, Article 12 of the International Covenant on Civil and Political Rights (ICCPR), which Israel has both signed and ratified, states that "[n]o one shall be arbitrarily deprived of the right to enter his own country." The United Nations Human Rights Committee, interpreting provisions of the ICCPR, has commented that "[t]he right to return is of the utmost importance for refugees seeking voluntary repatriation. It also implies prohibition of enforced population transfers or mass expulsions to other countries."[28]

The right of return is, for me, synonymous with my personal Palestinian national identity. There is probably no greater desire than for Palestinians to be able to return home to the land of our ancestors.

For Palestinians, it is an inalienable right; one that represents their struggle for justice and liberation from an enforced exile that began in 1948, with the expulsion of more than

750,000 Palestinians from their homes and which culminated in the destruction of their society. Most Palestinians had no control over the events of 1948 and the circumstances that continue to shape their lives in exile. There is significant moral strength in the Palestinian demand for an unlimited right of return to the homes from which they were forced. For Palestinians, it is the only way in which the historical injustices of 1948 and the ongoing injustice of exile can be truly rectified.

> Even though I am currently an American citizen, the desire to be able to go home, resides within me. This yearning is extended to all my fellow Palestinians who have not been as fortunate as I have. I feel it is my moral obligation to continue to be a voice for all Palestinians, who have suffered such great hardships over the course of the past century.
>
> It is a legal matter and it is also an emotional and moral issue for my people.
>
> I have been granted citizenship here in the United States. Having been "stateless" all my life, I am unable to describe the profound sense of happiness I felt when I attained American citizenship.
>
> With my American passport I was able to return to the land of my birth and that experience was extraordinary.
>
> As I've described in previous chapters, visiting my relatives who stayed in Haifa in 1948, and who I'd not seen for decades, was uplifting.
>
> I know that I am one of the lucky ones. But I also realize that many of my brethren continue to languish in Palestinian refugee camps. One, two and even three generations later, Palestinians continue to suffer.
>
> I continue to work to resolve this conflict so that they, too, can experience the fullness of life I have been granted.

Implicit in the right of return as a means of addressing an historical and ongoing injustice is the acknowledgment of responsibility by Israel for the displacement of Palestinians in 1948. It is this assumption of moral responsibility by Israel that lies at the core of the peace process, not only as a necessary precursor to any agreement on the right of return and compensation, but also as the first step in achieving true reconciliation between the parties.

It has been argued that the Palestinian demand for an unlimited right of return is unreasonable, given that few Palestinian refugees will actually seek to return to their former properties inside of Israel. For Palestinians however, this is irrelevant. It is about a shared collective identity and past, as well as a future existence; it is about "starting to live, answering the deep sense of belonging to the land from which refugees were torn decades ago, and about building relations between Palestinians and Jews that are based on justice and equality. Return is about the return of rights; all rights."[29]

The precarious situation of Palestinian refugees in their countries of refuge also reinforces the need for a right of return and resolution of the refugee issue. Despite the efforts of the League of Arab States to encourage its members to uphold the rights of Palestinian refugees, Arab host states have adopted, to varying degrees, a series of increasingly restrictive policies towards Palestinians. These policies include denial of residency rights, the right to own property and to engage in employment, as well as restrictions on freedom of movement and the ability to access government services.

The issue of compensation is an essential and central component of any final settlement of the refugee issue. Palestinian demands for compensation are grounded in UNGA Resolution 194 (discussed above), as well as in international law and equity.

Compensation takes two primary forms: the restitution of original properties confiscated by Israel, or where restitution is not possible (including where refugees elect not to return to their original homes), compensation for such properties, and compensation for the historical injustices and suffering undergone by Palestinian refugees. Israel should bear principal responsibility for the payment of compensation to Palestinian refugees, with claims assessed and paid on an individual basis. If Israel is unable to pay the full amount, the UN and the international community should also bear responsibility, given their role in the 1948 partition.

Although there is an understanding that compensation should be paid, at least for properties confiscated by Israel, there has been little discussion on the mechanisms for doing so, and the sources of funding for such compensation.

Any final resolution of the refugee issue must be perceived by the Palestinians to be just and fair, and address the historical and ongoing injustices perpetrated against the Palestinian people. Palestinians have stressed that the right of return is an individual choice, and that each refugee must be able to freely decide whether or not to return to Israel or a new Palestinian state, or whether to exercise their right to compensation.

Some Palestinians have adopted a softer, more "realistic" approach that favors a limited interpretation of the right of return, in which refugees would be entitled to return to the future Palestinian state in the West Bank and Gaza, rather than to their original homes inside of Israel. By enabling refugees to return to their "homelands," a just solution to their displacement would thus be achieved.

This approach has not been formally endorsed by the Palestinian Authority. Other Palestinians continue to insist on an unlimited right of return, arguing that the creation of a new Palestinian state without recognizing the right of refugees to return to former properties inside of Israel commits many Palestinians to a permanent state of exile.[30] The proposal for a more limited right of return has also received little support from Palestinian refugees themselves, who fear the Palestinian Authority will eventually compromise their rights to an unlimited return in exchange for a Palestinian state. Such fears are reinforced by the Palestinian leadership's failure to regularly solicit the views of refugees.

The absence of a unity government demonstrates political factionalism within the Palestinian leadership. This has presented obstacles to the peace process, as the legitimacy and acceptability of the positions advanced by the PA amongst the Palestinian people are by no means explicit. This is most evident in the rivalry between Fatah and Hamas between whom power in the Palestinian territories is divided. Hamas, which largely controls Gaza, has insisted on a One-State Solution and has refused to recognize Israel's right to exist. Although Hamas enjoys significant grassroots support among Palestinians, both Israel and the United States have refused to engage with Hamas since they consider Hamas to be a terrorist group.

Fatah, which controls the West Bank and represents the Palestinian moderates, has dominated the Palestinian Authority and has therefore assumed a central role in peace negotiations with Israel, to the exclusion of Hamas. Recent years however, have witnessed a sharp decline in public support for Fatah, prompting commentators to express concerns over the legitimacy of agreements concluded by the Palestinian Authority on behalf of the Palestinian people.

The release of 1,027 Palestinians from Israeli jails by Hamas in 2011 in exchange for the release of Israeli captured soldier, Gilad Shalit, has further demonstrated the effectiveness of Hamas in dealing with Israel. This, in turn, strengthens Hamas popularity within Palestinian society, thus, perhaps, lowering the status of the PLO and Fatah.

One State or Two States?

After 10 chapters spanning thousands of years of shared history, we have described divergent accounts of what has happened to two peoples who claim the same Land.

We also hope to illuminate the path to a viable and sustainable reconciliation between Palestinians and Israelis. Towards this end, this chapter assesses the two most prominent peace proposals—the One-State and the Two-State Solutions.

If the solution is to be one state, it would mean that Israel—barely six decades into its unique history and after 2,000 years of Jewish exile and persecution—would have to open its doors to millions of Muslim adversaries. Could Israel do that, and still be the Jewish homeland?

If the solution is to be two states, Palestinians would have to accept Israeli West Bank settlements being annexed by Israel, and accept Israeli security installations within their country. They would have to accept boundaries different from what they would prefer. And, they would have to accept Israel as the Jewish homeland. Can they do all this to realize a Palestinian homeland?

One State or Two States?

A Two-State Solution

In my opinion, the One-State Solution is *not* a viable solution to the Israeli-Palestinian conflict. Instead, the only path to realistic, sustainable peace for both peoples is two independent states living side by side: the State of Israel and the Palestinian State.

I firmly believe the Two-State Solution is a natural consequence of the unique origins of the Jewish homeland.

As you have read, Jewish suffering remains a central theme in our long and troubled history. Establishing and maintaining an independent Jewish state has intimately been connected not only to our spiritual survival, but also to our physical survival. After thousands of years of exile in countries that despised us, and the attendant persecution and murder fueled by that hatred, we hungered for the safety of a Jewish homeland. In this context, the enmity of Arabs and Palestinians is but the final hurdle in a perilous and multi-generational journey to that sacred end.

We have paid with our blood, perhaps more than any people in the world, to realize our dream. Now that our wanderings have come to rest in the State of Israel, we would never risk changing its essential democratic character, especially given how successful Israel has been—by any measure—since its inception.

In recent years, Israelis and Palestinians have made some progress towards a lasting peace. However, as is evidenced throughout this book, animosity and mistrust cloud our respective futures. The Palestinian narrative is endemic with references to al-Naqba. It emphasizes the plight of the refugees, Israel's overwhelming military might and the gradual annexation by Israel of Palestinian lands. Palestinians view themselves as innocent victims who are not responsible for their current plight. Instead, they place the full blame on Israel, which they demonize as a powerful and underhanded opponent determined to push the remaining Palestinian population into neighboring Arab states, or to imprison them within a truncated West Bank and Gaza.

To end the cycle of this conflict, a Two-State Solution must start now and continue unhindered over generations so that both sides can concentrate on building and perpetuating their separate economies and cultures. Over time, Israelis and Palestinians will learn to cooperate and eventually find a productive interdependence.

Is this a pipedream? I don't think so. Earlier in my life, I experienced years when Israelis and Palestinians lived in harmony. But I am not naïve. I have lived the second half of my life with the reality of radical Islamic threats against my people and my homeland. Even in "friendly" Arab states like Egypt and Jordan, the street rhetoric calls for the destruction of the Jewish state. In almost every instance, Israel's peace overtures have been met with violent responses.

This is why the tumultuous events spreading across the Middle East, known as the Arab Spring of 2011, do not encourage me to consider alternatives to the Two-State Solution. Many countries like Syria were reliably hostile towards Israel. Now the black-and-white realities of the past six decades are becoming "gray areas" of uncertainty. Even if many of these nations become democracies in the coming years, it is highly doubtful they will extend the hand of friendship to Israel. Free elections and free, emboldened speech circulating in social media and public forums don't automatically translate into an acceptance of Jews in the region. This leaves Israel vulnerable to changing governments and hostile factions from Morocco to Iran.

Physical Separation Needed

The pattern of Palestinian violence and Israeli military action has become a tragic cycle of threat and counter-threat; violence and counter-violence. It is a cycle that only seems to escalate. At this mutable point in time, the complete physical separation of the two sides is requisite to establishing the groundwork for coexistence, reconciliation, and ultimately, a sustainable peace.

But the tragic cycle is not limited to physical violence. The ongoing conflict has spun a narrative web of stereotypes and psychological conditioning that intractably separate Israelis and Palestinians.

Narratives create identities, and the identities the Israelis and Palestinians have carved out for each other are tangible reflections of the conflict. This is a significant barrier to lasting peace. Only when situational realities on the ground have been redefined and the physical cycle of violence ceases can Israelis and Palestinians author a new mutually inclusive narrative.

Demographics Demand Two States

On the eve of Israel's War of Independence in 1948, the area's population stood at approximately 2 million people. One-third was Jewish—mostly immigrants fleeing Europe. The remaining two-thirds were Muslims and Palestinian Christians.[1]

Today, this same arid, narrow strip of land between the Jordan River and the Mediterranean Sea is home to approximately 12 million people.[2] Fresh water shortages alone pose a continuous threat to the region. Add to this an abundance of economic hurdles, legal issues, military disputes and foreign interests—not to mention the status of hundreds of religious and historical sites—and it is clear why a real and lasting peace has eluded the most ardent of peacemakers.

Even in a climate conducive to peace, resolving conflict is an extremely delicate process. Finding viable solutions in a bitterly contested situation—where one minor concession can be manipulated by rejectionists on either side to sabotage all prior progress—is virtually impossible. This behavioral model exists on both sides of the Israeli-Palestinian conflict.

For this reason, the Two-State Solution is the only pragmatic choice. Not only would a Two-State Solution afford Palestinians the independence they demand, but it would also confer upon Israel the legitimacy and acceptance it has always desired—and still craves.

Equally important, the Two-State Solution would give deeply ingrained hatreds a "time out," giving negotiators and leaders more time and freedom to clearly focus on state-building efforts. Once the two peoples inhabit their own separate viable states, their efforts to forge real reconciliation and lasting peace can be successful.

Facts on the Ground

To compare the two proposed solutions, it's useful to recognize the relevant facts on the ground.

> The disputed land is under the control of Israel. Israel will be the entity that hands over the land for the creation of a Palestinian State—not the other way around.

> Israel is a democracy that values the vote of every man and woman.

> Israel does not have a constitution. This means that any law can be changed by a majority vote in the Knesset.

By 2012, the total population between the Mediterranean and the Jordan River was approximately 12 million. It is 52 percent Jewish and 48 percent Palestinian.[3] Israel has 7.8 million citizens, 5.9 million of whom are Jewish.

The Palestinian population is 5.4 million. 1.6 million citizens of Israel are of Palestinian descent. 2.1 million Palestinians live in the West Bank. 1.7 million Palestinians live in Gaza.

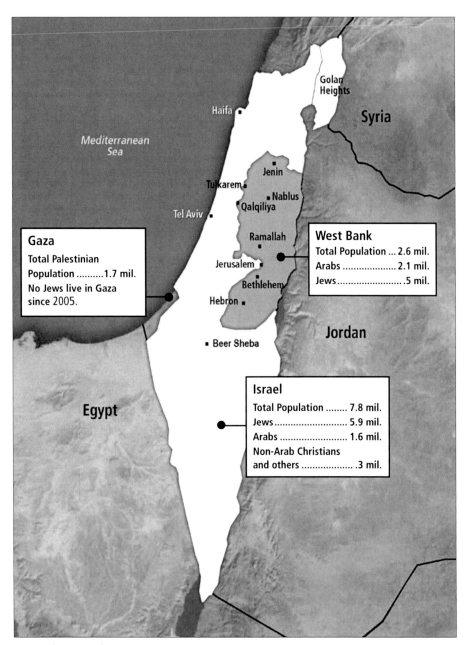

Map 29 | Demographics

Based upon an average four percent birth rate among the Palestinian population and a 1.5 percent growth rate among Israeli Jews, demographer Arnon Soffer predicts that by 2020, the Palestinian population will be approximately 8.8 million, while the Jewish population will be 6.3 million.[4]

As Aluf Benn points out, "Invading armies from neighboring countries seem a remote danger compared to the rapidly growing Arab population in Israel's midst."[5] That the non-Jewish population will outnumber the Jewish population in the Jewish state is the fundamental flaw with the One-State Solution.

The One-State Solution is a prescription for Zionist political suicide. To my people, the mere proposition of a One-State Solution is seen as a conspiracy to achieve through the ballot box what Arab bullets failed to accomplish. In other words, to many Israelis, the notion of a One-State Solution enables the Palestinians to achieve their goal of eliminating the Jewish homeland with demographics rather than with violence. As my friend Gadi Baltiansky, the head the Geneva Initiative, succinctly put it, "We Israelis want to *live* in peace—not to rest in peace."

Now let's combine these stark demographic trends with the issues of governance.

Israeli Laws

Proponents of the One-State Solution point to Israel's Declaration of Independence and to the array of Basic Laws that ostensibly guarantee fundamental rights, freedoms and equality to all citizens. Such rights have been guaranteed by every Israeli government since the country's inception. And this continuity is what One-State Solution proponents utilize to alleviate the fear that Jews would soon be dominated by a growing Arab majority.

Yet One-State proponents are overlooking a key weakness in this argument: Israel lacks a formal constitution. Therefore, each Israeli-elected government has to vote to protect these rights. As the Israel Supreme Court has ruled, that rights granted in the Israeli Declaration of Independence serve only as "guiding principles."[6] Moreover, Israel's existing Basic Laws can be overturned by a majority in the Knesset. Therefore, these rights would therefore be vulnerable to a popularly-elected, Arab majority government.

Accordingly, it is dubious that a government elected by an Arab majority under a One-State Solution would preserve the rights and freedoms currently given to all Israeli citizens today. Not only does history invite skepticism, but throughout the Arab world we still cannot find a single regime which provides democratic freedoms including: freedom of speech, or protecting the rights of minorities.[7]

In fact, of those Palestinians who are willing to accept a bi-national state, only 20 percent said they would allow it to be secular—and only as long as it was officially Muslim.[8] Given these attitudes, it is easy to envision those "fundamental guarantees"—those that One-State proponents are so fond of—being gradually and irrevocably dismantled and quickly replaced by Sharia law, notorious for its undemocratic principles. In fact, the history of minorities within Muslim regimes reveals that both Christians and Jews were coded as "Dhimmis," which relegated them to second-class citizenship.

One-State Solution Can't Succeed

Given the emerging demographic trends, the One-State Solution could only result in two possible outcomes. And both are undesirable.

The first outcome would be Israel becoming a Muslim state.

The second likely outcome of a One-State Solution would require abandoning the tenets of the Jewish state in order to save it. As former Israeli Prime Minister Ehud Olmert said in 2007:

> If the day comes when the Two-State Solution collapses, and we face a South African-style struggle for equal voting rights (also for the Palestinians in the territories), then as soon as that happens, the State of Israel is finished.[9]

In order to maintain the Jewish character of the State of Israel in a One-State Solution and also retain a Jewish homeland where Jews can freely practice their religion, Israel would be forced to curtail basic human rights of its Palestinian majority. This would undermine the founding principle of the State of Israel and severely contradict core Jewish values.

The Jewish population of Israel—or Jews worldwide, for that matter—would suddenly become subject to the will of the new Palestinian majority. Such a surrender would be totally unacceptable to Israelis. As we have seen, such arrangements have never benefited Jewish communities in the past and there is little reason to believe Jews would acquiesce to this situation without a fight. Like all sovereign nations, it is absurd to expect that the Jewish state would ever agree to its own demise.

When the modern State of Israel was within reach, Zionist leader Chaim Weizmann wrote these prescient words in his autobiography:

> I am certain that the world will judge the Jewish state by what it will do with the Arabs, just as the Jewish people at large will be judged by what we do or fail to do in this state where we have been given such a wonderful opportunity after thousands of years of wandering and suffering.[10]

The One-State Solution is not a solution at all. In any imaginable scenario, it is hard to believe that after decades of hostility, Israelis and Palestinians would suddenly treat each other with trust, dignity and respect. Forging positive relations from the ashes of such violent and deeply ingrained antagonism is a Herculean task.

Accordingly, the premature pursuit of a One-State Solution will only lead to further violence. It is for this reason that it must be abandoned in favor of the Two-State approach.

A Two-State Solution

The alternative—and what I believe is the best hope for creating a lasting peace—is the Two-State Solution. The Two-State Solution, presented at the 1991 Madrid Conference, has served as the basis for a peaceful solution to the Israeli-Palestinian dispute in the Oslo Process, the Camp David Accords and the current "Roadmap to Peace." Nearly all United Nations member states have pledged their support and considerable financial resources have been contributed by them to make it a reality.

A Two-State Solution should be pursued under the guiding principle of voluntary engagement. That is to say, the future of the region lies in two self-governing states with independent economies, security forces, educational systems and all other aspects of statehood. Incentives for cooperation and interdependent ties between the parties are vital and would function as sustaining mechanisms to bring about a lasting peace.[11]

The Two-State Solution avoids the problems inherent in forcing some form of national unity where none exists.

Aside from in the Americas and in Africa, nearly all the world's countries have been founded on the basis of some form of ethnic nationalism. This is also true of the Middle East. Rather than treating nationalism as a roadblock to co-existence, the parties should embrace it. It is only in the absence of contending narratives that the parties will effectively tackle the countless daunting tasks involved in establishing and maintaining a long-lasting sustainable peace. Physically and emotionally separated into two states, the parties can begin the healing process and come to view each other as neighbors rather than adversaries. Then Israel could see Palestinians as cooperative neighbors rather than terrorists, while Palestinians could view my people as allies rather than oppressors.

The Economic Factor

Under the Two-State Solution, each side would be free to engage the other at will. Free market forces would arise, providing incentives to push the parties towards engagement and mutual cooperation. While such areas of cooperation would likely extend well beyond the economic realm, it is in this area where cooperation is already being successfully implemented. This success can serve as a model for cooperation for other mutually beneficial activities and undertakings.

Many older Palestinians lament the "good old days" when a Palestinian worker could earn a decent middle class wage. All that vanished with the Second Intifada and the rise of Hamas.[12] Economic relations between Israel and the Palestinians deteriorated in an unprecedented manner following the eruption of the First and particularly the Second Intifada causing Israel to reduce its dependency on the Palestinian labor force. Israel formerly relied on day laborers from the Palestinian territories. Presently, it employs as many as 400,000 foreign workers from Thailand, the Philippines, the former Soviet Union and other countries. As opposed to Palestinian laborers who would work in Israel and then return to the West Bank and Gaza each day, foreign workers from other countries usually stay in Israel for years without their families and send most of their income home.

For Palestinians, the effect is obvious: every foreign worker in Israel takes a job away from a Palestinian laborer—a job that could be feeding his Palestinian family. The sharp rise in unemployment in the Palestinian territories, which some estimate as high as 70 percent, benefits no one.

The toll on the Israeli economy also is considerable. The average salary for a foreign worker in Israel is $1,300 a month. Typically, a foreign worker will spend $300 on living expenses in Israel and deposit $1,000 in family bank accounts in the nations where their families live. This approximates $3 billion in capital flight every year—about the same amount Israel receives in foreign aid annually from the United States. This places a destabilizing economic burden on Israel's relatively small economy.

Despite the enormous disparity between the two economies, a future Palestinian State is in no way chained to failure or exploitation. Even during the current unrest, attitudes about unskilled labor are beginning to change. Palestinians who understand the swiftly evolving labor market in Israel are acquiring the requisite skills to accommodate Israel's bustling high-tech economy. In response, Israeli companies have turned to Palestinian engineers and programmers who are valued for their skills, ambition, cultural similarity and geographical proximity.

According to one Palestinian economist, "In order to build a thriving economy and create new jobs, the Palestinians must put in place policies designed to increase local economic capabilities, encourage investment and create a legislative framework conducive to private sector activity."[13] Israel would gain access to Middle Eastern markets through a symbiotic bilateral relationship with Palestine. It would also benefit by providing Palestinians with technical and legal assistance to stabilize the Palestinian economy thereby attracting foreign investment. Additionally, Israel would be relieved of its growing foreign worker dilemma while Palestinians would gain the necessary training and technical support to compete in a global economy. This would include both low-tech technologies such as modern agricultural practices and high-tech training in computer programming and engineering.

The benefits of a symbiotic economic relationship based on market forces rather than one based on military confrontation will be advantageous for both peoples. Continued economic exchanges breed stability, trust and areas for further cooperation.[14] A Two-State approach would generate sorely needed capital, and internal stability would initiate joint ventures and locally produced innovations benefiting both sides. Reducing the need to employ workers from outside the region would result in increased local reinvestment. Not only would this spur the growth of indigenous industries, it would also greatly reduce dependence on foreign aid and capital.

In the same way the two-state model enables and even encourages cross-state cooperation, other areas of cooperation would follow and flourish—not because it would have been thrust upon the parties, which the One-State Solution advocates, but because it is logical, economical and prudent. Due to the two parties' close proximity and interconnected environment, cooperative networks in emergency response, disease control and the protection and distribution of natural resources has already been well established.

Accordingly, it is not difficult to extrapolate that in an atmosphere of stability and trust-building engendered by a Two-State approach, opportunities to expand mutually beneficial cooperation would be virtually limitless.

Why Are There Not Two States Now?

Given that the Two-State Solution is the most prudent way forward, the obvious question is, "Why hasn't it been implemented?" The short answer is that Palestinian society is not fully committed to peace.

While Palestinians may talk the language of peace, perusing a single Palestinian textbook that instills violence in young minds clearly demonstrates an alternate truth. Palestinian children are taught that Palestinian refugees will be returned to Israel proper. Arab political leaders refer to Israel as "Palestine," blatantly ignoring the legitimate existence of Israel. The most egregious proof is the denial of the historical right of the Jewish people to live anywhere in Israel, period.

As lead Palestinian negotiator Saeb Erekat explained, "Agreeing to the Israeli demand for recognition of Israel as a Jewish state would empty negotiations on the refugee problem of all content . . . and completely negate the Palestinian narrative."[15] The Palestinian position is "what's mine is mine and what's yours is also mine."[16] Jews are not part of the equation.

There is no doubt that an independent Palestinian State would serve as the best solution for both people, particularly my people. It would refocus Palestinian attention away from destructive acts toward the constructive endeavor of nation-building.

The newly established Palestinian state would be required to play by the rules of the game (i.e. international law.) The onus to stop terrorist attacks against Israel would be placed squarely upon the Palestinian government. It is a duty they could not afford to take lightly since any attack on Israel could then be legally interpreted as an act of war putting the Palestinian State at severe risk. If both sides exchange their swords for ploughshares, imagine the seeds of cooperation they could plant and reap together.

All this demonstrates that a Two-State Solution satisfies the needs of the Israelis and Palestinians without threatening either side with violence or annihilation. It allows Jews to maintain their homeland in Israel and live there in peace and security. For Palestinians, the Two-State Solution realizes their dream of building a state according to their needs and desires—whole, sovereign, and free from outside interference.

Unlike the One-State Solution, the Two-State Solution brings the parties into compliance with international law. Meeting the terms of this requirement would mend their respectively damaged images in the international community.

Finally, and most importantly, it is only with a Two-State Solution that true conflict resolution, through the process of voluntary engagement and trust-building, can transform an impossible dream into a probable reality.

Peace Is Possible

When the Two-State Solution is implemented, the quality of life for Israelis and Palestinians should vastly improve. This solution would allow both nations to flourish. Consequently the ideological barriers and geographic borders between the two cultures might eventually diminish in relevance. At some distant point in the future, they may even fade from memory.

This isn't as impossible as it sounds. History is replete with instances of unlikely and extraordinary reconciliation. Less than a century ago, Europe was embroiled in World War II. France and Germany were bitter enemies. Today, less than 70 years later, they are partners. Now that Europe is unified, the majority of European countries share a common currency. Borders are unobstructed. Former adversaries are allies.

I believe that a Two-State Solution could gradually lead to a similar relationship between Palestinians and Israelis.

I hope and pray for the day when our disparate narratives combine to tell a very different story—how two proud countries found the way to peace so their children could live unafraid, and free.

For a One-State Solution

> I see no other way than to begin now to speak of sharing the land that has thrust us together, sharing it in a truly democratic way, with equal rights for each citizen. There can be no reconciliation unless both peoples, two communities of suffering, resolve that their existence is a secular fact, and that it has to be dealt with as such.[1]

Many have raised the banner of the Two-State Solution—Palestinians, Israelis, Americans, even the United Nations. Since the days when the British Mandate controlled the historical land of Palestine, the Two-State model has been driven by the argument that it is the only option for a peaceful resolution between Palestinian Arabs and Jews.

I don't believe it.

In fact, the Two-State option has long been discredited because we have seen a version of it in action for decades, and it has utterly failed to resolve the conflict.

My belief in the One-State Solution reflects the sentiments of Edward Said. But my position is driven by personal experience as someone who has suffered from the calls for political division of the historical land of Palestine. And, it is driven by the failure intrinsic to various peace negotiations, six decades of violence and the increasingly complicated demographic mix in the land.

All these issues have led to me to believe the One-State Solution is the only way to ensure that both Arab Palestinians and Israeli Jews will live in peace and justly share one land that happens to be considered the ancestral land of both people.

The One-State Solution has many advantages. It gives equal citizenship and rights to all inhabitants of the land, regardless of ethnicity or religion. It abandons the cycle of violence that has gripped the Holy Land since the British imposed the divisive model of Two-States on the people of Palestine during the years of the colonial mandate. A single state in historic

Palestine between the Mediterranean and the Jordan River would mean that Jews, Muslims and Christians would have equal responsibilities for their shared, secular state. And as a secular state, it would be a multi-cultural and multi-religious society, designed to honor and uphold the rights of all individuals to practice their own religious beliefs as free peoples.

Not only is this idea visionary, but also it is sensible. A single, unified state will end the cycle of violence and discrimination that now exists between the peoples of the land and their collective prosperity. While this concept may be seen as anathema to some and unrealistic to others, the idea is neither new nor irrational. The proposal of a pluralistic democracy where Israeli Jews and Palestinian Arabs live together in one state stems from none other than the idealistic "father" of modern Israel, Theodor Herzl. When Herzl heralded the coming of political Zionism in the 1880s, his vision was of a pluralistic democracy where Jews and Arabs lived in one state with equal rights.

In his 1896 manifesto, *The Jewish State*, Herzl postulated that such a country would be at peace with its neighbors and would require no more than a small professional army. To this end, it can be similarly argued that the Arab States rejected UN Resolution 181 with the understanding that the land of Palestine could not be divided, but rather shared between the various peoples of this land.

David Ben-Gurion, before he became Israel's first Prime Minister, also entertained the idea of a bi-national plan.[2] Progressive Zionist organizations such as Brit Shalom and Agudat Ihud advocated the creation of a bi-national state in Palestine "whose identity would be equally Jewish and Arab and whose governance would be an Arab-Jewish condominium."[3]

Founded in 1926, Brit Shalom's mission was "to pave the way for understanding between Hebrews and Arabs [ivirim ve'arvim] cooperative ways of living in the Land of Israel on the basis of complete equality in the political rights of two nations [each] enjoying wide autonomy and for various types of joint enterprise in the interest of the development of the country."[4] In this effort Brit Shalom sought complete economic and political parity with the Arabs. Unfortunately, lukewarm support in the Jewish community, a lack of progress with the Arab population and rifts within the organization itself forced Brit Shalom to disband.

In 1942, some of the same activists established Agudat Ihud. According to its mission statement Agudat Ihud "stands for the union of Jews and Arabs in a bi-national Palestine based on parity of the two peoples; and for the union of the bi-national Palestine with neighboring countries."[5] Two of the famous Zionist founders, Martin Buber and Judah Magnes, were instrumental in spreading this message. Buber, a renowned Jewish philosopher and scholar wrote eloquently on the moral path that he felt would lead to compromise and lasting peace. In his 1947 essay, *The Bi-National Approach to Zionism*, he wrote,

We describe our programme as that of a bi-national state—that is, we aim at a social structure based on the reality of two peoples living together. The foundations of this structure cannot be the traditional ones of majority and minority, but must be different…This co-operation will allow development in accordance with an all embracing cultural perspective and on the basis of a feeling of at-oneness, tending to result in a new form of society.[6]

In addition to providing the moral framework to Agudat Ihud's program for peaceful coexistence, Buber delineated specific steps to realize the unified state he envisioned. He called for the respect of Israeli historical rights and Palestinian natural rights to the land and outlined policies to reach demographic parity between Jews and Palestinians. He also appealed for the immediate integration of Arabs into key government posts, the drafting of a basic constitution for a bi-national Palestine, and establishing governmental structures to help ensure equality and freedom between the Jews and Palestinians.[7]

Buber's contemporary, Judah Magnes, was Agudat Ihud's leading political figure. A skilled diplomat and orator, Magnes was admired by American Jews and the British Mandate government, as well as by David Ben-Gurion and other mainstream Zionists.[8] Magnes was in lockstep with Buber, and feared the ramifications of continued violence between Jews and Palestinians. He actively campaigned for a democratic bi-national state or a cooperative federation of states. He felt strongly that the land belonged to the peoples of all three monotheistic faiths and that "no code of morals can justify the persecution of one people in an attempt to relieve the persecution of another."[9]

A Zionist himself, Magnes fought for Jewish-Arab parity throughout his life. He even went so far as to "oppose the declaration of a Jewish state in favor of a federation or confederation of Jews and Arabs in Palestine… [and] actively opposed recognition by the United States of the Declaration of Israeli Statehood by lobbying in personal meetings with Secretary of State George Marshall and President Harry Truman."[10] Although Magnes ultimately failed, his words and warnings proved prophetic. As Jewish political philosopher Hannah Arendt stated, just as "Magnes and the small group of his followers in Palestine and Zionism had predicted there would either be Jewish-Arab cooperation or war, and there has been war…"[11]

More recently, the vision of a single-state entity with constitutional protections for all its citizens began to gain renewed interest in the aftermath of the failures of Oslo. In early 1999, Edward Said wrote in the New York Times against the Two-State option and called for a One-State confederation. Specifically, he questioned whether the entire process that began in Oslo in 1993 was the right instrument for bringing peace between the Palestinians and the Israelis. From Said's point of view, a real peace could not occur within the context of Israeli-Palestinian separation. During the 1917 Balfour Declaration and the British Mandate, the Palestinian Arabs consistently refused to compromise on any plan that would challenge their own demographic dominance in the region. Certainly, Said wrote, it is unfair to rebuke the Palestinians now for not accepting the 1947 Partition Plan. This is especially true in light of the fact that until that time, the Jewish population only held seven percent of the land. Why berate the Palestinians for responding negatively to this plan on the basis of their refusal to concede 55 percent of historic Palestine to a Jewish State when Jews were a small minority in the collective whole? From Said's perspective, the 1947 Partition Plan was an extension of the system of inequality between Jews and Arabs started by the British. Such inequality has been built into the policies of the Israelis and the United States ever since.

Said was not alone in his call for a single bi-national state. In 2003, Tony Judt published an article in *The New York Review of Books* entitled *Israel: The Alternative*. Responding to the failures of Oslo, Judt argued that the current "peace process is dead" and that a bi-national state based on democratic principles and equal rights was the only realistic option in which both Palestinians and Israelis could build a peaceful future. Judt acknowledged that "the very idea [of a bi-national state] is a mix of realism and utopia, hardly an auspicious place to begin." But, he noted, "the alternatives are far worse."[12]

Not surprisingly, Judt's article was harshly criticized. Michael Walzer of the Institute for Advanced Study in Princeton expressed concerns that a bi-national state, "would simply replace one nation-state with another."[13] From this perspective, because the Arab population of the bi-national state would soon outnumber that of the Jews, Judt's proposed bi-national polity would result in another Arab nation-state.[14] Elsewhere, Walzer derided the proposal for a bi-national state as an escapist fantasy that "offers no practical escape from the work of repressing the terrorist organizations and withdrawing from the Occupied Territories."[15]

Waltzer's critique disregards two important facts. First, the demographics of this disputed land have always favored the non-Jewish Palestinian population over the Jewish population; a non-Jewish majority is inevitable. Secondly, Jews and Palestinian Arabs have coexisted peacefully in the past and currently live in demographically mixed cities throughout Israel in relative peace and prosperity. As Said wrote, "Palestine is multicultural, multiethnic, multireligious. There is as little historical justification for homogeneity as there is for notions of national or ethnic and religious purity today."[16]

Between Said and Judt's similar perspectives, the prevailing fears shared by Israelis and Palestinians provide a strong and logical rationale for a One-State Solution. "Short of ethnic cleansing or 'mass transfer,' as in 1948, there is no way for Israel to get rid of the Palestinians or for the Palestinians to wish Israelis away," Said wrote.[17] Meanwhile, Judt dispelled the Israeli fear of a non-Jewish demographic threat to the "purity" of the Jewish state. Indeed, what truly threatens Israel itself is its anti-democratic obsession with Jewish purity rather than the perceived enemy of Palestinian citizens in its midst.

In a world where nations and peoples increasingly intermingle and intermarry at will; where cultural and national impediments to communication have all but collapsed; where more and more of us have multiple elective identities and would feel falsely constrained if we had to answer to just one of them; in such a world Israel is truly an anachronism. And not just an anachronism, but also a dysfunctional one. In today's "clash of cultures" between open, pluralist democracies and belligerent intolerant, faith-driven ethno-states, Israel actually risks falling into the wrong camp.[18]

The true threat to Israel's existence is its own intolerance, self-indulgence and pandering to the anti-democratic, faith-driven extremists in its own camp. Some on the Jewish and Israeli Left argue that the rise in extremist religiosity and continued military occupation of Palestinian lands captured in 1967, is causing Israel to lose its moral compass. To this end, the internal crisis within Israeli society is far worse than external threats to its existence. If this crisis continues, "The Jewish state would then no longer be Jewish on the ethno-demographic level but, by institutionalizing a new form of apartheid, would itself be cut off from any future and even from any moral right to its existence as such."[19]

While the One-State option is not at the forefront of the peace initiative today, it has gained significant support by those who see bi-nationality as a tangible example of equality between Jews and Palestinians. In June 2004, 200 scholars signed the Olga Document, which opened the debate for a bi-national future.[20] The document advocates for the acceptance of the Palestinian refugee's Right of Return, supports the idea of offering apologies for the expulsions and crimes committed in 1948, and cites the end of Israeli military occupation as foundational to any real negotiations between the Israelis and the Palestinians.[21]

Now, after over six decades of fighting for continuously failed resolutions, I propose that the time has come to resurrect and implement a One-State Solution. It is significant to identify reasons that allow us to offer this suggested model.

For many the Two-State Solution seems to be the most workable and just approach. Indeed, the Two-State model has become the only viable approach of the Oslo peace negotiations as it later became the cornerstone of the Quartet's "Road Map."

However, the Palestinian half of the Two-State Solution started to fade as Israel began to strengthen its political, economic and military grip over the Occupied Territories of the West Bank, and specifically around Jerusalem. Israel's expanding occupation of the West Bank and its all-out unjust policies against the Palestinian civilians is a constant provocation against a Palestinian State.

Why the Two-State Approach is Unworkable

First, it would adopt a process of independence, which would require abandoning the "Right of Return" of the Palestinian refugees of 1948. This Right has always been considered a "sacred" Palestinian principle and it has been the moral and legal center for any future resolution of the Palestinian-Israeli conflict. This principle holds that Palestinian refugees who were forced to leave the former British Mandate of Palestine as a result of the war between the Arab countries and Zionist Jews in the 1948 War have an inalienable right to return to their homes. The number of Arab Palestinians who fled the 1948 War is estimated at up to 800,000, among them, as many as 170,000 had to flee for a second time during the 1967 War. The issue of the "Right of Return" of the Palestinian refugees was recognized by the UN General Assembly, first in 1947 by Resolution 3236 and then again in 1948 by Resolution 194, which resolved that:

> ...the refugees wishing to return to their homes and live at peace with their neighbors should be permitted to do so at the earliest practicable date, and that compensation should be paid for the property of those choosing not to return and for the loss of or damage to property which, under principles of international law or in equity, should be made good by the Government or authorities responsible.[22]

Ruth Lapidoth from the Jerusalem Center for Public Affairs has claimed that the UN General Assembly Resolution 194 does not specify a "right" but rather says refugees "should" be allowed to return. She has also noted that General Assembly resolutions are not binding to member states, and that this particular resolution based its recommendations on two conditions: that refugees wish to return, and that they be willing to live at peace with their neighbors. Next, she argues that the latter condition is unfulfilled, citing actions of Palestinian militant groups. She concludes that Palestinian refugees have the right to seek a negotiated compensation, but not a "Right of Return."[23]

I would argue that most of criticisms of the Palestinian "Right of Return" were not based on the international legality of the UN resolution as much on the ideological and political concerns of the Israelis over the future condition of the Jewish character of the State of Israel if Palestinian refugees were allowed to return. Israeli novelist Amos Oz has argued the Palestinian "Right of Return" would make Arabs the majority in Israel. In Oz's view, such a step would amount to "abolishing the Jewish people's right to self-determination." Oz further claims that the Palestinian leaders claim a Right of Return while cynically ignoring the fate of hundreds of thousands of Israeli Jews who fled and were driven out of their homes in Arab countries, during the same war.[24]

It should be understood, however, that the Right of Return has always been regarded by the Palestinian people as the focal point and sacred principle of the Palestinian cause. Any attempt to disregard it would be a strong blow to the conflict's resolution. In fact, since day one, Israel has not taken the issue seriously. Israel views the admission of Palestinian refugees to their former homes as a political issue, one which should be resolved through negotiations as part of a final peace agreement.

Secondly, an independent Palestinian state in the West Bank (and Gaza) is impossible given the large numbers of Israeli Jewish settlements in the occupied territories of the West Bank. The continued expansion of Israeli settlements makes the creation of two viable states more difficult with each passing year.

In a recent interview on National Public Radio, Mustafa Barghouti described the Israeli settlements as "a situation where two sides are sitting negotiating over a piece of cheese, and while the Palestinians are talking, the Israeli side is eating the piece of cheese."[25] This simple, yet accurate, portrayal of the Israeli settlement movement highlights the illegal practices that are, in essence, an insurmountable hurdle in the creation of two states for two peoples. Similarly, Benvenisti warns, "at some point Israeli expansion will pass the point of no return, beyond which implementation of a Two-State Solution is not possible."[26]

To Human Rights Watch and other organizations, including the United Nations and Amnesty International, Israel's settlement program is an obvious form of government-sponsored discrimination. The results are demolished Palestinian homes, the displacement of Arab civilians, lack of access to water, food, basic utilities, and health care, and the illegal and immoral transfer of land from Palestinian owners to Jewish settlers.[27]

In 2010 alone, the UN estimates that at least 198 structures were demolished, and 300 Palestinians—half of whom are children—were displaced.[28]

This systematic displacement of one group of citizens for the benefit of another is blatantly discriminatory. It also progressively complicates the return of Palestinian refugees in a land swap or the relocation of Jewish settlers as part of an eventual Two-State peace agreement. An analysis of the data reveals that, in the vast majority of the settlements—about 75 percent—construction, sometimes on a large scale, has been carried out without the appropriate permits or contrary to the permits that were issued. The database also shows that in more than 30 West Bank settlements, entire neighborhoods have been built without permits or on private lands. The dissonance only intensifies when you find that municipal offices, police and fire stations were also built upon and currently operate on lands that belong to Palestinians.

The third reality that seriously hinders a Two-State Solution is the separation wall. This massive project was built both to protect Israeli citizens from suicide attacks and to enable settlers to acquire water and other natural resources. But its description as a wall is misleading. By 2010, the barrier had become a 650 km (400 mile) system of fortifications consisting of very high concrete walls, trenches, rows of barbed wire, and high steel fencing. Army patrols use restricted security roads that follow the barrier.

The separation wall divides families, cordons off communities, complicates travel and splits Palestinians from their land and resources. Instead of adhering to the 1967 boundaries, the separation wall weaves its way into Palestinian territory—a direct violation of an International Court of Justice ruling.

Israeli geographer, Arnon Soffer offers this damming account of what the wall is doing to Israeli-Palestinian relations:

> First of all, the fence is not built like the Berlin Wall. It's a fence that we will be guarding on either side… when 2.5 million people live in a closed off Gaza; it's going to be a human catastrophe. Those people will become even bigger animals than they are today, with the aid of an insane fundamentalist Islam. The pressure at the borders will be awful. It's going to be a terrible war. So, if we want to remain alive, we will have to kill and kill and kill.[29]

In a 2003 trip to the West Bank, *New York Times* columnist and author Thomas Friedman visited the separation wall, which had completely encircled the Arab city of Qalqilya. He had this to say: "Rather than create the outlines of a Two-State Solution, this wall will kill that idea for the Palestinians, and drive them, over time, to demand instead a One-State Solution—where they and the Jews have equal rights."[30]

The fourth and final fact on the ground that subverts the Two-State Solution is demographics. Jews are losing their numerical majority in Israel. The Arab birthrate continues to outgrow that of the Jewish population. Immigration into Israel has slowed as Jews in the Diaspora have chosen to remain overseas. And, emigration from Israel is increasing.

Haifa University estimates the total population west of the Jordan River will reach 15.5 million by 2020, with 6.4 million Jews and 8.8 Palestinian Arabs.[31] To Israeli Jews this is known as the "demographic threat." The fear of losing the demographic advantage in Israel and the imposition of a bi-national state is uniting both left and right wing Israeli leaders to find solutions, some of which are extreme.

One such radical "solution" proposed by right wing Israeli extremists is the relocation of Palestinian towns inside Israel to the future Palestinian State. While this seems like an inhumane tactic for removing unwanted people, a 2003 study by the Jaffee Center for Strategic Studies found that 57 percent of Israelis were in favor of forced expulsion or migration induced by material incentive, 46 percent supported the removal of Palestinians in the Occupied Territories and 33 percent supported the transfer of Palestinians who hold Israeli citizenship.[32]

This lack of concern for the "other" is deeply disturbing and could easily lead to brutality. The use of the term "apartheid state" is becoming a popular rallying cry for Palestinians who have shifted their struggle to a fight for civil, political, and human rights. The idea that Palestinians are being herded into South African style "bantustans" is an ugly prospect even for the staunchest supporter of Israel. Capitalizing on this sentiment, Palestinian leader Ahmed Queri spoke out against Israeli disengagement at the annual Herliza Conference "This is an apartheid solution to put the Palestinians in cantons. Who can accept this? We will go for a One-State Solution."[33]

It is important to note that some Israelis share this sentiment. Former Prime Minister, Ehud Olmert stated:

> We don't have unlimited time. More and more Palestinians are uninterested in a negotiated, Two-State Solution, because they want to change the essence of the conflict from an Algerian paradigm to a South African one...from a struggle against occupation, in their parlance to a struggle for one man, one vote. That is, of course, a much cleaner struggle, a much more popular struggle—and ultimately a much more powerful one.[34]

Doubts about the Two-State Solution increase the viability of the One-State Solution. Many of these Two-State doubters are Israeli. For example, Israeli political scientist and former Deputy Mayor of Jerusalem, Meron Benvenisti called for the formation of a bi-national state and denounced the Two-State Solution as "inapplicable" to the problem of Israel and Palestine.[35]

Daniel Gavron, a prominent Zionist, and Israeli immigrant, stated that partition between the two communities is no longer possible and "we are left with only one alternative: the Israeli-Palestinian coexistence in one nation."[36] A group of prominent Israeli artists supporting the One-State idea also is making inroads into the public Israeli consciousness. "If the State of Israel aspires to perceive itself as a democracy, it should abandon once and for all, the legal and ideological foundation of religious, ethnic, and demographic discrimination. The State of Israel should strive to become the state of all its citizens. We are calling for the annulment of all laws that make Israel an apartheid state."[37]

But what would this unified, bi-national state look like? How would a joint government work for the common good after decades of injustices perpetrated on both sides? How can Jews and Palestinians ensure their security if they share power rather than seek to dominate the other? How can each side have faith that the persecution by the other will end?

These questions must be debated and resolved.

Fortunately, the groundwork for a bi-national Israeli and Palestinian state has already begun. Academics, activists, government officials and others have outlined concrete measures to construct a government founded on human rights, which would guarantee protections for both the majority and minority populations.

Two frameworks in particular address the most salient issues. The first framework was developed by Palestinian professor and human rights activist, Mazin Qumsiyeh. In his book, *Sharing the Land of Canaan: Human Rights and the Israeli-Palestinian Struggle*, Qumsiyeh outlines a list of ultimate, intermediate and short-term goals to facilitate a social movement in Israel/Palestine:

Ultimate Goals:

The Right of Return for refugees

A pluralistic democracy in Israel/Palestine with equality and human rights for all

An end to all acts of violence

Intermediate Goals:

To develop more governmental and public support for the ultimate goals

To use economic and public relations tools of divestment and economic boycotts (the South African model)

To press foreign governments to stop military aid and link economic aid to international law and human rights

Short-term goals:

Community members and structures to identify with this vision

Engage in education and alliance building

Ensure fair news coverage with a concerted media strategy

Provide direct relief and humanitarian aid to those suffering from human rights abuses[38]

The second framework for a bi-national state was drafted by Amnesty International in 2002. Entitled, *Developing a Human Rights Agenda for Peace*, the report indicts the Oslo process for failing to ensure respect for human rights and therefore undermining the potential of the Two-State Solution. The Amnesty International report argues a pluralistic, secular, One-State Solution where each group is represented equally and has constitutional mechanisms in place for the protection of both the majority and minority as the method most likely to bring about a mutually agreeable compromise to the Israeli-Palestinian conflict. The group released a ten-point agenda to build peace between Israelis and Palestinians:

1. **The right to life, liberty, and security.** Extrajudicial executions, suicide bombings or other attacks against civilians, excessive lethal force and targeting of residential areas have violated the right to life of hundreds of people. The life of each individual

must be protected. The authorities must prohibit unlawful killings. Opposition groups also must reject unlawful killings. Every killing that does occur must be investigated and the perpetrators should be brought to justice in fair trials. The Palestinian Authority should abolish the death penalty.

2. **No subjection to torture or to cruel, inhumane or degrading treatment or punishment.** Torture, brutality by the security forces, and all other cruel treatment should be eradicated; any cases of torture or ill treatment should be immediately, independently and thoroughly investigated and the perpetrators brought to justice in fair trials. Incommunicado detention should be ended and all detainees should have prompt access to lawyers and family.

3. **No subjection to arbitrary arrest and detention.** In Israel detainees have been held without charge or a fair trial in administrative detention; under the Palestinian Authority, hundreds have been held without charge or trial even after the Palestinian High Court of Justice has ordered their release. Such arbitrary detention has often been carried out in the name of the fight against terrorism. All political prisoners held without charge or trial should be tried in fair trials or immediately released.

4. **The right to a fair trial.** In Israel, military courts have diminished defendants' rights to fair trials. Under the Palestinian Authority, the State Security Court hands down sentences in summary trials in flagrant violation of fair trial rights. Palestinian military courts have also held unfair trials. Laws must ensure respect for the right to fair trial as enshrined in international human rights standards.

5. **Free and equal treatment for dignity and rights.** No distinction or discrimination on the grounds of ethnic origin, religion, sex or other status in the enjoyment of human rights and freedoms. Discriminatory laws and practices should be abolished. The destruction of Palestinian houses and property should be abolished.

6. **The right to freedom of movement.** The past seven years have witnessed profound and flagrant denials of the right to freedom of movement. The Occupied Territories have become a land of barriers between towns and between villages. Palestinian towns and villages have been cut off from the outside world for days and often weeks; trenches have been dug around Jericho and Ramallah. Gaza has been enclosed for years like a prison. Palestinians from the Occupied Territories are unable to enter Jerusalem without a permit. The sick and injured frequently have been prevented from seeking medical treatment. These barriers to free movement should now be removed.

7. **The right to return to his or her country of origin.** The right to return is an individual human right, which cannot be given away as a political concession. Palestinians in exile should be given the choice to return to Israel, the West Bank

or Gaza Strip. Those who choose not to return are entitled to compensation. Those returning should also receive compensation for lost property. The same rights relating to return and compensation should also be given to Israelis who fled or were forced out of Arab and other countries.

8. **The right to freedom of thought, opinion and expression.** Under the Palestinian Authority, critics of the authority or the peace process have been harassed, arrested and imprisoned, often without charge or trial. The Israeli authorities have restricted the movement of human rights activists and journalists have been targeted. Peaceful expression of ideas and opinions should be guaranteed and any person detained solely for the expression of beliefs should be released immediately and unconditionally.

9. **Equality for women.** The freedom of women is limited by discriminatory codes and practices. Equality of women should be enshrined in laws and practices.

10. **No impunity for human rights abuses.** Allegations of human rights abuses should be promptly, impartially and thoroughly investigated and perpetrators brought to justice in fair proceedings.

Obviously, the One-State Solution has been a subject of serious consideration, even if it requires more vision to implement than a Two-State Solution, which capitulates to the momentum of Israel's unjust and discriminatory methods on the ground.

If self-defeating ideologies persist, if the realities on the ground become increasingly untenable, and if violence is allowed to infect new generations of young Palestinians and Jews, then peace in the Middle East will remain elusive. Israeli Jews and Palestinians need a new course. The situation brings to mind the famous remark by Einstein, who said, "Insanity is doing the same thing over and over again and expecting different results."

The way out of this destructive cycle is cooperation and respect. As time passes and violence continues unabated, the conflict continues to take root in new generations. Both sides are beginning to realize that after a century of dreams and conflict, the Zionist dream sits on the shoulders of its own contradictions. Israeli-Jewish, Israeli-Arab, and Palestinian populations are so interdependent and intertwined that their forced partition promises only a downward spiral toward disaster. Perhaps at some other time, two states were possible. But the Two-State option evaporated years ago. Perhaps as some voices have always argued, it never existed at all.[39]

While these frameworks are not all inclusive, they do provide an outline for how to proceed in a new direction. The bi-national One-State Solution is less of a solution than a process. Yet it is a process of hope and of peace, not of continued oppression and fear.

As Qumsiyeh so aptly states, "We can either remain locked in our old mythological and tribal ways, or we can envision a better future and work for it. The choice is obvious."[40]

As we now look to a One-State bi-national future, I can envision a state in which no group is forced to give up more land. This includes the Jewish settlers as much as it includes the Palestinian refugees who deserve restitution.

Now that *One Land Two Stories* has been published—clearly, in order to move forward, more collaborative work needs to be done. It is the authors' intention that their perspectives and personal insights contained in the book will generate greater understanding, encourage civil discourse and ultimately lead to better relations between Israelis and Palestinians. They intend to keep the conversation going through future research and dissemination of information.

Visit the website:
Drs. Gabbay and Kazak have created a growing repository of updated information pertaining to the conflict on their website at www.onelandtwostories.com.

For an e-book copy of this book go to www.onelandtwostories.com.

Schedule a presentation:
The professors are available to speak to groups interested in expanding their knowledge of this complex subject. To schedule a presentation contact the authors through the website.

Become part of the solution:
Knowing that many of their readers are committed to peaceful solutions, the authors ask that you sign up as *One Land Two Stories* Scholars. See the website at www. onelandtwostories.com.

To receive future correspondence:
Sign up to receive current information about book signings in your area, additional curricula and future publications.

CHAPTER 1 | ISRAEL

1. Bratcher, "Israelite Kings."
2. The Torah is comprised of five books, and is also known as the Five Books of Moses. The five books are titled; Genesis, Exodus, Leviticus, Numbers, and Deuteronomy. The whole of Jewish law, literature, and history is not contained solely in the five books of the Torah. Other important Jewish scriptures exist such as the Nevi'im (Prophets) and the Ketuvim (Writings). The Prophets is made up of 8 books. These books detail the time period from the time Israelites entered Israel until Judah was captured by the Babylonians. This time period is known as the "period of prophesy." "The Writings" is comprised of eleven books and includes the Five Scrolls. These books are sometimes divided into categories: "books of truth" of Psalms, Proverb and Job; the "wisdom books" of Job, Ecclesiastes, and Proverbs; the "poetry books" of Psalms, Lamentations, and Song of Songs; and the "historical books" of Ezra-Nehemiah and Chronicles.
3. Stand With Us, *Israel 101, 5.*
4. Genesis 12:1-3.
5. Genesis 13:14-15.
6. Genesis 17:8-9.
7. Genesis 21:12.
8. Genesis 26:24.
9. Genesis 28:14-15.
10. Exodus 6:2-8.

CHAPTER 1 | PALESTINE

1. Tamari, "Ishaq al-Shami."
2. Ali-Imran 3:67.
3. Al-Isra 17:1.
4. Al-Baqara 2:144.
5. Al-Sistanti, "Rules Regarding Waqf."
6. Siddiqi, "The Islamic Perspective of Jerusalem."

CHAPTER 2 | ISRAEL

1. Brecher, *Jewish Diaspora.*
2. The Book of Daniel is part of the Hebrew Bible. The Book of Ezra is also a book in the Hebrew Bible and describes the efforts of a rabbi to reestablish Jewish law and worship in Jerusalem once Babylonian control had ended. The book, likely written by Ezra, later details the events that took place in Jerusalem. The Book of Nehemiah describes the details of Nehemiah's return to Jerusalem.
3. Hooker, "After the Exile."
4. David, "History of Persecution."
5. Josephus, *The Jewish War,* 292.

ENDNOTES

6. Richman and The Temple Institute, "A Time to Weep."
7. Leviticus: 19:18.
8. *Fiddler on the Roof.*
9. Ibid.
10. Palestinian Media Watch, "Rewriting History."
11. Pinto, "Culture and Stereotypes."
12. Kniesmeyer and Brecher, "Life in the Pale."
13. Korn, *American Jewry and the Civil War*, 143.
14. "Aliyah through Sudan."
15. Wailer, "Protocols in 21st Century."
16. StandWithUs, "Quick Facts."
17. Anonymous, "Jewish Massacre Denounced," 6.
18. Herzel, The Jewish State.
19. "Immigration."
20. Goldman, "Dalai Lama."
21. The text comes from a poem by Naftali Hertz Imber called Tikvatenu, first published in Jerusalem in 1886. It soon became popular throughout the Jewish world and in 1933 was adapted as the anthem of the Zionist Movement by the 18th Zionist Congress. Upon establishment of the State of Israel in 1948, Hatikva became the national anthem.

CHAPTER 2 | PALESTINE

1. Hobsbawm and Ranger, *Invention of Tradition.*
2. Kimmerling and Migdal, *The Palestinian People*, xxvi-xxvii.
3. Smith, *The Early History of God*, 19.
4. Ibid. 36.
5. Kimmerling and Migdal, *The Palestinian People*, xxvii.
6. Muslih, *Origins of Palestinian Nationalism*, 211.
7. Doumani, Beshara, "Rediscovering Ottoman Palestine," 14.
8. Smith, *Palestine and the Palestinians*, 23.
9. Ibid., 24.
10. Ibid., 23.
11. Ibid., 22.
12. Sanbar, "Out of Place," 88.
13. Ibid.
14. Smith, *The Early History of God*, 38.
15. Gassner, "Survey of Palestinian Refugees," 6.
16. Khalidi, *Palestinian Identity*, 38.
17. Smith, *The Early History of God*, 70.
18. Ibid.
19. Sanbar, "Out of Place," 90.

20. Abboushu, *The Unmaking of Palestine.*
21. Kimmerling and Migdal, *The Palestinian People*, 104.
22. Cohn-Sherbok, *The Palestine – Israeli Conflict*, 105.
23. Ibid., 23.
24. Muslih, *Origins of Palestinian Nationalism*, 212.
25. Kimmerling and Migdal, *The Palestinian People*, 30-31.
26. Muslih, *Origins of Palestinian Nationalism*, 156.
27. Said, *Question of Palestine*, 117.
28. Khalidi, *Palestinian Identity*, 20.
29. Muslih, *Origins of Palestinian Nationalism*, 177.
30. Kimmerling and Migdal, *The Palestinian People*, 80.
31. Ibid.
32. Ibid., 84.
33. Muslih, *Origins of Palestinian Nationalism*, 210.
34. Ibid., 187.
35. Kimmerling and Migdal, *The Palestinian People*, 399.
36. Said, *Question of Palestine*,124-125.
37. Kimmerling and Migdal, *The Palestinian People*, 399.
38. Said, *Question of Palestine.*

CHAPTER 3 | ISRAEL

1. League of Nations, "An Interim Report."
2. Twain, *The Innocents Abroad*, 508-608.
3. Peretz, *Encyclopedia*, 235-239.
4. Meir-Levi, *History Upside Down*, 55.
5. Ibid.
6. Ibid., 56-57.
7. Simpson, *Palestine Report on Immigration.*
8. *Encyclopedia Britannica*, 11th edition, s.v. "Palestine."
9. Haim, *Education System*, 27.
10. Barkai, *Economic Affairs*, 493.
11. Meir-Levi, *History Upside Down*, 8.
12. Auman, *Land Ownership*, 25.
13. Winston Churchill, then Colonial Secretary, visited the Middle East in March 1921. There, he endorsed a deal in which the original territory of the British Mandate of Palestine would no longer include Trans-Jordan. Trans-Jordan was to be given to King Abdullah, who would serve as the Amir under the authority of the High Commissioner of Trans-Jordan. This arrangement left only 26% of the original territory of Palestine for the Balfour Declaration's call for a Jewish homeland. 74% of the British Mandate of Palestine became Trans-Jordan.
14. League of Nations, *The Palestine Mandate.*

ENDNOTES

15. Meir-Levi, *History Upside Down*, 58-59.
16. Ibid.
17. Scheindlin, *Short History*, 230.
18. Scheindlin, *Short History*, 200-208.
19. Dayan, *Pioneer*, 83.
20. Meir-Levi, *History Upside Down*, 8.
21. Morse, *Nazi Connection*, 59.
22. Meir-Levi, *History Upside Down*, 9.
23. United States Holocaust Memorial Museum, "Haj Amin al-Husayni: Arab Nationalist and Muslim Leader."
24. Meir-Levi, *History Upside Down*, 10.
25. Meir Levi, *History Upside Down*, 10.
26. *The Trial of Adolf Eichman*, Session 80.

CHAPTER 3 | PALESTINE

1. Linfield, "Statistics of Jews," 300.
2. Woodward, "The Middle East During World War I."
3. "McMahon-Hussein Correspondence."
4. Government of Palestine, *Supplement to Survey of Palestine*, 15.
5. "The Balfour Declaration."
6. Smith, *Palestine and the Palestinians*, 41.
7. Palestine in Focus, 26.
8. Khalidi, *Palestinian Identity*, 41.
9. Smith, *Palestine and the Palestinians*, 48.
10. Ibid., 45.
11. Ibid., 45.
12. Morris, *Righteous Victims*, 49.
13. Pappe, *A History of Modern Palestine*, 147.
14. Kimmerling and Migdal, *The Palestinian People*, 97.
15. Smith, *Palestine and the Palestinians*, 65.
16. Morris, *Righteous Victims*, 116.
17. Sela, Avraham. "The 'Wailing Wall' Riots (1929) As a Watershed."
18. Morris, *Righteous Victims*, 113.
19. Ibid., 116.
20. Ibid., 117.
21. Ibid., 122.
22. Smith, *Palestine and the Palestinians*, 31.
23. Ibid., 68-69.
24. Ibid., 69.
25. Khalidi, *Palestinian Identity*.

CHAPTER 4 | ISRAEL

1. Beschloss, *The Conquerors*, 212.
2. Ibid.
3. Hobbs, *Dear General*, 223.
4. "Holocaust Denial."
5. Nordling, *Holocaust Survivors*.
6. Kochavi, *Post Holocaust Politics*, 32-40.
7. Shlaim, "The Debate About 1948," 298.
8. Boyarin, "Palestine and Jewish History."
9. U.N. Resolution 181.
10. Bard, "Myths & Facts."
11. Meir-Levi, *History Upside Down*, 61-62.
12. U.N. Resolution 181.
13. Shalom Jerusalem, "The Grand Mufti of Jerusalem."
14. Kimmerling and Migdal, *The Palestinian People*, 156.
15. Meir-Levi, *History Upside Down*, 62-73.
16. Karsh, "1948-True Story," 27.
17. Bergman, *Israel's Wars*, 76.
18. Gold, *Fight for Jerusalem*, 137.
19. Morris, 1948, 128.
20. Porath, *Letters from Jerusalem*, 133.
21. Meir-Levi, *History Upside Down*, 71-72.
22. Declaration of the Establishment of the State of Israel.
23. Waage, "Miracle Called Israel."
24. Sachar, *History of Israel*, 333.
25. Dershowitz, *Case for Israel*, 75.
26. Ibid., 74.
27. Meir-Levi, *History Upside Down*, 69.
28. Ibid.
29. Ibid., 70.
30. Bard, "Myth and Fact: Flee in 1948?"
31. Steinberg, "Jerusalem 1948."
32. Lee, "Israel and Syria."
33. Caplan, "Tale of Two Cities," 21.
34. Meir-Levi, *History Upside Down*, 74.
35. Shields, "Jewish Refugees."
36. Meir-Levi, *History Upside Down*, 65.
37. Eretz Yisroel, "Palestinian Refugees."
38. Ibid.

39. UN Relief and Works Agency.
40. "Jews in the Arab World."
41. Meir-Levi, *History Upside Down*, 64.
42. Sachar, *History of Israel*, 395-405.

CHAPTER 4 | PALESTINE

1. Hilal, "Palestine: The Last Colonial Issue," 2.
2. Kimmerling and Migdal, *The Palestinian People*, 145.
3. Ibid., 153.
4. Ibid., 152-153.
5. Ibid., 153.
6. Pappe, "Zionism and the Two State Solution," 36.
7. Ibid., 9.
8. Tannous, *Enraging Story*, 19.
9. Pappe, "Zionism and the Two State Solution," 36.
10. Hogan, "The 1948 Massacre," 311.
11. Ibid.
12. Ibid.
13. Ibid.
14. "The Battle of Kastel."
15. Hogan, "The 1948 Massacre," 313.
16. Ibid., 314.
17. Ibid., 316.
18. Ibid., 324.
19. Ibid., 325.
20. Arbel, "I Was The Haganah Officer," cited in Hogan, "The 1948 Massacre at Deir Yassin Revisited," 328.
21. Morris, *Righteous Victims*, 208.
22. Ibid.
23. Hogan, "The 1948 Massacre at Deir Yassin Revisited," 330.
24. Kimmerling and Migdal, *The Palestinian People*, 161.
25. Pappe, 18.
26. Begin, M. *The Revolt: The Story of the Irgun*.
27. Hasso, "Modernity and Gender," 498.
28. Pappe, *The Ethnic Cleansing of Palestine*, xii.
29. Begin, M., The Revolt: *The Story of the Irgun*.
30. Ibid., 17.
31. Morris, *Righteous Victims*, 210.
32. Pappe, *The Ethnic Cleansing of Palestine*, 136.
33. Peteet, *Gender in Crisis*, 59.
34. Cypel, *Walled*, 161.

35. Ibid., 14.
36. Ibid., 171.
37. Smith, *Palestine and the Palestinians*, 88.
38. Ibid.
39. Ibid., 171-172.
40. Karsh, "The Palestinians Alone."
41. Smith, *Palestine and the Palestinians*, 88.
42. Karsh, "The Palestinians Alone."
43. Ibid.
44. Ibid.

CHAPTER 5 | ISRAEL

1. Tessler, *A History*, 393.
2. Dershowitz, *The Case for Israel*, 92.
3. Oren, *Six Days of War*, 293.
4. Nusseibeh and David, *Palestinian Life*, 87.
5. Zionism and Israel on the Web Project, "Six Day War."
6. Gilbert, Israel: *A History*, 381.
7. Ibid., 379.
8. Gilbert, *Routledge Atlas*, 66.
9. Bard, *Myths and Facts*, 53.
10. Oren, *Six Days of War*, 136.
11. Gilbert, *Routledge Atlas*, 67.
12. Meir-Levi, *History Upside Down*, 79.
13. Meir, "Lasting Peace," 447-461.
14. Meir-Levi, *History Upside Down*, 79.
15. "The Six-Day War-Introduction."
16. Meir-Levi, *History Upside Down*, 80.
17. Hart, *Arafat: Terrorist or Peacemaker?*, 239.
18. Zuckerman, "Opinion: Obama's Jerusalem Stonewall."
19. Pipes, "Ehud Olmert."
20. "Jordan's Desecration of Jerusalem," American-Israeli Cooperative Enterprise.
21. Zuckerman, "Opinion: Obama's Jerusalem Stonewall."
22. Meir-Levi, *History Upside Down*, 18.
23. UN Conference on Trade and Development 1994.
24. The World Bank, Developing the Occupied Territories, 4.
25. Meir-Levi, History Upside Down, 82.
26. Ibid.
27. Ibid., 19.
28. Glazov, "From Russia With Terror."

ENDNOTES

29. Meir-Levi, *History Upside Down*, 21.
30. Medoff, "Holocaust-Denier."
31. Meir-Levi, *History Upside Down*, 27.
32. "Yasser Arafat's Timeline of Terror."
33. Ibid.
34. Bard, "The Yom Kippur War."
35. Lorch, "The Arab-Israeli Wars."
36. Bard, "Facts About Settlements."
37. Levinson, "300,000 Settlers."

CHAPTER 5 | PALESTINE

1. See Article 3 of the "Palestinian National Charter."
2. Hammer, *Palestinians Born in Exile*, 35.
3. Kimmerling and Migdal, *The Palestinian People*, 223.
4. Ibid., 219.
5. Hammer, *Palestinians Born in Exile*, 35.
6. Kimmerling and Migdal, *The Palestinian People*, 235.
7. Lybarger, *Identity & Religion*, 22.
8. Kimmerling and Migdal, *The Palestinian People*, 238.
9. Ibid., 235.
10. Heacock, "Locals and Returnees," 3.
11. Lybarger, *Identity & Religion*, 22.
12. Ibid.
13. Ibid.
14. Iyad and Rouleau, *My Home, My Land*, 40.
15. Sayigh, *Armed Struggle*, 91.
16. Rubenberg, *The Palestinians*, 16.
17. Iyad, 40.
18. Hammer, *Palestinians Born in Exile*, 37.
19. Ibid.
20. Rubenberg, *The Palestinians*, 16.
21. Ibid.
22. See Article 10 of "Palestinian National Charter."
23. See Article 19 of "Palestinian National Charter."
24. Sayigh, *Armed Struggle*, 101.
25. Rubenberg, *The Palestinians*, 16.
26. Sayigh, *Armed Struggle*, 139.
27. Ibid., 140.
28. Rubenberg, *The Palestinians*, 16.
29. Ibid.

30. Morris, *Righteous Victims*.
31. Cypel, *Walled*, 189.
32. Ibid.
33. Khalaf (also known as Abu Iyad) Abu Iyad with Eric Rouleau, *My Home, My Land: A Narrative of the Palestinian Struggle*, 51.
34. Cypel, *Walled*, 214.
35. Nusseibeh and David, *Once Upon a Country*, 99.
36. Ibid., 101.
37. UN Security Council, "Resolution 242."
38. Ben-Ami, *Scars of War*, 129.
39. Ibid., 130.
40. Rubenberg, *The Palestinians*, 19.
41. Ben-Ami, *Scars of War*, 125.
42. Morris, *Righteous Victims*, 341.
43. Ben-Ami, *Scars of War*, 129.
44. Hammer, *Palestinians Born in Exile*, 37.
45. Ibid.
46. Ibid., 38.
47. Ben-Ami, *Scars of War*, 137.
48. Khalaf, (also known as Abu Iyad) Abu Iyad with Eric Rouleau, 59.
49. Ben-Ami, *Scars of War*, 138.
50. Ibid.
51. Gibson and Fanon, *The Post Colonial Imagination, 118.*
52. Ben-Ami, *Scars of War*, 138.

CHAPTER 6 | ISRAEL

1. Brenchley, *Six-Day War and Its Aftermath*, 91.
2. Bavly and Salpeter, *Fire in Beirut*, 26-27.
3. Israeli, *PLO in Lebanon*, 3.
4. Ibid.
5. Bavley and Salpeter, *Fire in Beirut*, 197.
6. Kerim and Samir, "Lebanon," 12.
7. Israeli, *PLO in Lebanon*, 230.
8. Bavley and Salpeter, *Fire in Beirut*, 42.
9. Gabriel, *Operation Peace*, 53.
10. Ibid., 37.
11. Ibid., 37.
12. Ibid. 42.
13. Israeli, *PLO in Lebanon*, 3.
14. Gabriel, *Operation Peace*, 52.

ENDNOTES

15. "A Sabbath of Terror," *Time Magazine*, March 20, 1978.
16. Menachem Begin, "Statement to the Knesset," March 13, 1978.
17. UNIFIL, "Mandate." UNIFIL,unifil.unmissions.org.
18. Chaim Herzog, "Statement to the UN Security Council," 1978.
19. Ibid.
20. Gabriel, *Operation Peace*, 57.
21. Smith, *Arab Israeli Conflict*, 354.
22. Gabriel, *Operation Peace*, 57.
23. Israel Ministry of Foreign Affairs, "Ambassador Blum on the Situation in Lebanon."
24. It should be noted that such a situation was made possible by the particular composition of the UN and its various bodies whereby the combined voting power of the Soviet Union and the Arab blocs all but assured a negative outcome for Israel-no matter what the case.
25. Israel Ministry of Foreign Affairs, "Ambassador Blum on the Situation in Lebanon."
26. Gabriel, *Operation Peace*, 58.
27. Eban, *The Beirut Massacre*, IX.
28. Palestine Facts, "Israeli Invasion of Lebanon 1982."
29. For a full accounting of the forces deployed in Lebanon on the eve of Operation Peace for the Galilee see: Katz, Samuel and Russell, Lee E. Armies in Lebanon: 1982-84, (Oxford: Osprey, 1985).
30. For a day-by-day account of events see Gabriel, Richard. Operation Peace for the Galilee. New York: Hill and Wang, 1984.
31. Gabriel, *Operation Peace*, 113.
32. The number of massacre victims is highly disputed. The Palestinian Red Crescent put the number at 2,000; according to the BBC the number was closer to 800. IDF intelligence reports estimated that 700-800 persons had been killed. In the end the Israeli Kahan Commission declared, "This may well be the number most closely corresponding with reality." See: "The Commission of Inquiry into the Events at the Refugee Camps in Beirut: Final Report." Panel Members: Kahn, Yitzhak; Barak, Aharon; and Efrat, Yona. The State of Israel (1983). p. 45.
33. Kahn, Barak, and Efrat, "Commission of Inquiry," 56.
34. Ibid., 73.
35. House Subcommittee on International Terrorism and Nonproliferation and the House Subcommittee on the Middle East and Central Asia of the Committee on International Relations, *Hezbollah's Global Reach*.
36. UN Security Council, "Report of the Secretary-General pursuant to Security Council Resolution 1559 (2004)," 2.
37. "Shamir Yitzhak."
38. In fact many older Palestinians now lament the 'good-old-days'-before the rise of Hamas- when a man could afford to by his own home and support his family. See: Slackman, M. and Bronner, E. "Trapped by Gaza Blockade, Locked in Despair," New York Times, July 13, 2010.
39. In fact many of these steps had already been established within the confines of the 1978 Camp David Accords.

40. Kreczko, "Support Reagan's Initiative."
41. Johnson, "Shadowplay," 43-46.
42. Sahliyeh, *Lebanon War*, 101.
43. Ibid., 222.
44. For a retrospective on Israel's decision to tacitly support Hamas see: Higgins, Andrew, "How Israel helped Spawn Hamas," *Washington Post*, January 24, 2009.
45. Palestine Facts, "Intifada from 1987-1993."
46. Ibid.
47. Ibid.
48. Ibid.
49. Arafat, "Arafat at the UN General Assembly."

CHAPTER 6 | PALESTINE

1. Moubayed, "Talal."
2. Kimmerling and Migdal, *The Palestinian People*.
3. Brynen, "PLO Policy," 51.
4. Ibid., 52.
5. Hudson, "Palestinians and Lebanon."
6. Sayigh, *Palestinians*.
7. Hudson, "Palestinians and Lebanon," 249.
8. Ibid., 253.
9. Khalidi, *Under Seige*, 29.
10. Hudson, "Palestinians and Lebanon," 254.
11. Cypel, *Walled*, 226.
12. Ibid.
13. The exact figures on the death toll in Sabra and Shatila camps cannot be determined because, in addition to the approximately 1,000 people who were buried in communal graves by the International Committee of the Red Cross (ICRC) or in Beirut cemeteries by family members, many corpses were buried beneath bulldozed buildings by militia members.
14. Schiff and Ya'ari, *Israel's Lebanon War*, 285.
15. Cypel, *Walled*, 441.
16. Hudson, "Palestinians and Lebanon," 255.
17. The War of the Camps was a sub-conflict within the Lebanese Civil War between Palestinians in Palestinian refugee camps and the Shi'ite Amal militia.
18. Khalidi, *Palestinian Identity*, 200.
19. King, *A Quiet Revolution*, 208.
20. Kimmerling and Migdal, *The Palestinian People*, 283.
21. Morris, *Righteous Victims*, 565.
22. Kimmerling and Migdal, *The Palestinian People*, 289.
23. Shlaim, *The Iron Wall*, 451.

ENDNOTES

24. Khalidi, *Palestinian Identity*, 200.
25. King, *A Quiet Revolution*, 263.
26. Ibid., 106.
27. Vitullo, "Uprising in Gaza."
28. Smerdon, "Israeli Army Fears."
29. Shlaim, *The Iron Wall*, 454.
30. Langer, "A Judicial System," 30.
31. King, *A Quiet Revolution*, 7.
32. Shlaim, *The Iron Wall*, 453.
33. King, A *Quiet Revolution*, 111.
34. Schiff and Ya'ari, *Intifada*, 378.
35. King, *A Quiet Revolution*, 223.
36. It seems that the media images of the powerful IDF retaliation against unarmed Palestinians propelled the cause for Palestinian self-determination more so than the numerous years of armed struggle.
37. King, *A Quiet Revolution*, 178.
38. King, *A Quiet Revolution*, 290.
39. Ashrawi, *This Side of Peace*, 10.
40. Ibid.
41. Arafat, "Statement."
42. Schiff and Ya'ari, *Intifada*, 3-4, 8.
43. Shlaim, *The Iron Wall*, 453.
44. Saleh, *History of Palestine*, 243.
45. Ibid., 244.

CHAPTER 7 | ISRAEL

1. "Declaration of the Establishment of the State of Israel."
2. "Statement to the General Assembly by Foreign Minister Eban."
3. Viorst, *Sands of Sorrow*, 100.
4. "Khartoum Resolutions."
5. Strober and Strober, *Israel at Sixty*, 197.
6. The historical moment when Golda Meir and Anwar Sadat met face-to face on the tarmac of Lod (now Ben-Gurion) Airport as witnessed and relayed by Yehuda Avner in: Strober, *Israel at Sixty*, 192.
7. Sadat, "Address to the Israeli Knesset: Peace with Justice."
8. Neff, "Sadat's Jerusalem Trip Begins Difficult Path of Egyptian-Israeli Peace," 83-85.
9. "Framework for Peace in the Middle East, Agreed at Camp David."
10. For the complete text of the Declaration of Principles and Oslo II, see the Appendix.
11. Ibid.
12. Reich, *Brief History*, 176.

13. "Black September Plea to Israel," BBC News, January 1, 2001.

14. Jung, *The Middle East and Palestine*, 190.

15. Palestine Facts, "Israel 1967-1991: Jordan Renounces Claims."

16. Satloff, "The Jordan-Israel Peace Treaty," 47.

17. "Treaty of Peace between the Hashemite Kingdom and the State of Israel."

18. Rabinovich, *Waging Peace*, 123.

19. Barak, "Plan for a Better Israel." Also see: Rabinovich, Waging Peace, 124.

20. Reich, *Brief History*, 196-97.

21. Katz, "Middle East Breakthrough Largely Illusion."

22. "President William J. Clinton Makes Announcement," Camp David, July 5, 2000.

23. Swisher, *The Truth About Camp David*, 207.

24. UN General Assembly, *Palestine—Progress Report*.

25. Horowitz, *Camp David*, 9.

26. Learner, *Healing Israeli/Palestine*, 120.

27. Enderlin, *Shattered Dreams*, 355-356.

28. Rabinovich, *Waging Peace*, 13.

29. Swisher, *The Truth*, 225.

30. Clinton, "The Clinton Parameters."

31. Ross, *The Missing Peace*, 755. For an explanation of these reservations see: Enderlin, *Shattered Dreams*, 339.

32. According to the agreement, the Palestinians would receive 100 percent of the Gaza Strip, 97 percent of the West Bank, an exchange of equally valued territories and a corridor providing safe passage between Gaza and the West Bank.

33. Shavit, "End of a Journey."

34. Enderlin, *Shattered Dreams*, 339-344.

35. The newly inaugurated Bush administration decided to take a hands-off approach.

36. Enderlin, *Shattered Dreams*, 348.

37. Pipes, "Ehud Olmert," 73.

38. Lapidoth, "Jerusalem and the Peace Process."

39. Parts of East Jerusalem came under Israeli jurisdiction with the passing of Israel's 1980 "Basic Law-Jerusalem-Capitol of Israel."

40. "The Status of Jerusalem."

41. "Basic Law: Jerusalem Capital of Israel."

42. Ross, *The Missing Peace*, 655.

43. Enderlin, *Shattered Dreams*, 181.

44. Clinton, "The Clinton Parameters."

45. Enderlin, *Shattered Dreams*, 352-354.

46. Rabinovich, *Waging Peace*, 172.

47. "President Interviewed by Israeli Television."

48. Haberman, "Dennis Ross's Exit Interview," 36.

ENDNOTES

49. Walsh, "The Prince," 48.
50. Prime Minister Benjamin Netanyahu, UN Address to the General Assembly, September 23, 2011.

CHAPTER 7 | PALESTINE

1. Ashrawi, *This Side of Peace*.
2. Basic Law of Israel–Jerusalem as Capitol.
3. UNGA Resolution 194, Article 11.
4. UNRWA, *The United Nations and Palestinian Refugees*.
5. Ben-Ami, *Scars of War*, 51.
6. Ibid.
7. Ashrawi, *This Side of Peace*, 111.
8. Shlaim, "The Oslo Accord," 26.
9. Ibid.
10. The Peoples Voice, "Israel's History in Quotes."
11. Shlaim, "The Oslo Accord," 24-40.
12. Ibid., 28.
13. Ibid., 29.
14. Ibid., 26.
15. Roy, "Why Peace Failed," 11.
16. Ibid.
17. Ibid.
18. Shikaki, "Palestinians Divided."
19. Ibid.
20. Butenschon, "The Paradox of Self-Determination in Palestine," 85.
21. Ibid., 88-89.
22. Said, "The Lost Liberation."
23. Shlaim, "The Oslo Accord," 35.
24. Roy, "Why Peace Failed," 11.
25. Ibid., 12.
26. Ibid., 12.
27. Ibid., 14.
28. Shlaim, "The Oslo Accord," 36.
29. Lustick, "The Oslo Agreement as an Obstacle to Peace," 61.
30. Roy, "Why Peace Failed," 8.
31. Ibid.
32. Ben-Ami, *Scars of War*, 247.
33. Ibid., 248.
34. Roy, "Why Peace Failed," 15.
35. Ibid.
36. "Al-Aqsa Intifada Timeline."

37. Ben-Ami, *Scars of War*, 291.
38. Ibid.
39. Aronson, "Settlement Freeze Redux," 9.
40. Palestinian Central Bureau of Statistics, *Impact of the Israeli Measures*, 5.
41. Harel, "Settlements Grow on Arab Land."
42. Ibid.
43. Ibid.
44. President Mahmoud Abbas, Address to the General Assembly of the United Nations, September 24, 2011.

CHAPTER 8 | ISRAEL

1. Bregman, *Israel's Wars*, 204-205.
2. Karsh, *Arafat's War*, 148.
3. Ibid.
4. Ibid., 150.
5. Ibid., 163.
6. Reich, *A Brief History of Israel*, 210.
7. Karsh, *Arafat's War*, 178.
8. Samuels, "In a Ruined Country," 77.
9. Tomeh, "Arafat Ordered Hamas Attacks against Israel in 2000."
10. "Interview by Marwan Barghouti," Al-Hayat, September 29, 2001.
11. Karsh, *Arafat's War*, 174.
12. IDF, Sgt. David Biri, September 27, 2000.
13. Katz, *Song of Spies*, 106.
14. Ibid.
15. Ibid.
16. Muravchik, *Covering the Intifada*.
17. Fallows, "Who Shot Mohammed al-Dura?" A detailed inventory of evidence demonstrating the Israeli soldiers could not have shot Mohammed and his father (pgs. 50-52) and suggests that there is good reason to believe that an unscrupulous plot was at play (53-55).
18. *Drei Kugeln und Ein Totes Kind* (*Three Bullets and a Dead Child*). See also Schapira's more recent documentary: *Das Kind, Der Tod, and die Wahrheit* (*The Child, the Death, and the Truth*).
19. "France 2 vs. Philippe Karsenty: The Appeal."
20. Meital, *Peace in Tatters*, 96.
21. Seager, "I'll Have Nightmares for the Rest of my Life."
22. Philps, "A Day of Rage, Revenge and Bloodshed."
23. "Barak Calls for Emergency Government." See also: Seager, "I'll Have Nightmares for the Rest of my Life."
24. "Coverage of Oct 12 Lynching in Ramallah by Italian TV Station RAI."
25. Carroll and Black, "TV Row over Mob Footage 'Betrayal'."

26. "Coverage of Oct 12 Lynching in Ramallah by Italian TV Station RAI."
27. Safian, "In the Palestinians' Pocket: Journalists Doing PR For the PA."
28. Muravchik, *Covering the Intifada*, 118.
29. Ibid., 121.
30. Isseroff, "Sharm El Sheikh Speech of President Clinton, October 2000."
31. Meital, *Peace in Tatters*, 97.
32. "Inauguration Speech of Prime Minister Ariel Sharon in the Knesset."
33. Harel, "Military Tribunal Convicts Three 'Santorini' Crew Members."
34. "PM Sharon Knesset Speech."
35. Data summary of Palestinian terrorism during the current conflict with Israel until the Sharm el-Sheikh summit, IIC, 2005.
36. Tucker, "Defensive Shield, Operation," 293.
37. Sharansky, *A Case for Democracy*, 214.
38. "Terrorist Attacks Against Israel (September 2000-2007)."
39. "Victims of Palestinian Terror since Sept 2000."
40. Chassay and Johnson, "Google Earth Used to Target Israel."
41. "Relentless Rocket Attacks Take Psychological Toll on Children in Sedrot," IRIN, 21 February 2012.

CHAPTER 8 | PALESTINE

1. Cypel, *Walled*, 316.
2. Greenberg, "Israel Police Question Two Rabbis."
3. Ibid.
4. The Washington Post, September 25, 1996.
5. Sosebee, "Attempts to Destroy the Haram al-Sharif," 16-17.
6. "Haram al-Shariff Killings," (Temple Mount), *Journal of Palestinian Studies*, XX,#2 (Winter 91), pp. 134-159.
7. Halper, "The Key to Peace," 21.
8. Ben-Ami, *Scars of War*, 265.
9. Ibid.
10. Ibid., 267.
11. B'Tselem, *On Human Rights*, 4.
12. Ibid., 3.
13. Ben-Ami, *Scars of War*, 269.
14. Ibid., 264.

CHAPTER 9 | ISRAEL

1. "Israel Gaza FAQ: The Background," Israel Ministry of Foreign Affairs.
2. Shachar, The *Gaza Strip*, 47-49.
3. Ibid., 49. Miller's aims were pragmatic not political—to grow oranges, not to extend Zionism.
4. The land was sold to the Jewish National Fund in 1946. It was renamed Kfar Darom and became the first Jewish settlement in Gaza when Israel reoccupied the territory in 1967.

5. The historical record supports the later view in that no permanent Jewish community was established in Gaza until the 11th Century. See: "The Jewish Claim to the Land of Israel." *Jewish Virtual Library*.
6. Shachar, *The Gaza Strip*, 57.
7. Ibid., 54-56.
8. Ibid., 58.
9. Nasr, *Arab and Israeli Terrorism*, 40.
10. Brynen, *Sanctuary and Survival*, 22.
11. Israel originally hoped that the religiously founded faction would not promote violence.
12. Rekhess, "The Rise of the Palestinian Islamic Jihad."
13. Meisels, "New Fundamentalist Group Challenges PLO in Israel."
14. Arafat, "Address to the United Nations General Assembly in Geneva."
15. U.S. Congressional Research Service, *Hamas*, E2430.
16. Schanzer, *Hamas vs. Fatah*, 41.
17. Ibid., 40.
18. Waak, "Violence Among Palestinians."
19. Tamimi, *Hamas*, 112.
20. U.S. Department of State, *Patterns of Global Terrorism 1999*.
21. Karmon, "Hamas' Terrorism Strategy."
22. Schanzer, *Hamas vs. Fatah*, 48.
23. Weiner, "Child Abuse in the Palestinian Authority."
24. Contenta, "Arafat's Regime in Shambles."
25. Prusher and Lynfield, "Killing of Yassin: A Turning Point."
26. Chassay and Johnson. "Google Earth Used to Target Israel."
27. "Relentless Rocket Attacks Take Psychological Toll on Children in Sderot," IRIN News, January, 2008.
28. Ibid.
29. "Q&A: Gaza Conflict."
30. Ibid.
31. Ibid.
32. "What are Qassam Rockets?"
33. Intelligence and Terrorism Information Center, "Rocket Threat from the Gaza Strip 2000 – 2007," 51.
34. "Hamas Rockets."
35. "Weapons Smuggling Tunnels in Rafah."
36. Ibid.
37. Sharon, "Address by Prime Minister Ariel Sharon."
38. "Prelude to Operation Cast Lead," 139.
39. Sharon, "Address by Prime Minister Ariel Sharon."
40. Ibid.
41. "The Disengagement Plan—General Outline."
42. Sharon, "Address by Prime Minister Ariel Sharon."

ENDNOTES

43. Johnston, "Chronology of Terrorist Attacks in Israel."
44. "Statement by Israel Ambassador Gillerman to the UN Security Council," March 25, 2008.
45. "Behind the headlines: Rafah Gateway to Terrorism," Israel Ministry of Foreign Affairs, 20 May 2004.
46. "Statement by Israel Ambassador Gillerman to the UN Security Council," March 25, 2008.
47. "Hamas exploitation of Civilians as Human Shields: Photographic Evidence," Israel Ministry of Foreign Affairs, March 6, 2008.
48. See for example: U.N. Security Council, "Resolution 1806: The Situation in the Middle East Including the Palestinian Question."
49. "Prelude to Operation Cast Lead: Israel's Unilateral Disengagement to the Eve of War," 139, *Journal of Palestine Studies*, Vol. XXXVIII, No. 3 (Spring, 2009).
50. "Exit of IDF Forces from Gaza Completed," Israel Ministry of Foreign Affairs, Sept 12, 2005.
51. Kuttab, "Gaza in Limbo."
52. Sharon, "Address PM Sharon addresses the United Nations General Assembly."
53. Tucker, "Gaza Strip Disengagement," 384.
54. Shachar, *The Gaza Strip*, 167.
55. Sharon, "Address PM Sharon addresses the United Nations General Assembly."
56. Ibid.
57. Usher, "Hamas Risen," 3.
58. Hroub, "Hamas after Shaykh Yasin and Rantisi," 21.
59. Usher, "Hamas Risen," 3.
60. Ibid.,11.
61. Ibid., 6.
62. "Gaza."
63. Usher, "Hamas Risen," 10.
64. "Gaza: Still No ICRC Access to Gilad Shalit."
65. "Q&A: Gaza Conflict."
66. "Gaza Facts – The Israeli Perspective."
67. Ibid.
68. Shacher, *The Gaza Strip*, 183.
69. Ibid.
70. "Operation Cast Lead," Globalsecurity.org.
71. Ibid.
72. Shacher, *The Gaza Strip*, 182.
73. Slackman and Bronner, "Trapped by Gaza Blockade."
74. Henkin, "How to Effectively Sanction Hamas."
75. Dershowitz, "The Case Against the Goldstone Report."
76. Goldstone, "Reconsidering the Goldstone Report on Israel and War Crimes."
77. "Behind the Headlines: Israel Designates Gaza a Hostile Territory."
78. "Gaza Facts–The Israeli Perspective."

CHAPTER 9 | PALESTINE

1. Sakran, *Palestine Dilemma*, 204.
2. Central Intelligence Agency, "Gaza," 2009.
3. Sanbar, "Out of Place," 88.
4. Smith, *Palestine and the Palestinians*, 36.
5. Jabotinsky, "The Iron Wall."
6. Kimmerling and Migdal, *The Palestinian People*, 96.
7. Rubenberg, *The Palestinians*, 14-15.
8. Ibid., 14.
9. Ibid., 14.
10. Shlaim, *The Iron Wall*, 81-81.
11. Rubenberg, *The Palestinians*, 15.
12. Ibid.
13. Lesch, "Gaza," 45.
14. Rubenberg, *The Palestinians*, 17.
15. Ibid.
16. Lesch, "Gaza," 46.
17. Ibid., 48.
18. Ibid., 49.
19. Ibid., 49.
20. Ibid., 49.
21. Ibid., 51.
22. Ibid., 55.
23. Said, *Politics of Dispossession*, 1994.
24. Lesch, "Gaza," 55.
25. Lesch, "Prelude," 3.
26. Ibid.
27. Ibid.
28. Shikaki, "Palestinians Divided," 90.
29. Ibid.
30. Turner, "Class," 141.
31. Lesch, "Prelude," 9.
32. Ibid.
33. Ibid., 10.
34. Abu-Amir, "Hamas," 167.
35. Ibid., 168-169.
36. Ageel, "Disengagement."
37. Amnesty International, *Israel/Gaza*.
38. UN Human Rights Council, *Human Rights in Palestine*.

ENDNOTES

39. Ibid.
40. Carter, "Goldstone and Gaza."
41. Finkelstein, "UN Inquiry."
42. "Sweet Freedom," Arab News.com, Editorial, October 22, 2011.

CHAPTER 10 | ISRAEL

1. Ayalon, "Ayalon addresses World Jewish Congress."
2. U.S. Congressional Research Service, *Israeli-Arab Negotiations*, 26.
3. Shragai, "Jerusalem," 20.
4. "Jerusalem Facts & Figures," Israel Ministry of Foreign Affairs.
5. Ibid.
6. Lapidoth, "Jerusalem and the Peace Process."
7. "Israel, the Conflict and Peace," Israel Ministry of Foreign Affairs, December, 2009.
8. Sherwood, "Palestinian Boycott."
9. Bard, "Myth and Facts," 295. Also: Bard, "Myth and Facts," 298.

CHAPTER 10 | PALESTINE

1. PLO Negotiations Affairs Department, *Negotiations Primer*, 38.
2. UN Security Council, Resolution 242, "The Situation in the Middle East."
3. PLO Negotiations Affairs Department, *Negotiations Primer*, 26.
4. UN Security Council, Resolution 465, "Territories Occupied."
5. UN General Assembly, Resolution 61/118, "Israeli Settlements."
6. ICJ, "Advisory Opinion."
7. UN General Assembly, Resolution 54/152, "The Right of the Palestinian People."
8. UN Security Council, Resolution 1397, "The Situation in the Middle East."
9. PLO Negotiations Affairs Department, *Negotiations Primer*,18-19.
10. Ibid., 19.
11. Ibid., 17.
12. Hassassian, "Jerusalem," 294.
13. Israel Central Bureau of Statistics, "Statistical Abstract," 2011.
14. B'Tselem, "Land Expropriation & Settlements: Statistics," 2011.
15. Ibid. Although established in violation of Israeli law, an official Israeli report indicates that state officials within the Israeli government were actively involved in establishing some of these outposts.
16. Foundation for Middle East Peace, "Settlement Information."
17. B'Tselem, "Land Expropriation & Settlements: Statistics." 2011.
18. PLO Negotiations Affairs Department, *Negotiations Primer*, 21.
19. UN Commission on Human Rights, "Question, " of the Violation of Human Rights in the Occupied Arab Territories, 2003.

20. PLO Negotiations Affairs Department, *Negotiations Primer*, 21.
21. OCHA, "Sharp Increase," 1, July 19, 2010.
22. OCHA, "Case of Sheikh Jarrah," 4. Also: OCHA, "Area C," 2, October 2010.
23. ICRC, "Commentary," Geneva Conventions.
24. UN Security Council, Resolution 465, "X."
25. UN General Assembly, Resolution 61/118, "X."
26. UN Commission on Human Rights. "Question," of the Violation of Human Rights in the Occupied Arab Territories, 2003.
27. ICJ, "Advisory Opinion," July 9, 2004.
28. UN Security Council, 4489th Meeting. Resolution 1397 of 2002 (S/RES/1397). 12 March 2002.
29. BADIL Resource Centre for Palestinian Residence and Refugee Rights, June, 1998.
30. Al-Husseini and Bocco 2010; Abu-Iyun and Murad 2006.

CHAPTER 11 | ISRAEL

1. Abunimah, "Palestinians on the Verge of a Majority."
2. Central Intelligence Agency, "Israel," 12 May 2008.
3. Ibid.
4. Defner, "Sound the Alarm."
5. Benn, "Trading Places."
6. Gutmann, "The Declaration."
7. Even though the Middle East is currently experiencing revolutions, scholars doubt that the "Arab Spring" will deliver secular democracy in the region in the near future due to the significant influence of Islamic laws.
8. Ibid.
9. Ravid, Landau, and Rosner, "Olmert to Haaretz."
10. Weizmann, *Trial and Error.*
11. Gabbay, S.M., 2007.
12. Slackman and Bronner, "Trapped by Gaza Blockade."
13. Shemala, "Palestinian Workers."
14. Keohane and Nye, *Power and Interdependence.* See in particular the author's discussion of Complex Interdependence.
15. Singer, "Who's Being Obstinate?"
16. Ibid.

CHAPTER 11 | PALESTINE

1. Said, "One-State Solution."
2. Sussman, "Challenge," 10.
3. Morris, *One State*, 44.
4. Ibid., 46.

ENDNOTES

5. Buber, *Palestine*, 7.
6. Buber, "Bi-National Approach," 10.
7. Buber, *Palestine*, 14-28.
8. Morris, *One State*, 50.
9. Magnes, "Toward Peace," 240.
10. Ellis, "Future of Israel/Palestine," 63.
11. Arendt, "Peace or Armistice," 76.
12. Judt, "Israel," 6.
13. Morris, *One State*, 11.
14. Ibid.
15. Walzer, 2003.
16. Said, "One-State Solution."
17. Ibid.
18. Judt, "Israel," 6.
19. Cypel, *Walled*, 476.
20. Ibid., 398.
21. Ibid., 398.
22. Resolution 194.
23. Lapidoth, "Legal Aspects," 485.
24. Oz, "Doves."
25. Amos, "Israeli Foreign Minister."
26. Sussman, "Challenge," 14.
27. Whitson, "Israel's Settlements."
28. Amnesty International, "Israel Intensifies," West Bank Home Demolitions," July 21, 2010.
29. Tilley, *One-State Solution*, 187.
30. Abunimah, *One Country*, 2010.
31. Morris, *One State*, 7.
32. Sussman, "Challenge," 19.
33. Ibid., 11.
34. Ibid., 12.
35. Lazare, "One-State Solution," 2.
36. Sussman, "Challenge," 9.
37. Qumsiyeh, *Sharing the Land*, 200.
38. Ibid., 215.
39. Tilley, *One-State Solution*, 183.
40. Qumsiyeh, *Sharing the Land*.

"1939 White Paper." In *A Documentary History of the Arab-Israeli Conflict*, edited by Charles Geddes. New York: Praeger Publishers, 1991.

Abu-Amir, Ziad. "Hamas: From Opposition to Rule." In *Where Now for Palestine?*, edited by Jamil Hilal, 167-187. London: Zed Books, 2007.

Abboushi, W.F. *The Unmaking of Palestine*, VT: Amana Books, 1990.

Abunimah, Ali. *One Country: A Bold Proposal to End the Israeli-Palestinian Impasse*. New York: Metropolitan Books, 2006.

---. "Palestinians on the Verge of a Majority: Population and Politics in Palestine-Israel." The Jerusalem Fund for Education and Community Development. http://www.thejerusalemfund.org/ht/display/ContentDetails/i/2244.

Ageel, Ghada. "The "Disengagement" As Seen From Gaza." Electronic Intifada. August 23, 2005. http://electronicintifada.net/content/disengagement-seen-gaza/5720.

"Al-Aqsa Intifada timeline." BBC News. Last modified September 29, 2004. http://news.bbc.co.uk/2/hi/middle_east/3677206.stm.

Al-Hayat, "Interview by Marwan Barghouti," September 29, 2001.

Alfassa, Shelomo. *Reference Guide to the Nazis and Arabs During the Holocaust*. New York: International Sephardic Leadership Council, 2006.

"Aliyah through Sudan." Israel Association for Ethiopian Jews. Accessed December 20, 2010. http://www.iaej.co.il/newsite/content.asp?pageid=449&lang=en.

American Memory. "Glossary-Saudi Arabia." Accessed May 27, 2010. http://memory.loc.gov/frd/cs/saudi_arabia/sa_glos.html.

Amnesty International. *Israel/Gaza: Operation 'Cast Lead': 22 Days of Death and Destruction*. London: Amnesty International Publications, 2009. http://www.amnesty.org/en/library/asset/MDE15/015/2009/en/8f299083-9a74-4853-860f-0563725e633a/mde150152009en.pdf.

---. "Israel Intensifies West Bank Home Demolitions." 2010. http://www.amnesty.org/en/news-and-updates/israel-intensifies-west-bank-palestinian-home-demolitions-2010-07-21.

Amos, Deborah. "Israeli Foreign Minister Touts Settlement Building." National Public Radio, September 7, 2010.

Anonymous. "Jewish Massacre Denounced." *New York Times*, April 28, 1903.

Arafat, Yasser "Address to the United Nations General Assembly in Geneva." Reprinted in *Le Monde Diplomatique*, December 13, 1988.

---. "Arafat at the UN General Assembly." Al-Bab. December 13, 1988. Accessed November 1, 2010. http://www.al-bab.com/arab/docs/pal/pal5.htm.

BIBLIOGRAPHY

---. "Statement by Yasser Arafat, 14 December 1998." In Vol. 9-10 of *Israel's Foreign Relations: Selected Documents*, edited by Meron Medzini. Jerusalem: Ministry of Foreign Affairs, 2002. http://www.mfa.gov.il/MFA/Foreign%20Relations/Israels%20Foreign%20Relations%20since%201947/1984-1988/419%20Statement%20by%20Yasser%20Arafat-%2014%20December%201988.

Arbel, Eliyahu. "I Was The Haganah Officer Who Inspected Deir Yassin The Day Following the Operation." Cited in Matthew Hogan, "The 1948 Massacre at Deir Yassin Revisted," *The Historian* 63, no. 3 (2001).

Arendt, Hannah. "Peace or Armistice in the Middle East?" *The Review of Politics* 12, no. 1 (1950): 56-82.

Arkadie, Brian Van. *Benefits and Burdens: A Report on the West Bank and Gaza Strip Economies since 1967*. New York: Carnegie Endowment for International Peace, 1977.

Aronson, Geoffry. "Settlement Freeze Redux." *Settlement Report* 19, no. 3 (May-June 2009).

Aruri, Naseer H. *Dishonest Broker: The U.S. Role in Israel and Palestine*. Cambridge: South End Press, 2003.

Ashrawi, Hanan. *This Side of Peace: A Personal Account*. New York: Simon & Schuster, 1995.

Auman, Moshe. "Land Ownership in Palestine 1800-1948." In *The Palestinians*, by Michael Curtis, 25. Piscataway: Transaction Publishers, 1975.

Ayalon, Danny. "Ayalon Addresses World Jewish Congress." Dannyayalon.com. June 21, 2011. http://dannyayalon.com/News/4070/.

BADIL Resource Centre for Palestinian Residence & Refugee Rights, Article 74, June, 1998.

"The Balfour Declaration." In *A Documentary History of the Arab-Israeli Conflict,* edited by Charles Geddes. New York: Praeger, 1991.

"Barak Calls for Emergency Government After Airstrikes." ABC News. October 12, 2000. http://abcnews.go.com/print?id=82403.

Barak, Ehud. "Ehud Barak's Plan for a Better Israel." Knesset. 1999. Accessed November 2, 2010. http://www.knesset.gov.il/elections/pm/ematza_pm_0.htm.

Bard, Mitchel G. "Facts About Settlements." *Jewish Virtual Library*. Accessed December 30, 2010. http://www.jewishvirtuallibrary.org/jsource/Peace/settlements.html.

---. "Myth and Fact: Did Arab Leaders Encourage Palestinians to Flee in 1948?" The Jewish Federation of North America. Accessed December 1, 2010. http://www.jewishfederations.org/page.aspx?id=121275.

---. *Myths and Facts: a Guide to the Arab-Israeli Conflict*. USA: American-Israeli Cooperative Enterprise, 2002.

---. "Myths & Facts Online: Partition." Jewish Virtual Library. Accessed December 1, 2010. http://www. jewishvirtuallibrary.org/jsource/myths2/Partition.html.

---. "The Yom Kippur War." *Jewish Virtual Library*. Accessed January 12, 2011. http://www.jewish virtuallibrary.org/jsource/History/73_War.html.

Barkai, Haim. "Land of Israel: Economic Affairs." In *Encyclopedia Judaica* 10, 493. Detroit: Macmillan Reference USA, 2007.

"The Battle of Kastel." Israel Defense Forces. Accessed July 24, 2010. http://dover.idf.il/IDF/English/ about/History/40s/1948/020401.htm.

Bavly, Dan, and Eliahu Salpeter. *Fire in Beirut: Israel's War in Lebanon with the PLO*. New York: Stein and Day, 1984.

Begin, Menachem, *The Revolt: Story of the Irgun*, Israel, Stimatzky Ltd., 1951.

Begin, Menachem, "Statement to the Knesset," March 13, 1978, Israel Ministry of Foreign Affairs.

"Behind the Headlines: Israel Designates Gaza a Hostile Territory." Israel Ministry of Foreign Affairs. September 24, 2007.

Beinin, Joel. "Marching toward Civil War." *MERIP Report* 136/137 (October-December 1985).

Bell, Matthew. "Jerusalem's Holiest of Holy Sites." *PRI's The World*. December 3, 2010. Accessed December 22, 2010. http://www.theworld.org/2010/12/03/jerusalems-holiest-of-holy-sites/.

Ben-Ami, Shlomo. "Diaries." *Ma'ariv*, April 6, 2001.

---. *Scars of War, Wounds of Peace: The Israeli-Arab Tragedy*. London: Phoenix, 2006.

Ben-Israel, Isaac. "The Crisis in the Oslo Process through the Prism of Israeli Deterrence." Strategic Assessment 5, no. 2 (August 2002).

Benn, Aluf. "Trading places; Can a Land Swap Keep Jews from Being a Minority in Their Own State?" *Washington Post*, August 14, 2005.

Beschloss, Michael. The Conquerors: *Roosevelt, Truman and the Destruction of Hitler*. New York: Simon & Schuster, 2002.

"Black September Plea to Israel." BBC News. January 1, 2001. Accessed November 1, 2010. http:// news.bbc.co.uk/2/hi/middle_east/1095221.stm.

Boyarin, Jonathan. "Palestine and Jewish History." *Peace Review* 3, no.2 (1991): 17-22.

Bratcher, Dennis. "Israelite Kings Date Chart (Based on the chronology of John Bright)." The Voice. Last modified April 11, 2011. http://www.crivoice.org/israelitekings.html.

Bregman, Ahron. *Israel's Wars: A History since 1947*. 3rd ed. London: Routledge, 2008.

BIBLIOGRAPHY

Brenchley, Frank. *Britain, the Six-Day War and Its Aftermath*. New York: I.B. Tauris and Co, 2005.

Brynen, Rex. "PLO Policy in Lebanon: Legacies and Lessons." *Journal of Palestine Studies* 18, no. 2 (Winter 1989).

---. *Sanctuary and Survival: The PLO in Lebanon*. London: Pinter, 1990.

B'Tselem. *On Human Rights in the Occupied Territories: Al-Aqsa Intifada*, June 2001. Jerusalem: B'Tselem, 2001.

Buber, Martin. "The Bi-National Approach to Zionism." In *Towards Union in Palestine: Essays on Zionism and Jewish-Arab Cooperation*, edited by Martin Buber, Judah Magnes and Ernst Simon. Jerusalem: Ihud Association, 1947.

---. *Palestine: A Bi-National State*. New York: Ihud Association of Palestine, 1946.

Bukhari, Muhammad ibn Ismail. "Merits of the Helpers in Madinah (Ansaar)." In *Sahih al-Bukhari*, translated by Muhammad Muhsin Khan. 58th ed. Alexandria, VA: Al-Saadawi Publications, 1996.

Bunch, Clea Lutz. "Strike at Samu: Jordan, Israel, the United States, and the Origins of the Six-Day War." *Diplomatic History* 32, no. 1 (2008): 55-76.

Butenschon, Nils, "The Paradox of Self-Determination in Palestine." In *Where Now for Palestine?*, by Jamil Hilal. London: Zed Books, 2007.

Caplan, Neil. "A Tale of Two Cities: The Rhodes and Lausanne Conferences, 1949." *Journal of Palestine Studies* 21, no. 3 (1992): 5-34.

Carroll, Rory, and Ian Black. "TV Row over Mob Footage 'Betrayal'." *The Guardian*, October 20, 2000. http://www.guardian.co.uk/world/2000/oct/20/israel2.

Carter, Jimmy. "Goldstone and Gaza." *New York Times*, November 5, 2009.

Central Intelligence Agency. "Israel." In *The World Factbook 2009*. Washington: Government Printing Office, 2010. Accessed January 12, 2011. https://www.cia.gov/library/publications/the-world-factbook/geos/is.html.

---. "Gaza" In *The World Factbook 2009*. Washington: Government Printing Office, 2009. Last updated August 16, 2011. https://www.cia.gov/library/publications/the-world-factbook/geos/gz.html.

Chassay, Clancy, and Bobby Johnson. "Google Earth Used to Target Israel." *The Guardian*, October 25, 2007. http://www.guardian.co.uk/technology/2007/oct/25/google.israel.

Cheema, Ashwarya. "Contemporary Relevance of India's Participation in UNSCOP." *Mainstream Weekly*, November 11, 2006.

Clinton, William J. "The Clinton Parameters." Israeli-Palestinian Conflict. December 23, 2000. Accessed November 1, 2010. http://israelipalestinian.procon.org/view.background-resource.php?resourceID=910.

Cohn-Sherbok, Dan and El-Alami, Dawoud. *The Palestine-Israeli Conflict*, Oxford, One World, 2006.

Contenta, Sandro. "Arafat's Regime in Shambles." *Toronto Star*, November 11, 2001.

"Coverage of Oct 12 Lynch in Ramallah by Italian TV Station RAI." Israel Ministry of Foreign Affairs. October 17, 2000. http://www.mfa.gov.il/MFA/MFAArchive/2000_2009/2000/10/Coverage%20of%20Oct%2012%20Lynch%20in%20Ramallah%20by%20Italian%20TV#letter.

Cypel, Sylvain. *Walled: Israeli Society at an Impasse*. New York: Other Press, 2006.

David, Levy. "A History of Persecution." ElijahNet. Accessed December 12, 2010. http://www.elijahnet.net/A%20History%20of%20Persecution.html.

Dawud, Abu. "Book 10, Number 1737." In *Sunan Abu Dawud*, translated by Ahmad Hasan. New Delhi: Kitab Bhavan, 1993.

Dayan, Deborah. *Pioneer*. New York: Massada, 1968.

"Declaration of the Establishment of the State of Israel." Israel Ministry of Foreign Affairs. May 14, 1948. Accessed December 1, 2010. http://www.mfa.gov.il/mfa/peace%20process/guide%20to%20the%20peace%20process/declaration%20of%20establishment%20of%20state%20of%20israel.

Defner, Larry. "Sounding the Alarm About Israel's Demographic Crisis." *Jewish Daily Forward*, January 9, 2004. http://www.forward.com/articles/6070/.

Dershowitz, Alan. "The Case Against the Goldstone Report." *Huffington Post*, February 1, 2010. http://www.huffingtonpost.com/alan-dershowitz/the-case-against-the-gold_b_442412.html.

---. The Case for Israel. Hoboken: John Wiley and Sons, 2003.

Drei Kugeln und ein totes Kind (Three Bullets and a Dead Child). Directed by Schapira, Esther. 2002.

"The Disengagement Plan—General Outline." Israel Ministry of Foreign Affairs. April 18, 2004. http://www.mfa.gov.il/MFA/Peace+Process/Reference+Documents/Disengagement+Plan+-+General+Outline.htm

Doumani, Beshara. "Rediscovering Ottoman Palestine: Writing Palestinians into History." Journal of *Palestine Studies* 21, no. 2. (1992).

Eban, Abba. "Introduction." In *The Beirut Massacre: The Complete Kahn Commission Report*. New York: Karz-Cohl, 1983.

"Ehud Olmert: "I am the Most Privileged Jew in the Universe." *Middle East Quarterly* 4, no. 4 (December 1997). Accessed December 30, 2010. http://www.meforum.org/376/ehud-olmert-i-am-the-most-privileged-jew-in.

BIBLIOGRAPHY

Ellis, Marc H. "The Future of Israel/Palestine: Embracing the Broken Middle." *Journal of Palestine Studies* 26, no. 3 (1997): 56-66.

Encyclopedia Britannica, 11th edition, s.v. "Palestine."

Enderlin, Charles. *Shattered Dreams: The Failure of the Peace Process in the Middle East* 1995-2002. New York: Other Press, 2002.

Eretz Yisroel. "Palestinian Refugees, Were Denied Resettlement Opportunities." Accessed December 1, 2010. http://www.eretzyisroel.org/~peters/resettlement.html.

"Exit of IDF Forces from Gaza Completed." Israel Ministry of Foreign Affairs. September 12, 2005.

Fallows, James. "Who Shot Mohammed al-Dura?" *Atlantic Monthly* 291, no. 5 (June 2003): 49-56.

Fiddler on the Roof. Directed by Norman Jewison. United Artists, 1971. VHS.

Finkelstein, Norman. "UN Inquiry Finds Israel 'Punished and Terrorized' Palestinian Civilians, Committed War Crimes During Gaza Assault: Interview with Norman Finkelstein." By Amy Goodman. Democracy Now!, September 16, 2009. http://www.democracynow.org/2009/9/16/un_inquiry_finds_israel_punished_and.

"Framework for Peace in the Middle East, Agreed at Camp David." *Jewish Virtual Library*. September 17, 1978. Accessed November 1, 2010. http://www.jewishvirtuallibrary.org/jsource/Peace/camp_david_accords.html.

"France 2 vs. Philippe Karsenty: The Appeal." CAMERA: Committee for Accuracy in Middle East Reporting in America. June 21, 2008. http://www.camera.org/index.asp?x_context=3&x_outlet=167&x_article=1364.

Gabbay, S.M., "Engineering Social Capital in the Middle East: Rebuilding Trust" in Corr, E.G., Ginat, J. and Gabbay, S.M., (Eds.) *The Search for Israeli-Arab Peace: Learning From the Past and Building Trust,* Portland, Sussex Academic Press, 2007.

Gabriel, Richard. *Operation Peace for the Galilee*. New York: Hill and Wang, 1984.

Gassner, Ingrid Jaradat, ed. "Survey of Palestinian Refugees and Internally Displaced Persons (2008-2009)." January 1, 2010. BADIL Resource Center for Palestinian Residency and Refugee Rights. http://www.badil.org/documents/category/35-publications?lang=en.

"Gaza." GlobalSecurity.org. http://www.globalsecurity.org/military/world/palestine/gaza.htm.

"Gaza Facts – The Israeli Perspective." Israel Ministry of Foreign Affairs. http://www.mfa.gov.il/GazaFacts/

"Gaza: Still No ICRC Access to Gilad Shalit." International Committee of the Red Cross. December 12, 2008. http://www.icrc.org/eng/resources/documents/interview/israel-interview-111208.htm.

Gaziel, Haim. *Politics and Policy-Making in Israel's Education System*. Eastbourne: Sussez Academic Press, 1996.

Gibson, Nigel C. Fanon: *The Postcolonial Imagination*. Cambridge: Polity, 2003.

Gilbert, Martin. *The Arab-Israeli Conflict: Its History in Maps*. London: Weidfield and Nicolson, 1975.

---. Israel: A History. New York: HarperCollins Publishers, 2008.

---. *The Routledge Atlas of the Arab-Israeli Conflict*. New York: Routledge, 2005.

Glazov, Jamie. "From Russia With Terror." *FrontPage*. Accessed December 30, 2010. http://archive.frontpagemag.com/readArticle.aspx?ARTID=13975.

Gold, Dore. *The Fight for Jerusalem: Radical Islam, the West, and the Future of the Holy City*. Washington: Regenry Publishing Inc., 2007.

Goldman, Ari L. "Dalai Lama Meets Jews From 4 Major Branches." *New York Times*, September 26, 1989.

Goldstone, Richard. "Reconsidering the Goldstone Report on Israel and War Crimes." *Washington Post*, April 1, 2011. http://www.washingtonpost.com/opinions/reconsidering-the-goldstone-report-on-israel-and-war-crimes/2011/04/01/AFg111JC_story.html.

Government of Palestine. *Supplement to Survey of Palestine, Notes Compiled for the Information of the United Nations Special Committee on Palestine*. Jerusalem: Palestine Government Printer, 1947.

Grabar, Oleg. "The Umayyad Dome of the Rock in Jerusalem." *Ars Orientalis* 3 (1959): 33-62.

Greenberg, Joel. "Israeli Police Question Two Rabbis in Rabin Assassination." *New York Times*, November 27, 1995.

Gutmann, E. "The Declaration of the Establishment of the State of Israel." Israel Ministry of Foreign Affairs. September 29, 2002. http://www.mfa.gov.il/NR/exeres/11364F53-F19B-4760-AA91-E066DDD0B29B.htm.

Haberman, Clyde. "Dennis Ross's Exit Interview." *New York Times Magazine*, March 25, 2001.

Halper, Jeff. "The Key to Peace: Dismantling the Matrix of Control." In *The Other Israel*, edited by Roane Carey and Jonathan Shainin, New York: The New Press, 2002.

"Hamas Exploitation of Civilians as Human Shields: Photographic Evidence." Israel Ministry of Foreign Affairs. May 19, 2009.

"Hamas Rockets." GlobalSecurity.org. http://www.globalsecurity.org/military/world/para/hamas-qassam.htm.

BIBLIOGRAPHY

Hammer, Juliane. *Palestinians Born in Exile: Diaspora and the Search for a Homeland*. Austin, TX: University of Texas Press, 2005.

"The Haram al-Sharif (Temple Mount) Killings." *Journal of Palestine Studies* 20, no. 2 (Winter 1991): 134-159.

Harel, Amos. "Military Tribunal Convicts Three 'Santorini' Crew Members." *Haaretz*, December 12, 2002. http://www.haaretz.com/news/military-tribunal-convicts-three-santorini-crew-members-1.25671.

---. "Settlements Grow on Arab Land, Despite Promises Made to U.S." *Haaretz*, October 24, 2006. http://www.haaretz.com/news/settlements-grow-on-arab-land-despite-promises-made-to-u-s-1.203258.

Hart, Alan. *Arafat: Terrorist or Peacemaker?* London: Sidgwick & Jackson, 1985.

Hasso, Frances S. "Modernity and Gender in Arab Accounts of the 1948 and 1967 Defeats." *International Journal of Middle East Studies* 32, no. 4 (November 2000).

"Hatikva." HebrewSongs. Accessed December 13, 2010. http://www.hebrewsongs.com/?song=hatikva.

Heacock, Roger. "Locals and Returnees in the Palestinians National Authority PNA: A Historical Perspective." In *The Becoming of Returnee States: Palestine, Armenia, Bosnia*. edited by The Graduate Institute of International Studies. Birzeit, Palestine: Birzeit University, 1993.

Henkin, Yagil. "How to Effectively Sanction Hamas." *Jerusalem Post*, August 9, 2009.

Herbert, Samuel. *An Interim Report on the Civil Administration of Palestine-League of Nations*. London: H.M. Stationary Office, 1921.

Herzl, Theodor. *The Jewish State*. New York: American Zionist Emergency Council, 1946.

---. *Theodor Herzl, Excerpts from his Diaries*. New York: Scopus Publishing Company, 1941.

Herzog, Chaim, "Statement to the UN Security Council," 1978.

Higgins, Andrew. "How Israel Helped Spawn Hamas." *Washington Post*, January 24, 2009.

Hilal, Jamil. "Palestine: the last colonial issue." In Hilal, *Where Now for Palestine?*.

---, ed. *Where Now for Palestine?: The Demise of the Two-State Solution*. London: Zed Books, 2007.

Hobbs, Joseph P. *Dear General: Eisenhower's Wartime Letters to Marshall*. Baltimore, MD: The John Hopkins University Press, 1999.

Hobsbawm, Eric, and Terrence Ranger. *The Invention of Tradition*. Cambridge, UK: Cambridge University Press, 1983.

"Holocaust Denial: An Online Guide to Exposing and Combating Anti-Semitic Propoganda." Anti-Defamation League. Accessed November 29, 2010. http://www.adl.org/holocaust/introduction.asp.

Hogan, Matthew. "The 1948 Massacre at Deir Yassin Revisited." *The Historian* 63, no. 3 (2001).

Hooker, Richard. "After the Exile: 538-332." The Hebrews: A Learning Module. Accessed December 13, 2010. http://www.wsu.edu:8080/~dee/HEBREWS/HEBREWS.HTM.

Horan, Deborah. "Israel: Assassin Whispers Confession as Israel is Silenced." *Inter Press Service*, November 6, 1995.

Horowitz, Uri. "Camp David 2 and President Clinton's Bridging Proposals-The Palestinian View." *Strategic Assessment* 3, no. 4 (January 2001).

Hroub, Khaled. "Hamas after Shaykh Yasin and Rantisi." *Journal of Palestine Studies* 33, no. 4 (Summer 2004).

Hudson, Michael C. "Palestinians and Lebanon: The Common Story." *Journal of Refugee Studies* 10, no. 3 (1997): 243-260.

"Immigration." *Jewish Virtual Library*. Accessed December 13, 2010. http://www.jewishvirtuallibrary.org/jsource/Immigration/immigtoc.html.

"Inauguration Speech of Prime Minister Ariel Sharon in the Knesset." Prime Minister's Office. March 7, 2001. http://webcache.googleusercontent.com/search?q=cache:KyE6_soZguAJ:www.pmo.gov.il/NR/rdonlyres/08D2FB02-08A7-4D14-8D7C-1B9BEDA04376/0/7008082592.doc+We+will+conduct+negotiations+with+the+Palestinians+to+achieve+political+agreements%E2%80%94but+not+under+the+pressure+of+terror+and+violence%E2%80%A6If+our+Palestinian+neighbors+choose+the+path+of+peace,+reconciliation+and+good+neighborly+relations+they+will+find+that+I+and+the+government+I+lead+are+honest+and+faithful+partners&cd=1&hl=en&ct=clnk&gl=us&client=firefox-a.

International Court of Justice (ICJ), Advisory Opinion, "Legal Consequences of the Construction of a Wall in the Occupied Palestinian Territory," 9 July, 2004.

Intelligence and Information Center (IIC), "Data summary of Palestinian terrorism during the current conflict with Israel until the Sharm el-Sheikh." September 28, 2005.

Intelligence and Terrorism Information Center. *Rocket Threat from the Gaza Strip 2000 – 2007*. Gelilot, Israel: Israel Intelligence Heritage & Commemoration Center, 2007.

International Committee of the Red Cross. *Geneva Convention Relative to the Protection of Civilian Persons in Time of War (Fourth Geneva Convention)*. August 12, 1949.

"Interview by Marwan Barghouti to Al-Hayat-29-Sep." Israel Ministry of Foreign Affairs. September 29, 2001. http://www.mfa.gov.il/MFA/MFAArchive/2000_2009/2001/9/Interview%20by%20Marwan%20Barghouti%20to%20Al%20Hayat%20-%2029-Sep.

BIBLIOGRAPHY

IRIN News, "Relentless Rocket Attacks Take Psychological Toll on Children in Sderot." January 27, 2008. http://www.irinnews.org/report.aspx?reportid=76438.

Islamic Resistance Movement (Hamas). *The Covenant of the Islamic Resistance Movement*. Translated by Raphaeli Israeli. The Avalon Project. August 18, 1988. Accessed May 12, 2010. http://avalon.law.yale.edu/20th_century/hamas.asp.

Israel Central Bureau of Statistics, Statistical Abstract, 2011.

"Israel Gaza FAQ: The Background." Israel Ministry of Foreign Affairs. http://www.mfa.gov.il/GazaFacts/FAQ/Background/israel-gaza-faq-the-background.htm

"Israel, the Conflict and Peace: Answers to Frequently Asked Questions." Israel Ministry of Foreign Affairs. December 30, 2009. Accessed December 8, 2010. http://www.mfa.gov.il/MFA/About+the+Ministry/Behind+the+Headlines/FAQ_Peace_process_with_Palestinians_Dec_2009.htm#Settlements.

Israeli, Raphael. PLO in Lebanon: Selected Documents. London: Weidenfeld and Nicolson, 1983.

Isseroff, Ami. "Israel War of Independence." *The Encyclopedia and Dictionary of Zionism and Israel*. Accessed December 1, 2010. http://www.zionism-israel.com/dic/War_of_Independence.htm.

---. "Sharm El Sheikh Speech of President Clinton, October 2000." MidEastWeb. 2005. http://www.mideastweb.org/sharm.htm.

Iyad, Abu, and Eric Rouleau. *My Home, My Land: A Narrative of the Palestinian Struggle*. Translated by Linda Butler Koseoglu. New York: Times Books, 1981.

Jabotinsky, Vladimir. "The Iron Wall." *Jewish Virtual Library*. November 3, 1923. Accessed July 1, 2011. http://www.jewishvirtuallibrary.org/jsource/Zionism/ironwall.html.

"Jerusalem Facts & Figures." The Jerusalem Municipality Website. 2008. Accessed December 2, 2010. http://www.jerusalem.muni.il/jer_main/TopSiteJeruEng.asp?newstr=5&src=/jer_sys/publish/HtmlFiles/1616/results_pub_id=6607.html&cont=1074.

"The Jewish Claim to the Land of Israel." *Jewish Virtual Library*.

"Jews in the Arab World." Al-Bab. June 18, 2009. Accessed December 1, 2010. http://www.al-bab.com/arab/background/jews.htm.

Jodeh, Mohamad. Interview by author. April 19, 2010.

Johnson, Penny. "Shadowplay: PLO Strategy in the Palestinian-Israeli Conflict." *MERIP Report* 136/137 (October-December 1985).

Johnston, William Robert. "Chronology of Terrorist Attacks in Israel—Part VIII: 2004." Last modified August 6, 2006. http://www.johnstonsarchive.net/terrorism/terrisrael-8.html.

"Jordan's Desecration of Jerusalem." *Jewish Virtual Library.* Accessed December 30, 2010. http://www.jewishvirtuallibrary.org/jsource/Peace/destoc.html.

Journal of Palestinian Studies, "Temple Mount," XX, #2 (Winter 91), pp. 134-159.

Josephus, Flavius. *The Jewish War.* London: The Penguin Group, 1981.

Ju'beh, Nazmi. "The Palestinian Attachment to Jerusalem." *Palestine-Israel Journal of Politics, Economics and Culture* 2, no. 2 (1995).

Judt, Tony. "Israel: The Alternative." *The New York Review of Books*, October 23, 2003.

Jung, Dietrich. *The Middle East and Palestine: Global Politics and Regional Conflict.* New York: Palgrave, 2004.

Kahn, Yitzak, Aharon Barak, and Yona Efrat. "The Commision of Inquiry into the Events at the Refugee Camps in Beirut: Final Report." *Journal of Palestine Studies* 12, no. 3 (Spring 1983).

Karmon, Ely. "Hamas' Terrorism Strategy: Operational Limitations and Political Restraints," *Middle East Review of International Affairs* 4, no. 1 (March 4, 2000).

Karsh, Efraim. "1948, Israel, and the Palestinians—The True Story." *Commentary Magazine*, May 2008, 23-29.

---. *Arafat's War: The Man and His Battle for Israeli Conquest.* New York: Grover Press, 2003.

---. "The Palestinians Alone." *New York Times*, August 1, 2010.

Katz, Lee M. "Middle East Breakthrough Largely Illusion." *United Press International*, September 4, 1999.

Katz, Mayn. *Song of Spies: A Novel of Israel., Its Mossad, and the Clash of Ideas.* San Francisco: Heliogrphica, 2005.

Katz, Samuel, and Lee E. Russell. *Armies in Lebanon: 1982-84.* Oxford: Osprey, 1985.

Keohane, Robert O., and Joseph S. Nye. *Power and Interdependence.* 3rd ed. New York: Longman, 2000.

Kerim, Mroueh, and Sabbagh Samir. "Lebanon Is Where the US and Israel Will Settle Accounts with the Palestinians." *MERIP Reports* 77 (1979).

Khalidi, Rashid. *Palestinian Identity: The Construction of Modern National Consciousness.* New York: Columbia University Press, 1997.

Khalidi, Rashid. *Under Seige: P.L.O. Decision Making During the 1982 War.* New York: Columbia University Press, 1986.

Kharchadourian, Haig. *The Quest for Peace Between Israel and the Palestinians.* New York: Peter Lang, 2000.

BIBLIOGRAPHY

"The Khartoum Resolutions." *The Avalon Project*. September 1, 1967. Accessed November 1, 2010. http://avalon.law.yale.edu/20th_century/khartoum.asp.

El Khazen, Farid. "Permanent Settlement of Palestinians in Lebanon: A Recipe for Conflict." *Journal of Refugee Studies* 10, no. 3 (1997).

Kimmerling, Baruch, and Joel S. Migdal. *The Palestinian People: a History*. Cambridge, MA: Harvard University Press, 1993.

King, Mary Elizabeth. *A Quiet Revolution: The First Palestinian Intifada and Nonviolent Resistance*. New York: Nation Books, 2007.

Knesset. "Basic Law: Jerusalem Capital of Israel." Israel Ministry of Foreign Affairs. July 30, 1980.

Kniesmeyer, J. and D. Brecher. "Life in the Pale of Settlement." *Beyond the Pale*. Accessed December 13, 2010. http://www.friends-partners.org/partners/beyond-the-pale/english/30.html.

---. "The Jewish Diaspora and Israel." *Beyond The Pale*. Accessed December 13, 2010. http://www.friends-partners.org/partners/beyond-the-pale/english/04.html.

Kochavi, Arieh J. *Post-Holocaust Politics: Britain, the United States & Jewish Refugees, 1945-1948: Jewish Displaced Persons in British Occupation Zones*. Chapel Hill, NC: University of North Carolina Press, 2001.

Korn, Bertram. *American Jewry and the Civil War*. Philadelphia: Jewish Publications Society, 2001.

Kreczko, Alan J. "Support Reagan's Initiative." *Foreign Policy*, Winter 1982-1983.

Kuttab, Daoud. "Gaza in Limbo," *The Jerusalem Post*, September 26, 2005.

Langer, Felicia. "A Judicial System Where Even Kafka Would Be Lost: An Interview with Felicia Langer." By George Moffett III. *Journal of Palestine Studies* 20, no. 1 (Autumn 1990): 24-36.

Lapidoth, Ruth. "Jerusalem and the Peace Process." *Israel Law Review* 28, no. 203 (Spring-Summer 1994). Accessed December 1, 2010. http://www.mfa.gov.il/MFA/MFAArchive/1990_1999/1994/7/JERUSALEM+AND+THE+PEACE+PROCESS+-+Jul-94.htm.

---. "Legal Aspects of the Palestinian Refugee Question." *Jerusalem Letter / Viewpoints*, September 1, 2002. http://www.jcpa.org/jl/vp485.htm.

Laqueur, Walter, and Barry Rubin, eds. *The Israel-Arab Reader: A Documentary History of the Middle East Conflict*. 6th ed. New York: Penguin, 2001.

Lazare, Danile. "The One-State Solution." *The Nation*, October 16, 2003.

League of Nations. "An Interim Report on the Civil Administration of Palestine, During the Period 1st July, 1921 - 30th June,1921." July 30, 1921.

---. "Mandate For Palestine." Mandate, 1917.

Learner, Rabbi Michael. *Healing Israel/Palestine: A Path to Peace and Reconciliation*. Berkeley: Tukkun, 2003.

Lee, Roger A. "Wars Between Israel and Syria: From 1948 to the Present." The History Guy. April 27, 2010. Accessed December 1, 2010. http://www.historyguy.com/israel_syria_wars.htm.

Lesch, Ann M. "Gaza: Forgotten Corner of Palestine." *Journal of Palestine Studies* 15, no. 1 (Autumn 1985): 43-61.

---. "Prelude to an Uprising in the Gaza Stip." *Journal of Palestine* Studies 20, no. 1 (Autumn 1990): 1-23.

Levinson, Chaim. "IDF: More than 300,000 Settlers Live in West Bank." *Haaretz*, July 7, 2009. Accessed December 30, 2010. http://www.haaretz.com/print-edition/news/idf-more-than-300-000-settlers-live-in-west-bank-1.280778.

Levy, Joshua. *The Agony of the Promised Land*. Lincoln, NE: iUniverse, 2004.

Linfield, Harry. "Statistics of Jews." In Vol. 25 of *The American Jewish Year Book* —5684. Philadelphia: X,1922.

Lorch, Netanel. "The Arab-Israeli Wars." Israel Ministry of Foreign Affairs. September 2, 2003. Accessed December 30, 2010. http://www.mfa.gov.il/MFA/History/Modern+History/Centenary+of+Zionism/The+Arab-Israeli+Wars.htm.

Lustick, Ian S. "The Oslo Agreement as an Obstacle to Peace." *Journal of Palestine Studies* 27, no. 1 (Autumn 1997): 61-66.

Lybarger, Loren D. *Identity & Religion in Palestine*. Princeton, NJ: Princeton University Press, 2007.

Magnes, Judah. "Toward Peace in Palestine." *Foreign Affairs* 21, no. 2 (1943): 239-49.

"McMahon-Hussein Correspondence: 1915-1916." In *A Documentary History of the Arab-Israeli Conflict,* edited by Charles Geddes, 23-28. New York: Praeger, 1991.

Medoff, Raphael. "Likely PA Prime Minister a Holocaust-Denier." *FrontPage*, February 26, 2003. Accessed December 30, 2010. http://archive.frontpagemag.com/readArticle.aspx?ARTID=19561.

Meir, Golda. "Israel in Search of Lasting Peace." *Foreign Affairs* 51, no. 3 (April 1973): 447-461.

Meir-Levi, David. *History Upside Down: The Roots of Palestinian Fascism and the Myth of Israeli Aggression*. New York: Encounter Books, 2007.

Meisels, Andrew. "New Fundamentalist Group Challenges PLO in Israel." *Sun Sentinel*, September 15, 1988.

Meital, Yoram. *Peace in Tatters: Israel, Palestine, and the Middle East*. Boulder, CO: Lynne Rienner Pub, 2006.

BIBLIOGRAPHY

Miskin, Maayana. "Poll: Young PA Arabs Want Sharia Law, Seek Iran as Ally." Arutz Sheva. October 27, 2010. http://www.israelnationalnews.com/news/news.aspx/140307.

Mitchell Bard, Mitchell. "Myths and Facts: A Guide to the Arab-Israeli Conflict." American-Israeli Cooperative Enterprise. Accessed December 10, 2010. http://www.jewishvirtuallibrary.org/jsource/myths2/myths2006.pdf.

Morris, Benny. *1948: The History of the First Arab-Israeli War*. New Haven: Yale University Press, 2008.
---. *One State, Two States: Resolving the Israel/Palestine Conflict*. New Haven, CT: Yale University Press, 2009.

---. *Righteous Victims: A History of the Zionist-Arab Conflict, 1881-2001*. New York: Vintage Books, 1999.

"Morrison-Grady Plan." In *The Encyclopedia of the Arab-Israeli Conflict: A Political, Social and Military History (Vol. II)*, edited by Spencer Tucker. Santa Barbara: ABC-CLIO, 2008.

Morse, Chuck. *The Nazi Connection to Islamic Terrorism: Adolf Hitler and Haj Amin al-Husseini*. Lincoln, NE: iUniverse, 2003.

"Most Palestinians Want Peace with Israel." *Haaretz,* June 20, 2010.

Moubayed, Sami. "Talal: The Sad Story of the King of Jordan." Mideastviews.com. February 21, 2006. Accessed August 18, 2010. http://mideastviews.com/articleview.php?art=88.

Muravchik, Joshua. *Covering the Intifada: How the Media Reported the Palestinian Uprising*. Washington, DC: Washington Institute for Near East Policy, 2003.

Muslih, Muhammad Y. *The Origins of Palestinian Nationalism*. New York: Columbia University Press, 1988.

Nasr, Kameel B. Arab and Israeli Terrorism. London: MacFarland, 1997.

Neff, Donald. "Sadat's Jerusalem Trip Begins Difficult Path of Egyptian-Israeli Peace." *Washington Report on Middle East Affairs*, October/November 1998.

Nordling, Carl O. "How Many Holocaust Survivors Were There in May 1945?" The Holocaust Historography Project. September 1, 1997. Accessed December 1, 2010. http://www.historiography-project.org/misc/19970901survivors.html.

Nusseibeh, Sari, and Anthony David. *Once Upon a Country: A Palestinian Life*. New York: Farrar, Straus, and Giroux, 2007.

"Operation Cast Lead." *GlobalSecurity.org.* http://www.globalsecurity.org/military/world/war/operation-cast-lead.htm.

Oren, Michael. *Six Days of War: June 1967 and the Making of the Modern Middle East*. Oxford: Oxford University Press, 2002.

Oz, Amos. "Doves Should Re-examine Their Perch." *The Guardian,* January 5, 2001. http://www.guardian.co.uk/comment/story/0,3604,417958,00.html.

Pacepa, Ion Mihai. "The Arafat I Knew." *Wall Street Journal,* January 12, 2002. Accessed December 30, 2010. http://www.weizmann.ac.il/home/comartin/israel/pacepa-wsj.html.

"Israel 1967-1991: Jordan Renounces Claims." Palestine Facts. Accessed November 1, 2010. http://www.palestinefacts.org/pf_1967to1991_jordan_renounce_claims.php.

---. "Israeli Invasion of Lebanon 1982." Accessed November 1, 2010. http://www.palestinefacts.org/pf_1967to1991_lebanon_198x_backgd.php

---. "Nature of the First Intifada, 1987-1993." Accessed November 1, 2010. http://www.palestinefacts.org/pf_1991to_now_intifada_nature.php

Impact of the Israeli Measures on the Economic Conditions of Palestinian Households. Palestinian Central Bureau of Statistics. April 2001.

"Rewriting History." 2010. Accessed December 22, 2010. Palestinian Media Watch. http://www.palwatch.org/main.aspx?fi=487.

"Palestinian National Charter (Covenant)." Mideastweb.org. Accessed July 1, 2011. http://www.mideastweb.org/palestinian_charter.htm.

Pappe, Ilan. *The Ethnic Cleansing of Palestine.* Oxford: Oneworld Publications Limited, 2006.

---. *A History of Modern Palestine: One Land, Two Peoples.* New York: Cambridge University Press, 2004.

---. "Zionism and the Two State Solution." In Hilal, *Where Now for Palestine?.*

"Israel's History in Quotes." The Peoples Voice. December 31, 2008. http://www.thepeoplesvoice.org/TPV3/Voices.php/2008/12/31/israel-s-history-in-quotes?tempskin=basic.

Peretz, Don. *Encyclopedia of the Modern Middle East and North Africa.* New York: Macmillan Reference USA, 2004.

Peteet, Julie. *Gender in Crisis: Women and the Palestinian Resistance Movement.* New York: Columbia University Press, 1991.

Philps, Alan. "A Day of Rage, Revenge and Bloodshed." *The Daily Telegraph,* October 13, 2000. http://www.telegraph.co.uk/news/worldnews/middleeast/israel/1370229/A-day-of-rage-revenge-and-bloodshed.html.

"Pilgrims' Progress." *National Geographic,* April 2008. Accessed May 2010. http://ngm.nationalgeographic.com/2008/04/religion-map/religion-map-interactive.

Pinsker, Leo. *Auto Emancipation: An Admonition to his Brethren by a Russian Jew.* Translated by D.S. Blondheim. New York: Maccabaean Publishing, 1906.

BIBLIOGRAPHY

Pinto, Nathan. "Jewish Culture and Stereotypes." About Jewishness. Accessed December 13, 2010. http://jewishness.bellevueholidayrentals.com/jewish_culture_and_stereotypes.html.

Pipes, Daniel. "Ehud Olmert: 'I am the Most Privileged Jew in the Universe'." *Middle East Quarterly* 4, no. 4 (December 1997).

"Negotiations and the Peace Process." PLO Negotiations Affairs Department. Accessed November 1, 2010. http://www.nadplo.org/inner.php?view=nego_permanent_security_hsecurityp.

"PM Sharon Knesset Speech-Vote on Disengagement Plan." Israel Ministry of Foreign Affairs. October 25, 2004. http://www.mfa.gov.il/MFA/Government/Speeches+by+Israeli+leaders/2004/PM+Sharon+Knesset+speech+-+Vote+on+Disengagement+Plan+25-Oct-2004.htm?DisplayMode=print.

Porath, Zipporah. *Letters From Jerusalem: 1947-1948.* New ed. Jerusalem: Association of Americans & Canadians in Israel, 1987.

"Prelude to Operation Cast Lead: Israel's Unilateral Disengagement to the Eve of War." *Journal of Palestine Studies* 38, no. 3. (Spring 2009).

"President Interviewed by Israeli Television." William J. Clinton Presidential Center. November 2, 1998. http://archives.clintonpresidentialcenter.org/?u=103198-president-interviewed-by-israeli-television.htm.

"President William J. Clinton Makes Announcement on the Upcoming Middle East Summit." *FCDH Political Transcripts.* July 5, 2000.

Prusher, Illene, and Ben Lynfield. "Killing of Yassin: A Turning Point." *Christian Science Monitor,* March 23, 2004.

"Q&A: Gaza Conflict." BBC News. January 18, 2009. http://news.bbc.co.uk/2/hi/7818022.stm.

Qumsiyeh, Mazin B. *Sharing the Land of Canaan.* Ann Arbor, MI: University of Michigan, 2004.

Rabinovich, Itamar. *Waging Peace: Israel and the Arabs 1948-2003.* Princeton: Princeton University Press, 2004.

Ravid, Barak, David Landau, and Samuel Rosner. "Olmert to Haaretz: Two-state Solution, or Israel is Done For." *Ha'aretz,* November 11, 2007. http://www.haaretz.com/news/olmert-to-haaretz-two-state-solution-or-israel-is-done-for-1.234201.

Reich, Bernard. *A Brief History of Israel.* 2nd ed. New York: Facts on File, 2008.

"Relentless Rocket Attacks Take Psychological Toll on Children in Sedrot." IRIN News. January 27, 2008. http://www.irinnews.org/report.aspx?reportid=76438.

Rekhess, Elie. "The Rise of the Palestinian Islamic Jihad." *Jerusalem Post,* October 21, 1987.

Richman, Chaim, and The Temple Institute. "A Time to Weep." Accessed December 22, 2010. http://www.templeinstitute.org/time_to_build.htm.

Ross, Dennis. *The Missing Peace*. New York: Farra, Straus and Giroux, 2004.

Roy, Sara. "Why Peace Failed: An Oslo Autopsy." *Current History* 101, no. 651 (January 2002).

Rubenberg, Cheryl. *The Palestinians: In Search of a Just Peace*. Boulder, CO: Lynne Reiner Publishers, Inc., 2003.

"A Sabbath of Terror (Palestinian Suicide Mission on Israel)." *Time*, 1978.

Sachar, Howard Morley. *A History of Israel: From the Rise of Zionism to Our Time*. New York: Knopf, 2007.

Sadat, Anwar. "Egyptian President Anwar Sadat, Address to the Israeli Knesset: Peace with Justice." In *The Israel-Arab Reader: A Documentary History of the Middle East Conflict,* edited by Walter Laqueur and Barry Rubin. New York: Penguin, 2001.

Safian, Alex. "In the Palestinians' Pocket: Journalists Doing PR For the PA." CAMERA: Committee for Accuracy in Middle East Reporting. October 19, 2000. http://www.camera.org/index.asp?x_context=3&x_outlet=13&x_article=193.

Safran, Nadav. *Israel Today: A Profile (Headline Series No. 170)*. New York: Foreign Policy Association, 1965.

Sahliyeh, Emile. The PLO *After the Lebanon War*. Boulder, CO: Westview Press, 1986.

Said, Edward. "The Lost Liberation." *The Guardian*, September 9, 1993.

---. "The One-State Solution." *New York Times*, January 10, 1999.

---. The Politics of Dispossession: *The Struggle for Palestinian Self-Determination, 1969-1994*. New York: Vintage Books, 1994.

---. *The Question of Palestine*. New York: Vintage Books, 1992.

Sakran, Frank C. *Palestine Dilemma: Arab Rights Versus Zionist Aspirations*. X: Public Affairs Press, 1948.

Saleh, Mohsen Mohammed. *History of Palestine: A Methodical Study of the Palestinian Struggle*. Cairo: Al-Falah Foundation, 2003.

Samuels, David. "In a Ruined Country." *The Atlantic Monthly* 296, no. 2 (2005): 60-91.

Sanbar, Elias. "Out of Place, Out of Time." *Mediterranean Historical Reviews* 16 (2001): 87-94.

Satloff, Robert. "The Jordan-Israel Peace Treaty: A Remarkable Document." *Middle East Quarterly* 2, no. 1 (March 1995).

BIBLIOGRAPHY

Sayigh, Rosemary. *Palestinians: From Peasants to Revolutionaries*. London: Zed Books, 1979.

Sayigh, Yezid. *Armed Struggle and the Search for State: The Palestinian National Movement*, 1949-1993. Oxford: Clarendon Press, 1997.

Schanzer, Jonathan. *Hamas vs. Fatah: The Struggle for Palestine*. New York: Palgrave Macmillan, 2008.

Scheindlin, Raymond P. *A Short History of the Jewish People: From Legendary Times to Modern Statehood*. New York : Macmillan, 1998.

Schiff, Ze'ev and Ehud Ya'ari. *Intifada: The Palestinian Uprising-Israel's Third Front*. New York: Simon & Schuster, 1989.

---. *Israel's Lebanon War*. New York: Touchstone, 1985.

Seager, Mark. "I'll Have Nightmares for the Rest of my Life." *The Daily Telegraph,* October 15, 2000.

Segev, Tom. *One Palestine Complete*. New York: Metropolitan Books/Henry Holt & Co., 2000.

Sela, Avraham. "The "Wailing Wall" Riots (1929) As a Watershed in the Palestinian Conflict." *The Muslim World* 84, no. 1-2 (April 1994).

"Sgt. David Biri." Israel Ministry of Foreign Affairs. September 27, 2000. http://www.mfa.gov.il/MFA/Terrorism-+Obstacle+to+Peace/Memorial/2000/Sgt+David+Biri.htm.

Shachar, Nathan. *The Gaza Strip: Its History and Politics from the Pharaohs to the Israeli Invasion of 2009*. Portland, OR: Sussex Academic Press, 2010.

"The Grand Mufti of Jerusalem and the Nazification of the Arab World." Shalom Jerusalem. Accessed December 1, 2010. http://www.shalomjerusalem.com/mohammedism/mohammedism21.html.

"Shamir Yitzhark." Israel Ministry of Foreign Affairs. July 26, 1988. http://www.mfa.gov.il/MFA/Facts+About+Israel/State/Yitzhak+Shamir.htm.

Sharansky, Natan. *A Case for Democracy: The Power of Freedom to Overcome Tyranny and Terror.* Green Forest, AR: Balfour Book, 2006.

Sharon, Ariel. "Address by Prime Minister Ariel Sharon at the Fourth Herzilya Conference." Israel Ministry of Foreign Affairs. December 18, 2003. http://www.mfa.gov.il/MFA/Government/Speeches+by+Israeli+leaders/2003/Adress+by+PM+Ariel+Sharon+at+the+Fourth+Herzliya.htm.

---. "PM Sharon addresses the United Nations General Assembly." Israel Ministry of Foreign Affairs. September 15, 2005. http://www.mfa.gov.il/MFA/Peace+Process/Key+Speeches/PM+Sharon+addresses+the+UN+General+Assembly+15-Sep-2005.htm.

Shavit, Ari. "End of a Journey." *Ha'aretz*, September 13, 2001.

Shemala, Nawaf Mahmoud Abu. "The Future of Palestinian Workers in Israel." *Al-Siyassa Al-Dawliya*, no. 165 (July 2006).

Sherwood, Harriet. "Palestinian Boycott of Israeli Settlement Goods Starts to Bite." *The Guardian*, June 29, 2010. Accessed 15 December 2010. http://www.guardian.co.uk/world/2010/jun/29/palestinian-boycott-israeli-settlement-goods.

Shields, Jacqueline. "Jewish Refugees from Arab Countries." *Jewish Virtual Library*. http://www.jewishvirtuallibrary.org/jsource/History/jewref.html.

Shikaki, Khalil. "Palestinians Divided." *Foreign Affairs* 81, no.1 (January/February 2002): 89-105.

Shlaim, Avi. "The Debate About 1948." *International Journal of Middle Eastern Studies* 27, no. 3 (1995): 287-304.

---. *The Iron Wall: Israel and the Arab World*. New York: W.W. Norton, 2000.

---. *Lion of Jordan*. London: Vintage Books, 2007.

---. "The Oslo Accord." *Journal of Palestine Studies* 23, no. 3 (Spring 1994): 24-40.

Shragai, Nadav. "Jerusalem: The Dangers of Division. An Alternative to Separation from the Arab Neighborhoods." Accessed December 1, 2010. http://www.jcpa.org/text/shragai_last2.pdf.

Siddiqi, Muzammil H. "The Islamic Perspective of Jerusalem." Speech for American Muslims for Jerusalem, Washington, DC, April 17, 1999.

Simpson, Sir John Hope. *Palestine, Report on Immigration, Land Settlement and Development*. London: His Majesty's Stationary Office, 1930.

Singer, Saul. "Who's Being Obstinate?" *Jerusalem Post*, December 21, 2010. http://www.jpost.com/Opinion/Op-EdContributors/Article.aspx?id=200486.

Al-Sistani, Ali. "Rules Regarding Waqf." Accessed July 1, 2011. http://www.al-islam.org/laws/waqf.html.

"The Six-Day War-Introduction." Israel Ministry of Foreign Affairs. November 3, 2003. Accessed December 30, 2010. http://www.mfa.gov.il/MFA/Foreign+Relations/Israels+Foreign+Relations+since+1947/1947-1974/THE+SIX-DAY+WAR+-+INTRODUCTION.htm.

Slackman, Micheal, and Ethan Bronner. "Trapped by Gaza Blockade, Locked in Despair." *New York Times*, July 13, 2010.

BIBLIOGRAPHY

Sosebee, Stephen J. "Attempts to Destroy the Haram al-Sharif Have a Long History." *Washington Report on Middle East Affairs*, November/December 1996.

Smerdon, Peter. "Israeli Army Fears Palestinian Rioters May Turn to Guns." *Jerusalem Post; Reuter Library Report*, February 9, 1988.

Smith, Charles D. *Palestine and the Arab Israeli Conflict*. 6th ed. New York: Bedford Books, 1988.

Smith, Mark S. *The Early History of God*. Dearborn, MI: Dove Booksellers, 2002.

Smith, Pamela Ann. *Palestine and the Palestinians 1876-1983*. New York: St. Martin's Press, 1984.

StandWithUs. Israel 101. Los Angeles: StandWithUs, 2007.

StandWithUs. "Quick Facts: Restoring the Land." Accessed December 13, 2010. http://www.askisrael. org/facts/qpt.asp?fid=19.

"Statement by Israel Ambassador Gillerman to the UN Security Council." Israel Ministry of Foreign Affairs. May 19, 2004. http://www.mfa.gov.il/MFA/Foreign+Relations/Israel+and+the+UN/ Speeches+-+statements/Statement+by+Amb+Gillerman+to+UN+Security+Council+19-May-2004.htm

"Statement to the General Assembly by Foreign Minister Eban." Israel Ministry of Foreign Affairs. June 17, 1967.

"Statement to the Knesset by Prime Minister Begin on the Terrorist Raid and the Knesset Resolution." Israel Ministry of Foreign Affairs. March 13, 1978.

"Statement to the Knesset by Prime Minsiter Begin Presenting Israel's Peace Plan." Israel Ministry of Foreign Affairs. December 28, 1977.

"Statement to the Security Council by Ambassador Herzog." Israel Ministry of Foreign Affairs. March 17, 1978.

"Status of Jerusalem." Israel Ministry of Foreign Affairs. March 14, 1999.

Stein, Leslie. *The Hope Fulfilled: The Rise of Modern Israel*. Westport: Praeger, 2003.

Steinberg, Gerald M. "Jerusalem-1948, 1967, 2000: Setting the Record Straight." Bar-Ilan University Faculty. Accessed December 1, 2010. http://faculty.biu.ac.il/~steing/conflict/oped/jerufact.htm.

Strober, Deborah, and Gerald Strober. *Israel at Sixty: A Pictorial and Oral History of a Nation Reborn*. Hoboken: John Wiley and Sons, 2008.

Sussman, Gary. "The Challenge to the Two-State Solution." *Middle East Report* 231 (2004): 8-15.

"Sweet Freedom", Arab News.com, Editorial, October 22, 2011.

Swisher, Clayton. *The Truth About Camp David: The Untold Story About the Collapse of the Middle East Peace Process.* New York: Nation Books, 2004.

Tamari, Salim. "Ishaq al-Shami and the Predicament of the Arab Jew in Palestine." *Jerusalem Quarterly* 21 (2004). http://www.jerusalemquarterly.org/ViewArticle.aspx?id=122.

Tamimi, Azzam. *Hamas: A History from Within.* Northampton, MA: Olive Branch Press, 2007.

Tannous, Izzat. *The Enraging Story of Palestine and Its People.* Jerusalem: Palestinian Liberation Organization, 1965.

"Terrorist Attacks Against Israel (September 2000-2007)." *Jewish Virtual Library.* 2010. http://www.jewishvirtuallibrary.org/jsource/Peace/aksagraph.html.

Tessler, Mark A. *A History of the Israeli-Palestinian Conflict.* Bloomington, IN: Indiana University Press, 1994.

Tilley, Virginia. *The One-State Solution: A Breakthrough for Peace in the Israeli-Palestinian Deadlock.* Ann Arbor, MI: University of Michigan, 2005.

Tomeh, Khaled Abu. "Arafat Ordered Hamas Attacks Against Israel in 2000." *Jerusalem Post,* September 29, 2010. http://www.jpost.com/MiddleEast/Article.aspx?id=189574.

"Treaty of Peace Between the Hashemite Kingdom and the State of Israel." In *Peacemaking: The Inside Story of the 1994 Jordanian-Israeli Treaty,* by Abdul Salam Majali and Munther J. Haddasin. Reading: Garnet, 2006.

"The Trial of Adolf Eichman." The Nizkor Project. Accessed November 2, 2010. http://www.nizkor.org/hweb/people/e/eichmann-adolf/transcripts/Sessions/.

Tucker, Spencer, ed. "Defensive Shield, Operation." In Vol. 5 of *The Encyclopedia of the Arab-Israeli Conflict: A Political, Social, and Military History.* Santa Barbra: ABC-CLIO, 2008.

---. "Gaza Strip Disengagement." In Vol. 1 of *The Encyclopedia of the Arab-Israeli Conflict: A Political, Social, and Military History.* Santa Barbra: ABC-CLIO, 2008.

Turner, Bryan S. "Class, Generation and Islamism: Towards a global Sociology of Political Islam." *British Journal of Sociology* 54, no. 1 (March 2003): 139-147.

Twain, Mark. *The Innocents Abroad.* Hartford, CT: American Publishing Company, 1869.

UN Commission on Human Rights, Question of the Violation of Human Rights in the Occupied Arab Territories, 2003.

UN Development Programme. *Human Development Report 2004: Cultural Liberty in Today's Diverse World.* New York N.Y.: Oxford University Press, 2004.

UN General Assembly. *Palestine-Progress Report.* December 11, 1948.

BIBLIOGRAPHY

UN General Assembly. "Resolution 181." *The Avalon Project.* Accessed December 1, 2010. http:/www. yale.edu/lawweb/avalon/un/res181.htm.

UN General Assembly. "Resolution 194." *Conditional Right of Return of Refugees.* Accessed December 11, 1948. http://www.yale.edu/lawweb/avalon/un/res1194.htm.

UN Human Rights Council. UN Fact-Finding Mission on the Gaza Conflict. *Human Rights in Palestine and Other Occupied Arab Territories.* September 25, 2009. http://www2.ohchr.org/english/bodies/ hrcouncil/docs/12session/A-HRC-12-48.pdf.

UN Interim Force in Lebanon. "Mandate." http://www.un.org/en/peacekeeping/missions/unifil/ mandate.shtml.

UN Relief and Works Agency. Accessed December 1, 2010. http://www.unrwa.org/.

---. *The United Nations and Palestinian Refugees.* January 2007. http://www.unrwa.org/userfiles /2010011791015.pdf.

UN Security Council. "Report of the Secretary-General pursuant to Security Council resolution 1559 (2004)." October 1, 2004. http://domino.un.org/unispal.nsf/1ce874ab1832a53e852570bb006dfaf6/ cf73fa2ed54ad56a85256f250054138c?OpenDocument.

---. "Resolution 242: The Situation in the Middle East." November 22, 1967.

---. "Resolution 1806: The Situation in the Middle East Including the Palestinian Question." January 8, 2009.

---. "Resolution 1397 of 2002 (S/RES/1397)." March 12, 2002.

UNIFIL Mandate, unifil.unmissions.org.

U.S. Congress. House. Subcommittee on International Terrorism and Nonproliferation and the Subcommittee on the Middle East and Central Asia of the Committee on International Relations. *Hezbollah's Global Reach.* 109th Cong., 2nd sess., September 28, 2006.

U.S. Congressional Research Service. *Hamas: The Organizations, Goals and Tactics of a Militant Palestinian Organization.* Washington: The Service, 1993.

---. *Israeli-Arab Negotiations: Background, Conflicts, and US Policy* (RL33530; Jan. 29, 2010), by Carol Migdalovitz. Text from: Federation of American Scientists. Accessed December 3, 2010. http://www. fas.org/sgp/crs/mideast/RL33530.pdf.

U.S. Department of State. *Patterns of Global Terrorism 1999.* Washington: Government Printing Office, 2000.

U.S. Holocaust Memorial Museum. "Haj Amin al-Husayni: Arab Nationalist and Muslim Leader" *Holocaust Encyclopedia.* Accessed November 2, 2010. http://www.ushmm.org/wlc/en/article. php?ModuleId=10007666.

Usher, Graham. "Hamas Risen." *Middle East Report* 238 (Spring 2006).

"Victims of Palestinian Terror since Sept 2000." Israel Ministry of Foreign Affairs. 2011. http://www.mfa.gov.il/MFA/Terrorism-+Obstacle+to+Peace/Palestinian+terror+since+2000/Victims+of+Palestinian+Violence+and+Terrorism+sinc.htm.

Viorst, Milton. *Sands of Sorrow: Israel's Journey from Independence*. London: I.B. Tauris, 1987.

Vitullo, Anita. "People Tied to Place: Strengthening Cultural Identity in Hebron's Old City." *Journal of Palestine Studies* 33, no. 1 (2003): 68-83.

---."Uprising in Gaza." *Middle East Report* 152 (May-June 1988).

Walzer, M., "Response to Israel: The Alternative by Tony Judt", *New York Review of Books* Volume 50, 14, 2003.

Waak, Erika. "Violence among Palestinians." *The Humanist,* January/February 2003.

Waage, John. "The Miracle Called Israel." *Christian World News*, May 16, 2008.

Wailer, Arthur. "The Protocols of the Elders of Zion" in the 21st Century." Holocaust Education & Archive Research Team. Accessed December 13, 2010. http://www.holocaustresearchproject.org/essays&editorials/protocols.html.

Walsh, Elsa. "The Prince." *The New Yorker*, March 23, 2003.

"Weapons Smuggling Tunnels in Rafah: Operation Rainbow." Israel Ministry of Foreign Affairs. May 17, 2004. http://www.mfa.gov.il/MFA/Terrorism-+Obstacle+to+Peace/Terror+Groups/Weapon+Smuggling+Tunnels+in+Rafah+May+2004.htm.

Weiner, Justus. "Child Abuse in the Palestinian Authority." *Jerusalem Post*, October 3, 2003.

Weizmann, Chaim. *Trial and Error; The Autobiography of Chaim Weizmann*. New York: Harper, 1949.

"What are Qassam Rockets?" The Jewish Policy Center. http://www.jewishpolicycenter.org/prr/qassams.php.

Wheeler, Brannon M. *Prophets in the Quran: An Introduction to the Quran and Muslim Exegesis*. London: Continuum, 2002.

Whitson, Sara Leah, "Israel's Settlements Are on Shaky Ground." *Los Angeles Times*, June 28, 2009. http://articles.latimes.com/2009/jun/28/opinion/oe-whitson28.

Woodward, David R. "The Middle East During World War I." BBC World Wars in Depth. http://www.bbc.co.uk/history/worldwars/wwone/middle_east_01.shtml.

The World Bank. *Developing the Occupied Territories: An Investment in Peace* 1. Washington, DC: World Bank Publications, 1993.

BIBLIOGRAPHY

"Yasser Arafat's Timeline of Terror." Committee for Accuracy in Middle East Reporting in America. November 13, 2004. Accessed December 30, 2010. http://www.camera.org/index.asp?x_article=795&x_context=7.

Zuckerman, Mortimer. "Opinion: Obama's Jerusalem Stonewall." *Wall Street Journal*, April 28, 2010. Accessed December 30, 2010. http://online.wsj.com/article/SB100014240527487034652045752087118465606650.html.

Zionism and Israel on the Web Project. "Six Day War." Accessed December 30, 2010. http://www.zionism-israel.com/dic/6daywar.htm.

LIST OF MAPS

CHAPTER 1 | TIES TO THE LAND

LIST OF VISUALS

LIST OF VISUALS

LIST OF VISUALS

CHAPTER 5 | 1967

LIST OF VISUALS

LIST OF VISUALS

1929 Palestine Riots: see Wailing Wall Riots.

1939 British White Paper: The British policy paper abandoned the Peel Commission recommendation of partitioning the British Mandate of Palestine into two states in favor of creating an independent state in which Jews and Arabs governed in proportion to their population. It limited future Jewish immigration into Palestine to 75,000 during the five-year period from 1940-1944, and placed restrictions on future Arab land sales to Jews.

1948 Arab-Israeli War (1948 War of Independence): The first Arab-Israeli war that began between Israel and neighboring Arab nations that rejected UN Resolution 181 (the Partition Plan) and Israel's Declaration of Independence.

1948 War of Independence: see 1948 Arab-Israeli War.

1949 Armistice Agreement: Agreement between Israel and Egypt, Lebanon, Jordan, and Syria that officially ended the official hostilities of the 1948 Arab-Israeli War and established armistice lines between Israeli and Arab forces in the West Bank.

1967 Arab-Israeli War: see Six-Day War.

1967 Armistice Lines: Not a permanent international border, the 1967 lines are based upon the 1949 Armistice Line established following the Arab-Israeli War in 1948. The 1967 lines make up the military border where troops from Israel, Egypt, Jordan, and Syria ceased fire following the Arab-Israeli Six Day War in 1967.

1967 Borders: Israeli border following the Six-Day War, encompassing the Gaza Strip and the Sinai Peninsula captured from Egypt, the West Bank (including East Jerusalem) from Jordan, and the Golan Heights from Syria.

1972 Olympic Massacre: Members of the Israeli Olympic team were taken hostage and killed by the Palestinian terrorist group, Black September, at the Olympic games in Munich in 1972.

1979 Israel-Egypt Peace Treaty: Ended the state of war between Egypt and Israel that had been ongoing since 1948, saw the withdrawal of Israel from the Sinai Peninsula, and led Egypt to become the first Arab nation to officially recognize Israel and establish a peace agreement with Israel.

1980 Basic Law (Jerusalem Law): Also known as the Jerusalem Law among the Basic Laws of Israel, declares that Jerusalem is Israel's "eternal and undivided capital."

1982 Lebanon War (Operation Peace for the Galilee): The War in Lebanon between Israel and the PLO.

Abbas, Mahmoud (Abu Mazan): Chairman of the Palestine Liberation Organization. Since November 2004, he has been the President of the Palestinian National Authority as the head of the Fatah Party.

GLOSSARY

AD (CE) (Anno Domini): Indicates years in the calendar 'After the Death of Christ', or CE (in the 'Common Era.')

ALA Liberation Army: Arab Liberation Army (Jaysh al-Inqadh al-Arabi) was an army of volunteers from Arab countries led by Fawzi al-Qawuqji which fought on the Arab side in the 1948 Arab-Israeli War.

Al-Hussayni, Abdal Qadir: (al-Husseini) Palestinian Arab nationalist and fighter who in late 1933 founded the militant group: Organization for Holy Struggle. He was a leader of the Palestinians from 1936 through the 1948 Arab-Israeli War, when he was killed in battle.

Al-Rantissi, Abdel Aziz: Co-founder of Hamas, a militant Palestinian Islamist organization, co-founded with Sheikh Ahmed Yassin.

Azzam, Abdel Rahman: Egyptian diplomat who served as the first secretary-general of the Arab League between 1945 and 1952.

Abraham: Jewish Patriarch regarded as the founder of both the Hebrew and Muslim people.

Mazan, Abu: see Mahmoud Abbas.

Abu Nidal Organization: A militant Palestinian group responsible for the attempted assassination of Shlomo Argov, the Israeli ambassador to Britain prior to the 1982 Lebanon War.

Al-Aqsa Intifada (Second Intifada): The Intifada, also known as the Second Intifada, was a period of violence between Israelis and Palestinians beginning in September of 2000 and lasting until 2005. The violence erupted following the breakdown of Palestinian-Israeli negotiations at Camp David between the United States, Israel, and the Palestinian Authority in July of 2000.

Al-Aqsa Martyrs Brigade: Palestinian terrorist organization founded by Yasser Arafat at the beginning of the Second Intifada.

Al-Aqsa Mosque (Al-Masjid Al-Aqsa): Sacred Mosque on the Haram al-Sharif (Temple Mount) in Jerusalem.

Al-Aqsa Tunnel: Israeli construction of tunnel(s) near the al-Aqsa Mosque have been contentious, as some Palestinians fear the construction jeopardizes the stability of their holy sites.

Al-Husseini (Haj Amin al-Husseini): Palestinian Arab nationalist and Muslim leader during the British Mandate of Palestine. He became the Grand Mufti of Jerusalem, led violent riots that opposed the establishment of a national homeland for the Jewish people in Palestine, and collaborated with the Nazis during World War II.

Al-Isra (Night Journey): First part of the Night Journey taken by Muhammad.

Al Jazeera: Arabic for "The Island," Al Jazeera is a prominent network of news and current affairs outlets headquartered in Doha, Qatar.

Al-Masjid Al-Aqsa: see Al-Aqsa Mosque.

Al-Masjid Al-Haram (Noble Sanctuary): See Dome of the Rock.

Al-Mi'raj: (Ascension) Second part of the Night Journey when Muhammad meets God.

Al-Naqba: From Arabic naqba, meaning "disaster" or "catastrophe." This term refers to the exodus of Arab Palestinians from Palestine in the wake of the creation of the State of Israel in 1948.

Al-Quds (The Holy One): see East Jerusalem.

Al-Sakhrah al-Musharrafah (Sacred Rock): see Dome of the Rock.

Allah (God): Name for God in the Islamic faith.

Allied Forces: The Allied Forces during WWI consisted of: the British Empire, France, Russia, Belgium, Serbia, Montenegro, and Japan, later joined by Italy, Portugal, Romania, the United States, Greece, and Brazil.

Aliyah: In Hebrew, aliyah means "going up." Aliyah refers to the act of Jewish immigration into Israel.

Anti-Semite: A person who is prejudiced against Jews as a religious, ethnic, or racial group.

Anwar Sadat: President of Egypt who met with Israel Prime Minister Begin at Camp David in 1979 responsible for the first Arab peace agreement with Israel.

Apartheid State: A nation that endorses an institutionalized system of domination and oppression by one ethnic or racial group over another group or groups in order to maintain its political or economic power.

Arab Great Revolt: see Great Revolt.

Arab League: Known officially as the League of Arab States, it serves as a regional organization of 22 member states and four observers to promote the interests of Arab states. Its first large action was the coordinated attack on Israel in 1948, following Israel's Declaration of Independence.

Arab Liberation Army (ALA): Led by Fawzi al-Qawuquji, the ALA was an army of Arab volunteers from Arab countries who joined the Palestinians to fight the 1948 Arab-Israeli War.

Arab Nationalists Movement (ANM): Arab Nationalist Organization that influenced much of the Arab world, particularly the Palestinian movement.

Arab Revolution, 1916-1918: Also known as the Arab Revolt (1916-1918), the Arab Revolution was a movement led by Sherif Hussein bin Ali that saw Arabs fight alongside British troops with the goal of defeating the Ottoman Empire. Arabs believed that aiding the British would lead to their being granted sovereignty over their own land, and the creation of a unified Arab state. However, this did not occur.

GLOSSARY

Arafat, Yasser: Founder of the Fatah Party and head of the Palestine Liberation Organization until his death in 2004.

Article 49 of the 1949 Fourth Geneva Convention: Protection of Civilian Persons in Time of War: Prohibits the forcible transfer or deportation of protected persons from occupied territory.

Ascension: see al-Miraj in Night Journey.

Ateret Cohanim: Hebrew for "Crown of the Priests," is a Zionist yeshiva, or Jewish educational organization, that encourages Israeli Jews to settle in Arab East Jerusalem by buying Arab property.

Axis Powers: Alliance of powers in WWII between Germany, Italy and Japan (as well as Romania, Bulgaria and Hungary) who fought against the Allied Powers.

BC: Time period before the birth of Christ. Also referred to as BCE.

BCE: Time period before the Common/Christian Era also referred to as BC.

Balfour Declaration, 1917: Was a declaration made on November 2, 1917, by the United Kingdom that, as a matter of policy, favored "the establishment in Palestine of a national home for the Jewish people." The declaration was contained in a letter from Foreign Secretary Arthur James Balfour to Baron Rothschild, a British Zionist leader, as part of an agreement proposed by the British Cabinet. Today, November 2 is celebrated as Balfour Day among the Jewish diaspora, but also serves as a day of mourning and protest for many Arabs.

Barak, Ehud: Prime Minister of Israel from 1999-2001. Negotiated with Yasser Arafat at the 2000 Camp David Summit.

Bar Mitzvah: A celebration of a Jewish boy when he reaches his 13th birthday thereby reaching the age of his adult religious duties and responsibilities.

Battle of Karameh: Was a battle on March 21, 1968, between the IDF and the Jordanian army against the PLO in the town of Karameh, Jordan. Both sides declared victory, but the Arab world has attached special significance to the battle after which the PLO's strength began to grow.

Beta Israel: A lost Hebrew tribe of Ethiopian Jews living in the bush of Ethiopia that were repatriated to Israel between the 1980s and 1990s. These Jews from Africa now have Israeli citizenship.

Bi-national State: A proposed solution to the Palestinian-Israeli conflict which would result in a single state composed of Israel, the West Bank and Gaza Strip or a single state composed of Israel and the West Bank with full citizenship for its inhabitants.

Black September: This refers to both the conflict, Black September, which began in September 1972 in Jordan, and to the Palestinian terrorist group that was responsible for the killing of eleven Israeli Olympians during the 1972 Munich Summer Olympics. The conflict erupted when King Hussein of Jordan initiated a military offensive following an attempt by militant Palestinians to take control of his kingdom. Thousands of people were killed, most of whom were Palestinians. The conflict ended in 1971, when the Palestinian Liberation Organization was expelled from Jordan.

The Black September terrorist group responsible for the massacre at the 1972 Munich Summer Olympics was formed in 1971 by members of Fatah.

British Detention Camps: Were British-run camps interning Jewish refugees who had attempted to immigrate into the British Mandate of Palestine in violation of British immigration policy in Palestine between 1946 and 1949. The camps in Israel and Cyprus operated from 1946 to January 1949. The British interned approximately 50,000 Jewish people in these camps.

Blue Flags: Were a non-violent group of Israeli citizens who supported the Israeli government 2005 plan to disengage and withdraw from Gaza. Orange Flags were those who opposed the Gaza Disengagement Plan.

British Mandate of Palestine: The League of Nations awarded temporary rule over Palestine, formerly a part of the Ottoman Empire, to Britain after WWI. The mandate ended on May 14, 1948. Also known as British Mandate for Palestine, Mandate Period and British Mandate.

Caliph: Title of a successor of Muhammad as temporal and spiritual head of Islam.

Cave of the Patriarchs: (Ma'arat Ha-Machpelah). In the city of Hebron, located in a series of underground chambers below a large structure where Abraham, Isaac and Jacob are buried. Palestinians refute the Jewish sanctity of the site.

CE (Common Era): see AD.

Camp David: United States presidential compound in Maryland where international conferences are frequently held.

Camp David Accords: Secret framework agreements between Egypt and Israel in 1978 that eventually resulted in the 1979 Egypt-Israel Peace Treaty.

Camp David Summit: Held in the U.S. in 2000, the Middle East Peace Summit at Camp David consisted of negotiations between United States President Bill Clinton, Israeli Prime Minister Ehud Barak, and Palestinian Authority Chairman Yasser Arafat on Final Status Issues.

Canaan: An ancient region between the Jordan River, the Dead Sea, and the Mediterranean conquered by biblical Israelites thousands of years ago. It is simultaneously claimed by Palestinians as their ancient homeland.

Christian Phalangists: Faction in Lebanon who allied themselves with Israel during the 1982 Lebanon War, directly responsible for carrying out the massacres in the Sabra and Shatila Palestinian Refugee Camps.

GLOSSARY

Church of the Holy Sepulchre: A sacred Christian church in Jerusalem on the burial site of Jesus Christ.

Clinton Parameters: Are the guidelines for the Permanent Status Agreement, as put forth by then-President Bill Clinton of the United States.

Coastal Road Massacre: 1978 hijacking of a bus on Israel's Coastal Highway in which 38 Israeli civilians were killed and 71 were wounded. The attack was planned by Abu Jihad and carried out by Fatah of the Palestine Liberation Organization.

Corpus Separatum: Latin for "separated body." This concept is used in reference to a city or place that is given different legal and political status from the territory around it. Not applied to independent city-states, the term was originally part of the UN's 1947 Partition Plan in reference to the jurisdiction of Jerusalem. This concept was never implemented, due to the outbreak of the 1948 Arab-Israeli War.

Dalai Lama: The spiritual head of Tibetan Buddhism.

Declaration of Principles (DOP) (Oslo Accords): The Declaration of Principles, signed by the PLO and Israel following the Oslo Accords, contains a set of mutually agreed-upon general principles regarding the 5 year interim period of Palestinian self-rule beginning in 1993.

Deir Yassin: Was a Palestinian village near Jerusalem where a contentious Israeli attack took place on April 9, 1948 during the 1948, Arab-Israeli War killing hundreds of Palestinians, including women and children. Following reports about this attack, Palestinians fled from Israel and became refugees.

Diaspora: Greek for "scattering" or "dispersion," this term is used for describing a group of people who have settled away from their ancestral homeland in multiple locations. The term originally applied only to Jews, but has since been used to describe the dispersions of other groups of people.

Disputed Territories: (Occupied Territories) Land captured by Israel during Arab-Israeli Wars, the status of which have not been successfully resolved by Israel and the Palestinians.

Dome of the Rock: (Al-Masjid Al-Haram) (al-Sakhrah) (al-Musharrafah) (Noble Sanctuary) (Sacred Rock) Built on the Haram al-Sharif in Jerusalem, the Dome is where Muslims believe Abraham readied Ishmael for sacrifice and where Muhammad ascended into heaven during his Night Journey.

Dreyfus Affair: A late nineteenth century French political scandal spawned by anti-Semitism. It involved a young artillery officer of Jewish descent, Alfred Dreyfus. He was convicted of treason in 1894, for communicating French military secrets to the German Embassy in Paris. Two years later, evidence that proved Dreyfus's innocence was covered up.

East Jerusalem: (al-Quds) (The Holy One) The part of Jerusalem that houses the Old City of Jerusalem including Jewish and Muslim Holy sites. Captured by Jordan in 1949, it was recaptured by Israel in the 1967 Six-Day War.

Edward Said: Palestinian American author and Columbia University professor who was a prominent advocate for Palestinian rights.

Eretz Yisrael: (Israel) (Land of Israel) (State of Israel) Hebrew for 'Land of Israel,' claimed by Jews as their homeland.

Effendi: Title of respect or courtesy given to government officials or learned professionals during the Ottoman Empire.

Ethnic Cleansing: Is the policy of intentionally and purposefully attacking, killing, and/or removing a specific ethnic or religious group from a given geographical location.

Etzion bloc: Collection of Israeli settlements in the West Bank destroyed after the 1948 Arab-Israeli War. Rebuilt following the Six-Day War, there is contention about their construction and legitimacy in the West Bank.

Faisal-Weizmann Agreement: Was a short-lived arrangement of Arab-Jewish cooperation created during the Paris Peace Conference in 1919 by Emir Faisal, son of the King of Hejaz, and Chaim Weizmann, a Zionist leader.

Farhoud: 1941 Pogrom against Iraqi Jews in Baghdad during which Jewish property was destroyed and Jewish civilians were killed. Often compared to Kristallnacht in Germany.

Fatah: (Movement for the National Liberation of Palestine) Is a Palestinian nationalist political party, as well as the largest faction in the PLO. Was created and led by Yasser Arafat until his death in 2004. After Arafat's death, Mahmoud Abbas became the head of Fatah.

Fatahland: PLO-controlled land in Lebanon under Yasser Arafat before the 1982 Lebanon War.

Fedayeen: Palestinian resistance groups formed following the 1948 Arab-Israeli War.

Fellahin: Arab peasant or farmer.

Fertile Crescent: The region in the Middle East known for its fertile land in an area mostly made up of deserts. This area consists of modern day Iraq, Jordan, Lebanon, and Israel/Palestine, Syria and parts of Egypt, Iran and Turkey.

Final Solution: Nazi Germany's plan for the systemic genocide of European Jews during WWII.

Final Status Issues: The unresolved issues between the Palestinians and Israelis delineated in the Oslo Accords, which include: borders, Jerusalem, refugees, and settlements.

First Intifada: The first uprising of the Palestinians from 1988-1995 against Israeli rule in the Occupied Territories (Disputed Territories).

GLOSSARY

First Jewish Holy Temple: Solomon's Temple built on the Temple Mount in Jerusalem around 950 BCE and destroyed by the Babylonians in 586 BCE.

First Qibla: The first direction of prayer for Muslims was Jerusalem. Subsequently, Muslims have faced Mecca (Mekkah) during their prayers.

Fourth Geneva Convention: (Geneva Convention relative to the Protection of Civilian Persons in Time of War) Was an international law adopted in August 1949, considered to be the quintessential piece of international legislation regarding the protection of civilians in a war zone.

Gaza (Gaza Strip): Territory along the Mediterranean Sea between Israel and Egypt.

Gaza Disengagement in 2005 (Unilateral withdrawal): Israel withdrew its troops and dismantled Jewish settlements in August 2005, leaving Gaza to the Palestinian people.

Gaza Strip: see Gaza.

German Third Reich: Government of Germany under Adolph Hitler and the National Socialist German Workers' Party (Nazi Party) from 1933-1945. Responsible for World War II, this government planned and implemented the Final Solution and the Holocaust in Europe.

Golan Heights: An area of land between the Syrian and Israeli border. Syria controlled this disputed territory from 1948 until 1967, when Israel took control over the territory following the Six-Day War. During the 1973 Yom Kippur War, Syria invaded the Golan. Israel and Syria signed a cease-fire agreement in 1974 which gave Israel control over most of the territory retaken by Israel during the war.

Goldstein Massacre: Israeli Baruch Goldstein opened fire on unarmed Palestinian Muslims praying inside the Ibrahim Mosque at the Cave of the Patriarchs in Hebron on February 25, 1994.

Goldstone Report: A September 2009 report prepared by a UN mission led by Justice Richard Goldstone. It controversially accused both the IDF and Hamas Palestinian militants of war crimes during the Gaza War (Operation Cast Lead) which took place in a three-week period from December 2008 to January 2009.

Grad Rockets: Russian-made, truck mounted rockets.

Grand Mufti: Head of the Muslim community in Jerusalem. This religious leader served as the political leader of the Palestinians during the British Mandate of Palestine. Also known as Grand Mufti of Jerusalem. See Hajj Amin Husseini and Hajj Amin al-Husseini.

Great Revolt of 1936-1939 (Arab Great Revolt): Nationalist series of organized strikes, boycotts, demonstrations, and armed struggles by Arabs against mass Jewish immigration in the British Mandate of Palestine.

Green Line: Named for the green ink used to draw the line during negotiations, is a demarcation line between Israel and its neighbors. It was established during the 1949 Armistice Agreements that followed the 1948 Arab-Israeli War, and is also used to differentiate between Israel and the territories it has occupied since the Six-Day War in 1967.

Hadith: Narrations used to understand the words of Muhammad in relation to Fiqh (Islamic jurisprudence). Shi'a and Sunni scholars use different collections of Hadith.

Haganah: Hebrew for "The Defense," Haganah was the primary paramilitary group that served as the underground army of the Jewish community from 1920 to 1948 during the British Mandate of Palestine. The group was later consolidated into the IDF following the Israeli War of Independence.

Haj Amin al-Husseini: (Hajj Amin) see Grand Mufti.

Hajj: The Fifth Pillar of Islam. The Hajj is an annual pilgrimage to Mecca that every able-bodied Muslim should make at least once in their lifetime.

Hamas (Harakat al-Muqawama al-Islamiyya) (Movement of the Islamic Resistance): Palestinians from the Muslim Brotherhood banded together to create the group Harakat al-Muqawama al-Islamiyya (Movement of the Islamic Resistance), which is known by the Arabic acronym, Hamas. Hamas was formed as a Palestinian nationalist-Islamist group, created as an alternative to the more secular Palestine Liberation Organization (PLO). Ruling Gaza since 2005, Hamas has committed itself to using violence to reach its goals. Hamas' goal is the creation of a theocratic state in all of Palestine and the elimination of Israel. Hamas is considered to be a terrorist organization by many western countries, including the United States.

Hanan Ashrawi: Palestinian Christian legislator and activist. Important leader during the First Intifada and first woman elected to the Palestinian National Council.

Hanif: An Arabian person in pre-Islamic times who followed a monotheistic faith but was not Jewish or Christian.

Harakat al-Muqawamat al-Islamiyyah: see Hamas.

Haram al-Sharif: Considered to be the third-holiest site in Islam, it is the place where Muhammad ascended to heaven during his Night Journey. The site is also home to the al-Aqsa Mosque and the Dome of the Rock. To Jews, the site is known as the Temple Mount, which is considered to be the holiest site in Judaism, as it is the site where the First and Second Holy Jewish Temples stood.

Haqq al-awda: see Right of Return.

Harakat al-tahrir al-watani al-filastini: meaning "Palestinian National Liberation Movement".

Hashemite tribe: A Bedouin tribe of Arabia who aided the British in WWI. The kings from the Hashemite Kingdom of Jordan are royalty who can trace their ancestry directly to Prophet Muhammad.

Hassan al-Banna: Schoolteacher and imam known for founding the Muslim Brotherhood.

GLOSSARY

Hebron: The largest city in the West Bank. As the burial site for Abraham, Isaac, Jacob, and their wives, Hebron is considered to be the second-holiest city in Judaism, after Jerusalem. It is also considered by many Muslims to be the fourth-holiest site in Islam. Some Muslims also believe the site was visited by Prophet Muhammad during his Night Journey.

Hebron Protocol: As part of the Interim Agreement, this protocol allowed for the redeployment of IDF forces in parts of Hebron. The protocol divided Hebron into two sections, H1 and H2, with most Palestinians living in H1. The downtown economic sector of the city controlled by Israel became H2.

Hectare: A metric measurement equal to 10,000 square meters.

Hejaz in Saudi Arabia: Hejaz is the western mountainous region in the Arabian Peninsula.

Hezbollah: A Shi'a Muslim militant group and political party based in Lebanon. Financially and politically supported by Iran and Syria, its paramilitary wing is regarded as a resistance movement throughout much of the Arab and Muslim worlds. Western countries including the United States consider Hezbollah to be a terrorist organization. Hezbollah formed in 1982 and calls for the annihilation of Israel.

Holocaust: Systematic genocide of six million Jews by the Nazis during WWII.

Holocaust Deniers: Those who deny the Holocaust occurred.

Holy Basin: The area surrounding the Old City of Jerusalem on the North South and East.

Holy of Holies: Phrase from the Hebrew Bible referring to the innermost sacred chamber of the Tabernacle and Holy Jewish Temples in Jerusalem where the Ark of the Covenant was kept. In modern times it refers to the Holy Ark, the place in each synagogue where Torah scrolls are kept.

Holy Sepulchre: Burial site of Jesus Christ.

Idolatry: The act of worshiping a material object as a god. Abrahamic religions consider idolatry a sin as followers of these religions believe there is only one God.

Illegal outpost: A Jewish community built within the West Bank without the authorization of the Israeli government.

Interim Agreement: see Oslo II.

Internally Displaced Persons: Often mistakenly referred to as refugees, internally displaced persons are those that are within their country's borders but have been forced out of their homes.

International City: A city-state that is independent of the direct supervision of a nation-state. The original UN Partition Plan designated Jerusalem as an International City. However, this never occurred. Sometimes referred to as an "Open City."

International Court of Justice: United Nations judiciary whose function is to settle legal disputes submitted by UN member States.

International Covenant on Civil and Political Rights (ICCPR): Article 12, which Israel has both signed and ratified, states that no one shall be arbitrarily deprived of the right to enter his own country.

International Criminal Court: Permanent tribunal prosecuting individuals for genocide, war crimes, and crimes against humanity.

Intifada: Arabic for "shaking off," used as a term for Palestinian resistance or uprising against Israeli occupation of the West Bank and Gaza. The First Intifada occurred from 1987 to 1993. The Second Intifada lasted from 2000 to 2005.

Irgun: Short for Ha'Irgun HaTzva'i HaLe'umi BeEretz Yisra'el, which means "National Military Organization in the Land of Israel." The Irgun was a Zionist paramilitary group from 1931 to 1948 during the British Mandate of Palestine. It was a splinter group of the Haganah. The IDF absorbed the Irgun members at the start of the 1948 Arab-Israeli War.

Irgun Zwei Leumi: Zionist paramilitary group founded by Avraham Stern during the British Mandate of Palestine to fight against British control of Palestine.

Isaac: The son of the patriarch Abraham and the father of Jacob.

Ishmael: The outcast first born son of the patriarch Abraham and a prophet of Islam in the Quran.

Islamic Jihad: A splinter group of the Muslim Brotherhood.

Islamism (Political Islam): A controversial term used to describe the belief that Islam is a political system in addition to being a religion. Many Islamist scholars encourage the enforcement of sharia law, promote political unity, and seek an end to non-Muslim influence in the Muslim sphere.

Israel: The ancient land occupied by biblical Israelites who followed Moses from Egypt to the "promised land." The modern State of Israel was established by the United Nations in 1948. It is also called the State of Israel, the modern State of Israel, Eretz Yisrael and Zion.

Israeli Defense Force (IDF): A combination of land, air and naval forces created to defend Israel.

Izz ad-Din al-Qassam Brigades: The military wing of Hamas and named for a famous Palestinian militant, the al-Qassam. Founded as an organization to effectively block the Oslo Accords, the group is responsible for numerous attacks against Israeli soldiers as well as civilians. The al-Qassam Brigades is listed as a terrorist organization by the United States, the European Union, the United Kingdom, and Australia.

Jenin: It is the largest town in the northern West Bank. A Palestinian refugee camp in Jenin was the site of a contentious battle between the IDF and Palestinian militants in 2000.

GLOSSARY

Jerusalem: The ancient city sacred to Jews, Christians and Arabs, continues to be a contentious Final Status Issue between Palestinians and Israelis who both claim it as their capital. Several holy sites for all three religions are situated near or within the Old City of Jerusalem. It is also known as the Old City and Masjid al-Aqsa.

Jewish Agency: Also known as the Jewish Agency for Israel, the Sochnut, or JAFI. The Jewish Agency was the pre-state authority for Jews prior to Israel's formal establishment in 1948. It was later recognized by the British Mandate as the organization responsible for Jewish immigration and the administration of economic, social, and other affairs related to the establishment of a Jewish national home.

Jewish Holy Temple: Sacred house of worship built in Jerusalem on the Temple Mount. Following the destruction of the First Jewish Holy Temple in 586 BCE, the Second Holy Temple was built. Later the Second Holy Temple was destroyed by the Romans in 70 CE. The Jewish Temple has since not been rebuilt. Also known as the Temple, Jewish Temple and Holy of Holies.

Jewish National Fund: An organization that was founded in 1901 for the purpose of acquiring and developing land for Jewish settlement in Palestine.

Jihad: The Quran calls for "jihad," meaning a military struggle on behalf of Islam. But the Quran also refers to jihad as an internal, individual, spiritual struggle toward self-improvement, moral cleansing and intellectual effort. It is said that Prophet Muhammad considered the armed-struggle version of holy war "the little jihad," but considered the spiritual, individual version of holy war- the war within oneself-as "the great jihad."

Jimmy Carter: President of the United States from 1976 to 1980.

Judaization of Jerusalem: An allegation by some Palestinians that Israel has tried to change the physical and demographic landscape of Jerusalem into a Jewish Jerusalem under Israeli sovereignty.

Judea: A successor to the biblical Jewish kingdom of Judah bordered by Samaria, the Jordan River, the Dead Sea, the Sinai Peninsula, and by the Mediterranean.

Kaaba: A building in Mecca which is considered Islam's most sacred site. According to the Quran, the Kaaba was built by Abraham and Ishmael. It is an integral part of the Hajj, which is one of the Five Pillars of Islam. Pilgrims are required to walk around the Kaaba seven times in an anti-clockwise direction. During prayer, Muslims around the world face the Kaaba regardless of where they are located.

Kadima: Hebrew for "forward" and the name of an Israeli political party formed by Ariel Sharon. It has attracted many career politicians from both the left-leaning Labor party and the right-leaning Likud party. It won the 2006 Israeli elections.

Kahan Commission: The Commission of Inquiry convened under the direction of the Israeli government following the Sabra and Shatila Massacre in Lebanon in 1982. Headed by the leader of the Israeli Supreme Court, Yitzhak Kahan, the commission set out to determine the role Israel played in the massacre.

Kangaroo Court: A 'sham' court case. The outcome is often determined before the trial is heard.

Keffiyeh: The traditional head covering of Bedouin Arab men.

Kibbutz: A collective Jewish community in Israel.

King Abdullah I: King of Jordan from 1946 to1952.

King Farouk of Egypt: King of Egypt from 1936 until he was overthrown in 1952.

Kippah: Yarmulke or head cap.

Knesset: The national legislature of the Israeli government.

Kosher: Kosher foods are those which conform to traditional Jewish dietary laws.

Labor Party: Political party established in Israel in 1968. All Israeli Prime Ministers were affiliated with this party until 1977.

Land-for-Peace: An interpretation of UN Security Council Resolution 242 derived from the resolution's first operative paragraph affirming that peace in the Middle East should involve the application of two principles: withdrawal of Israeli forces from the territories of the recent conflict, and termination of all claims and states of belligerency.

Land Swap: The notion that land in Occupied Territories may be annexed by Israel in exchange for comparable Israeli land added to the proposed Palestinian State.

Likud: A political party in Israel, led today by Benjamin Netanyahu.

Madrid Conference: An international meeting beginning the peace process between Israel and the Palestinians.

Mahmoud Abbas: see Abu Mazan.

Mandate Period: (British Mandate) (British Mandate of Palestine) see British Mandate of Palestine.

Ma'arat Ha-Machpelah: see Cave of the Patriarchs.

Masjid al-aqsa: (Jerusalem, Old City) see Jerusalem.

McMahon-Hussein Correspondence: Was a series of letters exchanged between the Sharif of Mecca and the British High Commissioner in Egypt. The subject of the letters was the future of Ottoman-held lands, and the British active encouragement of an Arab revolt against the Ottomans in exchange for a willingness by the British to recognize Arab sovereignty and independence movements.

GLOSSARY

Mein Kampf: Book written by Adolf Hitler claiming the existence of a Jewish conspiracy to control the world, expounding anti-Semitism and revealing Hitler's intentions to exterminate the Jews. The title translates as My Struggle.

Menachem Begin: Israeli Prime Minister who received the Nobel Peace Prize for signing a peace treaty with Anwar Sadat of Egypt in 1979. Leader of the pre-Israel Zionist group called the Irgun.

Middle East Quartet: United States, Russia, the European Union, and the United Nations established this group in 2002 to influence the peace process in the Middle East.

Modern State of Israel: (Israel, State of Israel, Modern State of Israel, Eretz Yisrael) see Israel.

Monotheism: The belief in and the worship of a single God. This term is most commonly used to describe the Abrahamic religions: Judaism, Christianity and Islam. In Judaism's holy book, the Torah, it is stated that God commands followers of the Jewish faith to worship only one God. Muslims believe that the foundation of Islamic teaching is based on the principle of Tawhid, or Oneness of God.

Mount of Olives: A mountain ridge on the east side of Jerusalem, used as a cemetery for thousands of years.

Movement for the National Liberation of Palestine: (Fatah) see Fatah.

Mughrabi Quarter: Is an Arab neighborhood in the southeast corner of the Old City of Jerusalem.

Muhammad: The founder of the religion of Islam whose followers are called Muslims. Muhammad was born in 578 BCE. His revelations were recorded in the Quran.

Muhammad al-Durrah Incident: A controversial incident in the Gaza Strip captured on film by the France 2 television network. Al-Dura was a 12-year old boy who died in a crossfire between Palestinians and Israelis at the beginning of the Second Intifada. The cause of his death remains controversial, with Palestinians accusing Israeli soldiers of intentionally shooting the unarmed boy.

Muhammad's Night Journey: see Night Journey.

Muslim Brotherhood: One of the world's oldest Islamic movements, the Brotherhood was formed in 1928 by Hassan al-Banna in Egypt.

Nationalism: An ideology of the 19th and early 20th centuries that believes in a national identity and political entity, often centered on a particular ethnic group. It may also involve the belief of national superiority, or the importance of the state above other aspects of life.

Naval Blockade: An effort to cut off food, supplies, war materials, or communications of a coastal area by force. Gaza has been under an Israeli naval blockade since Hamas has been in power.

Nasser, Gamal Abdel: The Egyptian army officer who overthrew King Farouk in a 1952 military coup and then became President of Egypt.

Netanyahu, Benjamin: Prime Minister of Israel from 1996-1999 and since 2009. He serves as the Chairman of the Likud Party.

Night Journey (al-Isra): According to Islamic tradition, Prophet Muhammad's journey is composed of two parts: al-Isra and al-Mi'raj. The first part, al-Isra, was when the Prophet Muhammad traveled from Mecca to Jerusalem. From there, he performed the second leg of his journey, al-Mi'raj, when he ascended into heaven. After meeting with Allah, Muhammad returned to Mecca to reveal the Second Pillar of Islam, stating that Muslims must pray five times each day. The Night Journey is believed to have taken place during the period of a single night.

Noble Sanctuary (Al-Masjid Al-Haram): see Dome of the Rock.

Occupied Territories: The Gaza and West Bank territories occupied by Israel at the conclusion of the Six Day War. Gaza was given back to the Palestinians in 2005. Also known as the Occupied Palestinian Territories and the Disputed Territories.

Old City: A walled section within the modern city of Jerusalem that, until the 1980s, formerly constituted the entire city. The Old City contains several important religious sites including the Temple Mount, the Western Wall, the al-Aqsa Mosque, the Dome of the Rock, and the Church of the Holy Sepulchre. After the 1948 Arab-Israeli War, the Old City became part of East Jerusalem under Jordanian rule. Israel has occupied the Old City since the Six Day War of 1967. Also known as Jerusalem and Masjid al-Aqsa.

Olim: Hebrew for Jewish immigrants in Israel.

Open City: (International City) A city that does not belong to a single nation. Jerusalem was deemed to be an Open City in the UN Partition Plan of 1947. It was to be governed by an international body. But Jordan seized East Jerusalem in the 1948 Israeli War of Independence.

Orange Flags: A non-violent group of Israeli citizens who opposed the 2005 Israeli Government summer plan to disengage and withdraw from Gaza. They were opposed by Blue Flags, who supported the withdrawal plan.

Operation Cast Lead: An Israeli military incursion into Gaza from December 27, 2008 until January 21, 2009 to stop rocket and mortar fire attacks into Israel from Gaza.

Operation Defensive Shield: An Israeli military action launched in 2002 to end the Second Intifada. It was the largest military action in the West Bank since the Six-Day War.

Operation Litani: An Israeli military operation into Southern Lebanon in 1978 against the PLO.

Operation Peace for the Galilee: see 1982 Lebanon War.

GLOSSARY

Oslo Accords: A historic series of agreements between Israel and the PLO that involved two phases: Oslo I in 1993 and Oslo II in 1995. The accords were the first agreements between Israel and the PLO to be negotiated face-to-face. They allowed for the establishment of the Palestinian National Authority.

Oslo I: The first of two phases of the Oslo Accords, this agreement involved two key features: the mutual recognition between Israel and the PLO, and the Declaration of Principles (DOP), which set an agenda for negotiations on Palestinian self-government in the occupied territories, beginning with Gaza and Jericho.

Oslo II: Also known as the Interim Agreement on the West Bank and the Gaza Strip, or simply the Interim Agreement, was the portion of the Oslo Accords that divided the West Bank and the Gaza Strip into three types of areas, each under varying degrees of control by the Palestinian Authority or Israel.

Ottoman Empire: A Turkish Empire (1453-1918) encompassing Turkey, Syria, Mesopotamia, Palestine, Arabia, Egypt, the Balkans, the Barbary States, and parts of Hungary and Russia.

Ottoman Turks: The rulers of the Ottoman Empire from 1453 to 1918.

Paganism: A general term used mainly to describe followers of polytheistic religions in antiquity, or pre-Abrahamic religions.

Palestinian Authority (PA): The Palestinian Authority, also known as the Palestinian National Authority and the PA, was formed in 1994, during the Oslo Accords peace negotiations between Israel and the Palestinian Liberation Organization. The PA was formed to serve as the governing body of the Palestinian Territories (West Bank and Gaza) while final status negotiations continued.

Palestinian Declaration of Independence: A document adopted by the Palestinian National Council on November 15, 1988. Read aloud by Yasser Arafat, the declaration announced the establishment of the State of Palestine. Arafat change this title from Chairman of the PLO to President of Palestine once the document was unilaterally proclaimed.

Palestinian Liberation Army (PLA): A group that was set up to be the military wing of the PLO. It was largely controlled by outside Arab governments, such as Syria.

Palestine Liberation Organization (PLO): A political and paramilitary organization founded in 1964. Since the Madrid Conference in 1991, it has largely been recognized to be the sole legitimate representative of the Palestinian people.

Palestinian National Authority (PNA): Originally founded as the Palestinian Authority, the PNA was formed after the Oslo Accords were agreed upon by Israel and the PLO.

Palestinian National Charter: Constitution of the Palestine Liberation Organization.

Palestinian National Congress: Met in May, 1964 in Jerusalem with an assembly of 422 Palestinians from ten Arab countries.

Palestinian National Council (PNC): The legislative body of the PLO, which meets every two years, and is responsible for the election of the Executive Committee. The PNC was first formed in Jerusalem in May 1964, where it adopted the Palestinian National Covenant.

Palestinian National Covenant (Palestine Charter): Charter declaring Palestine as the national homeland of the Arab Palestinian people.

Palmach: An elite force of the Haganah established in 1941.

Pan-Arabism: An ideology that calls for the unification of all Arab peoples from all Arab nations. The idea began as a union between Egypt and Syria whose aim was to unify the Arab world into a single nation stretching from Morocco to the Arabian Sea. Although Syria withdrew its membership in 1961, as an ideology, Pan Arabism remained strong well into the 1970s.

Paris Peace Conference, 1919: The meeting held at the end of World War I by the Allies where diplomats from more than 29 countries set the peace terms for the defeated nations. The treaties resulting from the conference dramatically reshaped the maps of both Europe and the Middle East.

The Faisal-Weizmann Agreement was forged during the conference.

Partition Plan: see United Nations Partition Plan.

Passover Massacre: Occurred on March 27, 2002, during the Second Intifada at a hotel in Netanya, Israel. The attack by Hamas consisted of a suicide bombing that killed thirty Israeli civilians during a Passover seder. Operation Defensive Shield occurred following this terrorist attack.

Peel Commission: Was a British Royal Commission of Inquiry headed by Lord Earl Peel that advocated altering the British Mandate of Palestine as a result of the 1936-1939 Arab revolt in Palestine. It was the first report to recommend the partition of the Mandate of Palestine. It was formally known as the Palestine Royal Commission during its existence from 1936 to1937.

Philadelphi Route: A narrow piece of land between Gaza and Egypt that contains a security corridor controlled by Israel. Smuggling tunnels beneath the route connect Egypt the Gaza Strip in order to move illegal items such as weapons and ammunition into the hands of Palestinian militants in Gaza.

Philistine: A native of ancient Philistia who lived on the coast of the eastern Mediterranean from about 1450 BCE until 723 CE when the Philistines were destroyed by the Assyrians.

Plan Dalet: Was a controversial plan executed by the Haganah in the spring of 1948. Its purpose has been heavily debated, but many Palestinians claim that it was designed to expel Palestinians from the Land of Israel.

Pogrom: Describes the organized massacre of helpless people; first used in Russia when whole Jewish villages were destroyed due to anti-Semitism.

Polytheism: The belief in and/or worship of more than one god.

GLOSSARY

Popular Front for the Liberation of Palestine (PFL): The second-largest group in the PLO, second only to Fatah. It is a national liberation movement founded on Marxist ideals that opposes negotiations with Israel, and is regarded as a terrorist organization by over 30 countries.

Pre-1967 Borders: see Green Line.

Promised Land: Phrase used in the Jewish scriptures to describe the land promised by God to Abraham and his descendants.

Qassam Rockets: A simple, small rocket developed by Hamas in Gaza.

Qibla: The Qibla is the direction Muslims must face while praying. The current direction is towards the Kaaba in Mecca, though the original direction was towards the Noble Sanctuary in Jerusalem. This change occurred after Muhammad made his migration (Hijra) from Mecca to Madina.

Quran: The central religious text of Islam which Muslims consider to be the verbatim word of God revealed to Muhummad by the angel Gabriel.

Ramallah: A city in the West Bank that is the headquarters for the Palestinian Authority.

Revisionist history: Reinterpretation of history which distorts or denies the historical record. For example, Holocaust deniers who claim the Holocaust never happened. There are also those who deny Jewish history in the Land of Israel.

Right of Return (Haqq al-awda): An international law principle that declares individuals have the right to return to or to re-enter their place of origin. It has been codified in the Universal Declaration of Human Rights (Article 13) and in the International Covenant on Civil and Political Rights (Article 12).

The Palestinian Right of Return is a Final Status Issue.

Road Map for Peace: A three-phase international plan developed by the UN, the United States, Russia, and the EU that proposes a two-state solution.

Rohan, Denis Michael: Australian citizen who attempted to set fire to the al-Aqsa Mosque in 1969. He was arrested in Israel for arson, tried, found insane and hospitalized in a mental institution.

Rosh Hashanah: Rosh Hashanah is the Jewish New Year. As the first of the Jewish High Holidays, it is observed ten days prior to Yom Kippur, the Jewish Day of Atonement—the holiest day of the year for Jewish people.

Sabra: A Jewish person born in Israel.

Sabra and Shatila Massacre: Took place on September 16 and September 18, 1982, in Palestinian refugee camps in Beirut. While the camps were surrounded by the IDF, a disputed number of civilians were killed (ranging from 328 to 3500) by Christian Lebanese Phalangists. The massacre took place during Operation Peace for Galilee, also known as the 1982 Lebanon War.

Sacred Rock (Dome of the Rock) (al-Sakhrah) (al-Musharrafah): see Dome of the Rock.

Salah: Five daily prayers for Muslims.

Samaria: A mountainous northern region of the West Bank.

Saudi Initiative: Also known as the Arab Peace Initiative, or Arab Peace Plan, this 2002 initiative, was reaffirmed in 2007 by the Arab League. It proposes the creation of a Palestinian state in the Gaza Strip and the West Bank with its capital in East Jerusalem. In return, Israel would be granted full recognition by all Arab countries allowing for the normalization of political and economic relations.

Sderot: An Israeli city near the border of the Gaza Strip that has been heavily attacked by an ongoing barrage of Qassam rockets from Gaza.

Second Intifada: see al-Aqsa Intifada.

Second Jewish Holy Temple: The Jewish Temple that was rebuilt by the Jews after the destruction of the First Jewish Holy Temple in 586 BCE. The Second Temple was destroyed by the Romans in 70 CE.

Second Lebanon War: Also called the 2006 Israel-Hezbollah War was a 34 day military conflict between Israel and Hezbollah in southern Lebanon.

Security Wall: (Separation Wall) (Security Barrier) (Security Fence) (The Wall) Built during the Second Intifada by Israel to prevent suicide bombers and terrorists from attacking its civilians. The Security Wall has been controversial for Palestinians whose lives have changed due to this structure dividing Israel from the West Bank.

Seder: A Jewish ceremonial dinner and service held on the first and second evenings of Passover.

Settlements: Israeli communities in the Occupied Territories.

Shimon Peres: Ninth President of Israel from 2007 to the present. Served twice as Prime Minister of Israel. He was first elected to the Knesset in 1959.

Semitic: A subdivision of early Caucasian people with linguistic commonalities, including the Akkadian, Assyrian, Aramaic, Moabite and Hebrew in its northern branch and Arabic, Sabaean, and Amharic in its southern branch.

Shalit, Gilad: Israeli soldier captured in 2006 by Hamas and held as a hostage for more than five years, was released by Hamas in 2011.

Sharon, Ariel: The Prime Minister of Israel who headed the Likud Party beginning in 2001, and who was responsible for the 2005 Unilateral Disengagement from Gaza.

Shi'ites: Muslims of the Shia branch of Islam.

GLOSSARY

Six-Day War: The Arab-Israeli War fought between June 5 and June 10, 1967. After the Israeli victory, Israel gained control and possession of the Gaza Strip, Sinai Peninsula, West Bank, East Jerusalem, and the Golan Heights. The West Bank and Jerusalem continue to be Final Status Issues.

Steadfastness Fund (Sunduq al-Sumud): Established at the Baghdad Arab Summit in 1978, a fund of $150 million dollars was to be donated by Arab countries and administered by Jordan and the PLO to assist Palestinians with social services, including unemployment benefits, retiree pensions and interest-free housing loans.

Stern Gang (ZL): A militia of fighters for Israel founded by a splinter group of the Irgun before the formation of the IDF. The founder of the Stern Gang was Avraham Stern.

Strait of Tiran: A 13-kilometer passage between the Sinai and Arabian peninsulas separating the Gulf of Aqaba from the Red Sea.

Suez Canal: A 100 mile long canal from the northeast coast of Egypt across the Isthmus of Suez that connects the Mediterranean and the Red Sea Gulf of Suez.

Sultan: The king or sovereign leader of a Muslim state.

Sunduq al-Sumud: see Steadfastness Fund.

Sunni (Sunni Islam) (Sunnism): The majority of Muslims. They are considered to represent the orthodox branch of the Islamic religion.

Sykes-Picot Agreement: A secret agreement between the United Kingdom and France in 1916 that divided future control and influence over Ottoman territories after World War I. This agreement paved the way for the Mandate System in the Middle East.

Taba: A town in Egypt on the Gulf of Aqaba.

Tallit: A Jewish prayer shawl worn over the outer clothes during prayers.

Tantura: A Palestinian Arab fishing village located 8 km northwest of Zikhron, on the Mediterranean coast of Israel, where a disputed attack took place against the villagers during the 1948 War.

Tanzim: Fatah's military wing.

Tanzimat Laws: The Tanzimat Laws changed land-ownership requirements within the Ottoman Empire during the rule of Sultan Mahmud II in the late 1800s.

The Holy One: (East Jerusalem) (al-Quds) see Jerusalem.

Temple (Jewish Holy Temple) (Jewish Temple) (Holy of Holies): The most sacred Jewish religious site of worship built by King Solomon in the tenth century BCE in ancient Jerusalem on the Temple Mount. It was destroyed in 586 BCE by the Babylonians. The Second Holy Temple was built on the same site in 515 BCE and later destroyed by the Romans in 70 CE.

Temple Mount (Sacred Rock) (al-Sakhrah) (al-Musharrafah): This is the site of the First and Second Jewish Temples. The Temple Mount is the holiest site in Judaism and it is where Jews face during prayer. In the Sunni Islamic faith, it is considered the third holiest site as it is the place where Muhammad ascended to heaven. Following the capture of Jerusalem by the Muslims in 637 CE, the Umayyad Caliphs ordered the construction of the al-Aqsa Mosque and Dome of the Rock in this location. During the 1948 Arab-Israeli War, Jordan took control of the Temple Mount. Since the 1967 Arab-Israeli Six Day War, Israel holds jurisdiction over the site. The site continues to be a source of contention between the Israelis and Palestinians and is a Final Status Issue for negotiation.

Temple Mount Faithful: Based in Jerusalem and founded in 1967, an Orthodox Jewish movement whose goal is to rebuild the Third Jewish Temple on the Temple Mount.

Tisha B'Av: Jewish holiday commemorating the destruction of both the First and Second Temples of Jerusalem.

Torah: The Torah, the most sacred Jewish text, contains Jewish law, literature, and teachings. The Torah contains the Five Books of Moses: Genesis, Exodus, Leviticus, Numbers, and Deuteronomy. Jewish faith asserts that the Torah was revealed to Moses by God at Mount Sinai. In the Christian faith, the Torah is referred to as the Old Testament.

Transjordan: Transjordan, the territory that makes up modern day Jordan, was previously a territory within the British Mandate of Palestine. In 1921, the territory was given to King Abdullah to found a new Arab country. Following the 1948 Arab-Israeli War, King Abdullah of Transjordan changed the country's name to the Hashemite Kingdom of Jordan.

UAR: UAR, or the United Arab Republic, existed from 1958 to 1961 as a union between Egypt and Syria. The union was Egyptian President Gamal Abdel Nasser's first step in his plan to create a pan-Arab state. Nasser became the president of the UAR and quickly moved to stamp out communists in Syria. Economic difficulties and political system disagreements led Syria to withdraw from the union in 1961.

UN Resolution 181: see United Nations Partition Plan for Palestine.

UN Resolution 194: Fully titled as United Nations General Assembly Resolution 194, this measure, passed in December 1948, provides for the return of refugees to their homes inside Israel and recognizes their right to receive compensation should they choose not to return, or if they have suffered loss of, or damage to, their original properties. Resolution 194 has, in turn, been reaffirmed by the UNGA every year since its passage.

UN Resolution 242: A unanimous resolution of the United Nations Security Council passed on November 22, 1967. The resolution called for a withdrawal of Israeli forces from territories occupied and acquired during the Six-Day War.

GLOSSARY

UN Resolution 338: United Nations Security Council Resolution 338 called for a ceasefire during the Yom Kippur War, and for the immediate implementation of Resolution 242.

UN Resolution 478: Also known as UN Security Council Resolution 478, this resolution declared Israel's 1980 Basic Law to be a violation of international law. The 1980 Basic Law established Jerusalem to be Israel's "eternal and undivided capital."

UN Resolution 1397: UN Security Council Resolution 1397 demanded an end to the Second Intifada and referred to the co-existence of the two states of Israel and Palestine, each with secure and recognized borders.

UN Resolution 3236: 1974 United Nations Resolution recognizing the Palestine Liberation Organization. It also added the "Question of Palestine" to the UN agenda.

UNRWA: United Nations Relief and Works Agency established to assist Palestinian refugees after the Arab-Israeli War of 1948. This United Nations (UN) organization continues to provide assistance to registered Palestinian refugees in Jordan, Lebanon, Syria and the Palestinian territories.

Umma (Ummah): Meaning "community" or "nation," umma is a concept derived from the phrase Ummah Wahida ("One Community") in the Quran, which was used in reference to a unified Muslim world.

Unilateral withdrawal (Gaza Disengagement): Israel gave the territory of Gaza to the Palestinian Authority without a negotiated peace agreement with Palestinians. Instead of "land for peace," through negotiations, Israel unilaterally withdrew from Gaza in 2005.

United Nations General Assembly: One of five principal sections of the United Nations and the only one in which all member nations have equal voting rights and representation.

United Nations Partition Plan (for the state of Israel and Palestine): The plan also is known as United Nations General Assembly Resolution 181. The UN Partition Plan was the original UN measure, adopted in 1947, that advocated splitting the British Mandate of Palestine into two states: one Jewish, and one Arab. It also called for the withdrawal of British forces two months before the states were to be created. War broke out during this period and the plan was never implemented.

United Nations Interim Force in Lebanon (UNIFIL): International UN forces originally were established by the UN Security Council in March, 1982 to confirm Israeli withdrawal from southern Lebanon, restore international peace and security and assist the Lebanese Government in restoring its effective authority in the area.

Universal Declaration of Human Rights Article 13: States the right of every individual to leave and return to his or her country.

United Nations Relief and Works Agency for Palestinian Refugees (UNRWA): see UNRWA.

United Nations Security Council: An international peace and security council, part of the United Nations. Its powers are outlined in the United Nations Charter. The Security Council consists of 15 members, including 5 permanent members who have veto power. It deals with the establishment of international sanctions, peacekeeping operations, and the authorization of military operations. It exercises these powers through the use of resolutions.

United Nations Special Committee on Palestine (UNSCOP): Was formed by the UN General Assembly at the behest of the United Kingdom in May 1947 to investigate and make recommendations in order to solve the conflict between Arabs and Jews in the British Mandate of Palestine. It recommended the termination of the British Mandate, and the creation of two independent nations: one for the Palestinian Arabs, and one for the Jewish people.

Wailing Wall (Western Wall): The only remnant of the Second Jewish Holy Temple destroyed by the Romans in the year 70 CE. The Wailing Wall, also known as the Western Wall, is located in Jerusalem at the base of the western side of the Temple Mount. The Wailing Wall is a place of prayer for Jews. The site is disputed between Israelis and Palestinians, as Palestinians argue that the Wailing Wall is a part of the holy al-Aqsa Mosque. During the 1948 Arab-Israeli War, Jordan took control of the Old City of Jerusalem and the Wailing Wall. Israel took control of the Wailing Wall when it captured the Old City of Jerusalem in the 1967 Arab-Israeli Six-Day War.

Wailing Wall Riots (Western Wall Uprising), (1929 Massacres), (Buraq Uprising): A series of violent conflicts that broke out in 1929 related to Jewish access to the Western Wall of the Second Temple in Jerusalem.

Wall (Security Wall) (West Bank Barrier) (Separation Wall): see Separation Wall.

West Bank: A territory that is disputed between Israelis and Palestinians. The West Bank lies between Israel and Jordan in the area west of the Jordan River. The territory was controlled by Jordan from 1949 until 1967, when Israel took control of it following the Arab-Israeli Six-Day War. Palestinians were given limited authority over the West Bank following the Oslo Accords signed by Israel and the Palestine Liberation Organization (PLO) in 1994.

West Bank Barrier: see Separation Wall.

Western Wall: see Wailing Wall.

Waqf: A concept of Islamic law that is similar to a common law trust. It is seen as an inalienable religious endowment (usually of land or property) in which the use and benefits are designated by the benefactor to the inheritor forever.

Yarmulkes: A skullcap worn by Jewish people, typically males.

GLOSSARY

Yishuv: Hebrew for "settlement." Yishuv is a term used for the Jewish population living in the Holy Land prior to Israel's establishment.

Yassin, Sheik Ahmed: A founder of Hamas and spiritual leader of the organization. He was assassinated by an Israeli airstrike in Gaza.

Yitzhak Rabin: Prime Minister of Israel who negotiated with Yasser Arafat. These negotiations led to the Oslo Accord in 1993. Both were awarded the Nobel Peace Prize. Rabin was assassinated on November 4, 1995.

Yom Kippur War: 1973 Arab-Israeli War fought in October 1973 between Israel and a coalition of Arab states led by Egypt and Syria. The war began when the Arab coalition launched a surprise attack on the Jewish Holy Day of Yom Kippur.

Zion: Mentioned 108 times in the Torah, Zion refers to the Holy Land, Jerusalem, the Land of Israel, and Israel.

Zionism: An international political, social, and nationalist movement supporting the establishment of a Jewish state in Palestine.

To access the documents listed below, please visit www.onelandtwostories.com.

Sykes-Picot Agreement
(16 May 1916)

Balfour Declaration 1917
(2 November 1917)

Faisal-Weizmann Agreement
(3 January 1919)

British Mandate of Palestine
(24 July 1922)

McMahon-Husain Correspondence
(16 March 1939)

British White Paper of 1939
(1 May 1939)

UN General Assembly Resolution 181/Palestine Partition Plan
(29 November 1947)

Article 13 of the Universal Declaration of Human Rights
(10 December 1948)

UN General Assembly Resolution 194
(11 December 1948)

Article 49 of the Fourth Geneva Convention Relative to the Protection of Civilian Persons in Time of War
(12 August 1949)

United Nations Security Council Resolution 54
(15 July 1948)

Article 12 of the International Covenant on Civil and Political Rights
(16 December 1966)

United Nations Security Council Resolution 242
(22 November 1967)

Palestinian National Charter
(1–17 July 1968)

APPENDIX I | DOCUMENTS

United Nations Security Council Resolution 338
(22 October 1973)

Camp David Accords
(17 September 1978)

Israeli-Egyptian Peace Treaty
(26 March 1979)

Basic Law: Jerusalem, Capital of Israel
(30 July 1980)

UN Security Council Resolution 478
(20 August 1980)

Military Order 947: "Concerning the Establishment of a Civilian Administration"
(8 November 1981)

Palestinian Declaration of Independence
(15 November 1988)

Israel-Palestine Liberation Organization Agreement: 1993 [Oslo I]
(13 September 1993)

Treaty of Peace Between the State of Israel and the Hashemite Kingdom of Jordan
(26 October 1994)

The Israeli-Palestinian Interim Agreement on the West Bank and the Gaza Strip
(25 September 1995)

A Performance-Based Roadmap to a Permanent Two-State Solution to the Israeli-Palestinian Conflict
(30 April 2003)

UN Security Council Resolution 1397
(12 March 2002)

Arab Peace Initiative [Saudi Initiative]
(2002)

Report of the United Nations Fact Finding Mission on the Gaza Conflict
(29 September 2009) Executive Summary:

Statement by Middle East Quartet SG2168
(5 February 2011)

Month	YEAR*	EVENT
	1800 BCE	Abraham settles in Canaan according to Jewish tradition (Genesis). His two sons, Isaac and Ishmael, had a rivalry believed to be the cause of many wars to come between Muslims, the descendent of Ishmael, and the Jews, the children of Isaac.
	1300 BCE	Philistines and Israelite tribes migrate to Canaan.
	1200–1100 BCE	Moses led the Jews out of Egypt. They wandered in the Sinai desert for 40 years before entering the Promised Land.
	1273 BCE	Joshua led the conquest of Canaan and delivered the land to the Israelites as promised by God to Abraham.
	1020 BCE	King Saul established a territorial state of Israel including Jerusalem, and came to be known as the first King of Israel. Jewish tradition recalls him as chosen by God to unify the nation under a kingdom.
	1004 BCE	The second King of Israel, King David, is appointed ruler after King Saul is killed by the Philistines. Islam considered David (Dawood) to be a prophet and the king of a nation.
	967 BCE	King Solomon is believed to have reigned in Israel's Golden Age and initiated the construction of the First Temple, which housed the Ark of the Covenant, and was completed in 960 BCE.
	920 BCE	The Kingdom splits into Israel in the north and Judea in the south.
	740 BCE	Isaiah prophesized that "a virgin shall conceive a son," interpreted by many Jews to be one of the many prophets, by Christians to be Jesus Christ and by Muslims to be the birth of Mohammed.
	722 BCE	Assyrians conquered Israel forcing many from their homeland.

APPENDIX II | CONFLICT TIMELINE

Month	YEAR*	EVENT
	586 BCE	Babylonians conquered Judea and destroyed the First Temple built by King Solomon.
	539 BCE	Persian King Cyrus allows Jews to return to Jerusalem.
	519 BCE	The Second Temple was built under Persian rule on its original site in Jerusalem to replace the destroyed First Temple.
	200 BCE	General Seleucids gained control of Palestine following Alexander the Great's death and permitted the practice of Judaism in the land.
	167 BCE	Led by the Maccabees, The Jews revolted against Antiochus IV of the Syrian Hellenic Dynasty, who had banned Judaism, and formed an independent kingdom with Jerusalem as its capital.
	61 BCE	Romans invaded Judea and conquered Jerusalem. The land was divided into several provinces.
	132–136 BCE	Bar Kochba leads the Jewish revolt, but the Jews lose and Judea is renamed "Palestine" by the Roman Empire in an attempt to delegitimize the Jewish people.
	70 CE	Titus and the Romans destroy the Second Temple and Jerusalem in order to end the Great Jewish Revolt.
	638 CE	Muslim Arab armies under Caliph Omar conquered Jerusalem, but allowed Christians and Jews to keep their religion.
	969 CE	Churches and Synagogues in Jerusalem were destroyed by the Fatimid conquest, a Muslim group from North Africa.
	1099 CE	The Crusaders invaded Palestine, killed many Jews and Muslims, and forbade Jews to reside in Jerusalem.

Month	YEAR*	EVENT
	1071 CE	The Seljuk Turks defeated the Byzantine emperor and demolish Jerusalem in the Battle of Manzikert.
	1244 CE	Ghengis Khan's army invaded and took over Jerusalem.
	1291 CE	After decades of trying to regain pieces of the land, the Crusaders were finally evicted when a Muslim group captured Acre in 1291.
	1831	Egyptians conquer Palestine under Mehmed Ali.
	1571	Palestine was taken over by the Ottoman Empire and the Turkish Sultan invited Jews fleeing the Spanish Inquisition to settle in the parts of Palestine.
	1740	Ottoman Sultan invites some rabbis to rebuild Tiberias, and thousands of Jews return to the land.
	1843	Rabbi Alcalay and Rabbi Kalisher produce the first Zionist writings, though the term "Zionist" isn't coined until 1890.
	1860	The first Jewish Jewish neighborhood (Mishkenot Sha'ananim) outside of Jerusalem's city walls, was built.
	1881	The Ottoman Empire imposed restrictions on the number of Jews settling in Palestine.
May	1916	The Sykes-Picot Agreement was signed between France and Britain to partition the land in the Middle East that was affected by WWI. This was seen as a promise by many Arabs as an exchange of the promise for Palestine in exchange for assisting the British against the Ottoman Empire.
November 2	1917	**Balfour Declaration** During the First World War, Britain committed to establishing a Jewish homeland in Palestine.

APPENDIX II | CONFLICT TIMELINE

Month	YEAR*	EVENT
August	1929	The Pogroms, or Hebron Massacres, by Palestinians against the "old-Yishuv" who had lived in Palestine for hundreds of years.
July	1937	The British first contemplated partition of Palestine Mandate into eventual Jewish and Arab states.
November	1947–1949	**Israeli War of Independence** follows the UN Partition on November 29, 1947. Israel defeats six invading Arab states. Transjordan occupies Jerusalem and the West Bank. Egypt occupies the Gaza Strip.
February–June	1949	Armistice boundaries agreed upon by Israel, Transjordan, Syria, Lebanon and Egypt. Israel maintains the Negev, Egypt the Gaza Strip and Transjordan controls Jerusalem and the West Bank.
October	1956–1957	Israel joined forces with Britain and France in an attack on Egypt over control of the Suez Canal. Under pressure from the United States and the UN, the attackers withdrew their forces ceding sovereignty over the Canal to Egypt.
February	1964	The PLO (Palestine Liberation Organization) was founded by Egyptian President Nasser to create a united Arab front against Israel based in Egypt, later the PLO was led by Yasser Arafat.
June 5	1967	**Six Day War (1967 War)** War of aggression by Arab countries against Israel, resulting in Israel taking control over Jerusalem and the West Bank, the Gaza Strip, the Sinai Peninsula, and the Golan Heights.
	1968–1970	**War of Attrition** Initiated by Egypt, this war along the Suez Canal against Israel, ended with a ceasefire without change to respective military positions.

Month	YEAR*	EVENT
October	1973	**Yom Kippur War** Egypt and Syria launched a surprise attack during a high holiday with the intention of regaining lost land from previous battles. The war lasted for 3 weeks and gave the Arab world a sense of victory.
September 17	1978	**The Camp David Accords** The meeting marked the first encounter between an Arab leader (Anwar Sadat) and an Israeli leader (Menachem Begin) who joined the U.S. and Egypt at a secret summit to negotiate agreements facilitated by President Jimmy Carter. Two agreements were signed that were based on UN Resolutions 242 and 338.
March 26	1979	**Israel-Egypt Peace Treaty** Signed in Washington following the Camp David Accords, its nine articles ultimately spelled out the role of the U.S. and the UN and the relationship between Israelis and Palestinians.
June– September	1982	**1982 Lebanon War** To stop terrorist attacks in Israel, the IDF invaded Lebanon to fight the PLO. After two months, the U.S. mediated a cease-fire, and the PLO moved to Tunisia.
September 16–18	1982	**Sabra and Shatila Massacre**, took place in Palestinian refugee campls near Beirut where Christian Phalangist militiamen killed hundreds of Palestinian refugees. Israel was indirectly held responsible.
December 8	1987	**The First Intifada** ("Shaking Off" in Arabic) This was a Palestinian uprising against Israeli occupation that lasted for four years.
May 14	1989	Israel's Peace Initiative was formulated by Prime Minister Shamir based on the Camp David Accords to strengthen peace with Egypt, promote peace with Arab states, resolve Palestinian self-rule, and improve refugee conditions.

Month	YEAR*	EVENT
October 30	1991	**Madrid Summit** This Peace conference attended by the U.S., the Soviet Union, Israel, Palestine, Jordan, Syria and Lebanon to resolve rival territorial claims over the West Bank, Gaza Strip and Jerusalem.
September 13	1993	**Oslo Accords (Declaration of Principles)** The agreements were intended for a mutual relationship between Israel and Palestine by creating the Palestinian National Authority and called for the withdrawal of Israeli military forces from parts of the West Bank and Gaza Strip.
May 4	1994	**Gaza-Jericho Agreement (Cairo Agreement)** This led to the establishment of the Palestinian Authority (PA) which was to fight terror and restrict violence, while Israel relinguished control over land to the PA.
July 25	1994	**The Washington Declaration** Signed by Jordan's King Hussein and Israel's Prime Minister Yitzhak Rabin to terminate a 46-year state of war between the two states. The pact also granted Muslims control over the Holy Muslim Sites of Jerusalem.
September 28	1995	**Oslo II (Taba)** This agreement divided the West Bank and the Gaza Strip into three areas, that differentiated distinct measures of Israeli/Palestinian control.
November	1995	**Assassination of Yitzhak Rabin** A member of a Jewish extremist group assassinated Prime Minister Rabin in a public square after Rabin initiated a peace process with Arafat and the PLO, considered risky by some Israelis.
October 26	1994	**Israel-Jordan Peace Treaty** The pact that established peace between Israel and Jordan. Primarily, it set the Jordan River as the natural border between the two states.

Month	YEAR*	EVENT
October	1998	**Wye River Talks** President Bill Clinton pursued easing tension between Arafat and Netanyahu six times until an agreement was signed. However, the memorandum was deemed a failure because Palestinian obligations were not considered to be fulfilled.
May	2000–2005 (approx.)	**Second Intifada** The Second Intifada resulted in the deaths of 5,000 Arab Palestinians and more than 1,000 Israelis. This Palestinian uprising against Israeli occupation precipitated the building of the Separation Barrier (Security Wall) to prevent terrorist attacks on Israeli civilians.
July 11-25	2000	**Camp David Summit** U.S. President Clinton convened a conference to continue the peace process. The summit ended in failure with Israelis and Palestinians blaming each other for the impasse.
January 22–27	2001	**Taba Conference** The PA and Israel hoped to reach a final resolution after a series of talks and came closest at this meeting to reaching a mutual arrangement , though the talks were dropped because of political shifts and time constraints.
March 28	2002	**The Arab Peace Initiative** The plan called for Israel to withdraw from all territories occupied since 1967 and the return of Palestinian refugees to their place of origin in exchange for peaceful relations and political recognition. The Initiative was unexpectedly dropped and has been re-adopted on several occasions.
April 12	2002	**Battle of Jenin** The IDF entered the Jenin Palestinian refugee camp to stop terrorist activities. Palestinians declared that a massacre took place, prompting investigations into the conflicting reports.

APPENDIX II | CONFLICT TIMELINE

Month	YEAR*	EVENT
April	2003	**The Road Map for Peace** This outlines an ongoing path towards a two-state solution and was proposed under the guidance of the EU, UN, Russia, and the U.S. As part of the process, the PA was required to abandon the use of violence and make steps toward democratic reform while Israel was to cease the construction of settlements in the West Bank and Gaza Strip.
June 4–20	2003	**Peace Summit at Aqaba** President George Bush, King Abdullah, Prime Minister Ariel Sharon and Prime Minister Mahmoud Abbas met in Jordan. Sharon vowed to dismantle illegal settlements while Abbas agreed to halt incitement to violence.
August 15–23	2005	**Gaza and West Bank Disengagement** Israeli citizens were prohibited from entering and remaining in areas to be evacuated as part of the new Disengagement Plan 2005 Law.
February	2005	**Sharm el-Sheikh Summit I** Following the death of Arafat, peace talks began to negotiate an end to the Second Intifada (al-Aqsa Intifada.)
July–August	2006	**Second Lebanon War** Israel attacked Hezbollah militants when Israeli soldiers were killed and others were taken hostage along the Lebanon-Israeli border. Israel responded with airstrikes and a 31-day ground invasion of southern Lebanon.
June 25	2007	During the Sharm el-Sheikh Summit II, leaders of Israel, the Palestinian Authority, Egypt and Jordan re-unite to discuss containing Hamas in the Gaza strip and supporting Fatah in the West bank.
June 7	2007	**Battle of Gaza** Hamas gained control of Gaza Strip from Fatah and removed its officials from the government.

Month	YEAR*	EVENT
May 14	2008	**Peace Valley Plan** The plan proposed to launch industrial and economic projects to promote growth and prosperity on both sides. This has been seen as a positive effort to promote reconciliation.
December– January	2008–2009	**Operation Cast Lead** In response to years of rocket and missile fire upon Israeli civilians from Gaza, the IDF launched a military incursion in the Gaza Strip. UN investigated this military action and released the Goldstone Report.

*Dates may not always align due to some discrepancies between Jewish, Christian and Muslim record keeping and calendars.

APPENDIX II | CONFLICT TIMELINE

INDEX

Dreyfus Affair: 52, 53, 54

Dura, Muhammad al-: 314, 315, 316, 334, 335, 466

East Jerusalem (al-Quds) (The Holy One): 5, 63,
71, 123, 160, 164, 174, 177, 190, 191, 194,
238, 239, 240, 241, 246, 253, 272, 273, 279,
282, 284, 297, 299, 303, 328, 331, 335, 338,
395, 397, 398, 399, 400, 402, 408, 410, 411,
412, 413, 414, 415, 416

Effendi: 78

Ethnic Cleansing: 25, 66, 135, 139, 141, 142,
331, 440, 457

Etzion Bloc: 396, 403

Faisal-Weizmann Agreement: 70

Fatah (Palestine National Liberation Movement):
166, 169, 170, 181, 182, 183, 188, 192, 193,
206, 217, 223, 234, 276, 299, 301, 302, 312,
313, 331, 347, 350, 351, 352, 364, 365, 367,
382, 384, 385, 388, 393, 394, 420, 468

Fatahland: 201, 203, 217

Fedayeen: 165, 193, 350

Fellahin: 78, 79, 80, 122

Final Solution: 17

Final Status Issues: 277, 291, Chapter 10–391-
420

First Intifada: 222, 225, 226, 227, 239, 244, 299,
310, 312, 340, 351, 380, 381, 398

First Jewish Holy Temple: see Temple

First Qibla: 34, 410

Fourth Geneva Convention: 402, 409

Gaza (Gaza Strip): 7, 31, 62, 71, 84, 121, 123,
126, 146, 147, 148, 151, 162, 163, 164,
165, 166, 173, 174, 177, 189, 190, 191,
194, 217, 222, 223, 224, 225, 227, 228,
237, 238, 239, 240, 246, 252, 257, 258,
260, 264, 268, 269, 271, 275, 276, 277,
283, 285, 286, 287, 291, 292, 293, 295,
297, 298, 299, 301, 302, 309, 311, 312,
313, 314, 320, 323, 324, 325, 329, 335,
336, 338, 341, Chapter 9–343-389, 393,
394, 395, 402, 403, 408, 409, 410, 412,
413, 415, 419, 420, 425, 427, 428, 432,
444, 447, 448, 461, 463, 464, 467, 468,
469, 470, 472, 474

Gaza Disengagement, 2005: 174, 359

Golan Heights: 83, 156, 160, 171, 266, 290

Goldstein, Baruch: 327, 330

Goldstein Massacre: 328

Goldstone Report: 367, 368, 386, 387, 469

Grand Mufti (Grand Mufti of Jerusalem) (Hajj
Amin Husseini) (Hajj Amin al-Husseini): 84,
88, 114, 456

Great Revolt of 1936-1939 (Arab Great
Revolt): 100

Green Line (Pre-1967 borders): 174, 245, 338,
395, 396, 397, 403, 409, 413

Hadith: 33, 34

Haganah: 23, 89, 113, 116, 117, 119, 122, 133,
134, 136,137, 138, 139, 140, 141

Husseini, Haj Amin al-: see Grand Mufti

INDEX

INDEX

INDEX